having

having

PROPERTY AND POSSESSION
IN RELIGIOUS AND SOCIAL LIFE

Edited by

William Schweiker & Charles Mathewes

WILLIAM B. EERDMANS PUBLISHING COMPANY
GRAND RAPIDS, MICHIGAN / CAMBRIDGE, U.K.

© 2004 Wm. B. Eerdmans Publishing Co.

Wm. B. Eerdmans Publishing Co.
255 Jefferson Ave. S.E., Grand Rapids, Michigan 49503 /
P.O. Box 163, Cambridge CB3 9PU U.K.

Printed in the United States of America

08 07 06 05 04   5 4 3 2 1

Library of Congress Cataloging-in-Publication Data

Having: property and possession in religious and social life /
    edited by William Schweiker & Charles Mathewes.
        p.   cm.
    Includes bibliographical references.
    ISBN 0-8028-2484-6 (alk. paper)
    1. Property — Religious aspects — Christianity — History of
doctrines. 2. Property — biblical teaching.   I. Schweiker, William.
II. Mathewes, Charles T., 1969-

BR115.E3H345   2004
178 — dc22

                                        2003064344

www.eerdmans.com

Contents

Acknowledgments

This book is the result of several years of intense scholarly collaboration, debate, and musing among the individuals whose work it represents. The book would not have been possible without a generous grant from the Lilly Endowment, which funded under the direction of William Schweiker the multiyear research project "Property, Possession, and the Theology of Culture." All of us are profoundly thankful for the support of Lilly and especially for the sage leadership of Dr. Craig Dykstra. As the project developed, we were able to present this material at various public conferences. Partly through the support of the Internationale Wissenschaftsforum at the University of Heidelberg, we were able to engage European scholars on this topic. Some of their work will be found in this book. We express our gratitude for the support and good graces of the IWF and the German colleagues who participated in that conference; without their vigorous conversations, this book would be far less than it is.

The project culminated at a public conference in Chicago in October 2000. In addition to support from Lilly, the conference was made possible through the support of the University of Chicago Divinity School. We give our thanks to Dean Richard Rosengarten of the Divinity School for his leadership in this event; to Ms. Sandra Peppers, administrator at the Divinity School, for advice and order; and to Ms. Molly Bartlett, Dean for External Relations at the Divinity School, for help planning and staging the conference. Finally, the conference and the project were aided by the support of the Martin Marty Center of the Divinity School of the University of Chicago. We give our thanks to Professor W. Clark Gilpin, director, and Ms. Sandy Crane, secretary. Without the support of these various institutions the massive work of this project would simply not have been possible.

All scholarly projects and books rely on the hard labor of many people to bring the work to completion. We were blessed to work with a group of scholars steeped in their own fields and yet deeply concerned about the pressing issues of our world. The group's unstinting intellectual attention to and meticulous care for each other's work are something that we know all members of the group individually felt, and still feel; in this case, the whole really was greater than the sum of its parts, and we are delighted to be able to thank the contributors here.

The co-editors each owe a debt of gratitude to the other. For William Schweiker, this project simply would not have been possible without the tireless labor, scholarly insight, and skillful reporting of the project assistant and now co-editor, Professor Charles Mathewes. Words of gratitude fail in this case! For Charles Mathewes, the opportunity to work on the project has been deeply formative for his education, and is simply one more manifestation of the great gifts Professor Schweiker has shared with him, for which he remains ever grateful.

Finally, we wish to thank Mr. Jonathan Rothchild and Ms. Aimee Burant for assistance during the final conference and Mr. Michael Johnson and Mr. Kevin Jung for their insight and diligence in the extensive work of preparing the manuscript for publication. And, finally, we would like to thank again each of the authors whose work graces the pages of this book. It is a true joy to work with women and men whose thought and commitments inspire one's own life.

WILLIAM SCHWEIKER
University of Chicago

CHARLES MATHEWES
University of Virginia

Introduction

WILLIAM SCHWEIKER AND CHARLES MATHEWES

The last few decades have seen the explosion and expansion of market economies into a complex global system. No one on this planet is untouched by these developments. From shantytowns in Africa and rural villages around the Black Sea to the high-tech worlds of Tokyo, Berlin, and New York, the people of this planet are living through massive changes in the concrete ordering of life. These changes take many forms, of course, including the fantastic spread of a consumerist mentality in the wealthy nations of the West, a mind-set especially found in the United States, that brings with it a host of related but unintended social consequences like rampant obesity, the commercialization of violence, and a society where spectacle and entertainment have replaced civil discourse. Yet in other places on the planet the present ordering of life is marked not by flagrant consumerism but by disease, grinding poverty, social breakdown, and the flourishing of manifold forms of fanaticism.

The global dynamics that currently structure much of life are novel in many respects, and, not surprisingly, these worldwide economic developments evoke intense and sometime violent response, as, for example, in demonstrations at various meeting of the global economic powers such as the World Bank, the IMF, the UN, and the G7. From the perspective of the demonstrators, "globalization" is an oppressive machine aimed at leveling all cultural differences in and through the systematic exploitation of poorer nations and the earth's resources. But for others, the global economic flow is the harbinger of increased prosperity and with it the possibility that more and more people will take control of their own political and social destinies. To say that we live in ambiguous times is no doubt an old truism. But it is, for all that, true.

1

While we must grant the novelty of the current age, it is also the case that people have always had to negotiate life in economic terms, perhaps most typically by gaining and losing things as property. People constitute much of their identity, their sense of self, in relation to the things they value. Communities facilitate social intercourse and survival by means of property relations. And given the importance of "having" in social and personal life, it is hardly surprising that the world's religions have pondered the moral and spiritual meanings of property and possession. Whether through a Hebrew prophet's criticism of the wealthy's exploitation of the poor, Jesus' teachings on the dangers of wealth, or Buddha's insights into craving and desire, the religions have wrestled with the place of property and possession — and, so, with having, losing, and gaining — in human existence. Property and possession constitute a field of basic human questions.

The Purpose of This Book

What, if anything, might the study of the biblical religions contribute to thinking about and responding to the facts of our present world situation, as they are bound to the humanly basic reality of "having"? The inquiries found in this book seek to provide some answers to that question. In order to do so, the authors reject the typical approaches that dominate theology and religious studies. One tactic, when theologians and scholars of religions turn to consider some contemporary question — say, war or human rights or ecological crises — is to accept the terms of the current discussion (political theory, cultural studies, or environmental science) and then apply these to the resources at the theologian's or scholar's disposal. It is as if religious resources — the ideas, practices, narratives, and institution of some religion — are nothing but data for examination under the microscope of a nonreligious method of inquiry. In the realm of economic life, this leads to the publication of endless books on things like "Christian faith and economic life" or "the economics of religious practices." These are important undertakings; we have all benefited from such inquiries. But the tactic of applying scholarly theory to "religious" data is not the purpose of this book.

The other customary strategy, found most often among theologians, is to assume that somehow the resources at the thinker's disposal — say, the Christian story — are perfectly free from the ambiguities, distortions, and legacies of violence found in all traditions and resources. Accordingly, the theologian does not need to use critical methods to study her or his own materials. The truth of the community's convictions pertaining to the realm of social existence is assumed. The tactic then is merely to announce the "truth" of the religious vision and to show how it enables us to escape the problems of the "world." And so we hear Christian theologians denounce the modern world in toto, castigate the market, and announce ideas like the biblical jubilee year as if that idea itself solved all our problems. As with the technological use of nonreligious methods on religious "data," the *confessional* tactic of thought, no matter how customary, is not by itself adequate to meet the challenges now facing people around the world or to confront openly and honestly the ambiguity found in all traditions.

The task of this book, *Having: Property and Possession in Religious and Social Life,* is not to accept the terms of contemporary economics or social sciences and then apply that manner of thinking to "religious resources"; we want to show that reflection on the biblical traditions provides new and unexplored resources for understanding cultural dynamics. We also do not assume, however, that somehow the biblical message is unambiguously pure and offers a simple counter-vision to the problems of "the world." Once we explore the real operative force of the biblical traditions in cultural processes, distortions come to light. And what is more, ideas like "the world" are leading abstractions that just as easily conceal as reveal truths about the actual working of human life.[1] The task of this book is audacious and therefore controversial. It sets forth a series of inquiries that aim to show the contribution religious studies and theological reflection can make to considering and responding to a humanly basic reality, namely, property and possession. The authors seek to uncover within the biblical traditions resources for thinking about the place of property and possession in cultural processes in ways that might be missed or distorted in a purely economic or political or social scientific approach to the topic. But we also want to isolate and criticize distortions within the biblical traditions and their long legacy of influence on Western civilization. As scholars, we understand ourselves to be in the service of wide humane purposes. We work as publicly engaged thinkers concerned about the current state of social existence.

In the remainder of this introduction we want to say something about this novel approach to "having" taken in the book and also to provide the

---

1. For an account of the importance and danger of abstractions in all thinking see Alfred North Whitehead, *Science and the Modern World* (Cambridge: Cambridge University Press, 1932). Whitehead is surely right that philosophy, or critical reflection, must explore, critique, and revise leading abstractions (the "isms") operative in a culture with the intent of providing a robust view of the world. In exploring "having," we are trying to break free of the domination of thought by economic abstractions while providing a richer and more complex account of this dynamic of human life.

reader with some context for engaging the essays to follow. Let us turn next, therefore, and explore this approach, what might be called a "material hermeneutics of culture."

Reflection on Property and Possession

While taking our orientation from the spread of the market in our age, the authors want to address a basic question about the very core of human life: *how do people find value in having things, and relatedly, how does having things give value to social life?* The idea of "having" is a relational concept. It denotes both what is possessed, things or property, and also the activity of having, of possession. The complex relation between possession and property denoted by the idea "having" is fraught with patterns of valuing. In every culture some things are seen as bearing worth in themselves; they are worthy of esteem and respect. Theorists call this intrinsic or non-instrumental value. Usually we encounter human beings in this way; a person makes a claim to be respected and esteemed. Other "things," including sometimes even human beings, have use or instrumental value. These two kinds of value — intrinsic and instrumental — are important in exploring the human dynamics of "having." Further, the "things" in which worth can be found or that provide meaning to human life need not be — and often are not — material entities, property in the usual sense of the word. People regularly experience the losing and gaining of love or faith or hope as well as of friends, family, and lovers. Our concern, accordingly, is broad. We focus both on forms of possession and on the manifold material and nonmaterial objects (i.e., property) that can be possessed. The idea of "property," we argue, specifies cultural practices of exchange and valuation of "things"; the term "possession" picks out within those practices the idea that persons can own and dispose of things but also be owned by them. What is at issue in the relation of property and possession is the complex yet humanly basic fact of "having."

The irony is that "things" can shift not just their value, but even the type of value they have within a culture. What was once valued as a bit of instrumental property can become esteemed and respected in its own right and vice versa. For instance, slavery — past and present — is a social practice in which a person is divested of esteem and respect and assigned worth within the social hierarchy of values as a "thing," as property, to be used. Conversely, sacred objects — relics, totems, and so forth — not to mention ancient tools now treasured as museum pieces can shift from holding a use-value to being held in esteem in their own right. This shifting in value status through which a mere "thing" takes on religious power and symbolism is often associated with distinctly religious and cultic acts or experiences marked by mystery, secrecy, and ritual authority. In this light, think of elements of bread and wine in the Christian Eucharist. Simple, material objects normally used to sustain life (bread, wine) shift in meaning and value within the act of worship so that they represent the body and blood of Christ.[2] This shifting between patterns of valuation is often subtle and driven by multiple purposes, yet in order to understand it, one must have a complex conception of the place of "having" in cultural existence.

From a cultural perspective, property and possession as the modes of "having" are thus primarily about matters of assigning worth. Strategies and tactics of assigning value to "things" are more intimately bound to cultural patterns of valuation than is often thought. And we are also interested in the "shifting" of valuations found in cultural practices, especially when those "shiftings" express deep social distortions (say, in slavery). This is why the approach or method taken in this book can be called a "material hermeneutics of culture." We explore how the understanding of *things,* hence a material focus, bears on the *meaning* of personal and social life within cultural practices of valuation. This is a hermeneutic insofar as meaning and understanding are the unique concern of inquiry. And we mean to explore *material meanings* and thus are decidedly not *materialist.* We deny the claim made by materialists that nothing exists but the universe of brute material objects, but we argue this precisely by showing how meaning and value are bound to and in fact transform the place of "things" in human life. We are interested in the interaction between cultural meanings and values and the universe of things that demarcate the arena of property and possession in a tradition or society. A material hermeneutics is a way to explore cultural artifacts, practices, and processes.

Now, to say that property and possession can usefully be approached from the perspective of cultural practices emblematically seen in religious sources is to make a simple but important claim. Like other cultural realities, property and possession are about how persons form their self-understandings, socially transmitted behavior, and ideals expressing a community's ethos, and they also inform the domain of social creativity and style. "Culture" is a reality

---

2. We are mindful, of course, of the manifold and profound differences among Christians in how to understand the Lord's Supper. Our only point is that no matter how interpreted, this act of worship is one in which things (bread, wine) normally used to sustain physical life take on new and profound significance, however that "taking on" and "significance" are variously understood. For a discussion of these matters see Michael Welker, *What Happens in Holy Communion?* (Grand Rapids: Eerdmans, 2000).

created through action and valuation that is important for the formation of distinct forms of human life. Our focus on the biblical traditions, accordingly, is not with "doctrines"; we attend to ideas, images, practices, and values arising in those traditions that continue to operate in Western societies. Insofar as the dawning global market reality is decisively shaped by the legacy of the West, charting and assessing the operative force of biblical impulses on Western cultures offers a new and important perspective on the current global reality.

Stated somewhat differently, our "method" requires that we explore the history of effects of biblical images and concepts in the cultural flow of the West and the ways in which those "effects" distort or illuminate perceptions of property and possession in viable social existence. The interest is not only in the place of "things" in cultural understandings; it is also focused on the concrete and particular rough and tumble of the historical legacies of biblical traditions in Western societies. We contend that one can learn something about property and possession by engaging the concrete workings and legacies of complex religious traditions. Religious traditions are not simply "data" the scholar manipulates and decodes from some other perspective. And this is the case simply because what makes a "thing" into property is not given by nature but is a matter of social practices, discourses, and patterns of value; and some of those practices — (perhaps) like the shifting of value — are distinctly religious. To consider property and possession within a material hermeneutics of culture means that the root issue is how social and religious practices demarcate human activities of having, losing, and the exchanging of "things" in the formation of complex social worlds.

Consider, for example, a wedding ring. In terms of cultural discourse about human relations, a ring can have significant, even life-defining, meaning. The same object is understood within alternate logics of economics, media, religion, and law. The media circulates manifold and conflicting images of marriage. Religious communities shaped by the biblical texts signify and demarcate profound human relations through symbolic acts. They define what counts as marriage. Religious marriage rites shift the very value of persons from unwed to wed. Economic value is often used to express deep affection; lovers shower each other with expensive gifts. Further, the ring has sign or symbolic value that circulates in a culture bearing subtle religious meanings and in that way saturates, or shapes, people's consciousness. Any understanding of the cultural "meaning" of property (say, the ring) must, by the nature of the case, explore it from interlocking perspectives. That is what our method of reflection, this "material hermeneutics of culture," aims to accomplish. In doing so, each author has tried to break through abstractions that isolate the meaning of property and possession with respect to just one sociocultural dynamic, logic, and pattern of valuation. To say that a ring is a symbol of love, for example, is, for Western societies, no doubt true. Yet that idea becomes a false abstraction if the meaning of property is set only within the logic of symbols about human affections. The same could be said about the domination of economic discourse; it too can become a leading abstraction.

The meaning of an object, the ring, is then the confluence of diverse discourses, and these discourses can be usefully explored through the idea of property. Furthermore, those relations defined by the cultural economy and social systems express other beliefs that are distinctly religious in character. To be sure, any "thing" will have many meanings. We have no desire to deny that fact and to claim that somehow property and possession are the most basic or most comprehensive cultural phenomena or that religious sources provide the only diagnostic perspective from which to understand them. Again, our hermeneutic, or practice of interpreting cultural practices, is decidedly not part of a *materialistic* philosophy. Exploring property and possession mindful of various points of reference allows us to examine comparatively the dynamics of cultural actions — present and past — and to activate insight into the complex interactions of dimensions of social and personal existence. In each case, what is at issue is how property enables us to show the contact points between dimensions of cultural existence.

Within the whirl of current global dynamics and the spread of market systems, why is this focus on cultural dynamics important? Why worry about the meanings of "property" and "possession" in the face of grinding and deadly poverty all about us? To be sure, careful reflection on social practices and meanings, even ones attentive to the material concerns of life, will not answer all social ills! But we believe that only a robust account of the importance of property and possession in human existence enables us to grasp and respond to the real depth of suffering brought about by systemic forms of injustice. And only with a robust understanding of the problem facing people around the planet can any adequate response begin to be formulated. In this sense, our labor is not the end point but rather a necessary step toward confronting injustice.

With some sense of the general purpose and method of this book, we can isolate the more particular forms of inquiry undertaken by the authors.

The Study of Religion and Culture

The scholars whose work constitutes this volume are dedicated to careful and critical reflection on the resources of specific traditions. Our orientation of thought means that different approaches to the study of religion can in fact work together. The collaborative labor among theologians, biblical scholars, political thinkers, ethicists, and economists has been one aspiration of the book. In fact, the book is the product of several years of joint research and untold hours of debate and conversation. Of course, it is often the case that scholarly approaches are set against each other. The scholar of religion avoids the theologian. Theologians disagree among themselves. Economists and ethicists challenge each other's perceptions of human action. Dispute rages about the relation between descriptive and normative claims. All of these disagreements are well known. Our point is not to rehash scholarly battles; it is simply to note that the cultural turn in thought means scholars can speak to the most pressing matters of life and also cooperate in new and important ways.

The linchpin of the project, as noted, has been to explore property and possession within cultural dynamics shaped (for good or ill) by the biblical traditions, to engage in a hermeneutics of "having." This unique focus has shaped how we approach our several scholarly disciplines. For instance, religious studies can be construed as a critical theory of culture. The scholar of religion is thereby interested in various cultural practices found in a civilization and the import of religious ideas, beliefs, and values on those practices. Many of the essays in this book can be seen in that light. They forge new and important approaches to their disciplines. Other essayists undertake the interpretation of culture in terms of explicit theological reflection. Insofar as that is the case, theology is transformed. What is called the theology of culture can be understood in various ways, of course.[3] For some thinkers among us it is the nondogmatic study of the interactions between cultural activities

---

3. This project stands, critically to be sure, in a long line of thinkers concerned to reflect religiously on culture. Many of the authors represented in this book have made their own contribution to the enterprise of the theology of culture. See, for example, Kathryn Tanner, *Theories of Culture: A New Agenda for Theology* (Minneapolis: Fortress, 1998); David E. Klemm and William Schweiker, eds., *Meanings in Texts and Actions: Questioning Paul Ricoeur* (Charlottesville, Va.: University of Virginia Press, 1993); Michael Welker, *God the Spirit* (Minneapolis: Fortress, 1994); Jean Bethke Elshtain, *Augustine and the Limits of Politics* (Notre Dame, Ind.: University of Notre Dame Press, 1997); Christine Firer Hinze, *Comprehending Power in Christian Social Ethics* (Atlanta: Scholars Press, 1996); and William Schweiker, *Power, Value, and Conviction: Theological Ethics in the Postmodern Age* (Cleveland: Pilgrim, 1998).

and the structures of human existence seeking to articulate, judge, and inform religious significance. Theological inquiry so defined focuses on the religious meanings, values, and ideals operative in actual social life. For other theologians represented in this book, the task is to reflect on the culture of Christian faith, to discern its operative contours and present meanings. The focus of our material hermeneutics has also transformed and energized the work of the political, economic, moral, and biblical thinkers among us. Scholars have discovered how basic questions of property and possession are to the life-world of the biblical texts. The economists, interestingly enough, argue that taking a cultural focus in their work requires attending closely to moral questions within the very dynamics of the market. Political thinkers have been moved to reflect on what it means to possess the "body" as a basic fact of political association. By focusing on a humanly basic fact of life, that reality of "having," we have enabled scholars to work together in mutually enlightening and transforming ways.

Once we focus our attention on cultural processes armed with rich concepts, we can also see how, in fact, distinctly religious ideas, symbols, and texts have already informed and shaped those same processes and concepts. This is certainly the case with property and possession. As various essays aptly show, it is exceedingly hard to understand contemporary ideas about property without a grasp of how they are encoded with ancient meanings and practices found among the biblical traditions. We aim to understand the meaning and social significance of "things" in personal and communal life attentive to these operative traditions. In this way, one no longer needs to rely on over-general ideas of "religion" in order to warrant religious reflection on culture. And because we are exploring how the biblical traditions and Christian ideas and practices shape sociocultural phenomena, our thinking is not delimited to dogmatic and ecclesial theology. The focus of our labor has been on the history of effects, as Hans-Georg Gadamer has called it — of beliefs, practices, texts, and symbols rather than religion in general. Insofar as we want to understand and even transform actual social and cultural life, this approach seems required. It means that one must give thick interpretations of cultures.

This book demonstrates both the ambiguity and the wealth of the resources that the biblical religions offer for reflection on property and possession. Various authors examine those traditions from the inside, as it were; other authors examine the impact of the biblical traditions on the wider flow of Western cultures and the postcolonial world. Granting that diversity of forms of inquiry — a diversity the reader will find in this volume — all of the essays do share some common points of reference. These are the following:

(1) inquiry into cultural practices of meaning and valuation; (2) the analysis of social dynamics, institutions, and structures; (3) an interpretation of the cultural significance of biblical ideas, texts, and traditions; (4) the critique of false, leading abstractions, a critique aimed at a more complete and subtle scheme of thought. These points of convergence in thinking about property and possession allow us to articulate a wide range of concerns in our practice of reflection on religion and culture. Our conviction is that by exploring property and possession along various lines of inquiry, we gain better understanding of how people find value in having things and how having things gives value to social relations.

Themes and Essays

It will be useful as a final step in this introduction to say a few words about the structure of the book and also each individual contribution. This is not meant to distract the reader from engaging each and every essay! It is meant to provide orientation in and through the rich banquet of inquiry found in the pages of this book.

Part 1: Biblical Trajectories and Theological Meanings

This book is divided into three parts, each of which explores the theme of property and possession in social and religious life from a unique perspective. Part 1 begins with an essay by Patrick Miller, a widely renowned scholar of Hebrew Scripture and Old Testament theology. Miller explores "Property and Possession in Light of the Ten Commandments," arguing that the Commandments set up a moral space and instigate a trajectory of thought that runs through the rest of the Bible. Importantly, Miller shows how the idea of "property" is basic to the whole Decalogue once we grasp how human beings are not to be "possessed." He not only traces this idea in terms of the Ten Commandments, but clarifies its trajectory throughout Scripture and beyond, revealing its importance for modern-day desires to foster human well-being and "good neighborhoods."

In his essay, the biblical theologian Andreas Schuele explores the theme of "love" as a social communicative process. Schuele shows how biblical discourse provides a rich conception of loving and sharing not often found in forms of thought that risk a reduction of "loving" to a property relation. In this way, Schuele's analysis finds an analogue in the work of Niklas Luhmann in social systems theory and thereby sheds light not just on love but on other social processes as well. In a contrasting way, the feminist biblical scholar Claudia Camp explores the ways in which much biblical thought reduces women to property. Entering debates about ancient Near Eastern cultures, Camp shows, in a way often missed in cultural studies, the close connection between cultural systems of honor/shame and their definition of "woman" as something that can, and indeed must, be possessed. She not only shows how this connection clarifies much biblical discourse, but also suggests that that discourse continues to resonate in the contemporary world.

The two remaining essays in Part 1 of the book move in decidedly different directions with respect to the biblical texts. In a sense, these two essays begin to chart the flow of biblical thought into the wider compass of Western life. In her contribution, "Silver Chamber Pots and Other Goods Which Are Not Good," Margaret Mitchell engages the thought of John Chrysostom, one of the most important early interpreters of St. Paul. Mitchell clarifies how this ancient Christian rhetorician is a resource for understanding the way in which the biblical texts were used in Late Antiquity, but also how they might help us today. Finally, theologian Michael Welker continues to develop a version of biblical theology. He shows how many modern Christian conceptions of "faith" are deeply subjectivist and, in fact, false abstractions (each person supposedly has some vague feeling of "dependence" on God). The typically "modern" account of faith actually manifests the same deep structure as property relations and thereby empties religious discourse of its social import. The theological task is to escape this conceptual "trap" by reclaiming a richer conception of faith found in the biblical traditions and demonstrating its significance for thought and life.

Part 2: Having and Using the Body and Material Meanings

Part 2 of this book begins with the essay "The Body and Projects of Self-Possession" by the well-known political ethicist Jean Bethke Elshtain. Elshtain examines the theme of the "body" in contemporary political discourse and suggests that increasingly we see the body as a matter of disposable property. This view of the body submits the materiality of existence to agendas of power bent on re-creating and perfecting the givenness of life. Elshtain seeks to counter this trend through the use of a richer set of concepts derived from Christian reflection. Those Christian resources, she argues, insist on the goodness of the quotidian and place limits on political power and ideals of perfection.

Elshtain's examination raises the question of how to determine when enough is enough. In her contribution, "What Is Enough? Catholic Social Thought, Consumption, and Material Sufficiency," the Roman Catholic social ethicist Christine Firer Hinze explores her own tradition's perspective on social issues. Hinze examines Roman Catholic social teaching (including the teachings of economist and ethicist John A. Ryan and liberationist social analyses) in order to respond to a culture of consumption.

Much as Part 1 of this book moved from biblical thought toward theology, so Part 2 concludes with theological reflection having traversed political, ethical, and economic reflection. The theological ethicist Charles Mathewes reclaims and revises a distinction first set forth by St. Augustine, namely, the distinction between what is to be used in life (use-value) and what is to be enjoyed (intrinsic good). Since only God can be the object of true human "enjoyment," Augustine thinks we are rightly called to "use" the world. Mathewes argues that the modern Western mind-set typically expects too much from worldly life, and that in order to curtail wanton consumption and the danger of a culture of commodified nihilism, we must reorient our affections and learn anew how rightly to use the world in relation to a higher, divine good that is enjoyed. Following Mathewes, philosophical theologian David Klemm undertakes an analysis of what it means to "possess" things and of the various forms in which "property" appears. He argues that "religious property," or grace, always appears within other forms of property, which leads him to formulate a conception of "material grace" that can be used to transform a consumerist mentality that all too often characterizes modern Western cultures. In this way, Klemm's essay deepens themes in the rest of the book by showing a distinctly theological perspective on property.

Part 3: Property and Possessions: Greed and Grace in the Social, Cultural, and Religious Imagination

The third part of the book begins, as did the previous parts, with an essay that orients the discussion around fundamental issues. William Schweiker, a theological ethicist, explores in his essay the disappearance of the language of greed in modern philosophies of commercialism. While not interested in a wholesale denunciation of capitalism, Schweiker does argue that we must "reconsider greed" in terms of moral motivation, and through his essay we come to understand the moral and religious depth of a basic human desire, the desire to "have."

Other essays in Part 3 continue the theme of "having" in the social, cultural, and religious imagination. Günter Thomas, theologian and media expert, argues in his essay that one of the crucial endangered resources in current society is human capital, especially "attention." Media culture continually seeks to capture and use human attention, while it is unable to renew that resource. Thomas reveals the Christian churches to be places where this crucial cultural resource can be regenerated, redirected, and invested outside the economy of attention. Following Thomas, Hebrew Scripture scholar David Gunn, in "Identity, Possession, and Myth on the Web: Yearning for Jerusalem," analyzes the story of possession found on the official website of the State of Israel. He demonstrates how biblical ideas about the divine right to possess "the Land" continue to fund contemporary political ideas, and how they continue to have real-life consequences as well.

Two essays conclude Part 3 by pressing the inquiry into the complex connection between economic and theological rationality. In "Avarice, Prudence, and the Bourgeois Virtues," world-renowned economic historian Deirdre McCloskey examines the connection between moral virtue and economic life. Seeking to overcome the contemporary divide between economics and ethics, she returns to the insights of Adam Smith and seeks to recall and, when necessary, revise Smith's moral theory. In the next essay, the Dutch economic historian Arjo Klamer broadens the notion of property and possession to include social and cultural as well as economic capital. In so doing, he seeks to find common ground for a dialogue between economists and theologians and to facilitate an exchange of the generally divergent perspectives held by these two groups. Finally, theologian Kathryn Tanner draws together many of the themes of Part 3 of the book in a way that parallels the discussion of David Klemm that ended Part 2 and Michael Welker's essay in Part 1. Specifically, Tanner seeks to isolate an "economy" of grace in Christian thought that reveals points of contact and also radical departure from modern economic theory, especially that of Locke. While the discourse of the "gift" has been used in much current thought in order to break overly economistic conceptions of human interaction (a concept we saw addressed in David Klemm's essay), for Tanner a different logic of Christian faith pertains. In this way, Tanner shows the distinctive contribution theological reflection makes to wider cultural and public concerns.

Conclusion

In this introduction we have tried to specify the basic purpose of this book, indicate its general approach, and provide a brief account of each contribution. But all of this is of course introductory. The reader is encouraged to work through the book, engage and challenge specific essays, and chart the complex connections between and among parts of the book and individual contributions. It is our hope that the reader bear in mind that the purpose of this book reaches well beyond its pages. Each and every contribution seeks to inspire reflection in the service of confronting challenges now facing people around the world. Some of the resources, but by no means all, needed to meet these challenges are to be found in the biblical religions. Our task is to show how those resources help us to understand the problems facing us and also offer some genuine possibilities for human life. For too long the examination of culture has neglected the decisive, if ambiguous, roles that religious beliefs and practices play in the social imagination. Our job is to overcome that neglect in the hope of thereby better understanding the place of having in human life.

Part 1   Property and Possession:
         Biblical Trajectories and
         Theological Meanings

Property and Possession in Light of the Ten Commandments

Patrick D. Miller

The Commandments As Cultural Code

Within the culture(s) where the Ten Commandments function, they do so as a kind of cultural code. The code character is suggested in at least two ways. One is reflected in their symbolic role. The Commandments are, in effect, a cultural icon, one that, like other icons, can be an object of true devotion and a relic on the wall — or in some instances both simultaneously, as would seem to be the case, for example, for the Alabama judge who has insisted that the Commandments be posted in his courtroom. They are immediately known by all members of the culture, even those who do not self-consciously identify themselves with the community for whom they are constitutive. They are the subject of sermons and jokes, books and cartoons. They are seen as both foundational and simplistic. Their normative and definitive character is assumed, again by the culture generally and often precisely because they are a cultural icon rather than because they have been appropriated as the formal teaching of a religious community, though that has contributed to their cultural status. There tends to be a general assumption that in the Commandments, the culture is given a set of universals — for which some case can be made, but primarily by way of the particular story out of which the Commandments come, a story that rarely functions as a part of the code. The disappearance of the story is a facet of the loss of cultural memory, or the loss of community memory in the experience of "historical oblivion" that characterizes contemporary culture with its "perpetual present amid perpetual change."[1] The imaginative power of the story

1. William Schweiker, unpublished working paper, p. 5.

that grounds and makes the Commandments intelligible has succumbed in large ways to the "infinity of images of possible worlds and lives" circulated by the media.[2] The power of the icon is deflated or the story is "mediaized" into a historical thriller or a cartoon.[3] Or, as happened in a cartoon that implicitly puts down the Alabama judge, the students who went on a murderous rampage in Littleton, Colorado (or their unidentified equivalents), are depicted as saying that if there had only been a set of the Ten Commandments on the wall, they, of course, would not have gone out and killed people. It speaks volumes that such a cartoon is probably reflective of a generally liberal moral perspective that has failed to perceive what the Alabama judge understood about the Commandments as a cultural icon.

A second way in which the Commandments function in the culture as a code lies in the fact that when the simple code language is deciphered or interpreted, important messages are thereby transmitted, some of which are not fully self-evident in the simple code. Those messages have everything to do with the character of life in the community, with its values, its relationships, its economy, and its identity.[4] It is in behalf of this dimension of the cultural code that this essay seeks to engage in an act of decipherment and interpretation toward reading the Commandments in thick fashion to recover the fulsome way in which they address the culture about goods, signs, valuation, and the way the culture in which they operate is meant to take on the character of a neighborhood. Human interrelationships in behalf of life and the valuing of life are articulated in complex ways so that property and possessions are defined, enhanced, and protected not only from encroachments by the neighbor but also from the greed that devises modes of economic oppression — legal and illegal — against those whose property makes them vulnerable to an intrusive acquisitiveness.[5]

---

2. William Schweiker, "Encounter, Character and Responsibility: Meaningful Texts on the Model of a Moral Outlook," a paper delivered at the Society of Biblical Literature Annual Meeting in November 1998.

3. In 1999, *Theology Today* included a strong critique by a prison inmate of the cartoon film "Prince of Egypt" for its distortion of the biblical story, which vitiates the story-telling role of the religious community by replacing its powerful story with a cartoon. See Leroy Gardner, "The Prince of Darkness," *Theology Today* 56 (1999): 396-98.

4. The issues of identity have to do both with the self-understanding of the culture as a whole, whose identity is articulated in a deceptively simple but enduring and strong way in the prologue to the Decalogue and the commandments that follow, and with matters of personal or self identity of its individual constituents.

5. It may be argued that the intention of the Book of Deuteronomy in its final redaction is to make an offer of life and good to the community (e.g., Deut. 30:15-20), one that is to be found in its living by the polity set forth in the book, a polity that is rooted in the Com-

The Commandments As Starting Point

In the Christian tradition, reflection on the place of property and its use and misuse takes its starting point from the Commandments. It can be argued — and such argument is implicit in the following — that the single largest issue or concern of the Commandments as a whole is the matter of property and possession. The aim of this essay is to ask how the Commandments help us think about property and possession as a significant dimension of human society and culture.

The specific starting point for this analysis is the most explicit connection between the Commandments and property: the prohibition against stealing.[6] While this commandment remains the focus throughout, other commandments will be brought into the picture to show how the Decalogue as a whole comes at the question of property and society from many angles. The process for discovering the Commandments' way of illumining human thought and action about property and culture involves the uncovering of a trajectory of meaning and effect, of thought and action, that flows out of the Commandments and serves to mark out and define a moral space for life with God and others or, to put it more concretely, to create a "good neighborhood."[7]

---

mandments. On Deuteronomy as a kind of polity for ordering community life, see S. Dean McBride, "The Polity of the Covenant People: The Book of Deuteronomy," *Interpretation* 41 (1987): 229-44.

6. In some religious traditions — for example, Lutheran and Jewish — this commandment is regarded as the seventh commandment, while in others — for example, Reformed and Orthodox — it is the eighth commandment. The numeration of the Commandments in this essay will be according to the Reformed tradition. There are various justifications for the different numerations and inferences that can be drawn from the variations, but they are not pertinent to the interpretation of the prohibition against stealing. For further discussion, see Eduard Nielsen, *The Ten Commandments in New Perspective: A Tradition-Historical Approach* (London: SCM, 1968), pp. 6-34.

7. Three spatial and structural images are used here: trajectory, moral space, and good neighborhood. All of them, and particularly the notion of trajectory, are fundamental to the approach that is laid out in the following pages. By that I mean to suggest that the Commandments begin to have their effect in an apparent simplicity, but as they are elaborated and specified, as they play themselves out in the life of the people Israel, as they are carried forward by the community into new situations and on into the New Testament and beyond, they open up and each one effects a dynamic, that is, a "trajectory," a flow of meaning, action, and effects to broaden in complex but coherent ways the possibilities or implications of the Commandments. With the notion of "moral space," for which I am indebted to Charles Taylor by way of William Schweiker, I have in mind the capacity, indeed the intention, of the Commandments to mark out the area in which life is to be lived. They define a locus for life, an inviting place that is filled

PATRICK D. MILLER

The Eighth Commandment: Against Stealing

The commandment, "you shall not steal" or "do not steal," is one whose force seems clear and whose moral pertinence is universally accepted.[8] The matter is a little more complicated than that, however, for this commandment has a specificity that opens up into a broader horizon of application from the beginning, and its trajectory of meaning and effect is already underway when we encounter it in the Decalogue. The substantive word of the commandment, "steal," means exactly what it suggests: to take from another and to do so by stealth, that is, under cover. There is an immediate problem, however, having to do with the implicit sanction or punishment for disobedience of this command. The other commandments are clearly identified as a kind of absolute law, for when we find forms of them in the Book of the Covenant or in the Deuteronomic law, they regularly are crimes for which the penalty is death. For example, Exodus 21:12 and 15:

> Whoever strikes a person mortally shall be put to death (sixth commandment);

> Whoever strikes father or mother shall be put to death (fifth commandment).

In the statutes of the Book of the Covenant, there are several cases in Exodus 22 that deal with theft of property — for example, a work animal or a food

---

with things that show us how to live and make us feel at home. Such spatial imagery is reflected in the way that others speak about the Commandments when they talk about their giving "latitude" or about their marking the "boundaries," serving as "fence posts," or providing large "areas" of freedom. The notion of "good neighborhood" is a specifying of the more neutral language of moral space, with particular reference to the Commandments' usage of the term neighbor and to the enshrining of the wholeness of the Commandments in the imperative of the Great Commandment to "love your neighbor." The Commandments specify what such neighbor love is like and thus lay out the design for a good neighborhood.

8. In one of the most recent studies of the Commandments, one hundred pages are devoted to discussion of the individual commandments and never less than five pages on any single commandment, except for the commandment against stealing, to which only two pages are given over (Werner Schmidt together with Holger Delkurt and Axel Graupner, *Die Zehn Gebote im Rahmen Alttestamentlicher Ethik* [Erträge der Forschung; Darmstadt: Wissenschaftliche Buchgesellschaft, 1993], pp. 122-24).

The Catholic biblical scholar Vincenz Hamp states the agreed-upon moral pertinence rather straightforwardly: "The ethical consciousness of all men concurs that stealing is wrong" (*Theological Dictionary of the Old Testament*, ed. G. Johannes Botterweck and Helmer Ringgren [Grand Rapids: Eerdmans, 1978], vol. 3, p. 45).

animal. In each case, there is economic restitution by the thief, not capital punishment. The one other case where an act of stealing is involved follows the two cases cited above about striking a person or striking father or mother and, like them, prescribes the death penalty: "Whoever steals a man, whether he sells him or is found in possession of him, shall be put to death" (Exod. 21:16 RSV). Deuteronomy reiterates this point in the only statute in the Deuteronomic Code that specifically refers to stealing: "If a man is found stealing one of his brethren, the people of Israel, and he treats him as a slave or sells him, then that thief shall die" (Deut. 24:7 RSV). The original force of the commandment, therefore, still operative by its specification in the two re-lated codes of law, is the freedom or protection of the individual, a prohibi-tion against the theft of a person and the conversion of the "personal" good into property for economic exploitation. No member of the community can appropriate any other member of the community illegally or against his or her will for economic gain or advantage.

The *story* of this commandment begins early in the Old Testament when Joseph says from prison in Egypt, "I was stolen out of the land of the Hebrews" (Gen. 40:15). That story is revealing for the way in which it depicts the effects of the stealing of Joseph: the loss of home and family, enslavement in Egypt, subjection to imprisonment through the false accusations of his master's wife. What is particularly noticeable in this story and in the laws that have to do with stealing persons is that stealing a person's freedom is virtually always a matter of economics, the theft of a person for economic gain, turning the stolen object into a human machine of productivity. Ju-dah's comment to his brothers is, "What *profit [beṣaʿ]* is it if we kill our brother. . .? Come, let us *sell* him . . ." (Gen. 37:26, italics added). The statutes prohibiting stealing a person assume in each instance that the purpose is to sell or ransom the individual. Thus every attempt to enslave, to restrict the freedom of, and to coerce and force economic production from one's brother or neighbor is a violation of the eighth commandment. The slave trade thus gets its first blow under the hammer of freedom and economic protection that is the eighth commandment, and the Commandments are seen to uncover a complex of legal and justice-shaped specifics about slavery that begin with the free Israelite but move out into other relationships that involve both the non-free and thus not-equal Israelite and the outsider or foreigner — for the question of persons as property is also taken up in the Sabbath Commandment and the complex of statutes that unfold its moral ethos.

In the Deuteronomic form of the Sabbath Commandment, the purpose of the Sabbath rest is "so that your male and female slave may rest as well as you" (Deut. 5:14). The trajectory of this commandment is best seen in the establishment of the *sabbatical principle,* articulated in Deuteronomy 15, which provides for release of debts and of slaves in the seventh year.[9] Not only do the sabbatical laws provide for release of the bondage of debt and servitude at regular intervals, but they insist that liberality must be the response to the person in need even if the sabbatical year is near (Deut. 15:9). The slave is to be released, and not just with ten dollars and a suit of clothes; the one who has benefited from the productivity of the bond servant is to "Provide liberally out of your flock, your threshing floor, and your wine press, thus giving to him some of the bounty with which the LORD your God has blessed you" (Deut. 15:14).

Furthermore, if the slave is well provided for in your home, he or she may *choose* to stay there and enjoy the benefit of your blessing forever. In Deuteronomy 15, of course, the issue is not the violent act of kidnapping for economic enslavement; it is the legal servitude of a person because of economic deprivation. The issue is still and even more so an economic one, however, and a further blow to economic enslavement or economic control of the life and productivity of another person is given. So the Commandments, as their complexity is spelled out in statute and story — and there is a narrative about the release of slaves in Jeremiah 34 — begin to open up a way of acting that transforms the servant who is in economic *bondage* into the recipient of economic *benefit,* while the recipient of the productivity, the master, becomes the dispenser of the benefit to the slave, who is either freed with economic goods or given a permanent place at the table of blessing and prosperity (Deut. 15:13, 16).

It is not to be denied that slavery in different forms existed in ancient Israel and is recognized in the laws. What is evident from the legal literature that may be connected to the Commandments, however, is that the legal tradition *implicitly* acknowledged the reality of persons coming into bondage of various sorts, either by capture in war or by bonded indebtedness because of financial obligations (practices that were standard in the world of ancient Israel's time), but *explicitly* was concerned particularly to provide procedures that humanized and restricted oppressive and permanent enslavement. The biblical narratives and stories attest to the way in which creditors could seize defaulting debtors or their dependents to exploit their labor or to sell them (e.g., 2 Kings 4:1; Neh. 5:5; Isa. 50:1; Amos 2:6; 8:6). The laws address the treatment of such persons so as to limit the possibility of exploitation

---

9. See Patrick D. Miller, "The Human Sabbath: A Study in Deuteronomic Theology," *The Princeton Seminary Bulletin* 6 (1985): 81-97.

and to protect against permanent enslavement. They also seek, especially in the Book of the Covenant, to preserve the interests of the creditor or master (e.g., Exod. 21:2-11). In the Deuteronomic form of the debt laws — probably a later development than the Book of the Covenant — the legal tradition is less concerned about the creditor's/master's continued economic benefit and more concerned about the renewal of economic possibility for the debtor servant (Deut. 15:7-17; see above). The selling of oneself, and especially the selling of one's children, was a practice in Israel as it was in other states, but this was an act *in extremis* (2 Kings 4:1; Neh. 5:5), and the legal tradition manifests a concern, already reflected in the Decalogue and continuing in the statutes and ordinances, for humane protection against oppressive enslavement. The concern of the laws was not to provide for bonded indebtedness, but to ensure that one could get out of it. The treatment of women in the slave law in Exodus 21:2-11 shows that they were more vulnerable to legal permanent enslavement than males, depending upon their status, but the laws also reflect some concerns both with regard to the captive slave who has become a wife and with regard to the enslaved daughter (Exod. 21:2-11; Deut. 21:10-14).[10]

10. In her important and comprehensive treatment of Exodus 21:2-11, Carolyn Pressler reaches the following conclusion:

> The exclusion of the enslaved daughter from the law of release in Exod. 21.2 has often been taken as the basis for sweepingly general statements about the status of women in the earliest period of Israelite history. That women were property, that women could not own property, that women were not part of the covenant community, or, at the least, that all slave women were concubines and therefore permanently bound to their masters. Recent discussions of women and the slave laws, perhaps partly in reaction to such negative generalizations, argue that the bondsmen and bondswomen were treated with marked parity; the bondswoman would either be freed under the law of release (v. 2) or by becoming the free wife of her master.
>
> The evidence does not justify either such negative or such positive generalizations. The wife's status follows that of her husband. The daughter is under her father's extensive control. Her ultimate status depends upon his decisions; still, she has some customary rights. The slave wife of a free man does not have the status of a free wife, but neither is she merely a chattel. The legal status of the slave wife of a bondsman does appear to be as a chattel, though even in her case there is a hint of her humanity in the bondsman's motivation [love of his wife and children] for choosing permanent servitude.

("Wives and Daughters, Bond and Free: Views of Women in the Slave Laws of Exodus 21.2-11," in *Gender and Law in the Hebrew Bible and the Ancient Near East,* ed. Victor H. Matthews, Bernard M. Levinson, and Tikva Frymer-Kensky, Journal for the Study of the Old Testament Suppl. Series 262 [Sheffield: Sheffield Academic, 1998], p. 172.) Pressler's work is especially attentive to the differences that a woman's role made in the way that the law worked, arguing cogently, for

The jubilee year law of Leviticus 25 is the most explicit in recognizing permanent slavery as an acceptable practice for captives taken in war or for resident aliens who became slaves (25:44-46). Such slaves may be passed on to the next generation, and there is no mechanism for their release. There is, thus, a limit to the effect on slavery of the commandment's trajectory.

Even here, however, the point is made in the context of a passage that is more explicit than any other in ensuring that no fellow Israelite ("your brother") shall be made into a slave even if he is forced to hire himself out for a time because of becoming impoverished. The divine deliverance from slavery in Egypt is the motivating force for the law (25:42). The jubilee law is there to protect against permanent slavery. The distinction between the treatment of the brother/neighbor and the foreigner in this context is the reason the identity of one's brother/neighbor is such a freighted moral issue in Scripture (Luke 10:29).

There is a kind of realism at work here that recognizes that human beings do become caught in economic bondage but insists that the legal system protect them from being permanently bound and provide opportunity for them to break free and resources to start afresh. It is revealing that these laws are regularly read in our time as a kind of utopianism, which is to say that we assume a moral world where economic bondage has to be permanent and the unreality is thinking one can get free of it.[11] The realism of the Commandments and the dynamic that flows from them is that economic bondage is real but not required and not perduring.[12]

A further development on the trajectory of this commandment is the brief statute in Deuteronomy 23:15-16, which forbids the return of a slave who

example, that widows, abandoned wives, and other women deprived of male protection were treated in the laws like male slaves and released in the year of release (pp. 167-72).

Further on slavery, see Victor H. Matthews, "The Anthropology of Slavery in the Covenant Code," in *Theory and Method in Biblical and Cuneiform Law: Revision, Interpolation, and Development*, ed. Bernard M. Levinson, Journal for the Study of the Old Testament Suppl. Series 181 (Sheffield: Sheffield Academic, 1994), p. 133; and more extensively, Carolyn Pressler, *The View of Women Found in the Deuteronomic Family Laws*, Beihefte zur Zeitschrift für die alttestamentliche Wissenschaft series, 216 (Berlin: W. de Gruyter, 1993), pp. 9-15.

11. There is hardly an instance in which I have discussed Deuteronomy 15 with students or others that someone has not asserted that what is reflected here must have been a utopian program that was surely never in effect.

12. Whatever judgment may be made about the viability of such provisions for release of debt and debt slavery, there are plenty of analogues to such provisions in ancient Mesopotamia in the form of royal edicts of release. For general discussion of these ancient Near Eastern analogues, see Jeffries M. Hamilton, *Social Justice and Deuteronomy: The Case of Deuteronomy 15*, Society of Biblical Literature Dissertation Series 136 (Atlanta: Scholars Press, 1992), pp. 45-72.

has escaped from his master to Israel. Not only is a forced return to the slave owner forbidden — and in this case the text may envision other kinds of servitude than bonded indebtedness, which is the primary focus of Deuteronomy 15 — but the escaped slave is given great possibility for new life. He (or she) can reside wherever he wishes anywhere in Israel. The expression that is used in this context — "in the place which he shall choose" (RSV) — is the same Deuteronomic expression as is used to speak of the freedom of the Lord of Israel "to choose" a place of dwelling for his people and his name (e.g., Deut. 12:5). The escaped slave from another country is as free to find a satisfactory place in Israel as the Lord is free to find a place for the name of the Lord to dwell. Thus begins the possibility of sanctuary in its truest sense, not merely a means of protection but the possibility for new life in freedom. And within the community that lives by this dynamic of freedom, such sanctuary is not an option; it is a part of the systemic structure by which the community orders its life.

The trajectory of meaning and action that is unfolded out of the eighth commandment, to which the Sabbath Commandment attaches itself, thus begins in a specific and critical safeguard of human freedom that is hidden but real. It is real, as the other laws indicate. It is hidden because we only discern it from the other statutes. For there is, obviously, no object to the word "steal" in the commandment itself. That absence of a restricting object opens up the trajectory to include the prohibition against the covert act to rob a person of his or her *property,* as well as of his or her *life.* So the law develops a body of casuistic law that identifies all sorts of ways in which one might steal from another and prohibits them or requires restitution when the theft happens and the thief is caught. Two illustrative examples, one complex of laws from the Book of the Covenant and one from the Deuteronomic Code, will help to make this point.

The Legal Trajectory of the Commandment against Stealing

The Book of the Covenant (Exodus 20:22–23:33)

In Exodus 22:1 and the verses that follow, the Book of the Covenant begins a set of laws, running through verse 15, that have to do with theft and restitution. This is where the word for "stealing" that we find in the eighth commandment comes into play most often in the Book of the Covenant. Several things may be observed:

1. The object of theft in one instance is "money or goods" (v. 7). In most

cases, the object is an ox, a donkey, a sheep, or a coat (once, in v. 9: "cloth-ing"). The reason for that repeated reference to animals is fairly obvious. These animals are the work and food and clothing animals, the means of economic support. The specifying of the eighth commandment is thus seen to focus particularly upon its protection not of property generally, though that is indicated in verse 9 with reference to "any other loss," but specifically of *the means of livelihood and production* for each member of the community. At least at this point on the trajectory and within the moral space created by the commandment, it is not a matter of general property rights but of what human beings, a family, need for support, need in order to provide food and clothing.

2. The concern for theft opens up more generally the matter of loss of property — loss again of the means of subsistence such as work and food and clothing animals but also grain in the field, whether by intention (that is, by theft) or by accident (for example, livestock grazing or fire, in verses 5-6). The eighth commandment thus leads into the large area of restitution and restoration as well as the maintenance of justice and fair dealing.

3. A series of these statutes has to do with safekeeping and borrowing the goods of another (vv. 10-13). In other words, relation to a neighbor's property and possession is not just a matter of possible theft or accidental damage but of the relationship of trust and what Michael Welker calls the "social virtue" of readiness to help and to assist a neighbor by, for example, loaning an animal to help in cultivation or keeping something for someone who is away on a trip. The endangerment of this social virtue is addressed in these statutes as cases are dealt with where one cannot easily determine what has happened. If goods kept for someone are stolen, how does the owner know this was not simply a theft by the neighbor who was keeping them? Statutes might have been set up saying the safekeeper was required to make full restitution. Then who would ever agree to help out in this way and risk loss? Or the practice might have been the other way: The one who asked for help put himself or herself at risk. Too bad. Bad luck. Either alternative, however, would create a communal climate of mistrust and reticence to help or seek help, breaking down the fabric of social trust on which a moral ethos depends. The difficult issue here is given a cultic and public mode of resolution: the persons are to be brought before God for a decision. In one statute (22:10-13), provision is made for "an oath before the LORD"; so the third commandment, against misusing the divine name, comes into play to undergird the protection of property further. Perjury can and did happen, but the danger of mistrust is addressed as the community knows now that the matter is also under divine sanction and the community can remember the divine decision. Further,

should mistrust be directed toward one who was truly innocent, that member of the community can live strengthened in the knowledge of his or her righteousness before God.[13]

4. The references to ox and donkey and sheep, which are central to the theft and property laws, carry us forward to the other references to these animals in statutes that follow. One statute provides for the giving of the first-born of sheep and oxen to the Lord, thus relativizing the possibility of setting an absolute worth on even those things that sustain and provide for life (Exod. 22:30). The members of the community are reminded in this act that their access to the land is through God's allotment, that property first belongs to the Lord and only, but importantly, secondarily to the family and the community. This is symbolized precisely in the relinquishment of the property that the statutes work so carefully to safeguard. Thus the eighth commandment is seen to lead not only to ad hoc protection of property but to regular relinquishment of it. In these statutes, inalienable right to property is given up while its protection is ensured in a pragmatic and coherent complex of individual, communal, and divine interaction. And the community is reminded that its access to property is not by any *right* at all but by God's gift and God's providence.

5. The ox and donkey, who are the primary focus of the theft cases, come in again in Exodus 23:4-5. These are two brief case laws having to do with the way in which one responds to the property not just of a neighbor but of one who is identified as an enemy (though this might be someone in the community). The second of the two laws has to do with finding an animal of one's enemy resting while carrying a load. It appears as if the statute is meant to instruct the person in such a situation to leave the animal alone and not to interfere with the property of someone with whom you have a hostile relationship.[14] The divine instruction about loving one's enemy thus begins not

13. Michael Welker, "Recht in den biblischen Überlieferungen in systematisch-theologischer Sicht," in *Das Recht der Kirche*, vol. 1: *Zur Theorie des Kirchenrechts*, ed. Gerhard Rau, Hans-Richard Reuter, and Klaus Schlaich (Gütersloh: Gütersloher Verlaghaus, 1997), pp. 398-401.

14. The interpretation of Exodus 23:5 is a notorious crux. It has typically been read as depicting an animal in distress because of its load and requiring the one encountering it to relieve the animal. Such a reading, however, which is as ancient as the Greek text, requires finding new roots in the text and ignoring what seems to be the plain reading of the text. No reading, however, is without its problems. For this reason, the interpretation of this text is dependent upon Exodus 23:4, where the text is much clearer. As will be seen below, the taking up of Exodus 23:5 in Deuteronomy 22:1-4 is much clearer and follows along the general direction of the statute in Exodus 23:4. On these verses, see Alan Cooper, "The Plain Sense of Exodus 23:5," *Hebrew Union College Annual* 59 (1988): 1-22; and Hans Joechen Boecker, "'Feindesliebe' im alttestamentlichen

in the New Testament but in the moral dynamic effected by the eighth commandment. Here, in effect, is a precursor to contemporary "Good Samaritan" laws, the legal accountability for attending to and not ignoring the need of one's neighbor.[15]

The trajectory of the eighth commandment continues as the Deuteronomic Code takes up the law of Exodus 23:4-5 in Deuteronomy 22:1-4 and elaborates it further. The Deuteronomic statute makes taking responsibility for property applicable explicitly to the brother or sister in the community, to one's compatriot now as well as to one's enemy. The Deuteronomic version expands the statute in two ways: (a) to include the coat or garment of one's neighbor or anything that is the neighbor's; and (b) to require that one take the straying animal into one's own safekeeping until it is possible to get it back to the neighbor.[16] It also clearly reads the second of the Exodus statutes as having to do with an animal that is not just resting under its burden but has fallen because of the load and so needs help. The Deuteronomic language is striking at one particular point. The term regularly translated as "ignore" is literally "hide oneself." The repetition of this term underscores the responsibility of the neighbor to move in positively and take actions to help secure the neighbor's property, to keep it safe and from harm, a facet of the trajectory that is developed in the Reformed tradition and elsewhere. *Passivity and inaction* are prohibited ("You may not withhold your help," v. 3), which means that positive action for the good is expected.[17] Nor is this simply responding to the neighbor's request for safekeeping of property. The eighth commandment thus does not simply inhibit us from mugging someone on the street or robbing a bank — exceedingly important inhibitions but responses to the commandment that work in a more passive way. It serves to effect a more systemic activity to ensure the economic sufficiency of our neighbor, a systemic

---

Recht? Überlegungen zu Ex 23,4-5," in *Verbindungslinien: Festschrift für Werner H. Schmidt zum 65. Geburtstag,* ed. Axel Graupner, Holger Delkurt, and Alexander B. Ernst (Neukirchen-Vluyn: Neukirchener Verlag, 2000), pp. 18-25.

15. Such accounting for the property of one's neighbor need not be elicited only by the legal system. It may come to play in a "neighborhood" by a Neighborhood Watch system. Or it may operate without any enforcement or formal system at all but as a practice among neighbors. An issue of *Newsweek* reported on a largely black neighborhood outside Washington, D.C., where a black couple watched the home of a newly arrived white couple while they were away for the holidays. "It helps validate the values we've established here as a community," said the husband of the black couple (January 17, 2000, p. 62).

16. On the way in which the Deuteronomic statute builds upon the text of Exodus 23:4, see Michael Fishbane, *Biblical Interpretation in Ancient Israel* (Oxford: Clarendon, 1985), pp. 177-79.

17. In fact, the hiding of oneself is already a kind of action but it is a *negative* action.

activity that is not even vulnerable to likes and dislikes, to favoritisms and antipathies, to hostilities and enmity between members of the community. One might call this "the economics of the straying ox." The force of the commandment is not simply that if I (that is, the one addressed by the statute) steal the property of my neighbor, I have to make restitution. It is also that if I find my neighbor's ox straying, *I cannot hide myself from the reality of my neighbor's economic endangerment.* I have to take the ox in, watch over it, and protect it, making sure that the property is returned so that my compatriot is able to use this ox to provide for the needs of life. The same applies with my brother or sister's donkey or a coat or any kind of property that belongs to them. I am drawn into active responsibility for securing my neighbor's economic well-being by securing and protecting his or her property, what Deirdre McCloskey calls "imaginative entry into the interests of others."[18] The eighth commandment here carries forward into the creation of a communal disposition to watch for the economic endangerment of other members of the community and not to hide from it behind gated communities and the walling-off, literally or figuratively, of the ghettos of the economically endangered.

The Deuteronomic Code (Deuteronomy 12–26)

The text just analyzed moves the discussion into the Deuteronomic Code as another example of the development of a trajectory of meaning and effect flowing out of the eighth commandment. In Deuteronomy 24:6 and the following verses, there are indications that some of the statutes in this group — not all of them — belong to the trajectory of the eighth commandment. One such indicator is the fact that scholars who have argued for viewing the Deuteronomic Code as structured according to the order of the Ten Commandments regard these statutes in Deuteronomy 24 as belonging to the section that explicates the commandment against stealing and moving into the sphere of the commandment against false witness.[19] The second indication

18. See Deirdre McCloskey's essay in this volume, p. 316.

19. See especially S. A. Kaufman, "The Structure of the Deuteronomic Law," *MAARAV* (1978-79): 105-58; Georg Braulik, "The Sequence of the Laws in Deuteronomy 12-16 and in the Decalogue," in *A Song of Power and the Power of Song: Essays on the Book of Deuteronomy*, ed. Duane L. Christensen (Winona Lake, Ind.: Eisenbrauns, 1993), pp. 313-35; Georg Braulik, *Die deuteronomischen Gesetze und der Dekalog: Studien zum Aufbau von Deuteronomium 12–26*, Stuttgarter Bibel-Studien series 145 (Stuttgart: Verlag Katholisches Bibelwerk, 1991); and Dennis J. Olson, *Deuteronomy and the Death of Moses: A Theological Reading*, Overtures to Biblical

that these statutes belong to the dynamic of the eighth commandment is that the statute against stealing persons and enslaving and selling them, which, as suggested above, is the starting point of the trajectory of the eighth commandment, is a part of this grouping, specifically Deuteronomy 24:7: "If someone is caught stealing the *nephesh*, the life, of his brother/sister, enslaving or selling him or her, that thief shall die" (my translation). In an associative process effected by "catchword,"[20] this statute is connected to the immediately preceding one by the reference there also to *nephesh* or "life": "No one shall take a mill or an upper millstone in pledge, for that would be taking a life in pledge." A close association is made between the theft of a person's life (the *nephesh*) and the economic deprivation of a person's life (the *nephesh*) by confiscating the primary means of providing bread on the table, millstones for grinding grain on which one may subsist. Here, of course, the statute is not talking about stealing but about legitimate financial dealings — loans and collateral. Alongside a basic statute that deals directly with stealing a life is set a corollary of the protection of life: the protection of the means of subsistence for life from *legal* deprivation. And the eighth commandment is seen to be open to a situation in which the neighbor may be in economic need and his or her property vulnerable to loss in legitimate but not moral ways.

The opening of the statutes to the question of loans and pledges as well as the protection of the means of subsistence as a sphere of moral space in which the eighth commandment is worked out connects then with other cases in these verses. So in verses 10-13, the economic advantage a member of the community has over another one by holding a pledge may not be used to encroach on the property of another ("you shall not go into the house to take the pledge" — v. 10) or to deprive another of the basic needs for life ("If the person is poor, you shall not sleep in the garment given you as the pledge. You shall give the pledge back by sunset, so that your neighbor may sleep in the cloak" — vv. 12-13).[21] And now it becomes clear why the coat or garment is included in the list of things that may be lost and must be returned if found (Exod. 22:9; Deut. 22:3). That this was a real issue is illustrated by a seventh-century Hebrew inscription in which a laborer, a grain harvester who speaks of himself as "your servant," petitions a higher-up to have his coat returned, a

---

Theology series (Minneapolis: Fortress, 1994). For other efforts to connect the statutes and the ordinances of Deuteronomy structurally to the Decalogue, see the essay by Braulik. No two persons see the arrangement in relation to the Decalogue exactly the same way, and the analysis given here is not precisely like any of the other proposals.

20. Note the comment of Braulik that "legal material is inserted according to key words or associative ideas" ("The Sequence of the Laws," p. 320).

21. See the related statute in Exodus 22:25-27.

coat that had been taken from him by Hoshaiah, presumably the overseer of the labor force.[22] There is no word of a loan or pledge but the right of the poor or laborer to have his or her basic needs protected is the inferred ground of the appeal.

The statute about the pledge of the *poor* in Deuteronomy 24:12 then leads into further statutes that have to do with the protection of the weaker members of the society and their material goods or means of life. So the "poor," whose collateral coat is protected, also have their wages covered in the statutes and with a similar motivation: verse 15 reads, "You shall pay them their wages daily before sunset, because they are poor and their livelihood [*nephesh,* also translated 'life'] depends on them" (cf. Jer. 22:13). The concern for the *nephesh,* the life, that is at the heart of the basic Deuteronomic formulation of the eighth commandment ("If a stealer of a *nephesh* is found . . ." — 24:7)[23] once again is the ground for further directive, this time about protection of wages.

The instruction about how to act vis-à-vis pledges continues, then, with reference to the pledge of a widow in verse 17 and thereby opens up the whole matter of appropriate justice for widow, orphan, and stranger or alien — appropriate justice being economic support rather than economic deprivation. Thus the final laws in Deuteronomy 24 have to do with leaving grain, olives, and grapes in the fields rather than scavenging every last one, so that the widow, orphan, and alien may have access to the productivity of the allotment of land that was given by God for the sustenance of the community as a whole and thus for each clan and, within each clan, for each individual. As time and circumstance have altered people's situation and pressed some into poverty, without goods and the fundamental possession of land on which to support themselves, the eighth commandment uncovers a process for accessing the land and its productivity.

A significant feature of this series of laws in Deuteronomy — and one also present in other statutes discussed above — is their *parenetic* character, specifically the presence of *motivation clauses* that encourage and rationalize

---

22. "A Letter from the Time of Josiah," in *The Ancient Near East: Supplementary Texts and Pictures Relating to the Old Testament,* ed. James B. Pritchard (Princeton, N.J.: Princeton University Press, 1968), p. 132.

23. This is my translation of the verse. The word *nephesh* in Deuteronomy 24:7, which provides a thematic word for connecting this statute to laws that precede and follow, is not used in the Book of the Covenant, where the expression is *'îš gōnēb.* The use of *gānab* only in 5:19 (the commandment) and 24:7 in Deuteronomy and in the parallel law in the Book of the Covenant (Exod. 21:16) confirms the clear connection between 24:7 and the eighth commandment. The rest of the formulation then provides a further linguistic chain of association among these statutes.

obedience. In the sequence of laws flowing out of the eighth commandment in Deuteronomy 24:10 and the following verses, motivation clauses of particular sorts are regularly included. They may be grouped into three categories:

1. In verse 13, the requirement to give back a garment taken in pledge from a poor person is undergirded by the promise that such action "shall be righteousness [ṣedāqâ] to you before the LORD your God" (RSV). The protection of property, which has to do not with a general view of property rights but with the daily need of the neighbor whose economic well-being is endangered, is specifically identified as a feature of the relationship with God, as a manifestation of one's conformity to the order that God wills for human life and for the world. The statute that prohibits a stripping clean of the fields and olive orchards (vv. 19-20) is reinforced with the promise that such provision for the sustenance of widow, orphan, and stranger will bring about God's blessing upon those who act in this way. Thus two of these statutes — returning a pledged garment and leaving remnants in the field — identify conformity to the system effected in these laws as bringing about two of the primary outcomes for human life before God: righteousness and blessing. Protection and provision of economic goods is not an end in itself; nor is it simply beneficial for those who are protected. There is a reciprocity here, but it is not between the obeyer of the statute and the beneficiary of that obedience. The one who obeys is enhanced, but that enhancement is a divine response to the keeping of the statute. While it is customary to think about the consequences of law in terms of the consequences of disobedience, these statutes focus upon the positive benefits of obedience and see the enhancement of the property-less and the property-endangered as effecting an enhancement of the one who so acts.

2. The statutes just described are then paralleled by those having to do with the pledge of a widow (vv. 17-18) and with the leaving of residue in vineyards as well as in grain fields and olive orchards (vv. 21-22). Here, the motivation to obedience is an appeal to memory, a paradigmatic example of what Jan Assmann has described as cultural memory, the "motor" memory (so Levi-Strauss) that funds present action.[24] The memory of the past — not the experience of the past but a memory that is held by those who did not experience the recollected past[25] but experience the past in recollection — effects a

---

24. Jan Assmann, *Das kulturelle Gedächtnis: Schrift, Errinerung und politische Identität in frühen Hochkulturen* (München: C. H. Beck, 1997).

25. Deuteronomy is specific about Moses' audience being a later generation after "the entire generation of warriors had perished from the camp," that is, those who had not trusted in the power of the Lord to enable them to stand against the mighty men and the great fortified cities of the land of Canaan (Deut. 2:14-15).

positive attitude toward the law. It is a form of sympathetic or empathetic response, the recollected past experience impelling the present community to treat those who are property-less and powerless as the Lord treated them in a similar situation.

3. The statute requiring proper payment of wages to the poor and the needy is given yet another grounding, in this case a negative one oriented toward the consequences of disobedience. The motivation is found in the sanction against disobedience, in this case, the possibility that the one whose wages are deprived may "cry to the LORD against you" (v. 15; cf. Exod. 22:21-27). Such outcry to the Lord is not to be regarded as a cultic process by which the law is supported. It is likely that such calling to the Lord is done in private and is not a public or cultic process, though this is a debated issue. The sanction is a reminder that the legal-juridical structure is undergirded by another structure, one that is present throughout the course of Scripture. When affliction and hurt occur, when the oppression of the poor is such that the cries of pain go up to God, the structure of human pain and divine compassion kicks in — a structured relationship most evident in the Psalms and other places where we encounter the prayers of those in trouble and here enfolded into the more formal structure of law and its obedience.[26]

This last motivation is duplicated in the parenesis around the laws of Deuteronomy 15 having to do with remission of debts and release of bonded slaves (15:9). In both cases, there is the further sanction that whoever acts to endanger the poor economically, either by refusing to lend willingly to the poor neighbor or by withholding the wages of a poor laborer, will be in a state of guilt or sin *(het')*. As Norbert Lohfink has noted, following the study of this word by Klaus Koch, "*het'* is a sin which can be expiated only by the death of the sinner."[27] Over against the positive reinforcement of the first category of motivation clauses above, there is now a massive sanction of a negative sort. Like the positive ones, however, it is a feature of the relationship to God, though it may have an ultimate outcome within the formal procedures of the society for punishment of the guilty.

Finally, this feature of the statutes having to do with the economic protection of the poor — that is, the cry of the poor effecting divine assistance — is set as the feature of Israelite law that indicates the greater justice or righ-

26. See Patrick D. Miller, "Prayer and Divine Action," in *God in the Fray: A Tribute to Walter Brueggemann*, ed. Timothy Beal and Tod Linafelt (Minneapolis: Fortress, 1998), pp. 211-32.

27. Norbert Lohfink, "Poverty in the Laws of the Ancient Near East and of the Bible," *Theological Studies* 52 (1991): 46. Koch's essay on *"ḥāṭaʾ"* is in the *Theological Dictionary of the Old Testament*, vol. 4, pp. 309-20.

teousness (ṣaddîq) of the ordinances and statutes of Israel. The only other time that there is any reference in Deuteronomy to "crying out" (qārā') to the Lord is in Deuteronomy 4:5-8:

> See, just as the LORD my God has charged me, I now teach you statutes and ordinances for you to observe in the land that you are about to enter and occupy. You must observe them diligently, for this will show your wisdom and discernment to the peoples, who, when they hear all these statutes, will say, "Surely this great nation is a wise and discerning people!" For what other great nation has a god so near to it as the LORD our God is whenever we call [qārā'] to him? And what other great nation has statutes and ordinances as just as this entire law that I am setting before you today?

As Lohfink has observed, the "calling out" or "crying out" in this text is to be understood, in light of the usage in the statutes, as the cry of the poor. That cry, which is not unknown elsewhere in ancient Near Eastern law, is here regarded as the primary testimony to the righteousness of Israelite law. An extra-legal protection against economic endangerment of the poor is the primary indicator of the righteousness of the system of justice set out in the statutes and ordinances. And, as elsewhere in Scripture, prayer is as much a moral act as it is a spiritual one.

What is to be noted in all of these statutes is that there continues to be the kind of negative or prohibitive formulation that we know from the Commandments — you shall not steal, you shall not watch your neighbor's ox straying, and the like — but around such formulations are other things that belong to the dynamic of the commandment against stealing: positive formulation of what you should do and what is needful, explanations of the situation and reasons for the statute that serve to motivate and undergird its function as policy for communal life, references to the deity whose word and way are embodied in these statutes and who places sanctions on disobedience of them and undergirds their protection of the weak, and associations of the experience of the weak and poor with the cultural memory of the community as a whole — Remember that you were slaves. This is how the commandment effects moral space and draws into a complex whole personal and situational dimensions, varying economic standings and interdependencies, reciprocal responses across situations of economic inequity (e.g., Deut. 15), and God's undergirding of communal and personal life in behalf of the routinizing of communal welfare and well-being when they are threatened by the vicissitudes (theft), contingencies (loss), and changes (economic) that inevitably but unpredictably happen. The sense of *coherence* and wholeness in all of this complexity is embodied and embedded in the constitutional directive of the Commandments.[28]

The Other Commandments

The issue of property and possessions as a center of cultural and personal value and economic significance does not rest simply on the central commandment about stealing. As already indicated, the Sabbath Commandment is fundamental to the valuing and signification of property and the relation between possession of the human person and possession of animals and material property, and the commandment guarding the divine name comes into play as a way of invoking divine decision and sanction. But other commandments directly engage this issue and continue to help the community of faith develop a realistic theology and a way of thinking and acting with regard to property and possessions.

The Ninth Commandment: Against False Witness

The most obvious of these are the last two commandments, against false witness and coveting, which follow the prohibition against stealing and with that commandment may be seen as part of a small grouping within the larger whole.[29] It may not be immediately self-evident what the prohibition against

---

28. For some indication of how the trajectory of this complex understanding of property rights, responsibilities, and protections has worked itself out in Christian theology and philosophy, see Kathryn Tanner's essay in this volume.

29. It has often been suggested that the Decalogue was formulated out of earlier groupings of two or three prohibitions, as one finds, for example, in Leviticus 19, where a number of prohibitions are clearly broken up into smaller groups by a repetitive conclusion, "I am the Lord." See Erhard Gerstenberger, *Wesen und Herkunft des "apodiktischen Rechts,"* Wissenschaftliche Monographien zum Alten und Neuen Testaments 20 (Neukirchen-Vluyn: Neukirchener Verlag, 1965). While that hypothesis is difficult to prove, it is possible to discern at this point an informal grouping, and others may be argued on various grounds — for example, the grouping of the Prologue and the three commandments that follow: worship of the Lord alone, prohibition of worship of images, prohibition of the violation of the name. Certainly one discerns groupings of commandments elsewhere in the Bible — for example, Jeremiah 7:9, Hosea 4:2, and the Sermon on the Mount, though in these instances there are usually four or five commandments in view.

false witness has to do with stealing, but the connections are both formal and material. They are *formally* associated in the sense that the two issues of theft and false witness are brought together in several instances within Old Testament literature, in legal (Lev. 6:1-5; 19:11-13), prophetic (Hos. 7:1; Zech. 5:3-4; Mal. 3:5), and psalmic/cultic (Ps. 50:16-20) literature. In some instances, stealing and false witness are present as part of a longer series, for example, Hosea 4:2 and Jeremiah 7:9. But in other cases, there is sufficient closeness of the two and focus on the two that a clear connection seems intended. That is evident, for example, in Hosea 7:1, where the prophet recounts the wicked deeds of Samaria: "they deal falsely, the thief breaks in, and the bandits raid outside." Lying and stealing are preeminently the sins of the northern kingdom. Even more direct in this regard is Zechariah 5:3-4 where a curse is directed against "everyone who steals" and "everyone who swears falsely," and the curse enters "the house of the thief" and "the house of anyone who swears falsely by my name."[30] And in Jeremiah 6:13 (and, in similar words, in Jeremiah 8:10) we read:

> For from the least to the greatest of them,
>   everyone is greedy for unjust gain;
> and from prophet to priest,
>   everyone deals falsely.

The significance of the connection is best seen, however, in some groupings in Leviticus 6 and 19. In the first instance, a list of sins is given, all of which have to do with property and possessions and for which a guilt or reparation offering is prescribed to make atonement and secure forgiveness:

> When any of you sin and commit a trespass against the LORD by deceiving [*kāhaš*] a neighbor in a matter of a deposit or a pledge, or by robbery [*gāzal*], or if you have defrauded [*'āšaq*] a neighbor, or have found something lost and lied about it — if you swear falsely regarding any of the various things that one may do and sin thereby — when you have sinned and realized your guilt, and would restore what you took by robbery or by fraud or the deposit that was committed to you, or the lost thing that you found, or anything else about which you have sworn falsely, you shall repay the principal amount and shall add one-fifth to it. (Lev. 6:2-5)

---

30. The clear overlap of the third and ninth commandments is evident in this formulation, which speaks of swearing *laššāqer*, that is, "falsely," as in the commandment prohibiting false witness, but adds *bišmî*, "by my name," as in the commandment prohibiting misuse of the divine names.

Two things are to be noted about this text. First, *lying or deceiving* in ways that do detriment to the neighbor's good, specifically to the neighbor's property and possessions, and *theft* are all bound up with one another in this formulation.[31] The theft can take place in various ways and the deception can be in regard to various kinds of property. The language of swearing falsely is only partially the language of the ninth commandment. In the reference to the neighbor and speaking falsely, one hears the language of the commandment, but the more formal "bear witness against" or "answer as a witness against" of the commandment, which points quite clearly to a court setting, is missing. The heart of the commandment's intent is evident, however, in the passage, and one begins to see the complexity of the commandment against false witness also. False words toward a neighbor that harm him or her may take place in the formal testimony of a court and may indeed lie behind these injunctions, as intimated by the reference to swearing falsely, which suggests a more formal process of lying.[32] But the deception against the neighbor to get at the neighbor's property is not confined to that formal setting. The Leviticus formulation lays open a variety of ways in which deception in behalf of the appropriation of a neighbor's property may take place, in or out of the court. In so doing, the text realistically identifies the complexity of the violation of the neighbor's possession and the inherent connection between theft and lying, the fact that appropriation of what belongs to another often, if not most often, involves fundamental deceptions.

The second thing one picks up from this passage is the connection to the cluster of legal formulations in Deuteronomy 24 discussed above, and also those in Exodus 21–23, which grow out of the eighth commandment: stealing, pledges, deposits entrusted to a neighbor, and withheld wages.[33] The term for "defraud"

31. The way in which this passage is to be seen as also a part of the trajectory of meaning developing out of the commandment against stealing is evident in the reference to possessions that had been left with or deposited with a neighbor and to a neighbor's lost property that someone had found and kept. These are moral aspects of the relation to property and possessions that are also dealt with in the section of the Book of the Covenant discussed above (Exod. 20:22–23:33).

32. See, for example, the comment on this by Gordon J. Wenham, who refers to the swearing falsely as "perjury in a public court" (*The Book of Leviticus,* New International Commentary on the Old Testament [Grand Rapids: Eerdmans, 1979], p. 108).

33. The terms for these different kinds of acts are not always the same in these three different contexts. Deuteronomy has a preference for 'bṭ for pledging, while Leviticus 6 has a *hapax legomenon (tĕśûmet yād).* The term for neighbor in the Leviticus text is not the customary *rēaʿ* but *ʿᵃmît,* a word used almost exclusively in Leviticus. So while terminology can provide some legitimate associations, as has been suggested above, one may not confine the associations simply to terminological identity.

in the Leviticus text has to do specifically with withholding the wages of a neighbor, as one can easily discern from the use of the same Hebrew term (ʿāšaq) in Deuteronomy 24:14. In a list of violations of covenant obligations in Malachi 3:5, somewhat reflective of the Decalogue but not including stealing, the sequence of sins is sorcery, adultery, swearing falsely, oppression of hired workers in their wages (specifically the widow and orphan), thrusting aside the alien, and not fearing God. It appears, in this instance, as if stealing (or coveting?) may be reflected in a specific and concrete instance — withholding wages of the poor[34] — as well as in the varied ways of oppressing widow, orphan, and alien, all of which may be assumed to be manifestations of economic oppression.[35]

That association is further reinforced in Leviticus 19:11-14:

> You shall not steal *[gānab];* you shall not deal falsely; and you shall not lie to one another [literally, each one to his neighbor]. And you shall not swear falsely by my name, profaning the name of your God: I am the LORD.
>
> You shall not defraud *[ʿāšaq]* your neighbor; you shall not steal *[gāzal];* and you shall not keep for yourself the wages of a laborer until morning. You shall not revile the deaf or put a stumbling block before the blind; you shall fear your God: I am the LORD.

To "deal falsely" is to use deception in gaining a neighbor's property — for example, denying that one had taken or possessed a neighbor's property. The swearing falsely again probably envisions more formal oaths, and the formulation here draws the third commandment, protecting the right invocation of the divine name, directly into view to undergird the proper handling of a neighbor's property. In the second complex, fraud, stealing, and withholding wages are probably all to be seen as variants of the same thing.

One does not have to look far in Scripture to find examples of the actual interplay of lying and stealing, of false witness and misappropriation of property. Amos 5:10 speaks of those who "hate the one who reproves in the gate [the court]" and "abhor the one who speaks the truth" (that is, does not bear false

---

34. In Deuteronomy 24:14-15, it is specifically the payment of wages to the *poor* laborer that is of concern.

35. A fairly literal translation of Malachi 3:5 would be something like the following: "I will draw near to you for judgment, and I will act as a swift witness against sorcerers, against adulterers, against those who bear false witness, and against oppressors of the hired worker in his wages, of the widow, and of the orphan, and the ones turning aside the alien, that is, those who do not fear me, said the Lord of Hosts." The preposition "against" (Heb. *b-*) identifies four categories of sins here, the last one extended but altogether referring to forms of stealing the property, the economic goods, and needs of the economically vulnerable.

witness). In the next verse, it becomes clear that the allusion is to the use of the court to get at the goods of the poor: "you trample on the poor and take from them levies of grain." The commandment against false witness is in view as it is designed to see that the community that lives by these signs and values does not let the court become a vehicle for misappropriation of the property of a neighbor. The paradigmatic story of this interplay of false witness and stealing is the account of the royal confiscation of Naboth's vineyard in 1 Kings 21.

The interplay of the eighth and ninth commandments thus identifies the close connection between property and theft of property and the legal system. Truth-telling in the large and complex interassociation of regulative agencies, courts, corporations, and individuals is a primary safeguard against the misappropriation of property. Distortion, slanting of facts, misrepresentation of issues — all these and other maneuvers are forms of deception that are prohibited because they do not effect the good neighborhood where the protection of a neighbor's property is part of the associative relationship.

As the juxtaposition of stealing with falsehood and deceit appears in Psalm 50:16-21, it becomes clear that the Commandments' attention to the question of property and possessions involves changing and shifting categories of goods:

> But to the wicked God says:
>   "What right have you to recite my statutes,
>   or take my covenant on your lips?
> For you hate discipline,
>   and you cast my words behind you.
> You make friends with a thief when you see one,
>   and you keep company with adulterers.
>
> "You give your mouth free rein for evil,
>   and your tongue frames deceit.
> You sit and speak against your kin;
>   you slander your own mother's child."[36]

The Commandments are clearly in view in this accusation of the wicked for rejection of "my statutes," "my covenant," "discipline," and "my words."[37] The

---

36. The expression here is unusual, literally "you set a fault/blemish against the child of your mother."

37. It is quite possible if not likely that the reference to "my words" would be heard as an explicit reference to the Commandments, whose only clear title is "ten words" (Exod. 34:28; Deut. 4:13; 10:4), though in Deuteronomy the term "decree" may have the Commandments in view (Deut. 6:17, 20), as may also the Hebrew word for "commandments."

references to stealing and adultery in verse 18 suggest that the commandment prohibiting false witness against one's neighbor is in view here. But the indictment is for the way the mouth and tongue have become instruments of deceit used for evil purposes against one's brother and sister, against one's own kin. Slander, ascription of faults, gossip, deceitful words that are used to hurt the neighbor are all in view. The deceit may involve material goods and economic values, as other texts have indicated, but the endangerment is also manifest with regard to one's name and reputation. What one "possesses" that is endangered by deceit is not only material property and personal goods but the standing of a person in the community. Against the assumption that "You cannot take away my good name," the Commandments recognize that it is quite possible to do so and seek a community devoted to truth in the recognition that its opposite often endangers the "goods" of the neighbor, material and nonmaterial.

In light of the above, it is not surprising that John Calvin saw in the ninth commandment a protection of both honor and property. One might put it as both *material good* and *good name*. The interaction of these two commandments thus invites further reflection on the interaction of the two kinds of property, material and name, and the way in which one undergirds the other, the good name being essential to the acquisition and protection of property, the presence of property and possessions accruing to one's reputation and honor.

The cultural significance of truth-telling to one another and about one another is underscored in the following comment by the ethicist Charles Swezey with regard to this commandment:

> Freedom of choice depends upon a knowledge of the case at hand, which lies take away. Integrity depends upon speaking from one's own perspective, which lies remove. When lies are habitual and the words of everyday discourse unreliable, we plunge into doubt and suspicion. Life together is not possible without a minimal trust in the veracity of words. An unwritten law exists: Unless checks are placed on the proclivity to evade truthfulness, corporate existence flounders and is altogether nasty and brutish.[38]

In the trajectory of both the commandment against stealing and the commandment against false witness, a text from the Letter to the Ephesians is an important reference point:

38. Charles Swezey, "Exodus 20:16 — 'Thou Shalt Not Bear False Witness against Thy Neighbor,'" *Interpretation* 34 (1980): 407.

So then, putting away falsehood, let all of us speak the truth to our neighbors, for we are members of one another. Be angry but do not sin; do not let the sun go down on your anger, and do not make room for the devil. Thieves must give up stealing; rather let them labor and work honestly with their own hands, so as to have something to share with the needy. Let no evil talk come out of your mouths, but only what is useful for building up, as there is need, so that your words may give grace to those who hear. And do not grieve the Holy Spirit of God, with which you were marked with a seal for the day of redemption. Put away from you all bitterness and wrath and anger and wrangling and slander, together with all malice, and be kind to one another, tenderhearted, forgiving one another, as God in Christ has forgiven you. Therefore be imitators of God, as beloved children, and live in love, as Christ loved us and gave himself up for us, a fragrant offering and sacrifice to God. (Eph. 4:25–5:2)

The admonition to the Ephesians is explicitly "directed toward maintaining the common life of the Christian community."[39] In this respect, it, like the Commandments, is instruction that has cultural significance. It has to do with the maintenance and enhancement of the way in which a community lives together, its language, its interactions, its values, its aims, its economy. What is most noticeable about the text is that it deals almost entirely with truth-telling and what Stephen Fowl has called "word-care," how Christians speak to and with one another, which includes truth to and about neighbors, words of anger and bitterness, and evil talk generally. But in the midst of all of this there is an injunction that those who steal must stop stealing and learn to do honest work with their hands so as to share with those in need. In other words, there is a juxtaposition here that is familiar from the Old Testament. Stealing threatened the truth and honesty essential to the common well-being of the community and vice versa.[40]

What also happens in this text is that Paul defines the opposite of stealing another's property and possessions: work in order to have something to share with those in need. In other words, the trajectory of the eighth commandment explicitly opens up from a narrow reading of the commandment as a guard of private property to a positive inducement to generosity. The

---

39. Stephen Fowl, "Making Stealing Possible: Criminal Thoughts on Building an Ecclesial Common Life," in his *Engaging Scripture: A Model for Theological Interpretation* (Oxford: Blackwell, 1998), p. 168.

40. The story part of this trajectory is the episode of Ananias and Sapphira in Acts 5, who come under the judgment of God not simply for holding back some of the proceeds of the property they sold, which was theirs to sell, but because they lied about it.

concern about stealing here is not focused so much on the property stolen as on the act of stealing to obtain things as an avoidance of working for what one gets. The latter — "work[ing] honestly . . . so as to have something to share" — creates possibilities of sharing for the good of others. In this way, the injunction to the Ephesian community follows out of and builds upon the various Old Testament regulations growing out of the eighth commandment that serve not only to protect the neighbor's economic well-being but to enhance it, and especially those statutes providing for the poor, that is, for those in need. The Scripture thus argues implicitly for a countercultural assumption that our aim is not the acquisition and protection (by legal and illegal means, by work and by stealing, by truth-telling and false witness) of our property and possessions but the sharing of the wealth that God provides.

The Tenth Commandment: Against Coveting[41]

The tenth commandment, prohibiting coveting what belongs to one's neighbor, obviously continues the Commandments' attention to the safeguarding of the property and possessions of the members of the community. In various ways, it also brings other commandments into the picture. The long discussion about the meaning of this commandment need not be rehearsed at length. The commandment's main thrust is to guard against that kind of lusting after what belongs to another that leads to acts of stealing. It has to do with specific *acts* against another's possessions but also moves into the domain of *inner desire* and *intention* lying behind acts of theft, fraud, and the like.[42] The protection of

---

41. Cf. William Schweiker, "Reconsidering Greed," pp. 249-71 in this volume.

42. The Hebrew word *ḥāmad,* which is the common word for covet in a way that leads to the act of taking, appears both times in the Exodus form of the commandment (Exod. 20:17). In Deuteronomy, *ḥāmad* occurs in the first reference to coveting, but in the second instance the word *hit'awweh* appears, a word that refers to a strong desire that does not necessarily involve explicit acting upon the desire. The double force of the commandment is summarized well in Mekhilta de Rabbi Simeon bar Yohai:

> The Commandment here reads "You shall not covet," but the text in Deuteronomy (5:8) goes on to say "nor shall you crave." The purpose is to make craving a separate offense, and coveting a separate offense. For if a person craves, he will end up by coveting. . . . Craving is in the heart, as Scripture says "if your soul craves" (Deut. 12.20), while coveting is an actual deed, as in the verse "You shall not covet the silver and gold on them and take it for yourselves" (Deut. 7.25).

(The quotation is taken from Alexander Rofe, "The Tenth Commandment in the Light of Four Deuteronomic Laws," in *The Ten Commandments in History and Tradition*, ed. Ben-Zion Segal [Jerusalem: Magnes, 1990], p. 45.)

the neighbor's property begins in the mind and heart, and the wrongful act is inhibited at its starting point when the neighborhood puts up a coveting watch over its life.

Erhard Gerstenberger has observed that that the commandment against coveting divides the property over which a "man" has authority into three categories: real estate, people under him, and animals.[43] This is evident in both forms of the commandment, although the Deuteronomic version mixes these categories up and does not follow the Exodus order. The threefold categorization is confirmed in Leviticus 27:1-25 and also in summary fashion in verses 28-29. The distinctions are important because of the way they help to provide an understanding of the categories of goods that belong to the realm of "property," that is, those "goods" that one has some claim over and that merit protection in the common life.

These include animals, but particularly those animals whose value and signification is their place in the culture's economy, that is, their potential for providing the "good" of livelihood and sustenance.[44] The issue is not property in the sense of ownership but property in its particular valuation, its potential for providing the needs of life. This is one large category of goods in the common culture. That the Commandments in this instance reflect an agricultural economy is no inhibition against recognizing the sort of goods intended as the trajectory or arc of understanding of the Commandments into other types of economies.[45]

A second category of property in the tenth commandment is persons. The complex understanding of personal goods, of property, is thereby further indicated because in very basic senses, the two types of persons mentioned in the commandment do not stand as property and possession in the same way, nor are they that in quite the same sense as either of the other two categories. Assuming that the male and female slave are bonded slaves — and that seems to be the category that the statutes and ordinances are most concerned about — these are persons who exist as the property and possession of another in only a temporary fashion. As such their valuation is economic in that, like the ox and donkey, they contribute to the productivity and economic value of the

---

43. Erhard Gerstenberger, *Leviticus,* The Old Testament Library (Louisville: Westminster, 1996), p. 441.

44. See the discussion of ox and donkey in the treatment of the Book of the Covenant above.

45. This is already evident in the move from the Commandments + Book of Covenant in Exodus to the Commandments + Deuteronomic regulations in Deuteronomy, since in the latter a more monied economy is in view. See Gerhard von Rad, *Deuteronomy,* The Old Testament Library (Philadelphia: Westminster, 1966), pp. 11-15.

master. But they can also make claims on the one under whose authority they come. The possession exists in a kind of reciprocal relationship with the possessor so that at the end of the period of servitude, according to the Deuteronomic Code, the male or female slave becomes a possessor of the possessions of the slave master (see above on Deuteronomy 15).

The other person whom one is prohibited from coveting in the tenth commandment is the wife of a neighbor. This commandment has been one of the grounds for interpreting the social system portrayed within the Old Testament as reflecting an understanding of women as property of their husbands. One response to such a commandment is to see it as indicating a biblical devaluing of women and wives. Another response is to hear in the commandment an understanding of possession that incorporates *personal relationships* as well as economic goods. The biblical stories and legislation indicate the complex relationships that husbands and wives have with one another, and rarely would one judge the stories of husbands and wives as indicating that the wife was primarily an economic good, though it is clear that the provision of sons is an important good for the economic well-being of the family. What was possessed or could be taken away from one incorporated, therefore, the family relationships and specifically the nurtured relationship between husband and wife that produced children and created a family. At this point, the commandment against adultery comes into play in the same relation to the commandment against coveting as has the prohibition of stealing.[46] The prohibition of adultery as a safeguard against the taking of a wife — or, as came to be the case, a husband also — is a pointer to the way in which human possessions incorporate significant human relationships. The definition of property as inferred from the Commandments is too narrowly conceived when it focuses simply upon economic goods or material goods. If the latter contribute to the self-understanding and self-worth of the individual member of the community, how much more is that the case for the familial relationships?

The third category of property envisioned in the coveting commandment and Leviticus 27 is a house. As Marvin Chaney has made clear, the "house" does not simply return one to a purely material and economic value. In the agricultural and peasant culture of early Israel, wherein each family unit was given an allotment of land upon which and by which to live,

> the *bayit* [house] referred variously to the extended family, their dwelling, the family plot which provided their common livelihood, and the whole gestalt of meaning and value which inhered in these technoenviron-

---

46. See the association of stealing and adultery in Psalm 50:18.

mental and socioeconomic realities. . . . [It] signaled both an extended family's means of sustenance and shelter and the network of human nurture which could grow only once these survival needs had been met securely.[47]

Here again, therefore, the commandment envisions a large understanding of property and possessions that is in a sense *structural*, incorporating various goods and categories of property that together make up the ingredients of the common life. The fullness of this notion of property is, of course, further indicated by the last clause of the commandment, "anything that belongs to your neighbor."

It is crucial at this point to recognize that whereas some would read the commandment against coveting as rising out of a propertied class protecting its material goods from the encroachment of the poor, that is not necessarily the case. Where one encounters instances of coveting in the Old Testament, they are largely acts of royalty and the wealthy. Coveting is not a problem of the poor. It is the king and the wealthy who lust after and take (for example, David's coveting of Bathsheba and Ahab's coveting of Naboth's vineyard). When the prophets inveigh against those who commit this sin, they clearly have in mind the wealthy who want to acquire more, as in the case of Isaiah's announcement of judgment:

> Ah, you who join house to house,
> who add field to field,
> until there is room for no one but you,
> and you are left to live alone
> in the midst of the land! (Isa. 5:8)

The point is made even more explicitly by Isaiah's eighth-century contemporary, Micah, who identifies coveting and taking as an act of the powerful:

> Alas for those who devise wickedness
> and evil deeds on their beds!
> When the morning dawns, they perform it,
> because it is in their power.
> They covet fields, and seize them;
> houses, and take them away;
> they oppress householder and house,
> people and their inheritance. (Micah 2:1-2)

47. Marvin L. Chaney, "You Shall Not Covet Your Neighbor's House," *Pacific Theological Review* (winter 1982): 8.

This does not mean that the poor do not steal. But the cultural problem is the acquisitiveness of the rich and powerful and the development of means — legal and illegal — to appropriate the property of others. The *internal* coveting is also of the wealthy, not necessarily for the property of the neighbor but for property *like* the neighbor's.

Finally, it is worth noting that over against an inappropriate desire for the property of a neighbor, there is a *proper* coveting of an immaterial good: the laws and precepts of the Lord. In Psalm 19:10, these are said to be coveted or desired more than gold, "even much fine gold." In other words, the psalmist suggests, in comparison with one of the usual objects of coveting, gold (Deut. 7:25; Josh. 7:21), that a property one may — and should — take to oneself is the precepts and ordinances of the Lord, the keeping of which brings great reward (Ps. 19:11).

The Prologue and the First and Second Commandment

In thinking about property and possessions from the perspective of the Commandments, one should say a word about the place of the initial section of the Decalogue, that is, the Prologue ("I am the LORD your God, who brought you out of the land of Egypt, out of the house of slavery," Exod. 20:2) and the prohibitions against having other gods and against making and worshiping images.

The Prologue, while seeming outside the field of interest, plays a critical role in that it sets the whole tone for how the issue of persons as property is to be dealt with. The Israelite experience of slavery and the redemption from it created an ethos about slavery that affected the way that matter is dealt with throughout. It is out of that experience and its outcome that the community learned about the oppressive character of slavery and bondage and the need to find ways to get free. That this connection is real and not simply imaginary is evident in the Sabbath Commandment about keeping the Sabbath. In the Deuteronomic form of this commandment, as indicated earlier, the primary purpose of rest on the Sabbath is to provide rest for slaves and servants. That is then grounded in the experience of being slaves in Egypt and being set free (Deut. 5:15). Not surprisingly, when the sabbatical laws are set forth, arising out of the sabbatical principle inherent in the fourth commandment, the remembrance of Israel's slavery and God's redemption is invoked again as a ground for liberality in setting free the bonded servant (Deut. 15:15). One more time, in the set of laws in Deuteronomy 24 discussed above, the remembrance of slavery in Egypt is the ground for carrying out a particular practice, in this case the leaving of some grain and fruit in the fields and vineyards for the alien, the orphan, and the widow to glean. And in the jubilee year law of Leviticus 25, the prohibition of permanent slavery of any Israelite is grounded in the claim of the Prologue to the Ten Commandments:

> For they are my servants, whom I brought out of the land of Egypt; they shall not be sold as slaves are sold. You shall not rule over them with harshness, but shall fear your God. (vv. 42-43)[48]

The experience of bondage *and* the divine redemption from that bondage are the primary impetus for the way in which the community deals with the plight of those who find themselves caught in some form of slavery. The Prologue sets that whole matter as a part of the identity of the deity who commands and as a presupposition out of which the Commandments arise.

The way in which the first commandment grounds all the rest means that its connection to the whole is complex and rich. It is the first commandment that pushes beyond all the matters discussed so far to raise questions about human love of property and the acquisitive instinct *in principle*. What human beings possess and the desire to possess more, whether in material goods, influence (a form of possession of persons), sex (the possession of persons), or other matters, have the potential to become the primary center of meaning and value in life, the ultimate value and thus the claim that has the force of another god. The danger here, against which the first commandment speaks, is set forth sharply in Jesus' injunction: You cannot serve God and mammon (Matt. 6:24; Luke 16:13); that is, you cannot serve God and property. The language is explicitly the language of the first and second commandments ("serve"). Jesus' saying functions both as a relativizing of any form of property so that it cannot ever be of ultimate value and as a warning that the instinct to make it so is ever with us. The making and worshiping of other gods begins with what one has and desires.[49]

A connection to the first commandment is indicated in the association of not stealing and not coveting with generosity as that is set forth by Luther

---

48. The injunction to "fear God" is an allusion to the first commandment, the positive form of which is to love or fear or serve God (see Deut. 6:4, 13).

49. This point is developed in more detail in Schweiker's "Reconsidering Greed": "In the formation of human desires, the believer is bid to love a reality that shatters sign value. One is to love God with heart and soul and mind, but God is precisely that reality which cannot be inscribed within any system of signs. The love of God, we might say, can limit the desire of acquisition precisely because what is desired exceeds objectification" (p. 269 in this volume). Cf. Charles Mathewes's argument for using the world rather than loving the world as a way of avoiding idolatry ("On Using the World," pp. 189-221 in this volume).

in his "Treatise on Good Works," where he says, "A man is generous because he trusts God and never doubts but that he will always have enough. In contrast a man is covetous and anxious because he does not trust God."[50] Luther also writes that "faith is the master workman and the motivating force behind the good work of generosity."[51] Coveting and stealing arise out of a lack of trust in the God who has made and provided for the human creature. They are ways of turning the accumulation of wealth into a god, of serving property rather than God, in sharp distinction from the generosity that lets go because of a trust that God will provide (Gen. 22:8, 14). The trust that one will have enough and does not need to covet or act to take from others what they have is a positive manifestation of the first commandment, articulated as the love and fear of God (Deut. 6:4, 13). As John Milbank has pointed out, following Luther, the propensity for illegal and legal acquisition is a fear that there will not be enough for us, a basic violation of the trust implicit in the love and fear of God, and thus a placing of the "more" — in whatever form it may take as a possession — "before me," before God (Exod. 20:3; Deut. 5:7), that is, "in front of me" or "alongside of me" or "over against me."[52] The prohibitions against stealing and coveting are thus safeguards in behalf of the primary commandment, the love of God alone, as much as they are safeguards in behalf of the neighbor's property.

In his final defense and articulation of his righteousness before God, Job sets out both a number of ways that he has not violated the commandments and the way he has acted as one who fears God, a primary characterization of Job in the Prologue to the book (1:1; 2:3). In the course of his "negative confessions" of innocence, Job contends:

> If I have made gold my trust,
>   or called fine gold my confidence;
> if I have rejoiced because my wealth was great,
>   or because my hand had gotten much;
> . . .
> this also would be an iniquity to be punished by the judges,
>   for I should have been false to God above. (Job 31:24-28)

---

50. Martin Luther, "Treatise on Good Works," in *Luther's Works*, vol. 44, ed. James Atkinson (Philadelphia: Fortress, 1966), p. 109. See also Schweiker, "Reconsidering Greed." In an oral communication, Schweiker has described his essay as "a meditation on the First Commandment." While it may be much more than that, it is at least that.

51. Luther, "Treatise on Good Works," p. 3.

52. Luther, "Treatise on Good Works," p. 3. (I owe the Luther citations to John Milbank, *The Word Made Strange: Theology, Language, Culture* [Oxford: Blackwell, 1997], p. 225.)

This claim on the part of the righteous but oppressed one does two things: It makes the enjoyment of riches a violation of the first commandment, and it indicates that the issue of that commandment is who and what do you trust. The acquisition of excessive wealth as it arises out of coveting and stealing is indeed a neighbor issue, but it is fundamentally a matter of the fear of God and the sole reliance on the Lord for the provision of life.[53]

Conclusion

In conclusion, the Commandments may be seen in all these ways to create a moral space that is rich and diverse. They do not effect a simple trajectory of things that one does and does not do, even though that is the traditional and catechetical way of explicating the Commandments. Negative and positive commands are indeed present throughout, but they do not exhaust what is on this trajectory. Reason and warning, explanation and encouragement, sanction and reward, social description and analysis of a primitive sort (class and category distinctions enfolded into the statutes), one-time acts (taking a pledge or lying against a neighbor) and continuing modes of behavior (not stripping the fields or vineyards or defrauding a neighbor by withholding wages), external acts (theft, swearing an oath falsely) and internal disposition (lusting after what belongs to a neighbor), historical recollection (remembering slavery), and the reliability of divine compassion (the poor crying out to the Lord) — these and other things serve to define the moral topography of the culture whose life is effected, nurtured, and protected by these commandments. In the process, the very character of property and possessions is seen to be complex and inclusive of material and nonmaterial goods, land and the means of living, honor and reputation, familial relationships and the nurtur-

---

53. The commandment against the making of images is in many ways tied to the prohibition of the worship of other gods, and various traditions identify these as a single commandment. Their shared focus relative to the issue of trusting in wealth rather than in God is indicated by the fact that there is a close association between the making of images and silver and gold. Indeed the Deuteronomist specifically associates coveting with the desire for the silver and gold of the Canaanite idols. The only times that Deuteronomy uses the word for "covet" (*hāmad*) are in the tenth commandment and in 7:25, where there occurs the prohibition, "Do not covet the silver or the gold that is on them and take it for yourself, because you could be ensnared by it; for it is abhorrent to the Lord your God." In this instance, coveting property for its wealth is not a sin against the neighbor but a temptation away from the full devotion to the Lord. See the brief discussion in Patrick D. Miller, *The Religion of Ancient Israel* (Louisville: Westminster/John Knox, 2000), pp. 22-23, and the essay by Walter Brueggemann referred to there.

PATRICK D. MILLER

ing of a way of life. In the directives of the Commandments and the trajectory of meaning and effects that grows out of legislation, story, prophecy, and song, a structure of valuation is discerned, one to be nurtured in and by the culture if it is to be a neighborhood as well.

Sharing and Loving: Love, Law, and the Ethics of Cultural Memory in the Pentateuch

ANDREAS SCHUELE

The Modern Understanding of Love As "Intimacy"

In an investigation of the sociology of love in modernity, Niklas Luhmann presented the thesis that, in modern society, love has become increasingly responsible for the communication of *intimacy*.[1] As a methodological axiom Luhmann assumes that social life consists primarily of communication or, more precisely, of a multitude of different forms of communication, to which belong legal, economic, political, aesthetic, and religious forms, as well as the communication of family life or that of self-referential "talking to oneself." All these forms occur in every society in one way or another and are indispensable because they mediate between the respective needs of the individual and that individual's integration into a given social unit.

Societies, however, differ considerably in the manner in which they coordinate these forms of communication with each other. According to Luhmann's often expressed conviction, modern societies stand out because of a high degree of specialization. That means, above all, that they no longer connect each contribution to social life in order to bring it into harmony with as many others as possible, as perhaps the case still was under the medieval feudal system. Hence, to take a few examples, for something to appear politically meaningful is not dependent on it also having a believable religious aspect; similarly, we consider it as elementary for the existence of a democracy that those principles are not dependent upon the opinions of markets and the

---

1. Niklas Luhmann, *Liebe als Passion: Zur Codierung von Intimität* (Frankfurt am Main: Suhrkamp, 1996), esp. pp. 49-56.

51

tastes of mass media; what is deemed as aesthetic need not also have "educational worth"; and finally, modern industrial nations take advantage of the fact that the idea of economic efficiency is not necessarily bound to the support of social rights. The way in which all of these contributions are to be connected into an overarching cultural semantic is not given from the outset; hence the increasing differentiation and individualization of the social sphere suggest both freedom and confusion — the virtue and vice of modern life.

According to Luhmann, the communication of love has also gone through this specialization process. To expect love, or to give love, is not always and in every instance appropriate. There is communication that is directed to love, and that which avoids it. Love can expect too much of communication; it can in wrong moments break down distance where distance would have promoted the success of communication rather than the "unreasonable demands" of love.[2] Whereas concepts such as "respect" and "esteem" are considered, especially in the modern age, as universally sturdy — in other words, as always fundamentally to be expected and demanded[3] (among marriage partners and siblings as much as between trading partners or opposition politicians) — love concentrates itself on a particular form of social life, namely, the communication of intimacy. As Luhmann once pointedly put it, love moves about "within the world of another to find meaning," to shape one's own desire, understanding, judgment, and action out of the experience of the other. This is not a form of the *unio mystica*, which focuses on a merger with the other. Love does not dissolve the boundary between the lover and the loved, despite the poetics of Romanticism that described the absorption in the other as that ultimate, albeit unobtainable, ideal. Love does not stand at the end of consciousness and identity, but enters into the risk of gaining identity within the world of someone else's experience;[4] and, on each occasion, it is precisely this preparedness that also stimulates the reciprocation of love.

"Within the world of another to find meaning" necessarily implies the idea of *other* people, people who always remain in approach and don't have to agree with one's own actual and, of itself in no way homogeneous, world of

---

2. Luhmann, *Liebe als Passion*, p. 172.

3. This is expressed in its most distinct form in Kant's notion of "esteem" as a "feeling *a priori*" (cf. his *Critique of Practical Reason*, trans. Louis Beck [Indianapolis: Bobbs-Merrill, 1956], pp. 74-92).

4. Cf. on the part of contemporary theology E. Jüngel's definition of love as an "event where even the highest degree of self-reference dissolves into an ever higher self-giving" ("Ereignis einer inmitten noch so großer Selbstbezüglichkeit immer noch größeren Selbstlosigkeit"); see Jüngel, *Gott als Geheimnis der Welt: Zur Begründung der Theologie des Gekreuzigten im Streit zwischen Theismus und Atheismus* (Tübingen: Mohr/Siebeck, 1986), p. 435.

experience. These approaches move about one another within a field of contact characterized by fulfillment and disappointment — an aspect explicitly, and to the greatest extent, focused upon within the medieval literature of courtly love. Love and its reciprocation constitute closeness, with the risk that the "world of the other" is misinterpreted, misunderstood, or that the whole is experienced ultimately as unattainable, disappointing, or simply closed off. Love is passion in the double sense of experience and suffering. In this regard it becomes clear without much further analysis that love is an enormously costly and uncertain form of communication, one that is actually able to enter into intimate togetherness for only a few, albeit particular and deep-reaching, relationships.[5]

Let us linger a moment with Luhmann's analysis and clarify a few observations that appear characteristic for contemporary culture. Modern societies are being experienced and described more and more as cold, impersonal, and loveless. With regard to love as a cultural theme, however, right across the spectrum from critical literature to the expressions of popular culture,[6] love appears in no way to have "cooled down."[7] Compared with other times, love has not become less important, and people are not unaware that the semantics of love are not wrapped up in physicality or the erotic, despite the eagerness of whole branches of industry to suggest that very thing. The consciousness of the lack of love with the simultaneous emphasis on its inalienability could, however, hang together with the fact that modern societies adapt themselves to the situation where it is true that love as intimacy possesses a high, even ideal status as seen within the whole field of social communication, but that it really gets attention in relatively few areas.

A further observation, one that will be important below, is that in modernity love represents one of the few communication forms that is not also reflected through the legal system of society. Whereas the concepts of *esteem* (for human dignity) and *respect* (for the property of the other) are anchored within fundamental human rights, love just cannot — and should not — be expected, let alone demanded or possibly even sanctioned. Understood as intimacy, love crosses the threshold where legality and morality find their

---

5. Cf. from a biological point of view *Attraktion und Liebe: Formen und Grundlagen partnerschaftlicher Beziehung,* ed. M. Amelang, H.-J. Ahrens, and H. W. Bierhoff (Göttingen: Hogrefe, 1995). The contributors examine the complexity of genetic, psychological, and social factors that encourage or hamper the emergence of love. Axiomatically, the notion of love is thereby located in the sphere of intimate togetherness.

6. On this aspect see J. Herrmann, *Sinnmaschine Kino: Sinndeutung und Religion im populären Film* (Gütersloh: Gütersloher Verlag, 2001), pp. 212-16.

7. Cf. Luhmann, *Liebe als Passion,* pp. 13-15.

limit.[8] That does not push love out of the terms of reference of social communication into the "purely private" spheres (as marriage and friendship are also at any time conceivable only within this frame), but it builds here a basis upon which it can evade legal and moral control.[9]

Love As a Commandment in Biblical Traditions

At this point, the function and status of love in modern societies can help us analyze the Old Testament commandment of love — help us to sense a contrast with a part of the biblical tradition. The Old Testament also has a concept of love that, at least at first sight, "encodes intimacy": the love poetry of the Song of Songs, one of the latest texts within the Old Testament canon, would be the best example. Such texts, however, only make it stand out that much more that the Hebraic 'ahab (to love) is also encountered in connections that lack any reference to the language of intimacy, namely, in the series of love commandments from the books of Leviticus and Deuteronomy, those commandments for compassion or fraternal love. In the Greek tradition of transmission, which became decisive for Christianity, the text reads, "love your neighbor as yourself" (Lev. 19:18). If one sticks to the idea of love essentially as intimacy, then one runs into a series of difficulties: love appears within the Torah in the form of a *commandment*. Love becomes an imperative: "You're supposed to love." In that regard, the command to love is met in the context of different legal systems — in Deuteronomy and in the so-called "holiness code" (Lev. 17–26) — and it stands there in both narrower and broader relations with familial, economic, and cultic regulations. Its character as commandment determines, therefore, more precisely that love possesses an ethical-legal and therefore normative character. To love or not to love is not a question of sympathy; it does not remain an issue left to the feeling of the individual, his emotional affinity, or her affection or even aversion in face of the other. Love is not that unavailable, exceptional thing that simply appears or fails to materialize; rather, it implies a behavior in relation to one's

8. In her reading of Henry James's novel *The Ambassadors*, Martha Nussbaum traces a similar tension between love as an intimate space and public morality: "What Strether senses is that what he calls the 'deep, deep truth' of sexual love is at odds with the morality of perception, in two ways. It asks for privacy, for others to avert their gaze; and on the inside it asks that focus be averted from all else that is outside." Cf. Martha C. Nussbaum, *Love's Knowledge: Essays on Philosophy and Literature* (New York: Oxford University Press, 1990), pp. 188-89.

9. Cf. U. Beck, "Die irdische Religion der Liebe," in *Das ganz normale Chaos der Liebe*, ed. U. Beck and E. Beck-Gernsheim (Frankfurt am Main: Suhrkamp, 1990), p. 248.

neighbor that can be required. And, at this point above all, the difference between the ethical-legal view of love in the biblical tradition and the romantic character of the modern understanding of love becomes thematic.[10]

That leads us to the persons who are supposed to be loved. Above all there are the *personae miserae* (the foreigner, the widow, and the orphan); then the *rēaʿ*, the "neighbor"; and, finally, outside the series of fellow human beings, God himself. The following reflections are aimed at unpacking the semantics of love that come to bear in relation to each of these target groups. It will be seen that this semantic is in no way uniform but rather contains throughout differing aspects that extensively avoid definitional homogenization. Perhaps it would be appropriate at this point, however, to give an indication of the developments in this area that will be met below. In regard to Luhmann's observation about modernity — that to love another means "to find meaning in his or her world" — the commandments of love within the Torah stand, in a certain way, in a complementary relationship: the semantics of love become crucial above all in those contexts where one opens one's "own world" to the other in order to create an environment that meets with his or her requirements for life. Even more pointedly formulated: love has something to do with the work of one's own experience and actual life for the benefit of the other. This in no way shuts out the understanding of intimacy as that deep, relational closeness, and as a closeness that is not simply at one's disposal. But the spectrum of a concept of love, understood in this way, becomes considerably broader. It potentially includes all the areas of structured and structurable life: law, property, and possession, and equally so the construction of personal identity and cultural memory. As we will see, all these themes are tied up in the series of love commandments found in the Torah.

Love and Law

Let us focus our examination of the commandment of love upon the *personae miserae* (the widow, the orphan, and the foreigner), beginning with a central passage of the book of Deuteronomy:

> For the LORD your God is God of gods and Lord of lords, the great God, mighty and awesome, who is not partial and takes no bribe, who executes justice for the orphan and the widow, and who loves the strangers, pro-

10. On this cf. Amelang et al., eds., *Attraktion und Liebe*, p. 203.

viding them food and clothing. You shall also love the stranger, for you were strangers in the land of Egypt. (Deut. 10:17-19)

In that age, as today, widows, orphans, and foreigners ("strangers") were people who typically appeared at the lower end of the social scale. It's true that one can also find in the Old Testament foreigners who had been able to establish themselves within the Judaic state. Under "foreigner" we do not have to think primarily of "ethnic minorities" that were suspended outside the power of the native hegemony. It may have been a matter of individuals, or at most small families, who for the same reasons as always left their homeland and had to build a new existence for themselves. And that could occur in all sorts of ways. For example, the Hittite Uriah, the husband of Bathsheba, rose within the military — a route often used by foreigners to establish themselves (2 Sam. 11). Widows, too, could establish themselves; occasionally we meet them in the role of the wise and, from time to time, even clairvoyant woman who was consulted in particular instances. The widow from Tekoa (2 Sam. 14) who was supposed to soften David's heart for Absalom is in this instance a striking example. The "normal case" may, however, have been much more prosaic. To be a widow, orphan, or stranger implied above all the lack of a primary group, which guaranteed economic security and social embeddedness, which in turn manifested itself in latent existential uncertainty. This is the foundational theme of the book of Ruth, which in many respects was both exemplified and criticized by the levitical and deuteronomic conceptions of law.

One could conclude that in these cases love stood primarily as a synonym for "mercifulness." It had to do with help for the helpless, with economic support without the thought of personal profiteering. In the broadest sense it had to do with the establishment of a protected sphere of existence for those who had lost such a space due to their particular biographical situation. The association with compassion is a practical result that is certainly applicable, but it does not yet fully embrace the peculiarity of the talk of "love." In that regard one sees clearly that widows, orphans, and foreigners were not *without rights*.[11] Their social status in this respect is deceptive in that even the *personae miserae* were in no way "outcasts" who no longer existed within the society and could manage to live only through the voluntary donations of others. The Old Testament contains a whole series of regulations in favor of the rights of these groups. Through the so-called Levirate marriage, for example, a widow in child-bearing years had somewhat of a claim to being rein-

---

11. Cf. G. Braulik, "Deuteronomium 1-16, 17," in *Neue Echter Bibel Lfg. 15* (Würzburg: Echter, 1986), p. 86.

tegrated into her husband's family. The commandment of love was not a reaction primarily to a *loss* of rights which through compassion had to be
offset, therefore; widows, orphans, and foreigners did indeed possess a status
to human rights. Their occasionally precarious situation resulted not from
the fact that they lacked rights but from the fact that they of themselves had
little or absolutely nothing at their disposal to make those rights effective.
Rather, they had to rely on someone respecting those rights. Again the book
of Ruth is the illustrating text: even the alien widow Ruth is entitled to be received into the family of her closest Israelite relatives. With regard to that
there is no doubt. The actual theme of the book, with its partly tragic, partly
risqué, and partly humorous developments deals with how Ruth finally
achieves that right.

Love becomes central, then, where not the right itself but rather its efficacy is questioned. It doesn't have to do with setting down absolutely what
must be done in favor of the weak; but it does have to do with contributing to
their rights and welfare precisely when there is no external compulsion to do
so. "To love" and "to help someone to gain his right" therefore become semantic correlates. In Deuteronomy 10:18, this connection is made explicit by
the usage of stylistic parallelism. The command is introduced by the indica-
tive that God himself is the one who helps (*ʿoseh mišpaṭ*) the widow and orphan to get their rights and the one who loves (*ʾōhēb*) the foreigner. The difference between this formulation and that of the command in the Book of the
Covenant is instructive. In Exodus we read,

> You shall not wrong or oppress a resident alien, for you were aliens in the
> land of Egypt. You shall not abuse any widow or orphan. If you do abuse
> them, when they cry out to me, I will surely heed their cry; my wrath will
> burn, and I will kill you with the sword, and your wives shall become wid-
> ows and your children orphans. (Exod. 22:21-24)

It is clear that in the Book of the Covenant, the rights of the *personae miserae*
are important, and it is also here presupposed that such individuals are not in
the position to stand up for their own rights. In distinction from Deuteronomy, however, love is not the issue in this instance. Rather, the motivation to
respect rights is based on the threat of retaliation, for God himself stands up
for the rights of this group. In a certain way this establishes the legal "normal
case" even for the weak of society. The question as to why one should fight
particularly for their interests can remain open in this case, because the validity and effectiveness of those rights are now secured only through the threat
of punishment.

To summarize the situation so far, we could emphasize two different points: On the one hand, love toward another requires no qualitative leap. In that respect, love can "simply" manifest itself to help the other get just that right to which he or she is actually entitled. That does not make the foreigner a native, and it also changes only partly the status of widows and orphans. The understanding of love here has strikingly low expectations — in distinction to the high expectations given to a romantic understanding of the "power of love." On the other hand, there is the comparison with the Book of the Covenant that intends love as a turning toward the other, a love whose impetus lies outside of reward or punishment, but which nevertheless is not arbitrary but is still bound up with social expectations.

That leads us to a decisive question: On what precisely are the motivations to such actions, so distinguished as love, based? The decisive evidence, to which we should now turn, lies in the memory of Israel's time in Egypt and of the Exodus, a memory that is recorded in Exodus 22:21-24 and Deuteronomy 10:17-19 and, in the case of the Deuteronomy text, tied in a double sense with the theme of love: as the love of God to the weak, and as the commandment of love to the foreigner.

Love and Cultural Memory in Deuteronomy

To comprehend the connection of love and memory is at first difficult if one understands love primarily as a state, as a sphere in which people find themselves caught up. This understanding, one that leads us again down the path of a romantically shaped concept of love, is above all an inheritance of the Greeks. The hypostatization of love within poetry, and its mythical deification in the form of the Olympic gods, had the origins of their cultural history much more in the Aegean than in the region of the Fertile Crescent. Accordingly one finds traces of this view in the Old Testament, above all in those texts that developed within the time of Hellenism — primarily Ecclesiastes, the Song of Songs,[12] and perhaps even Ruth. Above all in the language of Deuteronomy, however, in which the abstract concept of love is met with most frequency,[13] the meaning of love is highlighted as "to love," as an activity, as a mode of the

12. "Set me as a seal upon your heart, as a seal upon your arm; for love is strong as death, passion fierce as the grave. Its flashes are flashes of fire, a raging flame" (Song 8:6). Love, symbolized by divine insignia like arrows and flames, stands (like death) for that kind of power that humans cannot dispose of but that, nonetheless, determines their fate.

13. Cf. Deut 4:37; 5:9-10; 6:5; 7:8-9; 10:12, 15, 18-19; 11:1, 13, 22; 15:16; 19:9; 21:15-16; 23:6; 30:6, 16, 20.

form of shared reality rather than an emotional state. The same is also valid for memory, which the ancient rhetoric expressed through the imagery of a space furnished by memory.[14] The legislation of Deuteronomy and the holiness laws of Leviticus combine love and memory in view of the Exodus tradition, as we will see below. In other words, the memory of Egypt and the Exodus releases an ethics to which love belongs as one of the central concepts. How then is this relation of memory to the ethics of love formed?

Let us visualize the scenario of the narrative: Following the prologue of Deuteronomy (chaps. 1–4),[15] we find the people of Israel having exited Egypt, having crossed the desert, and, now in the east Jordan region, pausing before they enter into the promised land. At this point, Moses turns to the people and presents a great speech, which is essentially the book of Deuteronomy.[16] This speech is, as it were, built upon two pillars, the first being a historical account beginning with Israel's origins and leading up to the present shortly before the taking of the land, and the second being an announcement of the Law of God that should be valid after entry into the land.[17] The relationship of narrative and addressee is fundamental to understanding the sense of this connection between historical review and legal proclamation before the entry into the land.[18] Within the narrative, the Israelites are those

---

14. The classical text on memory as something that creates "spaces of recollection" is Cicero's *De oratore* 2.352-54, which plays a significant role in contemporary studies on the phenomenon of "collective" or "cultural" memory; cf. esp. the work of M. Halbwachs, *Les cadres sociaux de la mémoire* (1925) and *La mémoire collective* (1939); and J. Assmann, *Das kulturelle Gedächtnis: Schrift, Erinnerung und politische Identität in frühen Hochkulturen* (München: Beck, 1997).

15. In what follows I shall confine myself to a synchronic reading of Deuteronomy. As G. Braulik has convincingly shown, different concepts of "memory" and "learning" are, however, present in all the stages of literary development in Deuteronomy; cf. Braulik, "Das Deuteronomium und die Gedächtniskultur Israels. Redaktionsgeschichtliche Beobachtungen zur Verwendung von lmd," in Braulik, *Studien zum Buch Deuteronomium* (Stuttgart: Katholisches Bibelwerk, 1997), pp. 119-46. For the connection of the prologue (esp. chap. 4) with legal parts of Deuteronomy, cf. A. D. H. Mayes, "Deuteronomy 4 and the Literary Criticism of Deuteronomy," in *A Song of Power and the Power of Song: Essays on the book of Deuteronomy*, ed. Duane L. Christensen (Winona Lake, Ind.: Eisenbrauns, 1993), pp. 214-15.

16. On the literary form of Deuteronomy cf. N. Lohfink, "Bund als Vertrag im Deuteronomium," in Lohfink's *Studien zum Deuteronomium und zur deuteronomistischen Literatur IV* (Stuttgart: Katholisches Bibelwerk, 2000), p. 285.

17. In contrast to Deuteronomy, the Book of the Covenant and the holiness laws of Leviticus locate the giving of "Torah" not at the border of the promised land but at Mount Sinai, which prefigures the temple mountain in Jerusalem.

18. See T. Veijola, "'Der Mensch lebt nicht vom Brot allein': Zur literarischen Schichtung und theologischen Aussage von Deuteronomium 8," in *Bundesdokument und Gesetz. Studien zum Deuteronomium*, ed. G. Braulik (Freiburg i.B: Herder, 1995), p. 158.

people who have Egypt and the desert wanderings "deep in their bones." The actual addressee of the text of Deuteronomy, however, is the people Israel who, now long settled, have taken possession of the land and for whom slavery and desert wanderings are no longer present in living memory.[19] In this way, a peculiar form of historical representation and historiography is chosen. Which intentions would stand behind such a representation of history? Above all it transfers in an imaginative way those who have come into the possession of land and goods into the position of "not-yet-possessors." Whoever hears the Torah of Yahweh out of the mouth of Moses would be led, as it were, out of the middle of the land to its borders, brought to the point of looking at their possessions as if what they owned would have to be repeatedly acquired anew. And it is here precisely where the point of the Deuteronomic conception of property lies. "Possession" is accordingly the result of just and regulated social relations as well as of true knowledge and worship of God — it is not a presumption.

As a consequence, the possession of land, goods, and life is not actually viewed as "one's own possession," but rather as the material reality of a successful life before God and with humanity; and to possess something means then, more precisely, to have a share in this reality. Deuteronomy therefore contemplates a structure of interdependence in which is essentially embedded what it means "to possess something." Kathryn Tanner, in her contribution to this volume, has described through observations about modernity what this *cannot* mean:

> This logic of modern property brings with it a certain understanding of social relations. Social relations are, first of all, consensual in virtue of a freedom that is a function of wealth. Having property allows one's relations with others to be consensual. If one has property one is not at the mercy of one's fellows but can approach them on an equal footing. The freedom that having property involves is, moreover, primarily understood negatively — as freedom from others and their potentially unjust seizure or use of what is one's own. One has one's own person and the products of one's own labor without owing them to anyone else; one does not owe them, in particular, to society, and therefore no legitimate social controls determine what one might do with them. Freedom from others suggests in this way freedom from any rights of needy others to use or enjoy what one has. Exclusive property rights in things and negative freedom mean that the modern sense of property is not easily compatible with the idea of

19. On the basis of speech-act analysis this has been rightly emphasized by Lohfink, "Bund als Vertrag," pp. 293, 298.

rights to well-being on the part of the general populace, or with the idea of a social commitment to furthering the livelihood of all.[20]

From this perspective, property is left to the sovereign power of the owner. This is a power that serves to deny obligations to the "have nots" and to establish a social agenda exclusively according to one's own discretion

It has been noted, however, that such a conception of a sovereign possessor does in fact occur even within Deuteronomy. This sovereign, however, is no human being, but rather God. He is the actual owner of both the land that is loaned to Israel and all its goods (Deut. 8:6-20). God gives of his own free will, and the Israelites receive all of this under the condition that they follow the commands of God, which means shaping life according to the stipulations of God's Torah — land and property in return for obedience.[21] There exists a broad scholarly consensus that the book of Deuteronomy has, in all probability, reproduced this form of the double-sided obligation from the conditions of state-rule as they existed between the Assyrian king and his vassals at the time of the late Assyrian empire (eighth to sixth century BCE) — a political environment in which the Israelite northern kingdom and Judah also found themselves.[22] Deuteronomy adopted this political form and adapted it at the same time: no longer is there a king of a far-off land, but rather Yahweh whose word is close to Israel is the giver of the land; and no longer is the concern with the keeping of vassal treaties, but rather the keeping of the covenant of Yahweh decided whether Israel would remain in the land or be cast out among all the nations. (The latter was the "punishment" that Assur executed against rebellious vassals and which also extinguished the northern kingdom in 722 BCE.) Yet the dark side of such a covenantal theology has been also repeatedly raised. In the end, is not Yahweh simply stylized as a super-potentate who, though actually more powerful, is not really any different from the Mesopotamian overlord? Does that allow for the relationship between God and his people to be thought of appropriately as "covenant," as an arrangement where both sides have claims and duties?

One should note that to the political duties of the vassal, Deuteron-

---

20. Kathryn Tanner, "Economies of Grace," p. 359 in this volume.

21. Cf. R. Albertz, "Religionsgeschichte Israels in alttestamentlicher Zeit 1," *Das Alte Testament Deutsch* 8, no. 1 (Göttingen: Vandenhoeck und Ruprecht, 1992), pp. 356-57; T. Veijola, *Bundestheologische Redaktion im Deuteronomium*, in *Das Deuteronomium und seine Querbeziehungen*, ed. T. Veijola (Göttingen: Vandenhoeck und Ruprecht, 1996), pp. 242-76.

22. For an overview of recent studies in the historical background of Deuteronomy cf. Albertz, "Religionsgeschichte" 1, pp. 356-60.

omy adds love of one's king. The relevant formula within the vassal treaties is *ramu kima napishtika,* "to love [the Assyrian King] as one's own life." In no way is here demanded an especially deep emotional tie. Rather, the meaning of this formulation is essentially pragmatic: to love someone like one's own *nephesh,* one's own "life" or "soul," implies a willingness to devote these to the other. What is being demanded is an allegiance that holds nothing back. The underlying concept of "love" is an all-encompassing self-surrender to the person being loved. Loving means not holding anything back, but placing everything within the right of disposal of another. In Deuteronomy 6:5, Israel is commanded to love its God "with all [its] soul" *(nephesh),* "with all [its] heart" *(lēb),* and "with all [its] might" *(me'ōd).* *Nephesh* denotes physical existence, *lēb* denotes the cognitive and emotional centers of human existence, and *me'ōd* the material goods. The covenantal concept of love encircles all the defining characteristics of the person. Hence "the-placing-into-service" of oneself in favor of another becomes the core of love, which does not at all require that the "beloved" other behaves likewise — at any rate, the Assyrian emperor did not add "love" to his own list of political obligations.

This is, however, a point where Deuteronomy diverges significantly from the Assyrian model. Although "love" is not part of Yahweh's covenantal obligations, is not something that Israel receives in return for its own loyalty, the love of Yahweh for Israel is one of the most defining elements of deuteronomic theology. However one assesses the adequacy of "covenant" as a theological category, it is clear that Deuteronomy has its own particular version of it, making "love" the motivating force behind Yahweh's engaging in a covenant with Israel. And this is the crucial point: whenever Israel remembers its own past, the events that preceded the covenant, this memory is intimately tied to what could be called Yahweh's love story with Israel (Deut. 4:37; 7:8; 10:15; 23:5), a story that encompasses the three largest parts of Israel's history before the Israelites' acquisition of the land: the ancestral age (4:37), the time of captivity in Egypt and the Exodus (7:8), and finally the forty-year-long desert wanderings (23:5).

It is important to see that establishing cultural memory here implies more than just selecting certain events of the past and putting them in historical sequence. It is rather about disclosing and making explicit the peculiar logic inherent in these events, their meaning giving coherence that is hidden from a merely descriptive point of view. This is the case also in Deuteronomy: what connects, according to Deuteronomy, the different periods of the early history of Israel and eventually culminates in the covenant and the giving of the Torah is the continuous creating and saving work of Yahweh toward what would become his people. In its most explicit form this is expressed in a text that exegetes, following Gerhard von Rad, like to call the "historical creed" of Israel (Deut. 26:5-10). This text starts out "My father was a Syrian about to perish, [but] he went down to Egypt . . . " (NKJV), followed by the rest of the covenant story.[23] Having in mind that in Deuteronomy love is the most inclusive term for Yahweh's creating and saving activity, it becomes apparent that the constitution of memory through the text is linked inextricably with the rhetoric of love.

It should be mentioned that in Deuteronomy it is beyond doubt that this story is about a love that was never reciprocated. None of the "mighty deeds" of God could move the people to love him of their own accord — not the election of their ancestors, not the Exodus, and certainly not the time in the desert, a time during which Israel doubted the sense and goal of the Exodus, finally rebelling and in so doing tossing aside in their entirety Yahweh's salvific acts. And yet it is here that we see a concept of love (based in covenantal law) attain a definitive position: Yahweh's love toward Israel does not fall within the obligations of the covenant. Above all, that means that this love is not conditioned upon compliance to the Torah. Israel can neither acquire the love of God through such compliance nor lose it through its own disregard. In other words, Yahweh already loved Israel before the covenant was in place, and he can continue to love them even when they break that covenant.

Yahweh's love and Israel's memory, so we might summarize, frame the concept of covenant. The entire complex of covenant, law, possession of land and goods, and social life within that land is drawn up upon a history of love that precedes all acts of remembering the past, and it is this memory that shapes moral conduct at every point in Israel's subsequent historical presence. This brings us to a position to look again at the connection between Israel's cultural memory and the command to love the stranger, which is made at various points of Deuteronomy.[24] We can now grasp the deeper meaning of these texts, which lies in the fact that the history of love between Yahweh and Israel opens itself up in relation to the foreigner. Their fate is characterized in a way that at the same time deeply determines the historical identity of Israel, i.e.,

23. Today, however, relatively few scholars would still agree with von Rad's influential theory that Deuteronomy 26:5-10 is part of the oldest layers of historical writing in ancient Israel. The consensus is rather that the "creed" is to be understood as a summary that not only looks back on the historical events but synthesizes the related literary traditions of the Pentateuch from a specific point of view. (For an overview of the discussion, see A. Schuele, *Israels Sohn — Jahwes Prophet* [Münster: Lit, 2001], pp. 146-52.)

24. In addition to Deuteronomy 10:19, cf. also Deuteronomy 15:15, 16:12, and 24:18.

that the person and status of the foreigner is identified on the basis of Israel's own creative and salvific experience with God. It seems to me that it is precisely here that we find one of the most excellent cultural and historical achievements of Old Testament ethics. And it is in terms of this identification (which is the sense behind the character of the command of Deuteronomy 10:17-19) that the dispositions and actions toward the foreigner should be fashioned. These dispositions and actions are now described likewise as love, analogously to the relationship of love between Yahweh and Israel.

Another text (in this case outside of Deuteronomy, but possibly influenced by the tradition) that expresses this notion in equally exemplary fashion is Leviticus 19:34, within the context of the holiness code. To quote from the Revised Standard Version:

> The stranger who sojourns with you shall be to you as the native among you, and you shall love him as yourself; for you were strangers in the land of Egypt: I am the LORD your God.

The formulation "love him as yourself" does require clarification. The translation here follows primarily the Greek tradition of the Septuagint, which uses the reflexive personal pronoun. Yet in Hebrew, this is not the case. If one translates the text word for word (as far as possible), then the text reads: "Love him — like you." At the grammatical level, two translations are equally possible: "Love him as yourself," but also "Love him, he is like you."[25] In light of our considerations thus far, it is clear that the second translation is a better approximation of the sense of the text. What makes the foreigner an object of love is his or her particular fate, which wraps Israel up within its own cultural memory.

That leads us finally to Leviticus 19:18 and the command to love one's neighbor, one of the most fundamental texts in biblical ethics and a text formulated analogously to Leviticus 19:34.

"Love Thy Neighbor" (Leviticus 19:18)

Here too we run into the problem of translation that was discussed above all at the beginning of the twentieth century amongst Jewish and Christian in-

---

25. For a detailed philological analysis cf. A. Schuele, "Kamoka — der Nächste, der ist wie Du. Zur Philologie des Liebesgebots von Lev 19,18.34," *KUSATU* 2 (2001): 97-130; "Denn er ist wie Du. Zu Übersetzung und Verständnis des alttestamentlichen Liebesgebots Lev 19,18," *Zeitschrift für die alttestamentliche Wissenschaft* 113 (2001): 315-34.

terpreters. This problem of translation directly parallels that of Leviticus 19:34. In contrast to the translation of the Septuagint — "love your neighbor as yourself" — which also lies behind each of the New Testament instances (Matt. 22:39; Luke 10:27; Rom. 13:9; Gal. 5:14; James 2:8), the Hebrew is grammatically ambiguous. Once again, a possible word-for-word translation would result in a formulation of the command that reads "Love your neighbor — like you." The philological approach also yields the possibility of translating the text, "Love your neighbor, (for) he is like you." More than anyone else in recent times, Martin Buber displayed the advantages of this variant. Buber formulated this passage in such a way that it left multiple interpretations open, leaving it as close as possible to the Hebraic syntax: "Treat your companions kindly, like you" ("Halte lieb deinen Genossen, dir gleich");[26] yet what is intended, according to clarifications he makes elsewhere, is a view of the neighbor "who is your equal," "who is like you."[27] As H.-P. Mathys has shown, this interpretation is no invention of Buber's but reaches far back into the Jewish history of the interpretation of this command to love.[28] After Buber, this interpretation was taken up primarily by E. Ullendorf, to whose influence a variant found within the New English Bible can possibly be ascribed: "You shall love your neighbor as a man like yourself." This has nothing to do with a feeling of being close or distant that leads to the fostering of one's neighbors; rather, the Hebrew term *kāmôkā* ("like you") is much more a statement of an ontological quality that has no limitation whatsoever: The neighbor is your equal, and this equality does not depend upon emotion, recognition, or the mere opinions of the individual. He is your equal, but he is not you yourself — that in particular is Buber's point, which led him against the Greek tradition of interpretation of Leviticus 19:18. Equality can only be serious, then, if there is a definite "You" standing over against the "I," one that is not simply a projection or a subjective image of a neighbor. Equality as a genuine form of interpersonality must therefore be grounded somewhere other than in subjective consciousness; it must be imported from without. And it is precisely here that Buber recognizes the sense and meaning of the "he is like you" as a command out of the mouth of God. Here we learn the will of God and acquire the realization of the elementary equality of "I" and "You" which we cannot create by ourselves: "The You meets me by grace — by

26. Martin Buber and F. Rosenzweig, *Die fünf Bücher der Weisung* (Köln 1954), p. 326.

27. Martin Buber, *Zwei Glaubensweisen* (Zürich 1955), p. 69.

28. Mathys finds the earliest reference to the translation "he is like you" in Naftali Herz Wessely's commentary on Leviticus from 1782; cf. H.-P. Mathys, "Liebe deinen Nächsten wie dich selbst. Untersuchungen zum alttestamentlichen Gebot der Nächstenliebe (Lev 19,18)," *Orbis Biblicus et Orientalis* 71 (Freiburg/Göttingen: Vandenhoeck und Ruprecht, 1986), pp. 6-7.

seeking it is not found."[29] The command to love one's neighbor is a regulation of the will of God, which corresponds to the regulation of the existence of human beings.[30]

Regardless of Buber's ingenious feel for language, these interpretations admittedly appear not primarily thanks to philological and exegetical observations, but rather to his general ontological approach. It is important for the exegetical approach to the text, however, that Buber finds the aspect of *interpersonal equality* in Leviticus 19:18. The sense of the text develops with this into something quite different: the Greek version asks about the type and quality of the love, while bringing love of self and love of neighbor into relation. The second possible version, which arises out of the Hebraic text, asks, on the other hand, about the "why" that lies behind the love of one's neighbor. The connection to the command of love toward foreigners lies in this approach and in that respect displays at the same time an analogy to the Deuteronomic understanding of the love of God toward his people. Above all, it becomes interesting then in our context to take up Buber's translation.

The first thing then noticed is that in many diverse ways the entirety of Leviticus 19[31] stresses the inequality, the legally and socially differing levels of status, simply among the Israelites themselves. One could even go so far as to say that the whole chapter revolves around the theme of inequality among equals, around the partly public, partly private, and subtly cloaked social divides and hierarchical arrangements among the Israelites. Verses 9 and 10 contain laws of compassion: at the harvest, the corners of the field (which could not be immediately reached with the scythe) should not be reaped, and the remains of the harvest should not be gleaned. That is equally the case with the vineyard: there too,

---

29. Martin Buber, *Das dialogische Prinzip* (Gerlingen: Steiner, 1992), p. 15.

30. Cf. H. Gese, "Der Dekalog als Ganzheit betrachtet," *Zeitschrift für Theologie und Kirche* 64 (1967): 121-38.

31. Especially instructive on the role of Leviticus 19 within the holiness code is M. Douglas, "Justice As the Cornerstone: An Interpretation of Leviticus 18–20," *Interpretation* (1999): 341-49. The interpretation of Leviticus 19 has recently triggered a discussion on the relationship between narrative and legal traditions within the Torah. Calum M. Carmichael, "Laws of Leviticus," *Harvard Theological Review* 87 (1994): 239-56, finds a connection between Leviticus 19:18 and the story of Joseph (Gen. 37-50). Above all, it is the relationship between Joseph and his brothers that he sees to thematize, to show both what separates even those who belong to the same social units and what makes them "neighbors." For a critique of this approach cf. B. Levinson, "Calum M. Carmicheal's Approach to the Laws of Deuteronomy," *Harvard Theological Review* 83 (1990): 227-57, and J. Milgrom, "Law and Narrative and the Exegesis of Leviticus XIX 19," *Vetus Testamentum* 46 (1996): 544-47. On the issue in general cf. R. Cover, "Nomos and Narrative," *Harvard Law Review* 97 (1983): 4-68; J. Watts, "The Rhetorical Strategy in the Composition of the Pentateuch," *Journal for the Study of the Old Testament* 68 (1995): 3-22.

the harvest should not extend to the very last grape; rather, something should be left over for the poor. In verse 13, among the general regulations against theft and robbery, we find a command that the day-worker be paid on the same day and that his wages not be retained overnight. Here, an abstract idea of equality appears through the command to concentrate upon the needs of another: to be paid on the same day was in no way a general right, but especially in the case of day-workers, who lived from hand to mouth, this was absolutely necessary to ensure that their survival was not threatened. Finally, verses 13 and 14 forbid the cheating of the disadvantaged and weak: the deaf should not be cursed, no obstacle should be placed in the path of the blind, and the social status of the weak should not be turned to their disadvantage before the courts.

The poor, the stranger, the deaf, the blind are, among others, all "neighbors" who are repeatedly supported in Leviticus 19 (cf. Lev. 19:13, 15, 16). If one considers the context of the law of compassion, it becomes clear that the command to love fulfills a very precise function in connection to the Israelite conception of the law. Love supports a deep realism in the situation of tension and divide within one and the same social unit. Already, therefore, an understanding of love built primarily upon a self-relatedness remains behind the neatly ordered and differentiated understanding of Leviticus 19. Those who love the other only according to the way they see themselves, according to their own status and to an awareness of their own prestige, can actually only start out from and arrive back at themselves within a loop of empty self-reference. This love never really reaches the other. But in this way we would lose sight of the point that Leviticus 19 as a whole is trying to sharpen: that even among equals, some are more equal than others.

The command to love contains therefore an idea of equality that is simply not guaranteed by national, cultural, or religious affiliation. To be part of a people group with a given tradition, a particular self-understanding, a binding and regulated legal and social life, does not yet attain the idea of equality intended in Leviticus 19:18. The meaning discloses itself, rather, in the reverse direction: the neighbor, who is my equal, is a person who is dependent upon the protection of life-supporting legal and social forms just like me, a person who requires the closeness and intimate warmth of others just like I do, because she can't live without all this and because he cannot furnish all this of his own accord. Therefore, it revolves about a socio-anthropological sense of a fundamental nature. In regards to Old Testament anthropology, Hans-Walter Wolff once spoke of the person as a "needy being"[32] — an expression that very aptly describes the image of humanity that stands behind Leviticus 19:18: the person is not simply

---

32. Hans-Walter Wolff, *Anthropologie des Alten Testaments* (München: Kaiser, 1967), p. 25.

constituted as an organic being, but rather just as much a socially "needy" be-ing, dependent upon environments that must accommodate those different needs, but which can only partially (if at all) be influenced by the individual person. This recognition, that a person is dependent upon environments that are favorable for and supportive of life, and that in this all human beings are the same, regardless of which end of the social scale they find themselves on, can therefore in view of the ethical question "What should I do?" amount only to "Behave toward your fellow human being in such a way that he or she discovers in you an environment that is favorable and supportive to life." Or, in the words of the Old Testament, "Love your neighbor, he is like you."

The concept of love from Leviticus 19:18 possesses an adequately for-malized structure that can be applied to very different interpersonal relation-ships. Love is, according to the understanding of Leviticus 19:18, the funda-mental form of interpersonal care, of a "turning toward" one another, because it stirs up the elementary anthropological requirement of equality as equal neediness.

Conclusion

At the beginning of the essay, we introduced love — within the horizon of modern thought — as a "code of intimacy." In this view of loving, "turning toward" another person is accordingly an intentional act, which aims at "finding sense in the world of another" (Luhmann) and achieves one's own identity out of the world of experience of the other. If we look back at the dif-fering versions of the Old Testament command of love, the spectrum widens considerably: love has even more sources than the intimate relationship be-tween "you" and "me." The Old Testament version leads at first to the opening of one's own cultural memory and identity for the situation and support of another who does not belong to the same community (Lev. 19:34; Deut. 10:17-19). The command to love one's neighbor in Leviticus 19:18 goes even one step further: it formulates the fundamental anthropological sense of an equal neediness of all human beings for environments that support life. The form-ing of such environments to the favor of one's neighbors is the crux of what distinguishes acts of love. In each of these different versions of the command to love, it is clear that love comes into view less as an affect or emotion, and more as a special form of creativity, which can apply in transformative and al-ways new ways to all regions of social life. And, of particular interest in the context of the essays in this volume, this transformative view of love contrib-utes fundamentally to a conception of rights, acquisition, and ownership.

Possessing Wealth, Possessing Women, Possessing Self: The Shame of Biblical Discourse

CLAUDIA V. CAMP

What is the relationship of our sense of self, our identity, to what we possess? We like to think of ourselves as something other than what we have. It is one of the (easy) ways we frame the notion of equality: rich and poor alike, we all share the dignity of our common humanity, or, if one prefers more theological terms, we are all God's children. Yet this ideal is hardly realized in practice, whether today or in that complex of genres, processes, and conflicts we call the biblical/Jewish/Christian tradition(s). Indeed, a strong strand within the First Testament tapestry resists the notion absolutely: to be a member of God's people is precisely to have a land, and a man's personal righteousness will be evident in his possession of material comforts and the (male) progeny to pass them on to.[1] And one cannot simply advert to the Second Testament to "cure" the problem (if, indeed, one sees it as such). The resistance to material possessions there tends to be based on the problematic assumption that the world will end soon anyway. Likewise, the later Christian adoption of the ideal of poverty was not only often ignored but also based on a different but equally problematic assumption, namely, the dualism of body and spirit, whose invidious effects have been well documented.

Pointing to these difficulties in the Bible and the traditions that grow out of it is not to say that good cannot be drawn or created from it. The notion that God intends (and sometimes — though this is a trickier idea — pro-

---

1. Leviticus 25:23 refines the idea of land possession, styling God's people as mere resident aliens in a land owned by the deity. This metaphorical nuance is worth further consideration. On the other hand, the concern for heirs, alongside the fact that the land's previous inhabitants had to be killed in favor of Israel, together complicate any easy effort to de-materialize the meaning of land possession.

vides for) the material well-being of humans can contribute to a viable theological ethics, as can the notion that our ultimate treasure lies not in the things we possess.[2] These two ideas do, however, stand in tension with one another, creating a hermeneutical difficulty for using these traditions as a resource for contemporary imagination on property and possession. Even more problematic, in my view, is the taken-for-grantedness of the Bible in particular as such a resource. Taking the Bible for granted dangerously dehistoricizes it, failing to take seriously its rhetorical quality and its embeddedness in structures of power and ideology, both in its ancient context and in its use in contemporary discourse. My point is this: both the close association of God *with* possessions and the distinction of God *from* possessions have been used for both harm and good, depending on who's doing the using and in what situation. As bits of rhetoric, they cannot be evaluated as absolutely life-giving or as absolutely oppressive; their value depends on their context of use. The study of them in particular contexts of use may give us a sense of their likely functional range of value in historical discourse.

What, then, is the relationship of our sense of self, our identity, to what we possess? Perhaps the most radical case of defining identity by possessions (or lack thereof) is when a person, taking a vow of poverty, declares herself free from such entrapments to the material world. Clearly present in this situation are mediating symbols and rhetoric that make sense of such a choice. What is obvious in that instance is just as true, though covertly so, in the life of the average person caught more fully in the bind of, on the one hand, the assertion that she is not what she owns and, on the other, the powerful cultural messages that seek to make her so, not to mention the pleasure she feels in the things she acquires and lives with. Here, however, we need to articulate and unpack the symbols and rhetoric that tell the story, give us the picture, tie the knot of selves and possessions in particular cultural contexts.

The underlying question of this essay is how the systems of symbols and rhetoric of which we are a part help mediate both the fact of our constitution by our possessions and the contradictions involved therein; the tension, that is, between both being and not being what we possess. Consideration of this question in light of the biblical tradition is complicated by three factors. First is the problem, alluded to above, of the contradictory views on God's relationship to possessions, a problem closely linked with that of divine justice. To what extent are possessions understood as reward for righteousness, and

2. See, for example, in this volume, the analyses by Margaret Mitchell and Christine Firer Hinze of the respective social ethics of John Chrysostom and John Ryan.

what happens theologically when this linkage is denied? Second is the matter of gender. In the Bible, the constitution of female selves vis-à-vis possessions is not a problem because women *are* possessions. The historical legacy of men's possession of women persists in our contemporary rhetoric of possession despite our efforts to transcend patriarchal practice. To what extent does this pervasive aspect of biblical discourse impede the tradition's value as a resource for contemporary thought on the ethical construction of property and possession? The final issue is the function of the Bible itself in these dynamics of identity and possession — the Bible as icon, if you will. What does it mean to the rest of the picture of property, possession, and identity to "have the Bible" as one of our possessions?[3]

It is, of course, the hope of many analysts of past cultures that their work will shed some light on the present. That is certainly true for me in turning to the work of the early-second-century B.C.E. Jewish sage Jesus Ben Sira, whose literary remains (Sirach or Ecclesiasticus) are found in the Apocrypha, the deuterocanonical writings of the Roman and Orthodox traditions. Ben Sira is, on one level, an obscure point of departure, yet I hope it will contribute to exploration of the issues just mentioned. Analysis of the place of property in Ben Sira's religious system shows a remarkable interweaving of the rhetorics of the marketplace, of theology, and of gender, as well as the contradiction of identities both constituted by our possessions and not. Indeed, the book provides a virtual template for both the consistencies and the vicissitudes in biblical thought on the issues in question. Although Sirach did not make it into either the Jewish or the Protestant canon, it was widely read in antiquity by both Jews and Christians. It is of particular interest for its place in the development of the Jewish and Christian self-identification as peoples of the book. Ben Sira is the first person on extant record to articulate a complex sense of possessing and being possessed by a

---

3. These are questions that are, in my view, well worth study in the contemporary world. There would be tremendous value in a wide-ranging ideological-critical look at the history of interpretation of the Bible on property and possession, including at every point a meta-analysis of its own possessedness. Particularly important would be analysis of the range of contemporary situations where these issues emerge. Where and how do the rhetoric of the marketplace and the rhetoric of religion reinforce or resist each other? How does gender factor in? And why do persons choose one or another element of the religious tradition to weave into the fabric of their economic values? It would be my preference to have such a study well underway before attempting constructive theological work on the issue. On this issue, see the collection of essays edited by Vincent Wimbush, *The Bible and the American Myth: A Symposium on the Bible and the Construction of Meaning* (Macon, Ga.: Mercer University Press, 1999). These things said, I hope readers will indulge my inclination toward a hermeneutics of suspicion in my own approach to the topic.

scriptural canon, named as "the law, the prophets, and the other books of our fathers."[4]

Furthermore, the intellectual and moral web that binds Ben Sira's views on possession, women, God, and Scripture is stretched on an ideological framework that has relevance for today as well. In the ideology of shame, we shall find the thread that ties together the disparate elements in Sirach, as well as the unifying theme of this essay. It is my contention that the rhetoric of shame, whether ancient or modern, expresses a profound aspect of moral existence at the same time it serves as an easily manipulated tool for the construction and maintenance of systems of power. It is the task of this essay to examine the currency of shame in the marketplace of power, a marketplace that includes control of persons and ideas along with material wealth and status.

"Each decade," declares John Taylor in *Esquire*, "lets itself down in its own way; each age displays a unique ethical lapse, one that emerges from and reflects its particular priorities."[5] One might question in what sense "a decade" constitutes "an age," thus allowing for Taylor's rather global characterizations of the ethical failings of "the sixties," "the seventies," "the eighties," and "the nineties." It is nonetheless hard to argue with his assertion that shamelessness, presumably the "characteristic ethical lapse" of the twentieth century's final decade, is indeed alive and well. I suspect, however, that its immoral health today has more than a little to do with what Taylor catalogues as the definitive failure of "the eighties," namely, greed, as well as that of "the seventies," spiritual narcissism.[6] His analysis focuses on the shameless deploy-

---

4. This phrasing is found in the Prologue to the book, written by Ben Sira's grandson, who translated his work into Greek around 130 B.C.E. While it is unlikely that at the time Ben Sira wrote (ca. 180) he was working with a definitively closed canon, the similarity of the Prologue's terminology to the still-current threefold division of the Hebrew Bible into Law *(Torah)*, Prophets *(Nevi'im)*, and Writings *(Kethuvim)* has suggested to some that he knew already a compilation well on its way to its final state. Other scholars, however, have questioned whether these often more loosely used terms should be equated with the later understanding of Tanak. The fact that fragments of all the Hebrew Bible books (except Esther) later recognized as canonical were found at Qumran (165 B.C.E.–70 C.E.) does suggest some significant level of agreement about the scope of the canon by the late second century B.C.E. Whatever the case, Ben Sira is undeniably concerned with the interpretation, and perhaps, in his own writing, the creation, of a multifaceted body of authoritative literature.

5. John Taylor, "Spin, You Sinners: The Shame of Shamelessness," *Esquire* (December 1996): 74.

6. Contra Taylor, "spiritual narcissism" is hardly the unique provenance of the seventies' "personal-fulfillment movement." It easily characterizes much of what is called "Christianity" today, notably including Christian fundamentalism.

ment of political "spin" by top political consultants like Dick Morris and Ed Rollins. (An accompanying article[7] also includes Michael Deaver in an unholy trinity of shame.) But the story will not be complete without some attention to the interwoven economic and spiritual realities of a culture that accommodates — and pays well — men like these. The shameless greed for power we see in them is, in one sense, no more than a variation of the shameless greed for wealth. It is a particularly revealing variation, however, because in it the symbolic and rhetorical processes of shamelessness are evident. Possession of this sort of power is founded on controlling public rhetoric to such a degree that one can deceive with impunity. Not insignificantly, as we shall see in our subsequent analysis of shame, the shamelessness of the Big Lie is expressed in the metaphor of prostitution: the sale of male integrity is articulated in terms of economic transfer of women's bodies.

If shamelessness is the current problem, a text like Ben Sira's, with its rigorous tutelage in shame and honor, might seem to be the solution. In fact, I shall argue, this book and the theo-ideological system it represents only contribute to the problem. This is true with respect to each of the discourses I am concerned with here, whether that of theology, gender, or relationship to the Bible. Shame ideology links, in problematic ways, biblical thought on property and possession to each of these other discourses.

Shame and the Construction of the Moral Self

Shame has been studied by scholars from different disciplines, using different methodologies. An anthropological approach that analyzes Ben Sira's text as part of a more generalized code of shame and honor in Mediterranean society has provided significant insight into its logic.[8] Before turning to those results, however, a different perspective deserves attention. Bernard Williams, in *Shame and Necessity*,[9] uses a psychological model to analyze the operation

---

7. Randall Rothenberg, "The Age of Spin," *Esquire* (December 1996): 70-73, 76-77, 124-26.

8. Claudia V. Camp, "Understanding a Patriarchy: Women in Second Century Jerusalem Through the Eyes of Ben Sira," in *"Women Like This": New Perspectives on Jewish Women in the Greco-Roman World*, Early Judaism and Its Literature, vol. 1, ed. Amy-Jill Levine (Atlanta: Scholars Press, 1991), pp. 1-40; Claudia C. Camp, "Honor and Shame in Ben Sira: Anthropological and Theological Reflections," in *The Book of Ben Sira in Modern Research*, ed. P. C. Beentjes (Berlin: Walter de Gruyter, 1997), pp. 171-88; David A. deSilva, "The Wisdom of Ben Sira: Honor, Shame, and the Maintenance of the Values of a Minority Culture," *Catholic Biblical Quarterly* 58 (1996): 433-55.

9. Bernard Williams, *Shame and Necessity* (Berkeley: University of California Press, 1993).

of shame in the construction of moral identity. His work focuses on shame in Greek literature and thus also contributes to the larger question of drawing resources from antiquity to shed light on contemporary culture.

Williams's psychological model locates the root of the human experience of shame in the experience of exposure, being seen by the wrong people in the wrong circumstances. Shame *(aidos)* is bodily grounded in the experience of nakedness, especially as associated with sexuality (*aidoia* = genitals). While nakedness is, in many cultures, the most powerful expression of shame, it is not its sum. "The root of shame lies in exposure in a more general sense, in being at a disadvantage: in what I shall call, in a very general sense, a loss of power."[10]

Shame involves the gaze of another, but this does not mean it is entirely heteronomous. While shame can in certain circumstances operate with the blunt external force of social approbation, its more important, and for Williams more basic, function is as a structure that mediates between the character of the individual and the values of a culture. Shame serves both as a conduit of social values to the individual and as a psychological processing station within the individual that converts those social values to his or her own. There is a "reciprocal structure" at work in shame: "the relations between what [a person] expected of the world and what the world expects of a [person] who expects that of it."[11] This structure works by giving "through the emotions a sense of who one is and of what one hopes to be" while at the same time embodying "intimations of a genuine social reality — in particular, of how it will be for one's life with others if one acts in one way rather than another."[12] Shame, in other words, helps constitute for the individual an autonomous identity, however much its content may have been socially mediated. In this identity is grounded one's sense of necessary moral action.

Now we can begin to see the role of shame with respect to my question about how the identity of an individual comes to be, or not to be, constituted by his or her possessions. Shame helps to constitute identity by providing a structure of reciprocity between self and world. I propose we specify this notion one step further and examine the mediation shame provides between the self and that particular part of its world comprised of its possessions. At this point, Williams's analysis of shame becomes less helpful. Although he describes shame as a sense of a "loss of power," he does not connect that observation with his further discussion of real issues of social power, namely, the attitudes of Greek writers to slavery and women.

---

10. Williams, *Shame and Necessity,* p. 110.
11. Williams, *Shame and Necessity,* pp. 84-85.
12. Williams, *Shame and Necessity,* p. 102.

The typical Greek view of what it meant to be human entailed the notion that one human's attempt to force or constrain another was wrong. The Greek practice of slavery in this moral environment thus raises a crucial question regarding shame. Why is it that individuals in a culture that valued freedom as essential to the fully human life did not feel shame in the coercive possession and use of other humans? Williams explains this paradox by invoking one sense of the notion of "necessity." "[C]onsiderations of justice and injustice were immobilised by the demands of what was seen as social and economic necessity."[13] This sort of necessity, imposed by force, collides, however, with that sense of necessity in moral behavior, generated by shame, that both preserves individual autonomy and connects the individual to society. "Social and economic necessity" seems to have immobilized shame as well as justice. Greek acceptance of slavery, in other words, involved a form of shamelessness, understood as the failure by some persons to apply the same criteria of selfhood to others that they treasured for themselves. This failure of shame created a blinder (shame being, most fundamentally, a state of exposure), an inability to address, or even see the need for addressing, an important question concerning who they were and what (much less *whom*) they possessed.

Aristotle, for both better and worse, opened up the problem for view. Acknowledging that slavery, if imposed by force, was indeed wrong, he attempted to justify it by appeal to "necessary identity." Necessary identities are those understood by a society to involve no constraint or force, a "natural" identity. Aristotle tried to show that there are some people for whom slavery is not contrary to nature and thus involves no force. One argument to this effect was modeled on the culture's largely unquestioned assumption about women's natural inferiority to men and the naturalness of their assignment to certain roles in the division of labor. The Greeks often expressed thanks for not being a slave, a woman, or a barbarian. Extending this line of thought, Aristotle assimilated the otherwise apparently unnecessary identity of the slave to the necessary identity of the woman, thereby naturalizing slavery.[14]

The earlier Greeks avoided the problem of having to defend the essential justice of the world, not by claiming that slavery was just, but rather by invoking the social necessity of it, thus removing it from the discourse of justice.[15] They acknowledged the force involved, which Aristotle tried to deny.

13. Williams, *Shame and Necessity*, p. 125.

14. Williams, *Shame and Necessity*, pp. 117-22, citing the *Politics* 1260a12-13.

15. Other scholars object to Williams's rather sweeping contrast between Aristotle and (presumably all) earlier Greeks on the justice of slavery. My argument does not require, however, that his historical observations cover all the nuances of an undoubtedly more complex situation, only that there be evidence that this view was held by some.

On the other hand, Aristotle represents an arguable moral advance with respect to slavery insofar as his need to defend it suggests a sense of precisely that shame that much of the culture seems to have lacked. One of the effects of the sense of "exposure" so basic to the experience of shame — what marks, in fact, its function as producer of identity — is what we would call self-consciousness. Aristotle presumably feels the need to defend slavery because his self has become conscious on some level that it is a problem, that it *ought* to have a place within the discourse of justice and injustice, even though it had not. It is this self-consciousness that has him working overtime to fill in the gaps, explain the contradictions, that the ideology of shame had masked. Of course his effort is abominable. But it records an exposure from which, fortunately, Western culture never quite re-covers.

Although Williams fails to show the full linkage of shame to slavery in ancient Greek thought, he does set the hermeneutical issue powerfully. He asks, does the rejection of slavery by modern society make us morally superior to the ancient Greeks? And his answer is "no." The immobilization of considerations of justice and injustice by social and economic demands "has not so much been eliminated from modern life as shifted to different places." We see injustice and understand the structures that cause it, but we do not act, partly because "we have no settled opinion on the question about which Aristotle tried to contrive a settled opinion: *How far does the existence of a worthwhile life for some people involve the imposition of suffering on others?*"[16] This is a question, needless to say, concerned on a fundamental level with the matter of possessions, whether human or otherwise.

My analysis suggests, however, that the problem is not merely a lack of "settled opinion" today, but rather a blindness that impedes the intellectual process of forming opinions. The haves cannot look at the have-nots without feeling shame. The desire to avoid the feeling of shame leads the haves to close their eyes, much like ancient Greek slave owners, and pretend the problem does not exist. Thus we have a paradox: the mechanism of shame, which should lead to moral choices, in practice creates its own shamelessness when tied to particular circumstances of disparity in power and possession. Shame as a psychological mechanism, in other words, always functions in relationship to social power. Because of its relationship to power, a shame system will collude in masking inconsistencies between the self and its moral actions that ought to be, but will not be, experienced as shamelessness. In this sense, shame generates shamelessness. As we shall see in turning to Ben Sira, one of the devices through which shame masks such moral incoherence is through

16. Williams, *Shame and Necessity,* p. 125 (my emphasis).

affirmations of social honor according to the values of the elite and of the honor of God in the face of human suffering.

Ben Sira, Shame, and Possessions

We turn now to another point of departure, the analysis of shame and honor in Mediterranean culture that is the subject of a growing literature in anthropology.[17] Here, too, we find analysis of how shame mediates self and society, but played out in more mundane arenas of human existence: not the shame that rises to the surface to produce grand moments of self-revelatory necessity of Sophoclean tragedy or Thucydidean history, but that which permeates invisibly the waters of socially constructed selves. My interest was drawn to this anthropological study of shame and honor in order to understand better these issues in the second-century B.C.E. book of Ben Sira.

Ben Sira is a book of instructional poems, written by a member of the scribal class to his (male) students, whom he'd like to turn into wise men. It forms a part of what scholars refer to as the biblical "wisdom tradition" (along with Proverbs, Job, Ecclesiastes, and the Wisdom of Solomon), whose concerns cover a range of issues from the wisdom required for success in the world to speculation on what humans can know of the ways of God. Because of its instructional genre, it offers more direct insight than most Jewish and Christian writings into the practice as well as the ideology of the culture — including its grappling with the self and its possessions.[18] It was also widely read by both Jews and Christians in antiquity, and was thus an influential book in the formative period of both religions. The ideology of shame and honor is a determinative construct at work in his text. Honor and shame are inextricably linked with each other in a code that is both theologized and gendered, as well as class-related. But Ben Sira lacks confidence in this system that supports him, and it is his anxieties that make his book so interesting, revealing once more the problematic relationship of shame to power. I shall identify three areas in which anxiety plagues him.

17. For an excellent introduction, see the collection of essays edited by David Gilmore, *Honor and Shame and the Unity of the Mediterranean* (Washington, D.C.: American Anthropological Association, 1987).

18. As I have noted, Sirach is also written at an important phase in the development of canonical thought. He identifies the Torah with Wisdom personified as a woman (24:1-23), a woman to be desired (24:19). This is, indeed, the only woman who should be desired if one is to avoid shame (24:22). The question of the place of canonical Scripture in Ben Sira's gendered system of shame and possession is, thus, not an idle one.

1. Ben Sira is anxious about his ability to control his women, as well as his ability to control himself in relation to women. A man's wife is possession par excellence in the sense that she is a possession that defines the male self who possesses her. A man's honor depended on his ability to possess his wife properly, particularly with regard to his exclusive sexual rights over her, while failure in this regard was the fastest road to shame. The cuckold epitomized the unmanly man; the sexually autonomous woman (whether prostitute, adulteress, or unmarried nonvirgin) was the embodiment of shamelessness itself.

> Better is the wickedness of a man than a woman who does good;
>> it is woman who brings shame and disgrace. (42:14)

Shame is exposure, and a shameless wife, in exposing her own genitals, exposes her husband's as well.

> Where there is an untrustworthy wife, a seal is a good thing;
>> and where there are many hands, lock things up. (42:6)

The reader is left to ponder whether the problem is the wife's hands on the husband's treasure box or some other man's hands on hers.

2. Ben Sira's anxiety about the shame at stake in controlling women is matched by his self-contradictory attempts to make meaning of the relationship between material possessions and the work of God. Wealth and authority tend to be seen as the signs of honor — in religious terms, as signs of God's favor to the righteous (11:17; cf. 40:13). The sage does not condemn wealth; indeed, he sees it as something to be acquired through astute business practices (42:4-5) and enjoyed; he faults the miser for his self-denial as well as his stinginess to others (13:4-5, 13-14). Yet danger lurks precisely here: "One who loves gold will not be justified; one who pursues money will be led astray by it" (31:5). Wealth can be acquired by evil means as well as good, and sometimes it seems God's action comes in retrospect rather than prospect.

> Who has been tested by [gold] and been found perfect?
>> Let it be for him a ground for boasting.
> . . .
> His prosperity will be established,
>> And the assembly will proclaim his acts of charity. (31:10-11)

Hardly new to the biblical tradition is awareness of the fact that the righteous sometimes suffer. Like the tradition, Ben Sira avoids the logical conclusion that suffering and poverty imply unrighteousness; he even expresses grief over "the wealthy man reduced to want" (26:28 NAB). One might expect honor to fill the moral chasm left by the failure of obvious justice with respect to material reward and punishment for righteousness or mendacity. Indeed, this sage sometimes suggests that the poor man will be honored for his wisdom (10:30; 11:1). But such a hope does not bear too close an examination:

> One who is honored in poverty, how much more in wealth!
> And one dishonored in wealth, how much more in poverty! (10:31)

Ben Sira lives in a society that accords honor to the powerful, no matter their ethics or their religion, and regards poverty as shameful. Just as the rich man can be reduced to poverty, the intelligent man can be held in contempt (26:28). Honor is good; honor and wealth together are better; neither is guaranteed. Honor cannot fill the gap left by unfulfilled expectations of just retribution in the realm of wealth and power.

This unhinging of honor and righteousness constitutes an even greater ideological chasm than the loosening of either of those from wealth. It is an incoherence Ben Sira both sees and refuses to see. His work in one sense represents a culmination of his tradition's understanding of self and possessions, insofar as it brings to the surface the role of shame in this dynamic. He confronts the moral inconsistencies both in the social practice of possessing and in the ideology that supports it: not only might a good man fail to achieve his just material deserts, he may also suffer social shame for this lack. The honor-shame system, in other words, fails to compensate with a sense of personal integrity what it takes away at the social level. Here the connection of shame to power becomes apparent. One who lacks social power also lacks that "reciprocal structure" of shame to which Williams refers, which generates individual autonomy as well as social conformity. The mechanism of shame that Ben Sira inculcates supports the status quo, and he counts on this system to work for him and for his students, evidence to the contrary notwithstanding. The result is that his honor-shame system helps mask the degree to which his own honorable life rests on others' suffering. As long as he himself can win honor and avoid shame, awareness of the system's failure for others dims as fast as it appears.

3. There is, moreover, one further problem in all this, and that is God. The matter of divine honor, or glory — the difference comes only in English translation, not in the ancient languages — provides the ultimate contradiction that must be suppressed when it comes to wealth and poverty. A pair of verses condenses the issue.

> Good things and bad, life and death,
>> poverty and wealth, come from the Lord.
> The Lord's gift remains with the devout
>> and his favor brings lasting success. (11:14, 17)

But which is it really? The second verse, affirming God's gifts, implies a theologizing of wealth in the manner of Proverbs and the Torah. The first verse, on the other hand, is a sample of skeptical wisdom, akin to that of Ecclesiastes. In contrast both to the theological optimism of one part of his tradition and the worldly skepticism of another, Ben Sira seems to want it both ways. He knows the world does not work according to the divine justice of the tradition's master narrative, but he tries desperately to make himself and his readers believe it is so.

> Great as his mercy, so also is his chastisement;
>> he judges a person according to one's deeds.
> The sinner will not escape with plunder,
>> and the patience of the godly will not be frustrated. (16:12-13)

Such justice is especially reserved for the poor and their tormentors:

> Panic and insolence will waste away riches;
>> thus the house of the proud will be laid waste.
> The prayer of the poor goes from their lips to the ears of God,
>> and his judgment comes speedily. (21:4-5)

Except, of course, when it comes slowly. Or not at all.

On one way of looking at things, the lack of connection between righteousness and honor in the human realm simply reproduces itself in the divine. The two attributes are simply not causally related in either arena. Yet whereas Ben Sira wrestles with this breakdown at the social level, he seems unable to admit it as a theological problem. As he moves to the climax of his work, divine glory or honor finally blankets the conceptual field, suppressing the contradiction between honor and justice. The terminology appears some thirty-two times in the last chapters of the book (42–51) where, first, the honor/glory of God's creative power is praised (42:15–43:33), and then a paean is sung to the ancestral heroes who both glorified God and were glorified by him, culminating in the scene of ultimate glory, the high priest in the temple (50:1-21). The book concludes with an attribution of majesty to God for giving the sage wisdom, because of which he will never be put to shame (51:17-18). Ben Sira's struggles with theodicy have been left behind.

Ben Sira's reflections on wealth and poverty express a class ethic.[19] Although one must apply with caution the notion of a "middle class" in antiquity, Ben Sira's position as a scribe, a member of a retainer class, provides a close analogy in terms of a social psychology. Unlike the biblical prophets, but much like the middle class today, he by and large supports the values, status, and class distinctions of a wealthy elite, while at the same time feeling threatened by the power they have over him, as well as by God, should he adopt the worst of their ways. Ben Sira affirms wealth as acceptable, even desirable, if honestly acquired and shared with the poor through almsgiving. By the same token, he neither despises nor elevates the poor on account of their poverty. He sympathizes with their difficult plight, and suggests that God does likewise. More clearly than his wisdom tradition predecessors in Proverbs, this later sage articulates the class *conflict* between rich and poor; "What peace is there between them?" he asks in chapter 13. His recommended response of almsgiving is, however, predicated on an ideology of individual piety; there is no systemic critique of the responsibility of the wealthy for a system of class disparity. Ben Sira and his students are not agents of social change, a fact closely related to their social location as a retainer class in the employ of and dependent on the wealthy for their livelihood.[20]

The operation of honor-shame ideology in this social location challenges the sage on various levels. First, because his own status as a member of the scribal class is a materially precarious one, the vicissitudes of socially ascribed honor and shame threaten him personally, and, not coincidentally, screen off his heavily theologized inclination to give alms from any more critical analysis. His sense of identity, as well as his income, lies with the rich. At the same time, these same vicissitudes threaten his ability to affirm convincingly the activity of a just, and therefore honorable, God. God's patent arbitrariness, acknowledged at some points, is denied with renewed assertions of retribution at others, and finally subsumed in adulation of the "glory" of God's power and majesty and his association with the great men of the faith. By the end of the book, Ben Sira has given up the expectation that God will act like a man of honor and praises the God of glory instead.

19. Benjamin Wright and Claudia Camp, "'Who Has Been Tested by Gold and Found Perfect?' Ben Sira's Discourse of Riches and Poverty," *Henoch* 23 (2001): 1-24.
20. Wright and Camp, "Who Has Been Tested?"

Shame, Sex, and Possessions: The Problem of Appropriation

Where does this analysis of shame leave us with respect to the questions I have posed in this essay (how we might understand the relationship between who we are and what we possess; whether a renewal of shame might counter the shamelessness of greed; and whether the biblically based traditions provide a resource with respect to these issues)? I'd like to suggest three considerations:

Shame, Self, and Systems of Power

Williams's book makes clear the inescapability of the structure of shame, as well as its real value, in the development of ethical selves, selves that are both socially constructed and also capable of moral imagination and action that transcend mere reproduction of conventions. A society that loses the ability to produce this structure in its members will be a society of persons who are not only selfish and deceitful but who lack the possibility of envisioning anything beyond their own self-preservation.

Although shame and honor are often found, sociologically speaking, in a reciprocal relationship, they are not in fact equal and opposite terms. Honor is essentially an accolade given or withheld by society. Shame, on the other hand, is potentially more interesting and useful a category of analysis because, although it is always filled with specific cultural content, it also has the more processual aspect identified by Williams. As such, it is one of the discourses through which the self is connected with the world — for our purposes, specifically, the world of one's possessions.

Nonetheless, shame must be analyzed in relationship to power. Shame can, in fact, get reduced in certain circumstances to a concern for mere appearances and conventions, and these will always support the power status quo. Any given system of shame will, moreover, as part and parcel of its processual aspect, mask incoherencies between what it holds to be the honorable person and what ought — within its own system — to be seen as shameful actions. This is true whether we focus on the individual or on society. For the individual, the experience of shame is a moment of self-revelation, but a costly one, certainly in terms of one's own sense of self-respect and often in terms of social goods or standing. It is indeed so costly that the *fear of feeling shame*, while perhaps not strong enough to prevent a shameful act in the first place, may create a block to acknowledging it. Likewise, societal self-interest works to mask shameful inconsistencies either by systematically ignoring them, as in the typical Greek (non)thought on slavery, or by attempting, in the face of all common sense, to naturalize them, as did Aristotle. One way or another, the effect is to preserve power for those who have it.

It is, in my view, the sort of analysis provided by Williams that makes meaningful at all the question of whether the biblical tradition has anything of moral worth to offer on this score. Without some perception of shame as a socio-psychological mechanism — as distinct from any specific content — the ancient honor-shame system as represented by Ben Sira becomes a list of do's and don'ts from which we pick and choose according to our preferences. Given that the system ideologically supports a patriarchal family household in which women are suppressed, children are beaten, and slaves are kept, one would hope we would choose very little of it. It is not that there are no good values here. Certainly, generosity is better than stinginess and almsgiving is better than turning a blind eye to the poor. But one of the several deep problems in the book is that it is precisely the concern for gaining honor and avoiding shame that keeps the author's more admirable tendencies in check, preventing a more systemic critique and construing even almsgiving within a framework of retribution. The relationship of self and possessions constructed by this system is that of a definitively *male* self, definitively *in control* of his possessions. He lives in fear of others' power with respect to his possessions, for to lose control of them is in fact to lose himself.

The Gendered Rhetoric of Shame

One of the greatest problems for reclaiming shame as part of our lexicon of proper possession is the degree to which the rhetoric of shame has always been, and continues to be, the gendered rhetoric of male dominance. This is in part a function of the natural symbolization of shame. The definitive experience lies in exposure, specifically exposure of the body, being seen naked. In patriarchal culture, a man can control his own nakedness; the trick is controlling that of his women. Here lies one of the great contradictions of patriarchy (at least in its Western mode): women's subordination to men is the most profoundly naturalized of injustices, yet a woman can shame the man who possesses her with the flick of her skirt. If we think this is a problem only in ancient thought, we need to think again.

I referred toward the beginning of this essay to an article in *Esquire* that bemoans the shamelessness of famous (or infamous) political consultants and its effect on the body politic. The question I raise is whether the biblical traditions provide resources for an alternative discourse that could compete with that of the spin doctors for the power of cultural definition. A comparison of Ben Sira with Taylor's article will certainly show the power of biblical discourse on the subject of shame, but not, I fear, for the good; for the rhetoric of shamelessness that provides both structure and content to Taylor's piece is that of Ben Sira — the rhetoric of possessing women. Referring to the Washington prostitute, Sherry Rowlands, who "told all" in a book about her client, consultant Dick Morris, he writes:

> A prostitute, for a modest sum from a disreputable publisher, betrays a client who is in the habit of fondly comparing his own profession, political consulting, to prostitution. This client, instead of fleeing in shame, proceeds to exploit the scandal in which he finds himself by announcing his intention, for a much larger sum from a reputable publisher, to betray *his* client, the President of the United States.

Our fascination with this story, Taylor argues, goes beyond Rowlands's offering of the details of fetishistic sex.

> What drew us to the scandal was its intertwined themes: prostitution, betrayal, exhibitionism, and, most importantly, shamelessness — the underlying condition that makes prostitution and betrayal and exhibitionism possible. For these are the defining pathologies of the Age of Spin.[21]

What is the problem here? It is not Taylor's characterization of our age as one of shamelessness, but rather his unconscious collusion in the age-old equation of shamelessness and prostitution. Although he states only that shamelessness "underlies" prostitution (along with betrayal and exhibitionism), the rest of his essay goes on to collapse the two terms metaphorically, insofar as it takes up without critique Morris's own "fond" understanding of his profession, precisely in its shamelessness, as one of whoring. Among the many unnoticed problems in his rhetoric is the somewhat anti-intuitive (at least in practical terms) equation of prostitution and betrayal. Betrayal, in fact, is the one thing a "client" does *not* expect of a prostitute: both her shame and her shamelessness — in both meanings of both terms — inhere in her opening and closing her mouth at the proper times.

Because he does not expect her betrayal does not, of course, mean he does not fear it. A second way in which Taylor's rhetoric continues in the ancient tradition of the ideology of shame is in his further metaphorical collapse of woman-controlled sex and devious speech, a favorite device of the

21. Taylor, "Spin," p. 74.

biblical writers (Delilah and Jezebel come to mind). Betrayal is indeed the currency of the prostitute, not intentionally, because of what she says, but essentially, because of what she is, namely, one who defies the system in which men control both women's bodies and their pocketbooks, and are shamed if they fail. Taylor turns the metaphor back on itself: in his commentary, the selling of sex stands for the selling of words, first by the prostitute Rowlands, then by the prostitute Morris. In a pre-tabloid age, women who sold their bodies had little outlet for their words, however much forbidden knowledge they may have had. If money was to be made on deceit — or on telling hidden truths — it was men who made it. But now the tables are turned: the prostitute can make a buck (though hardly as much as her client) in more ways than one. The criticism of Sherry Rowlands for selling her words (!) manifests a dramatic reversal of the metaphor: the whore is now *really* a whore. And, as Morris's megabucks deal with a "reputable" publisher shows, the man is still exempt from shame, even when he's a whore.

In the dominant discourse, male shame is identified with female shamelessness: betrayal (of men by men) "is" prostitution. The problem — so runs the underlying logic of Taylor's essay — is that prostitution is no longer shameful; ergo, neither is betrayal. But what would remedy this situation? Would it help if shame could be returned to prostitution? This apparently obvious solution would in fact solve nothing because the purported "shame" of prostitution always involves a gender imbalance; it involves women's shame, not men's (unless the prostitute is the man's daughter). Men have always had a right to whores and, indeed, admired each other for prowess with the nominally forbidden; only for this reason can Morris use the idea "fondly." Prostitution is part of the system whereby men have controlled women's sexuality. It is, to use Williams's term, a necessary identity — one understood as part of the natural order — in a patriarchal world. It is also, of course, the underside of the system. According to the system's stated values, it should produce shame for men involved. But systemic shame produces systemic shamelessness. "Gentlemen," says Morris, commenting on seeing two "reputable" reporters run into each other coming and going from a spin session, "never acknowledge each other in a bordello." The potential shame involved for the men is — and has always been — short-circuited by agreement about turning away the shame-producing gaze. As a social necessity, prostitution both demands and creates the blind eye of the honorable self.

When "gentlemen" avoid each other's gaze in a bordello, they always have a convenient place to fix it: invoking women's shame makes an easy cover for their own exposure. To the extent Taylor has aimed his gaze at betraying men and named them "shameless," he has done a service. To the extent he expresses his view of their shame in the terms of *their* view of women's shame, failing to critique the rhetorical identification of greed-based shamelessness with male-generated female shame, he reproduces the problem he seeks to correct. Rather than smirking along with Morris's fond analogy, he would have done well to recast the shamelessness of the spin-meisters in a discourse other than the one in which men "naturally" possess women.

Shame, the Bible, and Theologies of Possession

A feminist-critical analysis of the honor-shame code in Ben Sira should, I would argue, give us pause in turning to the biblically based traditions as a resource with respect to self and possession, for the code functions as part of a rhetorical system with multiple moral defects. The book assumes without question the existence of a class system and the owning of slaves; further, its shame ideology shares in the rhetoric and practice of gender-based dominance and subordination. But I would go farther even than this. Ben Sira's text is a testament to how the work of shame in the shaping of ethical character can be deformed in the interest of monotheism, specifically, in the effort to preserve the idea of a (single) just God in a world of rich and poor.

The insistence on the existence of a just moral order controlled by an all-powerful deity, combined with the justification of one's status and possessions in the face of those in need, is a lethal theo-ethical cocktail. Such a belief system creates the conditions for blindness to the central ethical question of shamelessness posed by Williams: *how far does the existence of a worthwhile life for some people involve the imposition of suffering on others?* Ben Sira's honor-shame ideology is grounded in the impossibility of asking this question with respect to women and slaves, and in the possibility of considering it only marginally, from the standpoint of *noblesse oblige,* with respect to the poor.

The temptation for those who wish to use the Bible as a resource for modern values is to dismiss these unfortunate aspects of Ben Sira's text as "historically conditioned" and proceed to seek out its more desirable, universalizable wisdom. If the pernicious persistence of his gender bias is not enough to dissuade one from this effort, his theology should be. This is a person who sees clearly the injustice in the world with respect to wealth and poverty and who goes to great lengths to suppress the connection between this reality and the character of God. Important for the present discussion is the way in which the insistence on the honor/glory of God deflects all questions about divine justice. An unjust God should rank as a dishonorable one; but, just as wealth and power can pass for honor in the human world, so power and magnificence can shield the deity from nagging "why's." If Ben Sira's honor-shame system is at best a list of do's and don'ts from which we pick and choose, it is at worst a massive theological justification of the way the world is in order to justify one man's place in it. Thus is the potentially positive work of shame in the formation of moral character deformed by the theological system in which it is used. The spin-meisters of the nineties have nothing on Ben Sira.

The question raised by this critique is whether the shame system in Sirach is endemic to biblically derived thought on the constitution of the self with respect to property and possession. This book, though not in everyone's biblical canon, represents a constant and often actualized possibility in a biblically based worldview. Radical monotheism in an unjust world raises serious questions about the claim of divine justice. Such questions might well challenge the moral comfort (not to mention status security) of the economically privileged. But appeals to the glory/honor of God can easily — and often do in popular middle-class Christianity — desensitize consciousness of these disruptive elements in religious experience. It is certainly true that belief in a just and powerful God has in recent years been a source of liberating theology for the poor. On the other hand, such belief functions widely in middle-class America — which I take to be the audience for this essay — precisely as they did for our ancient sage: as a justification for what we have, as a security blanket covering our fear of losing it, and as a means of mystification for the profound tension between our own claim about God's character and the unjust suffering in the world. There is a dangerous difference, however, in that we now have a Scripture even more firmly entrenched as the unquestionable word of God and indisputable authority for these traditional claims about God.

This study of shame as medium between self and possessions suggests, then, the ease with which the discourse of shame in the construction of the self can be derailed, deformed, or co-opted by those with control of different aspects of human society, whether of wealth, women, or theology. Shame is a powerful dimension of human moral experience. A renewed discourse of shame, however, must attend carefully to the language in which it is couched and to the class and gender interests with which it is associated.

Silver Chamber Pots and Other Goods Which Are Not Good: John Chrysostom's Discourse against Wealth and Possessions

Margaret M. Mitchell

I have stood up before you today as an ambassador with a request that is just, advantageous, and fitting. I have been chosen for this task by none other than the poor who dwell in our city, selected not by speeches or votes or the judgment of a common council, but by the pitiful and bitter sights of poverty (I met on the way here).[1]

The self-appointed leader of an embassy[2] who spoke these words to his urban eastern congregation was John Chrysostom, the fourth-century (c. 349-407) priest at Antioch and later patriarch of Constantinople. He was a fervent champion of the poor throughout his ministry,[3] and the tools of his fictional ambassadorship on behalf of the voiceless were the same as those of any diplomat: words. My goal in this essay is to focus in on those tools and examine

---

1. *On Almsgiving* 1 (*PG* 51.261), my translation (as with all quotations from Chrysostom in this essay). *PG* refers to J. Migne, ed., *Patrologia Graeca* (hereafter *PG*).

In Chrysostom's writings, see especially *On Almsgiving* (*PG* 51.261-72), *On the Delights of the Future* (*PG* 51.347-54), and the seven homilies of *On Lazarus* (*PG* 48.963-1054), as well as exhortatory passages from throughout his exegetical (and other) homilies. Otto Plassmann notes the relative paucity of our topic in the rest of Chrysostom's writings, for it was especially suitable for his sermons (Plassmann, *Das Almosen bei Johannes Chrysostomus* [Münster: Aschendorff, 1961], pp. 89-90).

2. As the passage progresses he takes on as his "co-worker" in the embassy none other than the apostle Paul.

3. By one estimate, there are at least ninety to one hundred sermons on rich and poor in his vast corpus of writings (Chrysostomus Baur, *John Chrysostom and His Time*, 2 vols., trans. M. Gonzaga [Westminster, Md.: Newman, 1959], 1:217).

the rhetorical cast and potential effectiveness of his discourses about money and possessions, which contain abundant and enduring themes, images, and values concerning the proper human attitude toward possessions. Chrysostom, "The Golden Mouth," is famous for being one of the most eloquent preachers in the Christian tradition (as well as for his sermons vilifying Judaizing Christians, which lamentably provided later Christians with abundant anti-Judaistic ammunition). Furthermore, his sermons are conspicuous for their repeated and tireless exhortations against wealth, which tie in with Chrysostom's overall attempt to democratize monastic values and the necessity for only limited attachment to the things of this world onto the laity. He is an important figure for the theme of this consultation both because of his historical significance as an early Christian social critic of wealth and extravagant possession, and because of the rhetorical passion and strict contingency within which his utterances on the topic of possessions are cast. From a historical point of view, Chrysostom's views on wealth were influenced by the Syrian asceticism in which he was formed, by the Christianized Stoicism that pervades his thinking,[4] and by his own intense firsthand experiences with abjectly poor persons and their extravagantly wealthy counterparts in the urban centers in which he carried out his ministry. There have been debates about whether or not Chrysostom had a consistent position with regard to the fair distribution of goods in the social order, since he advocates almsgiving constantly, but also in places evinces glimmers of a vision of systemic overhaul in the pursuit of a just social order, based especially upon the communitarian example of the church in Acts chapters 2 and 4.[5] Though he did not conceive of or institute a plan for social revolution on the ground, *through his discourse* and the theological and philosophical ideas behind it he imagined and advocated in the strictest possible terms the requirement for individuals to relinquish their wealth and their privilege as part of their Christian responsibility to God, to themselves, and to others. It was Chrysostom's own power of *perception* that enabled him to see and feel (with the extramission theory of vision held in antiquity)[6] "the pitiful and bitter sights of poverty" that pro-

---

4. "Des Johannes Argumente gegen den Reichtum und für die Armut stammen durchweg aus dem Arsenale der stoisch-kynischen Popularphilosophie" (Plassmann, *Das Almosen bei Johannes Chrysostomus*, p. 93).

5. These debates were compounded in the nineteenth and twentieth centuries by the interests of the scholars involved, who sought either to defend or repudiate Communism through his example. For a general introduction to this literature, see Arnold Stötzel, *Kirche als "neue Gesellschaft": Die humanisierende Wirkung des Christentums nach Johannes Chrysostomus*, Münsterische Beiträge zur Theologie 51 (Münster: Aschendorff, 1984), pp. 1-13.

6. This theory holds that in seeing, rays come forth from the eye and touch that which is

pelled his oratory, the vehicle by which he sought to put his hearers face to face with the vision that haunted him,[7] in order to bring about change in the social order of the city.

Although his writings on the subject resist categorical systematization and consistency, Chrysostom's major and often-repeated message is crystal clear — an unremitting challenge to bloated consumption and consumerism. Chrysostom's strident rebukes of his audience of fourth-century citizens of the Christian imperium, who dwelt in an economy in which the most wealthy person's lifestyle would be unbearable for many of the world's poor today, leaves one breathless at the thought of what he would say to the Ted Turners, Bill Gateses, and Oprah Winfreys of twentieth-century America, whose amassed wealth exceeds the G.N.P. of many a developing nation. But what the two situations share is this gap, this tremendous separation of persons by material needs that so characterizes the twentieth- and now twenty-first-century planet, as well as the late-antique Roman city, when viewed both locally and globally. Yet, as a caution I should say at the outset that Chrysostom cannot be simply claimed as a comrade in arms as though he were a precisely contemporary commentator (though at times the convergence of his views and contemporary situations is quite striking).[8] For instance, the engine driving some of his invective against the rich is his deeply misogynist tendencies, since he blames women especially for the vices of extravagance, triviality, and greed. Within his mix of redemptive and troubling, of palatable and nonpalatable levels of critique and acceptance of the social order he knew, however, one can find illuminating and even stirring conceptions of the place of possessions in the life of persons, communities, and the cosmos. But despite the situational rootedness of these exhortations, they are not simply "from the hip" practical advice for everyday use of worldly goods (though they contain some marvelously concrete excoriations and requirements). In general his denunciations of wealth stem from theological and philosophical positions about human life; it is those in particular which we shall seek to un-

---

seen (see, e.g., Dale C. Allison Jr., "The Eye is the Lamp of the Body [Matthew 6.22-23 = Luke 11.34-36]," *New Testament Studies* 33 (1987): 61-83.

7. The rhetorical form Chrysostom uses for this is ἔκφρασις, "vivid description," by which a speaker turns the hearer into a spectator. (For full discussion of the form, and Chrysostom's use of it, see Margaret M. Mitchell, *The Heavenly Trumpet: John Chrysostom and the Art of Pauline Interpretation*, Hermeneutische Untersuchungen zur Theologie 40 [Tübingen: Mohr Siebeck, 2000; Louisville: Westminster/John Knox, 2002], pp. 101-4.)

8. I am thinking here in particular of one of his condemnations of extravagant excess at wedding receptions (*Homilies on Colossians* 12.7 [*PG* 62.389-92]), and also of the ways in which he describes the encounter between panhandlers and possible donors.

cover and critique for our contemporary conversation. I have organized my analysis of this enormous body of material around the following three focal questions: First, how does Chrysostom define and view "possessions" in all their different manifestations and referents? Second, how are his views about the meaning and proper use of property and possessions rooted in conceptions about each of the three partners in economic transactions: the individual, the community, and the cosmos? And, last, what does Chrysostom think Christians should do to inhabit, improve, transform, or transcend the current socioeconomic order?

Definitions: Possessions, Wealth, and "Goods"

One of the strongest statements against wealth and possessions in Chrysostom's corpus of writings is found in the twelfth of his *Homilies on First Timothy* 12.3-4,[9] a sermon that likely comes from his Antiochene period (c. 386-98). Most valuably, this exhortation, because it is cast in the form of a debate about Christian attitudes toward possessions, gives us insights into not only Chrysostom's own viewpoint but also that of an interlocutor whom he summons and addresses along the way. Because it opens up many of the issues that occupy us, especially the definitional ones, I shall represent the continuous argument here at length, hoping to convey also by doing so some of Chrysostom's rhetorical processes and power.

Chrysostom's central purpose in this exhortation within his homily on 1 Timothy 4:1-10 is to demonstrate the proposition that "goods" (ἀγαθά) are not "good" (ἀγαθόν).[10] The argument unfolds in this way. First, Chrysostom makes the sweeping statement, so obvious to him as to require no proof, that "worldly goods,[11] though perishable and corruptible, are never possessed without labors and sweat." But then he introduces the objection of an un-

---

9. *PG* 62.561-64.

10. In late antiquity as in modern English the word "goods" was a common synonym for "possessions" (Liddell-Scott-Jones, *Greek-English Lexicon* [2004], 4 [s.v. ἀγαθός]; *Oxford Latin Dictionary*, XX [s.v. bonum]; *Oxford English Dictionary* 4.291). Chrysostom makes the same argument in *On Lazarus* 7.5 (48.1052): "For even now many who are distracted by luxury and gluttony are accustomed to say, 'we have had many good things [πολλὰ ἀγαθά].' . . . Don't simply call these things good [ἀγαθά], people, considering that these things were given by the Master so that by enjoying them in moderation we might have sustenance of love, and we might bolster the weakness of our bodies. But other things are what are truly good [ἕτερα δέ ἐστι τὰ ὄντως ἀγαθά]. For none of these is good, not luxury, not wealth, not expensive clothing, but they only have the name [ὄνομα]."

11. τὰ βιωτικὰ πράγματα, literally, "the things of daily life."

named interlocutor (who may have been real or contrived, as rhetorically required) that there are indeed people in the world who have acquired "goods" without great labors. In response to this Chrysostom first gives a catalogue of these so-called "goods" (ἀγαθά) that the interlocutor (and the audience) would have had in mind: money, houses, large tracts of land, herds of slaves, and scales full of silver and gold.[12] But a person who has been called to the philosophical pursuits of heaven, yet still "gazes at earthly goods," he says, should be ashamed and hide himself or herself from view. Then Chrysostom constructs an argument by contraries: "For if these things are good, then it would be necessary to call those who have acquired them good, also." But this leads to a logical contradiction (Εἶδες τὴν ἐναντίωσιν), since it would mean that the more a person steals and defrauds, and thus acquires more and more wealth, the more "good" he or she would be. This leads to an even broader generalization than the one that occasioned this sub-argument: "the passion of greed [πλεονεξία] is so destructive that it is simply not possible to become rich by not doing injustice" (καὶ οὐκ ἔστιν, οὔκ ἔστι μὴ ἀδικοῦντα πλουτεῖν). This means that here Chrysostom is defending the viewpoint that possession of wealth is, in effect, theft,[13] because it must have resulted from some act of injustice.

The defense of this proposition leads Chrysostom into even more elaborate arguments. First he must address an objection about inheritance — what if someone had inherited money from his or her father, and thus didn't do any injustice to possess it? Chrysostom's (predictable) answer? That somewhere back in the chain of inheritance some injustice took place in the acquiring of that wealth. This leads him into biblical *exempla* that both help and hurt his cause, so he dances among them and moves on quickly. First he brings in Adam, arguing that since his own contemporaries did not inherit their goods directly from Adam, some intermediaries who handed on the wealth must have unjustly taken away and borne fruit from someone else's

12. See the similar list in *Homilies on First Corinthians* 34.5 (*PG* 61.292): "What then is wealth [πλοῦτος]? Gold and silver, and precious stones, and clothes that are silken, purple and gold-edged." This unpacking of the term with vivid visual imagery is important and raises for us the question of what mental pictures come to mind when one thinks of "property" or "possessions," especially in a stock market–based economic system, a mercantile exchange where one purchases "futures," stock options, etc.

13. Adolf Martin Ritter, "John Chrysostom As an Interpreter of Pauline Social Ethics," in *Paul and the Legacies of Paul*, ed. W. S. Babcock (Dallas: Southern Methodist University Press, 1990), pp. 183-99 (notes 360-69); see also his "Between 'Theocracy' and 'Simple Life': Dio Chrysostom, John Chrysostom, and the Problem of Humanizing Society," in *Studia Patristica* 22, ed. E. A. Livingstone (Louvain: Peeters, 1989), pp. 170-80.

property. But, second, once the ancients are brought in Chrysostom must reckon with the fact that they, of course, did own property. Two conspicuous cases, Abraham and Job,[14] are treated exegetically (since they were both called righteous, δίκαιος, the charge of theft could not possibly apply to them), and, rather sophistically, he excuses their cases with a cultural anachronism, on the grounds that their wealth was not in gold or silver or buildings, but in cattle (thus it was all right). And, in addition, Job was "made rich by God" (θεόπλουτος) in his restoration at the end of the book, and the text nowhere mentions his gold and silver being taken away. Chrysostom clearly gives a priority in his own mental image of possessions to "cash" and luxury items, as we see plainly in other discourses that excoriate against jewelry (especially on women), and, in one case, silver chamber pots, which he rails upon at length in one homily as the epitome of the foolishness and arrogance of the super-rich.[15] Such "goods" can never be "good."

Finding this scriptural argument rough going, Chrysostom returns to his provocateur with a direct address: "Tell me, from where did you become rich?"[16] To the expected answer — "from my father, who got it from his father," and so on — Chrysostom asks impossibly, "Can you, going back through many generations, show that its acquisition was just?" Then he answers himself: "No, you cannot, but of necessity the root and beginning [ἀρχή] of it must have come from an injustice against someone." This social explanation receives a theological boost, as Chrysostom returns to Genesis and points out that "from the beginning [ἐξ ἀρχῆς] God did not make one person rich and another poor, nor, passing by, did he show great treasures of gold to one, and rob the other of the chance to search for it, but he left the same earth to all." From this theology of creation Chrysostom derives contemporary social criticism: "Why, then, if the earth is a common thing

---

14. These same examples of biblical notables who possessed wealth are treated by Chrysostom in *Homilies on First Corinthians* 34.6 (*PG* 61.294-95).

15. *Homilies on Colossians* 7.4-5 (*PG* 62.349-52). He regards this as the most shameful act imaginable, creating a parallel with Paul's 1 Corinthians 11:21 to express his disgust: ὁ μὲν καὶ ἐν ἀργύρῳ ἀποπατεῖ, ὁ δὲ οὐδὲ ἄρτου μετέχει ("one defecates into silver, while another does not partake even of bread") (7.5 [*PG* 62.352]). The image of chamber pots has a long history in the kind of Stoic moralizing that Chrysostom embraces. See, for instance, Plutarch, *Moralia* 1048B-C *(De Stoicorum repugnantiis)*, where golden chamber pots are mocked as a sign of trivial vanity.

16. In *Homilies on First Corinthians* 34.5-6 (*PG* 61.292-96), Chrysostom compares two cities, one entirely of rich and one entirely of poor, to demonstrate that while the rich need the poor, the poor do not need the rich, and indeed are self-sufficient. In order to defend his assertion that God did not make people either rich or poor Chrysostom must explain away two scriptural passages that appear patently contrary: "The silver is mine, and the gold is mine, and I shall give it to whomever I wish" (Hag. 2:8), and "Wealth and poverty are from the LORD" (Sir. 11:14).

[κοινή], do you have such vast acres of it, and your neighbor doesn't even have an ounce of land?" To the expected response of an appeal to patrilineal descent of ownership, Chrysostom responds that one must go back and find the original owner of the land. A final jab to the opponent is the example of Jacob, who was wealthy, but had earned his wealth as a wage [μισθός], as opposed to merely receiving it by inheritance.

Then Chrysostom interjects a surprising concession in order to move off this line of argumentation: "But, however, I am not being exactly precise here." Consequently he poses a new question: even if I grant your contention, that your wealth was justly acquired — either because it in fact was (though this would require that the gold was acquired when it simply gushed forth from the earth) or because of the fact that you are not responsible for your father's greedy acts — even then, is wealth good? Chrysostom's answer is unequivocal: "No way" (οὐδαμῶς)! In what follows Chrysostom and his dialogue partner debate conditions under which wealth (πλοῦτος) might be considered good. The interlocutor says it can be good (or "a good") if the one who possesses it is not greedy; it is only bad if the possessor doesn't share it with those in need. But Chrysostom does not agree,[17] because

> isn't this bad — alone to possess the Master's property, to enjoy the benefit of things that are common property? Is not "the earth the Lord's and the fullness of it" (Ps 24:1)? Then if our possessions belong to the common Master, then also they belong to our fellow slaves. For all the Master's possessions are common property [τὰ γὰρ τοῦ Δεσπότου πάντα κοινά].[18]

Chrysostom follows this with the improbable examples of the "great houses" and imperial property of his day, which, he maintains, are held in common (citing such "public" possessions as the marketplace and sidewalks). Then he grounds this social arrangement in the providential ordering of God (θεοῦ οἰκονομία), who in creating the universe made some things common property (κοινά), like air, the sun, water, the earth, heaven, the sea, the light, the stars,[19] as well as a common dispensation of human bodily parts and basic

---

17. Though he himself espouses this very view in *On Lazarus* 7.5 (*PG* 48.1052): "For wealth might be good for its possessor [ὁ γὰρ πλοῦτος τότε ἂν γένοιτο ἀγαθὸς τῷ κεκτημένῳ] when he does not squander it solely in luxury, nor in drunkenness and harmful pleasures, but when enjoying luxury moderately [συμμέτρως] he distributes the rest for the bellies of the poor. Then wealth is good [τότε ἀγαθὸν ὁ πλοῦτος]."

18. *Homilies on First Timothy* 12.4 (*PG* 62.563).

19. For the same argument, see *Homilies on Ephesians* 20.9 (*PG* 62.148).

structure, and also other common things, like baths, cities, marketplaces, and walks. (This is a rather unusual attribution of creative responsibility for public civic works to the deity.) Finally Chrysostom concludes with some rhetorical commonplaces about social concord, which are rooted in a standard philosophical critique of human economies; the very root of human strife and contention (ἔρις and φιλονεικία) is private ownership (termed "making something one's own" [ἴδιον ποιεῖν]), which begins with the cold words "yours" (τὸ σόν) and "mine" (τὸ ἐμόν).[20] It is only about private property that fights break out, never about things that are common to all (τὰ κοινά), such as the marketplace; such things are always treated peaceably, "But whenever someone tries to separate something out and make it her or his own, then contention comes in, as though nature herself were indignant [ὥσπερ αὐτῆς τῆς φύσεως ἀγανακτούσης], because although God from everywhere brings us together, we contend to divide ourselves, and to chop things up by making them our private possession [ἰδιοποιεῖσθαι]." The created order was meant to be shared commonly by all; the desire (ἐπιθυμία) for individual appropriation, for possession, of what belongs to God and to all is the root of evil for Chrysostom.

Chrysostom now returns to his original question: "How can the one who possesses wealth be good?" His answer is a paradox: "One can only be good if one shares what one has with others. When one does not possess wealth, then one is good. When one gives it to others, then one is good.[21] But when one possesses it, then one could not be good." Therefore, rounding off the discourse, "to possess things is not good, but not to possess them makes one appear good. Therefore wealth is not a 'good.'"[22] Consequently, one

20. On the Jerusalem community of the early chapters of Acts as a community of friends, with no possessiveness, no "mine," see *Homilies on First Thessalonians* 2.4 (*PG* 62.404), as in many other places in Chrysostom's writings.

21. Compare also *Homilies on First Timothy* 7.3 (*PG* 62.538-39): "Is gold good? [καλὸν τὸ χρυσίον]. But it is good for almsgiving, good for the aid of the poor, not for unprofitable use, so that it be hidden away in the house, dug into the ground, or worn around hands and feet and heads. This is why it was discovered, not so that we might bind the image of God with it, but so that we might release those who have been bound [οὐχ ἵνα τὴν εἰκόνα τοῦ θεοῦ κάταδεν ὦμεν τούτῳ, ἀλλ' ἵνα λύωμεν τοὺς δεδεμένους]."

22. Other such maxims about possession (which he once calls τοῦ θεοῦ τὰ παράδοξα, "the paradoxes of God") are also found in Chrysostom's writings, as, for instance, the following: "wealth does not belong to those who possess it, but rather to those who try to steal it" (*Homilies in First Corinthians* 35.6 [*PG* 61.305]); "despise possessions if you wish to have possessions; if you wish to be rich, become poor"; "not possessing many things, but not needing many things, is what makes a rich person" (Οὐ γὰρ τὸ πολλὰ κεκτῆσθαι πλουτοῦντος, ἀλλὰ τὸ μὴ πολλῶν δεῖσθαι) (*Homilies on First Timothy* 11.2 [*PG* 62.556]); and "wealth is not a possession, but a loan for use, not a matter of ownership" (Οὐκ ἔστι κτῆσις τοῦτο, χρῆσίς ἐστιν, οὐκ ἔστι κυρία) (*Homilies on First Timothy* 11.2 [*PG* 62.556]).

should not call wealth a good, but should reserve that term for the things that are truly goods (τὰ ὄντως ἀγαθά): virtue and benevolence (ἀρετή, φιλανθρωπία). The discourse ends with a paradoxical eschatological refrain about the real "goods": "Therefore let us become good [ἀγαθοί], then, so that we might also be good [ἀγαθοί], and we might obtain the goods [τὰ ἀγαθά] that are coming in Jesus Christ."

This lengthy passage has demonstrated what for Chrysostom is the basic problem. Wealth cannot be a "good" because it depends upon, and further generates, injustice (ἀδικία). Thus "wealth" (πλοῦτος) and "luxury" (τρυφή) are always, uncompromisingly, bad, for they constitute inequitable possession, which depends upon some form of injustice.[23] Possibly though rarely neutral are the terms χρήματα, which means literally "things one needs" but is used to denote "goods, property," and κτῆσις, "acquisition, possession."[24] Chrysostom can use these terms to refer to the necessities, the sufficiencies of daily life (food, clothing, shelter), but very often also to refer to an overabundance of those necessities and a privatized hoarding of "goods" to oneself. This leads to the question of "private property" itself, which Chrysostom engaged in the middle of our passage in a manner that assigns the blame for all social evil — greed, defrauding, injustice, and oppression — to private acquisitiveness. Here Chrysostom stands in a long line of Greek philosophical thought that blamed the simple word ἐμός ("mine") for the evils of all human societies.[25] What lies behind this direct accusation is a myth of pristine ori-

23. In *Homilies on Ephesians* 13.3 (*PG* 62.97) Chrysostom uses the metaphor of clothing to demonstrate the incompatibility of wealth and justice, for he contrasts wealth with "the garment of righteousness," arguing that one cannot wear both at the same time. This is because "the wearing of riches destroys this garment. Riches are like the thorns; as much as we cover ourselves with lots of them, so much more are we naked.... Wealth is a moth [Σής ἐστι ὁ πλοῦτος]. Just as the moth eats through everything and does not spare even the silken ones, wealth is the same way."

24. Liddell-Scott-Jones, *Greek-English Lexicon*, p. 1002.

25. See Margaret M. Mitchell, *Paul and the Rhetoric of Reconciliation: An Exegetical Investigation of the Language and Composition of 1 Corinthians*, Hermeneutische Untersuchungen zur Theologie 28 (Tübingen: Mohr Siebeck, 1991; Louisville: Westminster/John Knox, 1993), p. 94, especially the quotation from the second-century orator Aelius Aristides: "For 'this is not yours, but mine' [οὐ σὸν τοῦτο, ἀλλ' ἐμόν] begins every argument. But where people believe that possessions belong to all in common [κοινά], they also have a common point of view about them" (*Or.* 23.65; compare Plato, *Republic* 5.462C). Elsewhere in Chrysostom's writings, see *On Virginity* 68 (*PG* 48.584-85), in which he exclaims that "mine" and "not mine" are, after all, only words (*PG* 48.584), and discussion and further references in Manfred Kertsch, *Exempla Chrysostomica: Zu Exegese, Stil und Bildersprache bei Johannes Chrysostomos*, Grazer Theologische Studien 18 (Graz: Institut für Ökumenische Theologie und Patrologie an der Universität Graz, 1995), pp. 63-66; see also Stötzel, *Kirche als "neue Gesellschaft,"* p. 55 n. 114, who traces the commonplace back to Plato (*Republic* 5.462).

gins, on the assumption that primordially, or at any rate before the first utterance of this hideous word, which effects private possession, human beings lived together in harmony, sharing what were for all "common" goods. Elsewhere Chrysostom provides the next episode in this myth of lapsed origins: it was the devil himself who created the destructive word "mine."[26] And as a counterpoint to the lost primordial society Chrysostom has an Edenic biblical example in the early church of Acts 2, an "angelic commonwealth," which functioned as the restoration of the pre-"mine" period (though sadly it, too, was not to last).[27] Further definitions and redefinitions occur in this passage in regard to the "common possessions" of the cosmos on the grounds that it belongs alike and wholesale to the deity, and in regard to the "spiritual" possessions, the virtues, which should be the object of human energies and appetites.

Another illustration (of very many within Chrysostom's corpus of writings) of these reconfigurations of common property and ideal possession can be seen in *On the Calends* 3 (PG 48.956), part of a sermon against the observance of festival days for new moons and new years.

26. In *Homilies on Ephesians* 20.9 (*PG* 62.148) he proposes that "this accursed and defiled word ['mine'] was brought in by the devil." On that basis he argues for common ownership and calls those who claim private possession essentially thieves: "ἡ μὲν γὰρ χρῆσις κοινὴ πάντων ἐστὶν, πλεονεκτοῦσι δὲ οἱ δοκοῦντες αὐτῶν εἶναι κύριοι τῶν οὐκ ὄντων τὴν ὑπὲρ αὐτῶν φροντίδα" ("For the use belongs to all in common, but those who think they are owners of things that are not theirs are greedy in their very thinking about them") (*On Virginity* 68 [PG 48.584]). Indeed, in *Homilies on First Timothy* 11.2, Chrysostom stresses that ownership itself is only a fiction we participate in, for "ownership only exists in word, but in fact we are all owners of things that belong to others" ('Ρήματι μόνον ἐστὶν ἡ δεσποτεία· τῷ δὲ ἔργῳ πάντες τῶν ἀλλοτρίων ἐσμὲν κύριοι) (text F. Field, *Joannis Chrysostomi* [Oxford: Parker, 1861], 6:90.

27. "This was an angelic commonwealth, with none of them saying anything was his or her own. From this the root of evils was cut out. . . . The cold expressions 'mine' and 'yours' were not found there. That is why there was great joy at their dining table. No one was disposed to eat as though partaking of her or his own food, and no one as though partaking of others'. Indeed this seems to be a puzzle [αἴνιγμα]. Nor did they consider their brothers' goods as belonging to others, for they were the master's goods. So nothing was privately held, but belonged to the brothers. Neither was the poor man put to shame, nor the rich wrapped in conceit. This is joy!" (*Homilies on the Acts of the Apostles* 7.2 [*PG* 60.66]). As for the fall from this utopia, later in this homily Chrysostom asks, "How was it that those people, the three and four thousand, immediately chose virtue, and at once became philosophers, but now hardly one can be found?" The answer? They fixed their eyes on the things of the next world and its value, not the present, and they did away with possessions, since "when possessions were taken away, then there was no evil" (ὅτε χρημάτων ἀναίρεσις ἦν, τότε οὐδὲ πονηρία ἦν) (*Homilies on the Acts of the Apostles* 7.3 [*PG* 60.67]). But there is still one place even now where these ideals are accomplished — the monastery — where "'mine' and 'yours' are not found" (τὸ ἐμὸν οὐκ ἔνι καὶ τὸ σὸν ἐκεῖ) (*Homilies on First Timothy* 14.3 [*PG* 62.575]).

The feast of which I spoke is the continual feast, which does not wait for a cycle of years, nor does it circumscribe days, and rich and poor will be able to conduct it in the same manner. For there is no need of possessions [χρήματα] there, nor of wealth [εὐπορία], but of virtue alone. Do you have no things? But you do have the fear of God, a treasure richer than all possessions, which is not squandered, nor changed, nor spent. Look into heaven, and heaven's heaven, the earth, the sea, the air, the species of animals, the various sorts of plants, the entire nature of human beings. Consider angels, and archangels, and the powers above. Remember that all these things are the possessions of your Master [ταῦτα πάντα τοῦ Δεσπότου σου ἐστι κτήματα].[28] And a slave of such a wealthy master cannot be poor, if she or he has a gracious person as her or his own master.

The comparison that we see in the above passage between human possessions or wealth and the natural order is accompanied elsewhere by another predominating contrast that governs Chrysostom's deliberations on property — his pervasive assumption that postmortem existence will bring for the righteous a bounty of possessions and attainments against which those of this earth fail miserably to compare. "There is great wealth there [in heaven]. If we compare those riches with the earthly, the earthly appear more worthless than crap."[29]

Such passages as these demonstrate nicely the paradoxical work of redefinition[30] of the Christian social economy that Chrysostom undertakes in order to get his congregants to adjust their behavior in the light of a newly envisioned, and not yet actually manifested, social order. The possessions that most people seek after — elaborate houses, gold and jewels, silk clothing, rich and superabundant food — are not even "goods." The true possessions, the true "goods," are fourfold: the things needed for daily subsistence that belong to all as slaves of a common master/household owner; the character virtues;[31] the es-

28. Migne notes that two manuscripts read κτίσματα, "creations," instead of κτήματα, "possessions."

29. *Homilies on First Timothy* 17.3 (*PG* 62.595).

30. See also the lexical argument in *Homilies on First Timothy* 11.3 (*PG* 62.556): Χρήματα λέγεται παρὰ τὸ κεχρῆσθαι, οὐ παρὰ τὸ κυρίος εἶναι· καὶ τὰ κτήματα δὲ αὐτὰ χρῆσίς ἐστιν, οὐ δεσποτεία. This doesn't quite translate into English, but here is one rendering: "'Goods' [*chrēmata*] are so called from the act of using [*kechrēsthai*], not possessing; and 'possessions' [*ktēmata*] themselves are not a matter of ownership [*despoteia*], but of use [*chrēsis*]."

31. In *Homilies on Second Timothy* 6.4 (*PG* 62.636) Chrysostom ends his exhortation on almsgiving with a critique of the very idea that anything, except virtue, can be possessed: "What is truly ours is this: virtue [ἀρετή]. Possessions, even our own, are not ours [see the nice play in the Greek: τὰ δὲ χρήματα οὐδὲ τὰ ἡμέτερα ἡμέτερα], much less others'. But today they are ours,

chatological rewards that await all who have "despised" wealth in this life; and the humble but magnificent creatures and features of the universe, which belong to no one. To those who say "fine possessions are pleasing to look at," he rejoins, "but many other things are able to provide such pleasure. For the flowers and the pure air and the sky and the sun are much more pleasing."[32]

The Different Partners in the Economic Order:
Individual, Community, Cosmos

Chrysostom's various treatments of possessions are rooted in the two different directions of his paranesis which always meet in the middle. He is very troubled by the concrete impact of economic injustice on the poor but is equally worried about the eschatological fate of the rich in his congregation. Thus his approaches to the use and abuse of possessions often vacillate between these two perspectives and purposes, which are not identical. First we shall begin with Chrysostom's diagnosis of the role of the individual in relation to possessions and the wider economic order, in order to discern the theological, philosophical, and anthropological assumptions that drive his invective and his incentives. These constitute the religious logic in which Chrysostom's discourse and larger vision are rooted.

The Individual

Chrysostom's treatments of possessions are strikingly individualistic, since he is engaged in homiletical exhortation to his congregants, which he hopes will affect their behavior and life choices.[33] In general Chrysostom is ambivalent

---

and tomorrow not ours. Yet virtuous things are ours. For virtue doesn't succumb to loss, like possessions, but it is completely at hand for everyone."

32. Chrysostom extends the comparison into the negative: "For silver has a lot of rust (tarnish), which is why many say that it is black, which is clear from the seals that have turned black with tarnish. But there is no black in the sun, the sky, or the stars. People have greater enjoyment from these things than they do from that money. For it is not really the hue that gives pleasure, but the greed, the injustice. This is what pleases the souls, not the silver" (*Homilies on First Timothy* 7.3 [*PG* 62.538]).

33. Often Chrysostom admits he knows well how the many discourses against wealth fall on deaf ears ("but there are thousands of accusations against greed, both in private and in public, but there is no correction of behavior"). The antidote? After listing his basic arguments against wealth (a nice summary), he says: "If we sing away continually about these things, and hear them from others, perhaps some health will result, and there will be some escape from this terrible punishment" (*Homilies on First Timothy* 17.3 [*PG* 62.596]).

on the question of whether or not it is goods in and of themselves that are evil, or the distorted and dangerous human attitudes toward them,[34] though his exhortatory purpose of course accents the latter, since it is the (at least potentially) changeable variable. But this leads, of course, to the question of where goods came from in the first place, what their purpose was, and what human beings have done with them. We shall see how he handles this tension in one homily where he is engaging the famous biblical sentiment, "the love of money is the root of all evils" (1 Tim. 6:10 RSV).

The Poor   First Chrysostom argues that Christians are to use money for several reasons: for the care of the poor (ἐπικουρία τῶν πενήτων), for consolation for the sins committed by us (εἰς παραμυθίαν τῶν ἡμαρτημένων ἡμῖν), and for a good test and a pleasing act to God (εἰς εὐδοκίμησιν καὶ ἀρέσκειαν θεοῦ). What is most strikingly new in Chrysostom's discourse, which he for the most part holds in common with other fourth-century Christian writers, is its redefinition of and new perspective on "the poor." Whereas in classical antiquity civic euergetism was understood as the responsibility of wealthy citizens to provide benefactions for the commonwealth, which was socially stratified in a range of recognizable ways, Christian charity took its foundation from an innovative delineation of "the poor" as a distinct group, the proper object of philanthropy.[35] In fact, by building upon the Old Testament and ancient Near Eastern concept of "the poor" (which was never a sociological category of the

---

34. See *Homilies on Ephesians* 20.9 (*PG* 62.148): "Let riches perish ten thousand times over! Or, rather, not the riches, but the human wills which do not know how rightly to employ riches, but honor them more than all things." This is a longstanding preoccupation, especially of the Stoics; see, e.g., Seneca, *Epistulae Morales* 17.12: "For the fault is not in the wealth, but in the mind itself" (*Non est enim in rebus vitium, sed in ipso animo*).

35. Peter Brown, *Power and Persuasion in Late Antiquity: Towards a Christian Empire* (Madison: University of Wisconsin Press, 1992), pp. 71-117; Averil Cameron, *The Later Roman Empire (AD 284-430)* (Cambridge, Mass.: Harvard University Press, 1993), pp. 126-27; J. H. W. G. Liebeschuetz, *Barbarians and Bishops: Army, Church, and State in the Age of Arcadius and Chrysostom* (Oxford: Clarendon, 1990), p. 187: "But Christian giving was different from the traditional munificence expected from the wealthy inhabitants of cities. Christian charity was not directed towards fellow citizens or political supporters but towards the poor, whoever they might be. It was given to them precisely because they were poor or sick, and because God wants Christians to look after those in need. In fact this was one way in which men might atone for the sins with which they were inevitably contaminated. The idea that the poor and the sick and the old ought to be helped because they were there, and were God's creatures, is not classical. Moreover, Christian charity did not provide the same range of services as had been — and to some extent were still — provided by *curiales* for their fellow citizens. Christian charity did not provide amenities like shows and baths and colonnades which were of benefit to rich and poor alike. It was focused on basic needs of food and shelter."

polis),[36] Christian bishops in the late fourth century created a new social category that cut across the old political forms of the polis.[37] As Peter Brown has argued, this stemmed from a distinctly new theological position: that the poor should be objects of concern because they share the same human body as the givers.[38] This can be seen in one memorable passage where Chrysostom says that poverty and wealth are mere "masks" that tell us nothing of a person's true identity, which will be revealed at the final judgment when the masks are stripped off.[39] Furthermore, in Chrysostom's discourse the poor are given a new status on economic grounds, because he depicts them as possessors of genuine, spiritual commodities, which they have the power to trade with the rich on the open market.[40] Such teaching was also, of course, a swiftly effective political move, which created a solid constituency of support for Christian leaders and the church, by putting them in its debt.[41]

36. Brown, *Power and Persuasion,* p. 99.

37. See Brown, *Power and Persuasion,* p. 91, on the "singling out for particular concern of a category of persons that had no place in the traditional model of the urban community"; also Cameron, *Later Roman Empire,* p. 127: "Between these and the charitable foundations of the early empire the fundamental difference lay in their purpose and in the identification of the beneficiaries, specifically designated as the poor and needy in contrast to those of the early imperial foundations, which were often restricted to those of higher social class."

38. "By preaching incessantly on such themes, John wished to create in Antioch a new, more all-embracing sense of community, based on a sense of solidarity with a shared human nature. As a result, his exhortations came to place a quite unusual weight on the human body. For the body was the most vocal spokesman of all, in its manifest vulnerability, of the common descent of all human beings from Adam. John preached a brotherhood of bodies at risk. The two great themes of sexuality and poverty gravitated together, in the rhetoric of John and many other Christians. Both spoke of a universal vulnerability of the body, to which all men and women were liable, independent of class and civic status. In his sermons, John made brilliantly explicit what was, in effect, a slow change in the climate of his age" (Peter Brown, *The Body and Society: Men, Women, and Sexual Renunciation in Early Christianity,* Lectures on the History of Religions, n.s. 13 [New York: Columbia University Press, 1988], p. 316).

39. *On Lazarus* 6 (*PG* 48.986): οὕτω δὴ καὶ ἐπὶ τοῦ παρόντος βίου καὶ πενία καὶ πλοῦτος προσωπεῖα μόνον εἰσίν.

40. "Chrysostom sketched an alternative economic system in which the rich had to acknowledge their indebtedness precisely to those who were poor and insignificant in the eyes of the world. His message was one of mutuality. He obtained this mutuality by investing the very poor, who had previously been excluded from patron-client relations because they had nothing to contribute, with a valuable commodity, namely, special access to God" (Blake Leyerle, "John Chrysostom on Almsgiving and the Use of Money," *Harvard Theological Review* 87 [1994]: 29-47, at p. 41).

41. See Brown's chapter "Poverty and Power," in *Power and Persuasion,* pp. 71-117; and Cameron, *Later Roman Empire,* p. 178: "Furthermore, the development of a theory of Christian almsgiving, a subject on which much was written during this period, itself focuses attention on

Chrysostom's writings on "the poor" are therefore part of a larger program of theological and social redefinition. He stresses over and over again that the poor are "of the same substance" as "we," sharing the same divine image.[42] He calls the poor (somewhat romantically) "philosophers" (φιλόσοφοι) since they meet the central criterion of the wise person — they seek after nothing in excess.[43] Here his own asceticism and longing for the monastic life affect his view of others' lifestyles and livelihoods. But elsewhere this sense of the superiority of the poor is given a theological rationale: he depicts the poor dramatically as "those who dwell in a furnace" (like the three children in Daniel 3) without being harmed by the flames, because they have refused to commit idolatry by worshiping the "golden image," which is "the tyranny of mammon" (εἰκὼν χρυσῆ, ἡ τοῦ μαμωνᾶ τυραννίς).[44]

The Rich Theologically, therefore, human beings were placed in a world with goods as a test of their capacity for virtue in the proper exercise of those gifts for the sake of the poor, as restitution for sin, and in order to do what God wants them to do. But instead people become "obsessed by this passion" (ὑπὸ τῆς ἐπιθυμίας ἐκείνης κατεχόμενοι) and overturn the laws of nature and

the category of 'the poor' and may give a false impression both as to its composition and its numbers. As Jesus said, 'the poor are always with us'; what was really different in this period was that consciousness of the poor changed dramatically. In a sense, the existence of the poor was required by Christian ideology in order to neutralize the fact that the church itself was not only growing rich but also actively courting wealthy patrons. Moreover, there were many subtle ways of interpreting and modifying the scriptural injunction to give up all that one had. Bishops, for instance, came into considerable disposable assets on election, even if they had officially adopted poverty themselves, while even the religious life offered possibilities of accommodation. The urban poor in the east were rather different from the rural poor in either east or west. Finally, while 'the poor', in Christian mentality, stood for all that was wrong in the fallen state of man, this recognition did not give rise to social revolution or to the attempt to remove poverty *tout court* (indeed, Christians argued that the division of society into rich and poor was divinely ordained), but rather to the practice of almsgiving, which offered at one and the same time a convenient palliative and a source of prestige for the givers."

42. E.g., *Explanations of the Psalms*, Ps. 4.2 (PG 55.41); *On Anna* 5.4 (PG 54.674)

43. *Homilies on First Corinthians* 34.5 (*PG* 61.292); *On the Calands* 4 (*PG* 48.958). The inverse is also true; it is the duty of a philosopher to despise both riches and glory. "Such a person is the philosopher, such is the rich person: she or he has everything, and has nothing. . . . The true philosopher [is] the one who has need of nothing" (*Homilies on Ephesians* 21.4 [*PG* 62.153-54]). The latter is, of course, a Stoic commonplace, which Plutarch, at least, regarded as being a deliberately contrary proposition: "But they want to say something paradoxical and excessive and original. Say that the wise person has need of nothing, nor asks for nothing" (λέγε τὸν σοφὸν μηδενὸς ἔχειν χρείαν μηδὲ δεῖσθαί τινος) (*Moralia* 1068B, *De communibus notitiis adversus Stoicos*).

44. *Homilies on the Gospel of Saint Matthew* 4.11-12 (*PG* 57.53-54).

the commands of God. The covetous do not know God, for they are "driven mad" by avaricious desire (οὐδὲ αὐτὸν τὸν θεὸν ἐπίσταται· ὑπὸ γὰρ τῆς ἐπιθυμίας ἐκείνης κατεχόμενος, μέμηνεν). Thus they are like the Titans who go out with swords in hand, but unlike them, they are not merely faking it, for the money lovers are really crazy, and beside themselves (ἀληθῶς μαινόμενοι καὶ ἐξεστηκότες).[45] He extends this *exemplum* in an interesting direction by comparing the forms of armament of the two groups (the wealthy are armed inside their souls with thousands of swords, and vent their rage against everyone). This avaricious desire is likened to a plague that destroys persons and, through them, the whole world.[46]

Chrysostom's writings include many such diagnoses of the wealthy. For instance, he invokes the Stoic commonplace that pursuit of wealth is folly in many of his texts, such as in his list of the "foolish desires" (ἐπιθυμίαι ἀνόητοι) of 1 Timothy 6:9, which catalogue ancient Antiochene conspicuous consumption:

> And how is it not a foolish desire, when they possess idiots, when they possess dwarfs, not for the sake of human kindness, but for (mere) enjoyment; when they enclose fish in their courts, when they nurse wild beasts, when they busy themselves about dogs, when they adorn horses, and care about them no less than for their children? All these things are foolish and superfluous, neither necessary, nor useful.[47]

Elsewhere the wealthy themselves are termed "useless" (οὐ χρήσιμοι),[48] or owners of a savage beast — their property,[49] or misanthropes who consider everyone else their enemies.[50] And very often Chrysostom will depict greed

---

45. *Homilies on the Gospel of Saint Matthew* 4:11-12 (*PG* 62.595). Chrysostom often depicts the wealthy as "insane" (see also, e.g., *Homilies on Colossians* 7.4 [*PG* 62.349]).

46. "Thus this is the plague [λοιμός] that takes possession of all, some more so, some less so, but all just the same. And just like some fire igniting wood destroys and desolates everything, thus also this love of money wrecks the world. Kings, rulers, unskilled, poor, women, men, children, all equally are possessed by this evil. As though a dark gloom had fallen upon the world, no one can see straight [or, is sober]" (*Homilies on First Timothy* 17.3 [*PG* 62.594]). On greed, the obsession with possessions, as an illness or disease (τὸ πάθος or ἡ νόσος), see also, among many examples, *Homilies on First Timothy* 7.3 (*PG* 62.538).

47. *Homilies on First Timothy* 17.2 (*PG* 62.593).

48. *Homilies on First Corinthians* 34.5, 6 (*PG* 61.292, 294).

49. *Homilies on First Corinthians* 35.6 (*PG* 61.306).

50. *Homilies on Second Timothy* 7.1-2 (*PG* 62.638). The greedy person wishes the entire world were desolate and unpopulated, so that she or he could own it all. In the same context he terms the love of money, because it is insatiable, "boulimia of the soul" (βουλιμία γὰρ ψυχῆς φιλαργυρία).

or avarice (πλεονεξία), the improper attitude toward possessions, as an instance of self-imposed slavery, with vivid depiction of "the tyranny of possessions" (ἡ τῶν χρημάτων τυραννίς), which he neatly symbolizes by the making of literal "chains" of gold:

> Gold is good, but good for almsgiving, for good succor for the poor, yet not for unprofitable use, so that it should be secretly stored up at home, that it be set in hiding places dug in the ground, that it should be placed around hands and feet and heads. It was discovered for this reason: not so that we might bind the image of God with it, but so that we might release those who are bound. Use the gold for this: release the bound, don't bind the one who has been freed. For why, tell me, do you prize that which is least useful of all? For is it the case, that since it is gold, that no longer makes it a chain? Is it the material that makes it a chain? If it is gold, or if iron, it is the same thing (although the former is heavier than the latter).[51]

In addition to these anthropological or psychological diagnoses of the condition of the wealthy as sick, insane, or enslaved, Chrysostom commonly gives them a theological interpretation, as well. His eighteenth homily on Ephesians includes an extended proof that the proposition "the covetous person is an idolator" (ὁ πλεονέκτης εἰδωλολάτρης ἐστιν) is not mere hyperbole. First he depicts money as the cruel tyrant (ὁ ὠμὸς τύραννος) one takes on oneself, and love of money (φιλαργυρία) as the "hard and difficult yoke" (τὸ σκληρὸν ζυγὸν καὶ χαλεπόν).[52] Then he spins a neat simile: the Christian who serves money is like a counterspy in the king's army, who is worse than a deserter to the enemy because he serves the other master while pretending to serve God. Then Chrysostom constructs a detailed comparison of Christian covetous persons with "pagan" idolators (worshipers of Aphrodite and Ares, in particular). The covetous, he ironically observes, are *true* worshipers of mammon, since they worship not just in words but also in deeds. They are slaves to this passion (τῷ πάθει καταδουλοῦν σαυτόν). And the comparison extends further still, for the covetous also serve at an altar of sacrifice in honor of their beloved god:

> If you go by this altar of idols, you will see it reeking with the blood of goats and bulls; but when you go by the altar of covetousness [ὁ τῆς πλεονεξίας βωμός], you will see it breaking out with the horror of human blood. And if you stand by here, you will not see the wings of birds burn-

51. *Homilies on First Timothy* 7.3 (*PG* 62.539).
52. *Homilies on Ephesians* 18.2 (*PG* 62.123).

ing, nor molten fat and smoke given off, but bodies of human beings being destroyed.[53]

And, even worse, on the altar of covetousness not only are bodies immolated, but souls, for the souls of both the defrauded and those who defraud are slaughtered in the process.[54] Ironically, Chrysostom contends that idol worship at least means worshiping something God created (cf. Rom. 1:25), whereas the idolatry of covetousness involves worshiping something of one's own creation, the insatiable appetite for acquisition, thus proving that the covetous Christian person is even more base than the "pagan" idolater. Chrysostom concludes this extended allegory of the covetous as the idolater par excellence with a tie-in to his usual, complementary psychological analysis: "For to wish to have more than one's neighbor in the things of life arises from no other place than from foolishness, misanthropy, and arrogance" (ἐξ ἀπονοίας καὶ μισανθρωπίας καὶ ὑπεροψίας).[55]

In addition to these penetrating analyses of the problem of possession-mania for genuine human existence, Chrysostom also includes in his discourses some very commonsense appeals against overconsumption and avarice. For example, in one homily his dissuading appeal is buttressed by pragmatic (and graphic!) wisdom about bodily health:

> Riches are vain, when they are squandered for luxury. But they are not vain, when they are dispersed for the poor (cf. Ps. 112:9). But when you squander them for luxury, we see what sort of end they have: fatness of body, belchings, panting, abundance of excrement, heavy-headedness, weakness of flesh, fever, and faintness. For as someone who draws water into a cup with a hole in it acts in vain, so also the one who lives in luxury draws water into a leaky cup.[56]

Elsewhere with such wisdom instructions he seeks to prohibit the wealthy from being consumed by concern for their possessions. He presents the ancient metaphor of life as a journey and possessions as baggage, and queries: "Why do you fill your ship with thousands of tons of cargo?[57] If you are trimly arrayed, then you will fear nothing, no envy, no robbers, no plots. For you are not so much rich in wealth as you are in burdens. Not so much do you prosper in pos-

---

53. *Homilies on Ephesians* 18.2 (*PG* 62.124).

54. *Homilies on Ephesians* 18.3 (*PG* 62.124]).

55. *Homilies on Ephesians* 18.3 (*PG* 62.125). In the same context he diagnoses that covetousness arises from "love waxing cold" (cf. Matt. 24:12).

56. *Homilies on Ephesians* 12.1 (*PG* 62.89).

57. For the same commonplace, see Seneca, *Epistulae Morales* 17.3.

sessions as in toils and dangers."[58] In the context of an exhortation to parents about how to raise their children to be indifferent to wealth (which he regards as just as important as teaching them a trade by which to support themselves), Chrysostom includes this haunting maxim: "Therefore conversely wealth causes harm, for it makes them unpracticed for the vicissitudes of life."[59] On a more comical note, Chrysostom in one place reviles the ostentatious display of riches in luxurious clothing by depicting the Christian life as a mud-wrestling bout with the devil, for which the rich are hardly appropriately attired![60]

The Community

Although Chrysostom's approach to the problem (as he sees it) of possessions is rigorously and consistently individualistic, he can also view the issue from the perspective of the wider community that is the arena for all economic transactions, be they buying, selling, stealing, or almsgiving. His view of the community is based upon his Christian presuppositions about the brother-hood and sisterhood of all Christians, and also of their common enslavement to the one master, God. Thus, as we saw in an earlier quoted passage, eco-nomic decisions, Chrysostom thinks, should be made on the basis of the fact that all should share equally in the possessions of the beneficent and wealthy master, God, who owns everything.[61] Likewise, Chrysostom assumes that the deity created human beings to live in community, not in isolation, and that it is only human predilection for greed that endangers that design: "although God from everywhere brings us together, we contend to divide ourselves, and to chop things up by making them our private possession [ἰδιοποιεῖσθαι]."[62] So private possessions and greed, for Chrysostom, are what destroy all human communities (as evidenced in the failure of the communitarian vision of the Jerusalem church to last beyond one generation).

58. *Homilies on Ephesians* 13.3 (*PG* 62.97-98), quoting 1 Timothy 6:9.

59. *Homilies on Ephesians* 21.4 (*PG* 62.154). The topic of wealth and poverty often comes up in Chrysostom's many instructions on child-rearing. See also, for instance, *Homilies on First Timothy* 9.2 (*PG* 62.547): "Do you wish to leave your son rich [πλούσιος]? Teach him to be good [χρηστός]. For thus he will be able to put together also possessions [κτήματα], and if he doesn't, then he will be no worse disposed than those who do have many possessions. But if he is evil, even if you leave him lots of money, you have not left him a guard over it, but have made him even worse than those in extreme poverty."

60. *Homilies on the Acts of the Apostles* 7.4 (*PG* 60.68).

61. *On the Calends* 3 (*PG* 48.956).

62. *Homilies on First Timothy* 12.4 (*PG* 62.564), full context quoted above.

But Chrysostom also analyzes the importance of the community in setting and maintaining standards of valuation. As such it, along with the weak individual, can be a cause, as well as a victim, of economic injustice. In this regard we shall look at some passages in which Chrysostom critiques the market economy of his day as arbitrary. For instance, in a marvelous discourse about the difference between natural beauty and artificial possessions (which is the extension of a homily we treated at length above), Chrysostom devalues the current standards of wealth and beauty:

> Is a pearl beautiful? But consider that it is sea water, that it was formerly tossed about in the bosoms of the sea. Are gold and silver beautiful? But consider that they were and still are dirt and ashes.[63] Are silk garments beautiful? But they are the webs of worms. It is an assumption and prejudice [ὑπόληψίς ἐστι καὶ πρόληψις] of humans; the beauty does not consist in its nature. For the things that have their beauty in nature do not require some to instruct others about it.[64]

The latter principle, that people change their minds on their estimation of things because of what others tell them about how valuable they are, Chrysostom will prove from common human experience. Thus the issue of possessions is not simply one of individual decision-making:

> When you see a copper coin which has been simply color-coated with gold, you admire it at first, calling it a gold coin. But when those who know about such things instruct you about the deception, the admiration disappears with the deception. So you see that the beauty does not reside in the nature. But neither is it the case with silver. For when you see tin, you admire it as silver, just as you do brass as gold. Thus you have such a need of instructors to tell you what you should admire! Therefore the eyes are not sufficient for our discernment.[65]

Next comes a comparison with the natural order, which serves to solidify this point further.

> It is not this way with the flowers, but they are much more beautiful than these (metals). If you see a rose, you do not need any to instruct you, but you know in yourself how to discern anemones from violets. The same as

---

63. Cf. *Homilies on First Timothy* 7.3 (*PG* 62.538): "if you see silver, consider it as tin. But you cannot? Then indeed consider it what it truly is — it is dirt!"

64. *Homilies on First Timothy* 17.3 (*PG* 62.596).

65. *Homilies on First Timothy* 17.3 (*PG* 62.596).

with lilies and each type of flower. What this is about is nothing more than prejudice [πρόληψις]. And that this destructive passion is a matter of prejudice, come, tell me, if the emperor decided to enact a law making silver more precious than gold, would you not transfer your admiration and affection?[66]

Thus for Chrysostom wealth and valued property depend upon nothing more than a communally held prejudice or preconception. And because it is just a preconception, then it could be changed, and would be changed, if the market were to alter its standard of valuation. But of course in his context, as he sees it, the one who could at least potentially control the market is the emperor, not the populace per se. This line of thought leads Chrysostom to provide a brief analysis of a market economy, based on truisms in his culture illustrating the principle of supply and demand:

> And it is indeed the case that something is honored by virtue of its rarity, and not because of its nature. Fruits that are cheap among us are expensive in the territory of the Cappadocians. And other things in the region of the Serians (whence these clothes come) are much more expensive than the things that are expensive here. Likewise with the spices in Arabia and India, where stones are found, we find many such things to be the case. Such things are a case thus of prejudice, a human suspicion [ὑπόνοια, also "an opinion"], and we do nothing from judgment, but simplemindedly and as chance dictates. Therefore, let's sober up now from this drunkenness. Let's see what is actually good [καλόν], that which is good by nature [τὸ φύσει καλόν] — piety, righteousness — so that we might attain the promised goods [τὰ ἐπηγγελμένα ἀγαθά].[67]

The conclusion to this discourse shows that, even as Chrysostom recognizes a community role in the promulgation and maintenance of market standards, nonetheless he addresses his energies for change toward individuals, toward their self-transformation rather than toward systemic alteration. He appears to regard the market as a matter of ill-defined and unsupported community caprice, open to change at will, and therefore not worthy of trust. But this does not lead him to consider its overhaul or its takeover to steer it in different directions. This is ultimately because the market for Chrysostom is just a symptom of the much larger problem: the misconception that the things of this world — any of them, arranged, marketed, or consumed in any

---

66. *Homilies on First Timothy* 17.3 (PG 62.596).
67. *Homilies on First Timothy* 17.3 (PG 62.596).

fashion — matter in the least within the larger sphere of human life and meaning in God's universe.

The Cosmos

As we have already seen in many different instances, for Chrysostom the axiomatic framework within which the individual and community interact with possessions is the universe, which was created by God, and which therefore belongs only to God. This theologoumenon decrees that human beings do not have idiosyncratic rights of possession, but rather only as shared "slaves" of the common master. It also serves to put the market standards that esteem gold, jewels, and other luxury items coveted by the rich to shame, in comparison with the "free" splendors of the created order: the sun, the moon, the stars, the sea, and so on. But the createdness of the cosmos also includes a fundamental reality of crucial importance for Chrysostom's understanding of possessions, and that is the fact that all human life on this planet was created finite. Many of Chrysostom's exhortations about possessions are founded on this basic, often paradoxical interaction between possessions and death.

Chrysostom often expounds upon the connection between the value of possessions and the mortality of the human person, as exemplified by the (especially Stoic) *topos* that "you can't take it with you" (found often already in the New Testament, as in 1 Tim. 6:6-10; cf. Luke 12:16-34), which serves to relativize completely the current strivings for earthly marketable goods.[68] A different take is found in his exposition of Christian necrotic existence (Col. 3:3, "you have died, and your life is hidden with Christ in God"). Since we are dead, Chrysostom counsels, and we don't buy things for dead people to eat and wear, therefore we shouldn't amass such possessions for ourselves.[69] Another passage, from yet another perspective, makes the case that the rich, by seeking to be honored for their external possessions, displace themselves, and in the process actually are destroying their own existence as human beings (τὸ ἄνθρωποι εἶναι ἀπώλεσαν).[70] This connection between possessions and

68. According to *Homilies on First Timothy* 11.2 (*PG* 62.556), all possession is only a loan, for how can it be otherwise given the fact that "when you expire, either willingly or unwillingly, others receive all your belongings, and they in turn give them to others, who give them to still others?"

69. *Homilies on Colossians* 7.2 (*PG* 62.346).

70. *Homilies on the Gospel of Saint Matthew* 4.10 (*PG* 57.51). The anthropology here is animated by the distinction between the living human "self" or "soul" (ψυχή) and "lifeless" or "soulless" material possessions (τὰ μὴ ζῶντα, ἄψυχα).

death is also used by Chrysostom to claim that possessions, unlike poverty, can harm one even after death, because of the real threat of tomb robbers who will steal the possessions and defile the corpse.[71] But this is only a minor threat compared to the punishment of everlasting damnation for hoarding one's goods and depriving others, the way in which possessions most can hurt one beyond the grave.[72] A neat summary of Chrysostom's varied interconnections between death and possessions is found in the following passage about wills:

> For the better thing, and what provides great boldness besides, is to correct poverty while one is alive [ζῶντα διορθοῦν πενίαν]. . . . Therefore I urge you while you are alive to give over the biggest share of your belongings to those in need. But if some might be so small-minded [lit. "small souled" (μικρόψυχοι)] that they will not put up with that, then even if as forced by necessity let them become benevolent [φιλάνθρωποι]. For when you were living you clung to your possessions as though you were never going to die [ἀθάνατος]. But now, since you have learned that you are going to die [θνητός], abolish this idea and deliberate about your belongings as one who is going to die [θνητός]. Or, instead, as one who should enjoy undying life [ἀθάνατος ζωή] continually.[73]

All of this for Chrysostom is played out within the framework provided by his overarching eschatology — that the present life is of no consequence in comparison with the real, true life to come.[74] Thus he relativizes the importance of any attainments in this life, especially material ones. For instance, he calls the earthly life a sojourn in "an entrenched camp" (φωσσάτον), and asks provocatively, "who would want to build opulent houses in an outpost?"[75]

---

71. *Homilies on First Corinthians* 35.6 (*PG* 61.304).

72. *Homilies on First Timothy* 17.3 (*PG* 62.595): "we should see that . . . wealth will not be able to go along with us (at death), and here it abandons us; that it remains here, though the wounds it inflicts come along with us."

73. *Homilies on Romans* 18.7 (*PG* 60.582).

74. "For one who can philosophize about the resurrection, and share himself or herself completely in the life there, will consider the things of the present to be nothing — not wealth, nor plenty, nor gold, nor silver, nor the wrappings of clothes, nor luxury, nor rich tables of food, nor any other of such things — nothing" (*On Almsgiving* 1 [*PG* 51.262]).

75. *Homilies on Ephesians* 23.3 (*PG* 62.168).

Responsible Christian Attitudes and Actions with Respect to Possessions

Having traced Chrysostom's essentially negative definitions of possessions and wealth and his attempts to redefine what "goods" should be for Christians, and analyzed some of the theological and philosophical positions that undergird his understandings of the individual, the community, and the cosmos in economic interactions, we now turn to the content of Chrysostom's positive advice for how Christians ought to conduct their lives in relation to possessions. We shall treat this advice under four categories: ascetic piety, almsgiving, solidarity, and utopian visions.

Asceticism

While it is tempting to treat almsgiving as Chrysostom's first and major initiative in response to both the over-abundance of one's own possessions and the utter lack of others', I think that, especially given our analysis of the theological underpinnings of Chrysostom's exhortations, pride of place in his thinking goes first to asceticism as the seedbed from which all else should come to restore the primordial order of divine cooperative ownership.[76] Because Chrysostom diagnoses the problem as not primarily due to an inadequate system of distribution of resources, but rather to perverse human attachment to the wrong things, what must come first is a conversion to an ascetic way of life, a concentration on the things of heaven, not those of this world. And this requires, for Chrysostom as for the Stoics before him, not just the willingness to share or even to do without, but rather the despising (καταφρόνησις) of riches and possessions. This is often given expression in a wordplay between τροφή, bare "sustenance," and its evil opposite τρυφή, "luxury." Only the ascetic rejection of earthly goods, coupled with prophetic outrage at the injustice their improper use causes, will suffice. Thereupon an outward sign of this correct inward attitude will be almsgiving.

---

76. The priority of asceticism in Chrysostom's thinking was emphasized especially by Plassmann (*Das Almosen*, p. 95: "Die wichtigste moralische Pflicht ist die Abkehr von der Habsucht. Der Zweck des Almosens ist es, diese Abkehr zu beweisen, nicht aber, die Armen zu ernähren"). He has, however, taken the comparison too far, for Chrysostom was interested in the real alleviation of the sufferings of the poor, also.

Almsgiving

Appeals to almsgiving predominate in Chrysostom's homilies, as well as direct confrontation with excuses and complaints others make for refusing to give alms. The appeal to give alms to the poor, as to Christ (Matt. 25:31-46),[77] is so ubiquitous in Chrysostom's homilies that one passage will suffice to illustrate the form of his appeal. Here, as so often, he bases his call for almsgiving on his own compassionate observations of those in need, whom he seeks by his rhetoric to place before the eyes of his congregation:

> I have said these things so that we might not despise adjurations, especially when people urge us to do good works, to give alms or show benevolence. Now when poor people sit, with feet that have been amputated, seeing you running by, since they are unable to follow you on foot, as though with a kind of hook they think they will detain you by the fear of an oath, and, stretching out their hands they adjure you that you give them only one or two coins. But you run on by, though adjured by the name of your Lord. And indeed if by the eyes of your husband who is out of town, or your son or your daughter, you are adjured, immediately you give in, and your mind leaps up and you are warmed. But if he adjures you in the name of the Lord, you run on by. And I know many women[78] who, when they hear the word Christ, run on by, but when they are praised for their beauty by those who approach them, fall to pieces and are softened and stretch out their hand. Indeed they have put the wretched poor in such a state that they must act like jesters. For since by saying vehement and bitter words they do not touch their souls, they come to this way by which they delight them abundantly. And our great meanness compels the one who is afflicted and strangled by hunger to pronounce encomia about the beauty of those they are asking. And I would wish that this was all, but there is another form of begging even worse than this. It compels the poor to be jugglers, foul mouths, and jesters.[79]

77. On the crucial importance of this passage for Chrysostom see Rudolf Brändle, *Matth. 25,31-46 im Werk des Johannes Chrysostomus*, Beiträge zur Geschichte der biblischen Exegese 22 (Tübingen: Mohr Siebeck, 1979).

78. Here is one of many examples of Chrysostom's misogyny, as mentioned in my introduction, and seen likewise in the case of the silver chamber pots mentioned above. He sees extravagance as a particular vice of women, and likewise vanity, which is his particular point in this caricature. Another area for careful critique and assessment is Chrysostom's own embeddedness in the social order as priest and bishop and recipient (at least as church officer) of benefactions from the wealthy (see Leyerle, "John Chrysostom on Almsgiving," pp. 29-47).

79. *Homilies on First Thessalonians* 11.3 (*PG* 62.465-66).

Chrysostom regards almsgiving as an ethical act of redistribution of wealth mandated by the gospel. In places he appears to regard it as the only necessary ingredient of a just society.[80] An optimistic statement of the efficacy of almsgiving to resolve social inequity is found, for instance, in his homily that takes its departure from Matthew's depiction (Matt. 26:15; 27:3) of the price paid to Jesus' betrayer, Judas: "For by the grace of God I suppose that the number of people gathered together here adds up to about 100,000. And if each one would share a loaf with some poor person, then all would be in plenty. And if each one shared a single coin, then no one would be poor."[81]

This same confidence about the power of almsgiving to alleviate poverty once and for all is also found elsewhere in his writings, sometimes even with some statistical calculations to back up his proposals.[82] He also has a vision of almsgiving as a double-sided exchange, one in which the giver gains more than the recipient: "You owe greater thanks to the poor person for receiving your alms. For if there were no poor, then you would not cast off from yourself the majority of your sins. The poor are the healers of your ills. They provide their hands as your medicines."[83] This in turn requires a proper disposition of the hands of the wealthy: "if you would stretch out your hands to the hands of the poor, then you would touch the very height of heaven."[84]

---

80. The main impediment of that transformation, most of the time, appears to be the resistance and stubbornness of the rich, who excuse themselves by appeal to the need to leave an inheritance to their children (e.g., *Homilies on the Gospel of Saint Matthew* 66.4 [*PG* 58.630]), or even through their suspicion about the veracity of the claims of beggars (on the question, see Leyerle, "John Chrysostom on Almsgiving," pp. 29-47), to which Chrysostom has a ready, and impatient, reply. He diagnoses their unwillingness to give as simply "savagery and misanthropy" (ὠμότης καὶ ἀπανθρωπία) (*Homilies on the Gospel of Saint Matthew* 66.3 [*PG* 58.630]).

81. *Homilies on the Gospel of Saint Matthew* 85.4 (*PG* 58.762-63).

82. See especially the simplified calculus in *Homilies on the Gospel of Saint Matthew* 66.3 (*PG* 58.630), which maintains that if the top 10 percent of the populace, who are rich, would join with the next 80 percent, who are "middle class," in aiding the bottom 10 percent of the population, who are abjectly poor ("have nothing at all"), there would be only one poor person per fifty or one hundred citizens.

83. *Homilies on First Timothy* 14.2 (*PG* 62.574). See also *Homilies on Second Timothy* 1.4 (*PG* 62.606), and 7.4 (*PG* 62.642), where almsgiving is said to protect a household from any harm.

84. *Homilies on Second Timothy* 1.4 (*PG* 62.606).

Solidarity

As Chrysostom understands it, almsgiving is an act of solidarity with the poor. In one very striking rhetorical passage (which today sounds conspicuously liberationist) he calls for the rich to abandon their lofty places and join the poor, in a way combining into one virtue the previous two requirements of asceticism and almsgiving. The context is an extended allegory of the poor as the three children in the "furnace of poverty" (πενίας κάμινος), and the rich as all people who worshiped the idol of money, like those who made obeisance to Nebuchadnezzar's statue rather than die. In treating this theme Chrysostom swells to a crescendo that the rich, who are kindling the flame of the furnace, had better watch out, for they will be prey to the very flames they prepare for others. The only remedy, he writes, is this:

> Let us go down via almsgiving into the furnace of poverty, let us see the people who walk in it, philosophizing and treading on the hot coals, let us see the strange and paradoxical marvel of a person in a furnace singing praise, a person amid flames giving thanks, a person bound in the most extreme poverty and yet bearing great praise to Christ. . . . Now, let's not stand outside of the furnace, with no mercy toward the poor, lest we suffer what happened to those executioners (in Daniel 3). But if you go down to them and stand with the children, no longer will the fire be harmful to you. But if you sit above, disregarding those in the flames of poverty, the flames will burn you up. Come down, then, into the fire, so that you might not be burned up by the fire. Don't sit outside of the fire, lest the flames snatch you up. But if it sees you with the poor, then it will stay away from you. But if you are alienated from the poor, the fire will chase you down quickly and snatch you up. Therefore don't stand apart from the ones who are being thrown into the furnace. For when the devil orders those who have not worshiped money to be thrown into the furnace of poverty, do not be with the ones who are throwing, but rather with those thrown, so that you might be among the saved, and not the burned.[85]

85. Interesting for a study of the importance and impact of such images in discourse on property and possessions in society is the reaction to this emotional finale recorded in the next sermon, where Chrysostom says he hears many saying that they are very moved when hearing the homily, but lose the "fire of desire" (τὸ πῦρ τῆς προθυμίας, pun intended!) (*Homilies on the Gospel of Saint Matthew* 5.1 [*PG* 57.55]). Chrysostom attributes this to two things: unsuitable pursuits (religious observance is compartmentalized into less than one day a week, he complains), and evil companions.

Utopian Discourse and the Social Order

While in some passages, notably the two often-cited passages from the homilies on Matthew quoted above, Chrysostom appears to consider almsgiving the sufficient means to transform the present, unjust economic order, there are other passages in his writings that have been interpreted by some scholars as evidence that Chrysostom also had a more radical vision for concrete social change. The most recent proponent of this viewpoint is Adolf Martin Ritter, who counters directly those who consider such passages in Chrysostom's homilies to be mere *"oratorische Kraftstellen,"* or nostalgic wishful thinking:[86]

> In my judgment, a sharp eye for social realities and an understanding of Christian "perfection" — according to which "perfection" also has essentially to do with social justice — led him, in the end, to the insight that the means of private almsgiving are hardly adequate, even if the aim is to address only the most grinding poverty. On the contrary, we must look in all earnestness for other possible solutions. Thus Chrysostom often, and publicly, pushed toward a comprehensive "social utopia."[87]

Ritter has astutely appreciated the theological underpinnings of Chrysostom's thinking about possessions, which we have examined above: that God did not create people rich and poor, that the earth is for all free, and that there should be no talk of "mine" and "yours" because God's intention is for community of goods as the most fitting and most effective system. Ritter does recognize the prominence of calls to give alms to the poor in Chrysostom's homilies, yet he argues that through reflection on harsh experiences in the course of his long ministry Chrysostom came to realize the limitations of almsgiving as a means for achieving a just social order:

> If Chrysostom seems here [*Homilies on the Gospel of Saint Matthew* 66.3] to present the solution to the social problem in such a way that he assigns particular poor individuals to particular rich individuals and thus wants

---

86. O. Schilling, *Der kirchliche Eigentumsbegriff* (Freiburg: Herder, 1930), p. 38. Note also Ernst Troeltsch (both of whom are discussed by Stötzel, *Kirche als "neue Gesellschaft,"* p. 9): "The same Chrysostom who utters these ideas would like, however, to turn Constantinople and Antioch into a communistic fellowship of love like the monastic life; at the same time he calms the fears of his wealthy hearers by assuring them that in the present situation it will not be possible to carry out these ideas in practice" (*The Social Teaching of the Christian Churches*, 2 vols., trans. O. Wyon [Chicago: University of Chicago Press, 1960], 1:127).

87. Ritter, "John Chrysostom As an Interpreter," p. 188.

to call to life something like a community poor-relief system with an honorary and individualistic character . . . *he later moves toward an even more radical social utopia.* In his homilies on Acts, delivered in Constantinople, he takes up the idea of community of goods as it was practiced, according to Luke, in the early Jerusalem community. There is no doubt that the bishop and preacher is entirely serious in his proposal, even though he likens it at first simply to an idea hastily thrown out. For at the end he calls for an attempt at the daring venture. If one was actually to do that, it would turn out that this was no mere utopian scheme — as the monasteries have long since proven.[88]

Although the developmental aspect of Ritter's thesis may perhaps be debated,[89] he is right to oppose those who belittle Chrysostom's utterances as "mere show rhetoric." But while he is probably correct in countering that claim by insisting that Chrysostom was completely serious about his proposal for social change, what Ritter has perhaps not sufficiently emphasized is the extent to which it is precisely *as rhetoric* that Chrysostom seeks to make his appeal. The rhetoric on property and possessions is not an alternative to an actual social plan, but is an instrument for its realization. In this case, Chrysostom is expounding upon the communistic social order of the early church in Jerusalem. Let us take another look at this text — and in particular at his rhetorical strategy in it — in order to appreciate fully what John is seeking to do here:

> And if this were to happen now, we would live with greater pleasure, both rich and poor. It would not bring greater pleasure to the poor than to the

88. Ritter, "John Chrysostom As an Interpreter," p. 365.

89. The issue concerns the date of *Homilies on First Timothy* 12.3-4 (Ritter's next example, p. 366) vis-à-vis *Homilies on the Acts of the Apostles* 11.3. Hans Lietzmann ("Johannes Chrysostomos," *Pauly-Wissowa* 9, no. 2 [1916]: 1811-28, 1818) and Max von Bonsdorff (*Zur Predigttätigkeit des Johannes Chrysostomus: Biographisch-chronologische Studien über seine Homilienserien zu neutestamentlichen Büchern* [Helsingfors, 1922], pp. 53-59) place the series *Homilies on First Timothy* in Antioch, ca. 394, thus a decade before *Homilies on the Acts of the Apostles*, which are clearly from Constantinople (post-398). But the dating of Chrysostom's homilies remains inexact; the methodological difficulties in these earlier attempts at dating have recently been pointed out by Wendy Mayer, "The Provenance of the Homilies of St John Chrysostom: Towards a New Assessment of Where He Preached What," Ph.D. diss., Queensland, 1996. I would argue that variations in Chrysostom's expressed attitudes toward wealth may be as much or more due to a particular rhetorical exigency than to an orderly progression in ideas toward greater radicalism. But in a valuable exchange on this point in our conference at Heidelberg, Professor Ritter emphasized what our views hold in common, which I should like to reecho here: "that John Chrysostom has a legitimate place within the history of Christian utopianism — like Paul."

rich. And if you wish, in the meantime let's sketch it out in words [τέως ὑπογράψωμεν αὐτὸ τῷ λόγῳ], and in this way let us reap the fruit of pleasure, since you do not wish it in deeds [ἐπειδὴ ἐν ἔργοις οὐ βούλεσθε]. For it is especially clear from the things that happened to them back then, that by selling their possessions they were not lacking, but they made the poor become rich. Yet also now let's sketch this in words [Πλὴν ἀλλὰ καὶ νῦν ὑπογράψωμεν τοῦτο τῷ λόγῳ], and let all sell all their possessions, and let them bring them into the middle — in words, I mean [τῷ λόγῳ λέγω] — don't let anyone get stirred up, neither rich nor poor. How much gold do you suppose would be collected? I estimate (for it is not possible to speak accurately here [οὐ γὰρ δὴ μετὰ ἀκριβείας δυνατὸν εἰπεῖν]), that if all men and women here emptied out their goods, and gave over their lands, possessions, and houses (for I cannot not speak of slaves, since it wasn't the case then, but they saw fit for them equally to be free), perhaps a million pounds of gold would be collected. Or rather twice or three times that much. For tell me, how many are there on the tax rolls of our city? And how many would you want to say are Christian? One hundred thousand, you say, and the rest Greeks and Jews? How many tens of thousands of pounds of gold would they collect? And what is the number of poor people [πόσας ἀριθμός ἐστι πενήτων]? I don't suppose more than fifty thousand. Now for all of these to be fed every day, what abundance would be needed? Well, if there was a common feeding, and they ate together, then it would not need a great expense. "What then," someone will say, "are we supposed to do after the money is spent up?" Do you suppose that it can ever be spent up? For wouldn't the grace of God be ten-thousand-fold greater? Wouldn't the grace of God be richly poured out? What, then, shouldn't we make earth into heaven? . . .⁹⁰ But nowadays people are more afraid of this [a communal purse] than they are of falling into an immense and boundless sea. But if we were to make a test of this, then we should dare to instate this plan [Εἰ δὲ πεῖραν ἐποιησάμεθα τούτου, τότε ἂν κατετολμήσαμεν τοῦ πράγματος]. And how much grace do you suppose there would be? If back then they dared to instate this plan [οὕτω δὴ κατετόλμησεν τοῦ πράγματος], when no one was a believer, except only

---

90. Space constraints prevent me from quoting the entire argument, but in the unquoted section Chrysostom argues the following points: (1) if there was such magnificence in the primitive Jerusalem church's communal life, how much greater would it not be if accomplished for a much larger multitude? (2) living communally is far more economical than living separately, as demonstrated by the example of a household with ten children, whom it would be devastatingly expensive to set up individually in their own domiciles, but far easier to accommodate under one roof; (3) the proof provided by the monasteries, where no one starves.

three thousand, and five thousand, when they were the enemies of the entire world, when they could expect comfort from no direction, how much more would it be now, when by the grace of God there are believers throughout the world? Who would remain a Greek then? I don't suppose anyone would, thus we would allure all and draw them to us. But if we go forward on this way (of communal living), I believe in God, that also this will come to be [Πλὴν ἀλλ᾽ ἐὰν ὁδῷ ταύτῃ προβαίνωμεν, πιστεύω τῷ θεῷ, ὅτι καὶ τοῦτο ἔσται]. For only believe me [Πείσθητέ μοι μόνον], and we shall bring this plan to success in good order [κατὰ τάξιν κατορθώσομεν τὰ πράγματα]. And if God gives life, as I believe he does, we shall lead you[91] quickly into this commonwealth [ταχέως εἰς ταύτην ἡμᾶς ἄξομεν τὴν πολιτείαν].[92]

Here Chrysostom provides a vision for a concordant economic order (ὑπογραφόμενον ἐν λόγῳ) "sketched in speech" (in the same manner as Plato has Socrates describe the ideal *politeia* in the *Respublica*).[93] Playing with his audience's expected resistance to adopting any communitarian scheme (given that the majority of his congregational audience was upper class),[94] Chrysostom uses language that on the surface undermines the "reality" of his undertaking (just words, not deeds), but it is nonetheless an attempt at social change through the imagination. He stacks up appeals of different types to acquiesce to this "plan" (τὸ πρᾶγμα): the historical example of success in the Jerusalem church; a social and economic analysis of the current scene, if admittedly based on rough estimates; an argument of practicality in home economics for communal rather than individual living; a call to seize the present opportunity provided by the success of Christianity in the empire; and ap-

91. The text reads "us" (ἡμᾶς), which is nonsensical, but the two pronouns are ubiquitously interchanged in manuscripts. ("You" is also how the *Nicene and Post-Nicene Fathers* translation, by J. Walker et al., translates the word [*NPNF* 11.75]).

92. *Homilies on the Acts of the Apostles* 11.3 (60.97-98).

93. "'I understand,' he said, 'you are speaking of the city in which we have now come to set up our dwelling, the city which is established in words [πόλει . . . τῇ ἐν λόγοις κειμένῃ], since I do not suppose it exists anywhere on earth' [ἐπεὶ γῆς γε οὐδαμοῦ οἶμαι αὐτὴν εἶναι]. 'But,' I said, 'perhaps a pattern of it is laid up in heaven for the person who wishes to look at it, and by gazing upon it to settle himself or herself there'" (ἐν οὐρανῷ ἴσως παράδειγμα ἀνάκειται τῷ βουλομένῳ ὁρᾶν καὶ ὁρῶντι ἑαυτὸν κατοικίζειν) (*Republic* 9.592B).

94. Brown, *Power and Persuasion*, p. 76: "By the end of the fourth century, the church, far from being a church of the lower classes, reflected the sharp divisions in Roman society: its upper echelons were occupied by highly cultivated persons, drawn from the class of urban notables. [Those] preaching tended to address the wealthier and more educated members of the congregation." Chrysostom does, however, urge both rich and poor not to get too upset by what he is saying.

peals to the "bravery" of his audience, to the grace of God, and to the auxiliary outcomes (evangelistic success) that can be expected from this course of action. The closing part of this passage is most interesting, because Chrysostom puts all the attention upon his own ἦθος (ethos) as speaker. He testifies in behalf of his plan that, just as he believes in God, he knows the implementation of a communitarian economic order will bring even untold benefits. And he names precisely what must happen for the change to take place: Πείσθητέ μοι μόνον, "only be persuaded by me!" Chrysostom's rhetoric must do the job of converting the minds of his audience to adopt a new vision for the socioeconomic order. Yet this is not a reckless venture, but is as secure as the very belief in God. If his discourse is successful, "we shall lead you quickly into this commonwealth."

This passage gives evidence of the power of the Jerusalem community's concordant communitarian life for Chrysostom's understanding of earthly social economies. While he does not provide a detailed blueprint for a full-scale transition from the market economy and individualized possession of his day to a communitarian system, Chrysostom does regard the existing structures as a distortion of God's created intention for human life and community. But the arena for a revision of the present conditions is entirely the human will for Chrysostom, for it is only there that the allure of riches can be met and countered, once and for all.[95] This may not be so much due to a hesitation about altering the civic order, however, as it is to his sense that the new order can come only by first being given life in the imagination of each hearer, "through words."

Rhetoric and the Economic Order

What does it mean that Chrysostom's statements on property and possessions are, after all, "just words"? First, we should recognize that words are indeed the main tool in the hands of an ambassador, especially a self-appointed one like Chrysostom, who was propelled to his post by the moral imperative he felt from observing the conditions of his neighbors (see the quotation with which we began). So our first learning from Chrysostom is that intervention begins with sight, and is followed by words.

---

95. With Wolf Dieter Hauschild, "Christentum und Eigentum: Zum Problem eines altkirchlichen 'Sozialismus,'" *Zeitschrift für evangelische Ethik* 16 (1972): 34-49, p. 46: "Allerdings setzt Chrysostomus diese Kritik nicht in ein grundsätzliches Urteil über die Gesellschaft, in der so etwas möglich ist, um, sondern beschränkt sich auf die *moralische Verurteilung der einzelnen.*"

Second, Chrysostom's words are intended directly to combat the "mere words" "yours" and "mine," which he holds responsible for the injustices and deceptive practices of the current order: "for what entirely are 'mine' and 'not mine'? When I examine them accurately I see that they are bare words."[96] Chrysostom is here denigrating the very power of language, which is paradoxically both his adversary and his own set of weapons.

Third, they are words that are rooted, we have argued, in concrete theological and philosophical beliefs about anthropology, cosmology, and divine activity. If our reconstruction of the scaffolding of his ideas is correct, then these "just words" are the expression of "just thoughts," or "just commitments," which, when enacted verbally, may change the social order. But how might this change come about? If all economic orders are created and sustained by discourse,[97] then Chrysostom's imaginings of a communistic, concordant, and just economic order need to be taken seriously as attempts to change the world, even if they are not accompanied by a full-fledged revolutionary or programmatic upheaval on the ground. If Peter Brown is right, Chrysostom actually had in mind, or at least was involved in, an even more systemic alteration of the social order of the late Roman city: from a civic-minded polity with its institutions for economic distribution, public works and welfare, and entertainment, to a Christian society in which the basic social unit of the ascetic household would govern social relations and responsibilities.[98] And he went about it quite deliberately with words as his tool, even as he was himself embedded in complex ways in that economic order, as a consumer (though a stringently ascetic one, as even his enemies granted), and as a bishop, who both depended on contributions from the rich and had the power to distribute them to the poor.[99]

---

96. Τί δέ ἐστιν ὅλως ἐμὸς καὶ οὐκ ἐμός. Ταῦτα γὰρ ὅταν μετὰ ἀκριβείας ἐξετάσω, ῥήματα μόνον ὁρῶ ψιλά (*On Virginity* 68.3-4 [*Sources chrétiennes* 125.340-42]).

97. Like empires, as insightfully studied by Brown, *Power and Persuasion,* and Averil Cameron, *Christianity and the Rhetoric of Empire,* Sather Classical Lectures 55 (Berkeley: University of California Press, 1991).

98. Brown, *Body and Society,* pp. 305-22.

99. This ambivalence is captured nicely by Leyerle, "John Chrysostom on Almsgiving," pp. 44-47. Yet Chrysostom also could urge his congregants not to give their alms to the leaders of the church to distribute, but to give them directly, themselves, to the poor, so as to have the reward of service and not just that of giving money (*Homilies on First Timothy* 14.3 [*PG* 62.574]). The ascetic Chrysostom's association with a rich patroness is one of many ironies in his relationship with Olympias, a wealthy woman ascetic. (See the fine study by Elizabeth A. Clark, "Friendship between the Sexes: Classical Theory and Christian Practice," in eadem, *Jerome, Chrysostom, and Friends: Essays and Translations,* Studies in Women and Religion 2 [New York: Mellen, 1979], pp. 35-106; esp. pp. 54 and 68 on Olympias's financial munificences, including those for Chrysostom's see in Constantinople.)

While opinions on the actual impact of Chrysostom's sermons on the life of the poor vary[100] (and data is lacking for a certain judgment), one thing is clear, and justifies the task of this essay: that language makes a difference. The late-fourth-century "invention" of "the poor" may serve as an example to inspire new, and even more effective, configurations for cognitive and social change.[101] The new social order begins with a vision, which is verbally articulated publicly by some speaker and appropriated privately in the consciousness of those who hear it (either consigned with approval to permanent memory or rejected). Chrysostom's particular power as an orator was his ability through words to create vivid descriptions and images, such as the silver chamber pot (the ancient equivalent of Imelda Marcos's shoes or Tammy Faye's air-conditioned doghouse), which combine social experience and moral evaluation in stunning, publicly verified ways. In the complex interrelating dynamic of thoughts, words, and images, a social world, indeed a social alternative, is born and dies. Since it is "mere words" that uphold economic orders, the quality and contexts of such discourses must be attended to, as must the conceptions and commitments that underlie them. The twenty-first-century definitions of wealth, poverty, possessions, and property, from whatever realms they arise, and from whatever persons they emerge (and such persons are themselves implicated in varied ways in the social order), will determine the menu of economic possibilities to be considered, just as the rhetorical forms in which those concepts are cast will largely dictate their palatability and consequent potential for successful implementation.

100. Opinions vary from Liebeschuetz's more positive assessment (Liebeschuetz, *Barbarians and Bishops*, p. 188: "The causal connection between these wider developments and the preaching of precisely John Chrysostom is of course very slight. But the fact that such profound changes of attitude [toward the poor] did take place suggests that regular and sustained preaching did not go without effect") to Frend's somewhat impatient one (W. H. C. Frend, *The Rise of Christianity* [Philadelphia: Fortress, 1984], p. 749: "He sympathized with their sufferings though his remedies went no further than to prick the consciences of the rich to provide ever more alms for relief").

101. Witness, for instance, the definition of "the homeless" in the last several decades in America.

Subjectivist "Faith" As a Religious Trap

MICHAEL WELKER

The Topic of Faith

One of the main goals of the Property and Possession Project was to start a comparative exploration of symbols and rationalities of "having, gaining, and losing" in economic and non-economic (especially religious) symbol-systems.[1] On the basis of such comparative exploration, it was the leading expectation that the rhetorical and rational constitution and maintenance of economic, social, and religious forms of communication and order could be studied and tested.[2] Interdependencies could be discovered and checked; alternatives could be ventured.[3] Connected with this expectation was, of course, the hope to gain perspectives on a post-consumerist social order[4] and a post–*lex talionis* rationality, and to work toward a "cultural re-imagination" of the basic configuration of late modern societies.[5] The following contribu-

1. Including, of course, transformations and distortions of "having, gaining, and losing," like greed, user mentalities, and dangerous modes of yearning; cf. in this volume William Schweiker, "Reconsidering Greed"; Charles Mathewes, "On Using the World"; and David M. Gunn, "Identity, Possession, and Myth on the Web: Yearning for Jerusalem."

2. Cf. in this volume Patrick D. Miller, "Property and Possession in Light of the Ten Commandments"; Claudia V. Camp, "Possessing Wealth, Possessing Women, Possessing Self: The Shame of Biblical Discourse"; and Margaret M. Mitchell, "Silver Chamber Pots and Other Goods Which Are Not Good: John Chrysostom's Discourse against Wealth and Possessions."

3. Cf. Christine Firer Hinzi, "What Is Enough? Catholic Social Thought, Consumption, and Material Sufficiency," and Jean Bethke Elshtain, "The Body and Projects of Self Possession," both in this volume.

4. Cf. esp. Christine Firer Hinzi's contribution to this volume.

5. Cf. Kathryn Tanner, "Economies of Grace," in this volume.

tion chooses the topic of *faith* — specifically, having, gaining, and losing faith — for a number of reasons.

First, since "faith" is to be seen as a spiritual "gift," its rationality of "having and losing" should offer some challenges to the rationalities and symbols that guide our dealing with physical gifts and objects of desire. This does not mean that I intend a dualistic approach, setting in opposition, for example, the gift of faith and the gifts in the economy. I rather intend a multi-systemic or multi-contextual approach, which is conscious of the fact that in late modernity we live in functionally differentiated societies that require the awareness that a specific multitude (not just a vague "plurality") of norma-tively coded rationalities guides our individual and common lives, our moral options and our cultural sensitivities and imaginations. Despite the genius of the theoretical efforts of Talcott Parsons, Niklas Luhmann, and others, we do not yet have a satisfactory theory of pluralistic societies. But the awareness that monosystemic, dualistic, and relativistic approaches are insufficient, that they can easily lead into distortive abstractions, and that we have to take countermeasures in our theoretical and practical orientations is already of great importance.

Second, the topic of faith challenges us to the awareness that, in dealing with the canonic traditions of the Bible, a multi-systemic, or multi-contextual, approach seems advisable. On the one hand, this does not mean, of course, that we should treat these traditions like late modern pluralistic so-cieties. But, on the other hand, we should also question notions about the ho-mogeneity, or the simple, stratified order, of ancient societies and cultures. Even many biblical texts reflect the awareness that market, politics, and reli-gion follow different patterns, morals, and rationalities. These morals and ra-tionalities can be brought into perspectives of conflict and incompatibility (e.g., "You can not serve God and Mammon!"). On the other hand, we notice that one sphere can use some of the same language, symbols, and reasoning of the attacked "other" (compare, for example, Jesus' parables on prudent and good housekeeping and his recommendation to watch the behavior of the "children of the world").

This leads to the guess that not just different virtues and values (faith in religion; prudence in economics; love in the family; etc.) but rather differ-ent configurations and "hierarchizations" of values and virtues separate and relate these spheres, contexts, and systems. This also leads to the guess that the different configurations and hierarchizations of values and virtues can change in the course of historical and cultural development, expressing changes in the relations between social systems. This would explain why we see in some historical and cultural settings friendly and mutually supportive constellations between specific social spheres and systems (for example, religion and science, or religion and law), whereas in other settings, we see stronger divisions, stronger oppositions, stronger alienations of the same systems.

A third reason for the choice of my topic is that although it is highly debatable — at least for a theologian — that faith is just a virtue, the concentration on the topic of faith allows for an approach toward a virtue-theory reading of pluralistic structures like that which Deirdre McCloskey seems to suggest in this volume.[6] The topic of faith, viewed as a binding power for a set of virtues, might offer some help in "decoding" and "reading" this multi-hierarchical pluralism of virtues. Seeing faith as a virtue is certainly one possible outside perspective in a nontheological anthropology. The interesting question would be how the transformation (or even deformation) of a set or hierarchy of virtues in one social sphere or system affects the others and their interplay.

Fourth, the problematic texture of the kind of faith dominant in late modern societies offers an interesting test case of an optimization and maximization process that collapsed in on itself. A form that was meant to secure the inescapability and ubiquity of faith seems to lead to the systematic and systemic self-emptying, self-banalization, and self-secularization (as Wolfgang Huber has put it) of faith, and even to the loss of faith. If this is correct, the topic of faith could provide a model to deal with the extremely difficult limit-questions of having and losing (such as "What is enough?").

Fifth, over against these efforts to relate faith to the formative processes of cultural development, many strands of modern theology focus on faith as a strictly subjective trust and certainty. They distance, or even disconnect, this trust and certainty from other virtues, except in the form of a highly individualized and finally romanticized person-to-person love. The assumption is that only in such immediate, culturally unconditioned encounters does faith reach its existential depth and profundity. Faith becomes a transcendental form, accompanying "all experience," with the potential to enter any encounter with another human being. Thus, on the one hand, faith seems to be the key to many or even every religious door. On the other hand, this same observation also explains the banalization and exhaustion of this subjectivist type of faith. It conditions a permanent longing and yearning for God, for "the other," and for the identity of the self, offering a dialectical certainty, which continually frustrates and re-stimulates on both ends. It offers what Hegel called the "bad infinity" *(schlechte Unendlichkeit)* of a transcendental form

---

6. Cf. her contribution, "Avarice, Prudence, and the Bourgeois Virtues."

connecting the feeling of abstract freedom with the feeling of abstract dependence.[7]

It is important to explain both the great evolutionary success of this transcendental form and the distortions it brings about. It is difficult to judge whether the dominant type of religiosity in the ailing classic mainline churches of Western industrialized societies should be understood as a loss of faith or not. On the one hand, church leaders and academic theologians assure us that this type of faith is an evolutionary product that has survived the challenges of modern culture — providing a large number of what Karl Rahner has called "anonymous Christians," patient supporters of the church, and a culture open to religion. On the other hand, we keep hearing that our societies and cultures are suffering a great "spiritual hunger," that the language of faith has become strange and sterile, that the majority is ashamed to speak about matters of faith, and that fundamentalist reactions against this situation fail to resonate with realistic experience.

Seeing that faith is a religious and cultural form shaped and reshaped in the course of history, we can certainly ask, "What are the alternatives then?" Obviously a superficial renaming of God (as "the inner other") and of the abstract self is not among the options — if the underlying empty structure of infinite longing and yearning is retained.[8] To the contrary, emptiness and infinity — often seen as religiously important and attractive figures — seem to be the crucial problem. The alternative is to replace the dominant empty subjective form of faith — to replace its emptiness and infinity — with a textured pluralism (not just a plurality) of the life of faith.

Subjectivist Faith As a Religious Trap

A commonly accepted understanding of faith in current Western societies is that a believing individual is utterly certain of something "wholly other," of a "transcendent" power, instance, or vaguely conceived transcendent person that, at the same time, however, is intimately close. The "Beyond," the "final point of reference of creaturely dependence," the "other side" of the "founding relation of

7. Georg Wilhelm Friedrich, *Phänomenologie des Geistes* (Hamburg: Felix Meiner, 1952).

8. Cf. David Gunn's essay with respect to "the Land"; the respecification of the modern self with respect to the body, and the publicized emotion in postmodern media-and-competitive-sports-culture, would be other examples. Cf. M. Welker, "Is the Autonomous Person of European Modernity a Sustainable Model of Human Personhood?" in *The Human Person in Science and Theology,* ed. N. H. Gregersen, W. B. Drees, and U. Görman (Edinburgh: T&T Clark, 1999), pp. 95-114.

our existence,"[9] is given in an utmost, although continuously challenged, certainty; and this gained, challenged, and regained certainty is called "faith." This conception of "faith" approximates, and even collapses into, however, an emphatic self-reference. Karl Barth rightly called it "indirect Cartesianism."[10] This indirect Cartesianism can be grasped by the formula "I feel somehow dependent — thus I am." And, "I feel somehow dependent — thus I believe."

Since this conception of "faith" approximates, and even collapses into, emphatic self-reference, religious communication and particularly Christian theology have strongly tried to differentiate this "faith" from all forms of self-reference. As much as the inner certainty named "faith" was treasured, just as much were all forms of self-reference stigmatized and denounced as "sin." Against this background, attempts to distinguish between innocent, trivial, and healthy forms of self-reference, on the one side, and distortive, traumatic, and even demonic forms of self-reference, on the other, seemed to be risky. A paradoxical and neuroticizing mentality accompanied this religious form, since it proved to be extremely difficult to distinguish this empty inner certainty of a "Wholly Other" from a very simple and basic form of "pure" human self-reference that had come to terms with its inner structure: namely, *that all self-reference has to include some element of difference if it wants to reach the level of experiencing "certainty."*

The upside of this form of constantly challenged and reaffirmed certainty, which can be understood both religiously and secularly, seemed to be that nobody could escape this type of "faith" — at least not in cultures and among mentalities for which the self-reference of the individual is central, that is, in cultures that belong to typically modern society. Seen from the outside, this form called "faith" combines the experiences of immediacy and negation, containing elements of intimate self-awareness/self-reference and difference. Since this form can appear both as a religious form and as a form of pure dialectical self-reference, it can be interpreted in a variety of ways.[11]

---

9. Gordon Kaufman uses the expression "God as ultimate point of reference" in almost all his writings. I take up the expression "founding relation of our existence" *(Existenzbegründungsrelation)* from Eilert Herms.

10. Karl Barth, *Kirchliche Dogmatik* I/1, pp. 223, 224.

11. This form could be used to render more complex religious, moral, and metaphysical positions accessible for common sense, reducing and trivializing them and stating that they all would finally offer nothing else than this dialectic of subjective immediacy and difference; for example,

- religiously as the *"Gefühl der schlechthinnigen Abhängigkeit"* ("the feeling of the utmost dependence," Schleiermacher), or

It was above all Søren Kierkegaard who again and again presented this form as "faith" and recommended it as a genuinely Christian attitude: "exactly this is . . . the formula for faith: by relating to itself and by wanting to be itself, the self founds itself transparently in the power which has it set," or: "Faith is: that the self, by being itself and wanting to be itself, transparently founds itself in God."[12] Since this form of "faith" and its vocabulary were coined and transmitted by mass culture through the popular and semi-popular academic *public receptions* of the writings of Kant, Schleiermacher, Kierkegaard, Rothe, Troeltsch, and other thinkers of the nineteenth and early twentieth centuries, one could label it "neo-Protestant faith" and regard it as a product primarily of the nineteenth century. But directly, and indirectly, it has also been represented and spread by the most diverse theological thinkers and styles of thought of the twentieth century[13] and has become a widespread form of religiosity in the Western industrialized nations, particularly among

---

- from the point of view of moral philosophy as the simultaneity of self-assurance and self-challenge in the encounter with the "You ought!" of the moral law (Kant), or
- metaphysically as the dialectical unity and tension of "essence and existence" (Tillich).

12. Søren Kierkegaard, *Die Krankheit zum Tode. Der Hohepriester — der Zöllner — die Sünderin, Gesammelte Werke 24./25. Abteilung* (Düsseldorf 1954), 47 und 81. Vgl. ders., *Furcht und Zittern [1843], Gesammelte Werke 4. Abteilung* (Düsseldorf 1956), p. 78: "Dem Glauben ist einerseits der Ausdruck für den höchsten Egoismus eigen (das Furchtbare, das er tut, um seiner selbst willen tun), andrerseits der Ausdruck für die absoluteste Hingabe: Es um Gott willen tun." This position is connected with an emphatic stress on the "inwardness" *(Innerlichkeit)* or, more exactly, the pure inwardness of faith and with a strong polemic against all objectivity of faith's insight and understanding: z.B. *Einübung im Christentum, Gesammelte Werke 26. Abteilung* (Düsseldorf/Köln 1955), p. 216: "die erste Bedingung für das Christ Werden ist, daß man unbedingt nach innen gekehrt sei"; and, *Abschließende unwissenschaftliche Nachschrift zu den Philosophischen Brocken [1846]. Erster Teil, Gesammelte Werke 16. Abteilung* (Düsseldorf/Köln 1959), p. 215: "denn das objektive Wissen von der Wahrheit des Christentums oder von seinen Wahrheiten ist gerade Unwahrheit; ein Glaubensbekenntnis auswendig können ist Heidentum, weil das Christentum die Innerlichkeit ist." It is a consequence of this thinking that faith becomes self-referential in the end: "Der Glaube selbst ist gleichsam des Glaubens Gegenstand" (*Erbauliche Reden 1834/44, Gesammelte Werke 7., 8., 9. Abteilung* [Düsseldorf/Köln 1956], p. 85).

13. A particularly clear version of it has been offered by Rudolf Bultmann, "Welchen Sinn hat es, von Gott zu reden?", *Glauben und Verstehen,* I (Tübingen 1933), pp. 26ff., 36: "Denn wenn es sich im Glauben um die Erfassung unserer Existenz handelt, und wenn unsere Existenz in Gott gegründet, d.h. außerhalb Gottes nicht vorhanden ist, so bedeutet die Erfassung unserer Existenz ja die Erfassung Gottes." Ders., "Das Problem der 'natürlichen Theologie,'" *Glauben und Verstehen,* I, pp. 294ff., 297: "Das glaubende Existieren vollzieht sich in einem neuen Verstehen der Existenz." The most drastic formula is offered by a text of 1929, which was published in 1984: "Wahrheit und Gewißheit," in *Theologische Enzyklopädie,* ed. E. Jüngel, trans. K. W. Müller (Tübingen 1984), pp. 183ff., 202: "ich verstehe Gott, indem ich mich selbst neu verstehe."

educated persons. I therefore prefer the systematic term "subjectivist faith" for it. Most of the theological attempts to understand this type of "empty faith" and to propagate it join in the endeavor to demonstrate that this inner-most and utmost certainty is, on one hand, a clearly anthropological phe-nomenon, whereas, on the other, it is also a God-given and grace-sponsored one, and by no means a trivial event or even the result of an everyday percep-tual enterprise.

This experience of immediacy and negation, this experience of a reli-gious or quasi-religious certainty called "faith," seems to be extremely pre-cious and powerful, for it seems to allow us to introduce religious communi-cation at practically any point. Nobody can escape this experience of immediacy and negation. As soon as a person tries to thematize his or her "inner self," he or she runs into this quasi-religious certainty. What is the ele-ment of the "Other" whom I encounter when I try to reach the utmost depth of my inner self? Is that God? In a form that appeals to the modern mind, we seem to have at hand what Calvin called the "natural awareness," the "presen-timent of the Divine."[14] To be sure, it is a culturally tamed and domesticated natural certainty. Where in the *sensus divinitatus* Calvin saw a vague awe in the face of aesthetic powers, cosmic laws, and social orders, the modern reli-gious variant has only a notion of a poor dialectic of empty self-awareness.

Many forms of theology, of teaching, and of proclamation in the classic mainline churches have treasured this form of abstract and empty "faith" very highly. Such churches have done much to shield this empty certainty from the discovery of its religious arbitrariness and ambivalence. They adopted the idealist assertion that this certainty is the "foundation" of self-consciousness and the key to all epistemological and moral worth and the true foundation of personality.[15] They clothed this poor form with all sorts of rhetorics of "wholeness." And they tried to reinforce the differentiation between a self-reference given by the divine and a self-reference of purely anthropological origin. On the basis of the underlying theoretical construction, however, it was impossible to rid these attempts at differentiation of a trait of the arbi-trary. As the long debates on the reflection theory of self-conciousness teach us, this basic dialectical relation admits only the arbitrary definition and pre-dominance of the "subjective and active" and the "passive and objective"

14. See the beginning of John Calvin's *Institutio* in M. Welker, *Creation and Reality: Theo-logical and Biblical Perspectives* (Philadelphia: Fortress, 1999), chap. 2, and the important differ-entiation between a natural awareness and a presentiment of the divine and a "natural theol-ogy" by Wolfhart Pannenberg, *Systematische Theologie*, vol. 1 (Göttingen: Vandenhoeck und Ruprecht, 1988).

15. Cf. M. Welker, "Is the Autonomous Person . . . ?"

sides. Both aspects co-emerge in this self-referential certainty.[16] In retrospect, however, the often-heated theological debates about the proper nature of the true and right order of giving and receiving, or of activity and passivity, in this presumed relation of God and human being were like the fight over whether "the emperor's new clothes" were black or white.

This critical analysis of the inner texture of a typically modern form of religiosity should not lead us, however, to underestimate its power. This form of "faith" enables us to comfortably fuse religious and secular mentalities. It allows us, for instance, to proceed in no time from religious to moral communication and vice versa. Above all, it provides an excellent background focus for a consumerist culture with its need to stimulate the greed-fulfillment mechanism as effectively and perfectly as possible: already — but not yet; not yet — but already; intimacy with myself, which, however, changes into the encounter with the "Other"; the utmost certainty and yet at the same time the dialectical difference . . . Furthermore, this type of faith permits for a religious coding of universalist mentalities. And, recursively, it seems to bless religious mentalities with a universalist aura. It continually signals the message, "In a latent way, no reasonable person can be anything but religious!"

Like Calvin, who emphasized the power of the "natural awareness" of the divine — despite its vagueness, its ambiguity, and its ambivalence — we should acknowledge the power of the subjectivist form of "faith." But even if we take this religious form and its, so to speak, catalytic potentials seriously, we must at the same time, for reasons of clear-headedness and honesty, make clear how it systematically prevents and discourages a content-laden and communicative piety, and that it has actually driven vast parts of the churches into a religious speechlessness and inability to communicate.

Subjectivist Faith As a Loss of Faith?

Despite the difficulties described above of the effort to keep apart religious and nonreligious forms of subjectivist faith, despite its notorious emptiness and almost arbitrary availability, this "faith" will still find its ready defenders. And not only in popular culture. As a universally available phenomenon, subjectivist faith seems to be an excellent antidote in religion and the churches to

---

16. See Dieter Henrich, *Fichtes ursprüngliche Einsicht*, Wissenschaft und Gegenwart 34 (Frankfurt 1967); Dieter Henrich, *Selbstverhältnisse* (Stuggart: Reclam, 1982); M. Welker, *Der Vorgang Autonomie. Philosophische Beiträge zur Einsicht in theologischer Rezeption und Kritik* (Neukirchen: Neukirchener Verlag, 1975).

all kinds of domination and formation of hierarchies. This, among other things, was extremely important to Schleiermacher.[17] The power and manifold capability to function catalytically that were already granted to this "faith" seemed to recommend it to many. And admirers of modern culture may even praise it as a form that has allowed modernity to rid itself of historical and cultural ballast and to finally center religiosity on "the essential." The critics of this form possibly appear as traditionalists, religious *Bildungsbürger*, and elitists, or even as theological Cold War warriors who want to deny successful modern achievements their due recognition.

Thus it is not enough, for instance, to set Luther's or Paul's understandings of faith in opposition to the modern emptied understanding of faith and observe that in these cases the subjective faith relation to God is always connected to objective faith — included in it, borne and nurtured by it. In these and other theological classics, we surely find the subjective relation to God always linked with a conviction that has passed through certainties examined in manifold ways and through manifold questions for truth. Paul can write to the different congregations that "their faith is known in all the world," that he rejoices in this faith, that he wants to learn more about it; he can speak of the "growth" in faith or of the mutual enrichment and strengthening of faith. Paul also sees a second (or rather ontologically first) level of objectivity by speaking of the faith that has "come with Christ" or come as a "gift of the Spirit."[18] But why is it that such observations do not simply support traditionalist or biblicist preferences? Why do these observations make it necessary to discuss profound objections to the subjectivist faith and its usual alternatives?

17. See the warning against a "Hierarchie der intellektuellen Bildung, ein(em) Priestertum der Spekulation . . . , welches ich meines Teils nicht allzu protestantisch finden kann," in Schleiermacher, *Über meine Glaubenslehre. Zwei Sendschreiben an Herrn Dr. Lücke,* in *KGA* 1/10 (Berlin 1990), pp. 307-94; quotation: Schleiermacher-Auswahl (Siebenstern, München, und Hamburg, 1968), p. 128.

18. In the first chapter of Romans, Paul clearly describes a complex spiritual exchange as "faith": "First, I thank my God through Jesus Christ for all of you, *because your faith is proclaimed throughout the world.* . . . For I am longing to see you so that I may share with you some spiritual gift to strengthen you — or rather so that we *may be mutually encouraged by each other's faith, both yours and mine*" (Rom. 1:8, 11-12, italics added). He also shares with the Thessalonians, at the beginning of the first of his letters that have been preserved, that "in every place your faith in God has become known" (1 Thess. 1:8). He tells them that he sent Timothy as a messenger to "strengthen . . . you for the sake of your faith" and "to find out about your faith." Finally, he tells them that he rejoices over "the good news of your faith" (1 Thess. 3:2-6; cf. 7ff.).

In Colossians, Ephesians, 2 Thessalonians, and Hebrews as well we find formulations that make thankful reference to the fact that the faith of a community is publicly known (cf. Eph. 1:15; Col. 1:4; 2 Thess. 1:3; Heb. 13:1). In Philemon and 2 Timothy the same thing occurs with regard to the faith of individuals that has "become known" (cf. Philem. 5; 2 Tim. 1:5).

Whoever has become sensitive to this field of problems cannot but perceive that a complex religious syndrome of suffering goes along with subjectivist faith. This syndrome of suffering demands a thorough self-examination and self-criticism of modern theology and piety. Not traditionalist preferences, but the perception of a complex set of factors from which the classical mainline churches in the Western industrialized nations, paralyzed and traumatized, obviously suffer at the beginning of the twenty-first century necessitates the examination and correction of a powerful and basic form of modern religiosity.

At least five factors must be named that, mutually strengthening each other, make subjectivist faith a power that not only blocks up faith but seems to destroy it systematically:

First, subjectivist faith comes in the form of a transcendental principle. It does not come — as faith should — as a form that directly animates or enlivens the communication of faith. It is individualizing and stale, a fact that is hidden by its universal arbitrary availability.

Second, subjectivist faith comes as a necessarily empty religious form. It does not come — as faith should — as a disclosing form that gains and promotes the knowledge of God and, in its light, stimulates content-laden knowledge of self and world.

Third, subjectivist faith comes as a (both challenged and restored) unconditional and utmost certainty. It is a self-sufficient religious form. Although this "faith" can and has to be activated again and again, it does not offer — as faith should — a regulative to pass or advance from mere certainty to the serious individual and communal search for truth.

Fourth, subjectivist faith comes as a paradoxical, self-inhibiting, even neuroticizing form in its combination of immediacy and negation. It does not promote — as faith should — joy, doxology, and the ennoblement of those who are seized by faith and spread it.

And fifth, subjectivist faith is of an escapist character. It conditions the withdrawal from expressive, festive, communicative, progressive forms of religious life or even counteracts them — as faith need not and should not do.

But these criticisms are not yet sufficient. They can be countered by the statement that faith may be very well grasped as an empty principle, but that this principle is open to infinitely many developments and shapings, and that exactly this fact is its power and its strength of conviction. Thinkers theoretically most well-versed have summed this up in the formula, *Faith is a communication medium.*

MICHAEL WELKER

Faith As a Communication Medium: A Solution,
or Merely a Continuation of the Problem?

Faith does not simply come as an individual, arbitrary certainty, but in an abundance of forms of religious dialectical certainty, forms that are stronger or weaker, more fleeting or steadier, as described above. Since these forms admit of communication and the knowledge of their likeness and relatedness, faith comes as a netted ensemble of such dialectic certainties. Thus this principle of religious certainty functions *as a communication medium*. Human beings can again and again join this medium, whether they themselves are religious or whether they come from insecurity, from attitudes and surroundings that are distant to faith, even without faith or hostile to faith.

In her important contribution, "Sünde: Ein Definitionsversuch,"[19] Sigrid Brandt has shown how faith (as well as love and hope) can be understood as a "communication medium." On the one hand, Brandt employs Pauline theology; on the other, insights of the sociologists Talcott Parsons and Niklas Luhmann. Following Luhmann, she writes that communication — even and especially communication of faith — "does not simply [designate] a communicative action that transfers information. Rather, communication is an act in which three components, namely information, communication and understanding, are at the same time differentiated and connected," in order to make the connection and flux of further communication possible.[20] Following Parsons, Luhmann called "communication media" those forms which transfer a "symbolically generalized code of selection" to secure the "transferability of achievements of selection over more or less long chains. Truth, love, power, and money are prominent, evolutionarily successful examples of this."[21] Faith, too, can be regarded as such a code of selection, which activates a "symbolically generalized communication medium."

In that the code of selection, "faith," is co-transferred in communications and information, it is guaranteed that the communications are "religiously" understood and religiously continued. The communication medium

---

19. Sigrid Brandt, "Sünde: Ein Definitionsversuch," in Sigrid Brandt, Marjorie Suchocki, and Michael Welker's *Sünde. Ein unverständlich gewordenes Thema* (Neukirchen: Neukirchener Verlag, 1997), pp. 13-34.

20. Brandt, "Ein Definitionsversuch," p. 22. See also two works by Niklas Luhmann: *Vertrauen. Ein Mechanismus der Reduktion sozialer Komplexität*, 3rd ed. (Stuttgart: F. Enke, 1989), pp. 50, 51; and *Ökologische Kommunikation. Kann die moderne Gesellschaft sich auf ökologische Gefährdungen einstellen?* 3rd ed. (Opladen: Westdeutscher Verlag, 1990), pp. 62ff., 267.

21. Luhmann, *Vertrauen*, p. 51.

"faith" ensures that certain human expressions are understood as expressions of piety and about piety, and not only as historical information or expressions that signal psychosomatic problems and cause worry. Completing Luhmann's thoughts, Sigrid Brandt shows that a communication medium like faith advances not only the general tone and frame for specific (in this case: religious) communication, but also makes possible very individual, typified shapings without destroying the religious security of communication. Communication media allow us to switch between the generalizing and the specifying tendencies and to give greater weight sometimes to the one tendency, sometimes to the other. Brandt is right when she states,

> Faith, hope and love mostly do not symbolize their general meaning in plain language. They rather look for vivid forms of communication, forms that concern human beings in their entirety and in their connections of life. They are noeto-psycho-somatic symbolizing media. Their forms of communication depend upon the creativity and originality of the person who communicates the message as well as upon the social forms of communication, the semantics of their time, and their cultural space.[22]

But what in fact does subjectivist faith achieve as a communication medium? Which signals of connection and continuation does it send and affirm as "religious"? In what way does it actually, as a code of selection and as a communication medium, counteract the above-mentioned syndrome of problems of subjectivist faith? The answer to this question is extremely disillusioning. It is true that subjectivist faith does in fact function not only as a form of individual religious experience but also as a communication medium. But as such it only heightens the loss of faith because, in line with our analysis of the figure of "the inner relation to a wholly other that is intimately close," it ultimately only passes off and communicates the form "perplexity *(Betroffenheit)*/sensitive susceptibility" as a comprehensive religious form.

This, however, initiates a sweeping process of self-secularization[23] of religiosity and piety, since "perplexity/sensitive susceptibility" is by no means stimulated only in the religious sphere but also in family life, in moral communication, in contact with the arts, and, above all, in the communication of the mass media (and here in great abundance). To be sure, similar experiences across diverse sociocultural areas can mutually strengthen each other.

22. Brandt, "Ein Definitionsversuch," p. 24.
23. I owe this expression to Wolfgang Huber.

This observation is confirmed by the continual interest of religious communication in situations of "passage" in the family, by the frequently close relationship of religion and morals, but also by the notorious love-and-hate relation, and the tension, between religion and the media.[24] Against this background, the decay of religious knowledge and the banalization of religious communication in the modern industrialized nations become understandable. These developments were only temporarily interrupted and turned back in situations of national crisis, such as postwar situations.

Faith Lost and Regained

With this background in mind, we will not be able to solve the problem of subjectivist faith by setting faith as a communication medium in opposition to faith as an individualized and emptied form of experience, for the emptied form of experience only reappears in the communication medium as a code of selection, with accelerated force of strengthening the above-mentioned syndrome of problems. Nor is it sufficient to simply conjure up the "contents" and, as many theologians of the first decades of the twentieth century have done, deplore religiosity's "colossal loss of reality," since it is not clear which contents are really able to lead us out of the crisis. Furthermore, it is insufficient to demand only increased individual or communal engagement, since it is not clear which kind of engagement we need to find a way out of the crisis.

Rather, we have to impute that the reason why subjectivist faith became an evolutionary success is that for many people it seemed to offer simply an optimal or, at least, in the history of culture, a superior religiosity. With regard to individual engagement, this is easily understood, because the communication medium "perplexity/sensitive susceptibility" can be attuned to the smallest and finest individual emotions. Subjectivist faith is to a high degree sensitive to and open for the concrete individual, for attunement to her or his emotional and affective forms of experience. More precisely, in principle unburdened by almost any content-related religious matter, it is mainly concerned with the individual in his or her relation of dependence. Subjectivist faith covers the content-related side in principle by an abstract theism and a

24. Cf. Günter Thomas, *Religion — Ritual — Medien. Zur religiösen Funktion des Fernsehens* (Frankfurt am Main: Suhrkamp, 1998); G. Thomas and M. Welker, "Einleitung: Religiöse Funktionen des Fernsehens?" in *Religiöse Funktionen des Fernsehens? Medien-, kultur- und religionswissenschaftliche Perspektiven,* ed. G. Thomas (Opladen: Westdeutscher Verlag, 2000).

totalitarian religious thought that relates everything — in fact in a seemingly thoughtless manner — to God, and God to everything.[25]

God is the "ground of all being," the "all-determining reality," the "cause of everything" — so run the corresponding ciphers and jargon phrases. Dependence and abstract *ubi*-presence/*omni*-potence, *figure of dependence and omni-quantor,* these are the modes of thought with which a theology attuned to subjectivist faith seems to secure the "content-related side." Totalitarian religious thought remains undeterred by everything from the ironic queries as to whether God created the button on my pants, or willed the staggering steps of the drunk, to the very serious questions of theodicy. It seems no less disturbed by the biblical traditions that contradict this form of religiosity. It systematically mixes up the power and possibility of God to act creatively, even out of the dust and in the greatest loneliness, with an omnipresence and omnipotence that causes "everything." Yet by simply relating all and everything to God, and God to all and everything, it leaves faith behind. It is by no means easy to make clear that such totalitarian religious thought suppresses or stultifies faith, for faith certainly sees the possibility that every event could in principle be related to God. *But faith's interest in God, in the knowledge of God, and in the knowledge of reality in the light of the knowledge of God, leads it to ask where that relationship becomes clear. In totalitarian religious thought's vague assurance that everything is somehow or other related to God, nothing becomes clear.*

With this observation we find a clue to the loss of faith in subjectivist faith. Subjectivist faith follows in a plainly parasitic manner a great discovery of modernity. This is the discovery that in all conscious situations of life the "consciousness of the 'I think'" can be aroused and that this "consciousness of the 'I think'" gives every person an abstract certainty of the steadiness of his or her own existing and of an interpersonal belonging together. Subjectivist faith *doubles* this certainty of steadiness and relates it to "an Other." It can do so since the "consciousness of the 'I think'" can appear as the feeling of

---

25. A whole theological network of critical encounters and movements of the twentieth century have collaborated in the collapse of this religious form of power. This has been a deliberate goal in Bonhoeffer and Moltmann, in many theologies of liberation, and in almost all feminist theologies. At least initial steps in this direction have been made by Barth, Pannenberg, Jüngel, and Tracy, in some process theologies, and in other thinkers and developments. Christological and Trinitarian insights and questions were determinative for the efforts to put an end to classical theism (not to be confused with monotheism of the living God). Also insights from the theology of law and from pneumatology, as well as metaphysical, moral, and political reasons, forced abstract theism to be called into question. Despite all its difficulties (cf. the introduction to my *Creation and Reality*) this development has to be supplemented and complemented by an equally serious critique of subjectivist faith.

freedom *and* as the feeling of dependence. Thus the "all-determining Other" in the "relation of dependence" is the perfect mirror or shadow of the modern "I."[26] The presence of this God is activated by the "consciousness of the 'I think'" in the form of the "alternative reading" or in the form of the ever new "message of dependence."

Probably following a remark by Kenneth Burke,[27] Niklas Luhmann once asked ironically whether "faith [could] not [be] organized like money," and thereby not only aroused pious indignation but also kindled literary theological activities.[28] Subjectivist faith *has* already in many respects "organized" God "like money." The experiences of the "Other" and the "perplexity" are, on the one hand, always the same and can, on the other, almost arbitrarily be measured out and heightened. Nontrivial "natural" experiences are scarce and become scarcer still with increasing accustoming. Therefore artificial perplexities are staged and scarcity is continually produced and eliminated, particularly efficiently in the area of electronic media, such as in connection with situations of "bad news," competitive sports, and entertainment music. Much can be said in favor of this supposition: Subjectivist faith and media piety get along together very well.

The recovery of faith presupposes the knowledge that cultural and religious "substance" cannot be gained via totalization and a "bad infinity" (to quote Hegel). Faith aims at knowing the coherence of the creative, life-supporting, and life-sustaining powers of God and aims at forever better understanding these powers and thus God's being and will. So faith, rightly understood, does want *to find something out and to know something,* even if, in the face of the living God and with regard to what it tries to say with expressions like God's "glory" and "holiness," it is conscious of the temporariness and possible inadequacy of all knowledge of God. Faith is *a special form of cultural knowledge,* which, however, with regard to its main object, the living God, is at all times conscious of its own temporariness and linked with a highly principled readiness to be questioned.

In the conviction of faith, God, by referring to the individual person through faith, does not only accept and take seriously the single person in her or his spiritual, bodily, sensory, and emotional singularity. In faith, people gain a universal dignity. For Christians, this dignity is that they become "one person with Christ," as Luther says. This means that they become bearers of

26. This God is, by the way, the personification of the power of a mechanistic universe.

27. In Kenneth Burke, *A Grammar of Motives* (Cleveland: World, 1962), pp. 355f.

28. See, for example, Falk Wagner, *Geld oder Gott? Zur Geldbestimmtheit der kulturellen und religiösen Lebenswelt* (Stuttgart: Klett, 1984).

God's presence on earth. Thus faith combines an interest in the protection and the development of the human personality with the interest in the knowledge of the living God. Wherever this interest is reduced through emptying and individualization, faith is also systematically weakened. One of the most important tasks in the interreligious dialogue in pluralistic societies is to understand how other religions try to ground the dignity of human beings and the protection of the personality (but in doing so to understand the weaknesses and dangers of the neo-Protestant style of piety).

The concentration on the living God and on God's freedom is accompanied by a principal sensitivity for the information and knowledge of all the participants in the life of faith. This holds true not only for the active participants or even those with intellectual master achievements but also for those who participate only more or less passively in it, and even for those who seem to enter into the life of faith only by attracting pity and sorrow and remembrance. Outsiders may try to book it as "high sensitivity for cultural contingency." They may even mix up faith with the "reduction of complexity and contingency."[29] The respect of God's freedom and liveliness combined with the burning interest in the knowledge of God is in fact linked with a pluralistic openness and a high sensitivity and readiness to break up as far as historical changes and shifts in the mentalities are concerned.[30] *The interest in "cultural learning" and "spiritual learning" is essential to faith.*

But over against knowledge, the weaknesses of faith that is penetrated by knowledge must be considered as well. Faith is in principle highly susceptible to being affected by emotions because of the above-mentioned sensitivity for God's freedom and liveliness, and the meaning of the manifold "testimonies" and the concrete personality of the faithful. Perhaps, in the current culture, many regard this as not problematic or even as a strength of faith (and, with the help of subjectivist faith, they may try to bring this in the "forms" of religious immediacy and a medium of communication). The dangers become evident, however, as soon as we understand that cultural and moral moods, media fashions, and many other forms of what the nineteenth century ciphered as "Zeitgeist" all too easily operate decisively on sensitive faith and distort or destroy it. The knowledge of the absolute powerlessness of subjectivist faith with regard to these problems is a presupposition for the search for productive alternatives.

29. Niklas Luhmann, *Funktion der Religion* (Frankfurt am Main: Suhrkamp, 1977).

30. The concept of "the witness" is most appropriate to express the relation of the individual believer and the acts of faith to faith in general. The conscious fragmentariness of the own knowledge of God and the simultaneous striving for certainty and authenticity is well expressed in it. I owe this insight to Hans-Georg Gadamer.

Part 2 Property and Possession:
        Having and Using the Body
        and Material Meanings

The Body and Projects of Self-Possession

Jean Bethke Elshtain

In thinking and rethinking the theme of the body as property and possession, even, at times, as a kind of messianic project, many issues demand thoughtful consideration, including our acquiescence in the grandiose and glamorous promises and premises of our fast-paced techno-culture. Interweaving those promises and premises with a meditation on the theme of excessive cultural absorption, defined in a rough and ready way as an inability to stand apart from our cultural preoccupations such that we can reflect on them critically and somewhat dispassionately, is called for. Why? Because those called by the name "Christian," those, therefore, who are (or ought to be) poised in a fruitful tension between *contra mundum* and *amor mundi,* often lose that tension by giving themselves over entirely to the world and its projects. Over-identification with the currents of one's own time is complex because this usually derives from a deformation of deep needs and desires that help to constitute our humanity, including loving regard for the self and respect for others. This loving regard and concern for others can easily go awry. Indeed, at least if one follows Martin Luther, all our needs are *bound* to be distorted in light of the fact that we are in rebellion against God, the source of undistorted love. Given that Christian anthropology presumes intrinsic relationality — there is no primordially free self — sifting our cherished and essential commonalities (and commune-alities) from excessive and unthinking absorption in dominant and often problematic forces is a delicate and complex matter.

Let me put a distinction on the table that may help to clarify. There is a chasm that separates Christian understandings of servanthood from mere slavishness. The one — servanthood — posits that we grow as selves as our capacities for servanthood widen and deepen. The other — slavishness —

141

means to be the possession of some other and, as well, to be caught in a scenario in which one's options are either slavery or domination, executioner or victim (to borrow Albert Camus's pithy phrase.) The terrible irony of the latter is that one doesn't require a task-master poised to administer blows should one fail to do the master's bidding in order to be enslaved. One is akin to Kafka's bird in search of a cage. And the master, of course, needn't be a single person or group of persons but, rather, a confluence of forces under whose sway one has fallen uncritically.

Let's take up an example of excessive cultural acquiescence and absorption as it seeps into the pores, sinews, and tissues of the ways in which we think about and treat the body in late modernity.[1] The overarching and framing thematic is a flight from finitude that implicates us in forms of "self-excision" that occlude recognition of the complexities and joys of embodiment — the "givens," if you will, of finitude and created being itself. One spin-off is widespread acquiescence in destruction of the bodies of others as part of our culture's panoply of rights and punishments.[2] If pride fetters us through inordinate self-absorption, the tentacles of cultural over-determination strangle us through forms of inappropriate self-loss. Either way, we abandon recognition of the many ways in which we are claimed by that which is other than ourselves, that which redeems us through works of love in and through freedom and faith.

A number of issues have been summarily adumbrated. Let's flesh matters out, beginning with reminders about the nature of Christian freedom and the fact that we are both creatures and creators. As creatures we are dependent. It follows that our creaturely freedom consists in our recognition that we are not abstractly free but free only in and through relationship. A limit lies at the very heart of our existence in freedom. Christian freedom turns on recognition of the limits to freedom.

Dietrich Bonhoeffer, in *Creation and Fall*, frets that man as creator easily transmogrifies into a destroyer as he and she misuse freedom.[3] At the same time, our freedom is a constitutive part of our natures. So: how do we understand this freedom? Christian freedom is not opposed to the natural order

---

1. The United States is clearly my focus, although much if not all of what I say is applicable to the developed or, in John Paul II's terms, "super-developed cultures of consumption" of the West.

2. Abortion-on-demand at any stage of pregnancy and the death penalty would be the two prime candidates for discussion here. The essay's length is such that I will not be able to discuss these in full.

3. Dietrich Bonhoeffer, *Creation and Fall: A Theological Exposition of Genesis 1–3* (Minneapolis: Fortress, 1997). This is volume 3 of Dietrich Bonhoeffer's Works, now in progress.

but acts in faithfulness to it.[4] We begin by taking human beings as they are, not as those fanciful entities sometimes conjured up by philosophers in what they themselves call "science fiction" examples.[5] To be sure, the freedom of a real, not a fanciful, human being means, among other things, that one can (to quote Robin Lovin) "project oneself imaginatively into a situation in which the constraints of present experience no longer hold."[6] One can strive to imagine states of perfection or nigh-perfection. At the same time, actual freedom is always situated; it is not an abstract position located nowhere in particular. Freedom is concrete, not free-floating. Freedom is a "basic human good. Life without freedom is not something we would choose, no matter how comfortable the material circumstances might be."[7] Our reasoning capacity is part and parcel of our freedom. But that reasoning isn't a separate faculty cut off from our embodied selves; instead, it is profoundly constituted by our embodied histories and memories. Christian freedom, in Lovin's words, consists in our ability to "avoid excessive identification with the surrounding culture, since that tends both to lower . . . moral expectations and to deprive [persons] of the witness to alternative possibility. . . ."[8] If the horizon lowers excessively and all is collapsed into immanence, the possibility that we might exercise our capacity for freedom is correlatively negated. So the denial of freedom consists, in part, in a refusal to accept the freedom that is the human inheritance of finite, limited creatures "whose capacities for change are

4. This is not the time and the place to unpack ethical naturalism and moral realism. Suffice it to say that I am committed to the view that there is a "there there," that there are truths to be discerned about the world, and that the world isn't just so much putty in our conceptually deft hands. The world exists independent of our minds but our minds possess the wonderful capacity to apprehend the world, up to a point given the fallibility of reason.

5. One example would be the work of philosopher Judith Jarvis Thompson, known for her current support of physician-assisted suicide, but who first made her reputation by providing justifications for abortion by analogizing from a woman hooked up during her sleep to a violinist for whom she was then required to provide life support, to a woman in relationship to the fetus she is carrying. Thompson claimed that the woman would be within her rights to unhook the violinist, even if it meant his or her death; similarly, a woman is not required to carry a fetus to term. I have never understood why a reasonable person would find this argument compelling. Fetuses do not get attached covertly but emerge as a result of action in which the woman is implicated. As well, the fetus's dependence on the mother for sustenance for nine months is part of the order of nature — it simply is the way humans reproduce. There are many ways to sustain violinists in need of life support, and an adult violinist is scarcely analogous in any way to the life of a human being *in situ*.

6. Robin W. Lovin, *Reinhold Niebuhr and Christian Realism* (Cambridge: Cambridge University Press, 1995), p. 123.

7. Lovin, *Reinhold Niebuhr and Christian Realism*, p. 126.

8. Lovin, *Reinhold Niebuhr and Christian Realism*, p. 94.

also limited, and who can only bring about new situations that are also themselves particular, local, and contingent."⁹ To presume more is problematic, launching us into a pridefulness; to presume less may well mean participating in the denial of finitude that helps to underwrite forms of un-freedom, often, of course, in the name of great ideals, like choice or justice. So our freedom is, at one and the same time, both real and limited.

With this as backdrop, let's examine current projects of self-overcoming that constitute examples of denial of finitude and rely on our continuing acquiescence and our lassitude where these cultural demands and trumpeted enthusiasms are concerned.¹⁰ Such projects are tricky to get at critically because they present themselves to us in the dominant language of our culture — choice, consent, control — and because they promise an escape from the human condition into a realm of near mastery. We are readily beguiled with the promise of a new self. In so doing, we may deny or harm the only self we've got. Consider, then, that we are in the throes of a structure of biological obsession underwritten by claims of absolute self-possession that erode recognition of both the fullness and limitations of embodiment.¹¹ We are bombarded daily with the promise that nearly every human ailment or condition can be overcome if we just have will and skill enough. (Money helps, too.) As we seek cures for the human condition, the desperate edge of that seeking bespeaks a conviction that our imperfect embodiment *is* the problem that must be overcome. For example: a premise — and promise — driving the Human Genome Project, the massive project that has mapped the genetic code of the human race, is that we might one day intervene decisively in order to guarantee better if not perfect human products.¹² Claims made by promoters and

9. Lovin, *Reinhold Niebuhr and Christian Realism*, p. 130.

10. This, too, is more complex than simply acquiescence. For example, where the matter of abortion is concerned, there is enormous popular support for some forms of restriction and restraint on the practice. The *elite* culture (the media, those with incomes over $50,000 per year, lawyers, as the most reliable social science studies demonstrate) long ago fell into lockstep with an absolute abortion "right," including partial birth abortion, a practice the American Medical Association itself has declared not to be a legitimate medical procedure. So on the level of opinion all is not homogeneous. But this opinion rarely translates into action of any sort. Thus, the atrophy of civic habits of the past four decades or so goes hand in hand with the triumph of projects that constitute flights from finitude.

11. Not ours alone, of course, but I will concentrate primarily on North American culture in depicting this obsession and grappling with its hold on the collective psyche.

12. Just to be clear at the outset, I do not intend to issue strictures against any and all attempts to intervene through modern forms of gene therapy in order to forestall, say, the development of devastating, inherited conditions or diseases. There is a huge difference between preventing an undeniable harm — say, a type of inherited condition that dooms a child to a short

advocates run to the ecstatic — for example, Walter Gilbert's 1986 pronouncement that "[The Human Genome Project] is the grail of human genetics . . . the ultimate answer to the commandment, 'Know thyself.'"[13] In the genome-enthusiast camp, some are already talking about Designer Genes — that *is* genes, not jeans. Do you want a blue-eyed, blond-haired, strapping youth with athletic tendencies, perfect teeth, and a seventy-five-year warranty? I exaggerate but not by much. Note that an advertisement reported by *The New York Times* in early spring, 1999, one that had appeared in college newspapers all over the country, reads as follows: "EGG DONOR NEEDED/ LARGE FINANCIAL INCENTIVE/INTELLIGENT, ATHLETIC EGG DONOR NEEDED/FOR LOVING FAMILY/YOU MUST BE AT LEAST 5'10"/ HAVE A 1400+ SAT SCORE/POSSESS NO MAJOR FAMILY MEDICAL ISSUES/$50,000/FREE MEDICAL SCREENING/ALL EXPENSES PAID."[14] As *Commonweal* noted in an editorial prompted by this advertisement, it brings back eerie reminders of earlier advertisements that involved trade in human flesh (the reference point being the slave trade) and suggests that "we are fast returning to a world where persons carry a price tag, and where the cash value of some persons . . . is far greater than that of others."[15] Soberer voices — including those within the scientific community that say, "Whoa. Let's slow down a bit," are drowned out by the clammering chorus of huzzahs.

Scientist Dorris T. Zallen, swimming against the cultural tide, after having noted that the early promises of genetic intervention to forestall "serious health problems, such as sickle-cell anemia, cystic fibrosis, and Huntington's

---

and painful life — and striving to create a blemish-less perfect human specimen. How one differentiates the one from the other is part of the burden of argument. One example of justifiable intervention would be a method of gene therapy that spares children "the devastating effects of a rare but deadly inherited disease. In the condition, Crigler-Najjar syndrome, a substance called bilirubin, a waste product from the destruction of worn-out red blood cells, builds up in the body. . . . Bilirubin accumulates, causing jaundice, a yellowing of the skin and the whites of the eyes. More important, bilirubin is toxic to the nervous system, and the children live in constant danger of brain damage. The only way they can survive is to spend ten to twelve hours a day under special lights that break down the bilirubin. But as they reach their teens, the light therapy becomes less effective. Unless they can get a liver transplant, they may suffer brain damage or die." Because previous attempts at gene therapy have all fallen far short of expectations, therapy to cure this disease might not work either. But this sort of intervention would spare a small number of children tremendous suffering, and it is entirely defensive — it involves no eugenics ideology of any kind. See Denise Grady, "At Gene Therapy's Frontier, the Amish Build a Clinic," *The New York Times*, Science Times, Tuesday, 29 June 1999, D1, 4, at p. D1.

13. Cited in Roger Shattuck, *Forbidden Knowledge* (New York: Harcourt Brace, 1996), p. 1973.

14. As reprinted in an editorial in *Commonweal* (26 March 1999): 5.

15. *Commonweal* editorial, p. 5.

disease," have thus far had only the meagerest success, takes up a booming genetic enterprise that promises not prevention of harm but the attainment of
perfection. This is called "genetic enhancement." One starts with a healthy
person and then moves to perfect. Zallen calls this the "genetic equivalent of
cosmetic surgery." The aim is to make people "taller, thinner, more athletic, or
more attractive." Zallen lists potential harms, including reinforcement of "irrational societal prejudices. For instance, what would happen to short people
if genetic enhancement were available to increase one's height?" The "historical record is not encouraging," she adds, noting earlier eugenics movement
with their hideous outcomes, most frighteningly in Nazi Germany, but evident in this country as well where policies of involuntary sterilization of persons with mental retardation and other measures went forward apace.[16]

It is important to take note of the fact that, although several kinds of responses to the *libido sciendi* run amok are possible, one dominates in this essay — the theological, philosophical, and ethical; but yet another response
comes from science itself. Here the calmer voices, by contrast to promotions
of the wildly optimistic sort, remind us that the scientific community at present has only the "vaguest understanding" of the details of genetic instruction
— unsurprising when one considers that each "single-celled conceptus immediately after fertilization" involves a "100-trillion-times miniaturized information system. . . ."[17] Yet those who proclaim that the benefits of genetic
manipulation are both unstoppable and entirely beneficial downplay any and
all controversies, and short-circuit any and all difficulties, playing up complexity *only so long as it works in their favor.* In this way, they can deflect any
and all "non-expert" criticism in a manner that "effectively precludes others
coming to an independent judgment about the validity of their claims."[18] So
we avoid the ethical and cultural discussion we need, and those who try to
promote such discussion — *including* scientists who remind other scientists
(as well as the public) of the obstacles to and danger of genetic transformation — are tagged with the label of techno-Luddites.

In the 1997 film *Gattaca,* not a very good film but an instructive one, the
protagonist (played by Ethan Hawke) is born the "old-fashioned way" (a
"faith-birth") to his parents, who had made love and taken their chances with
what sort of offspring might eventuate. In this terrible new world, when a
child is born an immediate genetic profile is done. The protagonist, Vincent,

16. Doris T. Zallen, "We Need a Moratorium on 'Genetic Enhancement,'" *The Chronicle of Higher Education* (27 March 1998), p. A64.

17. James LeFanu, "Genetics Are Not Gods," *The Tablet,* 12 December 1998, pp. 1645-46, at p. 1645.

18. LeFanu, "Genetics Are Not Gods," p. 1645.

is a beautiful but, it turns out, genetically hapless child (on the standards of the barren world that is to be his lot) who enters life not amidst awe and hopefulness but amidst misery and worry. His mother clutches the tiny newborn to her breast as his genetic quotient is coldly read off by the expert. "Cells tell all," the prophets of "genoism" intone. Because of his genetic flaws (for his was an unregulated birth) young Vincent isn't covered by insurance; he doesn't get to go to school past a certain age; and he is doomed to menial service. He is a de-generate. Or, as the scanners immediately pronounce it, an "Invalid."

Vincent contrives a way to fake out the system, as he yearns to go on a one-year manned mission to some truly far-out planet. Only "Valids" — genetically correct human beings — are eligible for such elite tasks. So Vincent pays off a "Valid" for the Valid's urine, blood, saliva, and fingerprints and begins his arduous, elaborate ruse. For this is a world in which any bodily scraping — a single eyelash, a single bit of skin sloughing — might betray you. Why would a Valid sell his bodily fluids and properties? Because the Valid is now "useless," a cripple, having been paralyzed in a car accident. Indeed, his life is so useless on society's standards (which he, in turn, has thoroughly internalized) that, at the film's conclusion, and after having stored sufficient urine and blood that Vincent can fool the system for years to come, the crippled Valid manages to ease himself into a blazing furnace — to incinerate himself — life not being worth living any longer for one who cannot use his legs.

As for Vincent, and despite some very tense moments, life is as good as it is ever going to get by film's end: he has made love to Uma Thurman, and he has faked his way (with the connivance of a sympathetic security officer) onto the mission to the really far-out planet of which he has dreamt since childhood, and this despite his genetically flawed condition. This is a bleak film. The *only* resistance Vincent can come up with is faking it. He has no language of protest and ethical distance available to him. This is just the world as he and others know it and presumably will always know it. Uma Thurman's intimacy with an Invalid is as close to resistance as she can get.[19] There are no alternative points of reference or resistance. There is a world no reasonable or minimally decent person would wish to inhabit.

Of course, we aren't in the *Gattaca* nightmare yet. But are we drawing uncomfortably close? There are many who believe so, including the mother of a Down syndrome child who wrote me after she had read one of my columns

---

19. A bit reminiscent of Julia, young female sexual revolutionary, in Orwell's *Brave New World*. She is, of course, defeated and comes to love Big Brother.

about genetic engineering in *The New Republic.* I had mused, in that piece, on what our quest for bodily perfection might mean over the long run for the developmentally different. My interlocutor, whose child died of a critical illness in his third year, wrote me that she and her husband were enormously grateful to have had "the joyous privilege of parenting a child with Down syndrome. . . . Tommy's [not his real name] birth truly transformed our lives in ways that we will cherish forever. But how could we have known in advance that we indeed possessed the fortitude to parent a child with special needs? And who would have told us of the rich rewards?" She continued:

> The function of prenatal tests, despite protestations to the contrary, is to provide parents the information necessary to assure that all pregnancies brought to term are "normal." I worry not only about the encouragement given to eliminating a "whole category of persons" (the point you make), but also about the prospects for respect and treatment of children who come to be brain-damaged either through unexpected birth traumas or later accidents. And what about the pressures to which parents like myself will be subject? How could you "choose" to burden society in this way?

She's right. In the name of expanding choice, we are narrowing our definition of humanity and, along the way, a felt responsibility to create welcoming environments for all children. If we can simply declare, "They made their bed (they chose to have an 'abnormal' child) and now they must lie in it," this declaration takes us, as individuals and as a society, off the hook. The proponents of a complex cluster of views that aim to diminish the sphere of the "unchosen," by stitching together a rubric of expanding *choice,* enhancing *control,* and extending *freedom,* have been enormously successful in their efforts to convince people that they *are incapable* of the work of care and love when it comes to a child with "special needs."

The needs of all children are special and particular, of course. The category of "special needs" sprang up in our recent past with concern and compassion in mind. We appear to have decided, however, that ordinary folks no longer possess competence in this area, thereby truncating the arena of our own free responsibility and falling into expert-sanctioned acquiescence in the judgments of the culture as to which life is worth living. Simultaneously, we have enlarged without limit (save whatever pragmatic cutoff points might pertain at any given moment) a notion that parents — or, more narrowly, the woman — possess absolute power of life and death over life *in situ* at any stage. We shrink the domain of hands-on, everyday competence of ordinary women and men by insisting that they must — for this is the direction "choice" takes at present — rid themselves of "wrongful life" in order to forestall "wrongful births" that will burden them and, even more importantly, the wider society. This, in turn, makes it more difficult than ever to consider the possibility that the present abortion "right" often embodies in practice a great burden for women who are told that they *alone* have the power to choose whether or not to have a child and that they *alone* are expected to bear the consequences if they choose to have the child.

The growing cultural conviction that children with disabilities ought never to be born and that prospective parents of such children ought always to abort undermines the felt skein of care and responsibility for *all* children.[20] This is at least a reasonable worry, especially when the machinery of technology now surrounding childbirth turns every pregnancy into what was once called "a crisis pregnancy." HMOs are in the process of standardizing prenatal testing and genetic screening procedures that were once used only when couples had a history of difficulties. The point of all this is to initiate a process — should a sign even be hinted at — "of cajoling and pressuring that terminates in an abortion. . . ."[21] Jeannie Hannemann, a family life minister, "sees a culture shift taking place moving away from supporting families with special-needs children toward resenting such families as creating a 'burden' on society. [She has] heard of HMOs refusing treatment to special needs children, arguing their mental or physical problem represented a 'preexisting condition' because their parents elected not to abort them after prenatal screening indicated a problem."[22]

The heart of the matter lies in our loss of appreciation of the nature of human embodiment. The social imaginary — which the dominant scientific voices in the area of genetic engineering, technology, and "enhancement" have joined — declares the body to be a construction, something we can invent. We are loath to grant the status of givenness to any aspect of ourselves, despite the fact that human babies are wriggling, complex little bodies pre-programmed with all sorts of delicately calibrated reactions to the human relationships "nature" presumes will be the matrix of child nurture. If we think of bodies concretely in this way, we are then propelled to ask ourselves questions about the world little bodies enter: is it welcoming, warm, responsive? But if we tilt in the biotech constructivist direction, one in which the body is

20. Please note that I do not want in any way to diminish the difficulties involved in parenting a child with disabilities. As the mother of an adult daughter with mental retardation, I understand this very well. Instead, I am trying to capture the present temperament that dictates that such births are calamitous and ought never occur.

21. "Search and Destroy Missions," *U.S. Catholic* (January 2000): 16.

22. "Search and Destroy Missions," p. 16.

so much raw material to be worked upon and worked over, the surround in which bodies are situated fades as the body itself is enshrined as a kind of messianic project.

The body we currently inhabit is represented by an imperfect body, the one subject to chance and the vagaries of life, including illness and aging. This body has become our foe. The new body to come — extolled in manifestos, promised by enthusiasts, embraced by many ordinary citizens — is to be our gleaming fabrication. For soon, we are told, we will have found a way around the fact that what our poor foremothers and forefathers, living in a less enlightened era than our own, took for granted — that the body must weaken and falter and one day pass from life to death — will itself be abolished. The future perfect body will not be permitted to falter. The body may grow older in a strictly chronological sense, but why should we? So we devise multiple strategies to fend off aging. And we represent aging bodies as those of teenagers with gleaming gray hair. A recent *New York Times Magazine* lead article on "The Recycled Generation" trumpeted the "promise of an endless supply of new body parts" via stem cell research, although that research is now "bogged down in abortion politics and corporate rivalries."[23] One of the entrepreneurs who stands to make even more millions of dollars in what the article calls the "scientific chase" for "the mother of all cells — the embryonic stem cell" — bemoans the fact that the rush toward this final frontier of finding out how to live forever is being slowed down by the "knee jerk reaction" on the part of many people to "words like 'fetal' and 'embryo.'" The image that comes bounding out of the piece is that of a cutting-edge go-getter who construes opposition or criticism as the atavistic outbursts of mostly religious people, those who go "completely irrational" when they hear certain words.[24] These strategies and concerns speak to our repudiation of finitude and to our longing for full self-possession. They offer ample testimony of how cultural and ethical criticism is bracketed or demeaned as atavistic. So, rather than approaching matters of life, death, and health with humility, knowing that we cannot cure the human condition, we seek cures in the assumption that the more we control the better — if only the irrational and superstitious among us will get out of the way once and for all.

There is strong similarity between this project and that which drives the marketization of everyday life, including the presupposition that nothing is good in itself, including embodied existence. Good is reduced to strictly

23. Stephen S. Hall, "The Recycled Generation," *The New York Times Magazine,* 30 January 2000, pp. 30-35, 46, 74-79.

24. Hall, "Recycled Generation," p. 32.

consequentialist criteria that we measure and compare in functionalistic terms. Thus, it becomes quite easy to be rather casual about devising and implementing strategies aimed at selective weeding out or destruction of the bodies of those considered imperfect or "abnormal." If we are even the least bit queasy about this sort of thing, the reaction is attributed to the lingering, residual effects of superstitious attitudes surrounding the human body, many sustained by religion. Should a concerned person raise the alarm and ask whether, if we continue down this road, at one point in the not-too-distant future old age might itself be considered anomalous when measured against blooming youth, the question is cast immediately as part of dystopian mentality. Other questions — such as, Will the unproductive elderly at that point be *encouraged,* in the interest of an overall social benefit, to permit themselves to be euthanized because they are extra mouths to feed and a nuisance to just about everybody? — are similarly treated; for in such matters a frame of mind holds sway that would have us see *only* the most benign effects of change, including or perhaps especially those that come to us enveloped in the shimmering mantle of scientific advance.

It is important to stress just how widely accepted this technocratic view is and how overwhelmingly we, as a culture, are acquiescing in its premises. In a review in the *Times Literary Supplement* of four new books on the genetic revolution, the reviewer opined matter-of-factly that one must inevitably start to choose one's descendants. We do this now in allowing or preventing the birth of children according to medical reasons, thus selecting lives. So long as society doesn't cramp our freedom of action, we will stay on the road of progress and exercise sovereign choice over birth by consigning to death those with a less than stellar potential for a life not "marred by an excess of pain or disability."[25] Despite the horrible events associated with the old eugenics, there are those, including molecular biologist Robert Sinsheimer, who call unabashedly for a "new eugenics." (Most, remember, try to avoid the word, one that Nazism and the notorious Supreme Court case *Buck v. Bell,* which permitted involuntary sterilization of "cretins," gave a bad name.) Sinsheimer writes: "The new eugenics would permit in principle the conversion of all the unfit to the highest genetic level."[26] We see this in widespread

25. But who defines excess? This is a squishy soft criterion that now come into play at present for such "abnormalities" as cleft palate.

26. Quoted from the *Journal of Engineering and Science* in Shattuck, *Forbidden Knowledge,* pp. 193-94. The literature of reportage, enthusiasm, concern, and so on is nearly out of control. A few magazine and newspaper pieces worth reading include: Jim Yardley, "Investigators Say Embryologist Knew He Erred in Egg Mix-Up," *The New York Times,* Saturday, 17 April 1999, p. A13; Martin Lupton, "Test-Tube Questions," *The Tablet,* 20 February 1999, pp. 259-60;

adoption of prenatal screening, now regarded as routine, so much so that prospective parents who *decline* this panoply of procedures are treated as both ignorant and irresponsible. And in litigation in which parents have sued on the basis of wrongful birth or, through proxy, when the child has sued on grounds of wrongful life, we once more see the widespread presumption that life should be wiped clean of any and all imperfection, inconvenience, and risk. Creation is hobbled and bobbled. We must put it right.

The New York Times alerted us to this fact in an essay by their science editor, Gina Kolata.[27] Kolata points out that, in the immediate aftermath of Dolly, the cloned sheep who stared out at us fetchingly from the covers of so many newspapers and magazines, there was much consternation and negative rumbling: I recall very well for I was one of the rumblers.[28] But opposition dissipated quickly, she continues, with fertility centers already conducting "experiments with human eggs that lay the groundwork for cloning. Moreover, the Federal Government is supporting new research on the cloning of monkeys, encouraging scientists to perfect techniques that could easily be transferred to humans."[29] A presidential ethics commission may have recommended a "limited ban on cloning humans," but, after all, she notes, "it is an American tradition to allow people the freedom to reproduce in any way they like."[30] Really? Since when? In any way they like? This is simply false to the historic and legal record. This society, in common with any society of which we have any knowledge, past or present, has built into its interstices a variety of limitations on "reproductive freedom." But the view that "freedom" means doing things in "any way one likes" pertains as a new cultural norm. Attempts

David L. Marcus, "Mothers with Another's Eggs," *U.S. News and World Report,* 12 April 1999, pp. 42-44; Nicholas Wade, "Panel Told of Vast Benefits of Embryo Cells," *The New York Times,* Thursday, 3 December 1998, p. A24; Anne Taylor Fleming, "Why I Can't Use Someone Else's Eggs," *Newsweek,* 12 April 1999, p. 12; Nicholas Wade, "Gene Study Bolsters Hope for Treating Diseases of Aging," *The New York Times,* Friday, 5 March 1999, p. A12; Lisa Belkiun, "Splice Einstein and Sammy Glick. Add a Little Magellan," *The New York Times Magazine,* 23 August 1998, pp. 26-31, 56-61, a chilling piece that shows the many ways in which geno-enthusiasm and commodification fuse; Stephanie Armour, "Could Your Genes Hold You Back?" *USA Today,* Wednesday, 5 May 1999, pp. B1-2. An example of how the bizarre becomes commonplace is Gina Kolata, "Scientists Place Jellyfish Genes into Monkeys," *The New York Times,* Thursday, 23 December 1999, pp. 1-20. We have normalized the preposterous and do not even ask, why on earth would anyone do that — put jellyfish genes into monkeys?

27. Gina Kolata, "Human Cloning: Yesterday's Never Is Today's Why Not?" *New York Times,* 2 December 1997, p. A1, A17.

28. This foreboding also comes through in Bryan Appleyard, *Brave New Worlds: Staying Human in the Genetic Future* (New York: Viking, 1998).

29. Kolata, "Human Cloning."

30. Kolata, "Human Cloning."

to counter such subjectivist construals tend to flounder — not because they are bad arguments, but because the tide of cultural affirmation in this matter runs so swift and so strong. As a result, opposition to "any way one likes" disappears like the morning's dew at first sun.[31]

The tenor has changed quickly, according to Kolata and *The New York Times*. It describes a "slow acceptance" of the idea of cloning in the scientific community — an acceptance that took all of six months, with opinion changing from horror and queasiness to acquiescence and approval. Besides, the article concludes, "some experts said the real question was not whether cloning is ethical but whether it is legal."[32] A doctor is quoted, at article's end, saying these words: "The fact is that, in America, cloning may be bad but telling people how they should reproduce is worse. . . . In the end . . . America is not ruled by ethics. It is ruled by law."[33] Law and ethics are here separated by a chasm, despite the dominant Western tradition of natural law, the implication being that no mere ethical norm or standard can be brought to bear, whether to criticize or to checkmate, statutory laws should they be unjust or unwise. Were the day to arrive when this were actually true, it would mean that we had given up on critical politico-ethical projects, thereby diminishing our arena of free responsibility. The point is that each new development is presented to us in the name of an entirely benign extension of human freedom and powers. When we acquiesce, we slowly but surely pave additional miles on the fast track toward eradication of any real integrity to the category of "the human." This is a likely outcome at any rate, given the fact that critical debate and discourse about such matters is by now predictable, as a few religious spokesmen or women are brought on board to fret a bit and everything goes on without major challenge.[34]

Professor Laurence Tribe of the Harvard Law School hastens to reassure us that all is well. He argues thus: If we ban cloning of humans, we diminish choice, and we do so illegitimately by appealing to divine commandment or

---

31. I cannot here deal with the commercialization of genetics but the huge profits to be made drive much of the scientific and technological work, alas. See, for example, Belkin, "Splice Einstein and Sammy Glick," pp. 26-31.

32. Kolata, "Human Cloning."

33. Kolata, "Human Cloning."

34. Think, by the way, of what this would have done to Martin Luther King's protest: simply stopped it dead in the tracks. The law of the Jim Crow South was the law of segregation. And no ethical argument can challenge the law. End of story. A comeback would be that you need to make a legal argument to change the law. But King's call for legal change was an ethical call. The reductive argument that law and ethics must never touch is a crude form of legal positivism, or command-obedience legal theory. What is *right* doesn't enter into the picture at all.

inspiration. Moreover, a ban on cloning would "criminalize" a method for "creating human babies." This blights human freedom and portends a "grave" evil, that of creating a "caste system" of the cloned. How so? Because if we ban cloning, we will make clones "a marginalized caste," so it follows that the "social costs of prohibition" are too high.[35] When I first read this piece, not having noted initially who was its author, I thought that I was reading a parody of rights-absolutism, rather along the lines of Jonathan Swift's proposal for how to deal with the Irish problem. Not so, as it turns out.

It is hard to imagine a stranger argument. All the heavy artillery — choice, freedom, marginalization, forbid — comes into play. The purveyors of progress favor this new freedom. By contrast, those who consider themselves under irrational divine sanction promote the "evil" of diminished choice and would "marginalize" clones. *They,* therefore, are reactionary and must be stopped before they negate an entirely abstract, hypothetical, invented freedom anyone has yet to exercise! Thus, we are enjoined to acquiesce in an entirely abstract "freedom" even as we take several additional strides in the direction of expunging even the merest intimation of our God-given embodiment. We relinquish the authentic freedom and responsibility that is ours in favor of an abstract ideal that feeds and fuels narcissistic imaginings of *radical sameness* — for one can see in cloning-enthusiasm a real fear of the different and unpredictable, a yearning for a world of guaranteed self-replication. As the Pontifical Academy noted in a statement on human cloning issued June 25, 1997,

> Human cloning belongs to the eugenics project and is thus subject to all the ethical and juridical observations that have amply condemned it. As Hans Jonas has already written, it is "both in method the most despotic and in aim the most slavish form of genetic manipulation; its objective is not an arbitrary modification of the hereditary material but precisely its equally arbitrary *fixation* in contrast to the dominant strategy of nature."[36]

35. Laurence H. Tribe, "Second Thoughts on Cloning," *The New York Times,* Friday, 5 December 1997, p. A23.

36. Pontifical Academy for Life, "Reflections on Cloning," *Origins* 28, no. 1 (21 May 1998): 14-16, at p. 15. The popular press has been filled with cloning articles. A few include Sheryl WuDunn, "South Korean Scientists Say They Cloned a Human Cell," *The New York Times,* Thursday, 17 December 1998, p. A12; Nicholas Wade, "Researchers Join in Effort on Cloning Repair Tissue," *New York Times,* Wednesday, 5 May 1999, p. A19; Tim Friend, "Merger Could Clone Bio-Companies' Creativity," *USA Today,* Wednesday, 5 May 1999, p. 13A. See also Lori B. Andrews, *The Clone Age: Adventures in the New World of Reproductive Technology* (New York: Henry Holt, 1999).

We are so easily bedazzled. If we *can* do it, we must do it, we believe. Ideas of strong self-possession lie at the heart of much of this triumphalism, the conviction that we can control everything in an entirely beneficial way. Better, it seems, to risk turning at least some children into products of our own self-replication. Better, it seems, to risk a damaging biogenetic uniformity, since much of the basic genetic information that goes into the creation of a child from two parents emerges as a result of sexual reproduction, something not replicable by definition when you pick one parent to clone. Better, it seems, to embark on an experimental course that would likely result in poor misbegotten children of our distorted imaginations, that don't quite make it to the end of the conveyor belt as nobody wants them, not in our brave new world.[37]

It is hard to see how this is much of an exaggeration on my part in light of the fantastic proposals being proffered every day in the name of science, progress, technological control, and being our own creators. In losing what Leon Kass has called "the wisdom of repugnance," we embark on a path that constitutes a violation of a basic sort. Let me share a bit of Kass's argument with you before I turn to xenotransplantation as another example of the excision of the barrier of repugnance. Kass calls upon us to pay close attention to what we find "offensive," "repulsive," or "distasteful," for such reactions often point to deeper realities. He writes:

> in this age in which everything is held to be permissible so long as it is freely done, in which our given human nature no longer commands respect, in which our bodies are regarded as mere instruments of our autonomous rational wills, repugnance may be the only voice left that speaks up to defend the central core of our humanity. Shallow are the souls that have forgotten how to shudder.[38]

---

37. But we have a solution to that one, too, don't we? We can be certain that the creatures nobody wants, whose lives are not "worth living," can be easily dispatched to spare their suffering. Physician-assisted suicide, the track down which we are moving, is, of course, part and parcel of the general tendencies I here discuss and criticize. Although I do not focus specifically on this matter, I recommend the following two essays for the general reader: Paul R. McHugh, "The Kevorkian Epidemic," *The American Scholar* (winter 1997): 15-27; Leon R. Kass and Nelson Lund, "Courting Death: Assisted Suicide, Doctors, and the Law," *Commentary* (December 1996): 17-29; and, as well, the late Cardinal Bernardin's "Letter to the Supreme Court," which was appended to a friend-of-the-court brief filed by the Catholic Health Association in a Supreme Court case testing the appeals of two lower court decisions that struck down laws prohibiting assisted suicide in Washington and New York states; and a brief by the U.S. Catholic Conference, "Assisted Suicide Issue Moves to Supreme Court," *Origins* 26, no. 26 (12 December 1996): 421-30.

38. Leon R. Kass, "The Wisdom of Repugnance," *The New Republic*, 2 June 1997, p. 20.

Remember, Kass is *not* arguing that repugnance is the *end* of the matter but, instead, a beginning. Those philosophies that see in such reactions only the detritus of the mind, or the churnings of irrational emotion, mistake our minds and our emotions. Our emotional reactions are complex, laced through and through and through with thought. The point is to bring forward such reactions and submit them to thought. Would we really want to live in a world in which the sight of anonymous corpses piled up elicited no strong revulsion, or a world in which the sight of a human being's body pierced through and through in dozens of places and riddled with pieces of metal was something we simply took for granted? Our reaction to the first image clearly gestures toward powerful condemnation of those responsible for creating mountains of corpses, as well as anguish and pity for the tortured and murdered and their families. In the case of the metal-pierced person, we may decide it is a matter of little import and yet ask ourselves why mutilation of the body that goes much beyond the decorative is now so popular? Does this tell us anything about how we think about our bodies?[39]

Kass points out that the "technical, liberal, and meliorist approaches all ignore the deeper anthropological, social and, indeed, ontological meanings of bringing forth new life. To this more fitting and profound point of view, cloning shows itself to be a major alteration, indeed, a major violation, of our given nature as embodied, gendered and engendering beings — and of the social relations built on this natural ground."[40] The upshot is that we cede the ground *in advance of any argument having been made* to the Laurence Tribes of the world when, in fact, it should work the other way around. "The burden of moral argument must fall entirely on those who want to declare the widespread repugnances of humankind to be mere timidity or superstition," Kass writes.[41] But we have become timid about defending the insights drawn from our tradition. In upending the ways we are bound and within which we are free, we do the following things, on Kass's view: we enter a world in which unethical experiments "upon the resulting child-to-be" are conducted; we deprive a cloned entity of a "distinctive identity not only because he will be in genotype and appearance identical to another human being, but, in this case, because he may also be twin to the person who is his 'father' or 'mother' — if

---

39. There is a big discussion here yearning to breathe free, of course, namely, the connection between beauty and truth. But it is one I cannot even begin to enter on at this point. The truth is often described as splendid and beautiful — Augustine's language — and God as beautiful in and through God's simplicity. The aesthetic dimension in theology and most certainly in ethics is underexplored.

40. Kass, "Wisdom of Repugnance," p. 20.

41. Kass, "Wisdom of Repugnance," p. 21.

one can still call them that"; we deliberately plan situations that we *know* — the empirical evidence is incontrovertible — are not optimal arenas for the rearing of children, namely, family fragments that deny relationality or shrink it; and we "enshrine and aggravate a profound and mischievous misunderstanding of the meaning of having children and of the parent-child relationship. . . . The child is given a genotype that has already lived. . . . Cloning is inherently despotic, for it seeks to make one's children . . . after one's own image . . . and their future according to one's will."[42] The many warnings embedded in the Western tradition, from its antique forms (pre-Christian), through Judaism and Christianity, apparently now lack the power necessary to stay the hand of arrogant anthropocentrism as a distortion, rather than an expression, of human freedom.[43]

Within the Hebrew and Christian traditions, a burden borne by human beings lies in discerning what is natural or given, presuming that that which is encoded into the very nature of things affords a standard, accessible to human reason, by which we can assess critically the claims and forces at work in our cultural time and place. (This isn't the only available standard, of course, but it was long believed an important feature of a whole complex of views.) Can "the natural" any longer serve as a standard? The great moral teachers, until relatively recently, believed so. It is worth reminding ourselves at this juncture of the irreducible fact of our embodiment on the Christian understanding of our natures. We are corporeal beings. We were created as such. According to Pope John Paul II, this account of our natures, including the ontological equality of male and female as corporeal beings, is "free from any trace whatsoever of subjectivism. It contains only the objective facts and defines the objective reality, both when it speaks of man's creation, male and female, in the image of God, and when it adds a little later the words of the first blessing: 'Be fruitful and multiply and fill the earth; subdue it and have dominion over it'" (Gen 1:28)."[44]

John Paul's account of Genesis looks forward to the encyclical *Veritatis Splendor* but is long presaged in his pre-papal writings. For example, in a series of spiritual exercises presented to Pope Paul VI, the papal household, and the cardinals and bishops of the Roman Curia during a Lenten Retreat in March 1976, Karol Cardinal Wojtyla argued that "one cannot understand ei-

---

42. Kass, "Wisdom of Repugnance," pp. 22-24.

43. See Roger Shattuck's wonderful discussion of Faust and Frankenstein in his *Forbidden Knowledge*.

44. Pope John Paul II, *Original Unity of Man and Woman: Catechesis on the Book of Genesis* (Boston: St. Paul Editions, 1981), p. 23.

ther Sartre or Marx without having first read and pondered very deeply the first three chapters of Genesis. These are the key to understanding the world of today, both its roots and its extremely radical — and therefore dramatic — affirmations and denials."[45] "From the beginning," in John Paul's account, is a guard against radical subjectivism, and subjectivism, remember, is "fundamentally different from subjectivity," as Wojtyla wrote in a 1960 essay on love. "Subjectivity is in the nature of love, which involves human beings, man and woman. Subjectivism, on the other hand, is a distortion of the true nature of love, a hypertrophy of the subjective element such that the objective value of love is partially or wholly swallowed up and lost in it."[46]

This subjectivism grounds what Colin E. Gunton has called "the rootless will" of late modernity that begins with an aggressive denial "of the possibility of objective meaning and truth."[47] We lose argumentation — what's to argue about if there is no truth to be found? — and "the demonstration" replaces the *disputatio.* The upshot, ironically, is "an overvaluation of the success of the scientific method and an undervaluation, if not complete relativization, of the methods of the humanities."[48] By contrast, an authentic appreciation of plurality, "in the sense of a diversity of voices contending for truth," is evidence against, not for, the postmodernist denial of objective meaning and truth.[49] For the "only *logos* underlying the postmodernist world is that of a dissipated and fragmented cultural pluralism," a world quite different from a robustly contesting plurality of voices. Gunton reiterates that the doctrine of creation is the very heart of the matter,[50] not only because it teaches about the origin of things but "as an articulation of the way things are by virtue of the relation they have with their creator."[51] Denying that relationship, we easily fall into subjectivism and a world of rootless wills.

Dietrich Bonhoeffer would agree. Too little has been made of Bonhoeffer's discussion of "The Natural" in his *Ethics,* including his conviction that this concept, having fallen "into discredit in Protestant ethics," had become the preserve almost exclusively of Catholic thought. Bonhoeffer aimed to resurrect "the natural" and, in so doing, he draws closer to the position unpacked by John Paul II in his catechesis on Genesis. Bonhoeffer claims

---

45. Karol Wojtyla, *Sign of Contradiction* (New York: Seabury, 1979), p. 24.

46. Karol Wojtyla, *Love and Responsibility* (New York: Farrar, Straus, Giroux, 1981), p. 153.

47. Colin E. Gunton, *The One, the Three, and the Many: God, Creation, and the Culture of Modernity* (Cambridge: Cambridge University Press, 1993), p. 102.

48. Gunton, *The One, the Three,* p. 103.

49. Gunton, *The One, the Three,* p. 105.

50. Gunton, *The One, the Three,* p. 107.

51. Gunton, *The One, the Three,* p. 124.

that fallen creation still has access to the natural, but only "on the basis of the gospel."[52] For the "natural is that which, after the Fall, is directed towards the coming of Christ." In his move to redeem the concept of the natural, Bonhoeffer argues that we enjoy a "relative freedom" in natural life. But there are "true and . . . mistaken" uses of this freedom and these mark "the difference between the natural and the unnatural." He throws down the gauntlet: "Destruction of the natural means destruction of life. . . . The unnatural is the enemy of life."

It is unnatural, argues Bonhoeffer, to approach life from a false "vitalism" or excessive idealism or, contrastingly, from an equally false "mechanization" and lassitude that shows "despair towards natural life," expressing as it does "a certain hostility to life, tiredness of life and incapacity for life." Our right to bodily life is a natural, not an invented, right and the basis of all other rights, given that Christians repudiate the view that the body is simply a prison for the immortal soul. Harming the body harms the self at its depth. "Bodilyness and human life belong inseparably together," in Bonhoeffer's words. Our bodies are ends in themselves and this has "very far-reaching consequences for the Christian appraisal of all the problems that have to do with the life of the body, housing, food, clothing, recreation, play and sex." We can use our bodies and the bodies of others well or ill.

The most striking and radical excision of the integrity and right of natural life is "arbitrary killing," the deliberate destruction of "innocent life." Bonhoeffer notes abortion, killing defenseless prisoners or wounded men, and destroying lives we do not find worth living — a clear reference to Nazi euthanasia and genocidal policies toward the ill, the infirm, and all persons with handicaps.[53] "The right to live is a matter of the essence" and not of any socially imposed or constructed values. Even "the most wretched life" is

---

52. This discussion in Bonhoeffer's *Ethics*, ed. Eberhard Bethge (New York: Macmillan, 1955), appears on pp. 142-85 and all quoted matter is drawn from those pages.

53. This is an area that deserves longer treatment than I can here give it. Fortunately, and at long last, there are texts in English on Nazi euthanasia as part of its general bio-politics. Of especial note is Michael Burleigh, *Death and Deliverance* (Cambridge: Cambridge University Press, 1994). This is a tremendously disquieting book for a contemporary American reader. So much of the language of our own genetic engineering and "assisted suicide" proponents seems echoes of National Socialist propaganda. The Nazis covered the waterfront, so to speak, justifying their programs of systematic selective elimination of the "unfit," of life unworthy of life (congenitically "diseased," handicapped, etc.), on a number of interrelated grounds, including cost-benefit criteria, perfecting the race, and compassion. The Nazis also controlled the media on this issue (it goes without saying), producing short propaganda films and full-length features, lavishly produced and starring German matinee idols, to promote their efforts toward euthanasia.

"worth living before God." Other violations of the liberty of the body include physical torture, arbitrary seizure and enslavement (American slavery is here referenced), and deportations, separation of persons from home and family — the full panoply of horrors the twentieth century dished up in superabundance. This fragment by Bonhoeffer on the natural is unfinished — as is the entirety of his *Ethics* — but it is suggestive and worth pondering as an alternative to cultural forces that make illegitimate *any* appeal to nature or the natural.

I submit that we fear our bodies and their vulnerabilities, and that the cultural project of fleeing finitude now shakes hands with a technocratic agenda, like cloning, but with many other agendas as well, including projects of radical excision of bodies deemed unworthy to appear or to remain among us.[54] We seek perfection in one realm; definitive excision in the other. These cultural urgencies should haunt us. A society that can no longer accept bodily limits, including natality and mortality, is a society in the throes of a moral muddle rather than sturdy enlightenment.

Surely those who embrace a doctrine of creation should extol the goodness and integrity of all bodies. As *The Book of Common Prayer* tells us, all the works of the Lord glorify, praise, and exalt the Lord. It is an incarnational sensibility that we are in danger of losing or that, perhaps, we have lost. We lose our amazement at life itself and the glory of the natural. We cannot exalt the Lord any longer (for that would seem a limit to our own freedom); instead, we worship at the altar of our own projects. If you haven't already, read P. D. James's novel *The Children of Men*.[55] The novel is set in Britain in the year 2021. No children have been born — none at all — on planet Earth since the year 1995. In that year, for reasons no one understands, all males became infertile. The world is dying. People are despondent, chagrined, violent. "Western science had been our god," writes the protagonist, Theodore Faron, an Oxford historian and cousin to the dictator of Great Britain. He "shares the disillusionment" of one whose god has died. Now overtaken by a "universal negativism," the human race lurches toward its certain demise. Because there will be no future, "all the pleasures of the mind and senses sometimes seem . . . no more than pathetic and crumbling defences shored up against our ruins." Children's playgrounds are dismantled. People disown commitments and responsibilities to one another save whatever serves some immediate purpose: what is chosen by contrast to what is given.

---

54. In a longer essay, the death penalty would come under critical scrutiny here as an act of such radical excision.

55. P. D. Jones, *The Children of Men* (New York: Alfred A. Knopf, 1993).

People thought they had eliminated evil, Faron notes, and all the churches in the 1990s "moved from the theology of sin and redemption" to a "sentimental humanism." In the name of compassion, the elderly, no longer needed or wanted, are conducted to a state-sponsored ceremony of group suicide called the Quietus. Faron concludes that human beings are "diminished" if we live without knowledge of the past and without hope of the future. In a world in which birth has ceased and death is managed and staged, "the very words 'justice,' 'compassion,' 'society,' 'struggle,' 'evil,' become unheard echoes on an empty air." To be sure, we can "experience nothing but the present moment." But our understanding of that moment is profoundly shaped and given meaning by our "ability to reach back through the centuries for the reassurance of our ancestry." This rich ancestry loses its meaning, in turn, "without the hope of posterity . . . without the assurance that we being dead yet live." For whom do we build? In whose behalf do we dream? If we are wrapped up in our own quest for self-possession, perfection, and control, we cannot even ask such questions much less answer them.

What Is Enough? Catholic Social Thought, Consumption, and Material Sufficiency

CHRISTINE FIRER HINZE

From a number of directions, modern Roman Catholic social thought[1] presses questions concerning "what is enough?" Social Catholicism, including papal social teaching, has emphasized each person's right to the minimum economic conditions necessary for living with human dignity. The grievous affronts to humanity wrought by economic marginalization and involuntary poverty are frequently highlighted. The excesses of selfishness and greed, and the unjust economic and social structures they breed, are denounced. A long-standing Catholic tradition reflects on the grounds for, and limits on, rights to acquire and possess private property. From Pope Leo XIII's 1891 encyclical *Rerum Novarum* forward, modern popes' championing of both the "working man" and workers' right to a family living wage have been

---

1. See, e.g., David O'Brien and Thomas Shannon, eds., *Modern Catholic Social Teaching: The Documentary Heritage* (Maryknoll, N.Y.: Orbis, 1992); Donal Dorr, *Option for the Poor: A Hundred Years of Catholic Social Teaching* (Maryknoll, N.Y.: Orbis, 1983); Michael Schuck, *That They Be One: The Social Teaching of the Papal Encyclicals 1740-1989* (Washington, D.C.: Georgetown University Press, 1991). The U.S. Bishops' 1991 statement on ecological responsibility offers a typical summary of major themes: *a God-centered and sacramental view of the universe,* which underpins human accountability for responsible use of the world's resources; a consistent *respect for human life,* which extends to respect for all creation; an emphasis on the ethical significance of *global interdependence and the common good; an ethics of solidarity* promoting cooperation and a just structure of sharing in the world community; an understanding of *the universal purpose of created things,* which requires equitable use of the earth's resources; *an option for the poor,* which prioritizes moral attention and motives in the quest for an equitable and sustainable world; and a conception of *authentic development,* which seeks directions for progress that respect human dignity and the limits to material growth (United States Catholic Bishops, "Renewing the Earth" [Washington, D.C.: U.S. Catholic Conference, 1991], pp. 5-6).

freighted with assumptions concerning economic sufficiency. And more recent papal treatments of authentic human development that criticize consumerism and materialist "overdevelopment" in the richer nations, along with nascent Catholic teachings on ecological responsibility, all imply judgments concerning how much material acquisition, possession, and use is too much, and how much is enough.

As the twentieth century moved to its close, new foci of concern for Catholic social thought emerged as scholars and leaders engaged in interdisciplinary dialogue and responded to changing ecclesial and cultural circumstances. In the years since the watershed Second Vatican Council (1962-65), some Catholics have brought a liberationist perspective to analyses of economic sufficiency and its acquisition and distribution within a globalizing capitalist order.[2] In other corners, there has been renewed interest in the ways Christian virtue ethics frame sufficiency in relation to personal and social practice.[3] A third site of reflection concerns ecology, and the profound consequences of human excess in a finite biosphere upon which the whole independent array of biological and material forms relies for survival.[4] These var-

---

2. "Liberationist" thought here refers to literature, beginning in the late 1960s, whose authors, responding to crises of massive human suffering caused by poverty, oppression, and exploitation among poor and marginalized groups, aim to re-articulate Christian faith and doctrine within an emancipatory hermeneutic. Liberationist approaches foreground biblical demands for social justice and solidarity with the poor; connect classic theological doctrines (especially sin and redemption) to dynamics of social suffering and transformation; engage in ideological and social-structural analysis (frequently indebted to critical social theory and other streams of revisionist Marxist thought); and work to unmask and combat oppressive social arrangements and practices. See, prominently, Gustavo Gutierrez, *A Theology of Liberation: History, Politics, and Salvation,* trans. and ed. Sister Caridad Inda and John Eagleson (Maryknoll, N.Y.: Orbis, 1973); Ignacio Ellacuria and Jon Sobrino, eds., *Mysterium Liberationis: Fundamental Concepts of Liberation Theology* (Maryknoll, N.Y.: Orbis, 1993). North American forms of liberationist thought have emerged among African-American, Hispanic, and feminist theologians. See, e.g., M. Shawn Copeland, "Black, Hispanic/Latino, and Native American Theologies," and Rebecca S. Chopp, "Feminist and Womanist Theologies," both in *The Modern Theologians,* ed. David F. Ford, 2nd ed. (Oxford: Blackwell, 1997), pp. 357-404.

3. See, e.g., Jean Porter, *The Recovery of Virtue* (Louisville: Westminster/John Knox, 1990); Jean Porter, *Moral Action and Christian Ethics* (London: Cambridge, 1995); Joseph J. Kotva Jr., *The Christian Case for Virtue Ethics* (Washington, D.C.: Georgetown University Press, 1996); Romanus Cessario, O.P., *The Moral Virtues and Theological Ethics* (Notre Dame, Ind.: University of Notre Dame Press, 1991); N. Murphy, B. Kallenberg, and N. T. Nation, eds., *Virtues and Practices in the Christian Tradition: Christian Ethics after MacIntyre* (Harrisburg, Pa.: Trinity Press International, 1997).

4. See, e.g., Walter E. Grazer and Drew Christiansen, S.J., eds., *The Earth is the Lord's: Catholic Theology and Ecology* (Washington, D.C.: United States Catholic Conference, 1997).

ied developments have brought fresh urgency to questions surrounding a Catholic ethics of sufficiency for the twenty-first century.

This essay seeks to identify the contours of a contemporary Catholic approach to moral limits on spending and consumption in affluent, market-oriented cultures like the United States. The claim I wish to advance is this: A constitutive moral effect of the mass consumer culture linked to contemporary market economies is culture's dismantling of personal and social temperance. Social Catholicism harbors a variety of resources — traditional, progressive, and radical — which, creatively combined, illumine this cultural dynamic and can contribute to a renewed ethic of economic sufficiency that addresses the question "what is enough?" in a manner appropriate to twenty-first-century circumstances.[5] This essay mines some of these resources in service of my argument. First, we will examine the contribution of priest-economist John A. Ryan (1869-1945), who integrated papal teaching, economic theory, and progressive-personalist politics to advance an original American Catholic position concerning economic sufficiency, within an agenda for large-scale political and social reform. Next we probe the underpinnings of Ryan's approach in Aristotelian-Thomistic understandings of virtue, relate Ryan's contribution to subsequent Catholic and secular critiques of materialism and consumerism, and set the stage for developments of this legacy that contemporary circumstances demand. The following section of the essay contributes to this needed development by introducing an argument concerning consumption and sufficiency that trades on a contentious alliance between two streams of recent Catholic and secular scholarship: Aristotelian-Thomist forms of virtue ethics, and critical-liberationist social analyses.[6] The first bequeaths classic Western articulations of the good human life and the motives, actions, and habituated practices required to attain it, which have decisively shaped Roman Catholic ethics. The second engages activists and scholars committed to solidarity with the poor in structural analysis and cultural criticism that explicitly places rigorous intellectual investigation in the service of movements for social transformation.

---

5. I am grateful to Dr. Regina Ammicht-Quinn, University of Frankfurt, for her "Critical Comments" on an earlier draft of this paper, delivered at the Internationalwissenchaftsforum, Heidelberg, Germany, April 2000. I shall be noting some of these in the course of what follows.

6. A method informed by the interplay between radical and traditional positions more effectively illumines consumer society's shaping of desire, by examining it from a vantage point shaped by *both* a finely grained analysis of virtues and vices *and* a critical analysis of ideology and social structure. Radical-traditional alliances can also help fortify transformative communal practices that challenge consumer capitalism's morally problematic features.

John A. Ryan on the Limits of Just Consumption[7]

A useful historical resource for mapping an economic ethic of "enough" informed by Catholic social thought is the work of the premier U.S. Catholic economic ethicist of the twentieth century, Monsignor John A. Ryan (1869-1945).[8] Ryan's work interpreted for an American economic context the papal social teachings of Leo XIII and Pius XI, forging a brand of social economics[9] that has continued to influence Catholic thought in the United States to the present day.[10] The centerpiece of Ryan's economic ethics was an understand-

7. Ryan's method, which correlates traditional theological and moral sources, economic science and analysis, and agendas for political and social change, merits emulation. A contemporary Catholic ethics of sufficiency must also look underneath and beyond Ryan's work: underneath, to critique and develop the theological and philosophical anthropology Ryan assumed; beyond, to address the ramifications and limitations of a Ryanesque approach for an ethic of "enough" in a new century. Ammicht-Quinn notes weaknesses and dangers in Ryan's interpretation of temperance, to be addressed below.

8. In his two major economic treatises, *A Living Wage* (London: Macmillan, 1906) and *Distributive Justice,* 3rd ed. (New York: Macmillan, 1942 [1916, 1927]), and in numerous other writings, Ryan articulates a comprehensive theory of the good economic order and of the rights and duties of its various members, with particular attention to the right of workers and their families to attain a decent livelihood, understood as the basic material conditions for reasonable degrees of human development.

9. "Social economics" and "Catholic social economics," of which John A. Ryan is considered one of the founders (Mark A. Lutz, ed., *Social Economics: Retrospect and Prospect* [Boston: Kluwer Academic Publishers, 1990], p. 262) refer to related, value-directed approaches within the field of economic science. Social economics resists dominant neoclassical economics' constricted depiction of the human agent and its eschewal of normative considerations in economic analysis. Ryan regularly acknowledged debts to major social economists of his day, including John Hobson, Richard Ely, and Sidney and Beatrice Webb. In the United States, the link between Catholic social economics and social economics is reflected in the evolution of the Association of Catholic Economics, founded in the 1940s, which became after 1965 the more pluralistic Association for Social Economics. The development and range of the field today is represented in the ASE's two scholarly journals, the *Review of Social Economy* and *Forum for Social Economics.* Contemporary social economists articulate a fuller anthropological basis and normative contextualization for economics, and "share a strong conviction that a meaningful economics capable of addressing social problems needs to be value-directed or normative and guided by such basic ideals as community, environmental sustainability, human fulfillment, and meaningful work" (Mark Lutz, in *Social Economics,* ed. Lutz, p. 423). For histories and descriptions of various strands within social economics, see essays by Lutz, Thomas O. Nitsch, and Edward J. O'Boyle, all in *Social Economics*; also John B. Davis and Edward J. O'Boyle, eds., *The Social Economics of Human Material Need* (Carbondale, Ill.: Southern Illinois University Press, 1994).

10. Unfortunately, later-twentieth-century Catholic social teaching in the United States displayed an attenuated engagement with this tradition of Catholic economic thought. There has also been a dearth of knowledgeable dialogue between social economics, Catholic or other,

ing of human dignity and welfare, grounded in a neo-scholastic anthropology and articulated within a Thomistic, teleological, natural law ethical approach.[11] His work reflects an abiding commitment to advancing a doctrinally faithful Catholic social ethic that is robustly interdisciplinary in method, ecumenically attuned in presentation, and publicly engaged in practice. The economic questions treated by Ryan ranged from macro-issues like the relative merits of capitalism versus socialism, and sophisticated matters of public policy, to the minutiae of individual families' spending habits and details of everyday social comportment. Ryan contributes to Catholic thinking about "enough" in relation to acquisition, spending, and consumption primarily in his writings concerning true and false human and economic welfare, and minimum and maximum standards of living.[12]

Ryan frequently warned against the particular ease with which inhabitants of advanced modern economies could fall prey to the temptation to seek happiness through material acquisition and consumption. In his eyes, this tendency augured profoundly deleterious outcomes, both spiritual and moral.[13] Among these are the surrender of a "reasonable" human life that values "thinking, knowing, communing, loving, serving, and giving," in favor of an impoverished ideal consisting in "having and enjoying."[14] Morals and

---

and important liberationist discussions. See Stephen Martin, *"Healing and Creating" in Catholic Economic Ethics: Bernard Lonergan and Social Economics in Dialogue* (Ph.D. diss., Marquette University, May 2000), esp. chaps. 1-3.

11. Historically contextualized expositions of Ryan's theological ethics are Charles E. Curran, *American Catholic Social Ethics: Twentieth-Century Approaches* (Notre Dame, Ind.: University of Notre Dame Press, 1982), pp. 26-92, and Harlan Beckley, *Passion for Justice: Retrieving the Legacies of Walter Rauschenbusch, John A. Ryan, and Reinhold Niebuhr* (Louisville: Westminster/John Knox, 1993), pp. 110-88.

12. A common objection to the Aristotelian/Thomistic moral schema that grounds Ryan's treatment is the obsolescence of the hierarchical, rationalist anthropology that it employs. With Jean Porter and others, I do not claim that all aspects of this tradition are applicable to present moral discourse. The distortion, however, of the *humanum* that Aristotle and Thomas describe in terms of the vices opposed to prudence, temperance, justice, and fortitude strikes an authentic chord when considered in relation to the effects of consumer capitalism on the perceptions and practices of its participants. See, e.g., Porter, *Recovery of Virtue;* Kotva, *The Christian Case for Virtue Ethics.*

13. See, e.g., John A. Ryan, "The Fallacy of Bettering One's Position," *Catholic World* (1907); *Distributive Justice,* esp. 1942 ed., chap. 18, "The Duty of Distributing Superfluous Wealth"; and "Minimum and Maximum Standards of Living," in his *Declining Liberty and Other Papers* (New York: Macmillan, 1927), pp. 315-29.

14. John A. Ryan, "False and True Welfare," in *The Church and Socialism and Other Essays* (Washington, D.C.: University Press, 1919), pp. 184-94. This economic critique continues to be found in official Catholic social teaching to this day; see, e.g., Pope John Paul II's critique of

character are damaged, Ryan argues, in the pursuit of "high society" activities such as entertaining whose chief goal is to outdo or keep up with others' sumptuousness of dress, food, and equipage. Excessive pursuit of material satisfactions easily leads to gluttony and drunkenness, as well as lust, as persons lower themselves to the servile control of their animal instincts. Materialistic consumerism also weakens the religious sense and the altruistic sense. Ryan adduces evidence that indicates that when people rise above a certain level of affluence, their contributions to the common welfare tend to decrease.

Going a step further, Ryan contends that even habitual and prolonged usage of modern conveniences that are not immoral in themselves (he lists streetcars and electric bells — we might list microwave ovens and laptop computers) can injure character. People become dependent on such conveniences and

> less capable of that measure of self-denial and of endurance which is indispensable to the highest achievement. These and many other contrivances of modern life are undoubtedly an obstacle to the development of the invaluable ingredient of character which consists in the *power to do without*. They contribute insensibly, yet effectively, to a certain softness of mind, will, and body which is no advantage in life's many-sided struggle. It does not follow that these conveniences ought not to be utilized at all; it follows that they are not the unmixed blessing which they are commonly assumed to be.[15]

Furthermore, "The indefinite pursuit of material satisfaction is, in considerable measure, injurious to health." Rich foods, sexual unchastity, intemper-

---

consumer culture as valuing "having" over "being," *Sollicitudo Rei Socialis* (1987), no. 28; following Pope Paul VI, *Populorum Progressio* (1967), no. 19; *Octogesima Adveniens* (1971), no. 4. Papal documents found in O'Brien and Shannon, eds., *Catholic Social Teaching*.

15. Ryan, "False and True Welfare," pp. 186-87. To Ryan, a lifestyle too dependent on creature comforts and conveniences led to the diminution of "mental powers and activities" ("False and True Welfare," pp. 188-89). As proof, Ryan points to the increasing proportion of college and university students who choose those courses of study that have a "practical" rather than a theoretical or academic aim and outcome; such students "will almost all devote their energies later to the business of money-getting. This means the exercise of the lower powers of the brain and intellect" ("False and True Welfare," p. 188). Ammicht-Quinn cautions against uncritically adopting Ryan's claims here; she emphasizes that a Christian approach to consumer asceticism must never be reduced to "praising what makes us hard" — a slogan of the Nazi-era *Hitlerjugend* ("Critical Comments," p. 4). She rethinks traditional Western understandings of asceticism in Regina Ammicht-Quinn, *Korper-Religion-Sexualitat: theologische Reflexionen zur Ethik der Geschlechter* (Mainz: Matthias-Grunewald-Verlag, 1999).

ance all take their toll. "Even the claim that a larger volume of happiness will result from the development and satisfaction of a larger volume of wants is unfounded." For, he holds, the greater number of wants that are activated, the greater the suffering and disappointment when these wants are unsatisfied. We are, in a sense, all slaves to the wants we habitually satisfy.[16]

Ryan's concern about excessive or conspicuous consumption should not be misread: he also condemned amassing superfluous wealth, even when one did maintain a simple and disciplined style of living. In his writings on the living wage and distributive justice, Ryan distinguished three separate levels of wealth: (1) wealth sufficient to provide the necessities of life; (2) wealth sufficient to provide the conventional necessities and comforts of one's own social plane or station in life; and (3) wealth that is superfluous to maintaining the standards of decent livelihood or one's station in life. Everyone, he argued, has a natural right to the first level of wealth, an estimation of which determines the normative living wage. Ryan attempts to enumerate the specifics included in this frugal, yet more-than-basic, level of material comfort and security, and to estimate the dollar amounts needed to acquire them at various times and in various geographical regions. He allocates, for instance, moderate amounts for amusement and recreation, for clothing that will allow one dignity in the society of one's peers, for organizational memberships, for periodicals and other literature, and for donations to charity.[17]

As for more economically advantaged households, Ryan seems to regard upper-middle-class wealth (or the lower reaches of it) as the utmost moral limit to ownership. In choosing housing, clothes, food, and recreation, advantaged householders ought to apply the tests of simplicity, moderation, and comparative inexpensiveness, and to observe a maximum limit on the amount any family may legitimately spend for comforts. Within these parameters, the second level of wealth could be morally tolerable in many, though not all, circumstances. Any wealth attained at the third level, however, Ryan deemed entirely subject to the call of grave necessity on the part of the neighbor.[18]

Ryan advanced his case against excessive acquisition and consumption on commonsense, philosophical, and religious grounds. He found ample

16. Ryan, "False and True Welfare," pp. 190-91. Appealing to the writings of Thorstein Veblen and Charlotte Perkins Gilman, Ryan goes on to deny that the pursuit of beauty and refinement requires ever-higher standards of living, arguing that upward mobility often attenuates refinement by making for gaudy display and weak accession to fashion fads.

17. In addition to *A Living Wage*, chap. 7, see Ryan, *Distributive Justice*, chap. 21.

18. Here I concur with John A. Coleman, *An American Strategic Theology* (New York: Paulist, 1982), pp. 85-97. Cf. Ryan, "Minimum and Maximum Standards of Living," pp. 328-29.

grounds within the New Testament, the teachings of the Fathers, and the continuous teaching of the church for exhorting Christians toward a suspicion of wealth, accompanied by "a certain asceticism." His neo-scholastic Thomist training and his study of social and economic "facts" also led Ryan to perceive strong ties between personal habits of economic intemperance, distorted cultural patterns of valuation and practice, and societal injustice. He frequently launches out against the intransigence that causes so many "good" Christians, in thrall to the idol of material pursuit and enjoyment, to spurn the moral conversion required for economic justice. Far too many Catholics, he contends, give only lip service to the serious moral obligations surrounding their economic lifestyles. Members of every class allow themselves to fall into the grip of the culture's illusion that "to be worthwhile life must include a continuous and indefinite increase in the number and variety of wants, and a corresponding growth and variation in the means of satisfying them," and they are seduced into valuing desires for purely physical gratification equally with the demands of the spiritual, moral, and intellectual faculties. Since physical satisfactions are susceptible to indefinite increase, variety, and cost, it is easy to assume that there can be no practical limit set to the amount of goods or income needed to keep life worth living. For the culture as well as for individuals, the category of "surplus" or of "superfluous goods," which one is obliged to distribute to the needy neighbor, effectively drops out. People who accept this "working creed of materialism" embrace propositions not only against right reason, but against scriptural revelation and centuries of church teaching.[19] Such persons, abetted by their communities, are seriously jeopardizing both their earthly and their eternal happiness. For what forms or deforms good human character simultaneously does so for spiritual character; the two are wholly intertwined.

Besides combining the personal and communal in his argument for material moderation, Ryan yokes together individual and social effort in his schemes for social betterment. He consistently refuses to designate either individual charity or social policy as the sole path to a decent economic livelihood for all.[20] Moral and religious conversion alone is insufficient to produce

---

19. Ryan, "False and True Welfare," pp. 192-97. Ryan cites a proposition condemned as "scandalous and pernicious" by Pope Innocent XI in 1679 to the effect that "It is scarcely possible to find among people engaged in worldly pursuits, even among kings, goods that are superfluous to social position. Therefore, hardly any one is bound to give alms from this source" (Ryan, *Distributive Justice*, p. 243; citing *Enchiridion Symbolorum*, prop. 12).

20. Ryan writes, "So long as men put senses above the soul, they will be unable to see clearly what is justice, and unwilling to practice the little that they are able to see. Those who exaggerate the value of sense gratifications cannot be truly charitable, and those who are not truly

justice; "social effort" through political, economic, and cultural associations and structures is also needed. Consonant with the teachings of Leo XIII and Pius XI on subsidiarity, Ryan perceives an important role for public policy, but a role balanced and limited by the integrity and proper domains of other social entities, of the church, and of the legitimate freedom of individuals and their families.

Regardless of one's place in the social organism, economic justice requires that each person have access to economic sufficiency under conditions that respect dignity and cultivate potentiality. Articulating a version of what theologians would later call the "option for the poor,"[21] Ryan contends that to attain this goal, a fundamental redistribution of power to the benefit of those who presently have the least clout in the industrial capitalist system is necessary. Worker justice must comprise "sufficiency, security, and status": sufficiency for labor in the present through a family living wage; security for labor in the future, through savings and social insurance; and a new status for labor that includes sharing in management, profits, and ownership.[22] Ryan thus summarizes a full-bodied understanding of what constitutes "enough" in complex industrialized settings, one that goes beyond moderate material *abundance* to include certain degrees of temporal *security* and a share in social *power* through genuine participation in guiding work's processes and outcomes.

Ryan's program was focused on the injustices facing the working class, was critical but not condemnatory of capitalism, and was strongly reformist in its agenda for change.[23] With other early-century social crit-

---

charitable cannot perform adequate justice. The achievement of social justice requires not merely changes in the social mechanism, but a change in the social spirit, a reformation in men's hearts. To this end nothing could be more immediately helpful than a comprehensive recognition of the stewardship of wealth, and the duty of distributing superfluous goods" (*Distributive Justice*, p. 245).

21. For the argument that this "option for the poor" is a theme found throughout modern Catholic social thought, see Dorr, *Option for the Poor*. Ryan directed his energy and attention not to the truly indigent, however, but to the struggling working person who is unable to garner a decent remuneration despite adequate efforts, the group that today is often called "the working poor." See also n. 23.

22. See "Democratizing Industry," in Ryan, *Declining Liberty*, pp. 224-38.

23. A more radical form of American social Catholicism emerged during these same years. Dorothy Day, Peter Maurin, and the Catholic Worker movement gathered small communities committed to Christian personalism, nonviolence, and the exercise of the corporal and spiritual works of mercy in service of the poor, homeless, and unemployed. Day and Maurin were sharply critical of capitalist economy for its militarism, exploitation of workers, and neglect of the vulnerable. The Catholic Worker's social agenda today retains anarchist and personalist priorities, which lead members to engage in civil disobedience and public actions

ics,[24] he inveighed against an ascendant creed of consumption and material satisfaction that he believed was contaminating and distorting the meaning of "the pursuit of happiness" in American life. Critics since Ryan's day have more systematically analyzed them, but the priest-economist clearly grasped some of the ideological power of consumer culture, and recognized the intertwining of social belief and structure that culture reflects and promotes. In these ways, Ryan charted for American Catholic leaders the century's most widely embraced plan for assessing and critiquing capitalist economy and the relationships to acquiring, having, and keeping it might entail.

After Ryan: Virtue, Structure, Power

In Ryan's presentation, economic justice demands both good institutions and virtuous economic actors, that is, persons who are habituated to proper judgments, desires, and practices with respect to the ends and rewards sought through economic activity. Economic and political institutions must provide access for all citizens to material sufficiency.[25] Actors within a political econ-

---

designed to expose and protest political and economic injustices. See June O'Connor, "Catholic Worker Movement," in *The New Dictionary of Catholic Social Thought,* ed. Judith Dwyer (Collegeville, Minn.: Liturgical, 1994), pp. 128-31. Recently, for example, the Los Angeles Catholic Worker community distributed one hundred new shopping carts to homeless persons, to protest ticketing, jailing, and police confiscation of supermarket-owned carts from homeless citizens who frequently use them to carry all their worldly belongings. Jeff Dietrich, "The Great Shopping Cart Caper," *Catholic Agitator,* 2 August 1998, p. 3, writes, "The real purpose of our free shopping carts is not simply to help the poor or to keep them out of jail, though it is definitely that. [It] is actually to insure that the poor, with the emblem of their poverty and suffering, will not be entirely invisible to the community."

24. Daniel Horowitz identifies two dominant traditions of thought on the morality of consumption and spending in *The Morality of Spending: Attitudes toward the Consumer Society in America, 1875-1940* (Baltimore: Johns Hopkins University Press, 1985). Ryan, whose career spans precisely the decades during which mass consumer society became firmly entrenched, bridges the two lines of critique Horowitz identifies. Like "traditional moralists," he advocated self-restraint and "Culture" as good codes for working class families. Like "modern" moralists, Ryan worried about the cultural degradation wrought by mass consumption, and the softening impact of consumerism on all citizens. See Horowitz, pp. xviii-xix. More recently, historian Susan J. Matt has analyzed consumerism's relation to shifting popular apprehensions of virtue in *Keeping Up with the Joneses: Envy in American Consumer Society, 1890-1930* (Philadelphia: University of Pennsylvania Press, 2003).

25. As Harlan Beckley states, in Ryan's virtuous economic order, need is the primary canon for distribution. See *Passion for Justice,* pp. 167-68.

omy need to be able to distinguish among and prioritize genuine needs versus superfluous wants. The primacy that Ryan accords virtue in a just economic order clearly reflects the Thomistic framework marking Catholic moral theology of his day.[26] Also characteristic of Catholic social thought is Ryan's conviction that, when they reduce the meaning and purpose of "economy" to market exchange, or human agents to self-interest-maximizing *homo economicus*, mainstream economists fall prey to a category mistake bound to distort both analysis and policy recommendations.[27]

Along with his reliance on Aristotelian-Thomistic virtue traditions with their accompanying understandings of human nature and sociality, two other analytic trajectories shape Ryan's economics. A second trajectory, the one most prominently featured in Ryan's work, attends to institutional arrangements and practices, employing social science tools to analyze and propose changes in laws and industrial policies that fail to meet standards of justice. A third line of investigation targets culture and ideology, examining the intimate interaction of social structure and personal agency in creating and maintaining virtuous or vicious social structures and power relations. This last remained mostly implicit in Ryan's work, as Marxian-inspired forms of ideology critique were eschewed by Catholic scholars until well after Vatican II. As his discussion of true and false welfare illustrates, however, Ryan was an astute observer of the psyche-shaping aspects of consumer economy and of the cultural and personal mores that such an economy reflected and nurtured.

Each of these three strands persisted and evolved in later-century American Catholic thought, though neither in the same literatures nor in any integrated fashion. Treatments of economy directly indebted to Thomistic natural law and virtue approaches continued among a small school of "Catholic economists," who, in the 1960s, joined other nonmainstream social economists to form the Association for Social Economics. Ryan's legacy of attention to "economic facts" in the service of advocacy for the economically vulnerable and public-policy reform was carried on in the

---

26. Beckley underscores the dignity of, and justice toward, individual persons as the central note that emerges in Ryan's work (*Passion for Justice,* esp. pp. 110-87), yet this stress on the individual remains firmly set within an affirmation of the common good.

27. Karl Polanyi would later name this error "the economistic fallacy," the logically fallacious identification of "economic phenomena" with "market phenomena," and "humanity" with the actor in market exchange. See Polanyi, *The Livelihood of Man,* ed. Harry W. Parson (New York: Academic Press, 1977), pp. 6-18. This conceptual fallacy has had practical consequences, as persons who embed social relations within market economy rather than vice versa begin to live in and create a world where the fallacy is naturalized and seems self-validating.

research, education, and lobbying work of the National Council of Catholic Bishops. The third, more radical and transformative strand, with its emphasis on ideology critique and thoroughgoing cultural renovation, flowered after Vatican II, becoming most closely identified with representatives of liberation theology.[28]

In the Catholic community and beyond, the years following 1965 were marked by growing attention to the material insufficiency afflicting much of the world's population, even as the United States and other nations experienced unprecedented and widespread economic growth, abundance, and, in many cases, the afflictions of excess. Liberation theologians made the questions arising out of this painful paradox their special focus; heightened concern with understanding and responding to unjust economic structures and practices is also clearly evident in papal and episcopal teaching. Paradoxically, this new stress on the option for the poor and active solidarity with — rather than simple charity toward — those lacking enough broke forth in Catholic thought just as, in the United States, a majority of European-American Catholics were transcending their working-class roots to become comfortably ensconced in the middle classes.

By the close of the century, these changing economic circumstances and developments in social doctrine had created a climate wherein a large, mostly European-American, and heavily bourgeois segment of the U.S. Catholic population faced a number of difficult moral questions. What ends, norms, and parameters distinguish a virtuous pattern of consumption and spending? What minimums and maximums are mandated or allowed? What particular economic dispositions and habits of judgment and action — what virtues — ought to be educed, cultivated, and maintained among the faithful, and by their institutional representatives in both ecclesial and public dealings? As the grandchildren of Ryan's generation grapple with such challenges, the three trajectories that characterized his economic ethics — a focus on personal and social virtue, practical agendas for institutional renovation, and intimations of radical ideological critique and deeper structural transformation — continue to delineate a promising context for forging the necessary responses.

Catholic social thought since the 1950s, including papal teaching, has maintained contact with these three trajectories, as is especially evident in the

28. In North America, the work of Bernard J. F. Lonergan, S.J., particularly his analyses of intellectual horizons, the operations of individual and group bias, and historical cycles of progress and decline, has provided another rich theoretical means for understanding virtuous and vicious social interactions and power relations. See esp. his *Insight: A Study of Human Understanding* (New York: Philosophical Library, 1957).

writings of Pope John Paul II.[29] But recent official teachings, while suggestive, stop short of a full ethical treatment of consumption and economic sufficiency. Effectively confronting questions surrounding consumption and sufficiency in globalizing twenty-first-century economies requires this more complete theoretical and practical position. Staking out the lines of such a position in conversation with Ryan's tri-dimensional legacy helps expose lacunae and control for biases to which any single trajectory, taken by itself, is prone.[30] Creatively counterpoised, these three mutually correcting directions of thought and action can frame a robust contemporary ethics of material sufficiency and consumption.

Traditional Virtue, Radical Social Analysis

Ryan's diatribe against consumer culture targeted the overstimulation of material wants and the debilitating effects this has on character. Developing this critique for a new century, we might ask: to what extent does consumer capitalism, especially that form practiced in contemporary North America, pro-

---

29. See Pope John Paul II, *Laborem Exercens* (1981), *Sollicitudo Rei Socialis* (1987), and especially *Centesimus Annus* (1991), in O'Brien and Shannon, eds., *Catholic Social Teaching*. On consumerism and its effects, the pope sounds remarkably like Ryan: "The manner in which new needs arise and are defined is always marked by a more or less appropriate concept of man and his true good. A given culture reveals its overall understanding of life through the choices it makes in production and consumption. . . . In singling out new needs and new means to meet them, one must be guided by a comprehensive picture of man which respects all the dimensions of his being and which subordinates his material and instinctive dimensions to his interior and spiritual ones. [If this is not done] . . . consumer attitudes and lifestyles can be created which are objectively improper and often damaging to his physical and spiritual health. . . . It is not wrong to want to live better; what is wrong is a style of life which is presumed to be better when it is directed toward "having" rather than "being" and which wants to have more not in order to be more, but in order to spend life in enjoyment as an end in itself. It is therefore necessary to create lifestyles in which the quest for truth, beauty, goodness and communion with others for the sake of common growth are the factors which determine consumer choices, savings and investments" (*Centesimus Annus,* no. 36).

30. Traditional virtue approaches are vulnerable to an overly personal orientation that stresses private virtue but is insufficiently critical or transformative with respect to ideology or social structures. Circumscribed attention to institutional analysis and public policy reform ignores the more profound anthropological, moral, and social-structural dimensions illumined by virtue and structural-ideology strands. Liberationist ideology critique, left on its own, fails to engage the practical workings of market economy, or to acknowledge its benefits. This third line of analysis is also ill-equipped to propose ameliorative or transformative agendas for redressing the evils it exposes.

voke or even require habituated patterns of social and personal intemperance whereby both the capacity to judge what is enough and the capacity to rest satisfied with sufficiency are severely attenuated, if not destroyed?[31] Prefatory to considering this question, a brief elaboration of how radical-analytic and virtue approaches might bear on an interpretation of these questions concerning consumer capitalism is in order.

Traditional Virtues and the Dynamics of Desire

Aristotle and Thomas Aquinas, magisterial representatives of Western virtue traditions, describe the good life within a finely grained analysis of proper and improper desires, objects of desire, and means and degrees of pursuing or satisfying desire.[32] For both, the moral virtues "shape the human agent as a desiring creature in such a way that he spontaneously desires and seeks what is in accordance with the truly good life that he is trying to lead." And because human desire pertains to the whole person, including the body, the passions, the rational appetite of the will, the intellect, and the spirit, "distinct moral virtues are needed to rectify these different aspects of human desire."[33]

For Aristotle and Aquinas, the cardinal virtues — prudence, temperance, fortitude, and justice — are pivotal in this work of ordering human judgments and desires, and shaping the dispositions and actions that flow

31. In focusing the following discussion on consumer capitalism in its contemporary North American forms, I take seriously anthropologist Daniel Miller's caution — a caveat shared by economist Deirdre McCloskey in the present volume — against an irresponsibly universalizing polemic that fails to recognize that consumption, embedded in different contemporary market and political contexts (e.g., Norway vs. the United States), does not inevitably exhibit the extreme moral and religious distortions suggested by Harvey Cox, David Loy, and others. See Miller's excellent introductory essay, "Consumption As the Vanguard of History," in *Acknowledging Consumption: A Review of New Studies,* ed. Daniel Miller (London: Routledge, 1995), pp. 1-57, at p. 27; cf. his treatment of myths concerning consumption, pp. 20-30. John A. Ryan's earlier polemic against consumerism, and modern Catholic social thought as a whole, regarded a certain degree of "temperate consumption" as not only tolerable but required for the dignified human life.

32. See Aristotle, *Nichomachean Ethics;* Thomas Aquinas, *Summa Theologiae,* Latin text and English translation (Cambridge: Blackfriars, 1964), 23 vols.

33. Porter, *Recovery of Virtue,* citing Thomas Aquinas, *Summa Theologiae* I-II, 1.55, art. iv. This understanding of virtue as "desiring aright" means that any retrieval of an ethic of enough will involve not the rejection or condemnation of desire but rather its redirection and reshaping toward authentic human well-being. Cf. Ammicht-Quinn, "Critical Comments," for a creative discussion of this point.

from them. The intellectual virtue of prudence empowers right decision-making and means-selection in particular and changing circumstances.[34] The virtues of fortitude and temperance form and bring rational direction to the subrational (or better, "conscious yet pre-rational")[35] affections or passions of concupiscence and attraction, fear and aversion in the various areas of life. Finally, the social virtue of justice (and in a different way, for Aquinas, the theological virtues of faith, hope, and charity),[36] "orient[s] the will toward goods that transcend the individual, without which orientation she could not achieve even her true individual good."[37]

Aristotle's insistence, largely shared by Thomas, that virtue is the habit of desiring and aiming for the mean between the extremes of excess and deficiency places understandings and practices of "enough" at the heart of a virtue-centered construal of the moral life. In this regard, virtuous persons and their just communities recognize that, as Mortimer Adler puts it,

> There are two modes of desire, not just one mode. There are acquired desires, differing from individual to individual, and there are natural desires, common to and inherent in all individuals who belong to the human species and so participate in one and the same human nature. The English names for these two radically different modes of desire are "wants" and "needs."[38]

34. So Philip Land speaks of prudence as the reasoning of practical wisdom. "[P]ractical knowledge . . . must proceed from a 'well ordered appetite' or desire for the end of moral life. Prudence, unlike other more speculative exercises of the intellect, is not concerned with affirming or denying, but rather *for pursuing and avoiding in accordance with desire*" (emphasis added; Philip Land, S.J., *Catholic Social Teaching* [Chicago: Loyola University Press, 1994], p. 231).

35. Porter, *Recovery of Virtue*, p. 113.

36. The essay does not consider how the infused virtues affect and sublate the acquired virtues. On this see Cessario, *The Moral Virtues and Theological Ethics;* and the overview and analysis in Renee Mirkes, O.S.F, *Aquinas on the Unity of Perfect Moral Virtue and Its Significance for the Nature-Grace Question,* (doctoral diss., Marquette University, 1995).

37. Porter, *Recovery of Virtue*, p. 103. James Keenan correctly notes that contemporary understandings of the cardinal virtues must take into account the impact of enculturation and of individual personal differences, and must also propose an anthropological setting for virtue that transcends the limits of faculty psychology. (I disagree, however, with his claim that the traditional list of four needs to substantially rewritten.) See James Keenan, S.J., "Proposing Cardinal Virtues," *Theological Studies* 56, no. 4 (December 1995): 709-29.

38. Mortimer Adler, *Desires: Right and Wrong: The Ethics of Enough* (New York: Macmillan, 1991), p. 14. Aquinas stresses that temperance concerns the capacity to identify and moderately enjoy pleasures connected with "the needs of the present life" (see *Summa Theologiae* II-II, q. 141, art. vi; q. 142, art. I).

The capacity to distinguish between wants and needs enables persons and communities to identify kinds and degrees of virtuous moderation — temperance — in economic matters, including in spending and consuming.

Yet, pursuit of the mean does not constitute the apotheosis of the moral life in every respect. The virtuous person judges and acts in the context of certain ultimate goods that are of inexhaustible worth, and do not themselves admit of a mean in their pursuit.[39] From a religious perspective, God and the goods of God (divine truth, goodness, life) stand as such inexhaustible and endlessly valuable ends. But the fact that philosophers and religionists can conceive of ends for which "enough" in effect loses its meaning recalls a danger endemic to human endeavor. The person or group striving to live and do well is always liable to a slippage of the moral gears whereby the human capacity to desire "more" in an unbounded way — the sort of desire that can be satiated only by an ultimate and infinite end — gets interpolated into dynamics of desire for limited, bounded goods. This slippage is at the heart of the ancient religious problem of idolatry, described by Augustine in terms of disordered loves. When people seek with ultimate ardor ends which are not the Chief Good, virtue becomes counterfeit, and sin and unhappiness result.[40] In market economies, the immaterial (and so interminably expandable) ends of money and profit are uniquely susceptible to this illegitimate transposition; but so are cyclical patterns of consumption.[41]

A virtue approach to consumer culture has a number of potential merits. It directs attention to social valuations and their impact on persons' dispositions to see, judge, and act in substantive and ongoing ways. Virtue discourse provides a vocabulary that can highlight the entrenched, *habituated* nature of these patterns once etched into the psyches and spirits of persons

39. Adler, *Desires*, p. 14. Aquinas takes this up in a number of places, including *Summa Theologiae* I-II, q. 64, art. iv.

40. Cf. St. Augustine, *Of the Morals of the Catholic Church*, esp. chaps. 3, 5, 6, 8, and 11; in Waldo Beach and H. Richard Niebuhr, eds., *Christian Ethics*, 2nd ed. (New York: John Wiley and Sons, 1973), pp. 110-18. Aquinas, *Summa Theologiae* II-II, q. 23, art. vii, states that one can speak of "virtue" within a limited sphere of action that aims at some particular good. "But if that particular good is not true good, but only apparent, then also the virtue that aims at that good will not be true virtue, but a counterfeit virtue. Thus, as Augustine says, 'the prudence of the covetous is not true prudence, which devises various ways and means of making money . . . and the same of the temperance of the covetous, by which they abstain from luxury as being an expensive taste. . . .'" If one seeks a limited, though genuine good, then the virtue that seeks it will be true virtue, but imperfect in reference to its final end in God.

41. Relevant to this line of argument are recent dialogues between theologians and psychologists concerning links between sin, vice, and the dynamics of addiction, and relations between personal and social sin. See, e.g., Gerald May, *Sin and Addiction* (San Francisco: Harper, 1988); Judith Merkle, "Sin," in *The New Dictionary of Catholic Social Thought*, ed. Dwyer, pp. 883-88.

and groups. Categories of virtue and vice provide ways to reflect on how these deep-seated patterns promote or detract from human flourishing.[42] Finally, a virtue approach offers tools for considering how destructive patterns of economic valuation and activity may be identified, resisted, and sometimes, through grace and arduous effort, changed.

Culture, Ideology, and Economy

Though traditional ethics assumes a socially embedded moral agent, virtue discourse tends to begin with and to accent the individual and his or her moral character. Modern radical social theory, and liberationist approaches indebted to radical traditions, proceed from the opposing starting point. According to these lines of analysis, human social constructs like a capitalist economy depend for their existence upon the maintenance of a network of beliefs, assumptions, and feelings (a common horizon or worldview) shared by a critical mass of their participants. This noetic web, this worldview, is *ideological* insofar as it also provides the framework within which thought, desire, and action are, in daily and multifarious ways, conformed to and conditioned to accept the continuance of the social system. In contemporary capitalist economies, this common set of perceptions and valuations creates a matrix within which certain issues and questions — those assuming or promoting the preservation of the status quo — tend to be regarded as significant, while others — those that might question or undermine it — are either ruled out of court or obscured from view.[43]

Anthropologist Pierre Bourdieu[44] weds the languages of virtue and ideology critique in the notion of *habitus,* his term for the modus operandi at the heart of participation in any social structure, its processes, and its perpetuation. Focusing on the "dialectical relationship between the objective structures and the cognitive and motivating structures which they produce and which tend to

42. Moreover, human flourishing and degradation are intimately intertwined with their ecological habitat and context.

43. On modern radical social theory, see Mary E. Hobgood, *Catholic Social Teaching and Economic Theory: Paradigms in Conflict* (Philadelphia: Temple University Press, 1991), pp. 26-69; cf. Christine Firer Hinze, *Comprehending Power in Christian Social Ethics* (Atlanta: Scholars Press, 1995), pp. 39-60, 153-80, 216-65.

44. Pierre Bourdieu, *Outline of a Theory of Practice,* trans. Richard Nice (Oxford: Cambridge University Press, 1977). See also J. M. Balkin, *Cultural Software: A Theory of Ideology* (New Haven, Conn.: Yale University Press, 1998); John C. Oliga, *Power, Ideology, and Control* (London and New York: Plenum, 1996); and the significant contributions of Paul Ricoeur, esp. *Lectures on Ideology and Utopia,* ed. George H. Taylor (New York: Columbia University Press, 1986).

reproduce them," Bourdieu portrays participation in social relations as decisively shaped by, and reflected in, a particular *habitus* that also identifies one as a member. Bourdieu's notion of *habitus,* described as "a system of lasting, transposable dispositions which, integrating past experiences, functions at every moment as a *matrix of perceptions, appreciations, and actions* and makes possible the achievement of infinitely diversified tasks,"[45] fruitfully blends traditional and radical forms of analysis to provide a helpful tool for understanding and critiquing complex contemporary social dynamics such as consumerism.

To cast consumer-market thinking, valuing, and practice under the light of ideological suspicion is not to deny that there are dispositions and habits (virtues) that make for successful market relations, and that involve more than simple interest maximization or Machiavellian power play. At their best, the habits that make for humane and robust commerce rely upon and confirm values such as human dignity, trust, creativity, and sociality.[46] But the market can neither generate nor guarantee respect for the more comprehensive anthropological and moral foundations on which these values rest. And insofar as market cultures operate in ways that conceal, corrode, detract attention from, or disempower practices and associations whereby such values are engendered and secured, market economy can become destructive not only of extra-market integuments but also of the moral foundations on which market economies' own continued success relies.

Such cumulatively deleterious patterns and consequences of large-scale social patterns have been referred to in recent Catholic thought as "structures of sin."[47] The emergence of this term in official and scholarly vocabulary signals a nascent awareness that a Catholic theology of culture, and economic ethics within that, must help believers perceive and analyze these structures, and point toward avenues for confronting, opposing, or transforming them.

---

45. The "infinitely diversified tasks" that *habitus* enables are due to "analogical transfers of schemes permitting the solution of similarly shaped problems," and also thanks to "the unceasing corrections of the results obtained, dialectically produced by those results. . . ." (Bourdieu, *Outline of a Theory of Practice,* pp. 82-83).

46. See, e.g., Deirdre McCloskey, "Bourgeois Virtue," *American Scholar* (spring 1994): 177-91. Aquinas acknowledges that genuine, though imperfect, virtues attach to the pursuit of particular temporal goods. See n. 38 above. This Thomistic heritage is evident in papal social teaching's approbation of virtues exercised in business economy, such as munificence and industriousness. See, e.g., Pope Pius XI, *Quadragesimo Anno,* no. 132, and Pope John Paul II, *Centesimus Annus,* no. 32, in O'Brien and Shannon, eds., *Catholic Social Teaching;* cf. Michael Naughton and Gene R. Laczniak, "A Theological Context of Work from the Catholic Social Encyclical Tradition," *Journal of Business Ethics* 12 (1993): 981-94.

47. This term enters papal social teaching in 1987 in Pope John Paul II, *Sollicitudo Rei Socialis,* nos. 36-37, in O'Brien and Shannon, eds., *Catholic Social Teaching.*

The Eclipse of Temperance in Mass Consumer Societies

All of the traditional religions teach that human beings are finite creatures and that there are limits to any earthly enterprise. A Japanese Zen
master once said to his disciples as he was dying, "I have learned only one
thing in life: how much is enough." He would find no niche in the chapel
of The Market, for whom the First Commandment is, "There is *never*
enough."[48]

We may now further explore the thesis that contemporary mass-market
economies tend to generate, and may require, a culture of consumption
wherein the meaning and value of sufficiency is obscured, and temperate
practices actively impeded. Evidence for the plausibility of this thesis comes
most clearly into view when the claim, and its applicability to American economic culture, are scrutinized from both traditional-virtue and radical-
ideological lenses.

The Virtue Lens For Thomas, the cardinal virtue dealing with possession
and money is justice, which orders one's relations with others; the chief vice
against justice is covetousness or greed.[49] John Ryan repeatedly warned that
should efforts to found a better economic order founder, "the main cause of
the failure will be a very ugly and very ancient vice. It is the vice that we call
avarice or greed."[50] The significance of covetousness or greed as it operates in
capitalist political economy, and its role in undermining communal consensus concerning sufficiency in various forms, cannot be gainsaid.

Yet temperance, the virtue that moderates desires for, and movements

48. Harvey Cox, "The Market As God," *Atlantic Monthly* 283, no. 3 (March 1999): 18-23, at
p. 23. Also analyzing the analogues between market economics and religions are David Loy, "Religion and the Market," in *Visions of a New Earth: Religious Perspectives on Population, Consumption, and the Environment,* ed. Harold Coward and Daniel C. Maguire (Albany, N.Y.: State University of New York Press, 2000), pp. 15-28, and A. Rodney Dobell, "Degradation and the
Religion of the Market," in *Population, Consumption, and the Environment,* ed. Harold Coward
(Albany: State University of New York Press, 1995). Miller and McCloskey (cf. n. 31 above) would
object to Cox's totalizing portrayal of The Market as inevitably removing any boundaries to
"enough." I seek to show that at least in the case of contemporary American economic culture,
this criticism largely applies.

49. Covetousness is the immoderate desire to possess material goods as well as the "immoderate straining for all the possessions which man thinks are needed to assure his own importance and status . . . a desperate self-preservation, overriding concern for confirmation and
security" (Josef Pieper, *Prudence* [New York: Pantheon, 1959], p. 41; cf. Aquinas, *Summa
Theologiae* II-II, q. 118, art. I).

50. John A. Ryan, *A Better Economic Order* (New York: Harper and Brothers, 1935), p. 190.

to attain, enjoy, or consume material goods and pleasures, is a virtue equally and perhaps more fundamentally at risk.[51] The dynamism of consumer markets begets a practical agnosticism concerning parameters or limits to material satisfaction. Members of consumer cultures are habituated to expect, desire, and enjoy a seemingly endless flow of new, improved, or increased material goods and comforts. Over time, this undermines members' capacities to discern, in any meaningful way, not only "what is enough," but rather, what "enough" could possibly mean in the first place. Absent that crucial rudder, participants in late capitalist culture are susceptible to life patterns that amount to well-packaged, high-technology versions of Thomas Hobbes's "endless seeking of power after power, that ceaseth only in death."

It would be wrong to claim that analyzing consumer economy from a virtue-oriented perspective reveals only personal and social vice and moral corruption. Contemporary Catholic social economists such as Peter Danner and Edward O'Boyle make this clear by arguing, in recognizably Thomistic-Aristotelian terms, that the appetite for gain-seeking, and the desire for and enjoyment of economic abundance, are not evil or sinful *in se*. On the contrary, these appetites and desires are of themselves benign, but in need of virtue's direction and discipline.[52]

While depicting gain-seeking and consumer desires as natural, potentially creative and useful human capacities, however, Danner and O'Boyle emphasize the normative limits of this claim. This is due to what they call the "spiritual poverty" at the heart of capitalist market economies. From their Catholic economic perspective, consumer markets not situated within and guided by a fuller anthropological, social, and moral worldview are inevitably subject to corruption. A particularly insidious form of such corruption occurs when familial, communal, and civic relations become embedded in and directed by the economic values and relations of the capitalist market, rather than vice versa.[53]

---

51. Aquinas, following Gregory, regards vices *deficient* of prudence as originating from intemperance, specifically the vice of lust, which carries one away and "entirely suppresses reason from exercising its act." Vices embodying *excess* or false similitude in relation to prudence are rooted in covetousness, which, as the immoderate love of possessing external things, is the chief vice opposed to justice (*Summa Theologiae* II-II, q. 55, art viii; cf. Pieper, *Prudence*, pp. 41-42).

52. See esp. Peter Danner, *An Ethics for the Affluent* (Lanham, Md.: University Press of America, 1980), and *Getting and Spending: A Primer on Economic Morality* (Kansas City, Mo.: Sheed and Ward, 1994); Edward O'Boyle, *Personalist Economics* (London: Routledge, 1996).

53. This is a major argument of Karl Polanyi, *The Great Transformation* (New York: Farrar and Rinehart, 1944). See also John Paul II, *Centesimus Annus*, no. 40: "The economy in fact is only one aspect and one dimension of the whole of human activity. If economic life is

Temperance has traditionally been regarded as the virtue directed toward regulating the self, and justice as the virtue regulating relations with others in society. In a contemporary development of the "unity of the virtues," the conjunctions between these self- and other-directed habits, *as these interactively reflect and reinforce social structures and power relations* in consumer market economies, need to be recognized and better understood.[54] Insight concerning such connections is a major development in Catholic teaching and thought over the twentieth century, but the practical and strategic implications of this dawning awareness remain notoriously difficult to effectively articulate, much less to act upon. In the attempt to do so, critical cultural and ideological analysis provide important tools.

The Ideological Lens   Reflecting the attention to sociology of knowledge that characterizes radical social theory, David Loy observes:

> [T]he industrial revolution was "in the end a revolution in demand" — or more precisely, "a transformation of desires." Since we have come to look upon our own insatiable desires as "natural" it is necessary to remember how much our present mode-of-desiring is also one particular, historically-conditioned system of values — a set of habits as manufactured as the goods supplied to satisfy it.[55]

In any society, getting, keeping, and consuming each involve a potential endlessness that can confound even the sincere aspirant to moderation. In contemporary market economies, the virtue of temperance must operate to determine what is enough in a context wherein these processes are remarkably accelerated and intensified.

---

absolutized, if the production and consumption of goods become the center of social life and society's only value, not subject to any other value, the reason is to be found not so much in the economic system itself as in the fact that the entire socio-cultural system, by ignoring the ethical and religious dimension, has been weakened and ends by limiting itself to the production of goods and services alone."

54. On sinful social structures, see, e.g., Gregory Baum, "Structures of Sin," in *The Logic of Solidarity*, ed. Gregory Baum and Robert Ellsberg (Maryknoll, N.Y.: Orbis, 1989), pp. 110-26; and expositions of Bernard Lonergan's contribution such as Matthew Lamb, *Solidarity with Victims: Toward a Theology of Social Transformation* (New York: Crossroad, 1982), chap. 1; M. Shawn Copeland, *A Genetic Study of the Idea of the Human Good in the Thought of Bernard Lonergan* (doctoral diss., Boston College, 1991), chap. 3; Kenneth R. Melchin, *Living with Other People* (Collegeville, Minn.: Liturgical, 1997).

55. David Loy, "The Religion of the Market," p. 25, citing Fernand Braudel, *The Wheels of Commerce*, trans. Sian Reynolds (New York: Harper and Row, 1982).

Capitalist culture is not wholly bereft of the discourse of economic moderation and sufficiency. Both Ryan's American Catholic social thought and the United States's tax and social welfare policies, for instance, appeal to general, if contentious, public consensus concerning parameters that do in fact identify "not enough" (e.g., homelessness) and, with a bit more difficulty, "too much" (e.g., access to unlimited funds for luxuries while nearby neighbors starve). And studies of American families and workers indicate that people commonly describe themselves as striving for sufficiency, as wanting "just enough." Linda Rothman, a forty-three-year-old head-of-household interviewed by Robert Wuthnow and his associates in 1992, articulates this widely shared American response to the question, what exactly does money mean to her?

> She says it mostly means *being comfortable* and *not having to worry.* These are two sides of the same coin. They define, within a fairly narrow range, the upper and lower limits of what money connotes. "Comfort" is having just enough money to feel some pleasure in the way one lives. . . . "Worrying," in contrast, means being in a situation where the money may not even be sufficient to cover necessities.[56]

This interviewee also expressed an aversion to "extravagance," an attitude frequently expressed by Americans.

If the views of Linda Rothman are typical they suggest that, in practice, Americans do have fairly clear, if dispositional, standards according to which they identify what is enough. This suggests that habits promoting temperance and deterring covetousness and profligacy are prevalent in contemporary American economic practice after all. As Wuthnow, Juliet Schor, and others show, however, Americans' specific interpretations of being comfortable and "not having to worry" on the one hand, and extravagance on the other, are strongly subject to continual amendment and upgrading in relation to the socioeconomic reference groups against which they are measured.[57] The upshot

56. Robert Wuthnow, *Poor Richard's Principle: Recovering the American Dream through the Moral Dimensions of Work, Business, and Money* (Princeton, N.J.: Princeton University Press, 1996), p. 172.

57. See esp. Juliet B. Schor, *The Overspent American: Upscaling, Downshifting, and the New Consumer* (New York: Basic, 1998); also Juliet B. Schor, *The Overworked American: The Unexpected Decline of Leisure* (New York: Basic, 1994). Cf. Wuthnow, *Poor Richard's Principle*, and *God and Mammon in America* (New York: Free Press, 1994). Economist Robert H. Frank insightfully considers dynamics of socioeconomic reference groups in *Choosing the Right Pond: Human Behavior and the Quest for Status* (New York: Oxford University Press, 1985), and *Luxury Fever: Why Money Fails to Satisfy in an Era of Excess* (New York: Free Press, 1999).

of this in a consumer-capitalist setting has been the extreme elasticity and continuous expansion of the meaning of "enough" that Ryan was already decrying in the 1920s.

This problem is illustrated when Wuthnow's interviewee goes on to define "comfortable" as being able to buy an $80 blouse or a $250 suit at a major department store in town without worrying she was spending too much. Spending $1,000 for a suit, she judges, would be extravagant. She estimates that in 1992, it would probably take an annual income of between $100,000 and $150,000 for her to feel comfortable. "Again she insists 'extravagant is not me,' but comfort is something she feels is a legitimate aspiration." The example suggests how decisively the culture in which we live (and the groups and positional goods against which we measure our relative standing) "set the moral context for our considerations about money."[58]

Besides illustrating the slipperiness of the term, Linda Rothman's criteria for enough, "being comfortable" and "not having to worry," suggest how an attraction-aversion couplet basic to legitimate aspirations for safety and security gets enlisted in service of the workings of consumer markets. Combined with the lure of the "new and improved," these twin motives are prime targets of the advertising industry. Innumerable products and services are sold daily on the implied promise that they will either reduce worry or increase comfort.[59] In our day as in Ryan's, fear of worry and attraction to comfort operate both in people's concerns for attaining material satisfactions and in responses to the insecurity and uncertainty that mark their employment status and prospects for empowerment in the workplace.[60] But rather than sparking resistance or collaboration for change, feelings of deprivation generated by insufficient economic security and power are more often sluiced into greater, rather than less, investment in the work-spend cycle.

What is more, the dynamics of consumer culture conspire to distract and overload the attention of its participants, thereby diminishing their capacity to pierce the corruptive or alienating aspects of consuming pat-

---

58. Wuthnow, *Poor Richard's Principle*, pp. 172-73.

59. Interestingly, the virtues Thomas associates with temperance are also the frequent object of attack by marketers and advertising. These associated virtues include *continentia*, continence that allows us to resist being swept away by intemperate desires even when we feel them strongly; *humilitas*, which restrains pushiness; *ornatus*, moderation in external apparel; *parcitas*, "self-containedness and sparseness about superfluities"; and *simplicitas*, "moderation and restraint about luxuries" (Thomas Gilby, O.P., "Temperance," *New Catholic Encyclopedia*, vol. 13 [Washington D.C.: Catholic University of America, 1967], p. 986).

60. See Barbara Hilkert Andolsen, *The New Job Contract: Economic Justice in an Age of Insecurity* (Cleveland: Pilgrim, 1998).

terns, and curtailing their effective freedom to resist or change. Consumers and wage-earners are neither robots nor drones. But the exponential growth in choices, products, stimulation, speed, and communication available to consumers today taxes finite human capacities for attention in unprecedented ways. One effect of this is to defer sustained critical reflection on it all, including on the socioeconomic apparatus that fuels the delivery systems. Once again in the modern period, technological expertise has outstripped moral wisdom, and here operates to keep us from even noticing that it does so.

The ideological growing edge in affluent societies is ever-higher expectation (and tolerance) of novelty, purported improvement, and increase. Children are trained for this from their first McDonald's Happy Meal and "free toy." Between money-producing work activities and the panoply of activities connected with consumption, participants in affluent market economies easily find their limited time, energy, and attention exhausted. With the patterns of daily life etched between workplace, private home, and shopping mall, there ensues a concomitant dulling of moral sensitivity or civic attention, a horizonal oblivion and moral callousness[61] concerning the plight of suffering others, who languish on the margins of, or are crushed beneath, this destructive superdevelopment loop.

Even with respect to personal well-being, the *habitus* of American consumer capitalism subtly encourages its members to notice diversion and novelty, often at the cost of overlooking essentials. One result is that leisure — in the classical sense of time devoted to activities making for genuine self- or communal development — may be squeezed out, replaced by recreation or idleness.[62] And when the economic culture succeeds well enough, consumers scarcely notice leisure's absence. In a variety of forms, this consumer-producer lifestyle is reified and experienced as natural. And as this comprehensive way of seeing, judging, and behaving sets the parameters of "the way

---

61. Peter Unger, *Living High and Letting Die: Our Illusion of Innocence* (New York: Oxford, 1996), exposes the false consciousness whereby those in affluent cultures dismiss their responsibilities to assist the many others who suffer in dire need today. On the notion of "harmful superdevelopment" in affluent countries and its implications, cf. Pope John Paul II, *Sollicitudo Rei Socialis: On Social Concern* (Washington, D.C.: U.S. Catholic Conference 1987), no. 28.

62. Texts that demonstrate this claim from philosophical and historical perspectives are Josef Pieper, *Leisure, the Basis of Culture* (New York: Harper, 1952), and Benjamin Kline Hunnicutt, *Kellogg's Six-Hour Day* (Philadelphia: Temple University Press, 1996). Impoverished civic life is another result. By the 1950s, mass consumer culture was susceptible to Hannah Arendt's judgment that it had bred, in place of a community of citizens, "a society of jobholders" (Hannah Arendt, *The Human Condition* [Chicago: University of Chicago Press, 1958]).

things are," its power is dramatically entrenched. Bourdieu expresses the ideological efficacy of this state of affairs with brutal precision:

> Every established order tends to produce . . . the naturalization of its own arbitrariness. Of all the mechanisms tending to produce this effect, the most important and the best concealed is undoubtedly the dialectic of the objective chances and the agents' aspirations, out which there arises the *sense of limits,* commonly called the *sense of reality,* i.e. the correspondence between the objective classes and the internalized classes, social structures and mental structures, which is the basis of the most ineradicable adherence to the established order.[63]

Woven into this pattern of distraction and comfort-seeking, finally, is a profound message concerning *suffering* and its ultimate incompatibility with the desirable life. Capitalist economy may applaud sacrifices of time and energy in the pursuit of material gain, but consumer culture beckons workers and families toward a world of products and practices that protect from and eliminate suffering and discomfort. Habituation to the avoidance of pain and suffering — hallmark of what some critics describe as an addictive system — is a powerfully alluring feature of consumerism. These various effects combine to make consumerism's economic-cultural *habitus* a heady, morally and religiously problematic brew.

Virtue and radical-interpretive lenses, we have seen, illumine moral and religious dangers in contemporary market economies by highlighting three social verities of consumer capitalist culture. First, this culture offers no stable guidelines for what constitutes sufficiency or excess in consuming, spending, or buying. Second, though "enough" has always been subject to positional evaluation, consumer economies raise the stakes with extraordinary speed and frequency, placing one's own position, and that of one's reference groups, in permanent motion toward what is deemed newer, better, or more. The paradoxical consequence is that amid unprecedented material abundance, people are afflicted by a pervasive sense of insufficiency: be it time, money, goods, or attention, there is never enough. Third, advanced market economies generate an intemperate culture of work and play that siphons attention and energy primarily into the labor-consumption cycle, with several pernicious results: Nonmarket relations, values, and practices are danger-

---

63. Bourdieu, *Outline of a Theory of Practice,* p. 164. The irony is that consumer culture enmeshes its members in cycles of intemperance, which then function as *limits* on imagining or doing anything different. Cf. Charles Mathewes, "On Using the World," pp. 189-221 in this collection.

ously weakened. Consumerist and economic relations, values, and practices override and threaten to replace nonmarket social relations and values. And the ideological features of consumer culture conspire to naturalize these processes, thereby deterring participants from resisting or even noticing them.

Conclusion: Religious Communities and a New Ethic of Sufficiency

If consumer capitalism is a not only a manner of conducting economic relations but also a social structure whose dynamics and ideology shape participants' gain-seeking and consuming appetites in fundamentally intemperate directions, then there is a crying need for counter-systems and ideologies wherein market participants can discover themselves and their relations as other and more than gain-seeking exchange and pleasure-seeking consumption. Extra-market communities are sites where the limits of consumerist morality at least have a chance of being perceived, and alternatives to it can be embraced. Traditionally, civic, family, and religious communities have provided crucial counterweights to economic logic. But the totalizing proclivities of market economic systems, the counterfeits of virtue and vice the system breeds, and the distracting and potentially all-consuming character of market-focused living intermingle to present these groups with a difficult task indeed.

Religious communities, in particular, seem well-positioned to unmask and resist the delusory features of untrammeled market morality.[64] One would also expect Christian communities to be congenial loci for critical reflection on the dangers of reference-group upscaling and the importance of "choosing the right pond" in which to judge what is sufficient.[65] But too often the opportunity to act as counter-publics in this regard remains unseized by Christian communities in the United States. The demographics of American Catholic communities over the twentieth century suggest that participation in upward class and housing mobility, so endemic to American culture, consistently trumps allegiance to particular parish communities. Especially at the

---

64. Useful recent Christian treatments of consumer and market culture include John Kavanaugh, S.J., *(Still) Following Christ in Consumer Culture* (Maryknoll, N.Y.: Orbis, 1991); John A. Coleman, "The Culture of Death," in *The Logic of Solidarity*, ed. Baum and Elsberg, pp. 90-109; Robert Wuthnow, ed., *Rethinking Materialism: Perspectives on the Spiritual Dimension of Economic Behavior* (Grand Rapids: Eerdmans, 1995); and Dietmar Mieth and Marciano Vidal, eds., *Outside the Market No Salvation?* Concilium 1997/2 (London: SCM, 1997).

65. Cf. Frank, *Choosing the Right Pond*.

local congregational level, continually rising standards of living and consumption are rarely self-consciously discussed within the arc of religious morality, and even less frequently effectively contested.

At the dawn of a new century, a great many middle-class Christians, having tasted the fruit of economic success, are comfortably enmeshed in consumer culture.[66] To what extent will cultural assimilation atrophy the capacity of Catholics (who now comprise over one quarter of the population of the United States) and other religious congregations to act as prophetic or transformative forces in the face of the vices that mar consumer market economies? More pointedly, what role can religious communities play in bringing economic and ecological intemperance to light, and in forging creative, life-affirming, and practicable twenty-first-century forms of socioeconomic and ecological temperance?[67]

One step toward responding to these questions involves an explicit ministry of education and consciousness-raising among everyday believers concerning the cultural dynamics described here. Along with providing contexts for recognizing and reflecting on questions concerning enough, local congregations must foster conversations wherein people can help each other discern what sufficiency concretely entails in their specific circumstances. Catholic teaching and Christian social thought can be of assistance here. But the most difficult task may be to enlist the participation of working, spending, and consuming parishioners whose energies appear chronically overextended. To the extent that Christians and their neighbors are consumed by all that market culture promises or delivers, demands or denies, strategies for habituation into new forms of economic temperance remain both a crying need and an unmet challenge.

66. In the case of Catholics, this demographic fact must be juxtaposed with two others: In the United States, a troubling trend toward socioeconomic and racial-ethnic separation between urban and suburban Catholic populations; and globally, the fact that more Roman Catholics remain economically marginalized than affluent.

67. As Ammicht-Quinn stresses, a new ethic of enough will required not an asceticism that glorifies self-denial or impugns the bodily, but a joyful and life-affirming engagement in and with the material world. See also Mathewes's insightful treatment of the relation between enjoyment and asceticism in "On Using the World," pp. 189-221 in this volume.

On Using the World

CHARLES MATHEWES

Introduction: On Being-in-the-World

Many thoughtful people fear that we are living so far beyond our means that our present existence threatens to consume our future. Whether we agree with these fears or not, it is clear that we are caught in patterns of consumption and production that seem excessive and destructive. Michel Foucault puts it well: "For millennia man remained what he was for Aristotle: A living animal with the additional capacity for a political existence. Modern man is an animal whose politics places his existence as a living being in question."[1] What has put us in this situation? How can we live better lives? I want in this essay to propose answers to these questions.

My proposal may, however, surprise readers. Most thinkers diagnose our root problem to be a residual "otherworldliness" surviving as a relic of an earlier religious worldview, and they prescribe as a purgative for this a more diligent worldliness, or love for material existence as a whole — a more emphatic affirmation of the intrinsic value and fragility of nonhuman nature and human society. In contrast, I think we have come to this situation because we have loved "the world" too much, because we seek to find all our values and meaning in it. The problem, that is, is not that we remain too religious, but that we are not religious, not "otherworldly," enough; we have come to our sorry state by expecting all our needs to be met by and in the world. The solution to our crisis is to care about the world not less, but

---

1. Michel Foucault, *The History of Sexuality,* vol. 1, trans. Robert Hurley (Harmondsworth: Penguin, 1981), p. 143.

in a different way than we do. By aiming to recover the practices Augustine once designated with the phrase "using the world," perhaps we can make ourselves less rapacious creatures and, one hopes, place less strain on our world.

But what does it mean to "use the world"? Perhaps such a claim is hopelessly vague, little more than a vacuous slogan. Such suspicions of vacuousness are at least partially right, for this slogan stands in opposition to another equally vacuous slogan, namely, "loving the world." In our time the slogan "using the world" has been understood to represent the nihilistic, world-hating, life-denying, ascetical, and metaphysical attitude of the pre-modern other, against which the slogan "loving the world" has been granted all the legitimacy and value ascribed to what is *not* so nihilistic. In other words, ironically enough, the slogan of "loving the world" gains its meaning in an act of what Nietzsche would call "nay-saying," an activity of externalizing and denouncing what one does not want. We must move to a more complex analysis of what it is that these two slogans in fact obscure.

That is what I want to do here. I want to make readers uncomfortable with the simple dichotomy of "loving the world" versus "using the world" — in part because what passes under each slogan incorporates important elements of the attitude that it imputes to the other. Concerns about the corrosive effects of religious attitudes toward the world have for too long been allowed to describe the situation in ways that so tilt the debate in their favor that the debate has become empty. We can recover some of the complexities at issue in this area of inquiry by offering a robust alternative to the usual appeals to this-worldly sociopolitical, economic, and ecological improvements. There's more to be said for what passes under the title of "otherworldliness" than people typically recognize. If we can articulate what that is, we'll have advanced the debate beyond the ritual recitations of difference so common today.

Doing this involves offering a far more theological reading of our situation than is common today. One of the members of our group, Deirdre McCloskey, has argued for a focus on the "bourgeois virtues" as central to our lives, and particularly for the importance of prudence in contrast to earlier emphases on pagan courage and Christian love.[2] But even so this-worldly a morality as one built upon a formation of bourgeois prudence hides theological valences; for, as the philosopher Peter Geach has argued, "'prudence' and 'providence' are in origin two forms of the same Latin word; etymologies are

2. In this volume, pp. 312-36.

often misleading, this one is not."[3] This essay attempts to detail the contributions of some classical Christian theological insights for a deeper understanding of the relation between *prudentia* and *providentia,* and unpacks some of the implications of that relation for understanding true prudence. True prudence is a deeply theologically informed approach to valuing and inhabiting our existence, one that much of the Christian tradition, following Augustine, calls "using the world." Against criticisms of this approach — an approach I shall call the "use paradigm" — for advancing an instrumentalizing mentality toward the world, I will argue that much insight is packed into this proposal, to which we would be wise to attend.

I'll begin by sketching an interpretation of our current situation in opposition to the dominant, broadly "Weberian" account. I'll argue, contra Weber, that our situation is not due to an ascetic attitude toward the world but to an attitude that expects too much of it, that expects salvation to be immanent in the world — an attitude, in brief, that seeks to *enjoy* the world. Then I'll argue that, in this context, the "use paradigm" remains valuable insofar as it acknowledges that our ends transcend any worldly achievement, but are yet vectored by this world toward a transcendent God beyond, and I'll sketch some of the basic building blocks of the alternative practical program this "use paradigm" recommends. I will conclude by briefly discussing how this model illuminates current anxieties about "owning" ourselves, anxieties most visible in our thinking about death.

Modernity's Enjoyment of the World

Before we begin to trace the right understanding of the theological roots of prudence, we must uncover and exorcise a false picture of prudence's relation to theology. "Prudence" has often (and incorrectly) been thought to be rooted in theological motivations — from the thin-lipped prudence (hard to distinguish from moralism) of the Puritans, through the rather flaccid prudence (hard to distinguish from timidity) of George H. W. Bush. But this picture of prudence's theological vectors is a misleading one. It rests on three beliefs, about the present, the past, and the future. The belief about our present is

3. Peter Geach, *The Virtues* (Cambridge: Cambridge University Press, 1977), p. 70, and Deirdre McCloskey, "Bourgeois Virtue," *The American Scholar* (spring 1994): 177-91. For further examples of the turn to prudence in contemporary thought see Daniel Mark Nelson, *The Priority of Prudence: Virtue and Natural Law in Thomas Aquinas and the Implications for Modern Ethics* (University Park, Pa.: Pennsylvania State University Press, 1992), and Annette Baier, *Moral Prejudices* (Cambridge, Mass.: Harvard University Press, 1994).

that the modern world is thoroughly "rationalized," governed by rigorously capitalist, scientific, and materialistically reductionistic systems; "modernity" (including the contemporary, supposedly "postmodern" world) is about the mastery of the world by our technical reason, itself enabled by the "disenchantment" (negatively speaking) and "rationalization" (positively speaking) of the world. But there remain yet vestigial theological, and presumably anti-worldly, beliefs. The belief about our past is essentially a diagnosis of how we came to be so "disenchanted," as the ironic and unintended consequence of the "Protestant Ethic." This *Weltanschauung* oriented humans, via a program of "inner-worldly asceticism," toward "otherworldly" (and, though this is a further step in the argument, *anti*-worldly) ends. But this inner-worldly asceticism altered the social and material conditions of our existence so dramatically as to propel us into a state of worldly disenchantment. Hence the third belief, often expressed as a practical program for the future, claims that, given the assessment of our current condition and our history, the basic direction of our thought and lives should be toward further participation in the world, politically, culturally, and ecologically. Ours should be a project of ever-greater world-participation, a project of more fully loving the world, by more completely finding ourselves, and seeking out ends, in it.[4] The "revaluation of values" recommended by this program begins by locating fault for our current crises in our historical religious commitments, and particularly in that tradition of Christian thought that promotes an attitude which treats all "created" things as instruments to be employed to achieve our otherworldly salvation.[5]

I want to sketch a reading of modernity that destabilizes this account, for this picture of our situation is not only wrong but exactly backwards: The problem we face is not our persistent and pernicious captivity to an essen-

---

4. The shape this world-participation should take differs depending on what modern thinker is speaking: it can cash out in a more activist world-transformation, as promoted by Enlightenment thinkers such as Hans Blumenberg and Donna Haraway, or it can promote a more quietistic world-involvement, as with many ecologically minded thinkers.

5. See Anders Nygren, *Agape and Eros: A Study of the Christian Idea of Love* (New York: Harper and Row, 1969), pp. 449-563, esp. 539-43; Max Weber, *The Sociology of Religion*, trans. E. Fischer (London: Methuen, 1965), pp. 166-68; and Lynn White, "The Historic Roots of Our Ecological Crisis," *Science* 155 (10 March 1967): 1203-7. Another account, this one damning Augustine for his political implications, is offered by Quentin Skinner, in his *Foundations of Modern Political Thought*, vol. 1: *The Renaissance* (New York: Cambridge University Press, 1978), p. 50: "Augustine's view of political society had merely been ancillary to an eschatology in which the life of the pilgrim on earth had been seen as little more than a preparation for the life to come." As my use of the phrase "revaluation of values" is meant to suggest, Nietzsche is important here too, though I will not discuss him.

tially religious otherworldliness, but rather our abandonment of what we erroneously describe as such, and its replacement by an attitude that expects to find all our ends met by and in the material world. The modern world (insofar as it is "modern")[6] is not the consummation of the Christian religious vision, but its renunciation. Against accounts of modernity as primordially "ascetical" or "nihilistic," our problem is not that we *mistreat* (much less *retreat from*) the world, but that we try fundamentally to *enjoy* it.

The Enchantment of the World

I begin with one central myth of modernization, namely, Max Weber's account of *The Protestant Ethic and the Spirit of Capitalism*. The impress Weber's text has made on our minds is incalculable; and, much as Nietzsche's *The Genealogy of Morals* has been said by some to be "a kind of *Civitas Dei* written back to front," Weber's *Protestant Ethic* can be seen as a counter-text to Augustine's *Confessions*, offering a radically alternative interpretation of our current malaise. Because I will eventually want to defend the interpretation set forth in the *Confessions* and its allied literature, I begin by trying to rewrite, in turn, Weber's narrative.[7]

In essence, Weber's account is straightforward (which is part of its attractiveness): Modern European industrial civilization, with its bifurcation of reason and passion and its hegemonic control over all aspects of social life, has its roots in an understanding of work that first appeared among sixteenth- and seventeenth-century Puritans through the idea of the "calling." For these Puritans, worldly success was a sign of election, and so they anointed worldly economic activity with profound soteriological significance, making it an "ascetic" practice of self-denial; wealth was not to be

---

6. I mean the qualifier quite seriously. As Jeffrey Stout has recently put it, "No categories require more careful handling these days than *tradition* and *modernity*" (p. 49 in "Commitments and Traditions in the Study of Religious Ethics," *The Journal of Religious Ethics* 25, no. 3, 25th Anniversary Supplement [1998]: 23-56). Furthermore, as Bruno Latour has forcefully put it, it is an open question whether we have ever been "modern" at all; see his *We Have Never Been Modern*, trans. Catherine Porter (Cambridge, Mass.: Harvard University Press, 1993). And cf. Bernard Yack, *The Fetishism of Modernities: Epochal Self-Consciousness in Contemporary Social and Political Thought* (Notre Dame, Ind.: University of Notre Dame Press, 1997).

7. John Milbank, *Theology and Social Theory: Beyond Secular Reason* (Oxford: Blackwell, 1990), p. 389. (I use "myth" here in a non-derogatory way.) I am not the first to undertake this engagement with Weber; Charles Taylor's *Sources of the Self: The Making of Modern Identity* (Cambridge, Mass.: Harvard University Press, 1989) does this as well, though it is not explicit about the engagement. It should be clear how much my argument owes to Taylor's book.

spent but saved. As time went on, and this attitude grew more pervasive with the economic success of its adherents, the theological motivation became superfluous and finally atrophied, a vestigial element of a self-sustaining system. Ironically, however, while the theological rationale was lost, the intensity of motivation remained, entrapping us in an "iron cage." Thus, we have achieved worldly success beyond the Puritans' wildest imaginings, and yet in the process have become, in Weber's famous phrase, "specialists without spirit, sensualists without heart." The irony at the heart of this vision is palpable: the deep cause for modernity's centuries-long "disenchantment" is the profoundly (if more recently covertly) psychological-theological motive to *use* the world to "signify" our salvation.[8]

Weber's narrative is quite compelling, and it seems fair to say that it retains a good deal of its force, even after a half-century and more of critical examination. But criticisms have qualified it in at least two important ways. First of all, it is not as clear as Weber suggests that theological motives led to unbridled capitalism; in seventeenth-century New England — surely a close approximation to the ideal type of a society governed by the Protestant ethic — religious reasons were actually often restraints, instrumental in *curbing* the scope of capitalist work practices. Second, Weber's account focuses on the Anglo-Saxon and Germanic (and Reformation) roots of modernity, to the detriment of other sources, especially the Italian Renaissance. But histo-

---

8. The Weber passage is from Max Weber, *The Protestant Ethic and the Spirit of Capitalism*, trans. Talcott Parsons (New York: Charles Scribner's Sons, 1958), p. 182. Weber's work has of course spawned much controversy; see Robert W. Green, ed., *Protestantism, Capitalism, and Social Science: The Weber Thesis Controversy*, 2nd ed. (Lexington, Mass.: D. C. Heath and Company, 1973); Winthrop S. Hudson, "The Weber Thesis Reexamined," *Church History* 30 (1961): 88-99; and Richard van Dülmen, "Protestantism and Capitalism: Weber's Thesis in Light of Recent Social History," *Telos* 78 (winter 1988-89): 71-80. For an interesting approach to Weber's thesis, one rooting it in Weber's life, see Arthur Mitzman, *The Iron Cage: An Historical Interpretation of Max Weber* (New York: Alfred A. Knopf, 1970).

I do not mean to suggest that, for Weber, "disenchantment" refers centrally to the loss of religious belief and the evacuation of mythology and belief in magic from our thought-worlds. Weber does not mean "disenchantment" merely or even centrally in this negative ideational sense. Rather, "disenchantment" refers positively to the fact that as society has become complex and social roles have become specialized, individuals have a harder time speaking about or effectively addressing "society" as a whole. This is seen not merely, or even (for Weber) most importantly, in the growing irrelevance to actual life of religious belief; for example, it is the root problem of ordering social life and generating political power, for while premodern societies could operate with an authority possessing a general "charisma," modern societies, insofar as they are modern, operate with highly bureaucratized "rationalities" that must be addressed individually, and that are essentially immune to the charms of charismatic individuals.

rians have argued that it was the Renaissance that introduced the rudiments of capitalism and consumerism into Europe — especially in the form of the increased production and consumption of "worldly goods." This account, highlighting an infinite number of small causes — mundane matters of trade routes, population growth (and urbanization), and new forms of reasoning and social organization such as double-entry bookkeeping and the corporation — lacks the grand tragic irony of Weber's narrative. But its dramatic flatness should not count against it.[9]

If we take seriously these critical emendations to Weber's account, a quite different narrative of the rise of modern industrial society emerges. Many of the rationalized capitalist practices that defined Puritan consciousness for Weber actually *preceded* the Puritans. And others developed simultaneously with the Puritans, though independently of them; thus political theorists have argued that the turn to markets served as a stabilizing device for early modern states.[10] (This is not, of course, to deny the Puritans' importance; but Augustinians will see Weber's locating of "worldly love" in the sixteenth and seventeenth centuries A.D. as a bit late in the game.) What led to the development of modern capitalist society was not a heretofore absent desire for things of this world, introduced by misguided theological reasoning,

---

9. On seventeenth-century New England, see Stephen Innes, *Creating the Commonwealth: The Economic Culture of Puritan New England* (New York: W. W. Norton, 1995), esp. chap. 3, "The Protestant Ethic and the Culture of Discipline"; on the Renaissance, see Lisa Jardine, *Worldly Goods: A New History of the Renaissance* (London: Macmillan, 1996). (It is noteworthy that Weber's *Protestant Ethic* contains exactly one reference to the influence of the Renaissance on Puritan thought, in which he notes the importance of Renaissance thought to forming the mental furniture, if not the theological assumptions, of the Puritan thinkers [p. 168]. He admits this influence only to go on to insist that Puritans were deeply opposed to the place of worldly joy and delight in Renaissance thinking. One might wonder whether our world is better described more as the unintended and ironic consequence of the Puritans' project, or more as the intended aim of the Renaissance.) For an argument that Weber *wrongly* locates the origins of "disenchantment" in the seventeenth century, whereas they are actually located in the Middle Ages, see Brian Stock, *Listening for the Text: On the Uses of the Past* (Baltimore: Johns Hopkins University Press, 1990), esp. pp. 116-39. For one compelling critique of the culturally specific picture implied by Weber's account, see Arjun Appadurai, *Modernity at Large: Cultural Implications of Globalization* (Minneapolis: University of Minnesota Press, 1996).

10. See Albert O. Hirschman, *The Passions and the Interests: Political Arguments for Capitalism before Its Triumph* (Princeton, N.J.: Princeton University Press, 1977), esp. pp. 129ff.; Hirschman sees capitalism as not just the ironically unintended consequence of a desperate search for individual salvation, but also as the result of "an equally desperate search for a way of *avoiding society's ruin*" (p. 130). For a general account of the origins of this "economic ideology," see Louis Dumont, *From Mandeville to Marx: The Genesis and Triumph of Economic Ideology* (Chicago: University of Chicago Press, 1977).

but rather a complex set of material practices, which enabled that desire to be fed (I do not say "met") with ever-increasing numbers of objects.

The effect of this increasing attention to meeting worldly desire — this increasing turn to the world — was anything but the "disenchantment" of the world. On the contrary, it infused the world with ever-greater value, and increasingly focused human desire on worldly goods. Far from leading to the disenchantment of the world, then, modern industrial society actually led to the world's ever-deepening enchantment. This shift was reinforced by capitalism's need to sustain a market for its products, which forced merchants and firms to excite desires for their goods, and thereby (if at times only inadvertently) fostered further desires and persons' proclivities to want more and different things.[11] Hence, people's desires increasingly focused upon material goods. However inadvertent, the effect of this was (and remains) to fix peoples' attention more and more securely upon worldly goods, and thereby to cause them to pay less and less attention to goals that cannot be described in terms of the consumption of worldly commodities. This "disenchantment" attempts to bend our longings back into the world, and so distorts them. The result is a situation in which we still have "theological" longings but must affix them to inevitably (and pathetically, not tragically) disappointing ends — namely, things of the world. The world becomes increasingly the locus of all our attention, and hence of all our valuing.

Desire, Excess, and Waste

The effects of this are manifold. The whole attitude toward time that we take is moving away from living in time as exclusively a matter of *waiting,* and toward living in time as a matter of industrious exploitation of time, of *making* time. And these psychological changes have resulted in large-scale sociological transformations. We meet our desires by overspending, and this overspending is supported by an increasingly complex latticework of debt on which our purchases rely, and which increasingly govern our economic concerns. This exacerbates the experience of the increasing compression of space-time, a perpetual shrinkage of our world, a closing-in of reality around us, even as we work ever more frantically at our lives. Psychologically speak-

11. Note that I am not arguing that the rapacity of our desires is due in any essential way to some bugaboo called "modern capitalism." Instead I am arguing that these rapacious desires pre-existed modern capitalism, and indeed are pervasive throughout human existence. The latter claim is properly Augustinian; the former, Marxist. For one formulation of it, see David Harvey, *The Condition of Postmodernity* (Oxford: Blackwell, 1990).

ing, we increasingly lack any way of conceiving of nonworking time, rest time, as anything but *wasted* time. We experience an increasingly rapid reduction in our "time off"; furthermore, this seems related to patterns of overspending and to the movement of our social center of gravity, our existential "home," from the home into the workplace itself. Sociologically, we increasingly live in a world of "total work," which, in the rare moments in which it reflects on itself, pictures the human good wholly in terms of being able to work, to occupy some space in the economic food chain. And the effect of this world of total work, of ever more production and consumption, on our environment, both natural and social, is disastrous: our attempts to satiate our excessive desires within the world transforms our excess longings into homogeneous *waste*, "goods" we turn into refuse when we realize that they do not satiate our needs. And this waste, and the ecological degradation that goes along with it, is the ultimate product of the consumer society, its greatest achievement.[12]

12. On the contrast between action and waiting see Stanley Cavell, "Ending the Waiting Game: A Reading of Beckett's *Endgame*," in his *Must We Mean What We Say? A Book of Essays* (New York: Cambridge University Press, 1969), pp. 115-62, and the work of Karl Barth, e.g., *Action in Waiting* (Rifton, N.Y.: Plough, 1969). The patience Barth requires is equally in danger of being lost; for a useful meditation on what "patience" is, see David Baily Harned, *Patience: How We Wait upon the World* (Cambridge, Mass.: Cowley, 1997). Needless to say, waiting, and the patience it relies upon, must also use hope, another phenomenon increasingly difficult to understand.

On the economic mania of contemporary culture, see Juliet Schor, *The Overworked American* (New York: Basic, 1992), and *The Overspent American* (New York: Basic, 1997); Arlie Russell Hochschild, *The Time Bind: When Work Becomes Home and Home Becomes Work* (New York: Metropolitan, 1997); and Josef Pieper, *Leisure the Basis of Culture*, trans. Gerald Malsbary (South Bend, Ind.: St. Augustine's, 1998). (For support of Schor's connection between overspending and increasing work, see David George, "Working Longer Hours: Pressure from the Boss or Pressure from the Marketers?" *Review of Social Economy* 55, no. 1 [spring 1997]: 33-65.) As Hannah Arendt argues, the very concept of "work," understood as "labor," is itself the result of a mongrelization of various interpretations of the human condition, and reflects our inability to imagine the fine-grained distinctions that are ideally definitive of these activities. See *The Human Condition* (Chicago: University of Chicago Press, 1958).

On the connection between consumer society and waste, see Jean Baudrillard, "Consumer Society," in *Selected Writings*, ed. Mark Poster (Cambridge: Polity, 1988), pp. 29-56, at pp. 34-35: "Everything is finally *digested* and reduced to the same homogeneous fecal matter (this occurs, of course, precisely under the sign of the disappearance of 'liquid' currency, the still too visible symbol of the *real* excretion *[fecalité]* of real life, and of the economic and social contradictions that previously haunted it). All that is past (passed): a *controlled*, lubricated, and *consumed* excretion *[fecalité]* is henceforth transferred into things, everywhere diffused in the indistinguishability of things and of social relations." This essay abridges Baudrillard's book *La Société de consommation* (Paris: Gallimard, 1970), which is translated into English in toto as Jean Baudrillard, *The Consumer Society: Myths and Structures* (London: Sage, 1998).

But the material consequences of our loving the world are not the only important ones; the impact of this attitude on our self-understanding is significant as well. Psychologically, we increasingly feel an abiding dissatisfaction, brought on by unmet desire, the psychological analogue to manufactured obsolescence. As we increasingly desire things, we increasingly focus our attention on satisfying our desires, and this shift in focus inevitably tends toward pervading all of our dealings with other people. This infinite desire comes to govern more and more of our handling of the world, leading to a generalized attitude of *consumption* toward the world and those within it. But this consumption is in fact another form of alienation, the realization that no matter how much we consume we will always want more. Jean Baudrillard puts it well:

> The acquisition of objects is *without an object.* . . . Consumer behavior, which appears to be focused and directed at the object and at pleasure, in fact, responds to quite different objectives: the metaphoric or displaced expression of desire, and the production of a code of social values through the use of differentiating signs. That which is determinant is not the function of individual interest within a corpus of objects, but rather the specifically social function of exchange, communication and distribution of values within a corpus of signs. . . . [Hence] consumption is defined as *exclusive of pleasure.* As a social logic, the system of consumption is established on the basis of the denial of pleasure. Pleasure no longer appears as an objective, as a rational end, but as the individual rationalization of a process whose objectives lie elsewhere. Pleasure would define consumption *for itself,* as autonomous and final. But consumption is never thus. Although we experience pleasure for ourselves, when we consume we never do it on our own (the isolated consumer is the carefully maintained illusion of the *ideological* discourse on consumption). Consumers are mutually implicated, despite themselves, in a general system of exchange and in the production of coded values.[13]

13. Baudrillard, "Consumer Society," p. 46. As Alasdair MacIntyre has been noting for several decades, *pleonexia* is the essence of this project; there is no "enough" in this account. See his *After Virtue,* 2nd ed. (Notre Dame, Ind.: University of Notre Dame Press, 1984), p. 137, and p. 227: pleonexia is "now the driving force of modern productive work." See also Lendol Calder, *Financing the American Dream: A Cultural History of Consumer Credit* (Princeton, N.J.: Princeton University Press, 1999), e.g., pp. 302-3: consumer debt has led people "to think of themselves as workers more than as consumers; and to consider their consumption more as a form of satisfying production — production of identity, production of well-being, production of meaning — than of wasteful destruction. . . . What Americans did on the installment plan was to transform consumer culture into a suitable province for more work." Calder seems to think that this

This focus on consumption reflects our fear of being unable to become the kinds of moral agents that past thinkers have suggested we should be; on this model, we are pictured as fountains of spontaneous power, yes, but the power "precedes" the "us" that we experience as ourselves, and we see ourselves as ravenous collections of wants. This interpersonal alteration inevitably becomes *intra*personal; we come increasingly to resemble what Harry Frankfurt calls "wantons," creatures who are driven by a set of unquestioned (and unquestionable) desires — not so much agents as epiphenomenal consequences of those more ontologically basic "wants." But as Mark Platts points out, these wants turn out to be not simply tyrannical but banal, for understanding our selves as captive to these wants "can be the end for a reflective being like us by being the beginning of a life that is empty, brutish, and long."[14]

In sum, then, against Weber's account, it is not an "innerworldly asceticism" spun wildly out of control, but modernity's insatiable desire for material things upon which blame for our situation must be laid. Seeing our situation in this way brings into focus a whole range of phenomena that otherwise go unarticulated in the dominant Weberian narrative. The increasing capacity of modernity to produce consumer goods has led to a deepening addiction to titillation in the psyches of modern consumers, which has in turn more tightly focused human activities around the pursuit of material goods, both directly — by fostering a deepening consumerist attitude about the world — and indirectly — by altering our moral self-understandings in certain significant ways. And the dominant model fails to explain why this has happened, why we have become the most *pleonectic* economy in the world while our subjective happiness is no greater now than it has been in the past. In part it fails to explain this because it is blind to the problem, because it takes demand (or "growth") to be *in se* a good thing, and cannot see any other sort of demand apart from the satisfaction of (typically punctual) desires; it cannot, that is, think outside of the economic paradigm. But it is clear that there are many concerns that cannot be framed from

---

transformation of bare consumption into "work" makes consumer culture slightly more approvable. I disagree. See also Robert H. Frank, *Luxury Fever: Why Money Fails to Satisfy in an Era of Excess* (New York: Free Press, 1999). (I discuss the exclusion of pleasure in consumer society under "Use, Enjoyment, and Play" below, in terms of our inability rightly to understand or inhabit the *joy* that is one central energy of the Christian gospel.)

14. See Mark Platts, "Moral Reality and the End of Desire," in *Reference, Truth, and Reality: Essays on the Philosophy of Language*, ed. Mark Platts (London: Routledge and Kegan Paul, 1980), pp. 69-82, at p. 80. For more on moral psychology, see my article "Agency, Nature, Transcendence, and Moralism: Recent Work in Moral Psychology," *The Journal of Religious Ethics* 28, no. 2 (June 2000): 297-328.

within that paradigm — among which are many of our most pressing difficulties.[15]

We do not lack for complaints about our situation, nor for descriptive critiques of our predicament; indeed, we have almost too many critiques. More appeals to "love of the world" will not help us in this most basic of problems; indeed, if this diagnosis is at all right, it can only make things worse. Our problem is that our focus on critique is just another attempt at such escapism, while we ignore the need to articulate an alternative positive vision. Weber's argument does not need to be condemned but replaced.

I nominate a broadly Augustinian Christian account as a helpful resource in this project. Augustinians take modernity to confirm one of their most basic premises, namely, that desire is a desire for *excess,* and that insofar as we attempt to *meet* our desires, we must expect that they will not be satisfied and that we will be, in this life, perpetual *peregrinatores,* wanderers from object to object, seeking ever new ways of excitation and leaving in our wake little but a cornucopia of "wasted" goods. And our current ecological depredations do suggest, for Augustinians, that such is happening: Our excessive desires are not met by the world's goods, but we expect them to be so met. We thus end up producing vast piles of refuse and waste, waste that we discard as

---

15. On the failure of economic frameworks, see Robert Kuttner, *Everything for Sale: The Virtues and Limits of Markets* (New York: Alfred A. Knopf, 1997).

A side note: People often attempt to dismiss criticisms of the contemporary world from the values of the past as nostalgic; typically the strategy is to ask whether we would rather live in our world or any past one. The assumption is that it is obviously better to live today. But this quick response obscures the shell game that the question actually is. There are two problems with it. First of all, insofar as I am *me* — with my values, my expectations, and my understanding of the world — there are certainly difficulties with transplanting me from now to the past; and this problem can be highlighted, and this dismissal at least partially subverted, by asking whether, by extension, I as *me* would want to live, say, three hundred years in the future. (I for one would not, I think.) Second, the question's arrogance lies in its obscuring of the dissimilarities of the objects of comparison. For we, the ones who ask and answer these questions, are Western, American academics, typically, and not at all typical of the ordinary human living today. The right comparison for us would be "Would you rather be an elite intellectual today or an elite intellectual then?" or, alternatively, "Would you rather be an average human living today or an average human living then?" The second formulation suggests a statistical answer, but we ought to consider their lives temporally; so the question should be whether a townsman in a city of Rus in, say, the thirteenth century, at the height of the Mongol raids, is better off than a townsman in the western Soviet Union in, say, 1939, just before World War II; or a peasant living today in the Punjab at the juncture of the world's two newest nuclear powers. The more realistic, in detail and in historical placement, the comparisons become, the less certain we are of an answer.

quickly as our fluctuating longings flit to the next thing desired. Driven by an incessant pressure to satisfy an ever-fluctuating desire, we can see that far from being helplessly "trapped" in Weber's "iron cage" (a quasi-gnostic image that suggests we are not to blame for our problems), a more appropriate image is one Augustine uses to describe his own suicide by libido, that of making of the self a *wasteland (regio egestasis)*.[16] So we ought to turn back to an Augustinian psychology, to see what we can make of it. Such is the topic I turn to next.

On Really Disenchanting the World

Let me be blunt: Really to disenchant the world, we need to get religion — or some sort of functional equivalent of religion. More cautiously, let me say that we need some system of thought, feeling, and understanding that makes available to us a way of organizing our desires in particular, and our lives more generally, so that we do not feel disappointed at the failure of worldly goods wholly to satisfy us. As I've said, this is unusual today, because many believe that religious commitments denigrate the world and at least indirectly support a consumerist mentality toward it. To defend my claim against these accusations, it will help to uncover some of the initial motives of one religious account and then sketch its implications for inhabiting the world. To do this I'll start with the pioneer of the "use paradigm," Augustine. Contrary to popular suspicions, Augustine's project is not world-denying but world-affirming; furthermore, the Augustinian proposal can help us resist the sort of reductionistically materialistic vision so powerful today, because it acknowledges that our ends transcend any worldly satisfaction, but are vectored by our loves in this world toward a transcendent God beyond.

Using Augustine's "Use"

Augustine uses the rhetoric of "use" to detail and promote the fundamental mode of comportment that he favors for our worldly existence. In order to use his account of use — to develop it for and deploy it in our own setting — I begin with a very brief summary of its initial formulation by Augustine himself and argue that he used it to go "against the grain" of the cultural

---

16. *Confessions*, II.10.

logics of his own day.[17] In doing this, I am not trying to repristinate Augustine but to use him — to contextualize his thought in order best to understand and most helpfully advance beyond his formulations. This will enable us to see more clearly how Augustine's example, imperfect as it is, still offers us much help today.

Augustine's account is quickly summarized: To enjoy something is to value it in itself, for itself; to use something is to value it for its instrumental value for another end. It is important to note that to use something does not mean *not* to love it, for some things that are to be used are also to be loved, albeit not all things.[18] The contrast between "enjoy" and "use" does not distinguish *what* should be loved from what should not be loved; it is rather a contrast in *how* one should value things. Augustine's anthropology makes it impossible not to think that we must orient ourselves to things in terms of our loves, in terms of how we value them. On this model, we are merely to use the material things of this world, and to enjoy only the wholly immaterial reality of God.

To many, this proposal seems dualistic, implying an ontological cleavage between this merely material world and the supremely spiritual next one, with nihilating consequences for the former. (Strong suggestions of such a dualism seem implicit in Augustine's famous contrasts between *amor mundi*

17. It is important to grasp a thinker's distinctiveness against her or his background, because theological discourse takes up the given intellectual commonplaces of the day and twists or disrupts them, rupturing their platitudinous placidities in order to open a space for the perpetually shocking, radically transforming, and liberating message of the *kerygma*. Methodologically, we ought to see Augustine as simultaneously both in his time and — precisely *as* he is "in his time" — in tension with it. See Kathryn Tanner, *Theories of Culture: A New Agenda for Theology* (Minneapolis: Augsburg Fortress, 1997). See also the last chapter of Tanner's *God and Creation in Christian Theology: Tyranny or Empowerment?* (Oxford: Basil Blackwell, 1988); the essays by and on Quentin Skinner collected in *Meaning and Context: Quentin Skinner and his Critics*, ed. James Tully (Cambridge: Cambridge University Press, 1988); and Nancy Struever, "Introduction: The Uses of the Present," in her *Theory As Practice: Ethical Inquiry in the Renaissance* (Chicago: University of Chicago Press, 1992).

18. *De doctrina Christiana* I.xxiii.22. This account is generally the one given *in nuce* in *De doctrina Christiana* I.iii.3–iv.4. There are interesting and complex questions about the status of other humans in this text; for a fascinating account of this, focusing on how hard Augustine found it to construct an adequate language within which to articulate the right relation to the neighbor in the world, see Oliver O'Donovan's fabulous "*Usus* and *Fruitio* in Augustine, *De doctrina Christiana* I," *Journal of Theological Studies*, n.s., vol. 33, pt. 2 (October 1982): 361-97. Also see John Burnaby, *Amor Dei: A Study in the Religion of St. Augustine* (London: Hodder and Stoughton, 1938), and "Amor in St. Augustine," in *The Philosophy and Theology of Anders Nygren*, ed. Charles W. Kegley (Carbondale, Ill.: Southern Illinois University Press, 1970), pp. 174-86. My account of Augustine is deeply informed by Burnaby's magnificent work.

and *amor Dei,* and also between the City of this world and the City of God.) But when contextualized, we can see that Augustine's proposal was meant to have quite the opposite effect; far from turning the Christian faith against the world, the "use paradigm" was his attempt to formulate, against the opposition of both the asceticism then popular in Christian circles and the puritanical conservativism prevalent among cultured pagans, a distinctly Christian rationale for appreciating and apprehending the world. It attempts to make intelligible how we can affirm the goodness of the created order as *created,* without treating it as the transcendental good. Augustine thus meant the "use paradigm" not to support ontological dualism but to undermine it: it was his central criticism of Manichaeanism that its commitment to dualism rendered it psychologically impracticable, morally paralyzing, and theologically impious.[19] Augustine held that the world is not really the problem — rather, the problem is with *us,* with our inordinate love of the world. For him, dualism is just a strategy for evading responsibility; he appealed to the "use paradigm" precisely to resist all escapisms, and to insist on the necessity of our engagement with the world, although, in our sinful state, it can only be a tragic, tortured engagement.

But Augustine's proposal could not be formulated in terms of a straightforward rejection of all things dualistic; it had to be expressed in conversation with his cultural setting. And this setting was, if not dualistic, at least far more focused on the sufferings attendant upon life in the world than it was affirmative of the goodness of the created order. Augustine worked in a culture experiencing a crisis of confidence in the "world." This crisis was built around the immediate presence of mortality and an overall feeling of social crisis in the face of the increasing urbanization of the Mediterranean world, exacerbated by the society's difficulties in sustaining its populace. Central to ordinary life was the presence of death: it was a world without refrigeration, where the presence of death constantly attended the most quotidian of tasks;[20] as Peter Brown remarks in *The Body and Society,* Augustine's was "a society more helplessly exposed to death than is even the most afflicted underdeveloped country in the modern world."[21] But the ever-present facts of corruption and mortality

19. Indeed, as Augustine recognized in his *Confessions,* a rigorously dualist and incommensurabilist account of evil does not allow for *any* conflict to take place between good and evil; see, e.g., his account of Nebridius's argument against the Manichees (in *Confessions* VII.ii).

20. I am grateful to William Schweiker for making this point to me.

21. Peter Brown, *The Body and Society: Men, Women, and Sexual Renunciation in Early Christianity* (New York: Columbia University Press, 1988), p. 6. See also his *Rise of Western Christendom: Triumph and Diversity, AD 200-1000* (Cambridge: Blackwell, 1996), esp. chap. 4, "*Virtuetes Sanctorum . . . Strages Gentium:* 'Deeds of Saints . . . Slaughter of Nations,'" pp. 54-

were not the only source of this cultural crisis, for the culture confronted a conceptual crisis brought on by external perils of a sort unknown to us: The *Imperium Romanum* was not just what we know as the Roman Empire; the *imperium* was more broadly the structures of rule, governance, and indeed order upon which that empire was built. Their political experience was not the experience of multiple and competing states, but of a conflict between *the* state and chaos: it was a world not so much with borders as with frontiers, and the barbarian hordes signaled to many not a change in political structure but the loss of order *tout court*. In the face of this chaos, the cultural authorities, and the world they epitomized, seemed not so much bankrupt as useless, their beauty "the fragile brilliance of glass," providing "a joy outweighed by the fear that it may be shattered in a moment."[22] Partly in response to this societal nervous breakdown, partly as a cause, and partly as a manifestation of it, new social structures were arising, structures built around ascetical practices that used the body to identify their adherents as not only different from, but directly opposed to, the status quo. The "retreat from the world" that marked much of Christian thought in this time was deeply political, if only by being *anti*-political (or, possibly, *counter*-political).[23] These structures affirmed the hu-

---

75, esp. pp. 54-57, for a vivid rendition of the deep apocalypticism that gripped Augustine's world.

Furthermore, in expressing this insistence on participating in the world, Augustine found himself vexed by his own choice of authorities; in his polished texts, meant for the Roman pagan "cultured despisers" of the Christian religion in his age, he "let in the hard male puritanism that Romans relished in their ancestors and in their favorite authors," which added "a peculiarly rigid note to Augustine's" theory of sexuality, and was largely responsible for the "darkened humanism" that is often understood as his sole gift to later generations. In contrast, Brown sees in Augustine's sermons (directed largely to the *rudes*) a voice "notably free of this icy tone" of thin-lipped Roman bodily *dominium*. See Brown, *The Body and Society*, pp. 426-27. On ancient Christian rhetoric in general, see Averil Cameron, *Christianity and the Rhetoric of Empire: The Development of Christian Discourse* (Berkeley: University of California Press, 1991). Cameron is not without the occasional howler, however; see p. 35 — Augustine's "concern for audience is amazingly modern." It is odd that Cameron thinks a concern for audience is restricted to the "moderns"; one would think that ancient rhetoricians might know something about it.

22. *De civitate Dei* iv.3 (p. 138 in Henry Bettenson's translation: *Concerning the City of God against the Pagans* [Harmondsworth: Penguin, 1972]).

23. See Ramsay MacMullen, *Enemies of the Roman Order: Treason, Unrest, and Alienation in the Empire* (Cambridge, Mass.: Harvard University Press, 1966), especially chap. 2, "Philosophers," pp. 46-94, esp. pp. 67-78, 70-71, and chap. 6, "The Outsiders," pp. 192-241, esp. pp. 209-13. It is important to note that at times asceticism could become a way of retaining the "old ways" when threatened by rapid change; thus James A. Francis, *Subversive Virtue: Asceticism and Authority in the Second-Century Pagan World* (University Park, Pa.: Pennsylvania State University Press, 1995), pp. 50-51: "Rather than reflecting any sort of radicalism, [Stoic] asceticism . . . was a vehicle for conforming to traditional standards of moral behavior."

man's place in the world to be one of quarantine, of fundamental avoidance, typically in some form of flight from the world, and it was within this setting, and to its inhabitants, that Augustine spoke.

Yet despite these larger cultural (and even perhaps ecclesial) tendencies, Augustine became "ever more deeply convinced that human beings had been created to embrace the material world."[24] His position grew like a pearl around his central, granular insight: We are part of the world, indeed we are in a way the vehicles of God's love for the world, and so we must participate in the world's redemption, just as we were the engines of its corruption. His proposal of the "use paradigm" was not meant rhetorically to restrict his contemporaries' excessively exuberant participation in the physical world; on the contrary, it was meant to urge them toward such participation, against their temptations at recoil from it, to flush them out of their safe caves (and, if not down from their ivory towers, off of their marble *styloi*) back out into the world. No straightforward dualism, neither the Manichees' evasion of responsibility nor the Pelagians' furiously juridical moralism, would do: The world cannot be simply avoided or easily managed. But Augustine meant also to *trouble* that involvement, to ensure that anyone's confidence in his or her own mode of participation would be troubled by questions about the character of that participation. Augustine knew that, were human persons given warrant to love things of the world *tout court*, the very character of their loves — their source and ultimate end in a transcendent and infinite good — would trap them in the finite, contingent, and all-too-mutable material realm.

The "use paradigm" should be understood in light of Augustine's philosophical theology, in particular the conceptual and metaphysical dialectic of God's transcendence and immanence, and the participatory ontology that this dialectic entails. For Augustine, God is "the cause which causes and is not caused" — the most real, indeed perfect, existence, *in which* all other realities, insofar as they exist, have their being.[25] But God is not captured within any such reality, but always transcends them. Thus God is simultaneously the absolutely transcendent source of all existence — because God is immune from the imperfections and mutations that mark all of our "this-worldly" existence

24. Brown, *The Body and Society*, p. 425. See Rowan Williams, "'Good for Nothing'? Augustine on Creation," *Augustinian Studies* 25 (1994): 9-24. Furthermore, it is important to realize that, despite his polemics with Pelagians, Augustine had an essentially positive view of sexuality. On this see especially Margaret E. Miles, *Augustine on the Body* (Missoula, Mont.: Scholars Press, 1979).

25. *De civitate Dei* v.9: "Causa itaque rerum, quae facit nec fit, Deus est." See further *De Genesi ad litteram* VIII.26: "Without any distance or measure of space, by His immanent and transcendent power He is interior to all things because they are all in Him."

CHARLES MATHEWES

— and yet (and yet *therefore*) the essentially immanent presence of all existence — because God is precisely the *life* and *truth* by which we participate in,
and know, existence.[26] (Indeed it is difficult to say how far Augustine was
even a soul/body dualist, in the sense of positing two entirely incommensura-
ble modes of existence; there are elements in his thought, in particular his
questions about the relationship between "spirit" and "flesh" in the inheritance of original sin, that would seem to pressure him to move toward acknowledging some form of interaction between soul and body.)[27] This dialectic of immanence and transcendence gives charges of dualism whatever
credence they possess, yet also forbids dualism any genuine place in an Augustinian schema. It underlies and connects the various terms Augustinians
use to describe sin, and gives that language its illuminative, analytic, and
practical power. It serves as the metaphysical basis for the connection between describing sin in the basically theological language of idolatry and in
the initially therapeutic language of disordered loves: Disordered loves are
centrally idolatrous, for they cause us to worship an idol of our own making
as God, and idolatry is necessarily a matter of disordered loves, for it calls us
to love and worship some partial end as the source of our true fulfillment. Because God is everywhere in creation, suffusing all things with being, to privilege some things within the world over against some others is implicitly to vi-
olate and defile God's order. God's immanence thus serves to remind us of
the enormous impiety of any ontological favoritism.[28] But if God is *in* all

26. God's creative action upon the world, and the action of created agents within it, thus operate on two different logical levels; they are, in Kathryn Tanner's formulation, "noncontrastive."
See Tanner's *God and Creation in Christian Theology,* esp. pp. 84-104; see also William Placher, *The
Domestication of Transcendence: How Modern Thinking about God Went Wrong* (Louisville: Westminster John Knox, 1996), esp. chap. 7, "Nearer Than We Are to Ourselves," pp. 111-27.

27. See the discussion in *De Genesi ad litteram,* bk. X, in which Augustine discusses the
generation of souls and the inheritance of original sin. He is torn between two theories
(Traducianism, which claims that souls are generated from an original soul, namely Adam's, in a
manner at least analogous to the generation of the body, and an alternate account, which argues
that all souls are created without mediation by God). In this discussion Augustine's supposed
pseudo-Neoplatonic dualism seems to conflict with centrally Christian exegetical and doctrinal
commitments, and Augustine himself is confessedly unsure which to affirm (cf. esp. X.21.37,
X.23.39). For an interesting and analogous argument with respect to Augustine's Pauline inheritance, see Paula Friedricksen, "Beyond the Body/Soul Dichotomy: Augustine's Answer to Mani,
Plotinus, and Juilan," in *Paul and the Legacies of Paul* (Dallas: Southern Methodist University
Press, 1990), pp. 227-51. See also Miles, *Augustine on the Body.*

28. I say "*ontological* favoritism" on purpose; to think that this means that we cannot
have "special attachments" to particular people is to miss the difference between the ontological
favoritism being decried here and the necessary psychological favoritism that attends our being
finite creatures.

things, God is not the *sum* of all things, and hence is not to be identified with creation as a whole; God's status as transcending all things ensures that to worship all things as God is to miss the point just as egregiously. It is dangerous to say that God is somewhere in particular, but it can be just as dangerous to say that God is everywhere, or nowhere. The dialectic of divine transcendence and divine immanence serves as a critical tool against all forms of idolatry, both those that implant God too immanently within the world and those that remove God too transcendently from it.[29]

The dialectic not only undergirds our conceptualization of sin; it equally, and perhaps more importantly, underlies and illuminates our conceptualization of love. Augustine's call for us not to shun the world, but to inhabit it in the right way, remains for him as a form of love. But what this love is, is not easily visible to us, in our current sinful state of grasping egoism. We should love the world *because* God loves it, and *in the way that* God loves it — which is a depth of love so great that God enters into the world in the person of the Son. But we must love the world *in God,* by participating in God's love of it. Indeed, as Augustine suggests in *De Trinitate* (especially Book VIII), it is especially by participating in God's love of the world (and in particular in God's love of the people of the world) that we come to know God. (This is because all love is God's love, and in a way all love just *is* God.) This is so because, for Augustine, we *always* act out of love, psychologically speaking; at no time are our dealings with anything done in a way that cannot be described as love. The role that the concept of "love" plays here reveals a (perhaps *the*) basic link between Augustine's ontology and his axiology. The world is love, because God is love. But this is not simply romantic praise of reality as a bunch of really good things; it has implications for the nature of reality itself. The universe we inhabit is not finally finite in the way that classical thinkers held, and our inhabitation of it is not finally a matter of knowing one's place, of fitting into a slot in the bureaucracy of natural categories. For

---

29. Augustine's concept of "world" involves all materiality, including human fabrications. See *Ten Homilies on the First Epistle of John,* trans. Rev. H. Browne, revised by Rev. Joseph H. Myers (in *A Select Library of the Nicene and Post-Nicene Fathers,* vol. 7: *St. Augustine: Homilies on the Gospel of John, Homilies on the First Epistle of John, Soliloquies,* ed. Philip Schaff [Grand Rapids: Eerdmans, 1991]), especially homily IV.4 and homily V.9 — the "world," used in a pejorative sense, includes in its reference those who love the world. Too often there is some sort of human/nature divide implied in ecology; see John Milbank, "Out of the Greenhouse," in his *The Word Made Strange: Theology, Language, Culture* (Oxford: Blackwell, 1997), pp. 257-67, and William Cronon, "The Trouble with Wilderness; or, Getting Back to the Wrong Nature," in *Uncommon Ground: Toward Reinventing Nature,* ed. William Cronon (New York: W. W. Norton, 1995), pp. 69-90.

Augustine, what changes things is the Christian concept of *grace:* Because everything is a gift, the problems we face are not about scarcity but about excess, about plenitudes, the excess of emotion and passion, of violence and desire, of goods and evils.[30] Augustine is not an axiological mercantilist: Love is not a scarce resource we parcel out parsimoniously, and ethics is not finally a zero-sum game, concerned with matters of *justice,* with the fair distribution of limited resources. Augustine's paradigm does not disallow love of the world; it simply attempts to tell us how best to inhabit that altogether appropriate love. And that is what we turn to next.

Practices of Using

While the language of Augustine's critiques of *amor mundi* and *amor sui* often tempts people to think that he locates the problem finally in the objects of our loves, Augustine treats each of these errors as formally identical manifestations of idolatry; this should make us see that the real problem with each form of sin is not the disparate objects but the sort of *amor* they manifest. The worry here is not metaphysical, but rather dispositional; the emphasis is not on love of the *world,* but rather on the *sort* of love we should have for the world — what kind of affective orientation we should have, what character our attachment to the world should be.[31] In reading his texts we must recognize their fundamentally practical and pastoral purposes.[32] The rhetoric of

30. This claim does not imply exclusivism, but simply particularism. There may be analogous ways, in other religious (and nonreligious) traditions, to think about excess, though I do not pursue them here. I aim to give a complex reading of what seems to me to be an oft-misunderstood account. That this is a legitimate project seems to me to be clear. For more on this matter see Charles T. Mathewes, "Pluralism, Otherness, and the Augustinian Tradition," in *Modern Theology* 14, no. 1 (January 1998): 83-112.

31. See Rowan Williams's discussion of the connections between Greek Orthodox understandings of *apatheia* and *ekstasis:* "dispassion is not a strategy of disengagement, but the condition for serious involvement with the world, unfettered from the fears and projections of the ego. No doubt this state remains an ideal goal, but it is an intelligible account of the direction in which a life might move. It may be that such an account of detachment might give some clues as to why it still matters to speak of God as passionless; let me refer you to the way in which some Eastern Christian writers, by the seventh century AD, had come virtually to identify *apatheia* with *ekstasis* and *kenosis,* outpouring and self-emptying love" (*Christianity and the Ideal of Detachment,* 1988 Frank Lake Memorial Lecture ([Oxford: Clinical Theology Association, 1989], p. 11).

32. See Pierre Hadot, *Philosophy As a Way of Life: Spiritual Exercises from Socrates to Foucault,* ed. Arnold I. Davidson, trans. Michael Chase (Oxford: Blackwell, 1995), and Ellen Charry, *By the Renewing of Your Minds: The Pastoral Function of Christian Doctrine* (New York: Oxford University Press, 1997).

Augustine's call for us to love God even to the contempt of the world is, in this light, a rhetorical aid to help us change our order of loves, grounded on his conviction that the most likely route to this conversion is to attack our excessive attraction to things of this world.[33] Augustine teaches practices, not centrally practices of discriminating or selecting among various objects of love, shunning some and worshiping others, but rather practices of transforming and harmonizing *all* of our various loves into an integral framework which will render our lives coherent and rightly ordered toward God. I'll discuss two facets of his recommendations here: how we should understand "possession" on this model, and how we should understand dispossession, or giving away. Both of these practices are intimately related, not only with each another but also with Augustine's broader theological picture, centered on the idea that the basic problem we face is one not of scarcity but rather of excess.

The first thing to note is that "using" objects does *not* mean not cherishing them in themselves. Indeed, one uses objects often by *treasuring* them, by respecting their autonomy from one's own particular interests; we respect the mundane goodness of things as they are separate from us (as they are in God). Here much work on aesthetic experience is helpful. The language of autonomy is at least as deeply at home in aesthetics as it is in ethics; as Iris Murdoch suggests, "virtue is *au fond* the same in the artist as in the good man in that it is a selfless attention to nature."[34] But in so treasuring objects — whether pieces of art, or beloved books, or what have you — one finds that their increased intrinsic value gives them more autonomy. They are, so to speak, less yours the more you love them. Value overflows your own subjective grasping of things, and inheres in the things themselves: You can love things so much, that is, that you *must* give them away, you must share them with others. Art is not art unless it is displayed; the object is made more valuable by being communicated to others. Material goods need not always operate within a zero-sum system, where the possession of a thing by one forbids its possession by others.[35]

33. A strategy employed elsewhere as well; see Calvin's *Institutes*, II.viii.54, on the role of "love of neighbor" as using our self-love against ourselves.

34. Iris Murdoch, *The Sovereignty of Good* (London: Routledge and Kegan Paul, 1970), p. 41; cf. pp. 86-91. But see Janet Martin Soskice, "Love and Attention" (in *Philosophy, Religion, and the Spiritual Life*, ed. Michael McGhee [New York: Cambridge University Press, 1992], pp. 59-72), which provides a useful and provocative challenge to this proposal.

35. Furthermore, ownership even of finite goods can be legitimate only insofar as we make *morally right use* of them; see D. J. MacQueen, "Saint Augustine's Concept of Property Ownership," *Recherches Augustiniennes* 8 (1972): 187-229, esp. pp. 221-26. Aquinas extends this in his discussion of how, in cases of extreme need, human right to property may be overridden by natural right to sustenance, and so what would ordinarily be theft (the stealing of apples from someone's orchard) is in fact nothing more than the right use of creation. See *Summa Theologiae*, II-II, q. 66, a. 7.

In this we have historical examples and intellectual pathfinders. Historically, we have the example of the Dutch Republic of the seventeenth century, which managed to be deeply religious and also deeply pleased by worldly goods. This was not accomplished without a good deal of anxiety on the part of the Burghers, but, given our sinful dispositions, such anxieties are probably morally quite helpful. Their love of material goods was their way to love the ordinary, to anchor themselves in extra-subjective realities, without losing touch with their own psychic selves (precisely because those selves found their pleasure in encountering what was *outside* of themselves). As the Polish poet Zbigniew Herbert (himself a witness, and victim, of an altogether different sort of materialism) suggests, the value of this bourgeois materialism is that it can support a democratic empiricism that resists the tyrannical tendencies of the human ego, unmoored from involvement or interest in the world it inhabits.[36]

In loving things in this way — a way that, as we saw, entails investing them with a certain degree of autonomy — one is already moving toward understanding how we might undertake various practices of *giving*. There is good and interesting historical work on how the Christian practice of *caritas* or charity differed from earlier Roman practices of gift-giving and especially euergetism, the practice that the Roman rich indulged in of giving elaborate parties for the poor. Most centrally, the difference was in the presence of the giver in the gift; whereas euergetism was a form of social capital for the Roman upper class — a way of simultaneously showing their magnanimity and ensuring that the poor would not hate them (not actively, anyway) — and thus was necessarily tied to *naming* or *knowing* the giver, for Christians charity was exemplified in (and idealized as) *anonymous* giving, a giving whose aim was realized not in the response of recipients or one's peers, but rather in the giving (which was always a sharing) itself.[37]

---

36. Zbigniew Herbert, *Still Life with a Bridle,* trans. John and Bogdana Carpenter (New York: Ecco, 1991). Cf. Simon Schama, *The Embarrassment of Riches: An Interpretation of Dutch Culture in the Golden Age* (Berkeley: University of California Press, 1988). See also Hannah Arendt, *The Human Condition,* "The Thing-Character of the World," pp. 93-96. I say *can;* note Herbert's account of "tulipomania" for the perennial perils of such materialisms.

37. Paul Veyne, *Bread and Circuses,* abridged and introduced by Oswyn Murray, trans. Brian Pearce (London: Penguin, 1990), pp. 19-34, esp. p. 26; see also Peter Brown, *Power and Persuasion in Late Antiquity: Towards a Christian Empire* (Madison, Wis.: University of Wisconsin Press, 1992), esp. pp. 89-91, 96, on the rivalry between the practice of euergetism and the charity of the churches as to how to handle urban masses. Compare *De civitate Dei* II.20, V.15. For the "imaginative structures" of grace and forgiveness that ultimately supported it, see Brown, *The Rise of Western Christendom,* pp. 30-31. For a general historical overview, see Scott Davis, "Philanthropy As a Virtue in Late Antiquity and the Middle Ages," in J. B.

In a curious way, this charity was less other-regarding than was euergetism, which sought the response of others' good opinion. But in a deeper way the reverse is the case: for the ultimate point of euergetism was the increased "glory" of the individual (where "glory" was really only a stand-in for some promise of security), while for Christians the point of *caritas* was the communal repetition and participation in God's gracious loving of creation (through the Trinity). You give because *you* wish to give, because you have been "given," and so you delight in giving; but the "yourself" whom you please would not be pleased were you to give *in order* to please yourself. This sort of prudential attitude imitates God's *ex nihilo* creation; it is a liturgical way of being-in-the-world, a form of *theurgy*, of active and practical participation in God's work, which is the world. It is in this way that we can see the connection between prudence and providence, *prudentia* and *providentia*, promised before. God-talk (theology) and God-work (theurgy) are two sides of the same coin; one who is prudent in the right sense loves the world not just as God loves it, but *in* God.[38]

But is such prudence really possible? All of this may sound attractive, and even plausible, as a way of managing our attachments to the world. But the image of control folded into the idea of "managing" is precisely what many find problematic about this account; any such attempt at managing our loves will undermine their profundity as *loves* — that is, as *pathe*, passions,

---

Schneewind, ed., *Giving: Western Ideas of Philanthropy* (Bloomington: Indiana University Press, 1996), pp. 1-23.

I am not claiming that one social practice (namely, euergetism) was simply replaced by another, wholly different, social practice (namely, charity), much as one component in a computer is removed from its slot and another slotted in; the transition took a long time, there are definite continuities between the two practices, and the reality of "almsgiving" and charity in the Christianizing Mediterranean was in no way innocent of desires for secular power or other interests. That the Christian practice was imperfectly manifest should neither surprise nor dismay anyone who has an operative concept of sin. All I am saying here is that the normative shape of these two practices, on the self-understanding of their practitioners, differed in significant and revealing ways.

38. On theurgy, see Gregory Shaw, *Theurgy and the Soul: The Neoplatonism of Iamblichus* (University Park, Pa.: Pennsylvania State University Press, 1995); for interestingly related proposals, see Catherine Pickstock, *After Writing: On the Liturgical Consummation of Philosophy* (Oxford: Blackwell, 1997), and William Schweiker, *Mimetic Reflections: A Study in Hermeneutics, Theology, and Ethics* (New York: Fordham University Press, 1990). The idea that an action's reality is in part determined by the self-understanding of the actor who undertakes it has a solid philosophical pedigree. As G. E. M. Anscombe puts it, action always takes place "under a description." See her *Intention* (Ithaca: Cornell University Press, 1958), §§ 23-26. I note that the crucifixion should inform our *imitatio Dei;* but I will not discuss that complex topic here.

things we suffer, things that we cannot command.[39] "Management" seems a way of cooling our passions until they are lukewarm at best. But this is impossible, critics argue: either the warmth of the attachments will decay ever further until they end in cold indifference, or (or perhaps alongside this) the attempt at management will fail to get at those passions which drive us most deeply and so contribute to our unknowing of ourselves. Either way, managing our passions seems problematic as a strategy for existence.

The Augustinian hears these concerns, but hears expressed in them a vision of the world profoundly inimical to the Augustinian account. The problem gestured at by these anxieties is a worry that "use" is identical to an overall grasping management similar to *autarkia* or, more extremely, *apatheia*. But the Augustinian position insists that use is always framed within a horizon of enjoyment. It is this that we have a hard time accepting — for us, work is primary and primordial: we must work in order to earn leisure, work in order to merit delight, work to deserve to enjoy; enjoyment is an endpoint to be attained, a vacation from the "real world," not a basis from which to work. The next section tries to suggest why such assumptions should be rejected, and what it would be like to reject them.

Use, Enjoyment, and Play

The real problem here, at the base of our resistance to the use proposal, is that we have no grasp of the real meaning, not of "use," but of joy, enjoyment, and happiness. We think that "joy" is simply *more:* More of what we want, an infinite supply of goods and pleasures. We operate within a framework governed wholly by a sense of purpose, means-ends reasoning that is focused on meeting our anxious, grasping needs. Our difficulty is, as Wendell Berry puts it, our "fundamentally ungenerous way of life," our captivity to a theology of endless (in several senses) acquisition. Our vocabulary is so infected with an instrumentalizing economic ideology that it affords us little leverage from within itself to imagine a world organized not around work, but instead around joy. It is difficult, if not altogether impossible, for us to acknowledge that a life lived in delight is anything but shallow. At times we seem to hope that we can admit it as a necessary part of relaxation (or "down time") under the misnomer of "frivolity"; but this gives away the game, and also gives away that what we mean by "joy" is not what joy should mean for us. Our age

---

39. As Martha Nussbaum argues in *The Therapy of Desire* (Princeton, N.J.: Princeton University Press, 1994).

makes it hard to sustain the belief that a desire to be happy is an appropriate desire by which to guide one's life. It is not only Kantians who have attacked eudaimonism as perilously egocentric. Others have suggested that an attitude of "the pursuit of happiness" is deeply inappropriate, given the extent of our century's crimes. For us there seems something scandalous, as Wendy Steiner has argued, in the idea of pleasure or beauty; as Theodor Adorno famously put it, "it is impossible to write poetry after Auschwitz."[40]

Given these challenges, it is not surprising that the Augustinian positions meet considerable resistance. For at the heart of the Augustinian proposal, as (one might argue) at the heart of the Christian vision itself, lies a

---

40. The Adorno quote is referenced in Lawrence Langer, *The Holocaust and the Literary Imagination* (New Haven: Yale University Press, 1975), p. 1; though I have been unable to locate this passage in Adorno's own writings. The Wendell Berry citation is from *What Are People For?* (San Francisco: North Point, 1990), p. 38; cf. his essay on "Economy and Pleasure," pp. 129-44. The literature on the problem of joy is rich; see Tibor Scitovsky, *The Joyless Economy: The Psychology of Human Satisfaction*, rev. ed. (New York: Oxford University Press, 1992), and his "How to Bring Joy into Economics," in his *Human Desire and Economic Satisfaction: Essays on the Frontiers of Economics* (New York: New York University Press, 1986), pp. 183-203. On beauty and pleasure see Wendy Steiner, *The Scandal of Pleasure: Art in an Age of Fundamentalism* (Chicago: The University of Chicago Press, 1995); Elaine Scarry, *On Beauty and Being Just* (Princeton, N.J.: Princeton University Press, 1999); Johan Huiziga, *Homo Ludens: A Study of the Play Element in Culture* (Boston: Beacon, 1955); and much of the writing of C. S. Lewis.

I disagree with Michael Welker's claim that our problem is rooted in our careless assumption that we have an "infinite" theological desire, which creates an infinite dissatisfaction with the world; this is a form of "worldliness" that this essay is meant to oppose. (For an account with some affinities to Welker, see Eugene Goodheart, *Desire and Its Discontents* [New York: Columbia University Press, 1991]; it offers good critique of worries about a "utopianism of desire," and a powerful expression of concerns about the ideology of desire becoming an external hegemonic discourse imposed on ourselves.) I think Welker's anxieties are rooted in a misconstrual of what I mean by "infinite desire," one that sees such a desire as an experience of sheer negativity, a nihilating longing that nullifies the value of all it touches, merely by being perpetually dissatisfied. I think this is a too-thin understanding of desire, one that allows the concept of foretaste (or another anticipatory concept) no purchase in it. It is, again, an understanding of desire tied into a modern attitude of impatience, refusing to wait, an attitude that demands all now. (My discussion relies on the intriguing difference between a "negative" and "positive sublime" as sketched out in John Milbank, "A Critique of the Theology of Right," in *The Word Made Strange*, pp. 7-35.) In contrast to Welker, I am claiming that the problem is that we have these desires which are "restless" outside of God, and that the claim that we must jettison this concept — the concept of a secularly restless desire — is (a) impossible to achieve (because that's in fact what we are), and (b) merely a further manifestation of the attempt to bend back into the world our theological longings. (For an interesting proposal to retain the idea of "restlessness" *within* the world, see Jonathan Lear's "Restlessness, Phantasy, and the Concept of Mind," in his *Open Minded: Working Out the Logic of the Soul* [Cambridge, Mass.: Harvard University Press, 1998], pp. 80-122.)

deep and abiding emphasis on joy and delight; eye has not seen, nor ear heard, the joys awaiting us in God's kingdom. Humans are created for the purpose of purposelessness, for delight — for God's delight, and for our own.[41] So it should come as no surprise that the Augustinian proposal has as its ultimate task the elaboration and defense of a worldview, an anthropology, and a theology all of which give pride of place to this emphasis on joy; the whole point of the "use paradigm," one might say, is to help us see how our real end in uselessness, how our half-faith in happiness, our partial intuitions that joy is our real home, can be validated and lived out. It is this general conviction, primordial to the Augustinian tradition, that most basically elicits suspicions and resistances today.

To overcome this resistance, we must understand the concept of joy, and to do this we must distinguish it from both frivolity and amusement. Frivolity is the attitude of the modern aesthete, whose genealogy stretches from Walter Pater and Bloomsbury to Richard Rorty and Derrida. While this aestheticism resists the purposefulness of life, it does so only in a way that reinforces it by retaining the endlessness of life, both as of infinite duration (in the literal sense of lacking any boundaries or structure) and as of lacking any overall goal. Frivolity is never quite able to forget its own inadequacy, and so ends up offering itself its own ironic knowingness as a consolation prize; but this consolation turns out to be cold comfort. The mode of being of the aesthete, then, is that of diversion and distraction, what Pascal called *divertissement*.[42] But this diversion is merely a form of boredom driven to desperation, attempting to escape its mode of life. While the need to escape is right, this diversion moves the aesthete in the wrong direction, as it were — further into the ephemeral and transient, a realm that they can never fully inhabit. Frivolity, thus, is anxious despair masquerading as action.

If frivolity revolves around wholly whimsical and superficial activity to distract people from their boredom, anxiety, and despair, amusement is the wholly passive and absorptive attitude cultivated in a society of media (and especially television) consumers. Amusement is equally ephemeral, equally transient, and equally reflects an essentially nihilistic attitude toward the world: constantly switching channels, the "amusee" seeks little but a momen-

41. Rowan Williams, "The Body's Grace," in *Our Selves, Our Souls and Bodies: Sexuality and the Household of God*, ed. Charles Hefling (Boston: Cowley, 1996).

42. On *divertissement*, see Pascal, *Pensées*, trans. with an introduction by A. J. Krailsheimer (New York: Penguin, 1966), esp. § 136 (Lafuma). Stanley Rosen, *Hermeneutics As Politics* (New York: Oxford University Press, 1987), esp. pp. 71-73, criticizes Derrida for frivolity, as opposed to Plato's "serious play." And see MacIntyre, *After Virtue*, pp. 24ff., for a discussion of the "aesthete" as a modern type.

tary distraction, one provided wholly by the flickering pictures, ever changing yet never satisfactory, on the screen. Baudrillard suggests this is driven by an oddly Kantian-deontological maxim to be happy:

> *Everything* must be tried: since man as consumer is haunted by the fear of "missing" something, any kind of pleasure. . . . It is no longer desire, nor even "taste" nor a specific preference which are at issue, but a generalized curiosity driven by a diffuse obsession, a *fun morality,* whose imperative is enjoyment and the complete exploitation of all the possibilities of being thrilled, experiencing pleasure, and being gratified.[43]

The passivity of amusement, merely camouflaged by the appearance of activity in watching, reveals not so much a desperate sense of endlessness to life as a refusal to begin it, a passive-aggressive refusal to accept connection to the world. If frivolity is our form of angst and despair, amusement is the contemporary manifestation of sloth.[44]

Joy differs from both amusement and frivolity as love does from despair and sloth. The aesthete's frivolity is finally self-referential; but the joyous soul roots its happiness elsewhere, in the love that is God. To seek amusement is ultimately to seek a way of avoiding time, and avoiding love, in favor of a form of ontological titillation; but joy plunges us into time and the world, without letting us think that the world can ever be an adequate locus of our delight. Joy does not seek satisfaction, equity, or indeed any form of *adequation* to the world. It does not seek "enough"; that is its point. Joy is al-

---

43. Baudrillard, "Consumer Society," pp. 48-49. Note that Baudrillard does not claim that no *actual* needs exist, but just that "consumption, as a concept specific to contemporary society, is not organized along these lines" (p. 47).

44. I have found the work of Neil Postman stimulating here; see especially his *Amusing Ourselves to Death: Public Discourse in the Age of Show Business* (New York: Penguin, 1985). See also Daniel Harris, "Quaintness," *Salmagundi,* no. 120 (fall 1998): 159-75, for a discussion of the phenomenon of "quaintness" as the impotent inverted mirror-image of consumerism. My discussion of sloth also has much overlap with the discussion of idleness in Christine Firer Hinze's essay.

For a stimulating and provocative defender of a position much like the one I am criticizing here, see Susan Sontag, "Notes on Camp," in her *Against Interpretation* (New York: Farrar, Strauss, and Giroux, 1966); esp. section 23: "In naive, or pure, Camp, the essential element is seriousness, a seriousness that fails. Of course, not all seriousness that fails can be redeemed as Camp. Only that which has the proper mixture of the exaggerated, the fantastic, the passionate, and the naive." See also section 24: "When something is just bad (rather than Camp), it's often because it is too mediocre in its ambition. The artist hasn't attempted to do anything really outlandish. ('It's just too much,' 'It's too fantastic,' 'It's not to be believed,' are standard phrases of Camp enthusiasm)."

ways already excessive, always already superabundant, and so is traduced by looking finally for a payoff or balance. To enjoy the world is to *not* expect it to meet our needs; it is to *play* with, by playing *in*, the world. Joy is a form of quite literally ecstatic play that moves the self ever more deeply into the rhythms or, as Augustine would say, the *ordo* of creation. In going "outside of oneself" in this playful ecstasy, one does not leave oneself behind, but rather one enters more fully into participation with the world. And we play with the world because God plays with it: In using the world we are enjoying it and loving it quite literally *in* the way that God loves it — we are participating in God's being-in-the-world.[45] In using the world we are loving it; and in loving the world we are becoming deified. To realize this is to realize that the "enjoyment" of God need not entail that the "use" of the world denigrates created things; rather, it consummates them.

Conclusion

Part of the difficulty with apprehending this vision is that, perhaps paradoxically, it still sounds so familiar to us: Its surface formulation — "using the world" — still seems intelligible to us, at least as what we do *not* want to endorse. But when we try to grasp its meaning, we realize that we have lost its content. It is essentially built around one basic metaphysical and theological premise, the premise of *gratuity*. Berry's suggestion that ours is a "fundamentally ungenerous way of life" is right. One route to overcoming this is realizing the gratuity of our lives. Creation is a gift, and the things in it are to be loved as gifts; we respond to gratuity with gratitude of our own. But even this gratitude is *not* finally our own: the use to which we put things is for our further participation in God's gratuitous loving of the world; so we use things in order to enjoy them, to participate in God's self-giving delight.[46]

45. See Hugo Rahner, *Man at Play*, trans. Brian Battershaw and Edward Quinn (New York: Herder and Herder, 1972), chap. 1, "The Playing of God." The idea of God delighting in, playing with, and enjoying the world suffuses the Bible; see Proverbs 8:30-31, in which "Wisdom" speaks: "I was beside him, like a master worker; and I was daily his delight, rejoicing before him always, rejoicing in his inhabited world and delighting in the human race." I am grateful to Patrick D. Miller for referring me to this passage. Also see David Klemm's discussion (in his essay) of the experience of grace as "most my own" and yet "not my own."

46. Thus, the basic problem humans confront is *excess*, not (as perhaps was the case with Aristotle and other classical theorists) *scarcity;* if grace does not abound, sin will. This explains, for Augustine, the Romans' desire for the infinite multiplication of gods, like the over-elaboration of a bad liar. For Augustine's critique of the rather promiscuous Roman pantheon, see *De civitate Dei* IV.8-29.

Alongside our ignorance, however, there is a deeper motive for our resistance to Augustine's program, one due to the matter of its proposal. The call to turn from wrong love of creation to right love of the Creator often meets with uncomprehending accusations of "dualism" and hostile resistance to the proposal as "life-denying." But Augustinians think such resistance serves merely to confirm the thesis in dispute, namely, that we humans remain too attached to the world, as is seen in our inability to conceive of any relationship to it between the extremes of total absorption or total renunciation. Our attachment to the world is so close to our hearts that at times it seems we would rather die than have it (and us) truly transformed.

But of course death is what is at issue here, in two ways. First, a conversion to right love of world, as Augustine construed it, can sound like a living death only to those who have not passed through it; to those who have undertaken it, it is no such thing, but rather conversion to true life, albeit imperfectly grasped. But second, and at least equally importantly, death is the root issue under debate. Those who call on us to love the world in all its finitude suggest that the world is the only good we seek. But our disappointments with the world serve to refute this thesis. For the fact is, all does change, all does pass away, all does die. This seems to be the final point on which such debates turn, and the Augustinian position looks strongest when one attends carefully to mortality.[47] Both I who write and you who read these words will pass away, decay; to live out our lives in blithe ignorance (or, more truthfully, desperate avoidance)[48] of this fact — or even to attempt to compartmentalize this truth, to put it in one part of our consciousness and quarantine it there — is our perennial temptation, from which no one is immune, and to which we all succumb from time to time. Hence not everyone really misunderstands what is at stake here: In the end, the issue of how to inhabit the world is not, for both Augustinians and their critics, merely a matter of an inadequate hermeneutic, to be handled by distinctions and conceptual finesse. There is a real difference between these positions, and we must choose.

Luther said that "man is more acted upon than acting," and this essay is essentially exegesis of that claim. There are two moments in which perhaps our passivity, our being "more acted upon than acting," is most apparent: birth and death. We did not ask for birth, and most of us do not ask to die. But our lives are lived between these two realities, and we must acknowledge

47. See Michael Ignatieff, *The Needs of Strangers: An Essay on Privacy, Solidarity, and the Politics of Being Human* (New York: Viking, 1985), p. 76, for a secular liberal appreciation of Augustine on this point.

48. See the discussion in Patrick Miller's essay in this volume on the connections between "ignoring" and "hiding ourselves" that he notes in Exodus.

them both. Our lives are ours to cherish and enact; but we can never presume to think that they are wholly ours, for they are in fact *given* to us. They will be taken away from us as well, at the hour of our death; but we should not despair to think that they are futile and folly, for our loves tell us otherwise. Thus we hang between birth and death, between presumption and despair, as on a cross. Rather than treat the world in a grasping manner, we would do better to love it as it is given, as a gift and not as our proper possession. We would do better — we would, indeed, be truly prudent — were we to remain alive to our death: not merely as a means of further treasuring the life we have now (though that is an important truth too often ignored) but also, and perhaps more importantly, as a means of giving our lives a form, so that, when it comes, we can meet our death, whatever that meeting entails, with grace.

Bibliographical Appendices

Consumerism and Materialism

Against the nostalgia of a long-gone age of economic virtue, see Lendol Calder, *Financing the American Dream: A Cultural History of Consumer Credit* (Princeton, N.J.: Princeton University Press, 1999), e.g., pp. 24-26. Consumer debt stood at a low point of 5.7 billion at the end of World War II (with credit restrictions), and it had risen to 1.266 trillion in July of 1998 (p. 291).

See also Richard Ohmann, *Selling Culture: Magazines, Markets, and Class at the Turn of the Century* (London: Verso, 1996), which offers a compelling though bleak picture of the role of magazines and their readers (especially in the period from 1890 to 1905) in dynamically creating the "mass culture" of the twentieth century. His insistence that the crucial determinants for our mass culture are the material conditions (and consumers' agency) of that period is helpful, but I should not want to miss the way that many of the important decisions were made well before that time for the culture as a whole.

For analyses of consumer society, see Eugene Linden, *Affluence and Discontent: The Anatomy of Consumer Societies* (New York: Viking, 1979); Ira Zepp, *The New Religious Image of Urban America: The Mall As Ceremonial Center* (Westminster Md.: Christian Classics, 1986); Stuart Ewen, *All Consuming Images: The Politics of Style in Contemporary Culture* (New York: Basic, 1988); and Marshall Berman, *All That Is Solid Melts into Air: The Experience of Modernity* (New York: Penguin, 1982), particularly pp. 74ff., regarding the "Faustian model of development." For a historical analysis of the rise of consumerism in eighteenth-century America, see Cary Carson, Ronald

Hoffman, and Peter J. Albert, eds., *Of Consuming Interests: The Style of Life in the Eighteenth Century* (Charlottesville, Va.: University Press of Virginia, 1994); this book argues that the origins of modern consumer society can be traced to a need for new ways to identify social distinction in an increasingly geographically mobile society, where one's physical movements can outrun one's reputation and status. See also William Leach, *Land of Desire: Merchants, Power, and the Rise of a New American Culture* (New York: Pantheon Books, 1993).

For a far more distorted picture, cf. James B. Twitchell, *Lead Us into Temptation: The Triumph of American Materialism* (New York: Columbia University Press, 1999), which is a rather extended, aggressive, and narcissistic rationalization (masquerading as celebration) for his purchase of a Miata when he neared age fifty (see pp. 274-83).

For an interesting discussion of the social, political, and economic changes happening in an increasingly globalizing world, see Saskia Sassen, *Losing Control? Sovereignty in an Age of Globalization* (New York: Columbia University Press, 1996), and Bill Maurer, "Forget Locke? From Proprietor to Risk-Bearer in New Logics of Finance" (in *Public Culture* 11, no. 2 [1999]: 47-67), which argues that a discourse of rights, deriving ultimately from Lockean property theory, is currently being replaced by a discourse of managed (and insured) risk.

Asceticism

The question of what is "asceticism" is a vexed one. I don't mean to defend the assumption here that "asceticism" is life-denying and world-destroying; indeed, my project is profoundly opposed to just this assumption. One deep aim of this essay, as with the essays of Margaret Mitchell and Christine Firer Hinze also included in this volume, is to redeem the Christian way of life as a legitimately world-valuing form of *askesis*. (This is not of course to claim that our proposals present a wholly unified front; differences should be apparent to the reader.)

For a discussion of the meanings that the term "asceticism" can take, see Vincent L. Wimbush and Richard Valantasis, eds., *Asceticism* (New York: Oxford University Press, 1995). Especially interesting are the essays by McGinn (on theory/practice), Dillon (on two trajectories toward the world in Plato's texts, one affirmative from Socrates, one negative from Plato himself, according to Dillon), and Cameron (on the role of asceticism in historical change at the end of antiquity). Valantasis's own essay, "A Theory of the Social Function of Asceticism," pp. 544-52, very interestingly shows how perilously inflated the concept of "asceticism" can become for scholars, by arguing that all forms of change are in some way "ascetical" (p. 548). See also Geoffrey Galt Harpham, *The Ascetic Imperative in Culture and Criticism* (Chicago: University of Chicago Press, 1987), for an equally global, and equally dubious, definition of asceticism.

For more historical work on Augustine's era, see Philip Rousseau, *Ascetics, Authority, and the Church in the Age of Jerome and Cassian* (New York: Oxford University Press, 1978), which is good on the transformation of asceticism from the East to the West (with Cassian), and in underscoring the way that we read back into the age rigid categories like "ascetic" and "bishop" — in fact all of these categories did exist, but they were in the midst of being worked out as to their definitive sense. See also David Brakke, *Athanasius and the Politics of Asceticism* (Oxford: Clarendon, 1995), which details how Athanasius constructed simultaneously a theoretical and theological account of monasticism and an ecclesio-political framework within which to capture it (see p. 12, n. 26). For a good picture of the political power of asceticism as exemplified in Late Antique Palestine, see John Binns, *Ascetics and Ambassadors of Christ: The Monasteries of Palestine 314-631* (Oxford: Clarendon, 1994). For an interesting comparison of John Chrysostom's relative rigorism and Augustine's relative laxism concerning their congregations, see Averil Cameron, *The Mediterranean World in Late Antiquity AD 395-600* (New York: Routledge, 1993), esp. p. 62. For a discussion of how bodily practices of asceticism were crucial in ways we do not yet fully recognize, see Theresa Shaw, *The Burden of the Flesh: Fasting and Sexuality in Early Christianity* (Minneapolis: Fortress, 1998), esp. chaps. 1 and 2. Cf. Peter Brown, *Authority and the Sacred: Aspects of the Christianization of the Roman World* (New York: Cambridge University Press, 1995), and especially his *Power and Persuasion in Late Antiquity: Towards a Christian Empire* (Madison, Wis.: University of Wisconsin Press, 1992). Chapter Three, "Poverty and Power," demonstrates that monastics were able to use what might be called "intellectual asceticism" as a form of power to counteract the brutal ideology of *dominium* and *imperium* supported by the pagan pedagogy of *paideia*. This was connected to the idea that Christian doctrine was universally apprehensible, and not simply the province of elites (pp. 73-75). Finally, see Brown's *Authority and the Sacred: Aspects of the Christianization of the Roman World* (New York: Cambridge University Press, 1995), pp. 77-78, for a moving description of the curious process whereby apparently radically anti-worldly monastics came to be seen, and to see themselves, as embracing the world, and thereby representing Christianity's loving creator God.

For a recent and very interesting post-Foucauldian analysis of how pleasure was understood in relation to power and control (both political control and self-control, though that distinction may be anachronistic here), see James Davidson, *Courtesans and Fishcakes: The Consuming Passions of Classical Athens* (New York: St. Martin's, 1998), esp. chap. 6, "Economies," and chap. 7, "Politics and Society."

Material Grace: The Paradox
of Property and Possession

David E. Klemm

Humans are constantly involved in the activities of acquiring, using, and exchanging property. But what does property *mean* to the people who acquire, use, and exchange it? By "property," I mean simply that which is one's own; consequently, that over which one has a right of disposal. In this essay, I propose to distinguish systematically among four kinds of property according to their different modes of being. A mode of being constitutes a fundamental way that humans relate to things in their world. When I speak about modes of being, I do not refer to different categories in which to sort out existing things. Rather, modes of being are different possibilities that any thing may assume in being what it is for individuals. Modes of being therefore ground the different meanings property may have for people.

I claim that human beings may give and receive property in the following modes of being: first as *commodity,* second as *gift,* third as *understanding,* and fourth as *material grace.* My purpose for drawing the ontological distinction among them is to show that acquiring, using, or exchanging property in the mode of being of material grace functions to overturn the common conception of the very nature of property and to reconstitute its meaning at a deeper level. My claim is that when property assumes the mode of being of grace, it takes on a paradoxical status relative to the common conception of property as that which is one's own. Property as material grace both is and is not one's property; it is a possession that is not one's possession. Moreover, I want to argue that the paradoxical experience of both owning and not owning one's own property precisely signifies the moment at which the divine depth of meaning and power breaks into the structure of acquiring, using, and exchanging property. Property as material grace is given and received as a living symbol of divinity.

In addition, I want to draw a further connection between such a possible conversion in thinking about the meaning of property and the real situation of violence that confronts us in our world as well as the opportunities for peace that we must seek. In that regard, I want to reflect on the changes in attitude and behavior that can follow from understanding the meaning of property as material grace. A systematic articulation of modes of being enables the mind to move sequentially from the surface level of commodity to the depth of property as material grace, a point that both signifies and makes present the being of God as the ultimate ground of all that is and is not. When such an in-breaking occurs, we undergo a conversion with important consequences, because it has the capacity to change our thinking about property in fundamental ways. In the light of grace, we can return to the everyday activities of understanding possibilities, giving gifts, and owning things with new eyes and a new attitude. I begin by orienting my reflections on property in the Platonic-Augustinian tradition of religious thought.[1]

Passions for Property

The concept of property has undergone a long and difficult development over the history of Western thought.[2] In some sense basic to most Western languages, property is what is proper to oneself or one's community; my property is what is my own. Individual claims to ownership, however, are always legitimized within the community. According to Plato, two principles found the human community (whether a state or household); both are variations on essential human finitude. First, there is the *principle of inadequacy or lack* — individual humans are not self-sufficient in a state of nature; we need the help of others in order to survive.[3] Second, there is the *principle of differentiation of talents* — all humans are equal in intrinsic value and dignity, but we each possess different abilities.[4] Hence humans band together into a republic, dividing and uniting their efforts to provide for the whole what each individual cannot provide for himself or herself. Already, at the very genesis of the

1. For a clear analysis of the Platonic-Augustinian tradition of religious philosophy in contrast to the Aristotelian-Thomistic one, see Paul Tillich, "The Two Types of Philosophy of Religion," in *Theology of Culture,* ed. Robert C. Kimball (London: Oxford University Press, 1959), pp. 10-29.
2. See Richard McKeon, "The Development of the Concept of Property in Political Philosophy: A Study of the Background of the Constitution," *Ethics* 48 (1937): 297-366.
3. Plato, *The Republic* 369b.
4. Plato, *The Republic* 370b.

state, the connection between property and violence appears. Lack of necessary materials for mutual flourishing in the community is a cause for war, and unequal property distribution is a cause for revolution.[5]

For Plato the essential question about property, subordinating all others, is this one: Which of the many goods that people desire and pursue are true goods, and which are mere appearances, and hence false goods? The typical Platonic answer to the question is that only knowledge as wisdom enables one to comprehend the differences between true and false goods. Hence pursuit of wisdom is the highest endeavor for an individual, and education is the highest responsibility for the community. For various reasons, however, few individuals and fewer communities can or will commit themselves to pursuit of the highest good. Most people strive for and defend their right to goods that flatter their sense of pride and increase their wealth, while renouncing the goods that would nourish the soul. To possess wisdom in this world is, therefore, both a blessing and a curse. It is a blessing to understand the true riches of life, but it is a curse to possess them; for knowledge of the Good entails recognition that it is better to suffer evil than to do evil, and all too often derision and persecution haunt the few wise and good people among us. Until all humans desire and pursue what is truly good, wise people will suffer violence from those who prefer pleasure and pride of ownership to a just mind, good will, and open heart. Such is the human plight.

St. Augustine's Christian theological thinking assigns the source of true and ultimate goods to the heavenly city of God, in distinction from the earthly city of humans. God gives to humans the very possibility of being, and to be is an ultimate good. Humans likewise produce goods — namely, the array of material and spiritual goods that are penultimate and less than divine, but are nonetheless real objects of desire within actual communities. Augustine asserts that the penultimate goods of this created world still reflect and participate in their uncreated divine source, which is also their ultimate goal. The desire that humans have for worldly possessions, however, is truly an expression of the desire that all creatures commonly have for their eternal creator. Nonetheless, under conditions of life in the earthly city, some human desires become distorted into concupiscence; rare is the love of goods that remains true to love of God as the final resting place of the heart's desire. So how can one distinguish between truth and falsehood in the realm of desire?

Augustine locates the criterion for distinguishing true from false loves according to the principle of proper use in relation to its end of enjoyment. The key distinction is between enjoying something *(frui)* for its own sake in

5. Plato, *Phaedo* 663, and *Republic* 464e; Aristotle, *Politics* II.7, 1266ff.

the sense of holding fast to it with an emotional attachment, and using something *(uti)* as a means to the end of obtaining what truly ought to be loved.[6] The former is the principle of a false love and a false sense of the Good; the latter is the principle of a true love for what is truly good in itself. In the nature of the case, humans are meant to enjoy God as the one "from whom, through whom, and in whom everything is," for God is the true object of the heart's desire.[7] Humans are meant to use worldly things for the purpose of enjoying God's eternal life. All created things are goods in themselves, because to be is to be good. But when humans enjoy worldly things for their own sake rather than use them to enjoy God's eternal life, their enjoyment becomes a form of abuse. Consequently their path toward true happiness is impaired.

At stake in this distinction between enjoying and using is the quality of desires or loves (motives) as well as the ends that people pursue. Augustine's principle is that one *is* as one *loves*.[8] The proper end of one's desire determines the morality of human actions. If I love money and the goods that I can enjoy with money for their own sake, then my love is distorted by being directed to the wrong end. I am improperly attached to worldly things. Such a distorted love can lead me only to frustration, anxiety, and unhappiness, because my being is disordered through my loving what ought not to be loved in itself, but rather ought to be used for a higher purpose. By contrast, if I assign the proper place to money and worldly goods as means by which both to enjoy and to share enjoyment of God's blessings, my love is rightly directed. I am consequently detached from worldly things without forsaking them. My love is no longer distorted, but is directed toward God as the one through whom comes true peace and happiness. In other words, for Augustine, the less I love money and worldly goods for their own sake, the more I am free to use them properly. Indeed, the greater is my claim to proper ownership in the moral sense. The more I love money and worldly goods for their own sake, the more I am enslaved by them and become miserable as a consequence. I cannot morally claim to own that which I do not use properly. Yet at the same time, my moral claim on property rests on my recognition that ultimately I do not own it. All of creation ultimately belongs to God, and as a creature endowed with reason I am assigned the task of using it well.

Augustine's image of two cities follows from the distinction between

---

6. Augustine, *On Christian Doctrine* 1.4.

7. Augustine, *On Christian Doctrine* 1.5.

8. See D. J. MacQueen, "St. Augustine's Concept of Property Ownership," *Récherches Augustiniennes* 7-8 (1971): 187-229, at 202.

rightly and wrongly ordered loves. The heavenly city, composed of the society of godly people, and the earthly city, composed of the society of ungodly people, are mutually exclusive human communities that nonetheless co-exist in time and space.[9] Citizens of God's city freely will to love God while forsaking ultimate ownership of worldly things. Citizens of the other city love worldly things that they claim or desire to own. Through the rightly ordered loves of God's society, universal peace arises. But through the distorted loves of the devil's society, a depraved social world arises. In it people strive against each other to acquire, own, and defend worldly goods. Violence ensues from self-serving loves. History is the battleground between these two competing cities. What lesson, then, should we draw from St. Augustine's thoughts on property in relation to love?

Augustine teaches us about what I call the paradox of property and possession. For Augustine possession of property has a paradoxical nature in the sense that those who correctly understand the meaning of property think about it in a way that runs contrary to the common opinion. Most people hold that owning property is an unqualified good, because property brings power, enjoyment, and prestige to its owner. They take delight in their possessions, become attached to the objects of their desire, and in this way are in fact possessed by them. A distorted desire for things of wealth and prestige replaces love of God. From such attachment to goods, various forms of evil result: attitudes of envy, greed, and enmity lead to scheming, treachery, feuds, unfounded lawsuits, thefts, forceful expropriation, injury, murder, and even war. By contrast, those who use their private property for the sake of enjoying God become detached from their goods and thereby possess them well.

At this point, I want to draw some distinctions that go beyond the Platonic-Augustinian legacy while continuing it. We need to understand the modes of being of the different kinds of property — commodity, gift, understanding, and material grace — in order to understand their true meaning. As we move through these four modes of being, we should recall that they are all susceptible to both proper and improper usage according to Augustine's criterion.

Property and Its Modes of Being

Modes of being are not classes of things but rather ways in which things come to be what they are. Modes of being are variations or species of "being." What

9. Augustine, *The City of God* 14.13.

is the being of a thing? Anything that is anything displays two fundamental elements: a conceptual or intellectual element and a perceptual or physical element. These two elements are basic: one cannot imagine a thing that altogether lacks either intelligible form or material content of some kind. The two elements are also irreducible to one another. The conceptual element is universal and hence predicable of many things; the perceptual element is particular and hence given to the senses or memory as a unique content within a determinate domain of space and time. In relating to a thing the mind conceives the conceptual element in accordance with its intelligible form. I conceive *what* it is. But at the same time, in relating to a thing the mind perceives the perceptual element in accordance with its material content. I perceive *that* it is. The being of a thing, however, neither is available within the lexicon of concepts under which we subsume particulars, nor appears to the senses or memory among the given contents of experience. The being of a thing is something else again.

By the being of a thing, I refer to what is between the universal and particular elements. The being of a thing is both the synthetic *connection* between a concept of the thing and a percept of the thing, and also the activity of *connecting* those two elements. As such, the being of a thing is the product of the imagination as it connects what I receive through the senses or memory with what I can conceive by the power of thought. So, whereas I conceive what a thing is, and I perceive that it is, I *understand* the being of a thing. That is, I understand *how* it is what it is, or I understand it *to be as* it is. Understanding in this sense is a dynamic, performative activity. Understanding is socially grounded and it can be changed. In understanding the being of anything, humans are all artists and poets and not merely passive receivers or abstract calculators. I create or construct the being of a thing by entering into a determinate relationship with the object. One and the same thing — for example, an automobile or a university degree — can therefore embody any number of modes of being at different times or for different people who relate to it. Modes of being are not exclusive or restrictive but are possibilities for understanding things in their being.[10]

10. For the idea of a mode of being deployed herein, I rely largely on the analysis of Martin Heidegger in *Being and Time*. To determine the modes of being of property, however, some modifications must be made to Heidegger's analysis. Heidegger articulated the modes of being of *Vorhandenheit, Zuhandenheit,* and *Wert,* on the basis of two principles. The first principle is that of subject-object separation, and the second principle is that of the direction of meaning from the subject to the object or vice versa. *Vorhandenheit* is the mode of being of things that are objectified for observation and scientific analysis; subject and object are maximally separated, and there is a stasis or equilibrium between them. *Zuhandenheit* is the mode of being of

DAVID E. KLEMM

Economic Property: Commodity

Property has the mode of being of a commodity when it is a valued entity —
a definite object with a price tag.[11] Things have the being of commodities
when they are acquired through monetary purchase or financial exchange
within a market system. The buyer wants something that the seller has (the
commodity), and the seller wants something that the buyer has (money). In
the market exchange through which the buyer acquires the commodity from
the seller, the operative concepts under which they come to agreement are a
definite description of the object to be exchanged along with its objective,
quantitative value.[12] A buyer wants to know what, exactly, she is purchasing
and what its objective value is. The operative percept is the image of the object as it appears to the senses. Usually the buyer wants to see and hold what
she is purchasing. Even with Internet or catalogue sales the deal is not complete until the commodity reaches the hands of the purchaser so that the image becomes real rather than merely virtual. Combine the image and description of a thing with a price, and you have a commodity. It is an object for sale.

With regard to the use of commodities, the intention of the buyer is to
enhance or improve life in certain predictable ways through the investment.
The thing purchased has a utility function, whether that utility is to transport
people from place to place or to promote the pride and honor of the owner.

---

tools that are an extension of the user's body; subject and object are minimally separated, and
there is a movement from the subject through the object, which is put to use as something at
hand. *Wert* is the mode of being of things that bespeak meaning or worth to someone; subject
and object are minimally separated, but the flow of meaning proceeds from the object to the
subject. *Dasein*, of course, is the mode of being human as both subject and object for oneself; it
is the mode of being that understands the meaning of being anything at all and thus is the condition of the possibility for all determinate modes of being. In his later writings, Heidegger
specifies other modes of being — such as the mode of being of a poetic word and of a work of
art — that will eventually concern us when we reflect on the idea of grace. See Martin
Heidegger, *Being and Time*, trans. John Macquarrie and Edward Robinson (New York and
Evanston: Harper and Row, 1962), pp. 74, 106.

11. The mode of being of a commodity appears at first blush to be analogous to
Heidegger's notion of *Vorhandenheit* — an object that is given to the analytical and objective
gaze as an entity. But there is a decisive difference between a commodity and an entity.
Heidegger's notion of entity does not include the element of desire that is ingredient in any
commodity acquisition. The buyer or seller of a commodity may put on an analytical gaze that
reduces the thing to an entity, but the gaze disguises a penetrating desire to own that is based on
the personal value of the commodity to the potential owner. No such personal value adheres to
Heidegger's notion of entity.

12. C. A. Gregory, *Gifts and Commodities*, as reported in *The Logic of the Gift*, ed. Alan
Schrift (New York and London: Routledge, 1997), p. 2.

The key idea here is profit in a broad sense: both buyer and seller want to profit from the converting money for goods or goods for money. Part of what an individual buyer or seller counts as profit is the purchase of freedom from a larger community or collective. What I own is at my own disposal; I am no longer lacking it and thus dependent on others to obtain it. Acquiring commodities loosens the ties that bind me as a dependent to the larger groups to which I belong: family, community, or state. What I own as commodity is mine to do with as I please. In making decisions about how to use or profit from my commodity goods, I am accountable only to myself as property owner (within the laws governing permitted use).

Social Property: Gift

Gifts are more complex and difficult to understand than are commodities.[13] An enormously rich and provocative interdisciplinary debate has arisen around the topic of the gift, inspired by the classic study of the French anthropologist Marcel Mauss (1872-1950).[14] Mauss's study produces an intellectual and emo-

---

13. In my view, no simple parallel exists between the peculiar mode of being of gift and any of the Heideggerian modes of being, although elements of several of them come into play with gifts. For one thing, the mode of being of gifts is much more highly determined by the social interactions among donors and recipients than is the case in any of Heidegger's determinate modes of being. Things have the being of gifts only when they are bestowed within the social context of gift exchange, and so they are quite different from either tools in individual use *(Zuhandenheit)* or things of individual worth *(Wert)*.

Nonetheless, because gifts are not merely isolated entities, but rather signify an entire network or world of interconnected meanings, each one of which refers to the being of *Dasein* as their final *um . . . zu* (for the sake of which, or purpose), gifts bear a likeness to tools. For example, a hammer refers to hammering, which refers to the building of a shed, which refers to the storing of grain, which refers to the need to prepare for the onset of winter, which refers to *Dasein's* finite being in the world. Through the system of significances *(Bedeutsamkeit)* in which it is embedded, a tool discloses the worldliness of the world in which *Dasein* dwells. A gift likewise refers to a network of socially determined meanings and discloses the worldliness of the social world. Similarly, because gifts bear meaning for their recipients, some likeness exists between gifts and things of *Wert*. For example, a souvenir that one brings back from a trip may become an object of worth and not merely a commodity. But the gift does not merely remind one of personal meaning; it refers to the intentions and expectations of another person, who is the gift-giver acting within a determined social context. The gift-giver may intend to give one something that has personal meaning. But the gift's origin in the thought and will of the giver, rather than the receiver, transforms the thing of *Wert* into something different — a gift.

14. See Marcel Mauss, *The Gift: The Form and Reason for Exchange in Archaic Societies*, trans. W. D. Halls, foreword by Mary Douglas (New York and London: W. W. Norton, 1990).

tional shock in many of its readers because it challenges and overturns some of their most cherished ideas and assumptions about gift-giving. Mauss challenges the commonplace that gifts are bestowed on someone freely and disinterestedly, with no strings attached, as a gesture of friendship or respect — possibly to commemorate a transition or rite of passage in life. Through detailed anthropological studies of gift exchange in traditional and archaic societies, Mauss shows that gift exchange is laden with social obligations and constraining reciprocal interests. Above all, the gift entails the following:

1. *an obligation to give* — acting as if I were a free and unconstrained agent, I bestow a gift on someone significant in my world at a crucial moment in his or her life; but I am in reality quite obligated to do so under penalty of having my inaction carry an insulting message;
2. *an obligation to receive* — the recipient apparently freely receives the gift, but he or she is likewise constrained to do so, else the refusal will be taken as a slight to the giver;
3. *an obligation to reciprocate* — once the gift has been received and acknowledged, the recipient must at the appropriate time make a return gift in kind, either directly to the donor or to other representatives of the donor's interests.

Although gift exchange is very different in archaic and modern societies, these three elements remain constant. In our highly gifted society, this threefold obligation holds in force at certain holidays and important events such as Christmas, birthdays, weddings, graduations, and so on. The gift is a material symbol of the giver's participation in social solidarity with the recipient and his or her family on the marked occasion. Complex rules govern the exchange: gifts call for return gifts in similar ritual circumstances, and one cannot "de-gift" (sell the gift) or "re-gift" (use the received gift as a gift for someone else) without insulting the original giver.

What is the mode of being of the gift? In what distinctive way are concepts and percepts combined in the acts of giving and receiving gifts? The crucial point is that gifts bind the giver and receiver together into an ordered system of social relationships. The gift embodies the meaning both of the personal relationship between giver and receiver and of the system of relationships within which their relationship is embedded. Moreover, the bind ties in two directions. The giver, and the whole social system through which he assumes his role, is bound to the receiver, who assumes power over the donor in receiving the gift (because the receiver is now free to respond as he or she chooses). At the same time, the receiver, along with his or her family or clan, is bound to the giver, who assumes power over the receiver in giving the gift (because the giver imposes the obligation to reciprocate on the receiver).[15] The being of the gift, then, is the living combination of the concept of the social group's identity or solidarity with the percept of individual object given, as mediated through the giver.

The being of the gift is therefore a profound and yet precise ambiguity. Gift exchange simultaneously both binds and liberates the giver and the receiver.[16] The binding is a matter of feeling; the obligation to reciprocate is first and foremost a felt obligation. Giving a gift, I bind myself to its symbolic value; the gift represents my understanding of the receiver and his or her situation in life. Receiving a gift and interpreting its meaning, I feel bound to acknowledge its symbolic value and to return the gesture in kind.

That is why Nietzsche's Zarathustra calls gift-giving an art.[17] One must know how to pick out a gift that captures the character of the recipient, marks the occasion with sensitivity, and expresses the unique relationship between the giver and receiver. One must also know how to receive a gift with grace and dignity, understanding both the intention embodied in the gift and the import of the social ritual it conveys. The synthetic power of gift both unites and divides people together into the social unit. And gift-giving does not occur only among equals. Ritual gift-giving establishes and respects the hierarchy of rank and power within the group.[18] Because of the ambiguous nature

---

15. According to Mauss, "the object received as a gift, the received object in general, engages, links magically, religiously, morally, juridically, the giver and the receiver. Coming from one person, made or appropriated by him, being from him, it gives him power over the other who accepts it." Similarly, the one who accepts the gift has power over the giver by virtue of the same ambiguous magical link. (Mauss, *The Gift*, quoted in *The Logic of the Gift*, ed. Schrift, pp. 29-32.)

16. For a sustained reflection on the simultaneously liberating and binding power of the gift, see the selections from Pierre Bourdieu's *The Logic of Practice* in *The Logic of the Gift*, ed. Schrift, pp. 190-230.

17. Friedrich Nietzsche, *Thus Spoke Zarathurstra*, trans. Walter Kaufmann (New York: Vintage, 1954), section on the gift-giving virtue, pp. 74-79.

18. In one of Mauss's most powerful reflections, he analyzes how the gift as symbol represents the spirit of the social group. Mauss takes the case of the Maori in Polynesia as paradigmatic of traditional and archaic societies. Mauss claims that one of the key ideas of Maori law and religion is that "What imposes obligation in the present received and exchanged, is the fact that the thing received is not inactive. Even when it has been abandoned by the giver, it still possesses something of him" (Mauss, *The Gift*, pp. 11-12). This force, which the Maori call *hau*, carries the spirit of the giver and, through him, the spirit of the group. Emil Beneviste glosses Mauss's comment to show how the gift is a floating signifier of the communal spirit. As such, to give and receive is always ambiguous, for to join the community is both a clear gain of solidarity and a clear loss of individual liberty. (Emil Beneviste, "Gift and Exchange in the Indo-European Vocabulary," in *The Logic of the Gift*, ed. Schrift, pp. 33-44.)

of the gift exchange, Mauss points out that in various European languages the etymology of gift connotes both present and poison, blessing and curse. As a form of property, the gift is odd. Once received, the gift is mine; I have dominion over it. But once received, what I do with it has clear social ramifications. I declare myself in relation to the others by my response to the gift.

Intellectual Property: Understanding

In articulating the modes of being that property can assume for people, we must not omit the obvious — namely, the capacity humans have to understand things (like property) in their being. Humans perceive things that appear to their senses, and we conceive universal ideas that clarify what these things are. When we combine percepts with concepts, we understand something in its being. Understanding is the capacity humans have to project an image of how or as what some thing or some situation is. As such, understanding is our most basic natural property: it is the ability that makes possible the other modes of being! Without the capacity to understand, humans would have concepts and percepts, but no ability to connect them into meaningful patterns. We *are* what we understand ourselves, other beings, and the whole of being to be. Because being is neither given to the senses as a percept nor given to thinking as a concept, but is rather the connection and connecting between them, understanding is in its essence always also a *self-understanding*. As such the operative concept of self-understanding is the "I" of our universal subjectivity, and the percept is the "this one here" of our personhood. In understanding anything, I understand how or as what "I" am "this person here."

Heidegger more than any other thinker illuminates understanding as the mode of being most characteristic of *Dasein,* or human being.[19] According to Heidegger's analysis, the human power of understanding determines human being as a being of possibilities. In understanding things as things, we project the possible modes of being that they may assume. We understand things in their *potentiality* to be. Understanding is the capacity to imagine how things could be or should be other than they actually are, because in understanding anything we connect what actually appears to our senses with a concept.

I am maintaining that understanding is the most fundamental piece of intellectual property we possess. Through the capacity to understand, we are

19. Heidegger, *Being and Time,* pp. 182-95.

linked to other kinds of intellectual property, which are so important to human beings. I am thinking of everything that Freud called the "mental assets of civilization."[20] These assets include the moral demands of society, its ideals of knowledge and good citizenship, as well as the cultural meanings of the creations of art. According to Freud, this kind of intellectual property compensates individuals for their necessary instinctual renunciations with higher psychological satisfactions. Freud also points out the volatile and fragile nature of such emotional compensation. Why is that?

Heidegger's answer is that we all too easily surrender our own capacity to understand — especially our capacity for self-understanding. That is say, we become fascinated with and absorbed in the world of commodities and social entanglements around us. We forget that each one of us as a singular "I" brings the light of understanding into the world and thereby assumes responsibility for the relationships both to commodities and to others. In other words, we lose sight of who we truly are as beings endowed with the capacity to understand.[21] The "who" of everyday self-understanding is not "I, myself," but the anonymous "they" of public opinion.[22] For the most part and from the beginning people are not the agents of their own actions. They are moved to act through advertising, convention, fashion, and the like. For Heidegger, this problem is the philosophical issue of human fallenness into inauthenticity. For much of Christian theology, this phenomenon of estrangement belongs to the doctrine of original sin. Augustine calls this initial state of lostness "concupiscence." It is like a window-shopping of the soul in which I lose myself in desires for shallow and untrue goods. By falling into the common desires in a self-forgetful way, I become disappropriated of my own true being, I turn away from God as highest good, and I disavow my responsibility to others. I forget that my proper name signifies me in my being, as one who can understand things in their being and can discriminate between true and false goods. I become nameless, and I lose the consciousness of being myself that makes my own capacity to understand my most valuable property.

For both Heidegger and Augustine, to possess genuine self-understanding is a task and not a given. The task of self-knowledge begins in the condition of "forgetfulness" or "fallenness." How, then, is it possible to recover my own true

20. Sigmund Freud, *The Future of an Illusion,* trans. James Strachey (London: W. W. Norton, 1961), p. 12.

21. Heidegger, *Being and Time,* sections 25-27.

22. Heidegger writes: "We take pleasure and enjoy ourselves as *they* take pleasure; we read, see, and judge about literature and art as *they* see and judge; likewise we shrink back from the 'great mass' as *they* shrink back; we find 'shocking' what *they* find shocking" (*Being and Time,* p. 164).

being from its estrangement in public opinion, to reclaim my own authentic self-understanding? Here I want to take a very different direction from Heidegger, who writes about the heroic decision to become myself in anticipating my own death. I want to talk instead about material grace as enabling the transition from fallenness to authentic self-understanding.

Religious Property: Material Grace

I want now to suggest that there is a fourth kind of property — a mode of being that is not captured by the notions of commodity, gift, or understanding. I propose to call this mode of being material grace. Recall that a mode of being is a determinate way of combining something abstract — a concept — and something concrete — a percept. The mode of being of a thing is a way of understanding *how* or *as what* this particular thing is the thing that it is.

As a mode of being, material grace denotes two meanings. First, I possess an object of material grace as something that is *most my own,* in the sense that the object becomes part of my being and enables me to become the one I truly am. By this I mean that objects of material grace reunite me with my own authentic self-understanding. Objects of material grace negate my fallenness into public opinion and restore me to the center of my own existence. Second, I possess an object of material grace at the same time as *not at all my own* — but God's own being of grace in relation to me. In other words, through objects of material grace I receive my own being as a gift from another — from God or the universe — but not from myself.

Received and possessed in this way, an object of grace becomes paradoxical. Things possessed in the mode of being of material grace constitute a species of property that formally overturns the genus "property" through the paradox that what is *most* my own is *least* my own. It is the presence of God within me. We can therefore call the mode of being of grace *spiritual presence.* What, then, are the elements involved in grace?

Objects of material grace are things like anything else — commodities, gifts, or objects of understanding. But at the same time, they are unlike other things. I want to call the object of material grace *religious* to indicate that it possesses a quality that transcends its economic value, its social significance, or its cultural meaning. This religious quality can, I insist, appear on, with, or through any other form of property. In other words, the religious quality transforms commodities, gifts, or objects of understanding into something other than themselves even while they remain themselves. This is the mode of being I call material grace.

For example, in the case of a commodity an object becomes material grace (and ceases merely to be a commodity) when it manifests and enables spiritual presence — the real presence of divine eternity experienced in and through a material object. Like the bread and wine of eucharistic Communion, the material object becomes a physical medium or symbol for the advent of God's being, precisely as it restores me to my own being. To refer to the eucharistic symbols is by no means out of place here, because the vision of religious property I am offering is profoundly sacramental in its essence. It is sacramental, but by no means confined to the sacramental system of the church. Rather, I am invoking the principle of *sacramentality* — namely, the principle that God is present in all of created reality, so that potentially anything whatsoever can at any time become a medium for the encounter with God's presence.[23]

An example of a commodity that has become an object of material grace could be an ancient stone I found and saved from the Irish Sea. The stone is black in color, smooth and round from centuries of lapping waves. Assuredly the market price for such a rock might not be very high, but such a stone might have priceless value for someone who was called back to himself or herself and thereby found the being of God in this common stone. Let me be clear. I am not talking about sentimental value. Nor am I talking about souvenirs taken as remembrances of things past, no matter how special they may be in someone's autobiography. I am talking about a natural object that confers selfhood on the self and has become a living symbol of God conceived of as the ground of all being.

Such a suggestion might sound absurd. What could be further from the self or from God than a stone? But with the principle of sacramentality in mind, it is not at all absurd. Let us assume that "God" means the living principle of the infinite unity of finite being and finite nonbeing. If so, then an ancient stone could assume the status of religious symbol if the concrete, material qualities of the stone can make present and perceptible to some owner the qualities of permanence, firmness, absoluteness, and fidelity that belong to the ultimate ground and power of being itself.[24]

---

23. Richard P. McBrien refers to the principle of sacramentality as central to the essence of Catholicism in *Catholicism* (Minneapolis: Winston, 1981), p. 1180. The principle of sacramentality is by no means exclusively Catholic, however. It also informs Protestant theologian Friedrich Schleiermacher's vision of the essence of religion and through Schleiermacher passes into Tillich and much contemporary theology. See Friedrich Schleiermacher, *On Religion: Speeches to Its Cultured Despisers,* trans. Richard D. Crouter (Cambridge: Cambridge University Press, 1988).

24. Of sacred stones, Eliade writes that "Rock shows him (i.e., archaic human being) something that transcends that precariousness of his humanity: an absolute mode of being. Its

Likewise, a gift offered and received ceases to be a gift and becomes material grace when it confers the spiritual presence of the giver rather than a social obligation.[25] Unlike the mode of being of gift as social property, a gift can assume the mode of being of material grace if its giving is purely donative in the sense that it imposes no obligation to receive and no obligation to reciprocate. True, the gift of grace typically elicits a labor of gratitude and the commitment of faith, but these responses arise freely and spontaneously from the transforming experience of grace — not from a felt sense of obligation. In so acquiring an object of grace, I receive the being of the other in sheer openness. And in my open receptivity, I become aware that I am here in relation to the other precisely as the one I am. I become aware that my simply being the finite and human one among others that I am is the most profound and precious gift imaginable. I become aware that I am the finite center of my finite world — literally the one who participates in the being of all that is through my creative acts of combining thought and experience.

In other words, things have the being of grace when they are received and possessed as transforming powers. They enable me to become the one I am. This kind of giving, a giving that is grace, calls forth the "I" of the receiver to respond to the living presence of the "I" of the giver. The "I" called forth in acknowledging and receiving the gift of grace is determined neither as the subject of economic valuation nor as the subject of social participation but as the pure subject of simple mindfulness in relation to others.

Now, a central claim of this essay is that the spiritual presence manifest in gift has a theological depth dimension. Through grace God breaks into my finite being in the world. The in-breaking of God is made possible by two things. First, there is the self-negating and self-transcending consciousness of the ones who give or receive grace. In the spiritual presence of grace, I become

---

strength, its motionlessness, its size and its strange outlines are none of them human; they indicate the presence of something that fascinates, terrifies, attracts and threatens, all at once. . . . We can hardly say that men have always adored stones simply as stones. The devotion of the primitive was in every case fastened on something beyond itself, which the stone incorporated and expressed" (Mircea Eliade, *Patterns in Comparative Religion,* trans. Rosemary Sheed [Cleveland: Meridian, 1963], p. 216).

25. Accordingly, the words and tune of a popular song (for example, Bob Dylan's "Not Dark Yet") may call to mind my finitude and disruption and thereby make me cognizant of the ubiquity of divine judgment. A photograph of my deceased father may combine with the concepts of understanding or wisdom, when that particular image enables me to still the turbulence of my soul and to recover the true center of my being in joyful, placid self-awareness. A baseball card of Sammy Sosa may combine with the concept of courage, when it empowers a child with the courage to be in spite of the anxiety of nonbeing. And so on. All of these are examples of real possessions through which grace breaks into one's world. Property becomes sacramental.

aware that as the finite center of my finite world, I am absolutely dependent on an absolute and infinite ground of both my being and the being of all that is.[26] I become aware that my being is one of openness to a depth that I cannot comprehend, but that I can gratefully receive in commitment and faith. When I say that the spiritual presence of grace has a self-negating quality, I mean that it points beyond itself to an infinite source and goal of meaning and power. In the fullness of being that is openness to grace, one's consciousness of self and other contains as well a consciousness of the depth dimension that infinitely transcends self and other. This quality in consciousness of openness to a divine depth is universal and innate in human beings because of their awareness of finitude.

Second, there is an element that we do not and cannot understand: the element of God's own agency. The in-breaking of God in grace — the divine presence in spiritual presence — is God's doing and not ours. It is true that we transcend the limits of human thinking when we use words that attribute agency or personality to the unthinkable divine being. Nonetheless, it is also true that the trope of formal paradox marks the location in human consciousness of the in-breaking of God's presence. When we speak of experiences of a having that is not a having, of a possessing that is not a possessing, we mark those places in our experience in which God's presence is most keenly felt. The reason that formal paradoxes in thinking mark the in-breaking of God in experience is that the idea of God is itself a formal paradox. To think God is to think the ultimate coincidence of opposites such as thinking and being, identity and difference, or being and nonbeing. As such, God is a *necessary* idea because it is as the final condition of the possibility of any thinking about being. Yet God is also an *impossible* idea (to think requires making distinctions that are ultimately effaced in the idea of God). When our experience registers something both necessary and impossible, such as the event of grace, the idea of God corresponds to the experience. We experience an in-breaking of God.

I am arguing that the event of grace is theological because when graced moments happen both giver and receiver recognize that a spiritual presence manifests itself in a self-negating way. When I give myself as grace to another, she or he receives the gift of my own being as a grace from God. When I am

26. Friedrich Schleiermacher, *The Christian Faith,* trans. H. R. Mackintosh and J. S. Stewart (Philadelphia: Fortress, 1928), pp. 5-18. For an explanation of religious self-consciousness, see David E. Klemm, "Schleiermacher on the Self: Immediate Self-Consciousness As Feeling and As Thinking," in *Figuring the Self: Subject, Absolute, and Others in Classical German Philosophy,* ed. David E. Klemm and Günter Zöller (Albany: State University of New York Press, 1997), pp. 169-90.

called forth and receive the gift of grace from another, I receive the gift of my own being as a grace from God. Both giver and receiver participate in the simple God-consciousness that is the feeling of absolute dependence on an infinite giver of all giving and creator of all being. This consciousness arises in the act of giving and receiving grace: "I," as origin point of all my thinking and doing, am not the origin point of my own capacity of thinking and doing. In the gift of grace, I give my own being to another as an offering. But in that very gift of grace I acknowledge that I do not own what is most my own; I am not my own property to give. The gift of grace makes tangible and perceptible what I both have and have not as my property — my own finite being as grounded in God's infinite being.

Anxiety, Material Grace, and the End of Violence

At the beginning of this essay I indicated how passions about property are linked with the legacy of human violence that should shame us all. The twentieth century was stained with violence of an unimaginable magnitude — from world wars to local ethnic cleansing, from nuclear explosions to letter bombs, from organized crime to gang warfare, from mass murder to child abuse. We have seen it all. Or have we? Surely continuing changes in social structures and rapid advancements in the technology of warfare and torture provide the violent imagination with new opportunities for evil inventions. The ancients knew that the passions of having — greed, avarice, envy — lie behind much violence. Any reflections on the problem of violence — its causes and possible cures — must include a reflection on the meanings of property. Can our distinctions among property's modes of being assist us in reflecting on the causes and end of violence? Let us make the attempt to see how passions about property arise and how they might be changed.

According to my foregoing analysis, property has four basic meanings for humans: commodity, gift, understanding, and grace. With regard to the first three of these modes of being (commodities, gifts, intellectual assets), humans relate to objects that are available to them through markets, social relationships, or education in the broad sense. These available objects can become real or potential possessions insofar as I produce my livelihood by working in the world.[27] And insofar as these things become possessions, I can

27. Paul Ricoeur, *Fallible Man*, trans. Charles Kelbley (Chicago: Henry Regnery Company, 1965), p. 173. See Ricoeur's reflections on the passions of having, power, and worth (pp. 161-91).

interiorize in feeling the possible relations to the thing. The relationship of "having" or "possessing" reverberates in the interior of my being, in the "I," which is affected by it. The lived attachment to things is a defining character-istic of human being — even when I am not being myself but have divested myself of myself by submitting to public opinion. I am always capable of ex-cessively wanting the available object, a wanting which makes me dependent on the object of desire. Once I possess the object, I am dependent on it as a thing, which can be lost or taken away. I feel anxiety about losing what is mine and thus losing part of myself. Ricoeur calls possession "the ensemble of forces which hold out against loss."[28] Let me trace the steps through which anxiety arises in connection with property.

The interior feelings of possessing what is "mine" occur together with the acts of differentiating between what is "mine" and what is "yours" in the domain of ownership. Beginning with feelings of attachment to my body, my thoughts, my things, my home, my place, by degrees I open up a space of dif-ference between my sphere of belongings and yours. The distinction between mine and yours is at the minimal threshold vis-à-vis myself and my family or my friends. Here things are largely held in common and boundaries are least tightly guarded, although disputes about what is mine and not yours can dis-rupt even the closest families and friends. The difference between mine and yours widens in the relationship to the surrounding community, but one hopes the bond of unity forged through recognition of common and public goods holds sway over divisiveness — else there is cause for civil violence or war. The difference between mine and yours can become an abyss, however, in relating my community to your community within the sphere of posses-sion. Vulnerable to loss in competition for available goods, and even to direct infringement on what is mine from others, passions of anger, envy, hatred, and revenge can attach themselves directly onto the other who stands be-tween me and the available goods of my desire. Wars between states can re-sult. In all of these cases, violence steams from the boiling water of the pas-sions of property.

The topic of the cause of violence is a difficult one for any thinker to ad-dress. In his remarkable study, *Reflections on Violence,* John Keane provides some theoretical assistance.[29] Keane points out that, in current public debate, we still tend to think in terms of "two cities." Today the distinction between the cities tends to be drawn politically and economically between two zones of habitation: "a democratic zone of peace, containing the comparatively

28. Ricoeur, *Fallible Man,* p. 174.
29. John Keane, *Reflections on Violence* (London: Verso, 1996).

open and prosperous parliamentary democracies" and "the rest of the world, a zone of violent anarchy, hopelessly entangled in war and warlordism, famine and lawlessness. . . ."[30] Keane rejects this distinction. Mass migrations, rapid dissemination and consumption of images and information, ease of transportation, and the like make permeable the boundaries between such fictive zones. Moreover, these facts about life in the twenty-first century ensure that "rootlessness, ethnic tensions and violent lawlessness are features of nearly every city of the developed democratic world."[31] In other words, the whole world feels threatened by potential violence. There are no safe zones.[32]

Keane points out the unsettling fact about life in the modern state: uncivil behavior shadows civil behavior at all levels of society.[33] For example, in Nazi Germany performances of Bach's organ music took place yards away from extermination camps. In the United States during the Vietnam Era, model suburban communities drew their economic lifeblood from companies manufacturing Agent Orange. In Columbine, teenagers shared a family meal one evening and opened gunfire against their schoolmates the next day. How can we conceive the relationship between the godly (or civil) society and the ungodly (or uncivil) society, when we are all implicated (individually and collectively) in both societies?

Two theories will not suffice. First, our century of violence belies the dogma of eighteenth-century optimism that the modern state in the nature of the case evolves teleologically toward a condition of perpetual peace (Kant), such that over time civility necessarily increases and incivility diminishes. Second, just as incredible are the equally dogmatic theories that the civ-

---

30. Keane attributes this thesis to Max Singer and Aaron Wildavsky, *The Real World Order: Zones of Peace, Zones of Turmoil* (Chatham, N.J.: Chatham House Publishers, 1993). See p. 4 of *Reflections on Violence*.

31. Keane, *Reflections on Violence*, p. 4.

32. Keane writes, "The democratic zone of peace feels more violent because within its boundaries images and stories of violence move ever closer to citizens who otherwise live in peace, due to the risk calculations and safety requirements of insurance companies; the eagerness for publicity of policing authorities; campaigns to publicize violence and to mobilize the criminal process (against rapists and child murderers, for instance); and the development of a global system of communications, parts of which know that violence attracts audiences and which are consequently driven by the editorial maxim, 'If it bleeds, it leads'" (*Reflections on Violence*, p. 5).

33. Keane cites Ernst Gellner's definition of civil society as "that set of diverse nongovernmental institutions which is strong enough to counterbalance the state and, while not preventing the state from fulfilling its role of keeper of the peace and arbitrator between major interests, can nevertheless prevent it from dominating and atomizing the rest of society" (*Reflections on Violence*, p. 10).

ilizing processes of the modern state necessarily produce increasingly horrible holocaust-style phenomena until we reach a war of all against all.[34] Keane rejects both extremes — the upward hike and the downward slide.

In their place Keane proposes that we live in the ironic situation that, although violence is the antithesis of civil society, every known form of civil society nonetheless tends to produce within itself a violent antithesis between civil and uncivil societies. The modern state will not of itself eliminate incivility, although specific institutional structural changes (e.g., along the lines of checks-and-balances within the American Constitution) can help. Nor will the modern state descend into barbarity; capitalism is not the problem. So why do the institutions of civil society, directed as they are against violence, tend to generate patterns of violence "that contradict the freedom, solidarity and civility which otherwise make them so attractive?"[35]

Keane's answer is startling. He says, "The openness that is characteristic of all civil societies — their nurturing of a plurality of forms of life that are themselves experienced as contingent — is arguably at the root of their tendency to violence."[36] The opening of markets around the world, followed by capital investments to expand business on a global scale, contribute just as much as the valued pluralism of society within our local neighborhoods to stresses and anxieties related to the encounter with Otherness. Anxiety increases with the legal and informal freedoms of citizens in the modern state in numerous ways. Civil societies are dynamic webs of social institutions and interactions in which "the opacity of the social ensemble — citizens' inability to conceive, let alone grasp, the totality of social life — combined with the chronic uncertainty of key aspects of life (employment and investment patterns, who will govern after the next elections, the contingent identity of one's self and one's household) makes their members prone to stress, anxiety, and revenge."[37]

In other words, we are all exposed to the fragile constitution of the world and the uncertainty of our place in it. As Søren Kierkegaard said, "Temporality, finitude — that is what it is all about."[38] At the same time, however,

---

34. Keane, *Reflections on Violence*, p. 36. The latter pessimistic theories assume that state power imposes renunciation of violent impulses, which store up and periodically explode in forms of state-sponsored barbarity. With reference to the latter thesis, Keane cites Zygmunt Bauman, *Modernity and the Holocaust* (London: Oxford University Press, 1993).

35. Keane, *Reflections on Violence*, p. 114.

36. Keane, *Reflections on Violence*, p. 114.

37. Keane, *Reflections on Violence*, pp. 114-15.

38. Søren Kierkegaard, *Fear and Trembling*, trans. Howard V. Hong and Edna H. Hong (Princeton, N.J.: Princeton University Press, 1983), p. 49.

we are losing the language in which to name the eternal ground of temporality, and thus the basis on which to recognize and accept anxiety as anxiety. The religious authority to define the power that founds the world loses credibility, but the feeling of the uncanny — our ultimate homelessness in the world — does not diminish.

The problem of violence confronts us at two levels. There is the structural or systemic level of introducing political constraints into the social and economic media of human interaction to assure just and fair transactions among humans. The structural level is vitally important, but I will bracket out this level for purposes of this discussion. There is also the personal and interpersonal level in which violence is related to distorted emotions and thought processes. At this level, the analysis of property as material grace becomes useful. No simple cure exists for the distorted passions concerning property that underlie violence in our society. There is no magical answer for the afflictions of the heart and will. Nonetheless, serious reflection on our possessions of material grace is an excellent starting point in the effort to transform the heart and will and thus to lessen in at least one location the unthinking impulses to violence in our world.

We recall the Augustinian principle that one is as one loves. It follows that if one can change one's loves — both the passionate motivations of desire and the objects of desire — then one can change one's being. To change oneself or another is an extremely difficult thing to do; if it were not, we would see examples of real conversion more frequently. Nonetheless, it is possible to change one's being, especially if that change is made in response to a real power in the world. The experience of material grace is empowering and healing, and it makes a great deal of sense to begin a reflection on conversion with reference to everyday experiences of material grace. I am assuming that all humans in fact do have experiences of property in the mode of being of material grace. If so, then we must develop a spiritual discipline to ensure that these experiences do not escape our recognition and attention, because they are potentially life-changing events.

There are two dimensions to any such spiritual discipline. First, too often an experience with spiritual depth, meaning, and power happens to us and we do not notice it or we forget it, because we lack the language with which to identify it and name it. In order to possess experiences of material grace, we need a vocabulary by means of which we can pick out these experiences and talk about them. To have such a vocabulary, we must learn to think theologically about depth meanings in culture. Theological discourse is too often narrowly associated with ecclesiastical symbols, rituals, and doctrines. We desperately need to be able to think theologically about the depth of meaning in everyday experiences of material objects — as well as the depth of meaning in the fine arts of painting, film, literature, and the like. If we wish to have the words and thoughts in which to reflect and interpret the depth of meaning in social life, we must work to create a new theology of culture for our time and to fight for its inclusion in the educational systems of the twenty-first century.

Second, in addition to possessing the words and thoughts by which to express the meaning of experiences of material grace, we must learn how to use these words and thoughts in the inner spiritual work with our own emotions. Otherwise, discrete experiences of material grace fade into memory and lose their potency. We recall them only as momentary events of meaning without lasting power to transform our being. The true gift of material grace is the appropriated feeling that the power of grace can enable us to change our distorted emotions and thoughts. The starting point is to learn to recognize our own dispositions and states of mind, so that we can comprehend when we are overly attached to property as commodity, gift, or understanding. Using Augustine's principle of right use of property as means to the end of true happiness versus wrong enjoyment of property as an end in itself, we can come to understand our own habitual tendencies toward indulgent attachment to goods. Distorted desires are infinite, and it takes vigilance to monitor the arising of greed, envy, anger, resentment, fear of loss, or need for revenge. In order to restrain these distorted emotions, it is necessary to understand their negative consequences — the fact that they become motives for actions that are destructive of well-being in the social world. It takes a conscious effort to replace negative emotions and thoughts with constructive ones. Here the capacity to remember experiences of material grace can be decisively important. It is never out of reach to return to the well of their original healing and empowering appearance by recalling such events or actually holding the grace-filled objects.

My point is that an intellectual analysis of true versus false goods is not enough to root out the disrupted emotions and negative thoughts that take hold in the human heart. No progress in changing bad habits of attaching oneself to things can be made without an inner struggle to restore peace and contentment with the true sources of happiness, when distorted emotions literally carry us away. Spiritual discipline is needed to restrain our impulses to have, hold, display, and protect our property for its own sake. The odd thing is that if you ask highly materialistic people whether they truly believe that happiness comes from possessing things, they will answer "No." Yet they seek happiness precisely in the things that cannot give it to them. Only a committed effort to change consumeristic attitudes can hope to succeed. Comprehending the meaning of objects of material grace can help, because these objects show us a mode of being of property that both is and is not my own. Objects of material grace give me a sense of my own most inner peace and contentment, yet they are not at my disposal as objects of possession. They happen to me as material events of meaning, and in that way invite me ever to return to them in order to overcome anxiety and confusion within the world of available goods.

Martin Heidegger captured the proper spiritual approach to property in a memorial address that he gave to his fellow villagers in Messkirch, Germany, in 1955. Heidegger spoke about humanity's increasing attachment to technical devices and technological progress, which he thought was turning the earth into a gigantic gasoline station. Heidegger warned that in attaching ourselves to all kinds of new technical devices we fall into bondage to them. He advised not turning back to a prior age but rather inculcating a comportment toward things that Heidegger called *Gelassenheit*. *Gelassenheit* reflects a composed and calm attitude toward things. This attitude has two components to it. First, *Gelassenheit* includes "releasement toward things," which means "We let technical devices enter our daily life, and at the same time leave them outside, that is, let them alone, as things which are nothing absolute but remain dependent upon something higher."[39] That is, we should consciously cultivate an attitude of detachment from things, learning to use them for higher purposes of achieving true human happiness without enjoying them as things which determine who we are. Second, *Gelassenheit* includes "openness to the mystery," which means that a depth of meaning pervades even technical things, hiding itself from us unless we open ourselves to its real spiritual presence. This depth of meaning both reveals itself in the materiality of the object of material grace and conceals its ultimate identity.

Objects of material grace invite us to relate to them with precisely the same releasement and openness. If, empowered by our experiences of material grace, we can generalize this attitude toward all modes of being of property, we can achieve a new and graced ground on which to stand in relating to goods of all kinds. The light bestowed in material grace can radiate into our engagements with all other things, persons, and places. Seen rightly, they are all divine gifts, which grant us the possibility of dwelling in the world together in a transformed way — through releasement toward things and openness to the mystery.

39. Martin Heidegger, "Memorial Address," in *Discourse on Thinking*, a translation of *Gelassenheit* by John M. Anderson and E. Hans Freund (New York: Harper and Row, 1966), pp. 54-55.

Finally, it should be clear that we should approach even the theological thinking and the inner spiritual work that I advocate in this essay in a constructive and yet critical way. Nothing protects experiences of material grace from becoming distorted, self-justifying experiences in their own turn except our own ability to think about them in a critical way. Human beings seem to have an incredible capacity for blindness when it comes to the objects of their own distorted desires. Even the desire to transform our own distorted desires can become distorted by the blindness within the human heart. Even the God who is the ultimate ground of mystery and meaning in the material world can become an idol under the ruses of the possessive desires. Objects of material grace restore a kind of openness to the immediate presence of ultimate meaning in things, but in enacting such openness we ought not to forsake the vigilant critical eye: Are we making idols of the invisible God?

Part 3   Property and Possession:
Greed and Grace in the Social,
Cultural, and Religious Imagination

Reconsidering Greed

William Schweiker

Gulliver's Complaint

Recounting his visit to the land of the Houyhnhnms, the country of gracious and virtuous horses, Gulliver, in his *Travels,* notes how despicable and vicious the Yahoos, or human beings, are in appearance and manner. Allowed to live among the Houyhnhnms, even to serve one as his master, Gulliver soon enjoyed a life mostly free of Yahoo vices. "I had no Occasion of bribing, flattering or pimping, to procure Favor of any great Man, or his Minion. I wanted no Fence against Fraud or Oppression."[1] But this was hardly a blissful "state of nature," as if the "horses" were more "natural" than human beings. The Yahoos — ignorant, violent, petty, lustful — also lived out their "nature."[2] The land of the Houyhnhnms was actually a country of virtues that curtailed viciousness and cultivated peace for "rational creatures." This country required no fences because cool reason ruled social interaction.

Gulliver is expelled from the land of the Houyhnhnms. The cause of his expulsion is proper fear by the Houyhnhnms that the odd mixture in his person of "some Rudiments of Reason" and "the natural Pravity of those Animals" (Yahoos) would work ill in their country. In a word, Gulliver's very being, his seeming inability to live a life of reason and virtue, meant that he was a threat to the fragile bonds of rational society. Rejected and brokenhearted,

1. Jonathan Swift, *Gulliver's Travels and Other Writings,* ed. Ricardo Quintana (New York: Modern Library, 1958), p. 226.
2. I hasten to add that some connection here is surely true for "Yahoo," the popular Internet search engine!

Gulliver departs by makeshift craft and some time later arrives back in native England. It took him years, he tells us, before he could tolerate the company of Yahoos, even his wife. Their actions, customs, and smells repulsed him. At last he is able to take supper at the same table with his wife and son.

Gulliver is never fully reintegrated into human company. In the final pages of his travels he tells us why. "My Reconcilement to the Yahoo-kind in general might not be so difficult, if they would be content with those Vices and Follies only which Nature hath entitled them to." The vices naturally allotted to Yahoos are theft, whoremongering, lying, deception, and the like. But, Gulliver continues, "when I behold a Lump of Deformity, and Diseases both in Body and Mind, smitten with *Pride,* it immediately breaks all the Measures of my Patience, neither shall I be ever able to comprehend how such an Animal and such a Vice could tally together."[3] Jonathan Swift thought, with good reason, that a certain dualism besets human beings, namely, our capacity for right action and our constant failure to do so. From this fact flows tragedy and comedy. And the greatest tragedy, Swift insists through the voice of Gulliver, is willful self-deception and self-aggrandizement, that is, pride.

Gulliver's complaint against Yahoo vices, and especially pride, is brilliant and timely satire. Writing amid the economic and political expansion of the British Empire, and mindful (no doubt) that John Locke had insisted "In the beginning all the world was *America,"* that is, a wasteland to be improved by human industry, Swift's satire joins interlocking debates in eighteenth-century Europe. Gulliver travels to strange and foreign lands to learn not the supremacy of the English Yahoo but the wisdom of the Houyhnhnms, the truly "other" — a rational creature seen by Europeans as mere "animal." Swift's picture of the Yahoos in their "state of nature" is part of the debate made famous by Jean-Jacques Rousseau about the conflict between nature and culture. Yahoos are hardly the free and peaceful "natural men" released from the corrupting force of society that Rousseau so dearly imagined. Gulliver's insistence that among the Houyhnhnms one needs no "Fence" against oppression and fraud dips into English political philosophy. He confirms Thomas Hobbes's insistence that political society is formed precisely to escape the war of each against each. Yet this is only true of Yahoos; one can imagine another creature, another way of social existence, not so brutish. Against Locke, Swift seems to be saying that the true "wasteland" is not untamed natural resources, but the human soul. The industry most needed is training in virtue, reason, and humility. And, finally, *Gulliver's Travels* ad-

3. Swift, *Gulliver's Travels,* p. 242.

vances a discussion among thinkers like Locke, Bernard Mandeville, and later David Hume and Adam Smith on the place of "vice" in the advance of culture and especially commercial society. Mandeville, we should recall, insisted that "Great Wealth and Foreign Treasure will ever scorn to come among Men, unless you'll admit their inseparable Companions, Avarice and Luxury."[4]

Are pride, greed, and want the engine of wealth? Is capitalism ignorant, violent, petty, and lustful? Is capitalism Yahoo to the bone? That is the question I want to explore in the following pages. This is hardly a dispassionate question. As the United Nations Development Program recently noted, "Global inequalities in income and living standards have reached grotesque proportions."[5] This is not to suggest, the United Nation report continues, that competitive markets should somehow be eliminated; markets have, in fact, stimulated growth. What is more, human beings have always engaged in patterns of exchange — barter, trade, and the like.[6] Mythically speaking, Eden is "pre-commercial," but as soon as Adam and Eve enter the world of history as actual agents, exchange is present. Ancient "economies" were usually agrarian and embedded in special social and cultural relations, often deeply religious and patriarchal in nature. In our situation, having traversed mercantile and industrial ages, we find highly differentiated and coordinated financial and credit systems as well as high-tech industries and even post-industrial information flows that are influencing all aspects of economic life. There is the emergence of new kinds of agencies (the World Bank, the International Monetary Fund, the World Trade Organization, as well as the North Atlantic Free Trade Agreement) and the collaboration of transnational corporations in the making of international law. What should we respond to this economic situation?

For many thinkers the task is to explore and specify rules and institutions that will ensure that the market serves persons and communities. I share that purpose, but, that said, the point of this essay is somewhat different. I do not intend to focus on strictly political and economic analysis, nor, for that matter, on institutional questions about the global economy. My project is more modest, socially speaking, but nevertheless morally and religiously crucial. While I suspect that self-aggrandizement and self-deception (pride) are probably interwoven with greed, my focus on matters of economy and morals

4. Bernard Mandeville, "The Fable of the Bees," in *Reflections on Commercial Life: An Anthology of Classic Texts from Plato to the Present,* ed. Patrick Murray (New York: Routledge, 1997), p. 150.

5. Cited in the lead story "A 'Grotesque' Gap" by R. C. Longworth in the *Chicago Tribune* 153, no. 193 (12 July 1999), section 1, p. 1.

6. I want to thank Max L. Stackhouse of Princeton Theological Seminary for providing helpful insight into these matters of definitions.

dictates closer attention to avarice. What is the morality of motives for wealth? In what follows, I want to probe our felt reactions, our love of wealth, and our revulsion, or lack of moral censure, over hideous inequalities in the distribution of the material necessities of life. Shifts in policy and institutions must be correlated with the development of profound moral sensibilities. And given this fact, I am concerned about the complex connection between human desires and culturally mediated schemes of value.

The timeliness of the topic can hardly be doubted. Throughout societies dominated by market capitalism there is, on the part of many, deep concern about how consumerism is shaping our lives. Automobile companies talk of installing refrigerated glove compartments so that drivers can consume at will. By some reports Americans snack virtually around the clock. Children are constantly bombarded with images of new games, new toys, new fashions. Perhaps it is fitting, then, to reconsider greed.

Greed Reconsidered

Much current reflection on property and possession forgoes any discussion of how to assess the motives for wealth, a question deemed basic by Swift, Locke, Mandeville, and Smith. There seem to be two reasons for this neglect. First, among Christian theologians in this century there has been profound suspicion of market economies. From popes like Leo XIII and American Social Gospel thinkers like Walter Rauschenbusch to current liberation theologians, the market has often been viewed as a profound impediment to the just distribution of material goods. In its most extreme form, this perspective has virtually identified economic injustice with capitalism. For such thinkers, capitalism is Yahoo to the bone; it is beyond the reach of Christian morals. Given this account, there has been little interest among such theologians in taking a new look at the market and human motivations.

During the 1980s this assessment changed somewhat. Protestant thinkers, including Max Stackhouse, David Krueger, and others, as well as the Roman Catholic bishops in the United States and moral theologians Dennis McCann and David Hollenbach, reopened the question of the moral assessment of the market.[7] Even Pope John Paul II, in his encyclicals on labor, made

---

7. See Max L. Stackhouse, *Public Theology and Political Economy: Christian Stewardship in Modern Society* (Grand Rapids: Eerdmans, 1987); Max L. Stackhouse et al., *Christian Social Ethics in a Global Era* (Nashville: Abingdon, 1995); David Krueger, *The Business Corporation and Productive Justice* (Nashville: Abingdon, 1997); and National Conference of Catholic Bishops, *Economic Justice for All.*

proper, if limited, place for the growth and expansion of the market.[8] Yet while all of this has been a welcome development, there has still been little exploration of matters of human motivation. Questions of social justice, not moral anthropology, have been central in recent years; the discourse of institutional and political analysis, values and motivations, has ruled the day.

What is interesting about Swift's century is that the focus was on how to account for the bonds of human society, and, especially, commercial culture. In order to understand those bonds rightly we must, Swift and others insisted, grasp the tenor and direction of human desires. This meant that economics was part of moral inquiry and, further, that an ethics demands a robust psychology. The second reason for the present neglect of this topic is, then, that, unlike Swift or Smith, political economy is no longer seen as part of the larger task of moral philosophy. The rise and differentiation of the "sciences" since the late eighteenth century has meant that economic and ethical reflection often move in rather diverse, even separate, orbits. Furthermore, too much contemporary ethics neglects work in psychology. It is typically argued, for instance, that the marks of moral agency are "rationality" and "freedom." But surely any informed account of behavior needs to provide a richer, more textured and culturally saturated picture of human existence.[9] I want to reopen the discussion about vice and capital, realizing that, at the level of validating claims, we are traversing disciplines.

With the title "Reconsidering Greed," I mean to suggest at least two things. First, I want to recap briefly earlier debates and explore why the idea of "greed" fell out of modern economic discourse. The loss of the language of greed, or avarice, is actually a shift in the assessment of human motivations and the question of just entitlement to goods among philosophers of commercialism. In other words, the loss of "greed" signals a change in how modern Western societies pictured human existence and the material needs of social life. Mindful of this shift, the second meaning of my title contends that we need to recover the idea of greed in order to have an adequate and robust understanding of human life and society. The idea of greed, properly understood, picks out a crucial dynamic and distortion of human life all too easily shaping current existence. That dynamic, I argue, hinges psychologically on the connection between desire and imagination in the human psyche. The ultimate purpose of this essay, accordingly, is to outline a revised account of

8. See, for example, John Paul II, *Centesimus Annus* (1991).

9. For an attempt to provide a richer picture of human existence see Iris Murdoch, *Metaphysics As a Guide to Morals* (London: Allen Lane/Penguin, 1993). Also see *Iris Murdoch and the Search for Human Goodness*, ed. Maria Antonaccio and William Schweiker (Chicago: University of Chicago Press, 1996).

greed and what it might mean for living morally and religiously in a culture of consumption. This will challenge the tactic of much traditional Christian morals that easily sees all human acquisitiveness as greed. Yet my argument also criticizes the loss of the concept of greed in economic thinking.

Given this agenda it ought to be clear that I deploy the resources for the Christian tradition not simply to speak to the Christian community but, rather, to engage wider debates about how we can and should live healthy, complex, and responsible lives.[10] On my account, responsibility is about respecting and enhancing the integrity of life. The moral and economic problem we face in commercial cultures is how to live rightly in an age of runaway consumption and the loss of any discourse about inordinate desires, the language of greed. Contemporary commercial cultures — the cultures of Imelda Marcos, Donald Trump, the global spread of McDonalds, and Nike shoes — have left us strangely mute about how to understand and assess the stimulation of desires necessary for the functioning of those societies. The two meanings of the title of this essay can thus be seen as different sides of the same coin; in other words, the task is to reclaim and revise a language of human desire necessary to live responsibly in a culture of consumption. I intend to draw freely on Western Christian resources in making this argument.

Let me be clear. The thrust of my argument — like the reports of the United Nations or the theologians cited above — is not to reject commerce or the market. Ideas about private property, creativity through production, increased wealth, the common good, and even the dynamics of the market cannot and ought not to be rejected out of hand. My concern is simply to secure the integrity of life — especially human life — as the aim of, not the means to, economic activity. The target of critique is not commerce or the market as such. Any realistic assessment of our situation has to accommodate the social goods the market in fact produces, goods like increased income across a wide spectrum of the society, innovation, international cooperation, and the like. The point, again, is to make these goods serve human ends rather than systemic purposes. We need a humane economy. The target of my criticisms in this essay is a culture of consumption that works within and through the market. One can only wonder if the strange inarticulacy about human desires seen in commercial societies is not itself necessary for those cultures. It is as if, as with the Yahoos, the rapacious drive of consumption shuns self-understanding. We good consumers do not want to know what and who we

10. This is an essay in Christian moral philosophy. On this, see William Schweiker, *Responsibility and Christian Ethics* (Cambridge: Cambridge University Press, 1995), and *Power, Value, and Conviction: Theological Ethics in the Postmodern Age* (Cleveland: Pilgrim, 1998).

are. We simply want to be satiated. Exploring the roots of moral dumbness remains on the margins of the present essay, even if I hope to combat the silence.[11] But it does suggest that the task of ethics ought not simply to be securing the foundations of moral norms and values; the purpose of moral inquiry is deeper understanding of our lives in order to live well.

That said, I want now to outline in broad stokes traditional assessments of avarice in commercial life. That discussion forms the backdrop for an engagement with the question that vexed Swift, Mandeville, and others, prompting complaints against or praise for Yahoo vices.

Assessing Avarice

Unless blinded by sheer ideology, most would admit that greed is a true and present reality. Many people on this planet are hungry; a minority of its inhabitants consumes resources at an increasing and alarming rate. As R. L. Longworth reports, the three richest officers of Microsoft, for instance, have more assets, approximately $140 billion, than the combined forty-three least-developed countries with populations in excess of 600 million! In about half of the world's nations, per capita income is now lower than it was ten or twenty years ago.[12] The desire for wealth and property is often mediated by a global media system, the flow of images that defines commercial hype. Furthermore, population is increasing at drastic rates in precisely those parts of the world with the least access to the earth's resources. This accentuates the division between "haves" and "have-nots," even as it signals the possibility of an age of global migration, social violence, and international conflict as persons and nations scramble for scarce resources. We live in an age of scarcity and runaway consumption bent on eating up cities, homes, human beings, and the earth. The cities and cultures we build — as well as our own sense of self — seem bound to property and consumption.

Greed is not only a present reality. It seems to be a constant feature of human life. It is hardly surprising, then, that voices of condemnation span the ages, reaching from ancient prophets to current advocates of economic rights. Buried deep within the moral imagination of the West is the assumption that greed enslaves and destroys persons and communities. But what is greed? Simply put, greed, or avarice (Latin: *avarus,* "greedy"; "to crave"; "to

11. On the idea of articulation and self-understanding see Charles Taylor, *Sources of the Self: The Making of Modern Identity* (Cambridge, Mass.: Harvard University Press, 1990).

12. See Longworth, "A 'Grotesque' Gap," p. 1.

desire"), is the inordinate love for riches. It is the rapacious desire for more goods or wealth than one needs or deserves.[13] The term greed designates, then, the relation between human craving and a specific object of that desiring, namely, culturally determined "riches," if and only if such craving exceeds basic human need and also the rightful limits on consumption. Of course, it is a difficult question to determine when those "limits" are exceeded; this seems, at least empirically, to be a matter of different social boundaries and projects. What counts as "greed" in one social context might well not in another. And this is why, we might imagine, the topic of greed has traditionally been situated at the intersection between the ethics of exchange, and thus the demands of commutative justice, and matters of personal morality, or the virtuous self.[14]

Greed is an exceedingly complex human desire. Phenomenologically, we can describe "greed" as a culturally defined craving, both in terms of "what is desired" and in terms of the rightful limits of possession, even as it is an attack on the limits of individual satiation and social relations. The greedy person wants, I propose, to possess all of a culture's highest riches and thus, implicitly, to have her or his desires absorbed into and defined by the society's value system even while exceeding the limits defined by that social system. Ironically, the life of the greedy undercuts participation in the very social network that defines her or his desires. This is why in traditional virtue theory greed is understood in relation to concupiscence and the demand for temperance. As Thomas Aquinas puts it, covetousness (hence greed or avarice) subjects the human will to a good lower than God, the true human end, and hence is sinful. Greed disorders the soul. Virtue puts the order of reason into passion, and, specifically, temperance curbs the passion that incites to anything against reason.[15] In our terms, greed is a passion, a human desire, to draw some socially defined material or ideal value (money, power, etc.) into the self and thereby to undercut the domain of social meaning itself. Greed

---

13. This same point could be made comparatively; namely, other religious traditions have also noted the problem of inordinate craving in human life. For examples of this see, in Buddhism, P. Payuot, *Buddhadharma,* trans. R. Olson (New York: State University of New York Press, 1995), and also, in Hinduism, Radharkrishnan, *The Hindu View of Life* (London: Mandala, 1960). Matters of social justice and the criticism of greed are also found in the great Hebrew prophets (e.g., Micah, Jeremiah, etc.). Sadly, it is not possible to explore these comparisons in this essay.

14. On the idea of commutative justice and the ethics of exchange, see Jon P. Gunneman, "Capitalism and Commutative Justice," in *The Annual of the Society of Christian Ethics* (Washington, D.C.: Georgetown University Press, 1985), pp. 101-23.

15. See Thomas Aquinas, *Summa Theologiae* II/II, q. 118 (covetousness); I/II, q. 61 (virtue).

works to isolate the self by breaking the necessary bonds of human community. One could see greed as a form of inverted narcissism in which the self is not elevated to the center of the world (pride), but, rather, seeks to consume the world and lose the self in what is desired and consumed. Yet in doing so, greed also undercuts the fragile bonds of social concord.

Gulliver is an apt example of this rough and ready phenomenology of greed. At one point in his stay with the Houyhnhnms, he learns that the Yahoos have found a treasure trove of diamonds. While these stones are worthless in the land of the Houyhnhnms, Gulliver himself craves them, and, in fact, seeks them out in the dead of night. His craving, in other words, is culturally defined by European images of "riches" that pit him against the Houyhnhnm society he (supposedly) wants to join. And his craving for the diamonds undercuts all his social relations: it involves theft from the Yahoos, and, for dread that he be seen as really Yahoo, the deception of the Houyhnhnm. Greed lives from while it also undermines social relations. It is a culturally formed craving riddled with excess. The excess is that the greedy person wants to subsume the socially defined wealth at the violation of the natural limits of satiation and normal communal bonds. This is why greed is one of the traditional vices, in terms of both individual moral failing and also a violation of the demands of distributive justice. "Greed" is a vice that links the person's self-relation to her or his interaction with a community.

If this is at all right, then one can easily understand why greed has long been condemned in Christian thought. The prohibition of covetousness is found in the Decalogue (Exod. 20:17) as well as New Testament texts (cf. Luke 12:15), and is specifically mentioned in lists of vices (Col. 3:5). We are even told that "the love of money is a root of all kinds of evil" (1 Tim. 6:10), and, in the Sermon on the Mount, Jesus insists that one cannot serve two masters, God and mammon (Matt. 6:24). This augments the claim, in Matthew 6:21, that where one's treasure is, there the heart — the core of one's being — will also be. Personal and communal identity is bound to what is possessed, and, accordingly, it is of grave moral and spiritual import not to be possessed by what one owns. In a word, Jesus' teaching concerns a doubleness in the property relation: it is necessary for and yet also potentially destructive of right self-understanding, social life, and relation to the divine.

Drawing on these biblical themes, traditional Christian thinkers taught that the malice of greed lies in the getting and keeping of money and possessions as the defining purpose of life. The greedy person does not see that these things are valuable only as instruments for an integral life. There is a confusion within greed between what is to be used for the necessities of life and what is to be sought as a good in itself. Martin Luther, for instance, endorsed traditional Christian teaching against usury. Yet he also thought, in a treatise on the "Common Chest," that the drive for wealth through investment was idolatrous. The investor trusts in something other than God as the true sovereign over time and life; the investor has faith in economic powers as sovereign. This allows us to see why greed was called a capital vice. Given its object, avarice can be the cause of many other sins. As the Hebrew prophet Amos put it, God will not revoke punishment of the people since

> they sell the righteous for silver,
>> and the needy for a pair of sandals . . .
> and in the house of their God they drink
>> wine bought with fines they imposed. (Amos 2:6, 8)

Idolatry, oppression, slavery, exploitation, and deception gather round and flow from greed. Furthermore, avarice can conceal itself as a virtue; it can commend itself under the pretext of making provision for future life. The excessive desire of, or pleasure in, riches has been seen throughout the history of Christian ethics as ruinous of the moral life.

This judgment about greed has meant a decided ambivalence about trade within traditional Christian ethics. Aquinas, in line with Aristotle (*Politics* 1.3), distinguishes, in *Summa Theologiae* II/II, question 77, two kinds of exchange. One kind, so-called "natural exchange," aims at satisfying the needs of life. This is the work of householders and civil servants whose responsibility is to care for home and state. The other kind of exchange, "profit exchange," aims not at satisfying the needs of life but is purely for profit. While natural exchange is commendable, the latter, in words similar to Luther's, "is justly deserving of blame, because, considered in itself, it satisfies the greed for gain, which knows no limit and tends to infinity." Importantly, Aquinas's argument centers on the "ends" sought through exchange (cf. *Summa Theologiae* II/II, q. 118). Since the end of greed is infinite gain, rather than satisfying basic human needs, it is morally condemned. Trading becomes "lawful" only when it is turned to serve some necessary or virtuous end. In their judgments, Luther and Thomas echo long-standing convictions held by Christians and "pagan" philosophers including Aristotle and Plato.

St. Ambrose put it well. In a letter to Bishop Constantius sometime in 379 C.E., he wrote, "Woe to him who has a fortune amassed by deceit, and builds in blood a city, in other words, his soul. For it is the soul which is built

---

16. St. Ambrose, *Saint Ambrose: Letters 1-91*, in *Fathers of the Church*, trans. Mary Melchior Beyenka, O.P. (New York: Fathers of the Church, 1954), p. 80.

like a city. Greed does not build it, but sets it on fire and burns it."[16] Greed crosses through social existence — the "city"; the ethics of exchange — and the integrity of personal life, the soul. It is potentially destructive of person and community. The Christian can, at best, accommodate trade for the necessities of life. Interestingly enough, the idea that greed is socially and personally destructive continues to find expression even in the popular imagination. Greed is a boundary phenomenon: it connects economics, politics, culture, and self. It gathers around it a host of images — hunger, fire, destruction, a primal insatiability.

In my judgment, what classical thinkers like Ambrose or Aquinas and current ones are saying is that one must consider the complex, reflexive connection between desire and commodification, that is, how a craving for things situated within patterns of economic exchange helps to shape and define the self and her or his desires. Desire is culturally saturated. Some desires — if not all — are not simply "given"; they do not arise in human life fully born. What you love, as Jesus might say, shapes who you are, but our loves are also shaped by cultural mediation. We have to understand how property matters to people, and this is a more complex issue than simply meeting basic needs like hunger, sex, or shelter, although it includes those needs as well. From this perspective, many philosophies of commercialism are deficient in failing to grasp how property is reflexively linked to the formation of a person's identity. The distinctively human fact is that "property" is a cultural construction and thus entangled with a culture's sense about and arrangements for human identity, dignity, and worth. What is at issue is how we build our souls and our cities.

It is not at all clear, however, that the moral designation "greed" is really apt for market-driven economies, or even for the formation of moral desires and identities. This is the point of the debate that Swift so brilliantly helped to advance. The debate marks a decisive shift from the perspective reaching from Aristotle to Ambrose, from Aquinas to Luther. There are, first, economic reasons why we might want to challenge an all too easy moral condemnation of human acquisitiveness, or desire for gain. After all, how is one to generate wealth, stimulate production, and enhance savings if a spirit of relentless acquisition is lacking? As Milton Friedman once put it, the social responsibility of business is to increase profits.[17] The idea that moral norms can and ought

17. Milton Friedman, "The Social Responsibility of Business Is to Increase Its Profits" in *New York Times Magazine* 13 (September 1970): 32ff. Also see Paul Weaver, "After Social Responsibility," in *The U.S. Business Corporation: An Institution in Transition*, ed. John R. Meyer and James M. Gustafson (Cambridge, Mass.: Ballinger, 1988), pp. 133-48. Also see C. Edward

to bear on the market is wrongheaded and economically dangerous. The wholesale condemnation of "greed" is nothing less than misplaced moralism. Second, Friedrich Nietzsche would say that moralism bespeaks the resentment of the poor for the power of the rich. The weak invert the tables of value established by the powerful and healthy to serve the purposes of the weak. While life, strength, and wealth are virtues for the powerful, in the eyes of the weak and outcast these "virtues" become vices that the evil — read: wealthy — work on the innocent — read: poor. So one might not only have a Friedman-like economic suspicion about the old vice of greed, but also advance a Nietzschean, psychological denial of moralism.

Nevertheless, in this history of ethics and even current discourse there seems to be little debate about how to define and understand greed. Yet for much Christian discourse, "greed," associated with covetousness, seems to cover all forms of human acquisitiveness indiscriminately, making it difficult, if not impossible, to speak of a morally right search for gain and wealth. Conversely, a good deal of current economic thought segregates the moral and the economic and thus banishes the very concept of greed from the domain of "exchange" to the realm of private life. The market requires the engine of human craving, but discourse about that desiring is oddly de-moralized. Mindful of this long condemnation of greed in Christian thought and the current economic reality, let us turn next, briefly to be sure, to earlier debates about avarice and commercial life. We must see how decisive that debate was for the modern "table of values" and the place of property in our lives. For the sake of brevity, I turn to Bernard Mandeville, in his "The Fable of the Bees," and to David Hume's essays as decisive for the question of avarice and commerce. The larger question, once again, is how to understand the loss of the discourse of "greed" within reflection on economic life.

The Vicious Yet Prosperous Hive

On Mandeville's account, in the "Fable of the Bees," society is driven by greed, envy, and discontent. Commerce is a matter of exchange, not production, and because of this there is constant revolution in tastes going on to further the market. Society is like a beehive. And, as Alan Ryan has noted, "Nobody can

---

Arrington and William Schweiker, "The Rhetoric and Rationality of Accounting Practice," in *Accounting, Organizations, and Society* 17, no. 6 (1992): 511-33, and William Schweiker, "Accounting for Ourselves: Accounting Practice and the Discourse of Ethics," in *Accounting, Organizations, and Society* 18, no. 2/3 (1993): 231-52.

exactly say the creatures in the hive are happy. . . . they are permanently discontent with what they have already. But the hive prospers. . . . they are well adapted to a peaceful and prosperous society."[18] Mandeville's point, and the force of his "fable," is to show that all the so-called vices — and only the vices — are in fact the foundation of a good social order. Private vices reap public good. While vice might mean moral ruin to the self, it is in fact economic salvation. Mandeville does not give wholesale endorsement of vice. Good results do not justify vicious conduct. His point, rather, is about the motivations necessary to run the market. This requires a very modern separation of the private and public realms. Economics as well as the morality of exchange must be evaluated on terms other than the discourse of personal virtue or viciousness. The market demands, for instance, not only avarice and pride, but also that the poor be ever kept in want. "When Men shew such an extraordinary proclivity to Idleness and Pleasure, what reason have we to think that they would ever work, unless they were oblig'd to it by immediate Necessity?"[19] A rich nation must make sure that most of the poor are always at work, spend what they get, and are thus always provoked to labor by necessity.

Mandeville's argument rests on a particular anthropology. He puts it like this:

> Man never exerts himself but when he is rous'd by his Desires:
> Whilst they lie dormant, and there is nothing to raise them, his
> Excellence and Abilities will be for ever undiscover'd, and the
> lumpish machine, without the Influence of his Passions, may
> justly be compar'd to a huge Wind-mill without a breath of air.[20]

The spring of human action is desire, and thus, if one wants economic production, one must provoke those cravings. Pride, avarice, and want drive persons to labor. And these same "vices" also keep consumption growing, a growth necessary for economic flourishing. Given this, one cannot aggrandize or enrich a nation if the very motives for prosperity and consumption are morally censured. This is important to see. For Mandeville, morality, in the strict sense of the term, aims at eradicating rather than directing the passions. His anthropology, in other words, undergirds what moral theorists call "non-naturalism" in ethics. Like Immanuel Kant after him and many Christian theologians before, he believed that moral duty and virtue stand against

18. Alan Ryan, *Property* (Minneapolis: University of Minnesota Press, 1987), pp. 99-100.
19. Mandeville, "Fable of the Bees," p. 151.
20. Mandeville, "Fable of the Bees," p. 149.

natural desires and wants, and not as their proper fulfillment. Accordingly, one must "de-moralize" economics in order to release motivations necessary for the generation of wealth.

It is, then, this assumption about the character of morality that demands Mandeville de-moralize economic life and give free reign to the vices as the engine of production and consumption. This has two important consequences. First, it forces the question of morals inward upon the self and aids other modern impulses to interiority, impulses like private religion, the growth of psychological inquiry, and the feeding of personal preference. Virtue and vice become disconnected from one's life as an economic agent. The self inhabits multiple roles each ruled by its own logic, discourse, and values. This compartmentalization of life leads, one suspects, to a certain public muteness about the depth and meaning of personal existence. Second, once the private and the public are so separated, economic activity and human exchange are ruled by no other value than simple utility. If the wealth of the nation requires the poor remain in want as a goad to labor and consumption, then poverty is a legitimate necessity of economic life. The principle of legitimation is no longer moral or even political; it is strictly economic in nature. One determines what is a tolerable degree of human depravation not in moral terms but on the grounds of economic calculation. In this respect, the division of private and public bears not only on the individual but also on social exchange. The nation is straddled between two different value systems. In personal life, the demands of duty and virtue reign; in the life of the nation, strict utility guides decision and policy.

In other words, the language of "greed," or avarice, no longer has relevance to economic life other than as a purely descriptive term about human motivation for wealth. Patrick Murray has noted that by drawing a stark line between hard-working poor and greedy rich, Mandeville "avoids the . . . paradox that crops up in twentieth-century capitalism, where the same persons are counted on to work hard and consume hard."[21] But we need to see that this separation is built on a certain conception of morality and also an account of desire. The upshot is that commerce is not a humanizing force, even if it generates wealth. In this respect, Mandeville continues, somewhat ironically, the long-standing censure, or reluctant accommodation, of trade running from Amos and Aristotle to Luther and the current papacy.

---

21. Murray, ed., *Reflections on Commercial Life*, p. 148.

Utility and Social Virtues

David Hume departs from the condemnation and accommodation of trade in traditional Christian thought; yet Hume also differs from Mandeville. He was critical of the "irreclaimable" passion of unmixed greed. And he even held that "a sense of humor and virtue" alone is able to "restrain or regulate the love of money." In spite of this, "Commerce, in Hume's view, is the great humanizing force in history. Moral consideration, joined to a host of others, weigh heavily in favor of commerce."[22] Unlike Mandeville, then, Hume believed that commerce serves not only economic ends but genuinely human ones. These human goods include increased knowledge, setting up law and order, softening human tempers, and even increased happiness. Against the hard and reductionistic vision of human beings and commerce, Hume presents a more capacious account of the economic activity. How does Hume make this argument?

Hume's decisive move, with respect to Mandeville and some (but not all) traditional Christian morals, is to reject non-naturalism in ethics. That is to say, for Hume the point of morality is to direct and tame natural desires, not to negate or transcend them under the call of duty. Mandeville's brand of non-naturalism in ethics, as we have seen, meant that "morality" was limited to the realm of the private. Hume insists that human beings have genuine sympathy for others. "The social virtues must, therefore, be allowed to have a natural beauty and amiableness, which, at first, antecedent to all precept or education, recommends them to the esteem of the uninstructed mankind, and engages their affections."[23] Human beings, uninstructed and natural, are hardly Swiftian-Yahoos; they have some untutored sympathy for the common good, for utility, and thus an appreciation of the social virtues.

Of course, persons need training in social virtue. This training is with respect to moral principle. Which moral principle?

> It appears to be matter of fact, that the circumstance of *utility*, in all subjects, is a source of praise and approbation: That it is constantly appealed to in all moral decisions concerning the merit or demerit of Actions: That it is the *sole* source of that high regard paid to justice, fidelity, honour, allegiance, and chastity: That it is inseparable from all the other social virtues, humanity, generosity, charity, affability, lenity, mercy, and modera-

---

22. Murray, ed., *Reflections on Commercial Life*, p. 155.
23. David Hume, *An Enquiry Concerning the Principle of Morals* (La Salle, Ill.: Open Court, 1966), p. 48.

tion: And, in a word, it is a foundation of the chief part of morals, which has a reference to mankind and our fellow-creatures.[24]

Having established the chief moral principle, utility, and its relation to fellow-feeling, the question Hume faced concerning commerce is whether or not it furthers utility and social virtues.

This much seems clear. Given his moral anthropology, Hume's basic point is that commerce as such advances social virtue, since it aims at utility. Further, this is "the natural course of things. Industry and arts and trade increase the power of the sovereign as well as the happiness of the subjects; and that policy is violent, which aggrandizes the public by the poverty of the individual."[25] Two things are asserted here. First, happiness, according to Hume, consists in action, pleasure, and indolence. "In times when industry and the arts flourish," Hume continues, "men are kept in perpetual occupation, and enjoy, as their reward, the occupation itself, as well as the pleasures which are the fruit of their labor. . . . Banish those arts from society, you deprive men both of action and of pleasure; and leaving nothing but indolence in their place, you even destroy the relish of indolence. . . ."[26] In a word, the more commerce and the arts advance, the further social virtue and happiness are to be found in a nation. Second, Hume cannot conceive, as Mandeville did, a utilitarian justification for the poverty of the individual. A thoroughgoing naturalism, that is, a careful look at actual human desires and affections, shows that we cannot approve policies that demean and destroy our fellow citizens. The shape of human social affection means that utility and personal happiness must go hand-in-glove if a nation's policies are to meet with approval and human life to advance. It also requires, as Hume knew, local communities to foster virtue and identities. Since there seem to be limits to how far fellow-feeling can extend, local communities are far better at enlarging affections than larger and more complex collectives. In terms of sentiment and affection, no one is a citizen of the world; such grand communities exist only at the level of principle.

Is this too optimistic a picture of human economic life? Hume does consider "vicious gratifications." Any particular form of gratification can become vicious, he writes, "when it engrosses all of a man's expense, and leaves no ability for such acts of duty and generosity as are required by his situation and fortune." And he continues, no doubt with Mandeville directly in sight:

24. Hume, *An Enquiry Concerning*, p. 66.

25. David Hume, *Essays: Moral, Political, and Literary*, Essay 1: "On Commerce," in *Reflections on Commercial Life*, ed. Murray, p. 159.

26. Hume, Essay 2: "On Refinement in the Arts," in *Reflections on Commercial Life*, pp. 164-65.

"To say that, without a vicious luxury, the labour would not be employed at all, is only to say, that there is some other defect in human nature . . . for which luxury, in some measure, provides a remedy. . . ."[27] Hume argues, against Mandeville, that one can never see vice as "advantageous." But this judgment, I am suggesting, flows from a different moral anthropology, one built on fellow-feeling, and also a naturalistic ethics in which the purpose of morality, and social institutions like commerce, is to direct rather than thwart human desires. Precisely for this reason, social utility can never in any simple sense override personal happiness. Commercial society was to further virtue and, when coupled with a sense of humor, enlarge sentiments beyond the "monstrously absurd" desire of unmixed avarice.

What Hume introduces back into the discussion of commercial society is the connection between trade and the sentiments of self, the "soul" as St. Ambrose put it. Unlike Mandeville, Hume declares that human sentiments can be tutored and enlarged; it is the special benefit of commerce to expand our fellow-feeling and love of utility. But of course this poses massive problems as well. As Murray has noted, "Hume had just an inkling of the question: Does the global economy erode the local conditions which form identities, loyalties, and virtues? Will the commercial 'enlargement' of our sentiments stretch them beyond the limits of their elasticity?"[28] More to the point, Hume seems to miss the force of Mandeville's real insight: that commercial society might need to foster "vice," greed, in order to balance production and consumption. How is it, we might ask, that "greed" itself is not a kind of enlargement of sentiment, not in terms of fellow-feeling but in the intensification of economic motive? Is it so easy to claim that commercial society transforms our sentiments, our inordinate desires, directing them to the proper end of happiness and social utility?

Conflict of Assessments

I have been following a rather complex path of reflection. This path has moved from an initial, and rather formal, phenomenological description of "greed," aided by Swift's wit and insight, through the condemnation of avarice by traditional moralists, and onward to the arguments of Mandeville and Hume. What we have seen is a conflict of assessments about greed. The arguments surveyed differ in their judgments about the Yahoo-nature of

27. Hume, "On Refinement," in *Reflections on Commercial Life*, p. 170.
28. Murray, ed., *Reflections on Commercial Life*, p. 156.

trading. Traditional Christian ethics denounces Yahoo vices that too easily dominate commerce. And yet, thinkers like Luther and Aquinas also hold that we can become better; we are not condemned to remain Yahoo. Mandeville praises Yahoo vices for their economic impulse. Realistic in his assessment of actual economic life, Mandeville is rather pessimistic about the possibilities for transformation, or human betterment. David Hume is quite optimistic about human betterment and that precisely through commerce. He believes that commerce is not Yahoo to the bone; somehow it transforms our vices into genuine virtues. We might put it like this: traditional Christian thought is more realistic than Hume about the motives driving commerce even as it is more hopeful than Mandeville about moral betterment. The reason for this is that Christian ethics must account for not only human vice and fault but also the created goodness of human life. In terms of an analysis of any human motivation, Christian thought will, by its own internal logic, weave a middle path between condemnation and simple endorsement.

The reason for my complex path of reflection is quite simple. It is important to clarify moral concepts since they enable us to articulate the shape of human lives. Yet moral concepts must be understood in terms of their descriptive power — their semantic and phenomenological structure — and also in terms of their historical and social indebtedness. Without such an analysis of moral concepts, we too easily fall prey to abstractions that blind us to the real dynamics of human life.[29] This path of thinking is intended to uncover some of the historical forces that have shaped our conceptions of greed, even as I hope to show how this concept picks out features of moral experience. The paradox of our situation, then, is that these strands of thought, and many others as well, flow into present conceptions and assessments of the marketplace. The question now is this: what have we learned, and what does it mean for living responsibly in a culture of consumption?

Two general conclusions can be drawn from our inquiry, conclusions that must factor into any normative response about how to live responsibly in a culture of consumption. First, it is clear that the very meaning of commercial society differs among the various traditions of thought we have explored. For the traditional Christian, to live responsibly in a commercial society one must labor for the necessities of life, curtail greed, and seek the higher goods of the spiritual life. Mandevillians, conversely, would argue, as some current rational-choice theorists in fact do, that we ought to seek, and seek unrelent-

---

29. On the problem of abstractions in theological and philosophical thinking see Michael Welker, *Creation and Reality,* trans. John Hoffmeyer (Minneapolis: Fortress, 1999).

ingly, the acquisition of wealth.[30] In the domain of commerce, the "vices" must be given free reign; virtue should pertain only to private relations. Finally, Humeans would argue that the responsible life entails the cultivation of social virtues and that, properly conducted, commerce is precisely the means to live such a life. In other words, we have seen that the basic question of our inquiry is not easily answered, since "a culture of consumption" admits of different construals with decidedly divergent implications for living morally. Little wonder, then, that societies deeply marked by these various traditions of thought, as well as others, seem at a loss for any coherent vision of responsibility in commercial life. Even if one were to understand life in (say) markedly Humean terms, the society in which one works, loves, and dies is nevertheless informed by different visions of life. This is merely to say that the question of moral diversity and pluralism besets matters of commercial existence as much as any other aspect of social life.

But, second, we have learned something else. I have suggested that greed is a human craving informed by social conceptions of "wealth." Greed, as pictured here, is imaginatively shaped by desire. A child might experience the pangs of greed for the latest video game; an adult for wealth, cars, clothes. Excessive craving is not in itself greed; it becomes greed if and only if the craving is imaginatively informed with respect to social conventions about what counts as "wealth." "Wealth" designates a social end or purpose the desire of which can be the efficient cause of human action and choice. But this is a unique kind of desire or cause of action. The greedy person is one who craves to have his or her desire so informed, wants to be absorbed into the social convention in the very act of consuming culturally defined goods. This was Aquinas's point in saying that avarice subjects the will to a good lower than the proper human end (*Summa Theologiae* II/II, q. 114, a. 5). Accordingly, we need to understand property in terms not simply of its use or exchange value, but also of what Jean Baudrillard has called the "sign value" of commodities.[31] A teenager, for instance, may crave a pair of GAP jeans not because of the market or exchange value of the pants but, more importantly, because the jeans have "sign value" among his friends, a value pertaining to status and social acceptance.

Greed is the desire to have one's self and most basic passions inscribed within the semiotics of a culture, its sign values. The phenomenology of

---

30. For this position see Robert Nozick, *Anarchy, State, and Utopia* (Cambridge, Mass.: Harvard University Press, 1974), and a criticism of it, Margaret Jane Radin, *Reinterpreting Property* (Chicago: University of Chicago Press, 1993).

31. See Jean Baudrillard, "Consumer Society," in *Reflections on Commercial Life*, ed. Murray, pp. 447-73.

greed, as I have called it, takes seriously the "sign value" of commodities in the formation of a person's sense of self. Something like it seems manifest in traditional Christian discourse, Swift's biting satire, and Hume's sensitivity for the need to enlarge sentiments. Only Mandeville, it would appear, fails to grasp this point, and that is because, given his non-naturalism in ethics, human passions are strictly untutorable. In other words, Mandeville does not grasp the reflexive structure of greed: how what is desired constitutes, through the mixing of imagination, sign value, and craving, a new order of desire best called greed. For Mandeville passions simply are given.

What then is the insight? How is this not simply a descriptive claim about the structure of one kind of human passion? The insight for an ethics of commercialism is this: the odd dynamics of the passion called greed are such that it feeds on cultural values, especially sign values, while simultaneously endangering the tranquility and justice of social life. Greed inscribes a person within a culture's table of values and yet, in the drive to subsume them into the self, also threatens the very bonds of society, bonds that require fairness, justice, and some concern for the common good. This is why, we might imagine, Ambrose drew the connection between the "city" and the "soul"; it is why Hume had to conceive of the means to enlarge sentiments; it is why Mandeville tried to separate morality and economy; it is why Luther and Aquinas, despite other differences, saw that greed is idolatrous and an attack on the common good. The paradox is that a commercial culture, through the power of its sign values, can and does foster excessive consumption and thus greed, but in the act of doing so threatens social stability and flourishing. Is it any wonder, then, that in advanced commercial cultures we see the breakdown of concern for the common good both among the wealthy, who consume at an alarming rate, and the poor, who desire that level of consumption? Traditional Christian thought was simply right on this point: greed is a capital vice because is gathers around it other forms of viciousness that undercut the possibility of sustainable social existence.

What then are we to do? Mindful of the diverse legacies of thought that have informed conceptions of property and acquisitiveness, how can persons live responsibly in a commercial culture? Mindful too of the phenomenology of greed and its real threat to social life, what pattern of thought will aid in so living? I turn next to those questions and thus to the final line of inquiry.

Imagination, Desire, and Consumption

If the above reflections are at all convincing, then the line that separates human aspiration and the acquisitiveness that motivates economic action from true greed in all of its destructiveness must be drawn with greater care than often is done in ethics. We must distinguish greed from acquisitiveness in terms of how the "sign value" of wealth functions in the formation of desire. On this account, commercial society is Yahoo to the bone if and only if it aims to form desire solely through the sign-value of commodities. This is a real and present possibility when a society is at loss for any alternate discourse through which to shape desire. In that case, commodification becomes totalistic; it infests all other realms of life with a seemingly limitless desire. Now we see the reason why I have been concerned to combat the removal of the discourse of greed from social life. The language of "greed" presupposes some table of values other than "commodities" and their sign value in the understanding and articulation of human desire and motivation. And this is so, since to call a desire "greedy" is already to make judgments about its destructiveness to the individual and to the society.

It is at this level of insight that I judge Christian discourse has a surprising contribution to make to reflection on property and possession. Stated abstractly, the contribution is this: In the formation of human desires, the believer is bid to love a reality that shatters sign value. One is to love God with heart and soul and mind, but God is precisely that reality which cannot be inscribed within any system of signs. The love of God, we might say, can limit the desire of acquisition precisely because what is desired exceeds objectification. Of course, it is also the case — given the human heart — that "God" has become the ultimate sign value in relation to which all else is valued. The labor of the social imaginary, in the need to fix an object of desire, fabricates idolatrous God-images that can and do legitimate other social structures and hierarchies. The destructiveness of this "theologizing of desire," if I may call it that, has been seen by many, ranging from the Hebrew prophets and their denunciation of the wealthy's exploitation of the poor to current feminist theologians. But the paradox is that the very demand to destroy idols can itself become an idol. Idolatry, that is, the reduction of the divine to our system of signs, is the inner meaning of greed theologically construed. This is what makes greed religiously dangerous, a "mortal" sin. Morally this means that "greed" is checked only when human desire is given a non-consumable object. Is this really possible? Perhaps what is needed is not an idea that somehow escapes the strange logic of iconoclasm so much as a discourse about inordinate and destructive desires. From this perspective, the loss of the discourse of greed within current social discourse means the triumph of commodification and the subsuming of a person's identity within a society's system of sign values.

The force of this argument should not be missed. The insight is to insist, unlike so much contemporary ethics, that moral matters are not piggybacked on a more or less neutral view of life. Moral claims are not explainable solely in terms of social conventions. Convictions about what is good, right, and virtuous afford light into reality, for the Christian tradition's claims about "God" are not simply imaginative constructions or symbols for "meaning" in life, although theological discourse does entail these functional dynamics. What is at stake are claims about reality. Faith in God, for instance, is a way of perceiving, interpreting, and evaluating the world. Theological ethics does not move from (say) economic and institutional analysis to trace out "ethical implications." Taking our lead from Christian ideas about "greed," we have thus been led to a profound moral and conceptual insight. At the very origins of human motivation is not a value-neutral set of blind impulses, but a complex, reflexive relation between desire and cultural valuations. (It is this too that explains the logic of iconoclasm in the theologizing of desire.) But this means that while human desires might be morally and psychologically recalcitrant, how they are culturally saturated, and thus rendered meaningful and understandable, depends on the "valuations" used to shape and inform desires. We must explore the symbolic and conceptual forms used to saturate desire and thus give rise to motivations. And this requires that there is some room for moral change, moral improvement in and through the rigorous examination of the reflexive relation of desire and valuations. In making this claim about motivations, we bridge "nature and nurture," simple naturalism and bald social-construction, in our account of "greed." My suggestion now is that the discourse of greed is one of those forms of "cultural saturation" needed to assess and shape human desire. The loss of this discourse is the loss of a crucial form of moral self-understanding.

There is irony in this, of course. I am suggesting that the contribution religious discourse can make to current economic life hinges on what is understood to exceed that discourse (i.e., "God") and yet is forever pulled into the circle of desire and cultural saturation. And given this, theological reflection makes its contribution by keeping a language of human viciousness alive! Put differently, the contribution a theological ethics of culture can make to commercial society is to designate what is "outside" of commodification and how that "outside" might form human motivations and self-understandings as well as expose moral failing, or viciousness. This is not to say that Christian discourse is the only means to check the commodification of desire, since, as just noted, it too continually falls into that enterprise. My point is merely that such discourse opens up reflection on human desire in a surprising way that can and ought to inform our reflection on economic existence. It provides a way to "reconsider greed" in terms of its dynamics and the importance of this discourse in social life.

Conclusion

What does this mean for living responsibly? More than anything else the focus of responsibility in our time concerns self-understanding in the exercise of power.[32] In terms of commercial life, this means that we are enabled and required to assess and even transform our self-understandings in the direction of economic power, the power to produce and to consume. The language of greed, I have been suggesting, is really a discourse about self-understanding at the level of human craving. By keeping this discourse in play within commercial society, we have one means to test self-understanding and the uses of economic power. The loss of this discourse, I have also suggested, means a return to a Yahoo world. It is against that possibility that the Christian tradition has something to contribute in sustaining a rich and complex moral discourse needed for a global, sustainable future.

---

32. On this see Hans Jonas, *The Imperative of Responsibility: In Search for an Ethics of the Technological Age,* trans. Hans Jonas and David Herr (Chicago: University of Chicago Press, 1984), and also Schweiker, *Responsibility and Christian Ethics,* esp. chap. 7.

The Cultural Contest for Our Attention: Observations on Media, Property, and Religion

GÜNTER THOMAS

Introduction

Times are changing. They are changing rapidly. In 1972 the first Report of the Club of Rome pointed out the limits of growth by describing the limitations of our natural resources as well the increasing pollution of our natural environment.[1] Since 1984 the annual State of the World reports of the Worldwatch Institute have provided information about the current trends in the world economy, the global use of scarce resources, and issues concerning a sustainable society.[2] Even though we have made great progress during the last decades in more efficient use of natural resources, all advanced industrial societies still depend heavily on them.

But do we depend only on natural resources like oil, gas, water, coal, wood, and metals? What is the most valuable resource, the most *contested* property of the information society? The most valuable and the scarcest resource of our society — saturated by television, the Internet, and cell phones — is *human attention*. Everyday, human attention is measured by "click-through-rates" and captured eyeballs, by the number of unique users and Nielsen ratings. Human attention is a property over which many forces fight. Billboards, newsstands, instant messages, and phone calls wrestle for our attention. This property, attention, is a resource needed by all communication

1. D. L. Meadows et al., *The Limits of Growth: A Report for the Club of Rome's Project on the Predicament of Mankind* (New York: Universe Books, 1972).

2. L. R. Brown et al., *State of the World: A Worldwatch Institute Report on Progress Toward a Sustainable Society* (New York: W. W. Norton, 1984-).

processes in which human beings are involved. Human attention belongs to a subgroup of cultural resources, a little-explored group but one that is necessary for the flourishing of human life and modern societies. The fact that those institutions and persons who attract and absorb lots of attention have cultural and often economic power underscores the importance of this cultural resource. Like natural resources, cultural resources can be used or exploited, but unlike many natural resources that can be found, cultural resources need to be regenerated and renewed. And in this struggle over the cultural resource of attention the religious communities cannot be silent.

This leads to the thesis of my essay: Human attention is a very much contested cultural property and resource. This struggle implies processes of having, gaining, and losing, and raises the question of where this resource is regenerated. The Christian churches are called to be places where the crucial cultural resource of attention is regenerated, redirected, and invested outside the contemporary economy of attention. So far the general thesis. Let's have a look at the details.

What Are Cultural Resources?

If anything has become apparent during the last three decades, it is that the way modern societies deal with their natural environments depends not only on the societal power structure but also on the mind-set of people, that is to say, on the complex cultural framework that influences political and economic action.[3] For better or worse, the functioning of society as well as the world of everyday life draws on cultural resources. As every reader of Max Weber's historical studies and Talcott Parsons's theories knows, the development of Western societies is heavily influenced by value systems, motivations, habits, and patterns stemming from certain strands of religious traditions. Specific value systems, latent patterns, an ethos sustaining and reshaping the legal system, and, eventually, everyday habits of behavior are cultural resources that are — for good and bad — at the basis of our individual and communal life. They are used in economical processes, in the legal system as well as in the political system. Not only knowledge transmitted and acquired in educational processes but also visions of a shared future and a good life are

3. This fact comes through occasionally in the "State of the World Reports" and lies at the basis of the churches' responses to the ecological crises. For an overview of the religious responses, see Barbara Kohler, *Die Überlebensfähige Gesellschaft angesichts der globalen ökosozialen Krise. Weltmodelle und Überlebenskonzeptionen des Worldwatch Institutes und thematisch verwandter kirchlicher Verlautbarungen* (diss., Heidelberg University, 1992).

necessary cultural resources for the development of a society. Such cultural resources are embedded in cultural institutions and in the individual beings who make up and support these institutions.[4]

Cultural resources are those "entities" that contribute to economic or political processes as necessary elements but are not the result of such processes. Yet are cultural resources only to be "found," like oil, air, and water? The whole set of cultural resources may be divided into roughly three groups. In one group are those that can be actively produced and built up, including certain skills and forms of knowledge. To the second group belong ethical orientations, habits, and values that need to be "edified" yet can only be "produced" in quite indirect and complex ways.[5] The third group consists of resources that can only be regenerated or nourished, such as curiosity or attention. Unlike natural resources, these cultural resources are not just "there" to be found and used but are themselves the result of cultural processes. Cultural resources in this third group emerge out of systemic and self-referential processes in which they are the "product" as well as the precondition. Like their "natural" counterpart, they are intrinsically limited, even though, unlike natural resources, they may seem to be unlimited.

Compared to natural resources these cultural resources are invisible properties that become most apparent when they are absent. These properties come to the center of attention only when they become one side of a distinction. Corruption in economic life, sociocultural brutalization, the lack of necessary types of knowledge, a breakdown of the legal system, the extinction of the arts — each of these phenomena can indicate the partial or total exhaustion or absence of cultural resources. And, in contrast to the natural resources, although the very absence of cultural resources might make them "present," they are not easily measured and quantified.

But of greater concern is the fact that many cultural resources need to be regenerated. For example, the basic trust that life is comprehensible, the ability to cope with life in the face to suffering, and the belief in justice — to name just a few — are all constantly being challenged.[6] Nevertheless, they are

---

4. The issue of cultural resources should not, however, be fused with the other issue of cultural institutions as it is outlined by William J. Bennett, *The Index of Leading Cultural Indicators: American Society at the End of the 20th Century* (New York: Broadway, 1994).

5. Such resources suffer from a paradox in communication: If, for instance, moral communication is recognized as intentional moral communication, its risk of being rejected rises extremely. These cultural resources can be built up only if they are not intended.

6. Clifford Geertz's theory of religion, for instance, can be read as an attempt to point out the ways religion helps to preserve and regenerate the cultural resources of knowledge, emotional stability, and ethical orientation — by working "at the limits of . . . analytic capacities, at

preconditions, or resources, for the flourishing of social and individual life. Within this broad range of cultural resources, one that has gone almost unnoticed by many social theorists up to now is human attention.

Human Attention: The Current Debate

The topic of human attention is moving to the forefront within the current debate about the international media culture.[7] In spite of this topic's apparent newness, it seems worthwhile to point out that the issue in some respects is a rather old one. Only if we comprehend key aspects of the older debate can we observe the dramatic shift that occurred at the end of the twentieth century.

The goal of catching someone's attention stands at the center of the rhetorical tradition. Moreover, early on the Roman poet Lucretius reasoned in *De rerum natura* about the need to have focused and selective attention *(attentio animi)* in order to gain real insight.[8] The connection between novelty and attention, that is to say, the issue of attracting attention through the novelty of an external stimulus, is also a matter of concern for a number of classical philosophers, even though they mention this issue only in passing. Johann G. Fichte, Johann G. Herder, and Jean-Jacques Rousseau are rather critical regarding the value of new insights and events that attract human attention. On the opposite side, David Hume and Gottfried W. Leibnitz value novelty as a way to channel people's interest in their philosophical programs. While all these references to attention point out the relation between novelty, individual attention, and successful communication, their peculiar premodern background becomes visible if one analyzes their shortcomings. Just as they cannot imagine our current overflow of (possibilities for) communication, they also do not envision an absolute scarcity of attention. For similar

---

the limits of . . . powers of endurance, and at the limits of . . . moral insight." See Clifford Geertz, "Religion As a Cultural System," in his *Interpretation of Cultures: Selected Essays* (New York: Basic, 1973), pp. 87-125, 100.

7. The present discussion is documented in Klaus Beck and Wolfgang Schweiger, eds., *Attention Please! Online-Kommunikation und Aufmerksamkeit* (München: Reinhard Fischer, 2001), and Florian Rötzer, ed., *Ressource Aufmerksamkeit. Ästhetik in der Informationsgesellschaft* (Kunstforum international, vol. 148, Jan. 2000), pp. 51-181. Rich historical material as well as a discussion of the concept is provided in Aleida Assmann and Jan Assmann, eds., *Aufmerksamkeiten* (München: Wilhelm Fink, 2001).

8. For this and the following historical references see Niels Werber, "Zweierlei Aufmerksamkeit in Medien, Kunst und Politik," in *Ressource Aufmerksamkeit*, ed. Rötzer, pp. 139-51.

reasons, the lack of attention is not considered to be a cultural problem but only an individual one.

The shift in the cultural economy of attention that occurred during the last decades has produced a lively debate, which takes as its starting point recent contributions from two individuals, Michael Goldhaber and Georg Franck, both of whom have written on the idea of an economy of attention.[9] Goldhaber and Franck share many insights regarding the phenomenon of attention, even though they differ in important respects. Despite these differences, they both develop this concept of attention in terms of two framing developments in modern society: (1) Economic models and concepts have become more and more important for decoding social and cultural processes. (2) Within the overall economy a further "dematerialization" in the production of value is occurring. Goldhaber, like Franck, takes as his starting point the overflow of information over against the scarcity of attention. For both, the Internet is the paradigm and the latest step in this development.[10] At the same time, they observe that in any given society the need for attention is even more widespread than money. Through a reciprocity of expectations, attention becomes something that can be traded: I am longing for attention and can give away attention. At the same time, I know that others are longing for attention and can give it away. Out of this reciprocity and exchange, an economy of attention emerges. Goldhaber and Franck do not, however, stop simply with a view of attention as a rare and highly valued tradable possession. Both move further by claiming that attention becomes a kind of currency that is the basis for the "attention economy." This move from an illuminating metaphor, or even a conceptual model, of an economy of attention to

9. See Georg Franck: *Ökonomie der Aufmerksamkeit. Ein Entwurf* (München: Karl Hanser, 1998); "Jenseits von Geld und Information," in *Ressource Aufmerksamkeit,* ed. Rötzer, pp. 84-94, also in *Telepolis* 09.11.1998 (http://www.heise.de/tp/deutsch/special/auf/6313/1.html); "Die neue Währung: Aufmerksamkeit," in *Merkur* 43 (1989): 688-701; "Ein Kampf um Aufmerksamkeit. Zur Organisation von Wissenschaft," in *Merkur* 51 (1997): 72-79. See Michael H. Goldhaber: "The Attention Economy and the Net," second draft version of a talk presented at the Conference on "Economics of Digital Information," Cambridge, Massachusetts, 23-26 January 1997 (http://www.well.com/user/mgoldh/AtEcandNet.html); "Kunst und die Aufmerksamkeitsökonomie im wirklichen Raum und im Cyberspace," in *Ressource Aufmerksamkeit,* ed. Rötzer, pp. 78-83.

10. One of the main arguments is that in the Worldwide Web most information is free, thus money is not any longer the main motive for the distribution of information. Whether this observation can hold true remains to be seen. The crises of the Web economy in 2000, 2001, and 2002 seem to invalidate this argument. In addition, this observation does not differentiate between relevant information and irrelevant information or, to be more specific, between data and information.

the claim that such an economy exists is a move that is very much debated among economists. While Franck suggests that there exists a "second economy" driven by attention and connected to the classical money economy, Goldhaber makes an even bolder claim.[11] He suggests that the attention economy will eventually replace the currently dominant monetarily based capitalist economy. Goldhaber believes the attention economy will eventually take the place of money as the driving force behind work. The transaction of products will finally be substituted by the transaction of attention.

Without any doubt, Goldhaber's strong substitution thesis is itself a questionable product of the attention economy. Not only is such a claim theoretically untenable, it even distracts from observing the powerful links between the money market and attention, an issue I will on touch later. It also diverts scholarly attention away from the crucial issue of an ecology of attention. The other idea of attention being something like a currency cannot be rejected wholesale but needs further sociological elaboration and theoretical scrutiny, particularly in the light of Talcott Parsons's theory of "symbolic media of interchange" and Niklas Luhmann's "symbolically generalized media of communication."[12] What seems to be most worthwhile, however, is the distinction made between attention as a *resource* and attention as a *property of exchange*. It will be valuable to explore the subtle dynamics between these two manifestations of attention.

Human Attention As Cultural Resource — Conceptual Clarifications

The public debate over Goldhaber's and Franck's theses clearly indicates the need for further conceptual clarification. The confusion about the concept is

---

11. Franck does, however, claim that attention might become more important than money for the social allocation and rationing of resources (*Ökonomie der Aufmerksamkeit*, p. 51).

12. Talcott Parsons, "Social Structure and the Symbolic Media of Interchange," in his *Social Systems and the Evolution of Action Theory* (New York: Free Press, 1974), pp. 204-28; Niklas Luhmann, *Die Gesellschaft der Gesellschaft* (Frankfurt am Main: Suhrkamp, 1997), pp. 316-97. Based on Parsons's and Luhmann's insights, the debate of Franck's and particularly of Goldhaber's proposal suffers from a theoretical confusion that overshadows already Goldhaber's texts: Assuming that attention becomes a kind of currency, a medium of exchange, does *not* necessarily mean that this currency can substitute for money. If, as the critics rightly affirm, attention can never substitute for money, we are left with the question: What is the system of which attention is the currency? Thus the critique from economists does not automatically invalidate the claim of attention being a "currency." Attention seems to be the currency of the media system.

intensified in the German discussion, since the German term *Aufmerksamkeit* can mean both awareness and attention. At the moment, I would like to differentiate the following concepts with the help of terminology borrowed from Niklas Luhmann.

Types of Attention

Awareness is not yet attention, since awareness requires only being awake and conscious with some kind of feeling, an intransitive state that includes the possibility of turning toward something. Attention is reached when awareness is combined with a focused intentionality. With this in mind, I would like to differentiate at least three types of attention.

First, attention can be directed toward the self, in the form of either self-reflection or daydreaming. This *self-reflexive attention* does not require a stimulus from the outside. Therefore it is not based on irritability but needs selectivity in order to achieve focused intentions. In cases when consciousness, or the cognitive-emotional system, turns to the outside, there are still two options.[13] But in both cases there is a highly complex process between the act of focusing attention through the cognitive-emotional system, on the one side, and the attraction of attention by the intended "object," on the other side. Due to the autopoietical nature of consciousness, attention can be directed by internal processes (intentions) or by outside irritations that mobilize and attract attention.

Attention can also be used to gain and to process selective perceptions. This type of *perceptive attention* should not be equated with passivity, since it can be very active in working through pattern recognitions and other forms of searching for and working through information. The binding of perceptive attention can occur by natural perception (such as the nonmediated environment present while driving a car or climbing in the mountains) or mediated perception (such as watching a film, listening to recorded music, and so on).

The third type of attention is based not only on awareness but also on perceptive attention. Since it includes the coupling with other cognitive-emotional or even social systems for the purpose of communication, I would like to call it *communicative attention*. Not all attention has to be directed to-

13. For Franck (*Ökonomie der Aufmerksamkeit*, p. 29), who is at this point more precise that Goldhaber, attention could be translated as "selective perception and goal-oriented processing of information." And yet, the latter seems to be too far-reaching. Active attention is already required in situations in which perception is intensified and has to face the *possibility* of information.

ward communication. This assumption is one of the most common mistakes made in the current debate, but for communication to occur, attention has to be very focused, and therefore this type of attention is easier to work out and understand. This type of binding of attention differs from perceptive attention since the double contingency of communication makes this process rather risky.

The much-debated case of accumulated attention[14] necessitates some kind of reciprocity, either in perceptive attention or in communicative attention or in the attribution of attention. Since the reciprocity of perception almost always leads to communication, however, accumulated attention is the result of direct or indirect communication that attributes attention.[15] If this accumulation of attention is centered on specific topics and attains some stability over time, it results in the creation of a public.[16]

Attention As Resource in Communication Theories

But why is human attention so important for modern societies, and in what sense is it a resource? Why is it such a valuable property, and — as I may add — why is its examination so important for the understanding of late modernity and so illuminating for theological reasoning about the church? To answer this question, one has to briefly look back at the shift in scholarly paradigms and how they are connected. Even this brief look at philosophical tradition reveals that attention is a resource because it is — to borrow a rather technical model — a dynamic interface. Research within the great tradition of German Idealism focused in many ways on the self, or the human person, and his or her consciousness. The potential of individual reason, the inner

14. Franck, *Ökonomie der Aufmerksamkeit*, chap. 4.

15. Two examples might illustrate the point: Mount Rushmore is not famous because the mountain realizes that it is the object of perceptive attention of many people, but because people talk about it and communicate their invested attention, thereby *attributing* attention. While communicative attention might include a reciprocity of attention between living beings, mediated communication makes it possible that even dead persons can accumulate attention through attribution processes. Many authors became "famous" only after their death, so they cannot perceive anymore in some meaningful sense the communicative attention they attract and receive.

16. This formal conception of "public" is broader than the Enlightenment concept connected to reason and rationality, yet it allows us to decode the so-called "decay of the public" as a transformation of publics through shifts in style, medium, and topics. See Günter Thomas, "Art: Öffentlichkeit," in *Metzler Lexikon Religion*, vol. 2, ed. Christoph Auffarth, Jutta Bernhard, and Hubert Mohr (Stuttgart: J. B. Metzler, 1999), pp. 586-89.

life, the "I," the individual subject, and the edification of a personality were at the center of interest. Although in many respects such ideas were already anticipated by Idealist thinkers such as Schleiermacher, Herder, and Humboldt, the twentieth century became the century of the linguistic turn. Language, shared symbolic systems, and patterns of discourse became the primary objects of intellectual inquiries. It seems to me that one link between both traditions is the role of human attention. Attention is the interface between objectified sociocultural processes, on the one side, and subjectivity and the whole complex of one's "inner life," on the other. By leaving out the place of attention, modern theories of communication are unable to point out their own presuppositions and are ill equipped to uncover the resources on which communication is dependent. At this point, I cannot elaborate this at length. Instead, the following three short references should illustrate my point.

Our first example: Hans-Georg Gadamer, whose work influenced much philosophical as well as theological hermeneutics, places the question of attention squarely at the center of the hermeneutical experience.[17] The logical structure of openness that characterizes hermeneutical consciousness rests on the priority of the question over against the answer. But why question? This is a question Gadamer never raised. Yet any act of questioning requires the investment of focused attention. In particular an act of questioning is based on highly selective attention that opens a horizon of questioning as the intellectual space within which this question makes sense. Therefore communicative attention is the interface between traditions, texts, and cultural objects, on the one side, and the understanding taking place in the hermeneutical experience of the person, on the other. Any reaching out to traditions and texts requires the delicate resource of attention. Seen in this way, Gadamer's work points toward the immense importance of attention for the whole human project of understanding.

In a similar vein, Jürgen Habermas concentrates in his theory of communicative action on the structure of linguistic expressions, their illocutionary power, and their semantic and pragmatic dimensions, which allow interlocutors to differentiate between instrumental, strategic, and communicative actions.[18] How do communicative acts contribute to the creation of interactions based on clearly articulated and negotiated normative claims? he asks.

17. Hans-Georg Gadamer, *Truth and Method* (New York: Seabury, 1975), chap. 2.3.c. Gadamer asks for the logical structure of openness which characterizes the hermeneutical consciousness, yet stops at the "question," without further questioning for the requirements for questioning.

18. See Jürgen Habermas, *Theory of Communicative Action*, vol. 1 (Boston: Beacon, 1984), chap. 3.

In raising such questions, however, Habermas explicitly rejects the examination of the dispositions leading to such linguistic behavior as merely a task of psychological inquiry. But, in so doing, Habermas cuts himself off from the question of the preconditions, or the cultural resources, required to engage in such communication. Communicative attention seems to be the invisible condition of possibility *(Bedingung der Möglichkeit)* for such linguistic engagement. By neglecting the issue of attention, Habermas also loses a valuable tool for analyzing the systemic colonization of the life-world, since this process could be decoded as an absorption of attention by other systems.

Let me turn quite briefly to a last example: Niklas Luhmann's theory of communication and of modern society which culminates in the — at first glance rather strange — dictum, "Not persons, only communication can communicate."[19] For Luhmann, society as a texture of autopoietical social systems consists of type-different forms of communication that emerge out of noise, that is to say the utterances of — among others — psychic systems. Both social and psychic systems operate interdependently and autonomously, yet they are connected by means of coupling. For Luhmann, the person is ultimately placed in the internal environment of society, even though he emphasizes the need for coupling in communication systems. While "viewing communication not as a phenomenon but as a problem," he wants "to ask how communication is possible at all."[20] He never concentrates, however, on the vital requirement of such coupling, that is to say, on the resource in the environment of attention.[21] Only attention makes understanding possible and enables the operation of communication, which is the unity of information, utterance, and understanding. What Luhmann calls coupling between the human consciousness as a psychic system and the social system happens to take place by means of human attention. While stressing difference, he never elaborates the selective exposure to communication as the construction of difference that operates by means of the selective distribution of attention.

What is the reason for such neglect by leading theorists of communication and language? In short, my hypothesis is that they do not realize the se-

---

19. Luhmann's complex social theory with his communication theory is best accessible in Niklas Luhmann, *Ecological Communication* (Chicago: University of Chicago Press, 1989), chap. 6. See also his *Social Systems*, trans. John Bednarz Jr. (Stanford: Stanford University Press, 1995), chap. 4.

20. Niklas Luhmann, "The Improbability of Communication," in *Essays on Self-Reference* (New York: Columbia University Press, 1990), pp. 86-98, at p. 87.

21. It should be noted that Luhmann clearly sees attention as the necessary requirement for communication, but it does not play a role in his communication theory. For his view on attention see Luhmann, "Improbability of Communication," p. 88.

vere imbalance between the overflowing possibilities of communication and the scarce property of attention that characterizes the information society of late modernity. Like economic theorists during the eighteenth and nineteenth centuries, they just assume that there is enough attention provided for in the communication process. The paradox that actual communication is severely restricted by the overflow of communication and that this constraint might become an issue in the future of modern societies is not taken into account in their theories.[22] Luhmann does reflect on the improbability of communication, but the dynamic that is unleashed in order to bind human attention is not considered in his approach.

Regenerating a Scarce Resource

Now I have to turn to the question: Why is attention a limited resource, and why does it need to be regenerated? If we look at the whole issue of attention with this concern in mind, two types of scarcity come into view. First, there is the scarcity of awareness, even though the limit can be neither measured nor understood as a natural given.[23] Human beings are finite beings in many respects. Not only in terms of the human life span, but also in terms of the limitations of time during a day, a week, or a year that define our natural and cultural rhythms, our attention is limited. It should be noted that all types of attention, even awareness, are limited. At least in terms of time, awareness is not without limits.

The second limitation can be found in the transformation of awareness into attention, as either self-reflexive attention, perceptive attention, or communicative attention. If we try to quantify attention in terms of time and persons, the natural limit of any kind of attention is the time of awareness. All types of attention taken together cannot exceed the time of awareness. As we shall see later, communicative attention is the object of social contests, so that the relation between perceptive attention and communicative attention becomes one of competition. Everyone knows situations where we are ex-

22. To be more precise: The issue is present in more media-oriented communication theories but not yet appropriately taken up by social theorists or social ethicists. For a remarkable exception see Orin E. Klapp: *Opening and Closing* (New York: Cambridge University Press, 1978); "Meaning Lack in Information Society," *Journal of Communication* 32 (1982): 56-66; and *Overload and Boredom: Essays on the Quality of Life in the Information Society* (New York: Greenwood, 1986), especially chaps. 2 and 7.

23. Compared to pre-modern times, artificial light as well as legal drugs such as coffee, tea, or cigarettes shift the limit.

hausted, tired, and not anymore able and willing to enter into deep communications, yet where we are still willing to engage in perception. The exhaustion of communicative attention is a clear marker that, even if we are awake and fully conscious, we have embodied minds and are bodily creatures. It should also be noticed that in the case of technologically mediated perception in perceptive attention, and in the case of communicative attention, *individual* attention becomes the basis of *social* phenomena.

Since the primary location of such attention (all three types — self-reflexive, perceptive, and communicative) is the individual cognitive-emotional system, the whole topic of attention is primarily dealt with within the field of psychology.[24] But since attention is required for the social process of communication, the psychologically given becomes a social resource and social property. The fact that attention inevitably becomes part of the sociocultural dynamic of having, gaining, and losing is nicely revealed in two linguistic expressions. Both point to communicative attention as the basis of social life. In English, you "*pay* attention to," indicating that attention is a valuable good like money, even a social currency. In German, you "*donate* attention" *(Aufmerksamkeit schenken)*, which clearly implies, on the one hand, the idea of giving something freely away by being attentive and, on the other, the idea of receiving a gift — the attention of another person. Since communicative attention is intrinsically a relational phenomenon, it becomes a social phenomenon within the sociocultural dynamic of having, gaining, and losing.

At the end of this section, I turn to the question of why attention needs to be regenerated. The topic of regeneration needs to be placed, however, within the broader context of an "ecology of attention."[25] At this point, I can only highlight essential aspects of such an ecology of attention. This wider context makes it apparent that the regeneration of attention has a formal as well as a qualitative side. While awareness can be taken for granted, attention in the form of self-reflexive attention, perceptive attention, and communicative attention cannot be taken for granted. The formal side concerns the bare presence of attention and the balance between the types of attention. Perceptive attention should not supersede communicative attention. Communicative attention in particular depends on individual as well as cultural memory and expectations. Any substantial change in the cultural memory will result

24. For an overview of the various theories see Werner Wirth, "Aufmerksamkeit. Ein Konzept- und Theorieüberblick aus psychologischer Perspektive mit Implikationen für die Kommunikationswissenschaft," in *Attention Please*, ed. Beck and Schweiger, pp. 69-89.

25. See Günter Thomas, *Medien — Ritual — Religion. Zur religiösen Funktion des Fernsehens* (Frankfurt am Main: Suhrkamp, 1998), p. 631ff.

in changed expectations. Another formal aspect is the relation between attention that is triggered and attracted primarily through irritations of the cognitive-emotional system and attention that is intentionally "invested" with interests, motivations, curiosity, or formed expectations. If more and more attention depends on external powers to attract attention, the result will be deep shifts in patterns of cultural reproduction. An additional aspect of an ecology of attention is the cultivation of sufficiently focused attention required for the communication of complex subjects, especially those that are not just "fun."[26] An angle I will touch on later is the cultivation of attention through interruption, which allows a process of refocusing.

The more qualitative side of the regeneration of attention takes as its starting point the fact that all attention is bound by something. Attention has to turn to something. Yet, to what objects and subjects of perception, to what topics and semantic fields of communication is attention to be turned? Since the degree of necessary selectivity is increasing in our media-saturated society, this question becomes pressing. The binding and management of attention becomes the primary social and political steering mechanism of media societies. In a media society the distribution of bound attention comes to be a discourse of power. It is further qualified by certain semantic realms, certain themes, and communicative practices. Where attention is a scarce resource, any binding of attention is at the same time a potential unbinding of some other attention. The public attention of a given culture can become so absorbed by certain themes that pressing issues for the flourishing of the communal life remain outside of the focus of attention. In such cases, the regeneration of attention is primarily a refocusing on relevant issues. The selective binding of attention becomes a question of individual and communal responsibility. One crucial issue within the ecology of attention is the possible commodification of attention, which increasingly takes place in an advertisement-driven culture. This process is closely linked to the other problem of a substitution of communicative attention by perceptive attention. When these processes come together in a media society, an exploitation of attention occurs.

26. One indicator for that claim may be the widespread phenomenon of attention disorders among children. Even though they might make a case for the social construction of diseases, they point to different types of attentions.

Audiovisual Media and the Exploitation of Attention

To see the link between the exploitation of attention and the growth of the media system one has to keep in mind three simultaneous tendencies that characterize late-modern information societies:

1. The construction of scarcity of attention by the overflow of possibilities of communication;
2. The substitution of money by attention; and
3. The attraction of attention through the physical stimulation of perception.

I turn now to explore in detail each of these tendencies of the attention economy.

The Construction of Scarcity

I already noted that natural as well as cultural resources come to the forefront of attention when they become scarce resources. In this regard, attention does not differ from clean water and clean air. Scarce resources are the most valuable properties. How did it come about that attention became a scarce resource? What makes it one of the most valuable properties of the information society? With the advent of the printing press, and the invention of the telegraph, the telephone, radio, and television, not to speak of the Internet, societies experienced a dramatic shift in the correspondence of attention and possibilities of communication. Without any doubt, the amount of leisure time available to people to use outside their everyday work also increased significantly during the last century. But what increased even more are the organized possibilities of communication. Not every possibility of communication can be actualized due to the limitations of human attention. In Luhmannian terms, the selectivity between an utterance and the following understanding that creates communication as its unity increased sharply. In this regard, the Worldwide Web again increases the possibilities of communication almost infinitely: in theory, one can now communicate simultaneously with everyone — a privilege in former times only the metaphysical Godhead could enjoy. Human attention in today's society is no longer overabundant, as in the past, but, relative to possible communication, rare. This is definitely a new situation that has emerged during modernity. Without any doubt, this process cannot just be perceived through the eyes of cultural pessimism. The

new situation came along with general education, democracy, and a liberation of cultural productivity. But at the end of this process, we face a strange
situation: Human attention becomes scarce even for the media system itself
in spite of the fact that the media already takes up most of our time outside of
work and sleep. The media system itself becomes trapped in a deadly paradox: The more media products there are on the market, the harder it becomes
to attract sufficient attention.[27] The only way to "solve" this problem is to am-
plify it. There exists a problem for the broader culture, however: the sheer
amount of time used for the consumption of audiovisual products makes human attention even more scarce for all those groups in the civil society who
rely on the availability of the time people spend outside work and sleep.

The Substitution of Money by Attention

This second tendency is manifested in an advertisement-driven media culture, which today includes such institutions as Yahoo and AOL. We all consume much more mediated communication in the form of newscasts, films,
soaps, stock-news, and instant messages than we can pay for with money.
Only a very few people could afford a newspaper, all the television programs,
and the Internet if they were required to pay with cash. What is actually taking place in our society is that more and more of the cost of communication
is paid for by advertisement. But what does this mean? What we don't pay
for with money, we pay for with attention. Attention becomes the "currency"
we exchange when we run out of money to get what we want — and we have
already run out of money relative to what we receive. Television networks,
newspaper and magazine publishers, as well as the net portals attract our attention with their offerings and sell it to advertisers who in turn pay for in
cash that which we cannot afford. At the very least, then, advertisement-
enabled communication is driven by the "currency" of attention. We don't
really get these things or services for free, we just pay in another "currency,"
that is to say, we trade some valuable property.[28] At the moment of this
trade, the perceptive or communicative attention is not a resource used for

27. See Siegfried J. Schmidt, "Aufmerksamkeit — revisited. Das Mediensystem verstrickt
sich in eine mörderische Paradoxie," in *Telepolis* 22.12.2000 (http://heise.de/tp/deutsch/special/
auf/4543/1.html).

28. The value of human attention attracted by advertisement is at least as much as the
amount paid for advertisement. But in that case the companies that advertise would still not
make money by advertising. Since they advertise because they can make more money by doing
it than by not doing it, the amount must be much higher.

actual perception or communication but becomes a property, or commodity, given away in order to get something beyond these moments of attention. And the rarer the property of attention grows, the more sophisticated become the means to attract it.

To point out these connections is not intended as just one more complaint about the media and their evil influence. One could easily turn the target of observation around: The economization of the cultural sphere — that is to say, the increasing tendency that monetary payment for cultural products is offset, or reduced, by the inclusion of advertisement — could also mean this: The danger that the civil society is weakened by an "attention-drain" may be a result of our drive to consume more than we can pay for with money. By doing this, we engage in a strange kind of self-exploitation.[29] But it may also raise questions of social justice, since people with more money can afford to pay less with attention. Due to their buying power, their attention, because harder to get, is more economically valuable.

Attraction of Attention through the Physical Stimulation of Perception

Politicians, advertisers, hardware producers, and analysts of contemporary culture mostly agree that we are living in a situation of vastly enhanced possibilities to communicate. This general impression has to be challenged, however. Over against this commonsense view, which I also picked up semantically in the essay so far, I would like to state the following thesis: The widespread use of audiovisual media primarily enhances the possibilities of mediated perception, yet possibly at the expense of communication. The widespread talk about communication technologies blurs the picture of the current cultural situation.

How is such a scenario possible? The media, ranging from radio and television to the Internet, must capture our attention in order to sell it to advertisers. But given the necessary selectivity on the user's side, this binding becomes more and more difficult. How, then, does it take place? The key to this process is the recognition that most so-called information (including the Internet in two or three years) is audiovisual communication. Yet I would like to ask further: Is most audiovisual communication really communication?

---

29. For this reason, any media ethics that does not encompass an ethics of consumption, an ethics of imagination and production, and an ethics of distribution falls short of the complexity of the whole communication process.

Drawing on a distinction in communication theory I have developed in some detail elsewhere, I want to suggest that television, film, and magazines, as well as the future Internet, primarily offer not communication but preconfigured spaces of perception.[30] The process of communication is always very slow and difficult, while perception can be very fast and deal with high degrees of complexity without decoding it completely. In order to effectively attract our attention between perhaps three to six hours a day, the media system does not primarily offer information and communication, but rather pre-arranged spaces of perception for experience-like consumption. This has far-reaching consequences for the attraction of attention. While communication binds attention through novelty and relevant themes, perception has other means to achieve this binding: perception can bind attention through attracting bodies. The use of film techniques to create the effect of speed (think about the

---

30. See Thomas, *Medien — Ritual — Religion,* pp. 434-43. At this point I am drawing on Niklas Luhmann's communication theory. He assumes that communication is the emergent unity of the differentiation of information, utterance, and understanding: (1) information as a selection of meaning out of an horizon of possibilities; (2) an act of utterance as a selection of this information; and (3) understanding as subsequent selection out of a second horizon of meaning, which is based on the difference between the information and the utterance. If communication is the emerging unity of this process, no single consciousness can capture or "see" all three aspects. If we look at the process from the perspective of an individual consciousness, an important task is to detect in the stream of perception units that carry the difference between information and utterance. To see someone blink her eyes can be just the perception of a physical behavior, or — seen as an utterance with information — a hint to adjust my tie. Among the various media some forms carry with them almost automatically this difference between utterance and information. Listening to vocal talk we are fine-tuned to such a difference and expect something other than noise. When we detect the difference between information and utterance, we attribute it to another cognitive-emotional system. Audiovisual media, moving pictures, don't carry with them this difference to such a degree as language.

Human consciousness is most of the time a perceiving consciousness rather than a communicating consciousness. Perception creates a compact unity of perception that does not imply passivity and is not without the making of distinctions. On the contrary, it implies the fast recognition of patterns, movements, and complex forms, which tend to be generalized. The differentiating marker of communication over against perception is the recognition of a selectivity, that is to say, the difference between information and utterance, which can be attributed to another self-referential system. Between just looking at a sunset and enjoying it, on the one hand, and looking at it and seeing in it a message of a communicating god, on the other, there is only a tiny difference: in the latter case, the sun is an utterance carrying an information coming from a self-referential godhead, not just a beautiful natural object of perception. Yet perceptions can be treated as communicative utterances. This phenomenon seems to be the basis of conversations with pets and of some mental diseases. But also the other way around, communicative utterances can be treated as mere perceptions, which is the case in the reception of audiovisual communication with moving pictures: cinema and television.

movie *Speed*); thematic orientation toward crime and violence and other basic human needs and drives; illusions of closeness — these are all means of attracting and binding bodies through perception. Of course, this observation should not be over-generalized. But it certainly highlights a paradoxical tendency in the so-called information society: to bind and attract more attention, one has to substitute perception for communication. If the media offered only communication in the strict sense of the word, they could never bind a person's attention for such a long time each day. In light of the distinction developed above, one can see that audiovisual media mobilize perceptive attention, not necessarily communicative attention.

Let me summarize the argument so far. I started out with the observation that we have today a clear sense of natural resources but still lack an equally developed sense of cultural resources necessary for the flourishing of individual and social life. Then I tried to cast some light on human attention, which I consider to be one of the most valuable properties of our information society, even though it is not yet considered to be a necessary cultural resource by leading communication theorists and even though few people realize the way in which it is in constant need of regeneration. To comprehend the exploitation of attention in the current media society, I pointed out three concurrent tendencies: first, the construction of scarcity through an over-abundance of possibilities to communicate and — for other cultural communication — through the factual absorption of most attention other than that in our work; second, the transformation of attention into a tradable property that can substitute for money; and third, the increasing tendency to attract attention not by communication but by perception. These three tendencies absorb, erode, and transform human attention — with far-reaching consequences for our culture. But, after all these considerations, you might ask yourself some questions: Where does religion come into the picture? Why is attention something that should be taken seriously by systematic theology? How should theological reflection react to this situation? These questions I want to address in the following section.

Religious Reflection, Theological Reasoning, and the Place of the Church in the Struggle for Attention

How does religion act to form culture, and how does the Christian church come into play? The first and most important reaction is to move beyond the competition principle. That means that religious reflection should explicate the specific contribution religions make in this situation. In addition, theological reasoning has to give theological reasons in what regard the Christian church can make a difference.[31]

Beyond the Competition Principle

Without any doubt, churches as religious communities operate within a market where there is stiff competition for attention. In many regards, the churches with good reason compete for their share in public and individual attention.[32] The churches in the modern period, not only in comparison to medieval times, have lost a considerable amount of mind-share and public attention. Many debates about the public role of the Christian churches document this perceived loss of attention, at least relative to the total amount of public attention. But this is, I want to point out, only one side of the issue. On the other side, churches are called to quit lamenting about the fact of competition and ask anew what it means to be the church in the current environment. The churches are called to move beyond what I would like to call the "competition principle" and ask what they are in this cultural environment of the twenty-first century and what their contribution to their cultural environments could be.

The question "What is the church?" cannot, however, be answered detached from any concrete cultural environment. The mission to which the church is called, the way it becomes a witness of Christ to the world, is tied to a specific time, to a specific cluster of cultures. And this relation of church, culture, and history is characterized by a double contingency: The social and cultural realities of a particular time challenge the church to see itself in a new light; and, at the same time, the church is challenged to contribute to the self-understanding and the flourishing of communal life. Even "resident aliens" interact with the cultural environments they inhabit as "residents."[33] For this

31. In doing that theological reflection and ecclesial practice face a paradox that should be acknowledged but that should not become an obstacle: Even the discourse about attention and even the life of the church needs attention. Not even the regeneration of attention is free from consuming attention.

32. The media not only absorb attention that could be directed to other groups of the civil society, but in some respects they have even taken over functions previously addressed by explicit religious communication. For a short overview of the current debate see Günter Thomas and Michael Welker, "Einleitung. Religiöse Funktionen des Fernsehens?" in *Religiöse Funktionen des Fernsehens? Medien-, kultur- und religionswissenschaftliche Perspektiven*, ed. Günter Thomas (Opladen: Westdeutscher Verlag, 2000), pp. 9-25.

33. Stanley Hauerwas and William H. Willimon, *Resident Aliens: Life in the Christian Colony* (Nashville: Abingdon, 1989). I agree with Hauerwas that we must begin by drawing a dis-

reason, I argue that the cultural battle for the property of human attention should be seen as a challenge to ask, What is the church's unique contribution, which at the same time can be the basis for a critical stance and an engagement in the public debate?[34] What can religious reflection discover in the life of religious communities — given this environment?

Religions and the Regeneration and Redirection of Attention

What difference does religion make in the fight for attention? At least three elements seem to be worth noting. First, religions use yet also regenerate, reallocate, and qualify attention. As many scholars of religion have elaborated, religious communication interrupts the rhythms of other activities, organizing a qualified "time-out." It decouples itself from other agendas and spheres of attention. The cultural institutions of Sabbath and Sunday embody social knowledge: Communal and individual life is best served when it is regularly interrupted to refocus attention. Religious communities give these interruptions the shape of festive celebrations, offer diverse forms of participation, and focus the attention on a commonly shared symbolic network. Ritualized communications combine the novelty of new events in life with the security of expectations provided by repetitions. The regeneration of attention happens in all these forms through a festive and shared deceleration of communication.

Second, this regeneration of attention occurs along with a reallocation of attention. By interpreting life outside the festive "time-out" in light of sacred texts, religions reframe or re-map the perception of reality. The appeal to some "real counter-reality" challenges the perception of reality together with its routine allocation of attention. This re-allocation of attention stimulates an active interplay between religions and other spheres of culture and allows one to differentiate styles of religiosity.

Finally, depending on the concrete content of its religious symbolism, religious communication also qualifies attention in ways leading to specific dispositions of action. By qualifying attention, such communication encour-

---

tinction. Yet the ways Christians relate to culture appear to be much more varied if we try to conceptualize these relations in the horizon of Trinitarian theology. The eclipse of any serious Trinitarian thinking in matters of culture is something Hauerwas shares with H. R. Niebuhr as well as J. H. Yoder.

34. To take the existence and contribution of the church as the starting point for reflection does not justify any retreat to the church as ethical realm. On the contrary, it prepares the church for its mission to "seek the welfare of the city . . ." (Jer. 29:7).

ages specific behavior and shapes everyday life, yet without determining completely certain behavior.

As many past and present religious conflicts vividly show, this process of regenerating, reallocating, and qualifying attention is highly ambiguous. It might be dangerous or life-enhancing — depending on the standpoint of the observer and the observed religious community. Therefore it is necessary to move on from a general functional perspective about religion to theological reasoning; in other words, we must develop a systematic-theological and Christian perspective on the church's being and place within the current culture.

Responsibility and Extravagance: The Breaking of the Logic of Attention

Together, this regeneration, reallocation, and qualification of attention within the Christian church follows a specific inner dynamic and is characterized by three elements. The inner dynamic of festive celebration does not consist simply in a turn to self-reference, closure, or introspection; this dynamic is not just the result of decoupling. It is characterized by three processes that are quite precisely spelled out in the Gospel of Matthew 18:20: "For where two or three are gathered in my name, I am there among them." The Christian community comes together with a clear thematic focus on the event and life of Jesus Christ. By doing this, Christians celebrate and recall the qualified attention God paid to them in Jesus Christ. This active remembrance in word and sacrament implies an active immersion into the canonical memory of Christ.[35] Yet this movement of their attention away from their present changes their present: Christ will be among them through the activity of the Spirit. "I am among them." By Christ's presence, they experience God's attentiveness to their present life. In Christ, God pays positive attention to our life regardless of human attentiveness, takes up the constant human search for attention and the ongoing need to pay attention to receive attention. What is called justification by faith is — among other things — a precise interruption and reorganization of one's own economy of attention.

---

35. Michael Welker, "Resurrection and Eternal Life: The Canonic Memory of the Resurrected Christ, His Reality, and His Glory," in *The End of the World and the Ends of God: Science and Eschatology in Dialogue*, ed. John Polkinghorne and Michael Welker (Harrisburg, Pa.: Trinity Press International, 2000), pp. 279-90. For the dependence of this process of remembrance on material media see Régis Debray, *Transmitting Culture* (New York: Columbia University Press, 2000).

By gathering in Christ's name, Christians try to see their reality and their involvement in the economy of attention from God's perspective. A critical observer might see there nothing but one of Gödel's strange loops: People trying to see the world from the inside as it would be possible to see it from the outside. Critics, the non-Christian as well as the theological, might see nothing but the construction of a Christian world following the mechanisms Nelson Goodman described: composition and decomposition, a specific weighting, ordering, some deletion and supplementation, as well as deformation.[36] But still, Christians hope and believe that God uses their constructions to make himself present. For this reason, faith in God becomes a serious matter of truly perceiving, interpreting, and evaluating the world in God's perspective.

The qualification and reallocation of attention from God's perspective is influenced by three elements: faith, hope, and love.[37] All three elements move the church's attention beyond its own boundaries. The reception or realization of God's attention in faith leads to a widening of human attention, temporally, socially, and in terms of its content orientation. Attention is widened in terms of time by the confrontation with the canonical memory of Christ and the perspective on what Christians hope for this world. Attention is widened in its social dimension, insofar as those gathered in Christ's name become part of the universal body of Christ, which spans over times and nations, and participate in the mission of Christ. Human attention is also qualified and reallocated by perceiving those to whom Christ paid attention.[38]

The reallocation and qualification of attention by love and hope challenges the economy of attention, because Christians are called to pay attention where it is needed, give attention as a gift, not as a social "currency." Without any doubt, the church as a social institution attracts and uses human attention. It is also, however, called to break the logic of the market of attention. At least locally and temporarily, it can call into question the logic of this

36. Nelson Goodman, *Ways of Worldmaking* (Indianapolis: Hackett, 1978), pp. 1-22. This constructionist perspective does not rule out some version of internal realism, which is guaranteed by God.

37. For a thorough treatment of this triad, see Thomas Söding, *Die Trias Glaube, Hoffnung, Liebe bei Paulus. Eine exegetische Studie* (Stuttgart: Katholisches Bibelwerk, 1992).

38. There is a sharp contrast between the way the media typically turn their attention to the dark and shadowy sides of life, and Christ's attentiveness. The media's "morbid curiosity" has to be contrasted with Christ's "caring attentiveness." For the former see Gannett Foundation, ed., *Morbid Curiosity and the Mass Media: Proceedings of a Symposium* (Knoxville: University of Tennessee, 1984). The media focus on the dark sides of life only insofar as the portrayal of these sides attracts attention that can be sold to advertisers. To put it into Kantian terms: Suffering people are not an end in themselves but are means to do business.

economy as it is so vividly exemplified in the media. According to this logic, the media pay "perceptive attention" to certain events and persons if and only if two conditions are fulfilled. First, there has to be a decent chance that by communicating this perceived event the media can attract more attention than they invest; and second, a considerable amount of the attention attracted has to be redirected back to, or re-invested in, the media itself. For this reason, good stories raise the ratings of a network, and, in turn, some journalists and filmmakers become celebrities. If the media pay attention, they have to get back more than they pay. For the media, to pay attention has to be a profitable investment.

Again, how can the churches not just mirror this economy of attention but challenge it? The proper practice of faith, love, and hope does not obey this logic. Why? The practice of faith, love, and hope turns attention to the issues and people who do not attract the attention they deserve (seen in Christ's perspective) or who just attract the fleeting attention of "morbid curiosity." Love and hope not only redirect attention but call for a responsible extravagance in paying attention. Love and hope invest attention in hopeless situations, events, and cases — without the hope of reciprocity in the currency of attention. By doing this, they not only gather but act in Christ's name.

Finally, academic reflection on religion and theological reasoning needs to focus not only on the life and responsibility of the church but also on what is needed for the flourishing of communal life. "Seek the welfare of the city where I have sent you" is a demand that also applies to responsible theological reflection. In the face of the current exploitation of human attention, theological reasoning has to work toward an "ecology of attention." Such a project cannot be carried out by theology alone, but needs to be developed in cooperation with other disciplines and in dialogue with other partners in the civil society. We still lack a thorough comprehension of the subtle mechanisms through which attention is built into the structures of our society. There is much debate about "dematerialization," "informatization," and "virtualization," but the basic resource for the processing of information in communication is still not thoroughly explored. An ecology of attention as part of theological anthropology and theological ethics takes seriously the finitude of human beings, their call to experience a real polyphony of life, as well as the human responsibility for the consumption of one's own media experiences.[39] Such an ecology of attention would have to consider the unavoidable side

39. For the preservation of a "multidimensional and polyphonic" life see Dietrich Bonhoeffer, *Widerstand und Ergebung. Briefe und Aufzeichnungen aus der Haft*, Dietrich Bonhoeffer Werke 8 (Gütersloh: Kaiser, 1998), p. 453

effects of the current distribution of attention. It would help us to see that late modernity replaces the forceful control of the human body as an exercise of social power with a more subtle control of persons — control, that is, by specific ways of attracting attention by the attraction of bodies by means of perception. Yet, an ecology of attention could not be developed without a vision of the good life that encompasses the human desire for pleasure and joy in the same way as the obligation to deal responsibly with our and other people's time — because life is both: a project and at the same time a gift. The creative tension between both is kept present by theological discourse.

Concluding Remarks

The real challenge for theological reflection concerned with our media culture is to understand the dynamics of having, gaining, and losing the property of attention, to understand the subtle processes by which this cultural resource is used, exploited, regenerated, and put to work in social life. Yet the observation of these dynamics should not trigger ecclesiological alarmism and lament about our culture. The current situation can instead challenge the church to discover the strengths and weaknesses of its own life and witness. My argument was that any new and deeper understanding of the culture in which the church lives, and the complex relationship between culture and church, can challenge the latter's self-understanding in a nondeterminate yet creative way. Hence, by taking up this challenge, the church can discover in what way it regenerates, reallocates, and qualifies human attention — in the light of God's own life-sustaining and graceful attentiveness. Over against the general economization of attention, the practice of faith, love, and hope embodies a responsible extravagance in the donation of attention. But, as part of the public responsibility of theological reasoning, theology has to stimulate the development of a constructive public discourse about an ecology of attention that unmasks the power of this economy. The contributions to this discourse will always be colored by God's own style of attentiveness and the Christian vision of the polyphony of life. Yet this might be what Christians owe to the public discussion.

Identity, Possession, and Myth on the Web:
Yearning for Jerusalem

DAVID M. GUNN

In July 2000, the parties to the Oslo Accords met at Camp David under President Clinton's auspices in talks that failed to reach a conclusion. By all accounts the status of Jerusalem was a major sticking point. Several days earlier my local newspaper had offered its editorial opinion on the matter:

> Arafat and the Palestinians have long insisted on regaining control over Arab portions of the ancient city. . . . Unfortunately, that demand can never be met. Barak can never surrender Israeli control over any portion of the city, nor should he be asked to do so. If Arafat's price for peace is a repartitioned Jerusalem, this precious opportunity must be grudgingly allowed to pass. . . . If Arafat and his people cling to their dream of reclaiming sovereignty over Jerusalem, peace is unattainable.[1]

As these and later talks have lurched their way toward dissolution, we have increasingly heard Jerusalem described as "the eternal and undivided capital of Israel." The epithet signals, of course, a claim to exclusive political possession or sovereignty as well as hinting at divine sanction. Yitzhak Shamir, former terrorist leader and prime minister, elaborates the claim: "Jerusalem was and is until today the eternal, national, heavenly, spiritual and physical symbol of the link, never to be broken, between the Jewish people and its land, the land of Israel."[2]

It is not surprising that this language of eternal possession passes largely unquestioned in American public political discourse: Jerusalem, the city that

1. *Atlanta Constitution,* 22 July 2000.
2. Associated Press, 27 April 2000.

always has existed and always will exist as Israel's capital. One might have supposed that a claim to eternity about a state barely fifty years old would prompt some query. But that would be to reckon without the power of the myth or master narrative sustaining the epithet, a narrative of "return" anchored in one of the West's most tenacious texts, the Bible.

The Zionist settlement of Israel and the establishment of the state have often been described in terms of European colonialism.[3] On the other hand, there is a dimension to the rhetoric of Zionist settlement that on the face of it runs directly counter to the usual rhetoric of colonial settlement. Jewish settlers and their "diaspora" supporters spoke, and still speak passionately, about "returning (or 'going up') to their homeland." The settlers *are* the indigenous people of the land, have always possessed it, as a dream, a destiny, a gift from the Holy One of Israel. Europeans developed a stock of legitimations for their encroachment on the land of others and Zionists shared this repertoire, including the claim that they were "transforming the wilderness." But while many of these justifications have been submerged before indigenous independence movements, the Zionist claim to "return" has proved to have remarkable staying power and influence, particularly where it mattered — namely, in the United States — and when married precisely to the language of independence. The rhetoric of "return," therefore, is worth special attention in any account of how the Bible has played a role in the possessing and dispossessing that characterize settlement. Here I explore one aspect of this singular rhetoric of return, namely, "yearning for Jerusalem."

1

As an entry point I go to the Israeli Ministry of Foreign Affairs website to find an "official" voice on the subject of "return." The "home" address (in August 2001) is http://www.mfa.gov.il/mfa/home.asp. I scroll down, choose the link *Facts about Israel* and click on *The State*. The address is http://www. mfa.gov.il/mfa/go.asp?MFAH00k90.[4] This link yields an introduction to Israel's Declaration of Independence: "Jews strove in every successive generation to reestablish themselves in their ancient homeland . . . they made deserts bloom, re-

3. Cf. Maxime Rodinson, *Israel: A Colonial-Settler State?* trans. David Thorstad (New York: Pathfinder, 1973); Gershon Shafir, *Land, Labor, and the Origins of the Israeli-Palestinian Conflict, 1882-1914* (Cambridge: Cambridge University Press, 1989); and Elia T. Zureik, *The Palestinians in Israel: A Study of Internal Colonialism* (London: Routledge and Kegan Paul, 1979).

4. Hereafter I shall cite in the text only the last part of the URL, beginning "MFA," which is the only part that changes.

vived the Hebrew language, built villages and towns, and created a thriving community. . . ." At the bottom of the page I find *Jerusalem — Capital of Israel,* and then under "Publications" I select *Jerusalem.* The new page opens (MFAH00j30) with words from the Talmud:

> Ten measures of beauty were bestowed upon the world;
> nine were taken by Jerusalem and one by the rest of the world.
> (Babylonian Talmud, Tractate Kiddushin 49:2)

I read further in romantic vein of "the capital of Israel, . . . located in the heart of the country," with its

> incandescent glow, golden in sunshine, silvery by moonlight, . . . rivaled in impact only by the kaleidoscope of its people — some the descendants of generations of Jerusalemites, others who have come from the four corners of the earth. Mingling with people wearing the spectrum of modern fashion are dark-suited ultra-Orthodox Jews, Arab women in brightly embroidered shifts and Christian clergy in somber robes.

Small wonder this multicolored marvel has been "praised by the Prophets, enshrined in literature and liturgy, and sung by poets, near and far, down through the generations" (MFAH00j30). I hesitate as I am reminded, with Amos Elon,[5] of Chateaubriand's description of "extraordinary desolation," or Edward Lear's phrase, "that vile place, the foulest and odiousest on earth." Instead I click on *Capital* at the top of the page to find a brief survey of "Jerusalem: The Capital of Israel" (MFAH00w40). The text begins with an epigraph:

> And the days that David reigned over Israel were forty years;
> seven years reigned he in Hebron, and thirty-three years reigned he in Jerusalem. (1 Kings 2:11)

The biblical epigraph from Kings provides the proof text for Jerusalem's political role as "capital of the Jewish people." This function, it would appear, is of the very essence of the city:

> With the establishment of the State of Israel in 1948, Jerusalem became once more the capital of a sovereign Jewish state. Throughout the millennia of its existence, Jerusalem has never been the capital of any other sovereign nation.

5. Amos Elon, *Jerusalem: Battlegrounds of Memory* (New York: Kodansha International, 1995), pp. 134, 42.

Jerusalem has stood at the center of the Jewish people's national and spiritual life since King David made it the capital of his kingdom in 1003 BCE. The city remained the capital of the Davidic dynasty for 400 years, until the kingdom was conquered by the Babylonians. Following the return from the Babylonian exile in 538 BCE, Jerusalem again served as the capital of the Jewish people in its land for the next five and a half centuries.

The Christian link with Jerusalem is essentially a religious one; under Muslim rule, Jerusalem was never the capital of any political entity. (MFAH00w40)

Then the western sector became Israel's capital in 1948 but the city was divided. Finally, in June 1967, the barriers were demolished and "the eastern sector was re-integrated into the nation's capital."

I click on *History* at the top of the page to open "Jerusalem: Through the Centuries" (MFAH00w50) and read from Psalm 137:

If I forget thee, O Jerusalem,
may my right hand forget it[s] cunning.
May my tongue cleave to the roof of my mouth,
if I do not set Jerusalem above my highest joy. (Psalm 137:5-6)

The "history" proceeds with brief biblical paraphrase, starting once more with David in "1003 BCE" but quickly moving to Solomon in order to configure the temple as "the religious and national center of the people of Israel" and the city as "the prosperous capital of an empire extending from the Euphrates to Egypt." The account comes to rest with the "reuniting" of the city in June 1967.

So Jerusalem's is a story of sovereign glory, displacement (exile), and restoration (redemption); in other words, it is the story of "Israel" in microcosm. That story, Jerusalem writ large, is repeated constantly throughout the website. In one form or another, the narrative runs as follows: The Jewish people/nation along with their religion and culture are born in the Land (Eretz-Israel). They are forcibly removed, however, exiled from the Land. They endure vicissitudes in far lands (prosperity, oppression), looking always with yearning to their lost Land. Then, after long centuries, the Zionist movement begins to forge for them a Return, an "ingathering of exiles," to their ancestral homeland. On return, they (are to) redeem Israel/the Land, establish law, and exercise justice.

One does not need the constant reminder of biblical quotations as webpage epigraphs to recognize how thoroughly "biblical" is this story. As the biblical story of return from Egypt (and possession of the land) is recapitulated in the return from Babylon (and possession of the land), so now a new post-biblical story of exile and return (and possession of the land) recapitulates both biblical stories.

What we have here might well be described as a "foundation myth"[6] or what Yael Zerubavel terms a "master commemorative narrative."[7] Indeed, one notable rendition of the narrative, to which others on the website make rhetorical allusion constantly and which may itself be found on the website, is the "Declaration of the Establishment of the State of Israel" (May 14, 1948).

While the myth or master narrative can be recounted in brief without mention of Jerusalem, the city frequently appears. Clearly, by way of synecdoche, Jerusalem/Zion is also the land or the state, so that Jerusalem's story is the story of the Land. And the city's freight as "capital" marks the myth of Exile and Return as a story of sovereignty lost (at Exile) and rightfully regained (at Return).

2

Jerusalem is a key element in the "living in exile" episode of the master narrative, inasmuch as it is cast as the object of desire whose attainment exile thwarts. If we move on, click on *Holy City* (MFAH0ow60), and bring up "Jerusalem: The Holy City," this function of the city becomes clearer. As usual, first comes the religious proof text, this time from Isaiah 66:

> Rejoice thee with Jerusalem, and be glad with her, all ye that love her: rejoice for joy with her, all that mourn for her. For thus saith the Lord, Behold, I will extend peace to her like a river and the glory of the nations like a flowing stream. (Isaiah 66:10-12)

Then follows the historical account, starting with an acknowledgment of Jewish, Christian, and Muslim religious connections to Jerusalem. It continues:

> The Jewish bond to Jerusalem was never broken. For three millennia, Jerusalem has been the center of the Jewish faith, retaining its symbolic value throughout the generations. The many Jews who had been exiled after the Roman conquest and scattered throughout the world never for-

6. Cf. Niels Peter Lemche, *The Israelites in History and Tradition*, Library of Ancient Israel (London: SPCK, 1995), pp. 86-97.

7. Yael Zerubavel, *Recovered Roots: Collective Memory and the Making of Israeli National Tradition* (Chicago: University of Chicago Press, 1995), pp. 3-12.

got Jerusalem. Year after year they repeated "Next year in Jerusalem." Jerusalem became the symbol off [*sic*] the desire of Jews everywhere to return to their land. It was invoked by the prophets, enshrined in daily prayer, and sung by Hebrew poets in far-flung lands. (MFAHoow60)

So here we have it: yearning for Jerusalem. This "topos" (or conventional rhetorical element) is, in fact, ubiquitous in accounts of the founding of modern Israel. In a brief article in the online journal *Ariel,* a few clicks away (MFAHo1o1o), Zusia Efron begins her account of longings for Jerusalem in Jewish folk art of Eastern Europe:

> Longings for Zion and Jerusalem have accompanied the Jewish people in their exile, for more than 2,500 years. . . . Longings for Jerusalem are mentioned more than 1,000 times in the Bible as well as in the Talmud, and in daily and holiday prayers — and are summed up in vision and hope at the end of the Passover Haggadah; in the supplicatory words, "Next Year in Jerusalem."[8]

Some of the most poignant expressions of these feelings were composed by the author of the Psalms:

> By the rivers of Babylon —
>   there we sat down and there we wept
>   when we remembered Zion.
> On the willows there
>   we hung up our harps. (Psalm 137:1-2)

> If I forget you, O Jerusalem . . . (Psalm 137:5)

In Meron Benvenisti's *City of Stone,* the topos even causes the author to desert his customary, more sanguine style:

> Year after year, for nearly 2,000 years, Jews vowed, "Next year in Jerusalem," mourning over its destruction and longing to work for its rebuilding. Time did not diminish their yearning, and it burst forth with irresistible force when the political conditions necessary for its fulfillment were attained.[9]

---

8. Zusia Efron, "'If I Forget Thee . . .': Longings for Jerusalem in the Jewish Folk Art of Eastern Europe," *Ariel: The Israel Review of Arts and Letters* 102 (1996).

9. Meron Benvenisti, *City of Stone: The Hidden History of Jerusalem,* trans. Maxine Kaufman Nunn (Berkeley: University of California Press, 1996), p. 145.

Amos Elon's offering in *Jerusalem: Battlegrounds of Memory* includes Jehudah Halevi's long-treasured language of love:

> Among the many vanquished capital cities of the ancient world, only Jerusalem survived in the imagination of her exiles and in that of their descendants from generation to generation. . . . As they wandered from land to land, they remained stubbornly a people of Jerusalem: "If I forget thee, O Jerusalem. . . . If I do not remember thee. . . ." Jerusalem became their great Capital of Memory. Memory gave them their culture and their identity. . . . Passover and Yom Kippur services ended with the exhortation "Next year in Jerusalem."[10]

The words of the Spanish-Hebrew poet Jehudah Halevi (c. 1075–1141) reaffirmed this devotion.

> Could I but kiss thy dust
> so would I fain expire.
> As sweet as honey then,
> My longing and desire.[11]

How long, indeed, could such longing be constrained? And what North American reader of this topos is not going to be swayed by the expression of such deep desire coming to fulfillment? Yearning not only drives the plot of return and rebuilding (redemption). At the same time, to an audience schooled in popular romance, it validates the outcome, namely possession of the yearned for, the beloved. Jerusalem/Zion/Israel is a woman, waiting for her lover's embrace.

3

That we are dealing with the language of romance is an observation of no small matter. Desire for Jerusalem is desire for Zion is desire for the Land. An American audience's enthusiasm for consummation in the plot of popular romance is certainly one dimension of the narrative's contemporary consumption. The language of romance also takes us to some historical roots of the narrative's formation in the wake of the romantic revival and the rise of "romantic" nationalism in the nineteenth century.

10. Elon, *Jerusalem: Battlegrounds of Memory*, pp. 33-34.
11. Jehudah Halevi, *Selected Poems of Jehudah Halevi*, trans. Nina Salaman (Philadelphia: Jewish Publication Society of America, 1924).

Writing of the Jewish student curriculum in Europe at the end of the eighteenth century, Moshe Halbertal observes the urgings of the Jewish Enlightenment for a turn toward the Bible and away from the Talmud, which had been central since medieval times.[12] He continues:

> With the rise of Jewish nationalism, the relationship of many Jews to the Bible and the Talmud took another turn. The Zionists preferred the Bible to the Talmud as the national literature, for the Bible tells a heroic story of the national drama whose focus is the Land of Israel. . . . Unlike the Talmud, they held, the Bible had the potential to become a national epic. Its drama unfolded in the hills of Judea, and it connected the national claim to the land with a historical past. Nothing in the Talmud, in contrast, appealed to the romanticism vital to national movements. It does not tell the glorious story of a nation; it has no warriors and heroes; no geography which arouses longing in the reader or a sense of connection to an ancient home.[13]

Zerubavel pinpoints the importance of "longing" in this context:

> For the Zionists the major yardstick to evaluate the past was the bond between the Jewish people and their ancient land. Influenced by European romantic nationalism on the one hand and drawing upon a long, distinctively Jewish tradition of longing to return to the ancient homeland on the other, Zionism assumed that an inherent bond between the Jewish people and their ancient land was a necessary condition for the development of Jewish nationhood.[14]

Let us look a little further at this connection between the language of longing and the construction of Jewish nationhood (and, in due course, the Jewish state). Nationalism assumed the need for a land in which "nationhood" could be fully realized. To some early (secular) Zionists, particularly those motivated by the desire to alleviate the predicament of Jews (and deal with issues of shame[15]

12. Moshe Halbertal, *People of the Book: Canon, Meaning, and Authority* (Cambridge, Mass.: Harvard University Press, 1997), p. 131.

13. Halbertal, *People of the Book*, p. 132.

14. Zerubavel, *Recovered Roots*, p. 15, cf. p. 22. Cf. Efron, "'If I Forget Thee . . .': Longings for Jerusalem in the Jewish Folk Art of Eastern Europe," pp. 61, 102.

15. Cf. Daniel Boyarin, "'An Imaginary and Desirable Converse': Moses and Monotheism As Family Romance," in *Reading Bibles, Writing Bodies: Identity and the Book*, ed. Timothy K. Beal and David M. Gunn (London: Routledge, 1997); Thomas J. Scheff, "Emotions and Identity: A Theory of Ethnic Nationalism," in *Social Theory and the Politics of Identity*, ed. Craig Calhoun (Oxford: Blackwell, 1994).

arising from the pogroms of the 1880s), the precise territory to be occupied was a debatable matter. Within a few years, however, the issue was settled: Palestine was to be the land of settlement. Jewish traditions of longing to return to Jerusalem were invoked to show that there had always been a desire to return to this particular geographical region. Hence the traditional language of longing was, and is, construed in terms of the innate desire of an exiled people to become a fully fledged nation-state. Longing becomes the motive power for a geopolitical venture in Eretz-Israel by those who, irrespective of their prosperity or oppression, construed themselves as "exiles."

Michael Seidel points us to a rich body of "exilic" writing with which, I suggest, the Zionist narrative has obvious affinities, from the *Odyssey* and the Argonauts to Huck Finn's river journey.[16] "In the exilic plot," Seidel argues, "the extraneous becomes foundational, the blighted and ill-fated from one sphere become instigators and originators in another. The powers of exilic imagining represent desired territory, lost or found, as narrative fate."[17] The Zionist narrative taps into this tradition. "Longing" then provides a bridge from this world of "exilic imaginings" to a narrative of national aspiration in which the desired is reified as actual land, configured politically.

4

Jehudah Halevi is invoked by Elon, as he is by many others, to buttress his exposition of the (geopolitical) Zionist master narrative. The assumption is that Halevi's yearning is one rendition of an ancient desire for possession of the Land/Jerusalem, which has been passed on from generation to generation of Jews until it has found its culmination in the romance of Zionist settlement and state-building. But Halevi is writing in a quite other vein of romance, typical of twelfth-century Spain (and elsewhere in western Europe) and not without its cognates in modern literature. He is as adept at penning love poetry for his imagined lovers as for any far-off holy city, perhaps rather more so. He is writing of yearning itself, and not simply of its object. The language of yearning has a peculiar power, which it draws from being situated in the space-time between desire and attainment, between passion (suffering) and consummation. As Seidel notes, speaking of exile and desire in Nabakov's writing, "As is the case with the homeland, the desire for the object of love

16. Michael Seidel, *Exile and the Narrative Imagination* (New Haven: Yale University Press, 1986).

17. Seidel, *Exile and the Narrative Imagination*, p. 8.

grows in proportion to the distance placed between it and the disorienting, displaced mind."[18] The power of yearning is represented in the space between Tristan and Isolde, a space occupied by a drawn sword.

That space "between," where desire can flourish as longing, is also the condition of religious yearning. Indeed the language of romantic love is often the language of adoration and worship even when its topic is not ostensibly religion: the yearning lover "adores" and "worships" the beloved. By the same token the language of religion draws on the language of love. Such metaphoric crossover makes it easy to understand how in the Middle Ages the yearning lover of the *Song of Songs* was the soul seeking the divine, the bride of Christ her husband, or Israel yearning for God.[19] Such a literary context is the location of Halevi's poetry and in such terms it would seem reasonable to interpret it.

As it happens, he did in fact set off on pilgrimage to Palestine, which suggests that he may indeed have attempted to collapse the space where yearning thrived by attaining the place of his desire. Yet were he to have reached the physical place, we could not be sure that he would have found his yearning space collapsed and a new space attained where yearning was absent. He might equally have found his yearning space simply displaced, since in losing yearning he risked losing himself. We do not know because he does not write of it. Halevi may have taken his poem sufficiently literally to have actually attempted to kiss the dust of Jerusalem (though it seems he tarried in Egypt and never reached his destination). He may also have taken a lover or two (perhaps that's why he tarried). But whether or not any of this happened, his poetry lived because its admirers found in its conjuring of yearning a conceit that they could easily transpose into many and various dimensions of their emotional and spiritual lives. Many Jews (and, indeed, many Christians) have regularly, over the centuries, understood "Jerusalem" metaphorically as a transcendent object of spiritual longing. Halevi was a master at constructing religious sensibility out of such conceits, as he did with his beautiful poem on the Sabbath as beloved. The Zionist co-option of his language into a geopolitical program envisioning the conquest and physical rebuilding of Jerusalem by Jews is then a remarkable one. Indeed, it is hardly surprising that by the end of the nineteenth century the apparent abandonment of traditional spiritual, metaphysical, or messianic meanings of exilic longing in favor of geopolitical/historical constructions prompted strong opposition to

18. Seidel, *Exile and the Narrative Imagination*, p. 176.
19. Cf. Ann Astell, *The Song of Songs in the Middle Ages* (Ithaca: Cornell University Press, 1990).

Zionism from Orthodox Jews.[20] Yet plucked thus from its former context, the language of yearning admits of this, as of any other, transposition, and now in these new clothes (which are not unlike Crusader clothes), lives on.

Once questions of metaphor and the functions of language are raised, the liturgical phrase so frequently cited in the myth's construction of yearning, namely, "next year in Jerusalem," becomes as problematic a witness as Halevi's poetry. The possibilities for understanding the phrase range from the purely performative, whereby the end of the service is enacted, to the literal, with boat passage in mind, and any number of metaphorical conjugations in between. Plainly the cryptic phrase has the potential to have meant a variety of things to a variety of people over a good many centuries and in many different places. Given, however, the relative dearth of literal action (travel to Jerusalem) subsequent upon the phrase's countless recitations over the times when it was actually in liturgical use (the subject of another discussion), it is not difficult to conclude that a literal meaning was the least prevalent of the possibilities. "Next year" ritually constitutes the present as being in the not-yet-there time; "Jerusalem" ritually constitutes the present as being in the not-yet-there place. Paradoxically the ritual places a value upon one's present time/place both as liminal, the in-between time, the not-yet-arrived-at place, and at the same time as the place and time to which one really belongs. "Now and not-then" and "here and not-there" is what one repeats. (The latter value is important to stress, since a simple focus on the liminal, in the context of nationalism, plays easily into anti-Semitism.)[21] Such a ritualized understanding of "where one is" may become a fundamental matter of identity. Attainment or possession, then, entails serious risk, as many Jewish thinkers well understood and argued in relation to Zionism in the years before the Holocaust radically shifted the grounds of the debate.

5

As the epigraphs and texts of the Israel Ministry of Foreign Affairs' website make clear, it is of the essence of the foundation myth that it is biblically warranted, and Efron, too, is eager to claim this stamp of approval. No less than one thousand times are longings for Jerusalem expressed in the Bible as well as in the Talmud, the writer tells us. But in fact the Bible's expression of such

20. Boas Evron, *Jewish State or Israeli Nation?* (Bloomington: Indiana University Press, 1995), pp. 54-55; Zerubavel, *Recovered Roots*, pp. 14-16.
21. Boyarin, "'An Imaginary and Desirable Converse,'" p. 199.

sentiments is sparse, to say the least. We have already mentioned most of them, since most appear on the website. Psalm 137 tops the list, and Lamentations is frequently invoked. The latter part of Isaiah is full of calls to return, of course, but contains curiously little "longing." In any event, it is becoming clear that relatively few did return. Perhaps others decided to stay where they were and get on with their lives, all the while learning to "yearn" as a ritual condition of their identity as "exilic" people, people of the God of Israel.

Both Psalm 137 and Lamentations are themselves witness to the complexity of "longing" as a literary construct since in neither case is it obvious that they are the direct product of "exile" (though I have not the time to develop this point here). But whatever the case on that score, there is an obvious difference between the modern (e.g., that of the website) and ancient literary contexts of the passages. These "longing" passages do not obviously specify political independence or sovereign "nationality" as objects of desire, whether past or future. But neither, for the most part, do the biblical (con)texts to which they belong. Indeed, it is notable that the literature that touches most the theme of political sovereignty, the accounts of the Maccabean revolt in the second century BCE, is not accorded canonical status within early Judaism. Hence, at least in this specific regard, the Zionist rallying song, "Hatikva," does not recapitulate the biblical topos of yearning as transparently as one might at first suppose.

> As long as deep in the heart,
> the soul of a Jew yearns,
> and towards the East
> an eye looks to Zion,
> our hope is not yet lost,
> the hope of two thousand years,
> to be a free people in our land,
> the land of Zion and Jerusalem. (MFAHook90)

As "The Hope" would have it, to be a "free people" in the land is the summation of desire. That is a concept certainly not explicit in the oft-cited biblical passages of yearning. Certainly, too, the orthodox community of Jerusalem at the end of the nineteenth century did not look kindly on such a conceit. Nor do many of their spiritual descendants today. Where, they would ask, is the singing of God's song?

Myths, master narratives, often mask structural social and ideological tensions. It may well be simplistic to speak of a divide in Jewish and Zionist thinking (and behavior) between the religious and the political, since those terms risk hiding the complexity of a "divide" that is in reality multiple "divisions." But, generally speaking, many share Boas Evron's analysis of a secularist versus religionist divide at the heart of Israeli society, his sense of deep fractures in Jewish identity. As I see it, the myth of exile, yearning, and return attempts to mask this ongoing and bitter struggle over Jewish identity. How so?

I return to the website and ask of the myth, Who is the subject of yearning in this particular narrative of exile and return? The answer, of course, is "the Jewish people." So yearning not only motivates the plot's transition from exile to return, it also constitutes the narrative's subject. (It is important to note that in both regards — motivation and subject construction — yearning, the affect of exile, works in tandem with suffering, the affect of persecution, specified, most often, as the Russian pogroms of the late nineteenth century and, ultimately, the great German destruction of the mid twentieth century.) This function of the topos — namely, subject construction — is of crucial importance for the myth, because without "yearning" the singularity and continuity of the subject would be less apparent.

Zerubavel and others have argued that while the Zionist myth from its beginnings in the nineteenth century has tended to make strenuous efforts to collapse all experience of Exile into the negative of persecution and suffering, this erasure of manifold positive dimensions of Jewish life over many centuries has proved a difficult eclipse to sustain.[22] As seen in more recent, post-state versions (like the website), the pressure of alternative memories of flourishing communities, distinctive ethnic customs, and rich cultural contributions has begun to make inroads into the myth, straining the Zionist characterization of Exile as only Disaster.[23] Under the strain, the singularity of the subject, the Jewish People Who Suffer in Exile, begins to break down. Yearning, on the other hand, unlike suffering, is an affect that unites the subject across all periods and places, and through the rough and the smooth. No matter what was happening, the myth could confidently assert, "the Jewish people" continually "yearned." Not that yearning has been wholly immune to contradiction. The Zionist movement has had to struggle, from its beginnings, to persuade people to come to Israel; most, even in the face of persecution, would rather have gone somewhere else, the United States most notably. Fifty years after the foundation of the state, however, this unitary, yearning (and/or suffering) subject is under even greater stress: as the website is forced

22. Zerubavel, *Recovered Roots,* pp. 16-20.
23. From "Facts About Israel" (http://www.israel.org/mfa/go.asp?MFAH00k90); click on *Culture* or *Society.* And see, on Jerusalem, Benvenisti, *City of Stone,* pp. 169-84.

to acknowledge, most of "the Jewish People" continue to live "in Exile" or in "Diaspora" (a term that nicely fudges the problem) or, as Zionist vocabulary would have it, in "voluntary Exile."[24] If this people is yearning to go, in actuality, to Jerusalem, it does not appear to be doing so too mightily. A puzzled reader of the myth might well wonder, Was it ever thus?

So yearning constitutes the unitary mythic subject. But, from my vantage point as a North American web viewer, the (ultra-Orthodox) men in black hats and dark suits "mingling with people wearing the spectrum of modern fashion" disturb this singularity. Here is a reconstitution of southwest Asian space as eighteenth- or nineteenth-century eastern Europe. At the same time, here and elsewhere on the website the space is being reconstituted as late-twentieth-century western Europe or North America; or Russia or Ethiopia. The Jewish People is a collective of myriad disparities, religious, ethnic, political, and cultural. According to the myth, however, the members of this people share both a name and a yearning (whether unfulfilled or assuaged). While "Israel" is a collective that attempts to supplant the disparities of the "People" with its own synthetic, "indigenous" culture, the men in black hats prove a stubborn reminder that the synthesis is a recent invention of immigrants sharing little (or nothing) in common — unless it be a name, a suffering, and, of course, a yearning. Yearning restores the people as it restores the romance.

6

The rhetoric of yearning is powerful and slippery. A narrative of yearning that issues in fulfillment — that is, possession — may engage its consumers for a time. But arrival risks dissipating the power that the "longing" generates. The master commemorative narrative of Zion, the more it becomes the narrative of the "eternal and undivided capital of Israel" — that is, the eternal possession — the more it risks becoming "passionless," its yearning empty, a hollow mask. By the same token, yearning's passionate imaginings may indeed empower, yet blind the yearning subject to an other subject's, as it were, "country."

Hidden from the great ethical thinker Emmanuel Levinas, the ponderer of the other, but only too apparent to master writer Amos Oz (perhaps because he actually looks into the face of the other) are the Arab inhabitants

---

24. Arnold M. Eisen, *Galut: Modern Jewish Reflection on Homelessness and Homecoming* (Bloomington: Indiana University Press, 1986), p. ix.

(possessors?) of the city/Land. Likewise with the website: it both hides and reveals these participants in the story. "Yearning" plays its part in the hiding. Indeed, in my view, it has overwhelmed Levinas's sense of justice.

Levinas wrote lyrically in 1951 of the religious genius of the Jewish people coming to flower in the foundation of the State of Israel — a genius that consisted "entirely in struggling against the intoxication of individual forms of enthusiasm for the sake of a difficult and erudite work of justice." Herein lay the yearning of the people for the Land.

> The thing that is special about the State of Israel is not that it fulfils an ancient promise, or heralds a new age of material security (one that is unfortunately problematic), but that it finally offers the opportunity to carry out the social law of Judaism. The Jewish people craved their own land and their own State not because of the abstract independence which they desired, but because they could then finally begin the work of their lives. Up until now they had obeyed the commandments, and later on they fashioned an art and a literature for themselves, but all these works of self-expression are merely the early attempts of an overlong adolescence. The masterpiece has now finally come.[25]

In 1967, Amos Oz, born and raised as a child in Jerusalem, found himself walking through the newly captured streets of the city:

> Their eyes hate me. They wish me dead. Accursed stranger. . . .

> I tried my hardest to feel in East Jerusalem like a man who had driven out his enemies and returned to his ancestral inheritance. The Bible came back to life for me: kings, prophets, the Temple Mount, Absalom's Pillar, the Mount of Olives. And also the Jerusalem of Abraham Mapu and Agnon's book Tmol Shilshom. I wanted to belong, I wanted to share in the general celebrations.

> But I couldn't, because of the people.

> I saw resentment and hostility, hypocrisy, bewilderment, obsequiousness, fear, humiliation and new plots being hatched. I walked the streets of East Jerusalem like a man who has broken into a forbidden city. City of my birth. City of my dreams. City of aspirations of my ancestors and my peo-

25. Emmanuel Levinas, "The State of Israel and the Religion of Israel," in his *Difficult Freedom: Essays on Judaism,* trans. Seán Hand (Baltimore: Johns Hopkins University Press, 1990), p. 218.

ple. And here I was, stalking its streets clutching a sub-machine-gun, like a figure in one of my childhood nightmares: an alien man in an alien city.[26]

Amos Oz, armed with his identity and an Uzi, had realized his people's ancient yearning, had returned and taken possession of the "eternal and undivided capital." Amos Oz had arrived.

26. Amos Oz, "An Alien City," *Ariel: The Israel Review of Arts and Letters* 102 (1996). On the Israel Ministry of Foreign Affairs website, at http://www.mfa.gov.il/mfa/go.asp?MFAH 01y10.

Avarice, Prudence, and the Bourgeois Virtues

DEIRDRE MCCLOSKEY

Introduction

What's an economy? The English economist Alfred Marshall gave in 1890 the simplest answer: it is the "ordinary business of life." Implicit in the answer is that love and faith and courage are not "ordinary." The business of saving one's immortal soul, for example, is counted extraordinary. So are romance and politics, clubs and churches, at any rate on their passionate side.

Definitions must leave out something. Yet Marshall's includes more than one might think. An economy is not merely the *bought and sold* business of life. And it is not, to mention a common misunderstanding of economics by non-economists, mainly about money. ("Money" understood as the medium of exchange, a temporary store of purchasing power, is viewed in economics as a veil, through which the economist discerns the ordinary business of making and consuming.) The economy includes, therefore, the household economy and the governmental economy, the provision for childcare in the home and the decision to make armies in Washington or Berlin.

Modern economics has defined itself, you see, as the science of the profane — at any rate "profane" in a theology that emphasizes asceticism and unworldliness as the path to the sacred; a more worldly theology is of course possible. Economics is the science of goods, understood in the economic sense as scarce sources of pleasure. The character of the pleasure is irrelevant, say the economists. If we get pleasure from priestly vestments in Communion, that's fine. The economist will turn to inquire about the supply and demand curves for vestments, which will determine their price.

The questions here are two: Can such an economics get along without a serious inquiry into the sacred? "Yes, by God!" the economists reply. And can a God-centered life get along without economics? "Yes," the theologians reply.

Both, I think, are mistaken.

Economics without God

The deep structure of modern economics, viewed from theology, is, so to speak, Augustinian. People are born in sin (that is, greed). By the grace of God, and of market forces, the sin is transformed into social good.

The invisible hand is not a vague or stupid argument, and most non-economist intellectuals would do well to try to understand it before turning away. The argument is fundamental to a logic of property and possession. For the moment leave the deep meaning of the words "property" and "possession" aside, ignoring their social construction. Consider what happens when anyway they exist.

Among the important things that happen is exchange. Jones exchanges what she possesses, her labor for bread, or her dog for a sheep, or her loan for interest. (The money prices of all these, I repeat, are merely a convenience for what is more fundamentally an exchange of goods and services for other goods and services.) Jones works an hour in the Starbucks at University Village, earning $8.00. She can buy with her hour's earnings four loaves of bread. (I anticipate another theme: a laborer in London in the 1770s earned a penny an hour, and would have needed the equivalent of *four hours* to earn even one loaf. It's a measure of how far capitalism has brought us in two centuries, 4:1 as against 1:4.) The grocer is made better off by the sale, or else he would raise the price of the loaf. He spends his "profit" on cappuccinos at Starbucks, perhaps, completing the circle rapidly. But, in any case, he is better off. So is she, the bread-buyer — or, again, she would not buy the loaves. So are the owners of the Starbucks, in accepting her offer to work for $8.00 an hour. So is she, in offering it. So are the customers, enjoying their cappuccinos. So, so, so: exchange is, as the economists express it, "mutually beneficial." Mainstream economists therefore cannot make sense of the Marxist claim that exchange is exploitation. From their point of view, the value of what each gets is always higher than the money price that each pays, or else the deal would not have gone through.

"Mutually beneficial" does not mean "idyllic for everyone involved." A "free market" does not for example mean "equal exchange," whatever exactly equality would mean. There is no reason for Starbucks and Jones to have the same amount of money in the bank for a mutually advantageous exchange to

313

take place between them. We do not live in the Garden of Eden and should not judge economic life against perfection, especially such an impossible perfection as "equal" exchange. Utopianism, making the best imaginable the enemy of the actually achievable good, has been a problem in social thinking since 1789, and Christian social thinking has not been an exception. We live in a world of scarcity, earning our bread from the sweat of our brows. The economist says in her grim way: grow up; face it.

Free exchange is better than theft or charity or hierarchy as a system of doling out what nature and our sweaty efforts have produced. If Jones the bread-buyer can simply pillage the grocer, or throw herself on his mercy, or get the bread by right of her high status, the outcome is worse than exchange. Why? Because only exchange among the systems is mutually productive. Value is "created" (as economists say) by putting the bread in the hands of the person who values it most, but along the way in free exchange the bread is voluntarily brought into existence. A regime of theft, or high taxes, by contrast, discourages production and makes the exchange of what is produced less likely. No one is going to run a grocery store that is regularly pillaged, whether by gangs of toughs or by hoards of tax gatherers. One can explain in such terms the poverty of the Scottish Highlands before their subjection to the rule of law, and of many sub-Saharan countries now, and of most communist countries, and of inner cities.

Make no mistake. Private ownership is essential for this mutual advantage in exchange and this encouragement to production in profit. "Stewardship" will not do, for the reason that a common park is littered because no one owns it and no one therefore has an incentive to keep it clean. That's another thing that happens when property and possession exist: people take care of what they own. For the earth to be treasured, it needs to *be* treasure.

A famous passage in Adam Smith's *The Wealth of Nations,* first published in 1776, is usually understood to mean that the engine of mutual advantage is this sinful, Augustinian greed. Smith writes:

> It is not from the benevolence of the butcher, the brewer, or the baker, that we expect our dinner, but from their regard to their own interest. We address ourselves, not to their humanity. But to their self-love, and never talk to them of our own necessities but of their advantages. Nobody but a beggar chuses to depend chiefly upon the benevolence of his fellow-citizens.[1]

1. Adam Smith, *An Inquiry into the Nature and Causes of the Wealth of Nations,* ed. Andrew S. Skinner and R. H. Campbell, vol. 1 (Oxford: Clarendon, 1979), pp. 26f.

Augustinians by the hundreds down to the Nobel laureate and leading misreader of Smith, the Chicago economist George Stigler, have supposed that "*The Wealth of Nations* is a stupendous palace erected upon the granite of self-interest."[2]

A structure as theological as this lurks just below the level of consciousness among economists.[3] But below: the economists and calculators are damned if they are going to call on any virtue. The economists, Marxist or bourgeois, insist on being theorists of anti-virtues, as they view them. Out of your sin shall come a goodness wholly undeserved. Out of your individual greed shall come market efficiency. Out of your class interest shall come The Revolution. Unintended. Grace.

My own view and that of a tiny minority of economists is heretical and Pelagian. People are born with an array of virtues, the Pelagian economists claim; or at any rate, children acquire the virtues at their mothers' knees or teachers' desks before they enter economic society. We Pelagians think that grace comes out of being children of God, as we all are, not from a paradox of fallenness.

For example, the realm of caring is outside the market, having nothing to do with butchers and bakers, and it, too, is mutually beneficial. It is a virtue, nongreedy. Its working does not require an original sin; rather an original virtue. A mother gives food to her child, and comes away from the "transaction" satisfied. I do not mean to reduce the satisfaction to utility. On the contrary, her satisfaction comes from an identity fulfilled, not from the "pleasures" directly and dubiously earned from making peanut-butter-and-jelly sandwiches for her son's lunchbox. She loves her child. So we feminist economists retort to Smith, if Smith is read as ignoring caring, "It's from the benevolence of your *mother,* my dear Dr. Smith, that you expect a *cooked* dinner," the elder Mrs. Smith being the woman in his household. The deeper point is David Klemm's: Property as grace is given and received as a living symbol of divinity.[4] The giver is enriched.

It needs to be realized how enormous the share of caring is in any econ-

---

2. Quoted in Samuel Fleischacker, "Talking to My Butcher: Self-Interest, Exchange, and Freedom in *The Wealth of Nations*," unpublished paper (Chicago: Department of Philosophy, University of Illinois, Chicago, 1999), p. 1.

3. Some other links between economics and theology have been brilliantly explored by Robert Nelson. See Robert H. Nelson, *Economics as Religion: From Samuelson to Chicago and Beyond* (University Park, Pa.: Pennsylvania State University Press, 2001), and his *Reaching for Heaven on Earth: The Theological Meaning of Economics* (Savage, Md.: Rowman and Littlefield, 1991).

4. See Klemm's essay, pp. 222-48 in this volume.

omy. After all, even most purchases in the marketplace and a great deal of income-earning are said to be for the benefit of someone other than the purchaser or earner. Parents, partners, children, friends, cousins, pets: we buy and sell for each other all day long. Something like a half of the marketed portion of national income is gotten on behalf of someone else. And massive amounts of caring labor, off the market books but not off the mind of economists nowadays, goes into every household of more than one loved one. Nancy Folbre, among other feminist economists, has emphasized the size of the caring sector, and has worried about its erosion by market substitutes.[5] As did Adam Smith: "Domestic education is the institution of nature — public education the contrivance of man. It is surely unnecessary to say which is likely to be the wisest."[6] One can argue about the matter. I would say that the market has widened the opportunities for caring; Smith thought so, too. But in any case the realm of grace is wider than secular economists believe.

The moral philosopher Samuel Fleischacker, however, has reinterpreted even the allegedly selfishness-recommending passage in Smith as Pelagian, as not supposing a sin in the original position of humankind. He notes that the very conventionality of the example — "Well, *of course* we address the butcher and baker in terms of what they can get from us!" — implies that Smith is not intent on stating the obvious, that butchers are in business for themselves.[7] This obvious point was Bernard Mandeville's only one, elaborated well before Smith into an all-purpose ethical theory that some economists like Stigler have found congenial. Smith took considerable trouble to attack Mandeville,[8] so his point can hardly be Mandeville's own.

On the contrary, Smith was pointing out that the *buyer,* who is the main character in Smith's parable, is "able to perceive, and address himself to, *other people's interests.*"[9] It is this faculty of imaginative entry into the interests of others that distinguishes in Smith's mind the human from the animal, and makes our form of cooperation in an economy so productive. A fair exchange does not show an impossible "equality" but simply the free speech to induce cooperation. The introduction of one satellite telephone into thousands of Bangladeshi villages (as a commercial service owned in each village by a local woman) has transformed their economies: now the farmers know if they are

---

5. See, for example, Nancy Folbre, *The Invisible Heart: Economics and Family Values* (New York: New Press, 2001).

6. Smith, *The Theory of the Moral Sentiments,* part 6, section 2, chap. 1.

7. Fleischacker, "Talking to My Butcher," pp. 1-2.

8. Adam Smith, *The Theory of Moral Sentiments,* ed. D. D. Raphael and A. L. Macfie (Indianapolis: Liberty Classics, 1982), pp. 308-13.

9. Fleischacker, "Talking to My Butcher," p. 4, italics his.

being cheated in a bargain, because they know the price in Dacca. According to Fleischacker, Smith "is interested in our capacity for being aware of other people's needs and feelings," the basis for commercial success. "Instead of an almost Ayn Randian exaltation of self-love, we may now see these famous lines as focusing on our capacity to be *other*-directed."[10]

Capitalism is commonly portrayed as selfish to the point of solipsism. It is nothing of the kind. It is the most social of systems. As Patrick Miller notes in his commentary in this volume on the trajectory of "Thou shalt not steal," "the economics of the straying ox" is more than a selfish matter. I have a religious obligation (foreshadowing, he notes, the New Testament obligation to love one's neighbor as oneself) to take care of another's goods: "I cannot hide myself from the reality of my neighbor's economic endangerment."[11] The "positive inducement to generosity" in the eighth commandment calls us to treat our neighbor as ourselves, requiring an imaginative leap that Smith called the impartial spectator.

*   *   *

Adam Smith and I, but no other economists, think of the place of an economy in a universe of good and evil in terms of the seven virtues Aquinas catalogued: the four "pagan" ones of courage, temperance, prudence (or wisdom), and justice, plus the three "theological" virtues of love, faith, and hope. The first four, the pagan virtues, glow in wily Odysseus or in the hero Gunnar of Njàl's Saga, men showing the virtues of a military aristocracy; the last glow in the life and words of St. Paul, "Faith, hope, and charity, these three. But the greatest is charity." The theological virtues, notice, have a stereotypically feminine air, or at any rate are not the virtues of the soldier.

Thus:

Courage	Temperance	Prudence	Justice	Love	Faith	Hope
Soldier					Saint	
	Inner-regard			Other-regard		
Aristocrat		Bourgeois			Peasant/Proletarian	

Economics since its invention as a system of thought in the eighteenth century has been very largely about that third virtue of the seven, prudence, an androgynous virtue counted good in both men and women stereotypically

10. Fleischacker, "Talking to My Butcher," p. 4.

11. In this volume, see pp. 17-50.

viewed. You can call it practical wisdom or *ratio* or know-how or self-interest or competence or rationality. The word "prudence" is a useful, long-period compromise among the wisdom-words from *phronesis* in Aristotle to "maximization" in the modern economists.

Prudence *is* a virtue, which is not something most moderns, Left or Right, are willing to see. In the last two centuries prudence has come to be viewed as mere selfishness, the Ayn-Randian sort of behavior one could assume as normal to a commercial society, hardly a "virtue." But the ancients, I think, had it right. We want to have people around us who are prudent, who can take care of themselves — every parent knows that. Of course, we also want our children or friends to be courageous, temperate, just, loving, faithful, and hopeful. The point is that ethics cannot be reduced without grave loss to The One, to an essential juice of goodness in the style of Plato. And among the Aristotelian Many, I say, the virtue of prudence is not to be scorned.

The way most economists do their job is to ask, Where's the prudence? Adam Smith asserted in 1776 that "what is prudence in the conduct of every private family can scarce be folly in that of a great kingdom."[12] A splendidly useful principle. The blessed Smith, however, understood that we do want people to have a balanced set of virtues, not merely prudence. He was not a very religious man, it seems, but was nevertheless a professor of moral philosophy, and took his job seriously. I believe he was forming in all his works an ethic for a commercial society. But his ethic was not Prudence Über Alles. After Smith's death his followers came to believe precisely this, that prudence, or utility, rules. Their single-mindedness was part of a wider rhetorical development beginning around 1700 that has elevated prudence to the master virtue, the Platonic juice. (This at the same time that in other circles prudence was being reduced to the master vice, drummed out of the virtue corps.) You will find people in business schools arguing that the reason to be loving or just is that it is prudent — it makes money, doing well by doing good.

Economics has lost its ethical bearings, which is no wonder considering its fierce secularism. The philosophical movement fashionable in the middle decades of the twentieth century, Positivism, has squeezed out ethical and theological reflection. Yet ethics and economics overlapped at its beginning. No one seriously disagrees that Adam Smith invented economics. (True, not out of nothing; but the field came to exist after Smith in the same way that geology came to exist after his Edinburgh friend James Hutton; or that modern philosophy came to exist after his greatest friend, David Hume.) But Smith

12. Smith, *An Inquiry into the Nature and Causes of the Wealth of Nations*, book 4, chap. 2.

was not, of course, a professor of "economics," or even of its older title (before about 1870), "political economy." His first book, the book he regarded as his masterpiece, the sixth edition of which he finished shortly before his death, was not *The Wealth of Nations* but *The Theory of Moral Sentiments.*[13]

After the promising Smithian beginning, economics and ethics, the prudent and the sacred, have become separate spheres. They have drifted apart to the extent that economists regard themselves as defined by their amorality (and likewise that moralists think it frightfully vulgar to mention considerations of prudence). It's not unreasonable to suppose that the separation of spheres into a bourgeois business-place and a Christian home, a man's world and a woman's, had something to do with the drifting apart. Jeremy Bentham and his school were important, too. By 1846, Charles Dickens was noting sardonically that "some philosophers tell us that selfishness is at the root of our best loves and affections."[14] Whatever caused it, the drift is fundamental to modern sensibilities. To be macho in the twenty-first century is to be some version of an economist. "Realists" in foreign policy, such as Henry Kissinger, scorn an interest in human rights for their own sake. One must have a utilitarian interest in everything. Oil, say.

My point is that Smith was right and later economists and calculators have been wrong. You can't run on prudence alone a family or a church or a community or a foreign policy or even — and this is the surprising point — a capitalist economy. Courage and love and the rest figure in any human group. You can't run human groups on love alone, either. Or on courage alone. It's the aloneness that's the problem. As Mary Midgley observes in her book *Wickedness,* evil comes from an unbalanced excess in what would in a balanced showing be a virtue.[15] Think of how dangerous it would be in a platoon with Medal-of-Honor types all around you; or how tiresome to be a nun with Mother Teresa types all around you.[16] Love alone is no excuse for an imprudent or unjust or intemperate act.

Prudent, economical, market-oriented, capitalist behavior *within a balanced set of virtues* is not merely harmless — it is virtuous; even, I am bold to say, in God's eyes. By contrast, the prudence-only behavior celebrated in economic fable is bad. Bad for business. Bad for life. Bad for the soul. We call it avarice.

13. The first edition of *The Theory of Moral Sentiments* was published in 1759, the last in 1790.

14. Charles Dickens, *Dombey and Son* (London: Penguin, 1985), p. 150.

15. Mary Midgley, *Wickedness: A Philosophical Essay* (London: New York, 2001).

16. Cf. Susan Wolf, "Moral Saints," in *Virtue Ethics,* ed. Roger Crisp and Michael A. Slote (New York: Oxford University Press, 1997).

This will not surprise an audience of theologians and biblical scholars. How does it change the economics? Radically. An economics that acknowledged the ethical wholeness of economic actors, in the style of the "social economics" described by Christine Hinze in this volume,[17] would come to different conclusions about prudential matters, too. To show this in factual detail would require a long book. The best brief example is the economistic theory of voting popular nowadays among American political scientists. People are supposed to vote their pocketbooks, to be wholly rational in choosing a Gore or a Haider. But wait. Voting is itself an irrational act. Once in the voting booth, fine, one might be imagined to choose which lever to pull by judging the effect of this or that candidate on one's income. It's not how you or I vote, but at least it is not self-contradictory. But any single act of voting is so trivial in most elections that the expected gain to the pocketbook (that is, the dollar gain multiplied by the probability that one's vote will affect the outcome) is a matter of a few pennies. *Going to the polls is much more expensive than a few pennies.* A rational theory of voter participation, then, is wholly inconsistent with the facts. No one but a madman would set off for the presidential election saying to himself, "That creep Gore will reduce my income. I must go to the polls to stop him, and I will." He won't. The "rational choice" framework for politics is a rational theory for a population of madmen. *Sic transit Gloria hominis economicae.*

What is most my own is not my own, David Klemm reminds us in his essay in this volume. I neither produce myself nor belong to myself.[18] Yes, and it is a truth that erodes the literally Godless utilitarianism of modern economics. A bizarre instance of what Klemm is referring to is the economic value of human life. Economists correctly observe that *some* valuation is necessary in designing, say, highways or air traffic controls. It is not literally the case that we design the autobahn with an infinite value of human life in view, or else we would require the BMWs to crawl down it at five kilometers per hour with a man waving a red flag in front of each. On the basis of *self* evaluations, such as how much one requires for entering dangerous jobs, the current value of life in the United States is one or two million dollars. But no one is an island; everyone's death diminishes me, for I am involved in humankind. The strictly correct economics, therefore, would include as well the values that *other people* place on me if I enter the profession of daredevil motorcycle jumping. This can be vastly more than the value I put. Technically speaking, lives are public goods, valued by the entire community. Even an apparently

17. See pp. 168-88.
18. See pp. 222-45.

bloodless calculation of the "worth" of a human life finds itself facing more than selfish prudence.

Economics needs a serious return to Smith and his preoccupation with character, and behind it an engagement with the sacred.

God without Economics

Any society, Christian or not, has both a sacred sphere and a profane sphere, a sphere in which love and obligation determine who gets what as against the sphere in which prudence and courage do so. And the two cannot be disentangled. We all live in families, and a church can be viewed from this social scientific perspective as a sort of family. Businesspeople cannot be routinely avaricious and remain in business, any more than a caretaker for a child can, or a dutiful daughter.

Many non-economists imagine that, on the contrary, avarice is necessary to keep the wheels of commerce turning, "creating jobs" or "keeping the money circulating"; that people must buy, buy, buy or else capitalism will collapse and all of us will be impoverished. It's a bubble theory of capitalism, that people must keep puffing, one version of the old claim that expenditure on luxuries at least employs workpeople. I say as an economist that it is mistaken. Nothing would befall the market economy in the long run if we tempered our desires down to one car and a small house and healthy foods from the Co-op. (And as the economist Robert Frank argues, taxing consumption to bring down rivalrous buying of Ferraris and other symbols of superiority would make us better off even without moderating our desires,[19] though I doubt that rivalrous consumption is a very long-lasting or very important feature of high capitalist economies; notice, for example, that it's always those other, silly people, not we, who are keeping up with the Joneses.) Workers in a temperate economy would not become permanently unemployed.

The mistake is to think that the relevant mental experiment is that tomorrow, suddenly, without warning, we all begin to follow Jesus in what we buy. No doubt such a conversion would be a shock to General Motors. But, the economist observes, people in the Christian Economy would find other employment, and would choose more nonwork activity. It would still be a fine thing to have lightbulbs and paved roads and other fruits of enterprise (the commercial version of courage). "In equilibrium," as economists say

19. Robert Frank, *Luxury Fever: Why Money Fails to Satisfy in an Era of Excess* (New York: Free Press, 1999).

when making this sort of point, the economy would encourage specialization to satisfy human desires in much the same way as it does now. People would buy Bibles and spirit-enhancing trips to Yosemite instead of *The Monica Story* and trips to Disney World, but we would still value high-speed presses for the books and airplanes for the trips. The desires would be different, but that doesn't change how the system works best: private property (such as your labor, your ideas) seeking its best employment; consumers (such as you) seeking the best deal. I agree with Benjamin Hunnicutt in his remarkable books on the leisure history of Americans that long hours are connected to our great Need-Love for commodities.[20] People following Jesus would by contrast make the plain pottery that an economy of moderation would demand and spend more time with their children. But the point is that the pottery would still be produced most efficiently in a marketing, free-trade, private property, enterprising, and energetic economy. We would be richer, not poorer, in the things and deeds we value.

This should be good news for Christians. We do not need to trim our demands for ethical consumption for fear that such a policy would hurt the poor. We do not need to accept avaricious behavior because of some wider social prudence it is supposed to serve, allegedly keeping us employed. A commercial society does *not* need to foster vice and greed "in order to balance production and consumption," as William Schweiker speculates in his essay in this volume.[21] The Dutch-English rhymester Bernard Mandeville, whom I have already introduced, articulated the mistaken supposition in 1705:

> Vast Number throng'd the fruitful Hive;
> Yet those vast Numbers made 'em thrive;
> Million endeavouring to supply
> Each other's Lust and Vanity
> Thus every Part was full of Vice,
> Yet the whole Mass a Paradise.[22]

---

20. See, for example, three works by Benjamin Kline Hunnicutt: *Kellogg's Six-Hour Day* (Philadelphia: Temple University Press, 1996); *Luxury or Leisure: The Dilemma of Prosperity in the 1920's* (Ann Arbor, Mich.: University Microfilms, 1976); *Work without End: Abandoning Shorter Hours for the Right to Work* (Philadelphia: Temple University Press, 1988). Cf. Juliet B. Schor, *Why Capitalism Underproduces Leisure: The Economics of Output-Bias* (Cambridge, Mass.: Harvard Institute of Economic Research, 1986); and Juliet Schor, Joshua Cohen, and Joel Rogers, *Do Americans Shop Too Much?* (Boston: Beacon, 2000).

21. See p. 265.

22. Bernard Mandeville, *The Fable of the Bees,* ed. Phillip Harth (Harmondsworth: Penguin, 1989), sections 3, 9.

Mandeville's economics is wrong, though ever since a comfort to the trickle-down school. "Such is the system of Dr. Mandeville," wrote Smith in 1759, "which once made so much noise in the world, and which, though, perhaps, it never gave occasion to more vice than would have been without it, at least taught that vice, which arose from other causes, to appear with more effrontery, and to avow the corruption of its motives with a profligate audaciousness which had never been heard of before."[23] The ethics of the country club could not be better characterized. What is wrong in the economics is that lust and vanity are no better springs for an economy than love and temperance: as I said.

To repeat, it is not the case that market capitalism requires avaricious people. More like the contrary. Markets, I now am claiming, exhibit behavior that Jesus would have approved of — in fact, behavior that he did, textually, once in a while, approve of. In any event, I want to claim that the imperfect economy we now inhabit contains in its very functioning a large amount of God-regarding virtue.

Consider your own workplace. How does your office or factory actually operate? Really, now. With monsters of prudence running around taking care of Numero Uno? No, not really. We find the cartoon strip *Dilbert* funny because the avaricious behavior of some of its characters is over the top, crazy funny, unacceptably prudent. Workplaces are in fact more like homeplaces. We are morally offended when our workmate complains about our dog in our office: what a nasty thing to do, we think; doesn't he realize that Janie is important to me; doesn't he care about me? A wholly prudential worker would not be capable of such sorrow and indignation.

The ethical wholeness of actors in a capitalist marketplace is not a minor, supplementary matter. The writer Don Snyder tried construction work to survive one winter in Maine:

> There were six of us working on the crew, but the house was so large that we seldom saw one another. . . . Once I walked right by a man in my haste to get back to a second story deck where I had been tearing down staging. [The contractor] saw this, and he climbed down from the third story to set me straight: "You can't just walk by people," he said. "It's going to be a long winter."[24]

Even in a workplace of men a tough, businesslike prudence cannot be all there is.

23. Smith, *The Theory of Moral Sentiments*, p. 313.
24. Don J. Snyder, "Winter Work," in *Survival Stories: Memoirs of Crisis*, ed. Kathryn Rhett (New York: Doubleday, 1997), p. 74.

I have a problem in making this point to my economist colleagues nowadays because they have forgotten that economics as an academic field and the market as an institution deal in fact with whole people. The economists since Jeremy Bentham in 1789 have posited a monster of prudence called *Homo economicus*. He is motivated by what C. S. Lewis calls "Need-Love," that is, an appetite that is satisfied by having a bite or getting a hug. (Economists since the 1880s have called the appetite a "utility function," and write down mathematical expressions for maximizing U [x,y] subject to a budget constraint.) It has nothing of Appreciative-Love, the delight even in the mere existence of the beloved, a call to admire: "He fathers-forth whose beauty is past change:/Praise him."[25] Some economists have reduced religion itself to a Need-Love itch, and speak of "explaining" church attendance as people scratching it. I think non-economists can understand the situation on the ground better, since they have not acquired an educated inability to see that prudence alone does not work.

The simple point I am making is that markets live in communities of virtue. Supply and demand, money and prices, would still go on working if people had identities more complex than the windup toys of standard economic theory. An ascetic "prefers" oatmeal in her bedsitter to a six-course breakfast at the Savoy Grill. Yet she will follow the economist's Law of Demand about oatmeal, buying less if its relative price goes up. She comes to her "tastes" through religious conviction, but in the market the tastes do what they also do in people motivated in other, unchristian ways — by keeping up with the Joneses, or commodity fetishism, or unthinking acquisitiveness. These too are identities, ethical decisions, though we think poorly of them.

Oddly, the prudence-obsessed economists have themselves been forced recently in their very mathematics to admit that *Homo economicus* must live with an identity formed in a family within a community of speech constrained by virtues (a nonbeliever would call it, in summary, "culture"; a Christian would call it "a moral universe"). For example, in "game theory," an aptly named part of high academic economics, it has been discovered that games (such as the nuclear arms race or participation in an economy) cannot be played with prudence-only rules. They break down, just as they do in Dilbert's office or on the construction site that does not attend to love and justice, too. This is true even if one does posit a *Homo economicus*, as a purely hypothetical idea to be pursued as social mathematics.

Off the blackboard it is clear that real economies depend on real virtues.

---

25. C. S. Lewis, *The Four Loves* (San Diego: Harcourt Brace Jovanovich, 1991). The quotation comes from "Pied Beauty," a poem by Gerard Manley Hopkins.

Economists have recently discovered such notions as trust and institutions, noting what the rest of us always knew, that a deal in a market (such as your employment with all its formal and informal clauses) depends on both prudence and the other virtues. One must belong to a community, since no contract can be explicit about every aspect of a difficult transaction and even in buying a newspaper the agent trusts that you won't suddenly snatch the money back and run out of the store. When I moved in 1980 from Hyde Park in Chicago to Iowa City, I was startled by the reduction in transaction costs. Every transaction was easier. Checks passed, cleaning ladies worked hard, auto mechanics did what they said they were going to do. Moving back to Chicago in 1999, I observed the contrast again. It is why co-religionists or co-ethnics are often so successful in business. Their communities of trust give them cheaper loans and cheaper supplies and even insurance in disaster. If you are not virtuous you get dumped. The overseas Chinese do better as a minority in Indonesia, where they have lived without marrying outside their group since the seventeenth century, than at "home" in Canton. Mennonites made fortunes in eighteenth-century Holland. The orthodox Jewish diamond dealers in Brooklyn trade stones worth thousands of dollars on a nod and a trusted word. Any economy depends on ethical behavior. The other virtues do not drive out prudence or make the New York Stock Exchange into a love fest. The honest workman is still worth his hire. The margin call still comes due. But actual, capitalist markets depend on more than prudence. If one performs economic experiments on students and other hired victims, it has recently been found, the love, justice, temperance, faith, hope, and courage come pouring even out of the laboratories.

*   *   *

So far I have said things that are unpopular with economists but not with Christians. Now I must in fairness turn the tables. I say: Envisioning prudence within the other virtues *does not entail abandoning prudence entirely.* The mistake of thinking that economics must concern either Only Prudence, on the one hand, or No Prudence at All, on the other, is shared by hard Right, hard Left, and soft center, politically speaking, which is to say that it is shared by most intellectuals. Most intellectuals think that introducing *any* element of cultural autonomy is devastating to a material explanation of class behavior, say. If movie plots have *any* effect on working-class consciousness, well, their factory jobs just don't matter at all (thus the Left).

A balanced regard for prudence among the virtues has a large effect on how a Christian views the market. The balance can be put so: the market, and the bourgeois ethic that supports it, must be given its due. It is not an invention of the devil. It is not intrinsically ungodly. In fact, as Max Weber noted a century ago, capitalism's practitioners have often enough been unusually godly folk. Yet the impulse among European intellectuals since 1848 has been never to give the market its due, and to feel in fact that one is being ethical only if one sneers at market outcomes.

The chain of reasoning against the intellectuals goes like this:

1. *Virtues underlay the market and its triumph c. 1830.*

Not vices, contrary to the cherished views of the intellectuals. Not imperialism, whether Iberian or Northern. Not the slave trade. Not the impoverishment of the working class. Not extractions from the Third World. Not the exploitation of women. As can be shown in statistical detail on each count.

2. *The triumph of the market was a necessary condition for modern economic growth.*

Marx and Engels say this, of course, in *The Communist Manifest* — though from a perspective of year 2000, or even 1948, even their fulsome praise for the accomplishments of the bourgeoisie in "scarce two hundred years" down to 1848 looks like understatement. Modern economic growth did not depend on central planning, nor corporate welfare, nor, again, any sort of theft from the poor. Modern economic growth was not a result of trade unions or government regulation or the welfare state. It was a result of letting markets work.

3. *Modern economic growth has been much greater than most intellectuals realize.*

Let me go beyond a telegraphic style on this one. It is not true, as many Christians with social concerns believe, that the world is getting poorer. In the past two centuries and especially in the past fifty years, and most especially since the fall of Communism, it has gotten much, much richer. Globalization encourages the capitalist engine of growth. If people understood how generous the engine has been they would have less enthusiasm for protectionism or socialism or environmentalism or economic nationalism in any of their varied forms. But most educated people believe that the gains to income from capitalism's triumph have been modest, that the poor have been left behind, that the Third World has been immiserized in aid of the enrichment of the First, that population growth *must* be controlled, that diminishing returns on the whole has been the main force in world economic history since 1800. All these notions are factually incorrect. But you will find all of them in the mind of the average professor of theology or biblical studies.

Angus Maddison's recent compilation of national income statistics worldwide, *Monitoring the World Economy, 1820-1992,* gives a way of measuring the generosity of the capitalist engine.[26] The central fact is well illustrated by the United States. From 1820 to 1994 the real per capita income of the United States increased by . . .

Well, take a guess. The exercise of guessing is important if you are to grasp the point. Do it, please, without examsmanship. What would you say? What is the rough magnitude of modern economic growth, 1820-1994, from Monroe to Clinton? What are we really talking about when we claim that globalization offers the world's poor a chance to be much better off? Take a guess, testing how close you come to the educated person's misunderstanding of the capitalist engine.

Fifty percent? A hundred percent? A doubling since the days of the Federalists? All right, two hundred percent, a tripling? Surely that is enough credit to give the bourgeois engines of economic growth?

No. *Sixteen hundred percent.* An increase by a factor of seventeen. (Recall our bread-buyers in Riverside, California, in 2000, and in London, England, in the 1770s: a factor of four times four — sixteen in that way of making the comparison.) In 1820 the average American, slave and free, produced $1290, expressed in 1990 dollars, a little below the present average for Africa. In 1995 she earned . . . $22,500.

If you do not find this figure impressive, I suggest you are not grasping it. It is utterly unprecedented. It dwarfs the impact of the invention of agriculture. It means that your great-great-great-grandmother had one dress for church, one for the week, if she were not in rags. Her children did not attend school, and probably could not read. She and her husband worked eighty hours a week for a diet of bread and milk (they were four inches shorter than you are). The scope of human life was radically narrowed — and is to this day in countries that have not experienced modern economic growth. You can say all you wish about the spiritual vacuum of modern life, and how we can't see the sunset in Los Angeles (in fact the environment has markedly *improved* in the past century: city air is cleaner after soft-coal and horse manure have been banished, and now auto and factory emissions are under attack; more people can get to the countryside; one *can* in fact see the sunset in Los Angeles nowadays: in fact I am looking at it right now). But the factor of seventeen represents an enormous freeing of people from drudgery and fear and insecurity.

26. Angus Maddison, *Monitoring the World Economy, 1820-1992* (Washington, D.C.: Paris Development Centre of the Organisation for Economic Co-operation and Development, 1995). The national income statistics cited below are all taken from Maddison's work.

Maddison's tables can be arranged this way:

The World Has Moved 1820-1992 from a Bangladeshi Living to a Mexican One

Year	World GDP/capita in 1990s US$ (p. 228)	Comparable country now (pp. 194-206)	World population in billions of people (p. 226)
1820	$650	Bangladesh	1.1
1870	900	(below Africa)	1.3
1913	1500	Pakistan	1.8
1950	2100	Philippines	2.5
1992	5100	Mexico	5.4

Source: A. Maddison, *Monitoring the World Economy*, 1820-1920

That is a very good thing, to go from the level of desperation to the level of hope. Notice the acceleration (greater in the past ten years) — except for 1913 to 1950, that era of de-globalization, of protection, of foreign policy governed by notions of economic nationalism now recommended by many progressives and conservatives together, and of the wars that come from the mercantilism of *Lebensraum* and the East Asian Co-Prosperity Sphere, the politics of a non-economic economics popular among realists.

As the first industrial nation and the champion of free trade Britain went from $1800 in 1820 to $3300 in 1870, nearly doubling in the face of exploding population — during precisely the half century in which the European avant-garde turned against free markets. British income per head was above all others until the New World's exceeded it (New Zealand in 1903, the United States in 1905, Australia in 1906: later the Antipodes slipped for a long while back into protectionist mediocrity). The rest of Europe did not catch up until after World War II — all the while the avant-garde complaining that Britain was "failing" economically. Now Britain wobbles upward with the other advanced industrial countries in a band plus or minus a few percentage points from the average, excepting the big, rich nation of churchgoers, which persists at 30 percent above the rest. So much for economic "failure" among the "Anglo-Saxon" leaders of industrialization.

Japan in 1870 was roughly at the present-day Bangladeshi level of income per head, the same as Brazil's in 1870. By 1939, it had attained the level of United States' income per head sixty years before (and was double Brazil's). In 1994, Japan had attained the United States' income level ten years before (four times Brazil's). It was a convergence through imitation, saving, education, and work — which then its former colony South Korea repeated. Korea's income in 1952 was a desperate $860 in 1990 prices. Now it is $10,000. So much for the lasting effects of even an especially brutal colonialism.

If we can hold off neo-socialist attempts to divide the wealth before it is created, the whole world can be rich. If India can restrain its Gandhian impulse to throttle the market, it can adopt American ways of retailing and Japanese ways of manufacturing and German ways of chemical-making and enter the modern world of a wider human scope. India does *not* need to repeat the stages through which Britain and France have traveled (contra the pessimism born of London-School-of-Economics educations among Congress Party politicians that India needs to go slow, to plan, to wait before leapfrogging into a post-computer world). Countries are *not* "like trees" or "like people growing up." There is no racial or cultural reason why India cannot in five or ten decades have an American standard of living. The twenty-first century can be a grand alternative to the Century of Protection (and Slaughter) just concluded.

4. **Modern economic growth has transformed the ethical universe for its beneficiaries, who are everyone involved.**

Contra the accepted view, there has in fact been no worsening of income distribution. The gap between rich and poor is smaller, not larger.

For example, modern economies are now able to indulge their tastes (as economists put it in their cold way) for environmental change, social justice, human rights. Sine qua non. It is emblematic that the first industrial nation was the first to abolish slavery, even its slaves in the West Indian colonies on which — a cynical view would say (mistakenly) — its wealth depended. Until the rise of a market and bourgeois ideology, until those devout Quaker traders — even slave traders — around 1780, it had occurred to no one that slavery was anything but God's plan.

5. **The Malthusian and now environmentalist notion that population growth is itself an evil and is the source of our poverty has been proven false.**

The zero-sum politics of the 1930s is ever popular, because pessimism always sounds wiser than optimism, but has been falsified again and again. It is not the case that the final struggle of capitalism, no more than Armageddon, is upon us. On the contrary, the century beginning offers a prospect of ever-widening enrichment: India is starting to see explosive growth; China has been experiencing it now for ten years. And in such countries the environment improves when the people want it to, that is, when they become well off.

*   *   *

I realize that saying such things brings a hard, un-Christian tone into the analysis. But surely it is incumbent upon a Christian heart to help the poor *prudently,* not in order to save money but in order to really save the poor. Prudence, I said, is a virtue. In such matters, practical wisdom, knowing how to achieve a spiritual end, proves itself.

Here is a disturbing example. Forgiving Third World debt, most economists would agree, will not much alleviate Third World poverty. It may help a little. But it is only prudent to grasp why economists are doubtful it will help much. It may well be a good spiritual exercise for the rich countries to make the gift. I do not deny the seriousness of such a Jubilee gesture. In fact, I support it (many economists would not). But what of its prudential force?

In the first place, *cui bono?* Are the poor of Tanzania, say, helped by forgiving debt owed by their government? The forgiving of debt has an "incidence," as economists put it, which may not correspond to its apparent legal placement. You help "the country." But wait: who gets the benefit? If the poor in the countryside get it, good; if the thieves running the government get it, no poor person has been helped. So forgiving debt may not accomplish its ethical intention. Here is a concrete example of what economists mean by "efficiency" and what I am calling prudence: enriching the rich in Tanzania simply does not accomplish what its label claims; it is inefficient, inefficacious, imprudent.

And, second, look at the other side of the transaction. Will big banks continue to make loans to poor countries if the debts are forgiven? Is lack of access to the international capital market a good thing for the poor of Bolivia?

And last, and most important, the magnitudes involved are trivial relative to the poverty to be relieved. If the poverty of the Third World was in fact caused by debt to the First World no one but the worst sort of Benthamite could reasonably object to forgiving it. But it is not so caused. It is caused chiefly by kleptocratic governments or private interests in league with governments that make market exchange unprofitable, that make investment in making something to exchange silly, that encourage achieving private wealth at the cost of other peoples' wealth instead of by working and saving and inventing (economists know this last by the odd term "rent seeking").

The plight of the world's poor *is* indeed caused by insufficient Christian charity. It *is* caused by greed. But the greed and lack of charity is not that of the First World. A Christian economics should concern itself with the ethical grounding not of Danish journalists or American college professors but of African politicians and Latin American generals.

A similarly surprising calculation of prudence can be defended about concern for the environment. It is conventional to believe that in every way the environment is under more pressure than in, say, 1900, that population growth is bound to continue toward catastrophe unless we adopt one-child policies, and the like. This is not factually correct. Birthrates have fallen extremely quickly in the modern world with rising incomes and standards of public health. Fertility has been falling like a stone in the Third World: from 6.2 live births per woman per lifetime in 1950-1955 to 3.3 in 1990-1995. (Over the same period it fell in more developed areas from 2.8 to 1.7.)[27] As economic growth accelerates, the number of mouths demanding it decelerates and then falls.

*   *   *

But if markets and capitalism and globalization make for riches, they also make rich people. (It should be pointed out, by the way, that *every* alternative economic system has also made some people rich: priests, say, or commissars, the emperor or the don.) Surely that is bad.

No. The indignation toward the rich — a strong theme, of course, in Christian and especially modern Catholic social thought — is based on a manna theory of riches. Riches fall from heaven, and it is only reasonable that heaven's rules be followed in its distribution. More for thee means less for me. Zero sum, as the economists have taught us to say.

But economists point out that the zero-sum manna theory is mistaken. To understand the mistakenness you need merely to grasp the first sentence of *The Wealth of Nations:* "The annual labour of every nation is the fund which originally supplies it with all the necessaries and conveniences of life which it annually consumes."[28] That is, people do not merely consume, as though manna were falling on them; they labor to make it. The economy has two sides, equal to the last penny as a mere consequence of double-entry bookkeeping: the consuming side; and the income earning, or goods-and-services-making, side. The economy is viewed by economists as a gigantic machine for making labor and capital and natural resources into consumable goods and services. Economists speak fondly of an "aggregate production function," $Q = F(L, K, T)$.

So what? This: We to some degree *choose* our incomes here on earth, and earthly rules are relevant if the encouragement to become educated and to work long hours is to be maintained. True, to be born into the American

---

27. Richard Easterlin, "The Worldwide Standard of Living since 1800," *Journal of Economic Perspectives* 14 (winter 2000): 17.

28. Smith, *An Inquiry into the Nature and Causes of the Wealth of Nations.*

economy as against that of, say, Afghanistan, is a large gift of God. But within any economy one earns per hour what one's accumulated (and, yes, God-given) skills warrant in view of what other people are willing to pay. This assertion is called "marginal productivity theory," and is among the best-attested generalizations of economics. One then chooses, within socially approved limits (which are of course subject to ethical criticism), the number of hours one works at the hourly earnings of marginal productivity. The result of the two choices — the long-run choice to invest in skills and the short-run choice of hours of work — is income. Income = MP x hours, according to this uncontroversial claim in modern economics. A doctor has studied hard and therefore gets paid a high hourly wage; being a workaholic type, she works many hours, too. So her income is immense.

Her income is immense, note, *because she offers services that her customers value highly.* In fact, by the logic of free exchange, the customers value the services *more* than what they pay — or else they wouldn't pay (setting aside for purposes of exposition the grotesque distortions that politically supported monopoly has introduced into the medical marketplace: unresponsive third-party payment, artificial scarcities of doctors, hospitals dominated by local medical societies). The wider point is that letting the doctor earn her immense income makes other people better off. (The point is known among political philosophers as the Wilt Chamberlain Example, after a hypothetical discussed by Robert Nozick.) One can therefore claim in a Rawlsian framework that leaving the rich worker alone (rich owners of unimproved land are another matter) does make the poor better off. They get the benefit of the skilled obstetrician. A society that does not expropriate rich workers will get more of them, "entry" into high-income fields. A society that, by contrast, "cuts down the tall poppies" (as Australians say) grows only stunted humans. The radical egalitarianism at the heart of much Christian social thinking is bad for the poor and bad especially for the rich and educated grandchildren of the poor.

Even in the Bill Gatesian extreme the inequality of incomes can be defended, and in such a religious society as America it has been especially easy to do so. We have been told since the muckraking journalists of the early 1900s that Andrew Carnegie and John D. Rockefeller were very nasty indeed — the equivalent of the evil global corporations or the evil computer millionaires of our own day. How else could they have gotten so rich?

The underlying notion is that the only way to get rich is to steal. But the theory is mistaken in a society that prevents most theft, whether with pistol or fountain pen. Property is *not* theft. If you buy your house low and sell it high, you are doing both of the people you deal with a favor. They didn't have to enter their house deals, and by their willingness they show they are made better off. True, you get the profit — at least until more buyers low enter and spoil your game, turning the former profit into consumer gain from your competition. But whoever earns it, national product goes up. That's one way that capitalism works.

The other and very important way it works (and most of the explanation of the seventeen or sixteen growth factors in the United States since the 1820s) is by invention, which in a large view is just another form of buying low and selling high.

The American economy in the late nineteenth century was a deal-making, inventive place, and so its national product went up (though at a slower rate than, say, India nowadays). If one looks into the way Carnegie and Rockefeller actually made their money it turns out that it was mainly not by cheating but by finding ways to make steel and oil cheaper than their competitors did. Steel rails sold for about $100 a hundredweight around 1870 and about $25 a hundredweight by 1900. Crude petroleum sold for about $3.50 a barrel around 1870 and about 90 cents a barrel by 1900. At the outset in 1870 the average American produced and consumed $2460-worth of goods and services (in 1990 prices), roughly what the average Latin American did in 1950.[29] By 1900, with Carnegie's fortune already made and Rockefeller's almost made, the figure was $4100. That's a rise of $1640, or 66 percent in thirty years (Latin America from 1950 to 1980 did better, about 100 percent in thirty years). To put it another way, the entire flow of goods and services increased in America by $214,000 million. Carnegie's $300 million when he sold out to J. P. Morgan and his consortium in 1901 made him the richest man in the world, a veritable Bill Gates. But it was only one-and-a-half *one thousandth* of the rise in production he helped deliver. To put it another way, this richest man in the world possessed on the order of $1 out of every $20,800 of American human and physical capital (I am capitalizing income at 5 percent). And then he gave every dime away, in accord with his Gospel of Wealth — to the library in Wakefield, Massachusetts, for example, where I first read as a child the socialist classics. So, of course, did Rockefeller (well, perhaps not every dime), as a devout Baptist who raised his children to a gospel of public service.

It needs to be recognized how peculiar and God-saturated the American experience with capitalist fortunes has been. In France or Britain or Germany a fortune starts a dynasty. In America — and only in America — rich people endow colleges, finance hospitals, support the opera, build the church. It is our private impulse, often tied (as in the thousands of colleges) to a reli-

29. Maddison, *Monitoring the World Economy*, p. 196.

gious impulse. A French millionaire assumes correctly that the state will provide. He is more interested in buying that castle or that vineyard, playing at aristocracy. Rich people in America have more often exhibited a bourgeois virtue.

How Commercial Societies Make Virtuous Citizens

"Bourgeois virtue"? Yes.[30] We have a vocabulary of the virtues that honors the soldier or the saint, but not the businessperson. And yet we are all bourgeois now, or getting to be. We need reflections on a virtuous life in a commercial society that do not define voluntary trade as evil. Our nostalgia for precommercial virtues has been disastrous, I would say, causing 1914 and 1917 and much of our twentieth-century woe.[31] It's been an odd development. People like Smith were devising a bourgeois ethic, but their project was abandoned in the nineteenth century and has never been restarted.

Modern capitalism is commonly seen, in the words of the legal philosopher James Boyd White, as "the expansion of the exchange system by the conversion of what is outside it into its terms. It is a kind of steam shovel chewing away at the natural and social world."[32] I don't think so. I do not deny that an amoral capitalism, recommended by the prudence-only folk, is damaging, though I would add that it often does its damage through an over-powerful government, such as the independent authorities in the New York area run by Robert Moses. But the growth of the market, I would claim, can be civilizing, too. It's not the worst ethic to be trained to smile at customers and do an honest day's work. Dr. Johnson said, "A man is not more innocently employed than in getting money."

Such an understanding was a commonplace in eighteenth-century European thinkers (and beyond Europe: one finds similar remarks in Japan at the time). William Schweiker writes that "Hume introduces back into the discussion of commercial society . . . the connection between trade and the sentiments of self, the 'soul' as St. Ambrose put it. Unlike Mandeville, Hume declares that human sentiments can be tutored and enlarged" by commerce.[33] Yes, they can, and have been.

---

30. See Deirdre McCloskey, "Bourgeois Virtue," *The American Scholar* 62, no. 2 (spring 1994).

31. McCloskey, "Bourgeois Virtue."

32. James Boyd White, *Justice As Translation: An Essay in Cultural and Legal Criticism* (Chicago: University of Chicago Press, 1990), p. 71.

33. This volume, p. 265.

Take the crudest of the ethical effects of bourgeois society, the enrichment of the people. We are rich by historical standards. In the poverty of the eighteenth century, we were less Christian. In 1700, brutality toward the poor, viewed as members of a separate race, was normal, as were slavery and public hanging and systematic wife beating. Contrary to a theme in the Gospels, being desperately poor has not proven helpful to a social gospel. Rich countries, not poor, engage in welfare statism and foreign aid. As economists would express it, charity and fellow feeling are "normal" goods like housing or education; that is, the amount we "consume" of them increases as our incomes do. Secularization was once thought to be an inevitable result of economic growth, or "modernization"; church attendance fell in France and England, to the anguish of Christians and the delight of anti-clericals. But such speculations, it seems clear by now, were not correct. Enrichment does not appear to lead necessarily away from the Kingdom of Heaven. Religion, in one or another of its many definitions, appears also to be a normal good.

But the ethical and spiritual effect of participation in a market is more than this economistic "income effect." Schweiker suggests that like other cultural practices, property and possession are about how people form their self-understandings. Indeed. The creativity that most of us are able to enjoy, creating ourselves in the process, is the making of children and the making of goods. Among the costs of sneering at the world's work is that it devalues the world's workers, making "mere" housewives and "mere" businesspeople feel inferior to artists and intellectuals and priests. The message of the Gospels is at least mixed in this regard. The honest workman is worth his hire and the manager is accounted shrewd who settles his master's debts at half their face value. True, the hostility to the rich in the Gospels is palpable, carrying on a Jewish prophetic tradition, and is notably more strident than in other religious traditions. (It is no accident, one supposes, that it was European Christians and Jews who in the nineteenth century invented socialism.) The message of literary modernism, by contrast, is unmixed. The only worthwhile life in Joyce's view is that of an impoverished artist. The European novel since 1848 has a bare handful of male bourgeois heroes working at their businesses: Silas Lapham in Howell's surprising novel, Tom in Mann's *Buddenbrooks*, Vic in David Lodge's *Nice Work*. Sinclair Lewis's *Babbitt* (1922) is only the most extreme and unrelenting of hundreds of literary assaults on economic life.

We intellectuals and artists should treat the bulk of the population with the respect due our fellow creatures. The respect, I have argued, has the practical advantage of the factor of sixteen or seventeen, and this has substantial and not obviously negative spiritual effects. But I am saying more: I am saying, as Montesquieu and Voltaire and other admirers of English liberties and

English commerce in the eighteenth century said, that *doux commerce* is no oxymoron. As Fleischacker puts it, speaking of one of Adam Smith's principal discoveries,

> That commerce is a form of speech, and that it thereby represents the force most opposed to the human tendency towards oppression and violence is, I think, a great philosophical insight. By speaking [and dealing] with our fellow human beings, we . . . show respect to them and to ourselves. . . . Smith goes Montesquieu one better: the virtues of commerce include not just peace among nations, but the moral bases of individual freedom and self-respect as well.[34]

I merely suggest here. I do not claim to have proven beyond the cavil that capitalism, markets, modern growth, globalization, free trade, and those bourgeois virtues are not the ethical and spiritual catastrophes that most intellectuals believe they are. To do so would take a book,[35] or more like a library. But I do wish to suggest that theology cannot get along without the systematic study of prudence; and economics cannot get along without the systematic study of God.

34. Fleischacker, "Talking to My Butcher," p. 17.

35. *The Vices of Economists — the Virtues of the Bourgeoisie* (Amsterdam: Amsterdam University Press, 1996).

Property and Possession:
The Moral Economy of Ownership

ARJO KLAMER

Economists versus Theologians

When theologians and biblical scholars turn their attention to the institution of property, they are inclined to focus on the vices that it promotes, and the contributions from such scholars in this book are no exception. Property makes them think of greed and injustice and inequality, among many other things. Deirdre McCloskey, in contrast, represents in this volume the voice of the economists at the table. Representative of all economists she may not be, as she is more than willing to entertain the notion of grace and to consider the meanings of the Ten Commandments; nevertheless, she is enough of an economist to stress the efficiency of the institution of property. In her argument she subsumes that institution under that of the market — a common move but problematic nevertheless as we shall see — and shows that the latter has brought unequalled growth, improving the lot of everyone, the least well-off included.[1] During her oral presentation for this project she confronted the skepticism of the others around the table by asking how much better-off the average American of today is than the average American of one hundred years ago. After some guessed a factor of two, and one person tried ten, she was able to surprise by pointing out that the average American is now seventeen times better-off. Case closed? Not quite. The others at the table remain with their concerns about massive poverty worldwide and the widening gap between the rich and the poor both within the rich countries and among

1. Deirdre McCloskey, "Avarice, Prudence, and the Bourgeois Virtues," pp. 313-36 in this volume.

countries. McCloskey's solution — less government, more market, and therefore more private property — does not convince them. Suspicions toward the market remain strong, her eloquent argument notwithstanding.

The dispute is an emotional one. On paper the emotions do not show quite as much as they do in the face-to-face encounters. It is not that fights erupt or that people get personal — these are academicians after all — but the irritations are easy to detect. Irritations indicate that values are at stake and in conflict. McCloskey highlights the virtues in the sphere of the market whereas the theologians stress the vices. The conflict goes deep; it also goes back a long time. Aristotle was already quite explicit in his condemnation of market exchange as unnatural. Charging interest was a taboo for him. His moral condemnation resonates in the words of John Chrysostom, the fourth-century priest who is the subject of Margaret Mitchell's contribution.[2] Only with the Scottish moral philosopher Adam Smith did a more positive perspective on the market come in vogue. His *Wealth of Nations* (1776) made it possible to think of the market as the realm of prudence. The twentieth-century economists Friedrich Hayek and Milton Friedman identified the market with freedom, in particular the freedom to choose. Now the market is commonly held to be heaven on earth, a place to celebrate not only free choice but also self-determination, enterprise, and welfare. Even so, those who cherish and stand for principles like dignity and faith are often appalled. To them the market is rather a place of self-enrichment, individualism gone mad, alienation, and injustice.

The opposition shows in the concerns people express. Whereas many outside the economic profession will prefer to think in terms of equity and desert, economists in general focus on the efficiency with which markets allocate scarce resources. In their view markets, more than any other mechanism, generate the right incentives for people to do the best they can and to consume whatever suits them best. McCloskey adds a twist to the economist's perspective by addressing the virtues of the market. Her argument is that the market cultivates the so important and commendable bourgeois virtues of prudence, temperance, foresight, entrepreneurship, and the like. Although her preoccupation with virtues brings her closer to the camp of theologians, the gap remains, and so does the suspicion.

Given the history and depth of the dispute, any claim for a resolution would be pretentious. Even so, I would like to make an attempt to find common ground. To that end I will broaden the notions of property and posses-

2. Margaret M. Mitchell, "Silver Chamber Pots and Other Goods Which Are Not Good: John Chrysostom's Discourse against Wealth and Possessions," pp. 88-121 in this volume.

sion. I do so in the light of a *cultural-economic* perspective. This means that I will consider whatever people do and possess in the light of values, as actions that are directed at the good life, the good community, or the good society. Economic processes, then, do not have ends in and of themselves but serve other ends. People earn money not for the sake of earning money but in order to realize goods such as friendship and membership in a group. People own an economic good like a car not for merely economic reasons but ultimately in order to better their life — the car may give them a sense of independence or more time with the family. Pursue this line of thought and the need arises to broaden the economic notion of property and to think in the more comprehensive term of possession: the wealth of people does not just consist of their economic properties but also of their nonmaterial possessions. People do not only own houses and other economic properties but can be said to be "have" or "possess" faith, friendship, and a certain kind of knowledge. Many such possessions they cannot own by themselves; certain goods are to be shared with others or held in common with a community or even humanity. When we think of the good life, the enlightened life, as our main concern, then the nonmaterial possessions are most likely far more meaningful than all the economic properties we can list. The latter are, at best, conditions for the other richness, but may just as well stand in the way.

With its focus on the good life, the cultural-economic perspective may also be labeled neo-Aristotelian.[3] The guiding question is "What are properties and, more generally, possessions good for?" (The "neo" alerts to the ongoing change.) Such a perspective may be more amenable to the theologians than to most economists. Then again, theologians may be deterred by the economic rhetoric in which I cast my argument. Whatever side you are on, please keep in mind that the objective is to indicate common ground for economists and theologians by broadening the notion of possession.

To Have and to Possess

Does it matter that one is rich or poor when hanging out at the beach? Recall the joke about the businessman who cajoles the poor man who is hanging out at the beach to pick up a business. When the poor man asks why he should do so, the businessman responds that when you are rich, you can afford hanging out at the beach, at which point the poor man observes that he is doing so al-

3. See, for instance, Irene van Staveren, *The Values of Economics* (London: Routledge, 2001).

ready. The joke makes us laugh at the paradox of richness. The poor man has already that for which the rich man had to work so hard. So he must be rich, too. The question is then, "Rich in what way?" What does the poor man have, or possess, that the rich man does not? Is it possible that he "has" more of what it takes to enjoy the hanging out? "Having" economic wealth may be neither a necessary nor a sufficient condition for enjoyment. Other capacities, personality traits, or values are called for.

"To have" is, I submit, "to own" or "to possess." This may seem strange at first; having a friend is not the same as owning him. Yet, having a friend implies having something like a companion, a friendly ear, loyalty, respect. Having a friend implies the ownership of a good called friendship, which is good for all of that. Others who do not have a friend will have to do without those "goods"; they do not possess, or own, or have what you have. We can "lose a friend" or "gain one." A friendship is worth something. (Mind you: that worth need not be validated in a market transaction. Valuation takes place outside the market, too, as I will stress later.) So the issue is to define goods in such a way that they comprise more than tangible things like cars and cupboards, and also more than all those commodities for sale, like haircuts and advice. Goods are all those tangible and intangible things that are good for something and therefore have value for one person or more.

The extension breaks with current conventions. In our capitalist societies we are inclined to reduce the issue of ownership to that of property rights to and possession of commodities (like houses, shares, and cash). The owner of the property right to a commodity is entitled to fruits of that commodity as well as to the right of selling it and appropriating the proceeds. Economists and lawyers have become very sophisticated in defining property rights. We can now even claim the rights to our ideas, inventions, and artistic creations, with the result that whoever enjoys them has to compensate us. In that way we can be said to "own" our ideas in the sense that they are our property. Property thus conceived is an institution that functions in and for the market. To define a thing, a good, or even a person as my property implies the possibility of selling the property on the market. The thing, good, or person is then a commodity.[4]

But why limit our possessions to commodities? So many other goods are of value even if we cannot trade them. When I speak of "my" child or "my" mother, I claim ownership in some sense. I do not legally own "my" child or "my" mother, of course, and certainly do not have the right to sell

4. Cf. Arjun Appadurai, ed., *The Life of a Thing* (Cambridge: Cambridge University Press, 1998).

them and keep the proceeds — at least not legally. Even so, I enjoy "my" child (at least most of the time); having a child entitles me to a sense of fatherhood. Likewise, I derive all kinds of values from still "having" a mother; some may argue that it is because I have such a good mother that I am doing so well economically and socially. To say that I "own" my child is to say that everybody else does not, her mother excepted of course. If you would claim "my" child, I would object vehemently and possibly violently. "Don't touch her; she is 'mine'!" If someone would claim my mother to be his, I will likely be confused, if not baffled, and subsequently, if I were to take him seriously, I would become angry.

Speaking of children, a mother, and a friend as if I possess them is strange. It is only strange, however, if we hold on to the economic and legal meanings of ownership. In the case of children and mothers, ownership has especially social and emotional returns. "Getting a child" gave me a sense of purpose in life as well as a sense of responsibility; it made me a father, and it has provided me with memories that can make me smile, laugh, and cry. Maybe having a good mother has been good for my career (the economic returns), but I prefer to think of the emotional stability, the trust, and the confidence that the "possession" has given me. (A therapist may see negative returns as well, but I prefer not to pay attention to those in this context.)

A broad notion of ownership is meaningful, and may alter our perspective on all kinds of issues. Say person A is economically rich but all alone and person B has no economic wealth to speak of but has a close family and good friends. Economically speaking, person A is the richer one; socially speaking, B is richer. Whom to envy? And what to say of person C who has little economic wealth and no friends but does have faith and spiritual awareness? Who would we say is the richest of them all? (Let me anticipate the standard criticism by noting that this is no excuse to give up the fight against economic poverty. Being deprived of economic goods is a sure bet for being without social goods as well. It is important to realize, however, that giving money and material things — the economic solution — does not suffice if the outcome does not include an increase in social goods.) Let us develop this.

Possessions Are Not Only Economic but Also Social and Cultural

Ask people about their possessions, and you most likely get a summation of things like compact disc players, cars, computers, bicycles, paintings, clothes, and appliances. "Possessions" make people think of tangible "goods"; people materialize their possessions. A neo-Aristotelian perspective compels us to probe further and ask, "what for?" or "what good do these things do?" We possess things to certain ends; "goods" have to be good for something. Mainstream economists are satisfied with utility as the end: we possess a compact disc player or a painting because its enjoyment adds to our total utility. Alternatively, we could consider the immaterial "goods" that the possession of a material thing generates. The picture in my living room may not only generate pleasure whenever I look at it; it also gives me status (among those who know about neo-expressionism), a sense of being cultured, and financial security (in dire times I can sell it). All these are positive "goods." To some the picture may, incidentally, also generate negative goods, like snobbery and waste. These immaterial goods are values. They are the qualities that we attach to things in order to place these things in the field of values that we have.

This extension of goods to include values will meet with resistance from the majority of economists, satisfied as they are with the notion of preference and utility. As some economists have pointed out, however, the notion of utility is without content.[5] Any utility will do; all utilities add up to form a single quantity. Such an abstraction permits an analysis that is focused on the constraints under which people operate and works well when "efficiency" is the overriding value. That more values are involved is the case made in an extensive literature.[6] The inclusion of values changes the analysis. A more interpretive approach is called for to make sense of why people consume what they consume. It may involve relationships, knowledge, status, reputation, identity, honor, grace, and so on.

This need to go beyond the vacuous notion of utility and to consider the substance of our choices led John Rawls to speak of primary goods such as self-respect and, more generally, "rights and liberties, powers and opportunities, income and wealth."[7] In his view we need to differentiate between

5. Cf. Marina Bianchi, ed., *The Active Consumer: Novelty and Surprise in Consumer Choice* (New York: Routledge, 1998).

6. See Jean Baudrillard, *Symbolic Exchange and Death* (London: Thousand Oaks, 1993); Pierre Bourdieu, *Distinction: A Social Critique of the Judgement of Taste* (London: Routledge and Kegan Paul, 1984); Colin Campbell, *The Romantic Ethic and the Spirit of Modern Consumerism* (Oxford: Basil Blackwell, 1987); Mary Tew Douglas and Baron C. Isherwood, *The World of Goods* (New York: Basic, 1979); Fred Hirsch, *Social Limits to Growth* (Cambridge, Mass.: Harvard University Press, 1976); Michael Hutter, "On the Consumption of Signs," in *The Active Consumer*, ed. Bianchi; Tibor Scivotsky, *The Joyless Economy: An Inquiry into Human Satisfaction and Consumer Dissatisfaction* (New York: Oxford University Press, 1976).

7. John Rawls, *A Theory of Justice* (Cambridge, Mass.: Harvard University Press, 1971), p. 62.

"goods" when we compare our possessions; the primary good of self-respect is to be valued most, regardless of individual preferences. Amartya Sen, too, argues that we should not just compare economic values (like income and wealth) when we assess distributive justice. He suggests we focus on differences in capabilities, or freedoms, like the liberty of political participation and dissent, the opportunity to receive basic education, and the freedom to live long and well.[8] African Americans may be economically quite rich in comparison with many people in developing countries yet have a lower life expectancy than many people in China and parts of India.

We might extend these arguments and work toward a different classification of possession. First of all, possessions are not just those things that an *individual* owns; communities, cities, nations, and organizations have possessions as well, and they are of various kinds. In general a possession is anything that an individual or social entity has that generates something of value for that individual or social entity. I will call a collection of possessions "capital." Those who dislike the economic vocabulary may think in terms of power or capacity. The basic idea is that any possession enables the generation of values. I propose to start with a distinction of three kinds of capital: economic, social, and cultural.

Economic capital denotes the capacity to generate economic income or economic values. It comprises the possessions of land, factories, durable goods, and machines, as well as the possession of knowledge. Economists call knowledge "human capital." It is typically the possession that students forget when they are asked to calculate their economic capital, even though it is their most prized possession. Human capital is part of economic capital insofar as it is responsible for additional income.

I will not dwell on the issue of measurement although it plays an important role. During the first half of the twentieth century economists invested a great deal in the development of measurements of economic capital. Those measurements are still quite unsatisfactory as they insufficiently account for the value of human and natural capitals. Nevertheless, they seem to work as magnets in policy discussions. The very fact of their existence seems to award economic capital an exceptional status, so much so that objectives are often stated in these terms. Because there are no measurements for the other capitals, they are conceived to be vague and abstract. As a consequence, they usually do not figure in the final count. Even so, the privileged status for economic capital is dubious in light of earlier remarks on the nature of goods. Economic values, like the balance in a checking account or the number of

8. See, for example, Amartya Sen, *Development As Freedom* (New York: Knopf, 1999).

343

shares of a stock, have meaning only insofar as they enable the realization of other values. Having a large balance is nice, of course, but only insofar as it enables me to achieve social status, security, freedom to do whatever I please, friendship, a meaningful life, or whatever else matters to me. Economic capital, therefore, enables the generation of other values, like social values.

Social capital is the capacity to generate social values like friendship, collegiality, trust, respect, and responsibility.[9] Pierre Bourdieu focuses on the benefits that people derive from participation in groups. Michael Walzer argues that membership in one or more groups is a person's most important possession.[10] Membership is a social good, as are friendship and solidarity. Social capital enables a person to have an identity and to receive recognition, attention, care, and the like. Like economic capital, social capital needs to be acquired. In the language of economists, people need to invest their time, resources, and energy to build up their social capital. We go out for dinner, attend Christmas gatherings, write notes, give compliments, and exchange gifts, all to bolster relationships with family, friends, and colleagues. Economic value, therefore, can be a means to general social capital, and vice versa, as when a relationship produces a job or a profitable tip. People possess social capital, but organizations, cities, or countries have it as well.[11]

Cultural capital is, in short, the capacity to inspire and be inspired. This, too, can be in the possession of organizations, cities, and nations as well as individuals. We may recognize cultural capital in the capacity to find meaning in a walk through the woods, a visit to a museum, or a church service.[12] Cultural capital enables us to award meanings to so-called symbolic goods and lifts us from the drudgery of daily life. It enables intellectuals to have those energizing sparks of insight and, if I understand the theologians well, enables us to experience the grace of God. Immeasurable as it is, cultural capital appears to generate the most important values of all, the values

9. Cf. Pierre Bourdieu, "The Forms of Capital," in *Handbook of Theory and Research for the Sociology of Education*, ed. J. G. Richardson (New York: Greenwood, 1985); James S. Coleman, "Social Capital in the Creation of Human Capital," *American Journal of Sociology* 94, supplement (1988); Alejandro Portes, "Social Capital: Its Origins and Application in Modern Sociology," *Annual Review of Sociology* 24 (1998); and Robert D. Putnam, *Bowling Alone* (New York: Simon and Schuster, 2000).

10. Michael Walzer, *Spheres of Justice: A Defense of Pluralism and Equality* (Oxford: Basil Blackwell, 1983).

11. The Human Development Index that the United Nations calculates for each country is a combination of social and economic indicators. Inspired by Sen's notion of capabilities, it does not come even close to being a measurement of social capital.

12. The concept of cultural capital gives rise to a great deal of confusion. I hope a general definition as given here suffices for the purposes of this exposition.

that can give meaning to our life.[13] It tends to be the main concern in the writings of theologians and biblical scholars in this volume. Charles Matthewes, for instance, wants us to see how "vestigial theological, and presumably anti-worldly, beliefs" still motivate much of modern rationalistic and consumerist behavior.[14] William Schweiker's concern is "simply to secure the integrity of life — especially human life — as the aim of, not the means to, economic activity."[15] I would consider "integrity" a cultural value as I would "grace," the subject of the contributions by Kathryn Tanner and David Klemm.[16]

I hasten to acknowledge the shortcomings of these descriptions. I realize full well the difficulties of making the notions of cultural and social capital more concrete. Their immeasurability, at least for now, does not signify their irrelevance. On the contrary, the cultural and social values that they generate are crucial for the worth of our lives and the communities we live in. In the future, we need to negotiate about the meanings of these concepts and possible measurements. For now, the main objective of their distinction is to pinpoint the different possessions that we have. We can gain economic values yet lose social and cultural values, or, to put it differently, we can build up economic capital while decreasing our social and cultural capital.

Considering the three forms of capital, we will less quickly claim to be rich or poor. When I suggested this to a church group that dealt with issues of poverty, I was criticized for downplaying poverty. Although they had earlier agreed on the importance of cultural capital, the participants insisted on an economic interpretation of poverty. I pointed out how strange it was that in spite of their suspicion of the economic sphere all they cared about was economic values (money!). But why not think in terms of social and cultural values? Surely, hunger and deprivation are serious impediments for the capacity to live a long and meaningful life. Money can solve such problems, but membership in a strong community (like a church, a family, or a country) can be as important, if not more, and that not only because of its economic values. The practical problems remain. It is still so much easier to talk in terms of

---

13. The UNESCO, along with various statistical agencies, is currently working on cultural indicators. The proposed measurements concern thus far mainly physical quantities like production and employment figures for the cultural sectors. Such figures are only superficially related to the notion of cultural capital as defined here. See UNESCO, *World Culture Report: Cultural Diversity, Conflict, and Pluralism* (Paris: UNESCO, 2000).

14. Charles Mathewes, "On Using the World," p. 192 in this volume.

15. William Schweiker, "Reconsidering Greed," p. 254 in this volume.

16. David E. Klemm, "Material Grace: The Paradox of Property and Possession," pp. 222-48 in this volume; Kathryn Tanner, "Economies of Grace," pp. 353-82 in this volume.

money than in the terms that really matter. And, surely, having money enables people (yet can distract them as well).

The importance of social and cultural capital is illustrated by the performance of a British artist. He succeeded in destroying everything he owned — all his material properties, that is. In a London gallery, he cut up all his books, his passport, his bed, his clothes, his car, everything. Does that mean that he was left without any possessions? Of course not. For one, he has the identity of an artist. Because of this action he received a great deal of attention and has become a much better known artist. He owns this piece, the performance, and very well might derive economic value from it. He still has his social capital, as nothing of that went through the grinder, and probably this was in fact increased because of this performance. His cultural capital probably increased, too. His poverty, therefore, exists only in an economic sense and also then is only short-term, as he has maintained his human capital and that part of social capital that is economically viable.

The Economic and Social Values of Property

Knowing what our possessions are is one thing; knowing why and how they increase and decrease is quite another. Economists are specialized in the inquiry into the causes of the wealth of people, organizations, and nations. For that reason they developed an interest in the institution of private property, which is a legal determination of possessions, when they realized that this institution might be a factor in the accumulation of economic capital. They sometimes justify the focus on economic capital on the grounds that its accumulation is a condition for overall wealth and as such usually implies increased social and cultural capabilities. Whether that assumption is correct remains to be seen. Sen, for one, questions it.

The discussion of the accumulation of economic capital usually comes in the economic literature under the heading of efficiency. Economists have made it their preoccupation to study when and how the least amount of inputs generates the maximum economic outcome (or value). That is why they talk about the rationalization of production processes but also about the advantages of allocation by means of markets versus alternative mechanisms. When it comes to the generation of economic value, they find markets generally to be most efficient, more so than governmental bureaucracies or barter. That motivates the institution of private property, since without it markets would not be able to exist. A market exchange, after all, is the transfer of property rights. When I buy an ice cream, I acquire the right to do with it whatever I please. I can eat it, throw it away, or, most likely, give it to my child. When I buy a property like a house I can occupy it or rent it to someone else. The transition toward a market society, as former Soviet countries are striving to accomplish, is mainly about establishing property rights. It remains a major issue in developed countries, as discussions on privatization and intellectual property rights indicate.

Privatization of public transport companies and distributors of energy serves the value of efficiency; at least, it does according to standard economic opinion. Privatization of property rights permits an exchange on the market. Privatized companies can be prized, and therefore they can be bought and sold. The claim is that the regime of the market stimulates efficient behavior of producers and accounts for better and cheaper products for the customers than would the case in a system that is controlled by governmental institutions.

The standard economic argumentation limits itself to economic values. As McCloskey argues, however, the argument can be extended to include the social and cultural dimension as well. Markets are social processes and as such can have an impact on social and cultural capital. Even Schweiker admits that markets can generate social goods like international cooperation and innovation, but stresses the social "bads" like avarice and greed. McCloskey's advocacy of the market does not only point at the tremendous gain in economic value but also at its importance for bourgeois virtues. It is in situations of markets that people learn to be prudent, entrepreneurial, diligent, and hard-working. In this extension of the argumentation we see how the institutions of private property and the market are socially and culturally embedded.[17]

When the infringement of copyright is the concern, the issue is usually not the damage in terms of economic value but a matter of desert: artists have worked for it and deserve to be compensated. Desert is a social value. It is the value to which Locke appealed in his justification of private property when he postulated labor as the condition of property. People earn the right to call a good their own because of the labor they have expended. Desert is a value that stresses effort and the importance of being recognized for it. This value also figures in Hegel's justification of private property. For Marx it was a reason to reject the capitalist mode of production as in that case those who produce the stuff, the workers, have no ownership of that stuff and so are robbed

---

17. Karl Polanyi, "The Economy As Instituted Process," in *Trade and Market in Early Empire*, ed. K. Polanyi, C. Arensberg, and H. Pearson (Chicago: Henry Regnery, 1971). This essay was first published in 1957.

of this essential human need to be affirmed in the possession of that which they created.

Another social value that figures in the justification of the institution of property is taking responsibility or taking care. As Aristotle already argued:

> That which is common to the greatest number has the least care bestowed upon it. Everyone thinks chiefly of his own, hardly at all of the common interest; and only when he is himself concerned as an individual. For besides other considerations, everybody is more inclined to neglect the duty which he expects another to fulfil; as in families many attendants are often less useful than a few.[18]

Owners of a house tend to attend to it better than renters. McCloskey would speak of the virtue of prudence in this case. The institution of private property also evokes that most important value of liberty. The possession of money coupled with the right to purchase property rights frees individuals from social ties and obligations and allows them to arrange their possessions according to their preferences. As Hegel noted, "a person must translate his freedom into a personal sphere in order that he may achieve his ideal existence."[19] Given its exalted status in modern life, liberty could be called a cultural value.

Collective and Communal Properties

Accordingly, the institution of private of property does not just serve the value of efficiency but is motivated by and embedded in a system of social and cultural values. Like any such system it encompasses goods and bads. The economists tend to focus on the goods, such as the incentives that the right to property gives and the sense of responsibility that it generates. Leave it to theologians to show the other side of the coin; the institution of private property may also stimulate greed and injustice and it may undermine social relations and destroy communities.

The negatives may extend to the context in which private property functions. For example, the institution of private property may be an impediment to the realization of all kinds of valuable possessions. Take the possession of being in an ongoing intellectual conversation: I happen to value such a

18. Aristotle, *Politics*, bk. 2.

19. Georg Wilhelm Friedrich Hegel, *Philosophy of Right*, ed. T. M. Knox, trans. T. M. Knox (London: Oxford University Press, 1967), sec. 41.

possession highly. It works when others who participate make an effort, are committed to the theme, and share certain codes and certain values. A conversation is a communal thing and continues to be valuable as long as it maintains its status of a *res nullens,* a thing belonging to no one. An explicit determination of private property is most likely the undoing of the conversation, as it violates the value of sharing that makes it work.

Cultural heritage is another good that needs to be shared in order to be meaningful. I can cherish a Caravaggio only because the appreciation of his work is shared by a community of scholars, art critics, and curators. I can be a Christian and experience Christian spirituality only by virtue of a Christian community that has sustained the Christian tradition and practices. Likewise, I have a national identity only because I share it with sixteen million other people. I can express social and political values by virtue of a national community that in my case happens to be the Netherlands. The possession of the Dutch passport allows me to be proud of being part of a caring society; it also gives me the right of being ashamed for Dutch actions in the former colony Indonesia and more recently for the drama of Srebenica. The shame is possible only because I can identify with and am part of the entity called the Netherlands.

Ownership, therefore, is not just an individual matter. Most of what we have, we own in common. In nature all things are held in common. On that principle nomadic people do not stake claims to territory. "Friends have all things in common," the Greeks told each other. When I claim that something is mine, I am telling you that it is not yours. With a good friend I would not make that claim, would I? Even if I can claim to have a friend, I do not own the friendship myself; at best my friend and I share the friendship.

For many goods the attribution of ownership is an issue subject to confusion and discussion. Take the university, an institution with which most readers will be intimately acquainted. Who owns it? Legally speaking, the university is a legal entity that is accountable in case one of "its" bricks hits one of "its" students. Yet, that does not settle the issue of ownership morally or socially. The settlement matters. When administrators act as if they are the owners of a business, they assume control, managing the business by hiring faculty to provide services to their customers, the students. When the faculty have a sense of ownership, they will act upon this sense by taking care of the research and the teaching, and they will be inclined to consider administrators as serving them, the actual owners. In that case the university is more like a cooperative, or an academic community. When politicians claim "our" university as a collective property, they will presume that they are responsible for its budget and its program (and will change the structure at will, as they recently did in Europe by deciding on the Anglo-Saxon BA/MA structure with virtually no consultation of the university community). I presume that most readers will opt for the second version of ownership and prefer to consider their university a communal good. Market-oriented strategies that administrators as well as politicians tend to advocate will be anathema to them.

The assignment of ownership also matters in cases of intellectual property. To what extent can I claim ownership of an idea? Most probably, I could have had my idea only because of the ideas of others. Even if an idea is original, it will invariably incorporate ideas of others. And what if the idea can circulate only because of a discursive context that others have brought about? Should it not make more sense to speak of communal property in that case and of the development of that idea of mine as a contribution to that communal property? If I were to do that, I may be more modest than if I were to cling to the idea of authorship and intellectual copyright.

And how about the ownership of a business? When a business issues shares, it is legally owned by the shareholders. As David Ellerman convincingly shows, this is a strange construction in the light of any moral or social sense of ownership.[20] For why assign ownership to people who have not expended labor, often have no ties with the corporation, may not ever have visited its physical locations, and only have supplied money? Why should they be privileged over and above those who invest their heart and soul in the corporation or, at least, spend a great deal of their time in its physical locations and contribute in one form or another to its production? The assignment of ownership may have instrumental reasons (without such a deal people may not be willing to surrender their savings), but it lacks a satisfactory moral or social justification. The assignment of ownership to the workers matters. It matters for the culture of the organization, for the sense of ownership on the part of the workers, and, with that, their sense of responsibility. (How to run such a company is another matter. Worker-managed companies do have troubles with the management, and are not always equipped to adjust to changing circumstances as the tough choices are avoided. Then again, quite a few professional organizations like law firms and accountant firms are worker-managed and generally do well.)

20. David P. Ellerman, *Property and Contract in Economics: The Case for Economic Democracy* (Oxford: Basil Blackwell, 1992).

Concluding Remarks

The conception of ownership over and beyond the legal sense of property serves several purposes. For instance, it calls attention to a sphere of human interaction besides the spheres of the market and the government. Not all values are realized in market settings. On the contrary, the most important social and cultural values will be realized in nonmarket settings, as in communities of friends and colleagues, in village and tribal life, in national settings, in schools and universities, in clubs — that is, in civil society. The refocusing will reactivate the notion of a moral economy and motivate a re-evaluation of the values that really matter in the end. It will also help to mediate in the tensions that emerge when economists and theologians discuss the virtues and vices connected with the institution of property.

Economists stand confirmed in their faith in markets. McCloskey is right to point out that markets have proven to be quite effective in the generation of economic values. She goes further, however, by pointing to the social values that are realized in market settings, such as prudence. Yet, we can extend her analysis to consider goods and possessions whose values are realized outside the spheres of the market. Friendship usually does not come about in markets; even if it does, it certainly is not sustained by means of market transactions. Moreover, friendship is not a commodity that can be bought and sold. Nevertheless, friendship is an important possession that can generate all kinds of values.

Another extension to the economists' story is the notion of common property. Economists do have the concept of a collective good; clean air is the usual example. Clean air is of great value, yet paying for the maintenance of its quality does not make a great deal of sense for an individual, as others cannot be excluded from its consumption. That's why we say that clean air is collective property. My argument extends the notion of collective property to include all kinds of immaterial goods. Think, for example, of the atmosphere of a town. All kinds of people contribute to it, nobody owns it, and everyone, including passers-by, benefits from it. The atmosphere is what the citizens of the town have in common. I'd say that the atmosphere is part of the cultural capital of that town.

"Common property" differs further from "collective property" in the sense that it is restricted to a group of people. This means that other people are excluded from sharing it even if no property rights are established or trades involved. The example is a discursive practice. When I want to write and talk about the cultural aspects of economics, I benefit tremendously from the existence of a literature on the subject and of scholars with the same interests. It matters a great deal whether these other scholars have already made efforts to set up an association, to organize conferences, and to publish journals. Such efforts bring about a common discourse that I can join and that may get me attention for what I am doing, a reputation, maybe, and, who knows, a job. I would not survive for very long without such a practice. If I do not want to be excluded and ignored, I will have to invest in the social and intellectual capital that are particular for that practice, such as a shared literature (the classics), a certain vocabulary, methods of research, and so on. Yet, no markets are involved directly in realizing this valuable possession, and no government either. It rather comes about in a network of informal, scholarly relations.[21] The same is the case for religious practices.

When we consider social and cultural values in addition to economic values, the disagreement on the institution of private property becomes a difference of opinion on the weighing of different spheres of value. The sphere of the market, in which the institution of private property has a seminal role, tends to favor the values of efficiency, liberty, and prudence; yet it may very well weaken and undermine other social and cultural values that do better in the public sphere where property is collective or in another sphere, the one that sustains common property.[22]

Many questions remain, including questions about the interactions between the various forms of possession, about the precise role of markets in the generation of social and cultural values (to what extent do markets stand in the way, really?), and about the spheres that are most amenable to generating the cultural values that we consider relevant. In this essay, however, my goal was simply to point out a space that would facilitate a constructive dialogue among economists and theologians, and in that task I hope I have succeeded.

21. For an impressive account of how discursive practices come about, see Randall Collins, *The Sociology of Philosophies: A Global Theory of Intellectual Change* (Cambridge, Mass.: Belknap, 1998).

22. Cf. Arjo Klamer, ed., *The Value of Culture* (Amsterdam: Amsterdam University Press, 1996).

Economies of Grace

KATHRYN TANNER

Modern times are marked by the recognition that social relations are susceptible to human influence; society is a human construction and therefore the shapes that social relations take are something less than inevitable givens to which one must be resigned.

In modern times, therefore, the really possible expands beyond the real or actual. This is evident in the way the present often appears as a narrowing and constriction of a more complex and variegated past, something that the historian must reconstruct — re-imagine — for us; the present appears against the horizon of a wider and fuller reality now lost. Thus, in the economic sphere, which is the subject of this essay, there is the increasing sense that commodity exchange has eclipsed other forms of social relation in modern life, thereby winnowing down the really possible to some much narrower subset of fact. Historians trace, for example, the intense political maneuvering by which personal relations — both labor relations and the marriage "contract" — came to be interpreted and regulated along the lines of commodity exchange, in a successful competition with previous and potentially realizable noncommodity and noncontractual understandings of what was at issue there.[1]

A sense that the really possible extends beyond the actual is also evident in the way the inevitable imperfections infecting any extant social arrangement occasion in modern times insistent expectations that things be different; the failings of the present set off reformist, even revolutionary, desire,

1. See, for example, Amy Dru Stanley, *From Bondage to Contract* (Cambridge: Cambridge University Press, 1998).

sparking efforts to envision and bring into being a different future. Thus, the failings of present global capitalism are not merely facts to be rued but provoke currents of restless dissatisfaction with an activist orientation. Such dissatisfaction fuels and is fueled by the social imaginary — a sense of possible ways of relating not restricted to those enforced in the present. Submerged in the dominant paradigms of the moment, but available for creative reinvigoration, are the subdued influences and the remains in fragmentary form of other ways of arranging social life, both past and present. Could, for example, traditions of common or inalienable property in pre-Enlightenment Europe, or forms of giving in Polynesian cultures colonized by the West, hint at new paradigms for patterning economic exchange in the United States and its global markets? A variety of loose symbol systems, moreover, circulate through the West and beckon as reservoirs for a creative rethinking of how to live together. While such symbol systems can be made to support extant social arrangements — and clearly are often made to do so, in fact — the very variety and internal complexity of symbol systems with sociocultural currency in the present permit their disentanglement from such uses. The possibility exists that any might be creatively reworked (against past and present uses) so as to be aligned with forces of social change.

I hope here to rework basic notions in Christian theology in the effort, specifically, to dislodge overly restrictive modern ideas about property and possession, and thereby suggest ways beyond the untoward socioeconomic consequences of the contemporary capitalist systems with which they are allied. I am therefore making constructive Christian theology perform as sociocultural criticism in much the way that cultural anthropology and histories of political and economic ideas often perform.[2] Providing alternatives to modern common sense in any of these ways reinforces the historically conditioned character of taken-for-granted ideas and underscores the impression that these ideas are, at least in principle, alterable. The existence of alternatives breaks up restrictive conventions of thinking about property in modern life, thereby broadening the contemporary imagination of discontent. Because conventional thinking is interwoven with the social practices it helps to make sense of and justify, the disruption or stretching of what contemporary people take for granted about property is at the same time a recommendation for changed practices; it provides hints about new ways of living.

---

2. As examples of the two sorts — examples, indeed, that are especially relevant as foils to my own argument to come — see James Tully, *An Approach to Political Philosophy* (Cambridge: Cambridge University Press, 1993), and Marshall Sahlins, *Stone Age Economics* (New York: Aldine and De Gruyter, 1972).

Re-imagining Christian theology for this project of sociocultural re-imagination has in its favor a heightened ability to startle, without the forfeiture thereby of its potential to demand attention from a Western audience. A trade-off, indeed, between commanding respect and expanding the imagination of discontent hampers the project of sociocultural criticism in its anthropological and historical forms. Thus, the anthropologist's description of practices of gift-giving among Fiji Islanders may be wild from a modern Western viewpoint and therefore enormously expansive of the Western imagination of economic relations; but why or how should we take these descriptions into account when re-imagining our own future, given their relative historical independence of Western economic practices?[3] Understandings of property in the pre-modern West and the patterns of social relations with which they were historically imbricated are obviously relevant to present Western practice — not just as historical influences but because these notions and their associated forms of social life continue to circulate in the West (for example, in the understandings of shared property that structure social relations in the family). In the present such notions are often simply downplayed or found in unsystematized tension with dominant ideas. They are therefore rather easily recoverable as a relevant focus for present discontent's social imaginary, especially when filled out by historical reconstruction of their provenance in previous noncapitalistic forms of exchange. For the same reason, however, there is nothing very surprising about these ideas; they are already considered, or readily made, nonthreatening to capitalistic forms of exchange, and therefore it is hard to see how they could amount to a real alternative.

Christian views concerning private property and wealth accumulation, for all the secularity and pluralism of modern Western societies, have been a major historical influence on contemporary economic practice and continue to have currency there, though one might argue that, with this advance of secularity and pluralism, they have become in many quarters almost as strange as the views of Fiji Islanders. This increasing strangeness combined with past and present influence might help avoid the trade-off I'm discussing, but at best no more than would be the case for any other set of presently marginalized, once more prominent historical influences on contemporary practice. As major positive historical influences on present practice — say, if Max Weber is at least partially right about Christianity's feeding the spirit of capitalism — such ideas cannot pretend to be much of an alternative to it; secularization is just more of the same with the religious motives and justifi-

---

3. I will argue additionally below that such practices are not as radically expansive of Western views as one might think — they are types of a debt economy.

cations for, say, private property accumulation gone. To the extent the substance of some Christian claims about property has been genuinely marginalized and submerged by the dominant paradigms of present practice — say, Christian prohibitions on usury or advocacy of a primitive communism like that supposedly in force in the garden of Eden — this represents their containment by present forces; it is a sign of how they have been rendered harmless, a sign of their historical defeat in the struggle against now dominant forces. Their resurrection therefore seems futile — a tired effort to re-prosecute a losing cause.

Christian theology regains its ability to startle, to expand the Western social imaginary in the present, when Christian views of economy are not limited to explicit Christian commentary on property and possession offered through the centuries — and not restricted either to familiar debates surrounding Christian norms like agape and their implications for social relations — but when basic Christian notions of God and God's relations to the world are themselves viewed as economic in nature. Relations of exchange and the circulation of goods, broadly construed, are at issue throughout the fundamental story that Christians tell about God, creation, providence, and salvation in Christ. This is a highly malleable story susceptible to multiple readings of the notions at issue and multiple accounts of how these notions are to be tied together to form a coherent story, as evidenced by the variability of Christian theology over the course of its two-thousand-year history. I will propose my own creative reworking of these notions and their interconnections, one that suggests a radical alternative to modern views of property and possession that underlie capitalist forms of exchange. Indeed, this reworking of a Christian symbol system is in part directed by that effort; an initial analysis of the shape that property takes and the functions it performs in modern market societies is the foil for my creative reworking of basic notions in Christian theology.

But first I employ that analysis to evaluate other contenders for a radical expansion of the social imaginary by theological means, and find them wanting — less radical, less disruptive, and therefore less significant as interventions on the present scene (besides being theologically suspect for reasons that will become apparent from my own construal of what Christianity is all about). These alternative logics of property center on forms of inalienable property, and are, I argue, logics of indebtedness or obligation. Locke's theologically informed treatment of property at a time in the West just prior to the dominance of modern markets is the starting point here. Criticism of Locke points in the direction of a more thoroughgoing economy of grace or gift, through Calvin who would seem to have done something like that, to those anthropological discussions of noncommodity gift exchanges in places like Fiji that have become a major influence on socially concerned contemporary Christian theologies and which I argue are only a logic of debt and loan writ large.

1

In modern life, one's value is determined by what one has — by one's possessions, by wealth — and in particular by what one has that can get one more — by forms of possession that amount to capital with its capacity to generate profit. Economic worth in this sense seems to establish worth of all sorts; without it one is hardly worthy of social concern or deserving of social benefits, hardly a player on the sociopolitical scene in any way that would make one's opinions and interests matter, or put one in a position to better oneself. In short, wealth has become the primary determinant of rights, liberties, and opportunities. The economy of free markets, characterized as it is by relations of buying and selling and contractual obligation, threatens, moreover, to dominate all relations. It is only with difficulty, for example, that relations between intimates are exempted, or that anything — say, a person's body (or body part) — is deemed an inadmissable object of commodity exchange. Despite the fact that they mean so much, only with great difficulty are inequalities in accumulated wealth subject to social restrictions. The haves are thought to deserve the more that having much makes easy; and the have-nots only with difficulty have much of anything at all.

Underlying this modern scenario is an understanding of property that is historically conditioned by the existence of capitalist markets and principles of production.[4] Under such conditions, as they developed in the industrialized West, property tends to be identified with wealth, with material stuff that might be traded or exchanged for money, or with capital in the sense of what is not to be consumed or used up to meet immediate human needs but used instead for purposes of accumulation, to yield more, to produce profit. To the extent property is not simply identified with what one has in one's physical possession, but involves a legitimate claim, property tends to mean simply a right to what one already possesses. Property in this sense does not include any right to what one does not have but deserves to, or any right to what is not a possible possession (say, rights to develop one's capacities and

4. See C. B. Macpherson, "Human Rights As Property Rights," *Dissent* (winter 1997): 72-77.

talents). Nor does it primarily concern rights in things short of possession (say, rights to use what one does not own).

Property is, moreover, private in the sense of exclusive ownership, the exclusive or negative right to keep others from the use and enjoyment of it. Only on that condition can property be bought and sold; it makes no sense to put up for sale what both parties to the exchange already have rights to use and enjoy. Property implies, besides rights to exclude others from the use or possession of what one has, rights to dispose and transfer by explicit contractual conditions of exchange; only private property, over which one has exclusive rights of possession and use, can be alienated in those ways.

Individually rather than communally defined, having property is not a function of social relations; social relations are instead the product of exchanges that (only) persons who already have property engage in freely, to further their self-interests. Nor does having property imply social obligations. Property involves an unconditional right of disposal: one has not just an exclusive right to use and enjoy what one has but the right to sell or alienate it freely. Freely means, in part, without thought of the social consequences and without being subject to social requirements. One can do with one's property as one likes (so long as one does not disturb thereby the private property rights of others). In this way the modern sense of property seems to bring with it unlimited rights of individual appropriation.

Having property in one's person is understood along these same lines. If one has nothing else, one still has one's own life and labor power; everyone possesses something — oneself and one's capacities for action. This is quintessentially private property in at least the sense of what is exclusively one's own: one's life and labor power are not owed to anybody else; one has the right to exclude others from the use or enjoyment of them; such rights can be given only through one's free consent. Exclusive property rights to one's person and capacities become the means of justifying all other forms of exclusive property — that is, property in material possessions. If one's labor is one's private or exclusive property, then so too are the products formed through its use. One has rights of exclusive possession with respect to what one has worked for.

Property in one's person is private property too, in that, at least with reference to one's labor power, it is disposable property — one can sell it and alienate ownership of the products of it. A modern capitalist market, indeed, requires persons with this sort of ownership relation to their own capacities to work since only on that condition are they free to contract to sell it in exchange for wages. Because one always owns oneself, the contracts in which one participates under conditions of extreme inequality can still be deemed ones into which one has freely entered. Inequalities in initial circumstances and results are, for that reason, not thought to make market exchanges less than genuine contracts. This connection between the idea of self-possession and market legitimacy means that rethinking self-possession threatens to make manifest the injustice of market relations in situations of economic inequality, that is, in situations where the institution of private property entails that some people will need to alienate their work and its products for the sake of a decent life.

This logic of modern property brings with it a certain understanding of social relations. Social relations are, first of all, consensual in virtue of a freedom that is a function of wealth. Having property allows one's relations with others to be consensual. If one has property one is not at the mercy of one's fellows but can approach them on an equal footing. The freedom that having property involves is, moreover, primarily understood negatively — as freedom from others and their potentially unjust seizure or use of what is one's own. One has one's own person and the products of one's own labor without owing them to anyone else; one does not owe them, in particular, to society, and therefore no legitimate social controls determine what one might do with them. Freedom from others suggests in this way freedom from any rights of needy others to use or enjoy what one has. Exclusive property rights in things and negative freedom mean that the modern sense of property is not easily compatible with the idea of rights to well-being on the part of the general populace, or with the idea of a social commitment to furthering the livelihood of all. What a society is all about, what it can be dedicated to, is in this way narrowed by modern understandings of property.

When a modern understanding of property — as an exclusive and unconditioned right to use and dispose of what one possesses — is combined with the rise and growing dominance of the competitive markets with which it was designed to work, the result is gross inequalities in wealth and all that wealth now buys in opportunities, respect, and responsibilities, without any apparent internal checks. In any reasonably free market that has expanded to include at least land and resources, exclusive property rights in things possessed fosters unequal distributions of wealth to the point where some people have so little that they are significantly disadvantaged relative to others and therefore ripe for exploitation or simple inhuman neglect by them. Under such conditions, a great many people, one can argue, are denied the opportunity to lead full and fulfilling lives.

2

While the position of John Locke is sufficiently similar to the modern understanding of property to be confused with it, his position represents a genuine second logic of property — and one that is informed by theological claims in an interesting way, in that it does not simply tinker with or subject modern property rights to certain constraints but gives a fundamentally unmodern understanding of property pride of place.[5]

First of all, if for Locke one has property in life, liberty, and the pursuit of happiness, then property is not easily identifiable with material wealth. Locke's position more clearly manifests the fact that property involves not mere physical possession but an enforceable claim, a right: for him rights of use to what one does not own — for example, rights to use of common lands — are a significant feature of property (in an economy in which land is only just becoming a rightful commodity of merely private possession).[6]

But of much greater significance is the fact that Locke makes inalienable property (property that is not at one's free disposal) and common property (involving positive rights of access on everyone's part to the means of subsistence and well-being) the bases of any exclusive rights of possession. For Locke (in keeping with the dominant Christian views of the ancient and medieval church) property rights are inclusive or common at their root: the world and everything in it has been given by God for the good of all and therefore all have a property right to use the natural resources of the earth so as to maintain their existence and further their well-being. Exclusive property rights are simply the way that this common property right is individuated so as to be actually enjoyed by particular people. In order for anyone to enjoy the common right to land and resources to satisfy personal needs and wants, one must make (usually through labor) a part of it one's own in an exclusive sense — no one has the right to take it from you or use it without your consent. Individual rights of exclusive appropriation are limited, however, by the same common rights that are their basis: private appropriation is legitimate only to the extent it continues to respect the rightful claims of others to what is necessary for them to exist and flourish.

The exclusiveness of one's property rights is also directly undercut because what one has a right to possess and use has not really been simply alien-

5. For this view of Locke, see Tully, *An Approach to Political Philosophy,* and Ruth Grant, *John Locke's Liberalism* (Chicago: University of Chicago Press, 1987).

6. For an expanded treatment of the ideas in this paragraph, see C. B. Macpherson, "The Meaning of Property," in *Property: Mainstream and Critical Positions,* ed. C. B. Macpherson (Toronto: University of Toronto Press, 1978), p. 7.

ated from its true owner, God, the one who made the earth and everything in it and therefore owns them. All private property is on loan or held in tenancy from God, who retains full possession (in some significant sense) and whose purposes — the good of all — must therefore be served if one is to maintain rightful possession. What cannot be made one's full or exclusive property cannot be alienated but only delegated or loaned, in political and economic contracts. One cannot, for example, sell what one does not fully own; one can only permit access to others on the same conditions extended to oneself by the real owner. Therefore what looks like a sale in a modern sense of free disposal or transfer of ownership is not really that but the transfer of rights of use with strings attached. Similarly on the political side of things, people delegate, rather than alienate, their property rights to institutions of government, with the understanding that these rights to existence and well-being will be preserved and furthered thereby. People retain these rights in some significant sense and therefore the powers entrusted to government are forfeited upon violation of the people's trust. One could therefore say that the people relate to their government the way God relates to them. In both cases someone is entrusted with something to carry out the intentions of the one handing it over, and violation of that trust brings retribution (through the revolt of the people against a corrupt government or God's punishment of you after death).

Locke is a famous proponent of property in one's person and capacities but this property, unlike the modern case, is inalienable. Because this property is inalienable, Locke denies that one can freely contract to be subject to a ruler with absolute power or freely contract to become a slave. Both slave labor and an absolute state require the alienation of property rights that cannot properly be alienated.

One can appeal again here to the idea of God's ownership of one's life and capacities. One cannot transfer to a slave owner or absolute ruler rights of unconditional disposal over one's life and capacities that one does not have oneself — in the same way one cannot sell (i.e., alienate by free and no-strings-attached transfer) an apartment one is only renting. Property rights come with God-given conditions — to serve the good of all through the exercise of such rights. One cannot give someone free disposal over oneself (or others) without contravening this sort of obligation to maintain and care for God's property; granting someone rights of free disposal simply means not holding him or her to such an obligation.

It is also the case that, for Locke, one's person and capacities are one's own (and not merely God's) in an inalienable way: giving someone else free disposal over them would therefore be to lose one's humanity. Loss of direct self-governance even with respect to one's capacities to act — labor power in the modern sense implied by the exchange of labor for wages — would seem then for Locke to slide uncomfortably close to slave labor. One's person certainly cannot be alienated as it is in slavery without the loss of one's humanity, but neither can one's labor power be alienated without a similarly demeaning cost if that means one exchanges for money the bare capacity to act in a way that puts it under the direction of another. One's humanity seems honored only in markets for labor where wages are exchanged for services that remain under the primary direction of the worker and presuppose the worker's own know-how (as is the case, say, in master/servant relations or pre-capitalist cottage industries).

While Locke's account of property rights goes some way toward undercutting the primacy of a modern understanding of property and the social relations it justifies, its effectiveness remains unclear. For example, in practice the relevance of appeal to common rights, rights of access to means of subsistence and well-being that one does not presently possess, is sharply curtailed. This is so, first of all, because the test of legitimate use of another's property rights is not positive approximation to the goal in accordance with which they were delegated — the subsistence and well-being of all. For example, the people do not have the right to overthrow one form of government simply to set up a better one. The original goal is merely a negative limit permitting the legitimacy of all sorts of governments that differ markedly in their ability to further, for example, the material happiness of the citizenry. The only legitimate revolution is one based, therefore, on a most egregious violation of trust. Human beings in serving God's purposes are similarly set loose. God's or the people's standard (the natural law to be furthered by the delegation of property rights) has very little critical bite, one might say.

Second, work as a requirement for private or exclusive rights undercuts the force of common right. The common right becomes a personal right only to the extent one mixes one's labor with the resources to which one has a common use right. Work is, in short, the condition for all private possession. Only physical incapacity or the scarcity of materials to work with (which results from others' efforts of private appropriation) justifies the transfer of unearned exclusive rights to those who do not work. This obligation to work is written into the conditions of God's original loan, or entrusting, of the earth and its resources to humans. Even though everyone has a right in common to the goods of the earth (and therefore one has a right to charity if one cannot work), one is obligated to work by the original contract between God and human beings: it is only in that way that one serves God's purposes and gains a legitimate right of use to some part of the earth for oneself. The result of all this is Locke's recommendations concerning poor laws: the state's disciplining of poor children to promote a work ethic and the forcing of the able-bodied poor to work.

Another major problem for Locke if he is to provide a genuine alternative to modern property rights is that talk of owning oneself and one's capacities oddly distances oneself from those capacities, and even more oddly from one's person, in a way that helps makes sense of their possible status as commodities. Although Locke maintains that they are inalienable at the cost of our humanity, having a proprietary relationship to them clearly suggests that they could be alienated. The individual seems to be separable from, to be in some external or contingent relation to, his or her own person and capacities; and therefore it might well be hard to see how the individual could be seriously diminished or injured through their sale. The individual in that case is no longer identified with the person directing the exercise and development of his or her own capacities; the individual becomes instead the mere repository of labor or talents susceptible to use by others for their own ends. Such a possibility of alienation or grant of free disposal is encouraged, too, by Locke's suggestion that the exercise of one's capacities is not the work of God but one's own work; God only owns — and therefore has the right to limit the use of — the substance of what one is (including what one is capable of doing) and the materials that one consumes and works on, not the actual exercise of one's powers through acts of one's own will. That exercise of capacities might seem, then, simply one's own to do with as one sees fit, and not what one holds as a loan subject to conditions set by the real owner, God.

Finally, the reward system behind Locke's understanding of the contract between God and human beings is religiously problematic; it is quite amenable to a two-covenant federal theology (which Locke himself espoused in *The Reasonableness of Christianity*). The primary covenant is one of works: God hands over something to you on the understanding that you will do what God wants with it; if you do, God will hand over more to you, but if you do not, you forfeit your rights and are subject to penalty. The covenant of grace *is* such a covenant of works modified or differently understood: the same covenant of works is a covenant of grace in that such a covenant exists at all by God's free choice and in that God has made it easy for you to serve God as God requires. Either what God requires is simply rather easy to perform in light of our God-given capacities (good intentions and right reason) or, if not easy to perform, then God (in virtue of what Christ does) mercifully accepts the best one can do in lieu of full performance. In short, the theology underpinning Locke's logic of property and exchange exhibits a rather deflated understanding of God's grace.

This absence of a strong sense of grace in Locke's theology might indeed suggest a new category upon which to build a genuine alternative to a modern logic of property: the category of gift. Ideas about property in one's person, common rights of use and work as a condition for individual appropriation of these rights of access, loan and obligation based on rights that have been entrusted or delegated — all seem too close to the modern logic of private property to hold out against it. The category of gift seems opposed to both a Lockean and a modern logic of property, and therefore to suggest the possibility of an interesting new one. Unlike private property in a modern sense or a conditional loan, gift suggests benefits offered freely and for nothing — benefits in the sense of what is for the recipient's good, offered freely in the sense that such benefits are not owed on account of the fulfillment of any previous condition, and for nothing in the sense of being offered apart from any expectation of a return. With such a category, theology and economy could be correlated in much the way they are for Locke. Now, however, the world and everything in it would be God's own because God is the giver (rather than the workman) of it. And presumably a human being would have a legitimate claim on what is in it not by virtue of a human God-like workmanship but by virtue of imitating (or participating in) this gift economy that God sets up as creator. One would have oneself as a gift of God and on that basis one could establish the proper character of relations of exchange with others.

For help in developing such an economy of grace or gift, one might turn, then, to a theologian who works with many of the same notions of tenancy, loan, and stewardship as Locke did when discussing human responsibility before God but who is committed to a much more robust account of grace. In the case of Calvin, for example — a Protestant reformer eager to emphasize the sovereignty of God's grace in a way thought by him to be lacking in theology previously — gift-giving from the ever-flowing fount of divine goodness accessible in Christ, God's fatherly beneficence to God's children, and human lives of gratitude for good gifts freely and liberally bestowed are arguably the dominant motif, within which this other quite common Christian vocabulary is set or with which it is set in tension.[7] On the one hand, there is only a single covenant of grace for Calvin that involves the free gift of mercy to the undeserving. God is not a harsh taskmaster paying wages to servants but a doting parent of wayward children who are lovingly chastised and rewarded despite their faults simply because they are God's own, the heirs to the parent's fortune in whom God wishes only

7. See Brian Gerrish, *Gift and Gratitude* (Minneapolis: Fortress, 1993).

to delight.[8] All that we do is by God's grace, and therefore the very notion of merit is destroyed (p. 790). We receive a reward not because our works earn it but because God out of kindness has simply set that value on what we do (p. 791). We are to keep the law as an act of honor, reverence, and gratitude, not as any simple obligation externally imposed by divine demand. On the other hand, however, God does seem to be setting us a task, to be greeted by either rewards or penalties. We should use God's gifts for the purpose for which he gave them to us (p. 840). They have been entrusted to our use as stewards, and we must one day render an account of them; a reckoning will one day be made of our use of them (pp. 723, 695, 720). God's gifts are held by us like "the usufruct of a field by another's liberality"; and therefore when we do what the owner of the title of the property requires of us, we "have only carried out services owed" (pp. 791, 790). We do not need to pay the debt of perfect performance of God's Law or the penalty for failure to so perform, but someone still has to — Christ (pp. 801-2, 796). Looking to that perfect payment, God overlooks our own failure to provide what is due; and upon that forgiveness, gives us the benefits that are the reward of it, the benefits that are properly owed to someone perfectly obedient (p. 805). One can put together these two sides of Calvin's theology so that they involve a fundamental disruption of the logic of debt and loan, but it is very hard to exclude the suggestion that here grace and liberality are simply being made to fit a context of legal requirement; legal requirement remains, one can easily argue, the dominant paradigm even while it is being contested.

If combining the language of grace with the language of tenancy and loan in the way Calvin does seems as prone to subvert the language of gift as to subvert the language of loan and debt, could one, instead, make the idea of grace the incontrovertible and perhaps exclusive organizing principle of a theological economy? Doing all one could to eschew language of ownership, even in the form of a loan, could one develop what it means to hold oneself and the whole of the world as gifts of God and then ask about the character that legitimate social (political/economic) exchanges might take on that basis?

Theologians who have suggested something like this — Stephen Webb, John Milbank, Catherine Pickstock, and Douglas Meeks to a lesser extent — have been quite drawn to models of noncommodity (gift) exchange in non-

---

8. John Calvin, *Institutes of the Christian Religion,* ed. John T. McNeill, trans. Ford Lewis Battles, vol. 1 (Philadelphia: Westminster, 1960 [1559]), pp. 822, 837. Further page references to the *Institutes* will be cited parenthetically in the text.

European locales not yet fully subject to market conditions.[9] In such economies of exchange, possessions seem always shared in a fluid circuit ever returning to their initiating source and flowing out again to meet needs in what
looks irresistibly to these theologians like some sort of this-worldly imitation
of (or participation in) the mutual love among Trinitarian persons. But to
what extent are such noncommodity gift exchanges really very different from
the logics of property we have previously discussed?

It is common, indeed, to simply contrast these non-Western gift exchanges with commodity exchanges in modern capitalist markets. Thus,
"commodity exchange is an exchange of alienable things between transactors
who are in a state of reciprocal independence . . . non-commodity (gift) exchange is an exchange of inalienable things between transactors who are in a
state of reciprocal dependence."[10] Unlike modern commodity exchange, gift
exchange occurs between familiars; it presupposes or brings about close relations of interdependence — relations of trust or agonistic personal claim —
that contrast with relations with strangers. Unlike the case of modern market
exchange in the West, in non-Western gift exchange one is not free to enter
into or refuse exchange. Instead, gift-giving is sustained through a system of
obligations: everyone must give when able, accept gifts offered, and give in return. Making a return "payment," even returning more than one has been
given as a sort of interest for benefits accrued through possession and use,
does not cancel debt but continues it; it merely increases obligation by making the original giver indebted as well. By such means gift relations are self-
sustaining, without the periodic or episodic and sequential character of commodity exchanges, one following another as the actual exchange of money for
goods or services (the completion of the deal) breaks off one's relations with
one person to make way for the next. The goal of exchange of the individual
giver is to maximize what one puts out — the more one gives the more one
benefits through the accrual of prestige — in contrast to commodity ex-

9. See John Milbank, "Can a Gift Be Given?" *Modern Theology* 11, no. 1 (January 1995):
119-61; Catherine Pickstock, *After Writing* (Oxford: Blackwell, 1998); Stephen Webb, *The Gifting
God* (Oxford: Oxford University Press, 1996); and Douglas Meeks, *God the Economist* (Minneapolis: Fortress, 1989). The exact nature of the respective appeals by these theologians to
noncommodity gift exchanges in non-Western "local" economies is a very complicated question, which I cannot go into here. These appeals are, for example, far from uncritical. But, using
Milbank as a kind of locus classicus, one can nevertheless say that the theological account of
grace is often proposed simply as a modified version of these exchanges. Milbank talks of them
as a kind of "advent" of his own Christian view of gift-giving; he is attempting to purify their
agonistic and closed character, while maintaining the priority on reciprocal relations and on
nonrepetitive, creative response that defines them.

10. C. A. Gregory, *Gifts and Commodities* (London: Academic Press, 1982), p. 12.

changes where the goal is to accumulate or take in as much as one can for oneself. Unlike modern commodity exchange, the persons who exchange rather than the objects of exchange are what are brought into relation through exchange. There is, moreover, no sharp distinction between the objects and persons of exchange, between objects and their owners, as in commodity exchange. Instead, objects themselves are personalized in ways that suggest they cannot be alienated from their givers. That objects personify their givers is the reason, indeed, why they obligate return. Finally, unlike commodity contract, return, though obligatory, should never be immediate, but always delayed; in the delay the gift's debt production is increased by being passed on to others so as to establish a longer string or stream of debt. Return giving should not be transparent in the search for equivalency (say, by return of the very same thing). Nor should the price of the gift (and the interest it brings) be calculated and thereby the character of a fair return established by explicit agreement.

These contrasts are, however, easily overblown. For example, gift exchange has some clear analogies with capitalist exchange. In both cases, the use-value of objects, their capacity to meet human needs, is not primarily at issue. (In non-Western gift exchange, these needs are met by alternative means of barter, cultivation of common or private property, or simple seizure.) Instead, what is often most at stake in both is prestige: one's status increases the more one gives or the more one gets through capitalist exchange. Rather than bringing about the meeting of needs, the primary effect of both is to create distinctive social relations — impersonal ones in capitalist exchange, personal ones in gift exchange. Exchange in both cases produces, moreover, a kind of increase or profit — that is the defining feature of capital, in the one case, and of giving across multiple recipients, in the other. Gifts in fact circulate similar to the way money does when it becomes capital: like the gift, money is not spent once and for all but only with the intention of getting it back through its passage from one hand to another; and its circulation is never finally closed or completed but constantly renewed, since in a capitalist circuit of commodity exchange money never fall outs of circulation through the purchase of a commodity for simple consumption of its use-value (e.g., one buys a coat never to wear, and wear out, and thereby meet one's personal need for warmth but in order to resell it, at, one hopes, a profit).[11] Capitalist markets are based on competition, but gift exchanges too have a competitive tendency. Gift-giving establishes relations of superiority and subordination: the gift-giver has status and is due a return gift or, short of that, return ser-

---

11. See Karl Marx, *Capital,* vol. 1, pt. II, chap. 4: "The General Formula for Capital."

vice. While gifts and return gifts can be balanced, the flexible, incalculable character of exchange, along with the tendency of increase through further giving, makes such balance very hard to achieve and rarely very clear. Competition among gift-givers is therefore not unusual: often an initial gift is more than matched by a return gift, setting off a chain reaction whereby each struggles to maintain the upper hand in relations of indebtedness.

One can argue, further, that gift exchanges simply *become* commodity contracts, when subject to conditions of capitalist markets and the cordial, nonhostile relations with strangers that characterize them, or, even more precisely, simply *become* loans when directed to outsiders.[12] Thus, gift exchanges are at bottom contractual in virtue of the obligations they enforce on all sides.[13] This contractual aspect is simply occluded by the participants — one cannot point it out without the loss of the gift character of the exchange. The contract is not spelled out but remains vague, and seems to depend on trust among intimates or, less charitably, on their awareness that they simply cannot do without each other and have no other choice. When such trust is lost and/or people have greater independence from one another, the terms of the contract now have to be made explicit and definite, immediate returns become preferable (since one cannot be certain that those indebted to you are trustworthy), and external reinforcement of obligation becomes necessary — for example, through codified law and the police. Focus shifts thereby to the objects — what they are worth — and away from the subjects who are parties to the exchange. And struggles for status do too.

To the extent the last major difference between the two remains — objects of exchange are inalienable from their givers — this simply means that gift exchanges turn into explicit loans. Recent work on noncommodity gift exchanges indeed plays up this connection.[14] Requirement of return to the giver, the fact that a gift is never finally alienated from its giver, does not require reference to some mysterious, spiritual quality of the gift — the *hau* that Mauss made famous. It simply means that gifts are common property or loans never fully possessed by the recipient. Locke's economy is therefore something very much like a gift economy — just one with explicit conditions,

12. See Lewis Hyde, *The Gift* (New York: Vintage, 1979), pp. 86, 88, 115, 134ff.

13. Pierre Bourdieu, *Outline of a Theory of Practice* (Cambridge: Cambridge University Press, 1977), is a famous proponent of this idea. This contractual feature does not mean that these gift exchanges are not genuinely such (that would assume an abstract or merely different account of gift's defining features); it just means that occlusion of obligation (among others things) defines this sort of giving.

14. See Maurice Godelier, *The Enigma of the Gift* (Chicago: University of Chicago Press, 1999).

more calculation, and special institutions of enforcement (and monetary payment for rights of use, or rent). They both envision a world that runs on debt and credit, in which primary obligations derive from the delegation, or holding in trust, of inalienable property.

If Locke's economy of inalienable property has problems, it is unclear why one should expect anything better from noncommodity gift economies. Indeed, far worse than anything we saw in Locke, all that the features distinguishing a gift economy from an explicit debt economy like Locke's produce is a world of infinite debt. Debts can never be completely paid off; they simply multiply without end. For similar reasons, once it starts up, competition for prestige, disconnected from the meeting of needs, presses on to absurd lengths; nothing curbs it. The result is potlatch: destruction of vast quantities of goods as proof of the giver's superiority. The relations between superiors and subordinates that giving establishes — the fact that getting a gift is never an entirely good thing, especially if you are poor and/or young and therefore without much to give back — promotes the ideal of an unpayable debt, one that would spell ineradicable domination. If God is such a giver, God is just the biggest of "big men."

Much as we saw with Locke, the lack of distinction between persons and things — holding one's person not in this case as inalienable property but in the form of a gift to be given to others — means here that some people, most often women, are very much treated as things, simple objects of exchange. Gifts become separable from the giver (much as we saw that for Locke person and capacities can become separable from oneself as one's property); some people then become the gifts that other people give and receive. Self-giving that one directs oneself is replaced by forms of exchange that could easily devolve into simple exploitation.[15]

Ironically confirming the point that gift economies are not all that dissimilar from loans or commodity contracts is the fact that what noncommodity gift exchange is most *unlike* is modern charitable giving. In modern charitable giving, gifts meet the needs of the recipient. Donor and recipient are commonly strangers, and giving does not establish ongoing relations between them. To the contrary, gift-giving often justifies the donor's not having anything further to do with the recipient, justifies, that is, the recipient's exclusion from the regular social or exchange relations that make up the majority of the donor's life. (For example, by charitable giving one justifies not empowering the recipient for participation in capitalist exchange.)

---

15. See Hyde, *The Gift*, pp. 101-2. This is not to say that women in gift economies have no power themselves as givers; cf. Annette Weiner, *Women of Value, Men of Renown* (Austin: University of Texas, 1976).

Giving is equated with the gift rather than the focus being on the relationship or act of giving and receiving. Gifts are alienated from their givers — they are often, for example, given anonymously. And no return is expected for them, besides perhaps gratitude, which might at its chilliest be expressed by the recipient's acknowledgment that the donor has already done more than enough, by an agreement not to subject the donor to further demands.

3

If an economy of grace that provides a genuine alternative to loan and capitalist exchange cannot be easily derived from gift economies, perhaps it is best to turn directly to theological traditions for help, with a selective eye. Searching through them with the knowledge we now have of other economic logics, what ideas about God's giving (and human giving on that basis) would appear to most expand the economic imagination of contemporary people?

In this light, the whole theological structure of things — moving from an account of God's triune nature through the whole host of gift-giving relations that God establishes with the world as its creator, covenant partner, and redeemer — can be viewed as a complex, multi-staged economy for distributing goods, one that abides by principles at odds with those characteristic of capitalist commodity exchange (such as theologically informed principles of unconditional giving, universal inclusion, and noncompetitive possession). The triune God is a God who communicates the goodness of Godself within the course of God's own dynamic life and outward in love to what is not God. In the history of God's dealings with the world, which culminate in Christ, God is seeking in ever more perfect ways to communicate to what is not God the fullness of gift relations that constitutes the perfection of God's own intra-Trinitarian life. Every stage of this history represents a greater effort to communicate God's own giftfulness as that is made possible by different but analogously structured relations between God and the world, relations differentiated in theological discussion by such terms as creation, covenant, redemption, and consummation in Christ. In creating the world, the triune God gives nondivine versions of, or substitutes for, God's own goodness. In covenant relations with Israel, God gives Godself as covenant partner. In Christ, God makes the human God's own and thereby incorporates the human within the intra-Trinitarian life. The human being Jesus is the Word of God in human form and therefore enjoys the Word's relations with the Father and Spirit in a form appropriate to a human life — the form of perfect fellowship or partnership. Jesus is the Trinitarian shape that human life takes in order to be the means of God's distribution of God's own goods to the world; in Christ, the human is purified, healed, and elevated beyond itself. United with Christ, human beings in their relations with others are to take on a similar Trinitarian structure; like Christ, but with differences from Christ reflected in their need for dependence on him, human beings are to become ministers of divine beneficence. The proper structure of a human economy for the distribution of goods is in this way established by situating it within a whole structure of oddly similar but materially different gift-giving relations between God and the world. The theological structure of things includes human beings and their responsibilities to others in that it recommends a shape or economy for their relations that abides by the same general principles variously instantiated throughout the whole structure of divine gift-giving.

If human relations are structured in a way that reflects the character of God's own giving, they should be marked by unconditional giving — that is, giving that is not obligated by prior performance and that is not conditional upon a return. This is a first principle that might cover both God's relations to us, in their diversity, and our relations with each other, within the same overall theological structure of things. This principle marks all these relations off from *do ut des* giving — "I give so that you will give," the alternative principle of conditional giving that covers barter, commodity exchanges, and debtor/creditor relations — ever the common currency of the distribution of goods in our world, which Christians are therefore called and empowered to revise.

In this theological structure of things, God doesn't give gifts to us because of what we have done to deserve them. They are not payments for services rendered. They are not owed by the fulfillment of some prior condition. This is so first of all because God gives us all that we are as creatures. The triune God as creator makes a total gift to creatures in the sense that there is nothing to creatures apart from God's giving; the whole of what they are is God's gift. Prior to these created gifts, there is therefore nothing to us to obligate God's giving them. This is so, in the second place, because of God's unilateral setting up of covenant relations with Israel; God gives Godself in partnership from sheer free beneficence and not because of this particular people's special merits.[16] Finally, gifts of unity with God in Christ, participa-

---

16. The Hebrew Bible includes, of course, a mix of unilateral and bilateral discussions of covenant; see, among others, Jon Levenson, *Sinai and Zion* (San Francisco: Harper, 1985). Any creative theological interpretation of this material must offer an ordering of the two different sorts of accounts. I am assuming a unilateral establishment of covenant that sets up a way of life for God's people. The blessings of covenant are conditional on the pursuit of that way of life, but not the covenant relation itself with God, who remains faithful to the covenant, ever calling Israel back to that way of life, which brings with it all the blessings of life.

tion in the triune life of God, are given because of our need, our sufferings and incapacities, not because of our righteousness and bountiful living in communities where justice and peace reign, not because of our good use of gifts already given.

Neither are God's gifts to us predicated upon a return being made for them. God does not give for the sake of a return since there is no return of which God is in need. This is a giving without need, a giving that though appropriate is not strictly required by God's own nature, since God's gift-giving character is already expressed in a more adequate or full fashion in relations among the Trinitarian persons.

Such a return is impossible in any case and therefore God does not give in expectation of it. We cannot pay God back for what has been given to us because God already has all that one might want to give back. The triune God already has, and in greater abundance, with a fullness unimaginable, all that we would like to present in exchange. In this way, God's giving to us is unconditioned by hopes of a return, in imitation of the gift-giving relations among Father, Son, and Spirit: the Father does not give to the Son and Spirit in hopes of a return since the Father already has everything that the Son or Spirit could possibly return.

One also cannot pay God back for what one has been given because there is nothing more for us to return than what God has already given us. The whole of creatures is God's gift in imitation of the way the whole of Son and Spirit are given by the Father. There is nothing more to us, we have nothing more that is simply our own, to give back as payment; we can only give back gifts received. All our gifts to God take on the character, then, of Eucharist offerings; we offer up to God the bread and wine that are already God's gifts to us as creator, empowered to do so by the gifts already received by humanity in Christ.

That God's giving is not conditional upon a return is reflected in the hidden character of God's gifts *as* gifts. If we *are* them we are not aware of having received them, as we generally would be in any case of gifts transferred from one hand to the next. God's act of giving is invisible; what we see is the fact of it, its issue in created goods, which appear to be simply our own. (As Derrida would like) God's gifts efface themselves in their very occurrence, in virtue of the fact of their difference from any other sort of gift exchange among creatures with which we are familiar — in which gift-giving is never total, never productive without remainder of its recipient.

God does give to the creature with the expectation that this giving will be reflected in all that the creature is and does. In the case of humans, this reflection is a matter of their intentional agency. Given the invisibility of God's action as creator, this reflection is not, however, forced, or put forward in a way that demands conscious response. Oriented around God's gift-giving relationship with us, our affections, cognitive faculties, volitions, and deeds should all become a register of that relationship. But this way of life is not an obligation, or the fulfillment of a debt, to God; it is simply the only way of life appropriate to the way things are; it is simply our effort, as Karl Barth would say, to be what we already are. Rather than anything God contracts from us through gifts to us, it is our free and joyful testimony and acknowledgment, our act of thankfulness and praise for what God already is in relation to us — the giftful fount of whatever it is about us that is good.

God does give to us in hopes that our lives will reflect this giving, but God's giving is not conditional on that sort of return being made by us. We don't forfeit God's gift-giving relations with us by not reflecting back to God what God gives, in even this most qualified form of payback. God maintains a gift-giving relation with us, however fragile the exhibition of those gifts in our lives or corrupt our performance in response to their being given. As God's creatures, a continuing relationship with God is the condition of our continuing to live, move, and breath; if we continue to have the time and space of this created existence, despite our failings and desperate lives, in which the reception of God's gifts is blocked, God must be maintaining this gift-giving relationship with us from God's side. Despite the fact that our lives do not reflect God's gift-giving, God still gives and is willing to give more. God indeed establishes a covenant with Israel — a gift greater than mere creation, more than anything that createdness requires — and maintains a steadfast faithfulness to it, again from God's side, whether or not we human partners manage to live in ways appropriate to it. Again, God gives unity with Godself in Christ even to sinners, indeed especially to them; they "deserve" these gifts simply because they need them. The gift of union with Christ remains ours, moreover, however short we come in the effort to reflect what it should mean for the lives we lead.

God's gifts can be blocked by our sins and the sins of others against us; but God doesn't stop giving to us because we have misused and squandered the gifts that have been given us. God's gifts are not on loan to us on the condition that we use them rightly, failures in attentive stewardship thereby bringing their forfeiture. Our sins interrupt the reception and distribution of God's gifts, bringing suffering and death in their train; but these effects are not God's punishment of us, an interruption of God's good favor in response to our failings. They are merely the natural consequences of a turning away from God's bounty, a bounty that continues to stream forth to us in the way it always has.

Properly reflecting relationship with God means, then, overcoming sin, becoming plastic once again (as Irenaeus would say) to God's giving of the good. Becoming this proper reflection requires, Christians affirm, more unmerited gifts in and through Christ; God supplies even the missing condition of blessings (holiness of life), which is to be our own contribution to the relationship. Rather than offer something in return, we are to remain open in gratitude for the reception of further gifts of God, inexhaustible in their fullness. God obliges, as Christians believe, offering gifts for gifts, gifts for squandered gifts, "rewarding" us anyway despite our inability to make a return, our inability to offer anything besides a willingness to receive more, "rewarding" us with new gifts that remedy even our failure to offer this non-offering of grateful openness to God's further gifts.

The fact that God cannot be repaid in principle and never by us sinners does not then establish an infinite, unpayable debt, one, say, that only God could pay on the cross. Jesus is not punished in our stead; God, as I've suggested, simply doesn't punish in response to sin. Nor does the cross save by paying back to God in a positive way the obedience that God's gift of the Law or a way of life requires, the Son of God in Christ taking our place as God's for once obedient partner. There is no such requirement of obedience as a condition of God's good favor. God saves through unity with the Son in Christ. Jesus' obedience to the Father — a life that reflects the Father's beneficent will for us — is an effect of that unity with the Son, not the very condition of our being saved by Christ. The humanity of Jesus is not blessed by God, in a way that extends the blessings of God to all of us, because Jesus is obedient; Jesus is obedient because his humanity has already been blessed. The cross simply doesn't save us from our debts to God by paying them. If anything, the cross saves us from the consequences of a debt economy in conflict with God's own economy of grace by canceling it. We are ransomed on the cross from the suffering and oppression in which a debt economy has thrown us; taken from the cross we are returned to our original owner God, to God's kingdom of unconditional giving, snatched out of a world of deprivation and injustice from which we suffer because of our poverty, our inability to pay what others demand of us. In Christ, we see the manner of divine action that the Jubilee traditions of the Hebrew Bible aimed to reflect: debts are forgiven rather than paid, debtors freed from the enslavement that accrues through nonpayment, land returned to its original owners despite their forfeiture of any claim to it through unpaid debt to the creditors who had seized it.

This unconditionality of God's giving implies the universal distribution of God's gifts, a second principle that distinguishes the theological structure of things from human economies as we know them. Because it has no preconditions, God's giving as creator is universal in scope; everything that is benefits. In Christ, God is clearly the God of sinners as well as of the righteous; of the Gentiles who lack God's gift of the covenant as well as of the Jews who have the benefit of the Law; of the suffering as well as of the fortunate, indeed the God especially of the former in that they are the ones in greatest need of God's gifts. There is nothing we need to do or to be in particular in order for God to be giving to us. The distinction between good and bad, between Jew and Gentile — all the distinctions that typically determine the boundaries of human love and concern — fall away in that God gives simply to those in need, in order to address every respect in which they are in need, without concern for anything they especially are or have done to deserve it.

God's giving indeed breaks all the usual boundaries of closed communities. In creating the world, God goes outside the community of the Trinity to offer gifts to the stranger, to what is not divine. God offers the gift of Godself in partnership with a people by choosing those who are deprived and enslaved strangers within the community in which they reside. Jesus aligns himself with those without favor or good standing within the community of God's people; and he brings all within the very life of the triune God despite all their differences, despite indeed the greatest difference of all that remains nonetheless between divine and nondivine.

In order to minister to God's own efforts to benefit the world in the way that God's own working for us establishes, we would therefore need to recognize the common right of all, simply as creatures, to the goods of God; we would have to recognize our obligation to advance the fortunes of that universal community of creatures that is the object of God's favor.

God's gifts of the goods of creation are not the exclusive possessions of particular persons (or creatures); recognizing the goods of one's own life as God's gifts entails recognizing God's efforts to give similarly to all others. The gifts of God's grace as creator in this way amount to an inclusive or common "positive" property right to life and all the goods of life (in a more or less Lockean sense of this, which does not imply that everyone has a property right to everyone else's life). But here (unlike what Locke says) rights of individual appropriation are also common, in the sense that the individual's rightful appropriation of what is due him or her on this common right to livelihood is not conditional upon work; rights of legitimate possession are based primarily on one's simple status as a creature in need.

The common character of such rights means that one does not hold one's gifts primarily in an exclusive sense against infringement by others; as a common "positive" property right, one has a right to life and livelihood to be shared with all others and not held against them or withheld from them. Exclusive possession as a negative, protective right against others is only at issue as a secondary, reactive measure to reinstitute common possession rights, in cases where others actively threaten to deny one's right to be included in the community of creatures gifted by God — when, that is, the extension to oneself of the common right to livelihood is being blocked by the possessiveness of others. The common aspect of God's gift-giving can be discussed, moreover, as a directly communal gift; part of what God is trying to give us is community with a certain shape. A covenant among human persons (the people of God) is itself God's gift, the gift of this very sort of community in which common or inclusive rights to well-being become a social priority.

God's giving is not owed to creatures, but, if those gifts are being given unconditionally by God to all in need, creatures are in fact owed the goods of God by those ministering such benefits, without being or having done anything in particular to deserve them. Our good works, in short, are not owed to God but they are to the world. There is an unconditioned obligation to give on our part because God's unobligated or gracious giving to the world is unconditioned by any differences of merit; God's giving follows only need, to the end of a complete distribution of the goods of God to all.

Those in need have a rightful claim on others, who are to be the ministers of divine beneficence to them, in imitation of the way the Son and Spirit have by rights of nature what the Father nonetheless gives to them. On an equal footing with the Father, the Son and the Spirit already are by nature what they are given by the Father; in this sense they have by rights of nature what they are given; they are given what is their very own. The human assumed by the Word in Christ, though in the needy situation of sin, has by rights of nature the gifts bestowed on it in virtue of its being the Word's very own. Though creatures are never owed anything by God — God's gifts are nothing but gracious here — God's decision to give them everything means an oddly analogous coming together of gift and right. In the creature's case, one is given that to which one has a right in that what one lacks is one's due; in contrast to a modern property right understood as a right to keep others from what is already in one's possession, here one has a property right to what one doesn't have. Because of God's unconditional beneficence, need determines a right here; we are only giving the needy their due when we try to meet their needs.

The community of concern to human beings as the ministers of divine benefit should therefore be as wide as God's gift-giving purview. In this universal community, humans should try to distribute the gifts of God as God does without concern for whether they are especially deserved by their recipients. Without bothering themselves, for example, with distinctions between the deserving or undeserving poor, human beings should give their full attention, instead, to the various needs of members of this worldwide community. They must offer special protections, moreover, as these become necessary, to those most likely to be left out of the community of concern at any point in time — the outcasts and strangers in their midst.

Again in imitation of God's relations with us, one gives to others with the hope that these gifts will be the basis for their activity as ministers of divine beneficence; one gives to them for their empowerment as givers in turn. Their failure to do so is not, however, cause for the forfeiture of such benefits; gifts to them were not conditional on such a return; the absence of it is not therefore grounds for discontinuing the gifts. Their becoming ministers of divine beneficence by way of our gifts is not, moreover, to be considered a return under threat, a payment of a debt, or the meeting of an obligation. It is rather to be hoped for as the natural concomitant of the joyful development of such gifts in thanks for gifts received. One expects dedication to the good of others to arise from the grateful sense that one has already been the recipient of benefit.

The reasonableness of such hopes gains support when the economic logic of a community dedicated to addressing the needs of all is further specified by a principle of noncompetitive relations that God's gift-giving abides by. So specified, unconditional giving in human relations to meet the needs of all takes on the shape of a community of mutual fulfillment.

Within God's intra-Trinitarian life and in God's relations with us, God's gift-giving is noncompetitive in that the giver's remaining giftful does not come at the expense of gifts to another, in that giving to others does not come at one's own expense, and in that being one's own and having for one's own do not begin where relations of active reception from another end. Indeed, we are, and have for, our own only as we, and what we have, are a beneficent other's.

These sorts of competitive relations are avoided because gift relations here are not in any usual sense exchanges or transfers. The Father needn't begrudge the Son or Spirit anything, the triune God needn't begrudge the world anything, the world needn't begrudge Jesus anything, Jesus needn't begrudge us anything, since in giving to all these others nothing is being given away. What is given remains the possession of the one giving. Nothing is transferred, as if these gifts involved the moving of material goods from one site to another. For example, creation involves no simple transfer because there is nothing to us prior to God's giving to receive such a transfer, no one exists prior to God's giving to take the gift in hand; we as a whole are the gift, rather than being the gift's already existing recipients. Moreover, we never take possession of what is given as if God's giving to us became at some point simply the given, the product of a completed transfer, and therefore simply ours. The gift is never separable from the giver: creatures would not remain what they are without a constant relation of dependence upon God; we are covenant partners with God only to the extent God remains present to us; we have gifts in Christ — say, eternal life — not in and of ourselves in the form of some new "supernatural" properties, but only as we remain one with Christ in faith and love by the gracious workings of the Holy Spirit. Our coming to be and to act independently of God is never the ground, then (as it is for Locke), of becoming, and making things, our own. We are our own and have for our own only as what we are and have are God's own.

Fundamentally at issue here is a sense of nonexclusive possession and nonexclusive rights of use. What the Father has the Son and Spirit also have, because in them the very same thing is repeated in different modes. The three work together as one in that the will to work — its particular shape, general capacities, and so on — is the very same among them in virtue of this identity of substance or essence. In Christ, what humanity has becomes the Son's own and the reverse, this time not because the very same thing is repeated in both in different modes but because the Word assumes humanity to itself, unites humanity with itself, becomes one with it. Because the human has become God's own by way of the Word's assumption of it, the triune God achieves God's ends — the fullest possible communication of goods to the creature — by appropriating human powers for that end: God saves in and through the living of a human life. Because the human is God's own in this way, the divine becomes the human's own in Christ — that is, Jesus acts by the power of God, with divine effects.

Following this same pattern of nonexclusive possession and rights of use in a way appropriate for human relations, what we have for our own good others should have as well. Wherever possible that would mean that rights of use to the very same things should be shared or common. Where that is not possible — and it is often not possible among finite creatures subject to fundamentally competitive limitations of time and space, creatures who are themselves by not being others — it means everyone having as far as possible in their own persons and lives the distinct goods that others also have in a distinct fashion in theirs. (For example, not everyone can live in my house; but they should be able to live in a comparable one of their own and my doing so should not come at their expense.) In every case, a community of mutual fulfillment would fundamentally mean that persons share their gifts with others as those others benefit in community from the effects of those gifts' employment. (For example, my development of my intellectual talents becomes the gift to others of my teaching and writing, gifts that those others react to and develop in turn in ways that become a gift to me — confirming, altering, radically realigning my own intellectual sense of things by way of their own teaching and writing.)

On this noncompetitive understanding of things, being ourselves as the persons we are and having all that we have for our own good should not come at the expense of our being our fellows' own in community. Son and Spirit are themselves, and all that they are for the good, just because they are the Son and Spirit of the Father, and the reverse. Apart from the grace of Christ, we are ourselves, and have all that we have for the good, just to the extent we continue to be the triune God's creatures, ever receiving from Father's hands of Son and Spirit. What the humanity of Jesus has beyond its created capacities is its own only as the Logos makes that humanity its own by assuming it to itself. What we have in Christ for our perfection and elevation becomes our own only as we are borne by Christ, only as Christ becomes the subject of our predicates, the agent of our own acts. United with Christ, we are ourselves only as we incorporate what is God's very own within ourselves; our acts are perfected only as we act along with and under the direction of God, whose powers become a kind of principle of our own now-compound operation, through the gift of Christ's Spirit. Similarly, our lives as individuals should be constituted and enhanced in their perfections as we share our lives with others in community, identifying ourselves thereby as persons in community with others and not simply persons for ourselves. We perfect one another in community as our operations to perfect our own gifts and talents enter into and supplement the operations of others in a combined venture for goods otherwise impossible.

Ideas about property in one's person are undercut in this way by the paradigm of perfected human lives in Christ — by Christian accounts of life in God, the life that we are to enjoy through Christ, our life in God's own eternal life. Like what happens in Christ, we, through Christ, are to be humans borne by God. We are no longer exclusively the subject of our predicates or the agent of our deeds; rather, all that we are, as the subject of those predicates and agent of those deeds, becomes the predicates of God's subject and the deeds of God's agency. Nothing hinges anymore on the distinction between ourselves and our capacities — the distinction that permitted an artificial alienation of ourselves from them in the labor contracts of capitalist exchange. Engrafted in Christ, we become — as the whole of ourselves — God's own, as the whole humanity of Jesus is the Logos's own and thereby the proper instrument or hand of the Father's working through the Son and in the Spirit. Though creatures and therefore what is not God, we lose our separability from God. Our sense of self is therefore expanded beyond anything simply our own; we are ourselves only as we incorporate what is God's very own within ourselves. Because we are united to God through Christ, Christ — and the Father and Holy Spirit as mutually inherent persons — dwells in us. We are ourselves and act according to our human nature only as we thereby act along with and under the direction of God. We in this way arrive at an expansive re-definition of self: one includes others within one's sense of self (which does not mean confusing them with oneself — any more than God and the human are to be confused in Christ) out of a recognition of one's own living in an essentially constitutive relation with them.

One must keep in mind, however, that these new understandings of nonexclusive possession and self-identification hold only under very particular preconditions. They presuppose, for example, a very unusual sense of possession or property in accordance with which you are the others' own by way of their giving to you. They own you, you are their own, only as they give to you for your own good, only as they make you the beneficiary of their own powers for the good, not in virtue of their abilities to restrict you, take from you, or do with you as they will.

While we may talk of our belonging to God as a form of divine ownership entailing rights of free disposal and protection against use by others, such talk is not true in the abstract but only when made concrete by talk of God's graciousness as gift-giver. Rather than having a claim on us by appropriation or primarily by rights of exclusive enjoyment, God has a claim on us by giving.[17] We are God's because God has given us all that we are for the good. What God gives is life and the means to its fulfillment — or, more formally, what God gives is the good and what promotes it. It is on this basis that one could say God has exclusive propriety rights and rights of disposal over and against others; those rights are exercised so as to hinder uses of God's creatures that run contrary to their livelihood.

Owning by giving is the way the Son is the Father's own, it is the way humanity is the Son's own, it is the way we are the Father's own. We are the Father's own as his children, not as his slaves, his children only through a gift and not by nature as the Son of God is, his children not in the sense of those of whom one has the right to make demands but children to whom the Father delights and wills to give his fortune, despite their follies and failings, indeed just for the sake of overcoming those follies and failings. We are to be each other's own in community in this same general sense of possession or property.

17. See Meeks, *God the Economist.* I try to enhance the theological specificity and systematic consistency of such a proposal.

Relations of nonexclusive possession and identification only make sense, too, where (as one remembers) giving to others and having oneself are not in competition with one another. The persons of the Trinity give to one another without suffering loss; each continues to have what it gives to the others. What the triune God gives to us does not lessen the inalienable fullness of God's own life. God gives to us without that giving being conditional upon a return, but God's giving, in short, is not self-sacrificial. What Jesus does for us — say, die on a cross — does not come at his own expense, but is part of the process of perfecting his own humanity to glory; our humanity is only perfected to the extent his is before us.

We too, then, should give to others out of our own fullness. It is not as the poor that we are to give to others but as those rich, to whatever extent we are, giving to those poor in what we have, in solidarity with them. Jesus entered into our poverty for the sake of the poor but he did so as someone rich with the Father's own love. We do not give of our poverty but of what we have already received so as to work for the good of others in response to their need. Having received gifts ourselves from God and from all those others in whom we are in community through Christ, we give to others, rather than withhold from them, rather than hold what we have simply as our own.

Rather than being in competition with our having something ourselves, having received gifts is in this way the very condition of our giving to others. Self-assertion, the effort to realize one's own perfection and good, therefore need not be at odds with concern for the needs of others. That sort of self-concern is not at odds with concern for others just to the extent one's own perfections are what enables gift-giving to others.

Following the same theological principle of noncompetition in our case, giving to others should not mean the impoverishment of ourselves. Though we are not ourselves as an exclusive possession, though we are not only our own, neither are we dispossessed in giving to others — self-evacuated, given away. In human relations, as elsewhere in the theological structure of things, giving should not be at odds with one's continuing to have. In a human community where others are not holding their gifts simply for themselves, presumably what one gave away would come back to one from others. But this is not quite what the theological structure of things suggests; it simply seems that what one gives does not come at one's own expense, that one isn't giving by a giving-away that leaves oneself bereft; what one gives remains in one's possession. A community conforming to this idea would be a community of mutual fulfillment in which each effort to perfect oneself enriches others' efforts at self-perfection. One perfects oneself by making one's own the efforts of others to perfect themselves, their efforts too being furthered in the same way by one's own. Something like that is happening all the time in community living, but it is rarely made a major principle of community reform and self-purification.

Indeed, I don't think either a principle of unconditional giving or this principle of noncompetitive relations in a community of mutual fulfillment is unrealistic for implementation in the present — at least as a principle for the reshaping of communities already on the ground. Human communities do not have to be divine ones; one need not pretend, for example, as many contemporary theologians do, that we're Trinitarian persons in community in order to see their point for the lives we already lead. This is not to say, however, that such implementation would be easy: the divine working for the benefit of the world that seeks to incorporate us as its ministers could be expected to meet resistance in our day just as it did in Jesus'. It is also not to say that specific recommendations for implementation would be easy to determine. The exact shape of such recommendations would depend on the particulars of the situation, according to a much more complex account of the present circumstances of global capitalism than I could hope to offer here.

Appendix: Bibliographic Resources on Property and Possession — A Critical Analysis

Jonathan R. Gangle

Language, money, God, and genetic engineering do not at first glance constitute a unified field of inquiry. More distinguishes than unites these categories, and a rudimentary survey of the recent published thought that has deliberated over the questions at stake in their investigation would seem at first glance to be served best by a clear disciplinary articulation into distinct fields: linguistics, economics, theology, genetics. After all, the great advantage of our contemporary, *debut-de-siècle* historical moment remains the power of vast cultural and technological resources regimented into clearly delimited tasks, the varied means of a complex society coordinated to specific, though various, ends. Today's economically powerful nations and the cultural and intellectual modes of production they enable possess enormous resources for the creation and distribution of well-differentiated knowledge. This sort of specialization may be very powerful, but it runs the danger of abstracting itself from the real texture of the social, cultural, and personal issues at stake. Much of the theoretical work gathered here from various disciplines under the broad heading of property and possession questions precisely the conditions and possible consequences of this ambiguous power at the heart of our shared sociohistorical moment — a power to make, to be, and to have.

The theme of property and possession does not itself constitute the object of an autonomous discipline. Instead, it serves as an important and often essential concept for a number of different fields. Any inquiry into the subject immediately finds itself faced with the vast array of already accomplished work in each of these areas. As especially relevant to the demands of the current study, notions of property and possession guide many of the everyday understandings and various modes of comportment toward the world that constitute our contemporary situation. Not only do we live in a world in which enormous emphasis is placed on what we *have* as individuals and communities, but economic structures — including conceptions of property — that serve to regulate the exchange of goods in society have come to define many of the most personal aspects of our daily lives. To the extent that our selves and worlds possess some form of unity (even if only the unity of a collection of fragments), interdisciplinary questioning of non–field-specific themes like property and possession can help shed light on the interrelatedness of various disciplines and, above all, their relevance to the demands of our contemporary social life.

The interrelationships between legal structures, social institutions, cultural patterns, and ecological processes that go into even so simple an example as a young person buying and owning a fuel-efficient new car (probably on credit) can only with great difficulty be sorted out and brought together into a coherent picture. No single discipline is able to assimilate all the information necessary to comprehend such a phenomenon or to process that information with an appropriately complex methodology. Perhaps for precisely this reason the subject of property and possession has become the site of much varied and provocative interdisciplinary work in recent years — although there has been almost no recognition of a field or discipline as such. Property and possession are conditioned by an almost limitless number of factors. It is an important element in such fields as economics, anthropology, sociology, history, and legal theory, as well as philosophy and theology. The present work is situated within a loosely organized but extremely busy and contemporary field of interdisciplinary work in the relations between social institutions, cultural practices, technological and political forces, and concrete human lives as they affect and are affected by different kinds of having. The theme of property and possession informs all of these areas of inquiry and is in many ways uniquely situated to demonstrate their commonalities and to resist the artificiality of clearly delineated, self-subsisting disciplines. This, then, is a work in dialogue with other recent works that have often themselves appeared between disciplines or at the places where two or more fields of inquiry overlap.

Any survey of the vast literature on property and possession in any of these fields must necessarily be selective. Within any one discipline the amount of material is overwhelming, and when it becomes a question of looking at the variety of perspectives taken on the subject from a set of largely heterogeneous disciplines, the quantity of material quickly becomes unmanageable. In the limits of this bibliography, therefore, the criteria for selection have been twofold. First of all, the focus has fallen primarily on recent works and

384

important canonical past works. A great deal of interesting work in the area has been accomplished in the past ten to fifteen years. This survey can in no way presume to cover the entire historical field of the issue of property and possession, but can instead suggest many of the most recent discussions in the area, while at the same time highlighting those texts within the literature that tend to be referred to again and again. Second, works of scholarship that themselves work between disciplines have been privileged. The present work is not only an interdisciplinary project in its own right, but it is also in dialogue with other similar border-crossing works. For this reason it seemed important to pick out research that challenges the clear disciplinary distinctions that often lead to the narrowness of specialization at the expense of dialogical possibilities and the important perspectival questions of context and relevance.

It would be impossible to present even the most rudimentary survey of a field that has yet to be charted and whose scope cannot be judged in advance. Instead, offered here will be something of a shopping trip through the scholarly supermarket of property and possession, a stroll through the tempting aisles of research in a variety of disciplines filled with a vast array of methodological and thematic styles from which one can choose — linked sometimes only tenuously to the fit and fashion of adjacent items. This shopping trip will inevitably gather many of the most important goods in the store, but it will also necessarily leave cartloads of valuable material on the shelves. If a complete inventory is impossible, at least the purpose will have been served of demonstrating an enormous potential for more detailed as well as more general exploration of a warehouse of research that resists easy compartmentalization or even clear, localized identification.

The division of this stockroom into the headings and subsections given below inevitably introduces an illusory element of organizational and disciplinary clarity into what is in fact the far messier and at times simply arbitrary process of presenting a complex and varied field. Many (if not all) of the works referred to could have been listed under more than one section, and some, while important, do not fit perfectly into any of them. The divisions themselves are there only to facilitate browsing — placing frozen foods and canned goods in separate aisles, as it were, in order to make shopping easier. In every case, the content disclosed in each of these works overflows the rigidity of any systematic demarcations. If there is no "essence" that might facilely answer the question *What is property?* neither is there any easy process of subdivision that might break the question down into its simple, component parts. The question of property and possession remains irreducibly complicated, heterogeneous, and provisional. Taken not as a complete whole, then, but rather as a loose aggregation of discrete parts and as the suggestion of a beginning for continuing investigations, the ensuing literature serves at least as part of that question's tentative and complex formulation.

Major Thinkers, Classic Texts

Taken together, the works listed below constitute something of a historical overview of the philosophical, economic, and sociological themes connected to the question of property and possession in modern Western culture. These books are among the most important within the literature, and each of them has spawned a significant body of secondary literature, of which a few relevant recent samples have been given in each case. This list does not try to provide a full canon of philosophical and economic thought on property by any means, but only to gather some of the most important theorists who tend to be referred to again and again throughout the contemporary literature on the subject and to point to one or two of each of their most influential texts. Almost every work cited in the various subsequent sections has been influenced heavily by one or more of the texts noted here, and often it is possible to get the sense of a contemporary thinker's working assumptions, general methodology, and ideological sympathies simply by knowing which tradition, broadly speaking, he or she stands in — whether Lockean, Hegelian, Durkheimian, or Weberian.

After Locke's description in the *Second Treatise* of a conception of property rights grounded in the productive power of one's own labor and the natural possession of oneself, which makes the products of one's labor one's own, there was the flourishing of a tradition in the eighteenth century of analyses of historical economic development beginning with Rousseau's account of the genesis of material inequality in the primordial social jealousy of small, fireside communities, which then eventually found its strongest voice in Hegel and the dialectical materialism of Marx. The work of Veblen, Durkheim, and Weber inherits this historical theoretical framework as well as a society in the midst of various kinds of cultural and economic upheaval in the late nineteenth and early twentieth centuries, and in a number of ways these thinkers begin to look more closely at the social and cultural components of economic development — the ways in which cultural and social formations both influence and are affected by economic structural change. Of course, the paradigmatic case is no doubt Weber's *The Protestant Ethic and the Spirit of Capitalism*. Polanyi carries through this tradition while critiquing some of its assumptions in his focus on institutional and cultural formations in both market and nonmarket economies and in his sustained critique of the presuppositions of neoclassical economics. Many of the works represented later will build on this foundation and continue to argue against the abstraction of economic models away from the cultural, political, and social contexts in which they occur. The editions listed for each work are generally the most recent available.

John Locke, 1632-1704

The Second Treatise of Government. Ed. Thomas P. Peardon. New York: Macmillan, 1986.

See also:

Vaughn, Karen I. *John Locke: Economist and Social Scientist.* Chicago: University of Chicago Press, 1980.

Jean-Jacques Rousseau, 1712-1778

Discourse on the Origin of Inequality. Trans. Franklin Philip. Ed. Patrick Coleman. Oxford, New York: Oxford University Press, 1994.

The Social Contract and Other Later Political Writings. Ed. and trans. Victor Gourevitch. New York: Cambridge University Press, 1997.

Adam Smith, 1723-1790

An Inquiry into the Nature and Causes of the Wealth of Nations. Ed. Edwin Cannan. New York: Modern Library, 1994.

The Theory of Moral Sentiments. Indianapolis: Liberty Classics, 1976.

See also:

Copley, Stephen, and Kathryn Sutherland, eds. *Adam Smith's Wealth of Nations : New Interdisciplinary Essays.* Manchester, New York: Manchester University Press, 1995.

Fry, Michael, ed. *Adam Smith's Legacy: His Place in the Development of Modern Economics.* London: Routledge, 1992.

G. W. F. Hegel, 1770-1831

Philosophy of Right. Trans. S. W. Dyde. Amherst, N.Y.: Prometheus, 1996.

See also:

Maker, William, ed. *Hegel on Economics and Freedom.* Macon, Ga.: Mercer University Press, 1987.

John Stuart Mill, 1806-1873

Principles of Political Economy: And Chapters on Socialism. Ed. Jonathan Riley. Oxford: Oxford University Press, 1994.

Utilitarianism. Ed. George Sher. Indianapolis: Hackett, 1979.

See also:

Lyons, David, ed. *Mill's Utilitarianism: Critical Essays.* Lanham, Md.: Rowman and Littlefield, 1997.

Pierre-Joseph Proudhon, 1809-1865

What Is Property? An Enquiry into the Principle of Right and of Government. Ed. and trans. Donald R. Kelley and Bonnie G. Smith. Cambridge: Cambridge University Press, 1993.

Karl Marx, 1818-1883

Capital: A Critique of Political Economy. Trans. Ben Fowkes. New York: Vintage, 1977.

The German Ideology: Including Theses on Feuerbach and Introduction to "The Critique of Political Economy." Amherst, N.Y.: Prometheus, 1998.

See also:

Neary, Michael, ed. *Global Humanization: Studies in the Manufacture of Labour.* New York: Mansell, 1999.

Thorstein Veblen, 1857-1929

The Instinct of Workmanship and the State of the Industrial Arts. New York: Kelley, 1964 (1914).

The Theory of the Leisure Class. New York: Transaction, 1992 (1899).

See also:

Brown, Doug, ed. *Thorstein Veblen in the Twenty-First Century: A Commemoration of "The Theory of the Leisure Class" (1899-1999).* Northampton, Mass.: Edward Elgar, 1998.

Tilman, Rick. *Thorstein Veblen and His Critics, 1891-1963: Conservative, Liberal, and Radical Perspectives.* Princeton, N.J.: Princeton University Press, 1992.

————. *The Intellectual Legacy of Thorstein Veblen: Unresolved Issues.* Westport, Conn.: Greenwood, 1996.

Emile Durkheim, 1858-1917

The Division of Labor in Society. Trans. W. D. Halls. New York: Free Press, 1984.

The Elementary Forms of Religious Life. Trans. Karen E. Fields. New York: Free Press, 1995.

See also:

Challenger, Douglas F. *Durkheim through the Lens of Aristotle: Durkheimian, Postmodernist, and Communitarian Responses to the Enlightenment.* Lanham, Md.: Rowman and Littlefield, 1994.

Nielsen, Donald A. *Three Faces of God: Society, Religion, and the Categories of Totality in the Philosophy of Emile Durkheim.* Albany: State University of New York Press, 1999.

Max Weber, 1864-1920

The Agrarian Sociology of Ancient Civilizations. Trans. R. I. Frank. London: Verso, 1998.

Essays in Economic Sociology. Ed. Richard Swedberg. Princeton, N.J.: Princeton University Press, 1999.

The Protestant Ethic and the Spirit of Capitalism. Trans. Talcott Parsons. London: Routledge, 1992 (1930).

The Theory of Social and Economic Organization. Trans. A. M. Henderson and Talcott Parsons. New York: Free Press, 1997.

See also:

Brennan, Catherine. *Max Weber on Power and Social Stratification: An Interpretation and Critique.* Brookfield, Vt.: Ashgate, 1997.

Schroeder, Ralph, ed. *Max Weber, Democracy, and Modernization.* Basingstoke: Macmillan, 1998.

Swedberg, Richard. *Max Weber and the Idea of Economic Sociology.* Princeton, N.J.: Princeton University Press, 1998.

Karl Polanyi, 1886-1964

The Great Transformation: The Political and Economic Origins of Our Times. New York: Farrar, Straus and Giroux, 1975.

The Livelihood of Man. New York: Academic, 1977.

See also:

Baum, Gregory. *Karl Polanyi on Ethics and Economics.* Montreal: McGill–Queen's University Press, 1996.

McRobbie, Kenneth, and Kari Polanyi Levitt, eds. *Karl Polanyi in Vienna: The Contemporary Significance of "The Great Transformation."* Montreal: Black Rose, 2000.

For an excellent anthology of excerpts from a number of these works (as well as several not listed here), see:

Murray, Patrick. *Reflections on Commercial Life: An Anthology of Classic Texts from Plato to the Present.* New York: Routledge, 1997.

For a collection of critical articles on some of these figures, see also:

Parel, Anthony, and Thomas Flanagan, eds. *Theories of Property: Aristotle to the Present.* Waterloo, Ont.: Wilfrid Laurier University Press, 1979.

The Legitimization and Limits of Property

Property rights are linked to conceptions of economic progress and the role of the state. Every system of exchange requires some kind of regulation — be it socially conventional, politically enforced, or some combination of the two

— which ensures the coherence of its own internal logic. The following works address, for example, the history of philosophical arguments for property rights (Grunebaum, Ryan, and Schlatter), the relation of property to larger social and economic institutions (Bethell, Konrad and Skaperdas, and Pejovich), and recent constructive work arguing for a balanced and culturally implicated notion of property such that the connection between private property and personal identity is not ignored (Radin). All of these texts engage property in terms of the idea of property rights guaranteed by laws and both maintained and challenged by social conventions and institutions. See:

Atiyah, Patrick S. *The Rise and Fall of Freedom of Contract.* Oxford: Clarendon, 1979.

Becker, Lawrence C. *Property Rights.* London: Routledge and Kegan Paul, 1977.

Bethell, Tom. *The Noblest Triumph: Property and Prosperity through the Ages.* New York: St. Martin's, 1998.

Grunebaum, James O. *Private Ownership.* London: Routledge and Kegan Paul, 1986.

Konrad, Kai Andreas, and Stergios Skaperdas. *The Market for Protection and the Origin of the State.* London: Centre for Economic Policy Research, 1999.

Macpherson, C. B., ed. *Property: Mainstream and Critical Positions.* Oxford: Blackwell, 1978.

Pejovich, Svetozar. *The Economics of Property Rights: Towards a Theory of Comparative Systems.* Dordrecht, Netherlands: Kluwer, 1990.

Radin, Margaret Jane. *Reinterpreting Property.* Chicago: University of Chicago Press, 1993.

————. *Contested Commodities.* Cambridge, Mass.: Harvard University Press, 1996.

Reeve, Andrew. *Property.* London: Macmillan, 1986.

Rose, Carol M. *Property and Persuasion: Essays on the History, Theory, and Rhetoric of Ownership.* Boulder, Col.: Westview, 1994.

Rowley, Charles K., ed. *Property Rights and the Limits of Democracy.* Brookfield, Vt.: Edward Elgar, 1993.

Ryan, Alan. *Property and Political Theory.* Oxford: Basil Blackwell, 1984.

————. *Property.* Minneapolis: University of Minnesota Press, 1987.

Schlatter, Richard. *Private Property: The History of an Idea.* New Brunswick, N.J.: Rutgers University Press, 1951.

Identity and the Individual

Possessing Self

We speak of possessing a self. Not only *am* I myself, my self is also *mine*. It becomes such in the same way that all property does — as situated within a particular social and cultural context. Self-ownership and identity are thus conditioned by inherited notions of property at the same time that they make property possible as something possessed by *someone*. In recent decades personal identity has itself become a much-discussed theme that, like property, has tended to extend itself across various disciplines, often challenging their presuppositions and self-understandings while legitimating new and different theoretical and social practices. It is no longer possible to speak innocently of an identifiable "we," and since the sixties, notions of the de-centered self heavily influenced by French post-structuralism have been, ironically enough, at the center of much academic discourse. See the following for considerations of self-ownership:

Carrithers, M., et al., eds. *The Category of the Person: Anthropology, Philosophy, History.* Cambridge: Cambridge University Press, 1985.
Cohen, Gerald A. *Self-Ownership, Freedom, and Equality.* New York: Cambridge University Press, 1995.
Fischer, Norman. *Economy and Self: Philosophy and Economics from the Mercantilists to Marx.* Westport, Conn.: Greenwood Press, 1979.
Wikse, John R. *About Possession: The Self As Private Property.* University Park, Pa.: Pennsylvania State University Press, 1977.

The following works trace the genealogy of the modern self and its social representations. Modernity has been characterized by many as a process of secularization, and, as Blumenberg points out, the concept of secularization itself is rooted in the transfer of ecclesial property rights of various kinds to worldly powers. His work examines the claim that modern society's characteristic features are transformations of medieval Christian doctrines, and he shows that any simple notion of an underlying sociocultural substance that might find itself unconsciously manifested in a new form is problematic. Habermas engages the question of social public life, its changing representations and consequent political ramifications in the transition to the modern era. Taylor's important book traces the development of modern moral self-understandings through careful examination of conceptions of the good, the development of a sense of inwardness, the increasing focus on everyday experience, and the interpretation of nature. See also Myers for a good discussion of the concept of self-interest in the early modern period as well as the collection edited by Lash and Friedman.

Blumenberg, Hans. *The Legitimacy of the Modern Age.* Cambridge, Mass.: MIT Press, 1985.

Habermas, Jurgen. *The Structural Transformation of the Public Sphere: An Inquiry into a Category of Bourgeois Society.* Cambridge, Mass.: MIT Press, 1989 (1964?).

Lash, Scott, and Jonathan Friedman, eds. *Modernity and Identity.* Oxford: Blackwell, 1992.

Myers, Milton L. *The Soul of Modern Economic Man: Ideas of Self-Interest, Thomas Hobbes to Adam Smith.* Chicago: University of Chicago Press, 1983.

Taylor, Charles. *Sources of the Self: The Making of the Modern Identity.* Cambridge, Mass.: Harvard University Press, 1989.

Possessing Body

The fact that one possesses one's body is held up by many as the prototypical instance of what it is to possess anything at all. At the same time, the body resists easy assimilation under the category of property. The issues of embodiment are at the same time issues of identity and self-possession (Baker, Burkitt), and the vulnerabilities of embodiment point to the limits of any simple notion of self-identity. Bodies are formed and maintained in social spaces, and a number of studies have looked at the complex relations between the body and society (Canguilhem, Foucault, Scarry, Schilling). For the classic phenomenological account of the role of the body in the constitution of experience of the world and of others, see Husserl's fifth Cartesian meditation, especially sections 42-56, as well as the work of Merleau-Ponty.

Baker, Lynne Rudder. *Persons and Bodies: A Constitution View.* New York: Cambridge University Press, 2000.

Burkitt, Ian. *Bodies of Thought: Embodiment, Identity and Modernity.* London: Sage, 1999.

Canguilhem, Georges. *The Normal and the Pathological.* New York: Zone, 1991.

Cataldi, Sue L. *Emotion, Depth, and Flesh: A Study of Sensitive Space: Reflections on Merleau-Ponty's Philosophy of Embodiment.* Albany, N.Y.: State University of New York Press, 1993.

Foucault, Michel. *Discipline and Punish: The Birth of the Prison,* trans. Alan Sheridan. New York: Random House, 1977.

Husserl, Edmund. *Cartesian Meditations: An Introduction to Phenomenology,* trans. Dorion Cairns. The Hague: M. Nijhoff, 1977.

Merleau-Ponty, Maurice. *Phenomenology of Perception.* London: Routledge and Kegan Paul, 1962.

Scarry, Elaine. *The Body in Pain: The Making and Unmaking of the World.* New York: Oxford University Press, 1985.

Schilling, Chris. *The Body and Social Theory.* London: Sage, 1993.

Scott, Russel. *The Body As Property.* New York: Viking, 1981.

Being Possessed

The strange phenomena of spirit and demoniacal possession might seem out of place in a discussion of economics and identity, but in fact the use of the term "possession" to describe the inexplicable event in which the integrity of a human individual is overcome by some alien force — be it called a spirit, a demon, or a god — is more than merely coincidental. In the same way that it is possible to possess oneself, it becomes possible (at least conceptually) to be possessed. Spirit possession and the cultural mediations that interpret it and make it possible throw social conceptions of the self and the body into relief (Lewis and Mageo). The very questions of identity and self-ownership find themselves pushed to their limits in the cases discussed in the literature below, whether they occur in ancient cultures or in the present day (Brown, Goodman, and Oesterreich), or in literary representation (Stock).

Brown, Michael F. *The Channeling Zone: American Spirituality in an Anxious Age.* Cambridge, Mass.: Harvard University Press, 1997.
Crapanzano, Vivian G., ed. *Case Studies in Spirit Possession.* New York: Wiley, 1977.
Goodman, Felicitas D. *How about Demons? Possession and Exorcism in the Modern World.* Bloomington: Indiana University Press, 1988.
Levack, Brian P., ed. *Possession and Exorcism.* New York: Garland, 1992.
Lewis, I. M. *Ecstatic Religion: A Study of Shamanism and Spirit Possession.* Second ed. London: Routledge, 1989.
Mageo, Jeannette M., and Alan Howard, eds. *Spirits in Culture, History, and Mind.* New York: Routledge, 1996.
Oesterreich, Traugott K. *Possession, Demoniacal and Other: Among Primitive Races in Antiquity, the Middle Ages, and Modern Times,* trans. D. Ibberson. Seacaucus, N.J.: Citadel, 1974 (1966).
Rodewy, Adolf. *Possessed by Satan: The Church's Teaching on the Devil, Possession, and Exorcism.* Garden City, N.Y.: Doubleday, 1975.
Stock, Robert D. *The Flutes of Dionysus: Daemonic Enthrallment in Literature.* Lincoln: University of Nebraska Press, 1989.

Possessing Virtue

Issues concerned with identity and self-possession quickly become involved with concerns about the ways in which character is formed and the social context of moral life in which this occurs. If the body is a kind of possession, moral action can be understood at least partly as the rights and responsibilities the utilization of that possession entails. The resurgence of virtue ethics in recent decades — focused especially on the development of certain habits and moral characteristics rather than abstract moral choice — has produced a large and growing literature, of which the work of MacIntyre and Nussbaum is well-known (see also Hursthouse and Statman). Williams has investigated the concept of shame as a site where moral issues, social worlds, and the "necessary identities" of individual bodies intersect. See also Claudia V. Camp's contribution to the present volume.

Gilmore, David. *Honor and Shame and the Unity of the Mediterranean*. Washington, D.C.: American Anthropological Association, 1987.

Hirschman, Albert O. *Shifting Involvements: Private Interest and Public Action*. Princeton, N.J.: Princeton University Press, 1982.

Hursthouse, Rosalind. *On Virtue Ethics*. Oxford: Oxford University Press, 1999.

MacIntyre, Alasdair. *After Virtue: A Study in Moral Theory*. Second ed. Notre Dame, Ind.: University of Notre Dame Press, 1984.

Nussbaum, Martha C. *The Fragility of Goodness: Luck and Ethics in Greek Tragedy and Philosophy*. Cambridge: Cambridge University Press, 1986.

Ross, Stephen David. *The Gift of Touch: Embodying the Good*. Albany, N.Y.: State University of New York Press, 1998.

Statman, Daniel, ed. *Virtue Ethics*. Washington, D.C.: Georgetown University Press, 1997.

Williams, Bernard. *Shame and Necessity*. Berkeley, Calif.: University of California Press, 1993.

The Social Context of Property: Owning and Exchanging

Property is always embedded in social practices and systems of cultural value. The sociological and anthropological studies of property and possession listed below examine the values that different forms of possession take in various cultures and time-periods and look at the structures of exchange that allow society to circulate property and to function as a field for the transfer of values and goods.

Society and Exchange

Economics is more than just a subset of social practices that it would be possible to abstract away from society as a whole. The works represented below demonstrate the complexity of the relationships between economic themes and those elements of social life that might not appear at first glance to be in any way economic. The collection edited by Appadurai is a good example of comparative, cross-cultural studies of goods as situated within a cultural context. See Hann, Narotsky, and Wilk for introductions to the methods and findings of economic anthropology. For analyses of social change and development which take into account the dynamics of exchange systems, see Archer, Boudon, Castoriadis, and Hodgson.

Albert, Michael, and Robert Hahnel. *The Political Economy of Participatory Economics.* Princeton, N.J.: Princeton University Press, 1990.

Appadurai, Arjun, ed. *The Social Life of Things: Commodities in Cultural Perspective.* New York: Cambridge University Press, 1986.

Archer, Margaret S. *Realist Social Theory: The Morphogenetic Approach.* Cambridge: Cambridge University Press, 1995.

Bloch, M., and J. Parry, eds. *Money and the Morality of Exchange.* Cambridge: Cambridge University Press, 1989.

Boudon, Raymond. *The Logic of Social Action.* New York: Routledge and Kegan Paul, 1981.

Bowles, Samuel, et al., eds. *Markets and Democracy: Participation, Accountability, and Efficiency.* Cambridge: Cambridge University Press, 1993.

Carrier, James G. *Gifts and Commodities: Exchange and Western Capitalism since 1700.* London: Routledge, 1994.

Castoriadis, Cornelius. *The Imaginary Institution of Society.* Cambridge, Mass.: MIT Press, 1987.

Etzioni, Amitai, and Pau R. Lawrence, eds. *Socio-Economics: Toward a New Synthesis.* Armonk, N.Y.: M. E. Sharpe, 1991.

Giddens, Anthony. *The Constitution of Society: Outline of the Theory of Structuration.* Cambridge: Polity, 1984.

Hann, C. M., ed. *Property Relations: Renewing the Anthropological Tradition.* Cambridge: Cambridge University Press, 1998.

Hodgson, Geoffrey M., ed. *The Economics of Institutions.* Aldershot: Edward Elgar, 1993.

Humphrey, C., and S. Hugh-Jones, eds. *Barter, Exchange, and Value.* Cambridge: Cambridge University Press, 1992.

Hutchinson, Frances, and Brian Burkitt. *The Political Economy of Social Credit and Guild Socialism.* London: Routledge, 1997.

Narotzky, Susana. *New Directions in Economic Anthropology.* London: Pluto, 1997.

Wilk, Richard R. *Economies and Cultures: Foundations of Economic Anthropology.* Boulder, Colo.: Westview, 1996.

Material Culture

With concerns overlapping those shown above, anthropologists have examined the ways in which concrete objects exist in social contexts. They investigate the ways we understand ourselves through the artifacts we use, create, and share. "Material culture" as a subdiscipline of anthropology looks at the things we possess as instances and expressions of cultural meaning. Much important work in this field has been published in recent years, implicitly reacting against the abstract focus of much contemporary economic thought. See particularly Berger, Dant, Miller, and Riggins. Issues of personal and social identity are reflected here through the objects we possess and utilize. See in this regard Cohen, Hoskins, and the psychological analyses of Miklitsch.

Berger, Arthur Asa. *Reading Matter: Multidisciplinary Perspectives on Material Culture*. New Brunswick: Transaction, 1992.

Buchli, Victor. *An Archaeology of Socialism*. New York: Berg, 1999.

Cohen, Leah H. *Glass, Paper, Beans: Revelations on the Nature and Value of Ordinary Things*. New York: Doubleday/Currency, 1997.

Dant, Tim. *Material Culture in the Social World: Values, Activities, Lifestyles*. Philadelphia: Open University Press, 1999.

Hoskins, Janet. *Biographical Objects: How Things Tell the Stories of People's Lives*. New York: Routledge, 1998.

Johnson, Matthew. *An Archaeology of Capitalism*. Oxford: Blackwell, 1996.

Miklitsch, Robert. *From Hegel to Madonna: Towards a General Economy of "Commodity Fetishism."* Albany, N.Y.: State University of New York Press, 1998.

Miller, Daniel. *Artifacts As Categories*. Cambridge: Cambridge University Press, 1985.

——. *Material Culture and Mass Consumption*. Oxford: Blackwell, 1987.

——, ed. *Material Cultures: Why Some Things Matter*. Chicago: University of Chicago Press, 1998.

Riggins, Stephen, ed. *The Socialness of Things: Essays on the Socio-Semiotics of Objects*. New York: Mouton de Gruyter, 1994.

Sahlins, Marshall D. *Culture and Practical Reason*. Chicago: University of Chicago Press, 1976.

Schiffer, Michael B. *The Material Life of Human Beings: Artifacts, Behavior, and Communication*. New York: Routledge, 1999.

Tilley, Christopher. *Metaphor and Material Culture*. Malden, Mass.: Blackwell, 1999.

——, ed. *Reading Material Culture: Structuralism, Hermeneutics, and Post-Structuralism*. Cambridge, Mass.: Basil Blackwell, 1989.

Theories of Economic Evolution

In addition to more static and comparative accounts of property and property rights, many important texts address explicitly the dynamics of change involved in the progress of economic history and trace the development of systems of exchange and the cultural structures that support them from their origins in hunter/gatherer societies and the transition to agriculture and to the complexities of modern capitalism (see North). These studies demonstrate that property has not been a static concept through history; instead, individuals and societies have possessed things and regulated the limits of property in almost as many ways as they themselves have existed. Notions of what it is to own and what kinds of ownership are appropriate have been almost continually contested, and at the same time, the economic structures that underlie so many of the issues addressed above have changed significantly over time. See especially:

McFarland, Floyd B. *Economic Philosophy and American Problems: Classical Mechanism, Marxist Dialectic, and Cultural Evolution.* Savage, Md.: Rowman and Littlefield, 1991.

North, Douglass C. *Structure and Change in Economic History.* New York: Norton, 1981.

Schumpeter, Joseph A. *The Theory of Economic Development.* Cambridge, Mass.: Harvard University Press, 1934.

As history progresses, social forms of property come into contact with other natural and cultural factors — be they religious, ecological, colonialist, or technological. In each case there is an exchange of influence. Marxian thinking generally relates all cultural phenomena back to a material substructure. Much important work of the past fifty years or so has tried to reassert the importance of culture and inherited traditions as in fact grounding our very conception of the material realm and in that way being implicated just as much as if not more than the material substructure in social and economic change. Of course this shift can itself be understood as largely determined by the large-scale economic changes that have occurred over the past century. In the end, it is probably impossible to argue conclusively for anything like the clear logical priority of material dialectics to culture or culture to economics. The actual situation is far too messy to ever ground one absolutely in the other. The transition to capitalism certainly was conditioned (at least in certain geographically distinct areas) by certain religious beliefs and practices, but it is equally true that economic processes have always influenced the direction of religious development. See the following for discussions of the interplay between culture and economics in various periods of history:

397

Ancient Economies

Claassen, Cheryl, and Rosemary A. Joyce. *Women in Prehistory: North America and Mesoamerica.* Philadelphia: University of Pennsylvania Press, 1997.
Robb, John E., ed. *Material Symbols: Culture and Economy in Prehistory.* Carbondale, Ill.: Center for Archaeological Investigations, Southern Illinois University at Carbondale, 1999.
Weber, Max. *The Agrarian Sociology of Ancient Civilizations,* trans. R. I. Frank. London: Verso, 1998.

Antiquity

Dougherty, Carol. *The Poetics of Colonization: From City to Text in Archaic Greece.* New York: Oxford University Press, 1993.
Dougherty, Carol, and Leslie Kurke, eds. *Cultural Poetics in Archaic Greece: Cult, Performance, Politics.* New York: Oxford University Press, 1998.
Kurke, Leslie. *The Traffic in Praise: Pindar and the Poetics of Social Economy.* Ithaca, N.Y.: Cornell University Press, 1991.
Rauh, Nicholas K. *The Sacred Bonds of Commerce: Religion, Economy, and Trade Society at Hellenistic Roman Delos, 166-87 B.C.* Amsterdam: J. C. Gieben, 1993.

Christian Antiquity

Avila, Charles. *Ownership: Early Christian Teaching.* Maryknoll, N.Y.: Orbis, 1983.

Medieval Culture

De Roover, Raymond. *Business, Banking, and Economic Thought in Late Medieval and Early Modern Europe.* Chicago: University of Chicago Press, 1974.
Kümin, Beat A., ed. *Reformations Old and New: Essays on the Socio-Economic Impact of Religious Change, c. 1470-1630.* Aldershot, England: Scolar, 1996.
Le Goff, Jacques. *Your Money or Your Life: Economy and Religion in the Middle Ages,* trans. Patricia Ranum. New York: Zone, 1988.
Little, Lester K. *Religious Poverty and Profit Economy in Medieval Europe.* Ithaca, N.Y.: Cornell University Press, 1978.
Lynch, Joseph H. *Simoniacal Entry into Religious Life from 1000 to 1260: A Social, Economic, and Legal Study.* Columbus, Ohio: Ohio State University Press, 1976.

Early Modernity

Adshead, Samuel A. M. *Material Culture in Europe and China, 1400-1800: The Rise of Consumerism.* New York: St. Martin's, 1997.

St. George, Robert B. *Material Culture in America, 1600-1860.* Boston: Northeastern University Press, 1988.

Religion and Modern Culture

Boulding, Kenneth E. *Beyond Economics: Essays on Society, Religion, and Ethics.* Ann Arbor: University of Michigan Press, 1968.

Grelle, Bruce, and David A. Krueger, eds. *Christianity and Capitalism: Perspectives on Religion, Liberalism, and the Economy.* Chicago: Center for the Scientific Study of Religion, 1986.

Preston, Ronald H. *Religion and the Ambiguities of Capitalism.* Worcester: Billings and Sons, 1991.

Taylor, Mark C. *About Religion: Economies of Faith in Virtual Culture.* Chicago: University of Chicago Press, 1999.

Waterman, Anthony Michael C. *Revolution, Economics, and Religion: Christian Political Economy, 1798-1833.* New York: Cambridge University Press, 1991.

The Culture(s) of Capitalism

Few would disagree with the thesis that capitalism has had enormous transformative effects on the societies that have embraced it or been embraced (often violently) by it. But as to the nature of these effects, the logic of their causes, and whether they are to be evaluated negatively or positively there is considerable argument. Many thinkers have pointed to the negative cultural consequences of contemporary economic practices, although often coming from very different cultural and ideological perspectives (Bell, De Bord, Ritzer, Schor, Scitovsky). For comparative accounts of capitalism as it appears in diverse social and cultural contexts, see Clegg, Hampden-Turner and Trompenaars, Kotkin, and Miller. Campbell's book is interesting as a trope on Weber's classic work on the Protestant ethic; he reads modern consumer society as grounded in the self-poetizing values established in late-eighteenth- and early-nineteenth-century romanticism. Also, see Hofstadter for a classic account of the ideology of social Darwinism, which has driven economic development and social policy in America.

Beck, Ulrich. *The Risk Society.* London: Sage, 1992.

Bell, Daniel. *The Coming of Post-Industrial Society: A Venture in Social Forecasting.* New York: Basic, 1973.

———. *The Cultural Contradictions of Capitalism: Twentieth Anniversary Edition.* New York: Basic, 1996 (1976).

Campbell, Colin. *The Romantic Ethic and the Spirit of Modern Consumerism.* Oxford: Blackwell, 1987.

Chase-Dunn, Christopher K. *Global Formation: Structures of the World-Economy.* Lanham, Md.: Rowman and Littlefield, 1998.

Clegg, Stuart R., and S. Gordon Redding. *Capitalism in Contrasting Cultures.* New York: de Gruyter, 1990.

De Bord, Guy. *The Society of the Spectacle.* New York: Zone, 1995.

Fine, Ben. *Women's Employment and the Capitalist Family.* London: Routledge, 1992.

Friedman, Milton. *Capitalism and Freedom.* Chicago: University of Chicago Press, 1962.

Galbraith, John Kenneth. *The New Industrial State.* Third ed., rev. Boston: Houghton Mifflin, 1978.

Hampden-Turner, Charles, and Alfons Trompenaars. *The Seven Cultures of Capitalism: Value Systems for Creating Wealth in the United States, Japan, Germany, France, Britain, Sweden, and the Netherlands.* New York: Currency Doubleday, 1993.

Hodgson, Geoffrey M. *Economics and Utopia: Why the Learning Economy Is Not the End of History.* New York: Routledge, 1999.

Hofstadter, Richard. *Social Darwinism in American Thought.* Boston: Beacon, 1955.

Kotkin, Joel. *Tribes: How Race, Religion, and Identity Determine Success in the New Global Economy.* New York: Random House, 1993.

Lash, Scott, and John Urry. *The End of Organized Capitalism.* Madison: University of Wisconsin Press, 1987.

Lebergott, Stanley. *Pursuing Happiness: American Consumers in the Twentieth Century.* Princeton, N.J.: Princeton University Press, 1993.

Macpherson, C. B. *The Political Theory of Possessive Individualism: From Hobbes to Locke.* London: Oxford University Press, 1962.

Miller, Daniel. *Modernity: An Ethnographic Approach.* Oxford: Berg, 1994.

Ritzer, George. *The McDonaldization of Society.* Rev. ed. Thousand Oaks, Calif.: Pine Forge, 1996.

Schor, Juliet B. *The Overworked American.* New York: Basic, 1992.

Scitovsky, Tibor. *The Joyless Economy: An Inquiry into Human Satisfaction and Consumer Dissatisfaction.* New York: Oxford University Press, 1976.

Waters, Malcolm. *Globalization.* London: Routledge, 1995.

Theories of Consumption

An emphasis on consumption has characterized a number of sociological studies since the early seventies. De Certeau's work has been crucial in marking this theoretical shift from production and producers to consumption and consumers. For De Certeau consumption — the usages to which products are put — has a subversive potential within the dominant social forces of production. Personal identities and opportunities may be expressed and actualized in the "secondary production" involved in a product's use. The notion of consumption includes a more internalized relation than that of property. Consumption fosters individual identities at the same time that it participates in the surrounding culture and propagates and/or subverts that culture's values. Important, too, have been the writings of Jean Baudrillard, who has carried further Veblen's insight that consumption serves primarily as an index of social rank — the process of "prestation" — rather than the more or less complete satisfaction of basic human needs. See Benjamin's enormous unfinished study of the Parisian arcades for a sprawling portrait that draws together thousands of quotations, economic facts, and fragmented images in order not only to represent, but in some fashion to embody, the complex intersections making up socioeconomic life for the consumers of the nineteenth century. Other more recent studies have looked at the implications of a consumer society from ethical (Crocker and Linden), anthropological (Douglas and Isherwood), and identity-forming (Friedman, Lunt and Livingstone, and Tomlinson) perspectives. In a contemporary consumer society, even time comes to have the status of a commodity to be consumed like any other market good (Antonides).

Antonides, Gerrit, et al., eds. *The Consumption of Time and the Timing of Consumption: Towards a New Behavioral and Socio-Economics.* Amsterdam: Royal Netherlands Academy of Arts and Sciences, 1991.

Baudrillard, Jean. *The Mirror of Production.* St. Louis: Telos, 1975.

———. *For a Critique of the Political Economy of the Sign.* St. Louis: Telos, 1981.

———. *The Consumer Society: Myths and Structures.* Thousand Oaks, Calif.: Sage, 1998.

Benjamin, Walter. *The Arcades Project.* Cambridge, Mass.: Belknap, 1999.

Bourdieu, Pierre. *Outline of a Theory of Practice.* Oxford: Cambridge University Press, 1977.

———. *Distinction: A Social Critique of the Judgement of Taste.* London: Routledge and Kegan Paul, 1984.

———. *Practical Reason.* Stanford, Calif.: Stanford University Press, 1998.

Brewer, John, and Roy Porter, eds. *Consumption and the World of Goods.* New York: Routledge, 1993.

Crocker, David A., and Toby Linden, eds. *Ethics of Consumption: The Good Life, Justice, and Global Stewardship*. Lanham, Md.: Rowman and Littlefield, 1998.

De Certeau, Michel. *The Practice of Everyday Life*. Berkeley: University of California Press, 1984.

Douglas, Mary, and Baron Isherwood. *The World of Goods: Towards an Anthropology of Consumption*. London: Allen Lane, 1979.

Dumm, Thomas L. *A Politics of the Ordinary*. New York: New York University, 1999.

Fine, Ben, and Ellen Leopold. *The World of Consumption*. New York: Routledge, 1993.

Friedman, Jonathan, ed. *Consumption and Identity*. Chur, Switzerland: Harwood, 1994.

Lunt, Peter K., and Sonia Livingstone. *Mass Consumption and Personal Identity: Everyday Economic Experience*. Philadelphia: Open University Press, 1992.

Mason, Roger. *Conspicuous Consumption: A Study of Exceptional Consumer Behavior*. New York: St. Martin's, 1981.

McCracken, Grant. *Culture and Consumption: New Approaches to the Symbolic Character of Consumer Goods and Activities*. Bloomington, Ind.: Indiana University Press, 1988.

McGovern, Charles, Susan Strasser, and Matthias Judt, eds. *Getting and Spending: European and American Consumer Societies in the Twentieth Century*. Cambridge: Cambridge University Press, 1998.

Miller, Daniel, ed. *Acknowledging Consumption: A Review of New Studies*. London: Routledge, 1995.

Rutz, H., and B. Orlove, eds. *The Social Economy of Consumption*. Lanham, Md.: University Press of America, 1989.

Silverstone, R., and E. Hirsch, eds. *Consuming Technologies*. London: Routledge, 1992.

Slater, Don. *Consumer Culture and Modernity*. Oxford: Polity, 1997.

Storey, John. *Cultural Consumption and Everyday Life*. London: Oxford University Press, 1999.

Tomlinson, Alan, ed. *Consumption, Identity and Style: Marketing, Meanings, and the Packaging of Pleasure*. London: Routledge, 1990.

Whiteley, Nigel, et al., eds. *The Authority of the Consumer*. London: Routledge, 1994.

For interesting discussions of the role of advertising in promoting and mediating consumerism within the broader field of cultural values, see:

Cross, Mary, ed. *Advertising and Culture: Theoretical Perspectives*. Westport, Conn.: Praeger, 1996.

Jhally, Sut. *The Codes of Advertising: Fetishism and the Political Economy of Meaning in the Consumer Society*. New York: Routledge, 1990.

Sivulka, Juliann. *Soap, Sex, and Cigarettes: A Cultural History of American Advertising*. Belmont, Calif.: Wadsworth, 1998.

Turow, Joseph. *Breaking Up America: Advertisers and the New Media World*. Chicago: University of Chicago Press, 1997.

Twitchell, James B. *Adcult USA: The Triumph of Advertising in American Culture*. New York: Columbia University Press, 1996.

Economics and Ethics

Entwined intimately with the concept of property is the concept of the proper. The various arguments for and against the very existence of private property have always themselves been caught up in notions of what is or is not proper for human individuals and societies. Natural rights law theorists and human rights activists have argued for the propriety of certain rights possessed by all. At the same time one of the most common designations of property involves freedom of utilization — what is mine is what I am free to use in whatever way I see fit. Inevitably, the freedom to use things as one wishes runs up against the limits of others' rights and the integrity of common goods (such as the environment, public civic space, cultural heritage sites, and so on). The next sections look at ethical concerns related to property and exchange from a number of perspectives: economic, feminist, religious, biotechnological, and ecological.

The Ethics of the Market

Neo-classical economics, with its focus on rational choice, marginal utility, and self-interest, has had to address the "free rider problem" — why should any rational, economic actor act altruistically or for a collective goal when his or her own personal interests would be equally well served by not doing so? As modern capitalist societies — and increasingly the entire globe — become more and more market-driven, the place of ethics within the discipline of economics as well as its right to critique it from outside has become hotly contested. For broad introductions to the arguments and issues at stake, see Rothschild, Sen, and Vickers. For more focused studies, see Haslett, Koslowski and Shionoya, Lunati, and Mulberg. See, too, the recent collections by Brittan and Hamlin, Groenewegen, Koslowski, and Wilber for relevant articles by many of the most important contemporary thinkers in the field. Fukuyama's discussion of the ways in which ethical behavior grounds economic success at the larger level of society remains one of the most thoughtful considerations of social values and their influence on the economic realm. See also the work by Christine Firer Hinze, Charles Mathewes, William Schweiker, and Deirdre McCloskey in this volume.

Brittan, Samuel, and Alan Hamlin, eds. *Market Capitalism and Moral Values.* Aldershot, England: Edward Elgar, 1995.

Bruyn, Severyn T. *A Civil Economy: Transforming the Market in the Twenty-First Century.* Ann Arbor: University of Michigan Press, 2000.

Collard, David. *Altruism and Economy: A Study in Non-Selfish Economics.* Oxford: Martin Robertson, 1978.

Fukuyama, Francis. *Trust: The Social Virtues and the Creation of Prosperity.* New York: Free Press, 1995.

Groenewegen, Peter D., ed. *Economics and Ethics?* London: Routledge, 1996.

Haslett, D. W. *Capitalism with Morality.* Oxford: Clarendon, 1994.

Koslowski, Peter, ed. *Contemporary Economic Ethics and Business Ethics.* Berlin: Springer, 2000.

Koslowski, Peter, and Yuichi Shionoya, eds. *The Good and the Economical: Ethical Choices in Economics and Management.* Berlin: Springer, 1993.

Lunati, M. Theresa. *Ethical Issues in Economics: From Altruism to Cooperation to Equity.* Houndmills: Macmillan, 1997.

Mulberg, Jon. *Social Limits to Economic Theory.* London: Routledge, 1995.

Pocock, J. G. A. *Virtue, Commerce, and History.* Cambridge: Cambridge University Press, 1985.

Rothschild, K. W. *Ethics and Economic Theory: Ideas — Models — Dilemmas.* Aldershot, England: Edward Elgar, 1993.

Sen, Amartya. *On Ethics and Economics.* Oxford: Basil Blackwell, 1987.

———. *Inequality Re-examined.* Cambridge, Mass.: Harvard University Press, 1992.

Vickers, Douglas. *Economics and Ethics: An Introduction to Theory, Institutions, and Policy.* Westport, Conn.: Praeger, 1997.

Wilber, Charles K., ed. *Economics, Ethics, and Public Policy.* Lanham, Md.: Rowman and Littlefield, 1998.

For a consideration of the ethical and legal issues at stake in protecting objects of cultural heritage, see:

Sax, Joseph L. *Playing Darts with a Rembrandt: Public and Private Rights in Cultural Treasures.* Ann Arbor: University of Michigan Press, 1999.

Feminist Critiques

Look to the following for feminist critiques of capitalism and the relations of women and economics — in various ways these works all address the place in the economic system that women have possessed, struggled to possess, and sought to have recognized as their own. While the inequalities and social transformations of women in the workplace have for some time been recognized and studied, at least by some (see Aslanbeigui, Gilman, and Kessler-Harris), only recently has the work traditionally done by women in the home been recognized as an integral part of larger economic processes (Matthaie and Reskin and Hartmann). For the labor experiences of black women in America, see Jones's work. For an excellent Marxist/feminist critique of capitalism see Gibson-Graham. See, too, Ferber and Nelson, Hartsock, and the collection edited by Kuiper and Sap for other up-to-date applications of feminist theory to economic issues.

Amsden, Alice H., ed. *The Economics of Women and Work.* Harmondsworth: Penguin, 1980.

Aslanbeigui, Nahid, et al. *Women in the Age of Economic Transformation.* London: Routledge, 1994.

Blau, Francine D., and Marianne A. Ferber. *The Economics of Women and Work.* Englewood Cliffs, N.J.: Prentice-Hall, 1986.

Ferber, Marianne, and Julie Nelson, eds. *Beyond Economic Man: Feminist Theory and Economics.* Chicago: University of Chicago Press, 1993.

Gibson-Graham, J. K. *The End of Capitalism (As We Know It): A Feminist Critique of Political Economy.* Oxford: Blackwell, 1996.

Gilman, Charlotte Perkins. *Women and Economics: The Economic Relation between Women and Men.* Amherst, N.Y.: Prometheus, 1994 (1898).

Hartsock, Nancy. *Money, Sex and Power: Toward a Feminist Historical Materialism.* New York: Longman, 1983.

Jones, Jennifer. *Labor of Love, Labor of Sorrow: Black Women, Work, and the Family, from Slavery to the Present.* New York: Vintage, 1986.

Kessler-Harris, Alice. *Out to Work: A History of Wage-Earning Women in the U.S.* New York: Oxford University Press, 1982.

Kuiper, Edith, and Jolande Sap, eds. *Out of the Margin: Feminist Perspectives on Economics.* New York: Routledge, 1995.

Martinez, Katharine, and Kenneth Ames. *The Material Culture of Gender, the Gender of Material Culture.* Winterthur, Del.: Henry Francis du Pont Winterthur Museum, Distributed by University Press of New England, 1997.

Matthaei, Julie. *An Economic History of Women in America: Women's Work, the Sexual Division of Labor, and the Development of Capitalism.* New York: Schocken, 1982.

Mutari, Ellen, et al., eds. *Gender and Political Economy.* Armonk, N.Y.: M. E. Sharpe, 1997.

Peterson, Janice, and Doug Brown, eds. *The Economic Status of Women under Capitalism.* Cheltenham, England: Edward Elgar, 1994.

Reskin, Barbara, and Heidi Hartmann, eds. *Women's Work, Men's Work.* Washington, D.C.: National Academy Press, 1986.

Religious Critiques

The following texts examine ethical questions in economics from a religious perspective. Several, including especially Ryan's classic work and the more recent work by Speiser, present religion as a necessary critique of the excesses and abuses of capitalism. See also Atherton, De Vries, Hinkelammert, and Hobgood for similar positions. Block, Brennan and Waterman, and Finn present broader analyses of economics within a religious context. Although slightly dated, Berg's study brings together and organizes thematically the various encyclicals, public letters, and so forth that various Christian churches worldwide released between 1979 and 1992 on economic questions of various kinds. See on this general topic:

Atherton, John. *Christianity and the Market: Christian Social Thought for Our Times.* London: SPCK, 1992.

Berg, Aart Nicolass van den. *God and the Economy: Analysis and Typology of Roman Catholic, Protestant, Orthodox, Ecumenical, and Evangelical Theological Documents on the Economy, 1979-1992.* Delft, Netherlands: Eburon, 1998.

Block, Walter, et al., eds. *Morality of the Market: Religious and Economic Perspectives.* Vancouver, B.C.: Fraser Institute, 1985.

Block, Walter, and Irving Hexham, eds. *Religion, Economics, and Social Thought.* Vancouver, B.C.: Fraser Institute, 1986.

Brennan, H. Geoffrey, and A. M. C. Waterman. *Economics and Religion: Are They Distinct?* Boston: Kluwer Academic, 1994.

Dean, James M., and A. M. C. Waterman, eds. *Religion and Economics: Normative Social Theory.* Boston: Kluwer Academic, 1999.

De Vries, Barend A. *Champions of the Poor: The Economic Consequences of Judeo-Christian Values.* Washington, D.C.: Georgetown University Press, 1998.

Finn, James, ed. *Global Economics and Religion.* New Brunswick, N.J.: Transaction, 1983.

Gower, Joseph F., ed. *Religion and Economic Ethics.* Lanham, Md.: University Press of America, 1990.

Hinkelammert, R. J. *The Ideological Weapons of Death: A Theological Critique of Capitalism.* Maryknoll, N.Y.: Orbis, 1986.

Hobgood, Mary E. *Catholic Social Teaching and Economic Theory: Paradigms in Conflict.* Philadelphia: Temple University Press, 1991.

Lenski, Gerhard E. *The Religious Factor: A Sociological Study of Religion's Impact on Politics, Economics, and Family Life.* Westport, Conn.: Greenwood, 1977 (1961).

Meeks, M. Douglas. *God the Economist: The Doctrine of God and Political Economy.* Minneapolis: Fortress, 1989.

Monsma, George N. *Economic Theory and Practice in Biblical Perspective.* Potchefstroom: Potchefstroomse Universiteit vir Christelike Hoer Onderwys, 1998.

Muelder, Walter G. *Religion and Economic Responsibility.* New York: Scribner, 1953.

Neusner, Jacob, ed. *Religious Belief and Economic Behavior: Ancient Israel, Classical Christianity, Islam, and Judaism, and Contemporary Ireland and Africa.* Atlanta, Ga.: Scholars Press, 1999.

Rieger, Joerg, ed. *Liberating the Future: God, Mammon, and Theology.* Minneapolis: Fortress, 1998.

Ryan, John A. *Economic Justice: Selections from "Distributive Justice" and "A Living Wage,"* ed. Harlan R. Beckley. Louisville: Westminster John Knox, 1996 (1906 and 1916).

Samuelsson, Kurt. *Religion and Economic Action: A Critique of Max Weber,* trans. E. Geoffrey French, ed. D. C. Coleman. New York: Harper and Row, 1964.

Sedgwick, Peter H. *The Market Economy and Christian Ethics.* New York: Cambridge University Press, 1999.

Speiser, Stuart M. *Ethical Economics and the Faith Community: How We Can Have Work and Ownership for All.* Bloomington, Ind.: Meyer Stone Books, 1989.

Stackhouse, Max L., et al. *Christian Social Ethics in a Global Era.* Nashville: Abingdon, 1995.

Viner, Jacob. *Religious Thought and Economic Society: Four Chapters of an Unfinished Work,* ed. Jacques Melitz and Donald Winch. Durham, N.C.: Duke University Press, 1978.

Wilson, Rodney. *Economics, Ethics, and Religion: Jewish, Christian, and Muslim Economic Thought.* Basingstoke: Macmillan, 1997.

Zweig, Michael, ed. *Religion and Economic Justice.* Philadelphia: Temple University Press, 1991.

The Ethics of Bodies and Technology

Some of the most controversial issues in today's culture are caught up with technological capabilities and their relation to the integrity of human bodies and communities. When society gains the technologies that allow it to intervene in the "natural" order of the body that was previously outside the strict economic domain, ethical concerns arise that cannot be separated from the issues addressed above as to body- and self-possession and the proper role of the state in regulating markets of various kinds. When body parts and tissues can be bought and sold like other commodities (Welie et al.), it would seem that almost no room is left — at least in the material realm — for the existence of anything that escapes the relativization of exchange-value. These issues are also brought to bear on a variety of health and social policies, especially with the rapidly advancing technologies in gene manipulation and cloning. For questions specifically concerning the screening and diagnosis of genetic disorders, see Harper and Clarke and the recent collection edited by Chadwick. See, too, the work by Jean Bethke Elshtain in the present volume.

Appleyard, Bryan. *Brave New Worlds: Staying Human in the Genetic Future.* New York: Viking, 1998.

Bayertz, Kurt. *GenEthics: Technological Intervention in Human Reproduction As a Philosophical Problem,* trans. Sarah L. Kirby. Cambridge, N.Y.: Cambridge University Press, 1994.

Buchanan, Allen, et al. *From Chance to Choice: Genetics and Justice.* Cambridge, N.Y.: Cambridge University Press, 2000.

Chadwick, Ruth, et al., eds. *The Ethics of Genetic Screening.* Dordrecht, Netherlands: Kluwer Academic, 1999.

Coulter, Angela, and Chris Ham, eds. *The Global Challenge of Health Care Rationing.* Philadelphia: Open University Press, 2000.

Edwards, J., et al., eds. *Technologies of Procreation: Kinship in the Age of Assisted Conception.* Manchester: Manchester University Press, 1993.

Elshtain, Jean Bethke, and J. Timothy Cloyd, eds. *Politics and the Human Body: Assault on Dignity.* Nashville: Vanderbilt University Press, 1995.

Gold, E. Richard. *Body Parts: Property Rights and the Ownership of Human Biological Materials.* Washington, D.C.: Georgetown University Press, 1996.

Harper, Peter S., and Angus J. Clarke. *Genetics, Society, and Clinical Practice.* Oxford: BIOS Scientific, 1997.

Harris, John. *Clones, Genes, and Immortality: Ethics and the Genetic Revolution.* Rev. ed. New York: Oxford University Press, 1998 (1992).

Junker-Kenny, Maureen, ed. *Designing Life? Genetics, Procreation, and Ethics.* Aldershot, England: Ashgate, 1999.

Kilner, John F., et al., eds. *Genetic Ethics: Do the Ends Justify the Genes?* Grand Rapids, Mich.: W. B. Eerdmans, 1997.

Martin, Emily. *The Woman in the Body: A Cultural Analysis of Reproduction.* Boston: Beacon, 1991.

Shannon, Thomas A. *Made in Whose Image? Genetic Engineering and Christian Ethics.* Amherst, N.Y.: Humanity, 2000.

Titmuss, Richard M. *The Gift Relationship: From Human Blood to Social Policy.* London: Allen and Unwin, 1970.

Welie, Jos V. M., et al., eds. *Ownership of the Human Body: Philosophical Considerations on the Use of the Human Body and Its Parts in Healthcare.* Dordrecht: Kluwer Academic, 1998.

Wheale, Peter, et al., eds. *The Social Management of Genetic Engineering.* Aldershot, England: Ashgate, 1998.

Ecology and Economics

The increasing scarcity of natural resources, a growing world population, and the environmental consequences of industrialization have brought to consideration the economic role of humanity's most concrete shared possession, the earth. See the following as an introduction to the field of economic and environmental policy arguments.

Bartelmus, Peter. *Environment, Growth, and Development: The Concepts and Strategies of Sustainability.* London: Routledge, 1994.

Baumol, William J., and Wallace E. Oates. *The Theory of Environmental Policy.* Second ed. Cambridge: Cambridge University Press, 1988.

Block, Walter, ed. *Economics and the Environment: A Reconciliation.* Vancouver, B.C.: Fraser Institute, 1989.

Bromley, Daniel W. *Environment and Economy: Property Rights and Public Policy.* Cambridge, Mass.: Basil Blackwell, 1991.

Coward, Harold, and Daniel C. Maguire, eds. *Visions of a New Earth: Religious Perspectives on Population, Consumption, and Ecology.* Albany: State University of New York Press, 2000.

Daly, Herman E., and John B. Cobb Jr. *For the Common Good: Redirecting the Economy towards Community, the Environment, and a Sustainable Future.* London: Green Print, 1990.

Hampson, Fen Osler, and Judith Reppy, eds. *Earthly Goods: Environmental Change and Social Justice.* Ithaca, N.Y.: Cornell University Press, 1996.

Jacobs, Michael. *The Green Economy: Environment, Sustainable Development, and the Politics of the Future.* London: Pluto, 1991.

Simpson, R. David, and Norman L. Christensen, eds. *Ecosystem Function and Human Activities: Reconciling Economics and Ecology.* New York: Chapman and Hall, 1997.

Applying Economics

Property rights are not only caught up in cultural practices and theories of the state, but also have produced economic models that have been applied to situations that go beyond what is commonly considered economic. Becker is perhaps the best-known proponent of applying economic theory to "non-economic" situations such as violent crime. The contributors to the collection edited by Carrier and Miller oppose this trend, especially in its broad application of universal abstract models within different concrete cultural and economic contexts, such as use of the model of the abstract "virtual consumer" — the pure rational agent posited by neoclassical economics — in organizing structural adjustment policies for developing economies. See Polanyi's work for a classic critique of these neoclassical economic assumptions.

Becker, Gary S. *The Economic Approach to Human Behavior.* Chicago: University of Chicago Press, 1976.

Carrier, James G., and Daniel Miller. *Virtualism: A New Political Economy.* New York: Berg, 1998.

Dumont, Louis. *From Mandeville to Marx: The Genesis and Triumph of Economic Ideology.* Chicago: University of Chicago Press, 1977.

Hochschild, Arlie. *The Managed Heart: Commercialization of Human Feeling.* Berkeley: University of California Press, 1983.

Hurst, Charles E. *Living Theory: The Application of Classical Social Theory to Contemporary Life.* Boston: Allyn and Bacon, 2000.

King, S., and P. Lloyd, eds. *Economic Rationalism: Dead End or Way Forward?* Sydney: Allen and Unwin, 1993.

Polanyi, Karl. *The Livelihood of Man.* New York: Academic, 1977.

Self, Peter. *Econocrats and the Policy Process: The Politics and Philosophy of Cost-Benefit Analysis.* London: Macmillan, 1975.

Sen, Amartya. *Choice, Welfare, and Measurement.* Oxford: Basil Blackwell, 1982.

Strange Economies: Sacrifice, Gift, Icon

Property is generally understood according the logic of a market economy in which goods are commensurable with each other, and consumption takes place within a socially circumscribed system of meaning and value. The categories listed below challenge this conception, revealing systems of exchange very different from the conventional, capitalist model. In the social practices of sacrifice and gift-giving and the cultural interpretations of the icon it is possible to see alternatives to the strict quid pro quo of market economies. Instead, these practices can disclose complex economies in which a divine or supramundane order participates. See also David Klemm's and Kathryn Tanner's contributions to this volume.

Sacrifice

Sacrifice may seem the antithesis of possession. In the ancient Hindu horse sacrifice, Greek ritual practices, and Abraham's near-sacrifice of his son we see the image of something given up, a possession consumed and destroyed. The short study by Hubert and Mauss first published over one hundred years ago remains an important introduction to the field. A wide-ranging literature has grown up since that time focusing on many different aspects of sacrifice and sacrificial rites. It seems the modern mind remains fascinated by the practice. Rowan Williams's book is a good place to start for discussions of the sacrificial nature and meaning of the Christian Mass. For other discussions of sacrifice, see:

Bataille, Georges. *Theory of Religion,* trans. Robert Hurley. New York: Zone, 1992 (1973).

Beckwith, Roger T., and Martin J. Selman, eds. *Sacrifice in the Bible.* Grand Rapids: Baker, 1995.

Bloch, Maurice. *Prey into Hunter: The Politics of Religious Experience.* Cambridge: Cambridge University Press, 1992.

Burkert, Walter, et al. *Violent Origins.* Stanford, Calif.: Stanford University Press, 1987.

Delaney, Carol L. *Abraham on Trial: The Social Legacy of Biblical Myth.* Princeton, N.J.: Princeton University Press, 1998.

Derrida, Jacques. *The Gift of Death,* trans. David Wills. Chicago: University of Chicago Press, 1995 (1992).

Girard, René. *Violence and the Sacred,* trans. Patrick Gregory. Baltimore: Johns Hopkins University Press, 1977 (1972).

―――. *Things Hidden since the Foundation of the World,* trans. Stephen Bann and Michael Metteer. London: Athlone, 1987.

Heger, Paul. *The Three Biblical Altar Laws: Developments in the Sacrificial Cult in Practice and Theology: Political and Economic Background.* New York: De Gruyter, 1999.

Hubert, Henri, and Marcel Mauss. *Sacrifice: Its Nature and Functions,* trans. W. D. Halls. Chicago: University of Chicago Press, 1981 (1898).

Williams, Rowan. *Eucharistic Sacrifice: The Roots of a Metaphor.* Bramcote, England: Grove, 1982.

Gift

Ever since Marcel Mauss's influential comparative study of gift-giving and exchange in parts of Polynesia, ancient Rome, and other societies appeared half a century ago, scholars in a number of fields have drawn upon his work and extended it both in empirical breadth and theoretical depth. Many anthropological studies have appeared in response to and building upon Mauss's work. Maurice Godelier has focused on the role of sacred objects, particularly those which "must not be given but must be kept." Their social role as objects of value held in common sheds further light on the phenomenon of exchange. See also Bataille, Sahlins, and the collection edited by Schrift. See Hyde's book for a discussion of art and literature within the framework of the gift. Givenness is also a category of the phenomenon in general as analyzed in its experiential structures by phenomenology. A number of philosophical and theological thinkers — particularly here Marion and Levinas — have drawn upon Heidegger's analysis of the German *Es Gibt* in elucidating the structure of being as gift. Marion has even in a certain sense raised the gift above being, as both Being and beings are given together in the same movement. For a good recent discussion of the gift in relation to theology and postmodernism in which Marion participates, see the collection edited by Caputo and Scanlon based on a conference at Villanova given in 1997.

Bataille, Georges. *The Accursed Share.* Vols. 1-3. New York: Zone, 1993.

Caputo, John D., and Michael J. Scanlon, eds. *God, the Gift, and Postmodernism.* Bloomington: Indiana University Press, 1999.

Godelier, Maurice. *The Enigma of the Gift.* Chicago: University of Chicago Press, 1999.

Hyde, Lewis. *The Gift: Imagination and the Erotic Life of Property.* New York: Random House.

Levinas, Emmanuel. *Totality and Infinity: An Essay on Exteriority.* Pittsburgh: Duquesne University Press, 1969.

———. *Basic Philosophical Writings.* Bloomington: Indiana University Press, 1996.

Mauss, Marcel. *The Gift: The Form and Reason for Exchange in Archaic Societies,* trans. W. D. Halls. New York: Norton, 1990 (1950).

Sahlins, Marshall. *Stone Age Economics.* New York: Aldine and De Gruyter, 1972.

Schrift, Alan D., ed. *The Logic of the Gift: Toward an Ethic of Generosity.* New York: Routledge, 1997.

Ythier, Jean M., et al. *The Economics of Reciprocity, Giving, and Altruism.* Basingstoke: Macmillan, 2000.

Icon

The icon is a religious image that can possess and be possessed. In Eastern Europe there is a large, often underground, market in icons that are bought and sold to collectors. Nevertheless, the meaning of the icon is such that in making the divine present in the gaze of the image, the viewer is himself or herself possessed by what the image represents. In this way the icon stands ambiguously in two economies — the everyday economy of goods exchangeable in terms of their relative value and the economy of grace that establishes infinite relations that exceed any possible relativization. By standing in the second, the icon to some extent escapes and challenges the first. The history of iconographic production and interpretation is continually caught up in this ambiguity. See Barasch, Dixon, Nichols, and Sendler for discussion and analysis of this history. See Marion for an excellent phenomenological and theological discussion of the distinction between the idol and the icon and the meaning of the icon in relation to Christian charity.

Barasch, Moshe. *Icon: Studies in the History of an Idea.* New York: New York University Press, 1992.

Dixon, John W., Jr. *Images of Truth: Religion and the Art of Seeing.* Atlanta, Ga.: Scholars Press, 1996.

Marion, Jean-Luc. *God without Being.* Chicago: University of Chicago Press, 1991.

Nichols, Aidan. *The Art of God Incarnate: Theology and Image in Christian Tradition.* New York: Paulist, 1980.

Sendler, Egon. *The Icon, Image of the Invisible: Elements of Theology, Aesthetics, and Technique,* trans. Steven Bigham. Redondo Beach, Calif.: Oakwood, 1988.

The Economics of Language and the Language of Economics

Perhaps our most complex and ambiguous possession (both individually and collectively) is language. Language possesses us before we possess it. It structures our experiences and mediates our relations to the world and to each other. Out of language we construct the narratives that order our individual and collective lives, and perhaps the most general form of exchange upon which all other socioeconomic orders are grounded is the interchange of words and ideas expressed in discourse. The centrality of language for twentieth-century philosophy does not seem to have exhausted itself yet (Lafont), and, if anything, a concern with rhetoric has increasingly occupied many of the most recent debates in a number of fields possessing intellectual territory most distant from and seemingly impregnable to the methods and insights of literary criticism and the "soft" humanities. Concerns within the scientific community since Kuhn's influential work have focused on the linguistic paradigms within which scientific inquiry and discussion move (Knorr-Cetina). A number of studies have also looked into the particular forms of rhetoric used in the human sciences (Foucault, Nelson, Ricoeur).

Ezell, Margaret J. M., and Katherine O'Brien O'Keefe. *Cultural Artifacts and the Production of Meaning: The Page, the Image, and the Body.* Ann Arbor: University of Michigan Press, 1994.

Fishman, Joshua A. *The Sociology of Language.* Rowley, Mass.: Newbury, 1972.

Foucault, Michel. *The Order of Things: An Archaeology of the Human Sciences.* New York: Pantheon, 1970.

Goux, Jean-Joseph. *Symbolic Economies after Marx and Freud,* trans. Jennifer C. Gage. Ithaca, N.Y.: Cornell University Press, 1990 (1973 and 1978).

Knorr-Cetina, K. *The Manufacture of Knowledge: An Essay on the Constructivist and Contextual Nature of Science*. Oxford: Pergamon, 1981.

Kuhn, Thomas S. *The Structure of Scientific Revolutions*. Third ed. Chicago: University of Chicago Press, 1996.

Lafont, Cristina. *The Linguistic Turn in Hermeneutic Philosophy*, trans. Jose Medina. Cambridge, Mass.: MIT Press, 1999.

Leroi-Gourhan, Andre. *Gesture and Speech*, trans. Anna Bostock Berger. Cambridge, Mass.: MIT Press, 1993 (1964).

Nelson, John, et al. *The Rhetoric of the Human Sciences*. Madison: University of Wisconsin Press, 1987.

Pecheux, Michel. *Language, Semantics, and Ideology*. New York: St. Martin's, 1982.

Ricoeur, Paul. *Hermeneutics and the Human Sciences: Essays on Languages, Action, and Interpretation*, trans. J. B. Thompson. Cambridge: Cambridge University Press, 1981.

It is often overlooked that Adam Smith, one of the founders of classical economic theory, was also concerned with the issue of rhetoric. Recently, there has been increased interest in the forms of language used by economists to express their findings and to argue for the validity of their theories. Because so much current economic research and thought is expressed through abstract mathematical or game-theory modeling, many economists ignore the questions of rhetoric that have engaged the other social sciences (as listed above). Several works in the past decade or so have tried to ameliorate this lack of disciplinary self-awareness. The work of Blaug, Henderson, McCloskey, and Samuels has in several ways addressed the question of how different forms of economic rhetoric matter in shaping the content they express, as well as how exactly economists communicate with each other, both in formal, published work and through informal discussions. See Shell's book for a historical picture of commerce in literary texts, and Voloshinov as a good starting point for looking at language through the lens of Marxist analysis.

Blaug, Mark. *The Methodology of Economics; Or How Economists Explain*. Cambridge: Cambridge University Press, 1980.

Hausman, D. *The Inexact and Separate Science of Economics*. Cambridge: Cambridge University Press, 1992.

Henderson, Willie. *Reading Economics: How Text Helps or Hinders*. London: British Library, 1987.

Henderson, Willie, and Anthony Dudley-Evans, eds. *The Language of Economics: The Analysis of Economic Discourse*. ELT Documents, no. 134. London: Modern English Publications in assoc. with The British Council, 1990.

Henderson, Willie, et al., eds. *Economics and Language.* London: Routledge, 1993.

Klamer, Arjo, et al., eds. *The Consequences of Economic Rhetoric.* New York: Cambridge University Press, 1988.

Lavoie, Don, ed. *Economics and Hermeneutics.* London: Routledge, 1990.

McCloskey, Deirdre. *If You're So Smart: The Narrative of Economic Expertise.* Chicago: University of Chicago Press, 1990.

————. *The Rhetoric of Economics.* Second ed. Madison: University of Wisconsin Press, 1998 (1985).

Rossi-Landi, Feruccio. *Language As Work and Trade: A Semiotic Homology for Linguistics and Economics.* South Hadley, Mass.: Bergin and Garvey, 1983.

Samuels, Warren J., ed. *Economics As Discourse: An Analysis of the Language of Economists.* Boston: Kluwer Academic, 1990.

Shell, Marc. *Money, Language, and Thought: Literary and Philosophical Economies from the Medieval to the Modern Era.* Berkeley: University of California Press, 1982.

Smith, Adam. *Lectures on Rhetoric and Belles Lettres,* ed. J. C. Bryce. New York: Oxford University Press, 1983.

Voloshinov, V. N. *Marxism and the Philosophy of Language,* trans. Ladislav Matejka and I. R. Titunik. Cambridge, Mass.: Harvard University Press, 1986 (1973).